THE BIBLE AS
HISTORY

THE BIBLE AS HISTORY

by

WERNER KELLER

Translated from the German by
William Neil

Revised and with a postscript by
Joachim Rehork

New material translated from the German by
B. H. Rasmussen

BARNES
& NOBLE
BOOKS
NEW YORK

This edition published by Barnes & Noble, Inc.,
by arrangement with William Morrow and Company.

1995 Barnes & Noble Books

ISBN 1-56619-801-1

Printed and bound in the United States of America

M   19   18   17   16   15   14   13

To my parents and
my friend Th. Ruth

CONTENTS

CONTENTS

CONTENTS

CONTENTS

INTRODUCTION TO THE
NEW REVISED EDITION

My book *The Bible as History* was first published in 1955. It was translated into 24 languages and used for religious instruction in schools, for Bible Seminars in Universities as well as by Bible Study Groups both Christian and Jewish. More than ten million copies have been printed throughout the world.

Since that time Biblical archaeology has brought to light hitherto undiscovered facts by the use of new techniques and the most up-to-date methods of investigation. It has been possible to confirm and reinforce a number of theories, while other accepted opinions, previously considered to be scientifically established, have had to be called into question and the conclusions even of well-known scholars revised. In order to preserve the scholarly reliability of my book, it has become necessary to include the most recent research results. One cannot and should not shut oneself off from new discoveries even if they are inconvenient.

I would have liked to bring my book into line with the most recent research myself, but a serious illness of some years' duration has unfortunately prevented me from undertaking this costly and responsible task. I have consequently been obliged, much against my will, to entrust this project to another. I am happy, however, to have obtained the collaboration of Dr. Joachim Rehork. In his appendix he has explained the principles according to which we agreed that the revision should be carried out.

To him I tender my sincere thanks.

WERNER KELLER

INTRODUCTION

"The greatest happiness of the thinking man is to have fathomed what can be fathomed, and quietly to reverence what is unfathomable."

GOETHE

WHEN a non-theologian writes a book about the Bible it is a rare enough occurrence to entitle the reader to ask for some explanation of how the writer managed to make himself master of his subject.

As a journalist I have been for many years exclusively concerned with the results of modern science and research. In 1950 in the course of my ordinary routine work I came across the reports of the French archaeologists Professors Parrot and Schaeffer on their excavations at Mari and Ugarit. Cuneiform tablets discovered at Mari on the Euphrates were found to contain Biblical names. As a result, narratives of the patriarchs which had been for a long time regarded as merely pious tales were unexpectedly transferred into the realm of history. At Ugarit on the Mediterranean, evidence of the Canaanite worship of Baal had for the first time come to light. By a coincidence, a scroll of Isaiah discovered in a cave by the Dead Sea was in the same year dated as pre-Christian. These sensational reports—and indeed in view of the significance of these finds it is not too much to use the word "sensational"—awakened in me the desire to come to closer grips with Biblical archaeology, the most recent and, generally speaking, least known province in the field of investigation into the ancient world. I therefore ransacked German and foreign literature for a comprehensive and intelligible summary of the results of previous research. I found none for there was none to find. So I went to the sources myself in the libraries of many lands—aided in this bit of real detective work by my wife's enthusiasm—and collected all the hitherto scientifically established results of investigations which were to be found in the learned works of Biblical archaeologists. The deeper I went into the matter the more exciting it became.

The door into the historical world of the Old Testament had been already thrown open by a Frenchman, Paul-Emile Botta, in 1843. In the course of excavations at Khorsabad in Mesopotamia he suddenly found himself confronted by reliefs of King Sargon II of Assyria, who ravaged Israel and led its people off into captivity. Accounts of this conqueror's campaigns deal with the conquest of Samaria, which is also described in the Bible.

For a century now, American, English, French and German scholars have been digging in the Middle East, in Mesopotamia, Palestine and Egypt. All the great nations have founded institutes and schools specifically for this type of research. The Palestine Exploration Fund began in 1869, the German Palestine Association in 1877, the Dominican Ecole Biblique de St. Etienne in 1892. The German Oriental Society followed in 1898: then in 1900 the American Schools of Oriental Research and in 1901 the German Protestant Institute of Archaeology.

In Palestine, places and towns which are frequently mentioned in the Bible are being brought back once more into the light of day. They look exactly as the Bible describes them and lie exactly where the Bible locates them. On ancient inscriptions and monuments scholars encounter more and more characters from the Old and New Testaments. Contemporary reliefs depict people whom we have hitherto only known by name. Their features, their clothes, their armour take shape before our eyes. Colossal figures and sculptures show us the Hittites with their big noses; the slim tall Philistines; the elegant Canaanite chiefs with their "chariots of iron" which struck terror into the hearts of the Israelites; the kings of Mari, contemporary with Abraham, with their gentle smiles. During the thousands of years that divide us from them the Assyrian kings have lost nothing of their fierce and forbidding appearance: Tiglath-Pileser III, well known as the Old Testament "Pul"; Sennacherib who destroyed Lachish and laid siege to Jerusalem; Esarhaddon who put King Manasseh in chains, and Ashurbanipal the "great and noble Asnapper" of the book of Ezra.

As they have done to Nineveh and Nimrud—old-time Calah—or to Ashur and Thebes, which the prophets called No-Amon, the scholars have also awakened from its ancient slumber the notorious Babel of Biblical story with its legendary tower. In the Nile Delta archaeologists have found the cities of Pithom and Raamses, where the resentful Hebrews toiled as slaves. They have laid bare strata which tell of the flames and destruction which accompanied the children of Israel on their conquering march into Canaan. In Gibeah they found Saul's mountain stronghold, whose walls once echoed to the strains of David's harp. At Megiddo they came upon the vast stables of King Solomon, who had "12,000 horsemen".

From the world of the New Testament reappeared the palatial edifices of King Herod. In the heart of Old Jerusalem The Pavement was discovered, where Jesus stood before Pilate, as is mentioned in St. John's gospel. Assyriologists deciphered on the astronomical tables of the Babylonians the exact dates on which the Star of Bethlehem was observed.

These breathtaking discoveries, whose significance it is impossible to grasp all at once, make it necessary for us to revise our views about the Bible. Many events which previously passed for "pious tales" must now be judged to be historical. Often the results of investigation correspond in detail with the Biblical narratives. They do not only confirm them, but also illumine the historical situations out of which the Old Testament and the Gospels grew. At the same time the chances and changes of the people of Israel are woven into a lively colourful tapestry of daily life in the age in which they lived, as well as being caught up into the political, cultural and economic disputes of the nations and empires which struggled for power in Mesopotamia and on the Nile, from which the inhabitants of the tiny buffer state of Palestine were never able completely to detach themselves for over 2,000 years.

The opinion has been, and still is widely held that the Bible is nothing but the story of man's salvation, a guarantee of the validity of their faith for Christians everywhere. It is however at the same time a book about things that actually happened. Admittedly in this sense it has limitations, in that the Jewish people wrote their history in the light of their relationship to Yahweh, which meant writing it from the point of view of their own guilt and expiation. Nevertheless the events themselves are historical facts and have been recorded with an accuracy that is nothing less than startling.

Thanks to the findings of the archaeologists many of the Biblical narratives can be better understood now than ever before. There are, of course, theological insights which can only be dealt with in terms of the Word of God. But as Professor André Parrot, the world-famous French archaeologist, has said: "How can we understand the Word, unless we see it in its proper chronological, historical and geographical setting?"

Until now, knowledge of these extraordinary discoveries was confined to a small circle of experts. Only fifty years ago Professor Friedrich Delitzsch of Berlin was asking "Why all this effort in these distant barren and dangerous lands? Why all this costly rummaging among the rubble of past ages when we know there is neither gold nor silver to be found there? Why this mad competition among different countries to get control of these dreary looking mounds for the sole purpose of digging them up?" The German scholar Gustav Dalman gave him the right answer from Jerusalem itself when he expressed the hope that one day all that the archaeologists had "experienced and seen in their scientific labours would be turned to good account and would help to solve the practical problems of school and church". This latter hope has so far however remained unfulfilled.

No book in the whole history of mankind has had such a revolutionary influence, has so decisively affected the development of the western world, or had such a world-wide effect as the "Book of Books", the Bible. Today it is translated into 1,120 languages and dialects

(1,660 in 1979), and after 2,000 years gives no sign of having exhausted its triumphal progress.

In gathering together and working over the material for this book, which I in no way claim to be complete, it seemed to me that the time had come to share with those who read their Bibles and those who do not, with churchmen and agnostics alike, the exciting discoveries which have resulted from a careful examination of the combined results of scientific investigation along many different lines. In view of the over-whelming mass of authentic and well-attested evidence now available, as I thought of the sceptical criticism which from the eighteenth century onwards would fain have demolished the Bible altogether, there kept hammering on my brain this one sentence: "The Bible is right after all!"

WERNER KELLER

Hamburg,
    September 1955

DIGGING UP THE OLD TESTAMENT

I

The coming of the Patriarchs
From Abraham to Jacob

CHAPTER 1

IN THE "FERTILE CRESCENT"

Four thousand years ago—Continents asleep—The great cradle of our civilisation—Culture in the Ancient East—Staged towers and pyramids had been built long before—Giant plantations on the banks of canals—Arab tribes attack from the desert.

IF we draw a line from Egypt through the Mediterranean lands of Palestine and Syria, then following the Tigris and Euphrates, through Mesopotamia to the Persian Gulf, the result is an unmistakable crescent.

Four thousand years ago this mighty semi-circle around the Arabian Desert, which is called the "Fertile Crescent", embraced a multiplicity of civilisations lying side by side like a lustrous string of pearls. Rays of light streamed out from them into the surrounding darkness of mankind. Here lay the centre of civilisation from the Stone Age right up to the Golden Age of Graeco-Roman culture.

About 2000 B.C., the further we look beyond the "Fertile Crescent", the deeper grows the darkness and signs of civilisation and culture decrease. It is as if the people of the other continents were like children awaiting their awakening. Over the Eastern Mediterranean already a light is shining—it is the heyday of the Minoan kings of Crete, founders of the first sea-power known to history. For 1,000 years the fortress of Mycenae had protected its citizens, and a second Troy had long been standing upon the ruins of the first. In the nearby Balkans, however, the Early Bronze Age had just begun. In Sardinia and Western France the dead were being buried in vast stone tombs. These megalithic graves are the last great manifestation of the Stone Age.

In Britain they were building the most famous sanctuary of the Megalithic Age—the Temple of the Sun at Stonehenge—that giant circle of stones near Salisbury which is still one of the sights of England about which many tales are told. In Germany they were tilling the soil with wooden ploughs.

At the foot of the Himalayas the flickering lamp of an isolated outpost of civilisation in the Indus valley was fast going out. Over China, over the vast steppes of Russia, over Africa, darkness reigned supreme. And beyond the waters of the Atlantic lay the Americas in twilight gloom.

But in the "Fertile Crescent" and in Egypt, on the other hand, cultured and highly developed civilisations jostled each other in colourful and bewildering array. For 1,000 years the Pharaohs had sat upon the throne. About 2000 B.C. it was occupied by the founder of the XII Dynasty, Amenemhet I. His sphere of influence ranged from Nubia, south of the second cataract of the Nile, beyond the Sinai peninsula to Canaan and Syria, a stretch of territory as big as Norway. Along the Mediterranean coast lay the wealthy seaports of the Phoenicians. In Asia Minor, in the heart of present day Turkey, the powerful kingdom of the ancient Hittites stood on the threshold of its history. In Mesopotamia, between Tigris and Euphrates, reigned the kings of Sumer and Akkad, who held in tribute all the smaller kingdoms from the Persian Gulf to the sources of the Euphrates.

Egypt's mighty pyramids and Mesopotamia's massive temples had for centuries watched the busy life around them. For 2,000 years farms and plantations, as big as any large modern concern, had been exporting corn, vegetables and choice fruits from the artificially irrigated valleys of the Nile, the Euphrates and the Tigris. Everywhere throughout the "Fertile Crescent" and in the empire of the Pharaohs the art of cuneiform and hieroglyphic writing was commonly known. Poets, court officials and civil servants practised it. For commerce it had long been a necessity.

The endless traffic in commodities of all sorts which the great import and export firms of Mesopotamia and Egypt despatched by caravan routes or by sea from the Persian Gulf to Syria and Asia Minor, from the Nile to Cyprus and Crete and as far as the Black Sea, is reflected in their business correspondence, which they conducted on clay tablets or papyrus. Out of all the rich variety of costly wares the most keenly sought after were copper from the Egyptian mines in the mountains of Sinai, silver from the Taurus mines in Asia Minor, gold and ivory from Somaliland in East Africa and from Nubia on the Nile, purple dyes from the Phoenician cities on the coast of Canaan, incense and rare spices from South Arabia, the magnificent linens which came from the Egyptian looms and the wonderful vases from the island of Crete.

Literature and learning were flourishing. In Egypt the first novels and secular poetry were making their appearance. Mesopotamia was experiencing a Renaissance. Philologists in Akkad, the great kingdom on the lower Euphrates, were compiling the first grammar and the first bilingual dictionary. The story of Gilgamesh, and the old Sumerian legends of Creation and Flood were being woven into epics of dramatic power in the Akkadian tongue which was the language of the world. Egyptian doctors were producing their medicines in accordance with text-book methods from herbal compounds which had proved their worth. Their surgeons were no strangers to anatomical science. The mathematicians of the Nile by empirical means reached the conclusion

FIG. 1.—The "Fertile Crescent" and Egypt—the great centres of civilisation about 2000 B.C.

about the sides of a triangle which 1,500 years later Pythagoras in Greece embodied in the theorem which bears his name. Mesopotamian engineers were solving the problem of square measurement by trial and error. Astronomers, admittedly with an eye solely on astrological prediction, were making their calculations based on accurate observations of the course of the planets.

Peace and prosperity must have reigned in this world of Nile, Euphrates and Tigris, for we have never yet discovered an inscription dating from this period which records any large-scale warlike activities.

Then suddenly from the heart of this great "Fertile Crescent", from the sandy sterile wastes of the Arabian desert whose shores are lashed by the waters of the Indian Ocean, there burst in violent assaults on the north, on the north-west, on Mesopotamia, Syria and Palestine a horde of nomadic tribes of Semitic stock. In endless waves these Amorites, "Westerners" as their name implies, surged against the kingdoms of the "Fertile Crescent".

The empire of the kings of Sumer and Akkad collapsed in 1960 B.C. under their irresistible attack. The Amorites founded a number of states and dynasties. One of them was eventually to become supreme: the first dynasty of Babylon, which was the great centre of power from 1830 to 1530 B.C. Its sixth king was the famous Hammurabi.

Meantime one of these tribes of Semitic nomads was destined to be of fateful significance for millions upon millions throughout the world up to the present day. It was a little group, perhaps only a family, as unknown and unimportant as a tiny grain of sand in a desert storm: the family of Abraham, forefather of the patriarchs.

CHAPTER 2

UR OF THE CHALDEES

Station on the Bagdad railway—A staged tower of bricks—Ruins with Bibli-cal names—Archaeologists in search of scriptural sites—A consul with a pick—The archaeologist on the throne of Babylon—Expedition to Tell al Muqayyar—History books from rubble—Tax receipts on clay—Was Abraham a city dweller?

"And Terah took Abram his son, and Lot the son of Haran, his son's son, and Sarai, his daughter in law, his son Abram's wife; and they went forth with them from Ur of the Chaldees" (Gen. 11^{31}).

... and they went forth with them from Ur of the Chaldees—Christians have been hearing these words for almost 2,000 years. Ur, a name as mysterious and legendary as the bewildering variety of names of kings and conquerors, powerful empires, temples and golden palaces, with which the Bible regales us. Nobody knew where Ur lay. Chaldea certainly pointed to Mesopotamia. Sixty years ago no one could have guessed that the quest for the Ur which is mentioned in the Bible would lead to the discovery of a civilisation which would take us farther into the twilight of prehistoric times than even the oldest traces of man which had been found in Egypt.

Today Ur is a railway station about 120 miles north of Basra, near the Persian Gulf, and one of the many stops on the famous Bagdad railway. Punctually the train makes a halt there in the grey light of early morning. When the noise of the wheels on their northward journey has died away, the traveller who has alighted here is surrounded by the silence of the desert.

His glance roams over the monotonous yellowish-brown of the end-less stretch of sand. He seems to be standing in the middle of an enormous flat dish which is only intersected by the railway line. Only at one point is the shimmering expanse of desolation broken. As the rays of the rising sun grow stronger they pick out a massive dull red stump. It looks as if some Titan had hewn great notches in it.

To the Bedouins this solitary mound is an old friend. High up in its crevices the owls make their nests. From time immemorial the Arabs have known it and have given it the name Tell al Muqayyar, "Mound of Pitch". Their forefathers pitched their tents at its base. Still as from time immemorial it offers welcome protection from the danger of sandstorms. Still today they feed their flocks at its base when the rains suddenly charm blades of grass out of the ground.

Once upon a time—4,000 years ago—broad fields of corn and barley swayed here. Market gardens, groves of date-palms and fig trees stretched as far as the eye could see. These spacious estates could cheerfully bear comparison with Canadian wheat farms or the market gardens and fruit farms of California. The lush green fields and beds were interlaced by a system of dead straight canals and ditches, a masterpiece of irrigation. Away back in the Stone Age experts among the natives had utilised the water of the great rivers. Skilfully and methodically they diverted the precious moisture at the river banks and thereby converted desert wastes into rich and fruitful farmland.

Almost hidden by forests of shady palms the Euphrates flowed in those days past this spot. This great life-giving river carried a heavy traffic between Ur and the sea. At that time the Persian Gulf cut much deeper into the estuary of the Euphrates and the Tigris. Even before the first pyramid was built on the Nile Tell al Muqayyar was towering into the blue skies. Four mighty cubes, built one upon the other in diminishing size, rose up into a 75 feet tower of gaily coloured brick. Above the black of the square foundation block, its sides 120 feet long, shone the red and blue of the upper stages, each studded with trees. The uppermost stage provided a small plateau, on which was enthroned a Holy Place shaded by a golden roof.

Silence reigned over this sanctuary, where priests performed their offices at the shrine of Nannar, the moon-god. The stir and noise of wealthy metropolitan Ur, one of the oldest cities of the world, hardly penetrated into it.

In the year 1854 a caravan of camels and donkeys, laden with an unusual cargo of spades, picks and surveyor's instruments, approached the lonely red mound, under the leadership of the British consul in Basra. Mr. J. E. Taylor was inspired neither by a lust for adventure nor indeed by any motive of his own. He had undertaken the journey at the instigation of the Foreign Office, which in its turn was complying with the request from the British Museum that a search should be made for ancient monuments in Southern Mesopotamia, where the Euphrates and the Tigris came closest together just before entering the Persian Gulf. Taylor had often heard in Basra about the strange great heap of stones that his expedition was now approaching. It seemed to him a suitable site to investigate.

About the middle of the 19th century all over Egypt, Mesopotamia and Palestine investigations and excavations had started in response to a suddenly awakened desire to get a scientifically reliable picture of man's history in this part of the world. The goal of a long succession of expeditions was the Middle East.

Up till then the Bible had been the only historical source for our knowledge of that part of Asia before about 550 B.C. Only the Bible had anything to say about a period of history which stretched back into the dim twilight of the past. Peoples and names cropped up in the Bible about which even the Greeks and the Romans no longer knew anything.

FIG. 2.—The great staged tower at Ur (Reconst.).

Scholars swarmed impetuously into these lands of the Ancient East about the middle of last century. Nobody then knew names that were soon to be in everyone's mouth. With astonishment the age of progress and enlightenment heard of their finds and discoveries. What these men with infinite pains extracted from the desert sand by the great rivers of Mesopotamia and Egypt deserved indeed the attention of mankind. Here for the first time science had forced open the door into the mysterious world of the Bible.

The French vice-consul in Mosul, Paul-Emile Botta, was an enthusiastic archaeologist. In 1843 he began to dig at Khorsabad on the Tigris and from the ruins of a 4,000 year old capital proudly brought to light the first witness to the Bible: Sargon, the fabulous ruler of Assyria. "In the year that Tartan came unto Ashdod, when Sargon the king of Assyria sent him ..." says Isaiah 20[1].

Two years later a young English diplomat and excavator, A. H. Layard, uncovered Nimrud (Kalchu), the city which the Bible calls Calah (Gen. 10[11]) and which now bears the name of the Nimrod of the Bible, "a mighty hunter before the Lord. And the beginning of his kingdom was Babel and Erech, and Accad and Calneh in the land of Shinar. Out of that land he went forth into Assyria and builded Nineveh and Rehoboth-Ir and Calah...." (Gen. 10[10-11]).

Shortly after that, excavations under the direction of an English major, Henry Creswicke Rawlinson, one of the foremost Assyriologists, unearthed Nineveh, the Assyrian capital with the famous library of king Ashurbanipal. This is the Nineveh whose wickedness the Biblical prophets constantly denounced (Jonah I[2]).

In Palestine the American scholar Edward Robinson devoted himself in 1838 and 1852 to the reconstruction of the topography of the ancient world.

From Germany, Richard Lepsius, later director of the Egyptian Museum in Berlin, recorded the monuments of the Nile area during an expedition which lasted from 1842–46.

Just as the Frenchman Champollion had the good fortune to decipher Egyptian hieroglyphics, so Rawlinson, the discoverer of Nineveh, was, among others, successful in solving the riddle of cuneiform writing. The ancient documents were beginning to talk!

Let us return to the caravan which is approaching Tell al Muqayyar.

Taylor pitches his tents at the foot of the red mound. He had neither scientific ambitions nor previous knowledge. Where is he to begin? Where is the best spot to deploy his native diggers? The great brick mound, architectural masterpiece of a shadowy past though it might be, conveys nothing to him. Perhaps in the heart of it lies something which might eventually be exhibited in the museum and might interest the London experts. He thinks vaguely of old statues, armour, ornaments or even perhaps buried treasure. He takes a closer look at the curious mound. Step by step he taps its surface. No indication of a hollow cavity within. The great edifice appears to be completely solid. Thirty feet above him the wall of the lowest block rises straight and sheer out of the sand. Two broad stone ramps lead to the next and smaller cone above, then above them rise the third and fourth stages.

Taylor clambers up and down, crawls along the ledges on hands and knees in the broiling sun, finding only broken tiles. One day, bathed in sweat, he reaches the topmost platform and a few owls fly startled from the dilapidated walls. Nothing more. However he is not discouraged. In his efforts to get to the heart of the secrets of the mound he makes a decision which today we can only deeply regret. He takes his labour gangs away from the base of the mound and sets them to work at the top.

What had survived for centuries, what had withstood sandstorm and blazing sun alike, became now the victim of tireless pickaxes. Taylor gives orders to pull down the top story. The work of destruction begins at the four corners simultaneously. Day after day masses of bricks crash dully down the sides to the ground. After many weeks the chattering voices on the top of the mound are suddenly hushed, the clanging and banging of the pickaxes stop abruptly. Falling over each other in their haste a few men rush down the side of the mound and up to Taylor's tent. In their hands they hold little bars, cylinders made of baked clay. Taylor is disappointed. He had expected more. As he carefully cleans his finds he recognises that the clay rolls are covered over and over with inscriptions—cuneiform writing! He understands none of it but he is highly delighted. The cylinders, carefully packed, are despatched to London. The scholars on Thames-side are however not impressed—and small wonder. These were the years when the experts were looking to North Mesopotamia, where, under their fascinated gaze, the emergence from the hills of Nineveh and Khorsabad on the upper Tigris of the palaces and colossal reliefs of the Assyrians, as well as thousands of clay tablets and statues, was enough to put everything else in the shade. What significance compared with them had the little clay cylinders from Tell al Muqayyar? For two years more Taylor hopefully continued his search. But there were no further results from Tell al Muqayyar and the expedition was abandoned.

It was seventy-five years later before the world learned what priceless treasures were still lying under that ancient mound.

As far as the experts were concerned Tell al Muqayyar was once more forgotten. But it was by no means neglected. No sooner had Taylor left than hordes of other visitors arrived. The broken walls and above all the top tier of the mound, which Taylor's gangs had shattered, provided a welcome and inexhaustible supply of inexpensive building material for the Arabs who over the years came from far and near and departed with as many bricks as their pack-mules could carry. These bricks, fashioned by men's hands thousands of years before, still bore plainly the names of Ur-Nammu, the first great builder, and of Nabonidus, the Babylonian conqueror who restored the staged tower which they called the Ziggurat. Sandstorms, rain, wind and the heat of the sun have all added their quota to the process of destruction.

During the First World War when British troops on the march to Bagdad in 1915 camped near this ancient structure they found that its former appearance had been completely altered. It had become so flat due to dilapidation and theft in the intervening years since 1854 that one of the soldiers was able to indulge in a piece of daredevilry. The step-formation of the tower which had previously been so clearly marked had disappeared so completely that he was able to ride his mule right to the summit of the mound.

By a lucky chance there was an expert among the officers of the party, R. Campbell Thompson, of the Intelligence Staff of the army in Mesopotamia. In peace time he had been an assistant in the British Museum. Thompson rummaged with an expert eye through the huge heap of bricks and was shocked at the deterioration of the material. Examination of the terrain led him to suppose that there were further areas worth investigating in the neighbourhood of the Tell, ruins of settlements which lay buried under the sand. Thompson recorded all this with great care and sent an urgent message to London. This prompted them to blow the dust off the insignificant looking little clay cylinders which had almost been forgotten and to look at them again with greater attention. The inscriptions on them were then found to contain some extremely important information as well as a curious story.

Almost 2,500 years before Taylor someone else had been searching and rummaging on the same spot with the same concern—Nabonidus, king of Babylon in the 6th century B.C., venerator of the past, man of renown, ruler of a mighty kingdom and archaeologist rolled into one. In his day he established that "the Ziggurat was now old". But his tactics were different from Taylor's. "I restored this Ziggurat to its former state with mortar and baked bricks." When the weakened structure of the staged tower had been restored he had caused the name of the first builder, which he had discovered, to be cut out on these little clay cylinders. His name, as the Babylonian had been able to decipher from a damaged inscription, had been King Ur-Nammu. Ur-Nammu? Was the builder of the great staged tower king of the Ur that the Bible mentions? Was he the ruler of Ur of the Chaldees?

It seemed highly probable. The same Biblical name had cropped up several times since then. Ancient records which had been recovered from other sites in Mesopotamia also mentioned Ur. It appeared from these cuneiform writings that it was the capital city of the great Sumerian people. At once the battered remnants of Tell al Muqayyar aroused eager interest. Scholars from the Museum of Pennsylvania University joined the archaeologists from the British Museum in fresh investigations. The staged tower on the lower Euphrates might hold the secret of this unknown Sumerian people—and of the Ur of the Bible. But it was not until 1923 that a joint American and British team of archaeologists could set out. They were spared the tiresome journey on the backs of swaying camels. They went by the Bagdad railway. Their equipment likewise went by train: trucks, rails, picks, spades, baskets.

The archaeologists had enough funds at their disposal to turn up the whole countryside. They begin their carefully planned excavation on a large scale. Since considerable finds might be expected, they reckon on taking several years. In charge of the expedition is Sir Charles Leonard Woolley. The forty-three year old Englishman had already won his spurs on expeditions and digs in Egypt, Nubia and Carchemish on the upper Euphrates. Now this talented and successful man makes Tell al Muqayyar his life's work. Unlike the zealous but unsuspecting Taylor several decades before, his chief aim is not directed to the staged tower at all. He is possessed with a desire above all to investigate these flat mounds which rise all around him out of the vast sandy plain.

Woolley's trained eye had not failed to note their striking configuration. They look like little Table Mountains. Flat on top, they slope downwards in an almost uniform pattern. Similar mounds exist in great numbers, large and small, in the Middle East, on the banks of the great rivers, in the midst of fertile plains, by the wayside on the routes followed by caravans from time immemorial. No one has yet been able to count them. We find them from the delta of the Euphrates and Tigris on the Persian Gulf to the highlands of Asia Minor where the river Halys tumbles into the Black Sea, on the eastern shores of the Mediterranean, in the valleys of the Lebanon, on the Orontes in Syria and in Palestine by the Jordan.

These little eminences are the great quarries for archaeological finds, eagerly sought and often inexhaustible. They are not formed by the hand of Nature, but are artificially created, piled high with the legacy of countless generations before us; vast masses of rubble and rubbish from a bygone age which have accumulated from the remains of huts and houses, town walls, temples or palaces. Each one of these hills took shape gradually in the same way through a period of centuries or even millennia. At some point after men had first settled there the place was destroyed by war or was burned down or was deserted by its inhabitants. Then came the conquerors or new settlers and built upon the selfsame spot. Generation after generation built their settlements and cities, one on top of the other, on the identical site. In the course of time the ruins and rubble of countless dwellings grew, layer by layer, foot by foot, into a sizeable hill. The Arabs of today call such an artificial mound a Tell. The same word was used even in ancient Babylon. Tell means "mound". We come across the word in the Bible in Josh. 11[13]. During the conquest of Canaan, where cities "that stood on their mounds" are spoken of, it is these Tulul, which is the plural of Tell, which are meant. The Arabs make a clear distinction between a Tell and a natural eminence, which they call a Jebel.

Every Tell is at the same time a silent history book. Its strata are for the archaeologist like the leaves of a calendar. Page by page he can make the past come to life again. Every layer, if we read it aright, tells of its own times, its life and customs, the craftsmanship and manners of its people. This skill on the part of excavators in deciphering the message of the strata has reached astonishing heights of achievement.

Stones, hewn or rough, bricks or traces of clay betray the nature of the building. Even decayed and weathered stones or the remains of brick dust can indicate exactly the ground plan of a building. Dark shadows show where once a fireplace radiated its warming glow.

Broken pottery, armour, household utensils and tools which are to be found everywhere among the ruins, afford further help in this detective work on the past. How grateful are the scholars of today that the ancient world knew nothing of municipal cleansing departments! Anything that had become unusable or superfluous was simply thrown out and left to the tender mercies of time and the weather.

Today the different shapes, colours and patterns of pots and vases can be so clearly distinguished that pottery has become archaeology's Number One measurement of time. Single potsherds, sometimes only fragments, make it possible to give a precise dating. As far back as the second millennium B.C. the greatest margin of error in establishing a date in this way is at the outside about fifty years.

Priceless information was lost in the course of the first great excavations of last century because no one paid any attention to these apparently worthless bits of broken pottery. They were thrown aside. The only important things seemed to be great monuments, reliefs, statues or jewels. Much that was of value was thus lost for ever. The activities of

Heinrich Schliemann, the antiquary, are an example of this sort of thing. Fired with ambition he had only one end in view: to find Homer's Troy. He set his gangs of labourers on to digging straight down. Strata, which might have been of great value in establishing dates, were thrown aside as useless rubbish. At length Schliemann unearthed a valuable treasure amid general acclamation. But it was not, as he thought, the treasure of Priam. His find belonged to a period several centuries earlier. Schliemann had missed the reward of his labours, that would have meant so much to him, by digging past it and going far too deep. Being a business man Schliemann was an amateur, a layman. But the professionals were, to begin with, no better. It is only during this century that the archaeologists have been working in accordance with approved methods. Beginning at the top and working down through the Tell they examine every square inch of the ground. Every tiny object, every piece of pottery is scrutinised. First they dig a trench deep into the mound. The different coloured strata lie open like a cut cake and the trained eye of the expert is able at a rough glance to place in their historical perspective whatever ancient human habitations lie embedded there. It was in accordance with this tried method that the Anglo-American expedition started work at Tell al-Muqayyar in 1923.

In early December there arose a cloud of dust over the rubble heap which lay east of the Ziggurat and only a few steps from the broad ramp up which ancient priests in solemn procession had approached the shrine of Nannar the moon-god. Fanned by a light wind it spread across the site until it seemed as if the whole area around the old staged tower was shrouded in fine mist. Powdery sand whirling up from hundreds of spades indicated that the great dig had started.

From the moment when the first spade struck the ground an atmosphere of excitement hovered over every shovelful. Each spadeful was like a journey into an unknown land where no-one knew beforehand what surprises lay ahead. Excitement gripped even Woolley and his companions. Would some important find richly reward them for their toil and sweat upon the hill? Would Ur give up its secrets to them? None of these men could guess that for six long winter seasons, till the spring of 1929, they would be kept in suspense. This large-scale excavation deep in Southern Mesopotamia was to reveal bit by bit those far off days when a new land arose out of the delta of the two great rivers and the first human settlers made their home there. Out of their painstaking research, carrying them back to a time 7,000 years before, events and names recorded in the Bible were more than once to take solid shape.

The first thing they brought to light was a sacred precinct with the remains of five temples, which had once surrounded king Ur-Nammu's Ziggurat in a semi-circle. They were like fortresses, so thick were their walls. The biggest one, which was 100 × 60 yards square, was dedicated to the moon-god. Another temple was in honour of Nin-Gal, goddess of the moon and wife of Nannar. Every temple had an inner court surrounded by a series of rooms. The old fountains were still standing, with long water troughs coated with bitumen. Deep grooves made with knives on the great brick tables showed where the sacrificial animals had been dissected. They were cooked as a common sacrificial meal on the hearths of the temple kitchens. Even the ovens for baking bread were there. "After 3,800 years," noted Woolley in his diary, "we were able to light the fire again and put into commission once more the oldest kitchen in the world."

Nowadays churches, law courts, tax offices and factories are quite separate establishments. It was otherwise in Ur. The sacred area, the Temple precinct, was not reserved exclusively for the worship of the gods. The priests had many other things to do besides their holy office. As well as receiving the sacrifices they collected the tithes and the taxes. That did not take place however without written confirmation. Every payment was noted on a little clay tablet—probably the first tax receipts ever issued. The amounts received were entered by scribes in weekly, monthly and yearly totals.

Minted currency was as yet unknown. Taxes were paid in kind: every inhabitant of Ur paid in his own coin. Oil, cereals, fruit, wool and cattle made their way into vast warehouses, perishable articles went to the temple shops. Many goods were manufactured in factories owned by the temple, for example in the spinning-mills which the priests managed. One workshop produced twelve different kinds of fashionable clothing. Tablets found in this place gave the names of the mill-girls and their quota of rations. Even the weight of the wool given to each worker and the number of garments made from it were meticulously recorded. In one of the legal buildings they found copies of the sentences carefully stacked exactly as they are in the administrative offices of modern law courts.

For three winter seasons the Anglo-American expedition worked on at the site of ancient Ur, and still this extraordinary museum of man's early history had not yielded up all its secrets. Outside the temple area the excavators had a further unprecedented surprise.

South of the staged tower, as they were clearing away a series of mounds, there suddenly emerged from the rubble solid structures: row upon row of walls and façades one after the other. As the sand was cleared away it revealed a complete checkerboard of dwelling-houses whose ruins were in places still 10 feet high. Between them ran little alleyways. Here and there open squares broke the line of the streets.

Several weeks of hard work were necessary and endless loads of rubble had to be removed before the diggers were faced with an unforgettable sight.

Under the red slopes of Tell al-Muqayyar lay a whole city, bathed in the bright sunshine, awakened from its long sleep after many thousand years by the patient burrowing of the archaeologists. Woolley and his companions were beside themselves with joy. For before them lay Ur, the "Ur of the Chaldees" to which the Bible refers.

And how well its citizens lived, and in what spacious homes! No other Mesopotamian city has revealed such handsome and comfortable houses.

Compared with them the dwelling-houses which have been preserved in Babylon are modest, in fact miserable. Professor Koldewey, during German excavations there at the beginning of this century, found nothing but simple mud brick erections, one story high with three or four rooms surrounding an open courtyard. That was how people lived about 600 B.C. in the much admired and extolled metropolis of Nebuchadnezzar the Great of Babylon. But 1,500 years before that the citizens of Ur were living in large two-storied villas with thirteen or fourteen rooms. The lower floor was solidly built of burnt brick, the upper floor of mud brick. The walls were neatly coated with plaster and whitewashed.

A visitor would pass through the door into a small entrance hall where there was a basin to wash the dust off hands and feet. He then continued into the inner court, which was laid out in attractive paving. Round it were grouped the reception room, the kitchen, living rooms and private rooms and the domestic chapel. Up a stone staircase, which concealed a lavatory, he would reach a gallery from which branched off the rooms belonging to members of the family and the guest rooms.

From beneath the debris of brick and plaster there emerged into the light of day all the things that these patrician houses had contained in the way of domestic appliances for ordinary use. Countless sherds of pots, jugs, vases and small clay tablets covered with writing combined to form a mosaic from which piece by piece a picture of everyday life in Ur could be reconstructed. Ur of the Chaldees was a powerful, prosperous, colourful and busy capital city at the beginning of the second millennium B.C.

One idea was very much in Woolley's mind. Abraham is said to have come from Ur of the Chaldees—he must therefore have been born in one of these two-storied patrician houses and must have grown up there. Woolley wandered through these alleyways, past the walls of the great temple, and as he looked up he glimpsed this huge staged tower with its black, red and blue blocks and its fringe of trees. "We must radically alter", he writes enthusiastically, "our view of the Hebrew patriarch when we see that his earlier years were passed in such sophisticated surroundings. He was the citizen of a great city and inherited the traditions of an old and highly organised civilisation. The houses themselves reveal comfort and even luxury. We found copies of the hymns which were used in the services of the temples and together with them mathematical tables. On these tables were anything from plain addition sums to formulae for the extraction of square and cube roots. In other texts the writers had copied out the old building inscriptions to be found in the city and had compiled in this way a short history of the temples."

Abraham—no simple nomad, this Abraham, but son of a great city of the second millennium B.C.

That was a sensational discovery and one difficult to grasp. Newspapers and magazines carried photographs of the crumbling old staged tower and the ruins of the metropolis. They caused a tremendous sensation. People looked with astonishment at a drawing which bore the title: "A House of the time of Abraham". Woolley had had this done by an artist. It is a genuine reconstruction in accordance with the finds. It shows the inner court of a villa-type house; two tall jars stand on a tiled pavement; a wooden balustrade running round the upper story shuts off the rooms from the courtyard. Was the old familiar picture of the patriarch Abraham, as it had been held for generations, which saw him surrounded by his family and his cattle, suddenly to be called in question?

Woolley's idea did not remain unchallenged. Very soon theologians and even archaeologists registered their dissent.

In favour of Woolley's idea were the words of Gen. 11[31]: "And Terah took Abram his son and Lot ... and they went forth ... from Ur of the Chaldees." But there are other references in the Bible which point to somewhere else. When Abraham sends his old servant from Canaan to the city of Nahor, to fetch a wife for his son Isaac, he calls this place Nahor his "country" (Gen. 24[4]), his "father's house" and "the land of my kindred" (Gen. 24[7]). Nahor lay in the north of Mesopotamia. After the conquest of the Promised Land Joshua addressed the people in these words: "Your fathers dwelt on the other side of the flood in old time, even Terah the father of Abraham and the father of Nahor" (Josh. 24[2]). In this case the "flood" means as in other places in the Bible, the Euphrates. The city of Ur was excavated on the right bank of the Euphrates: looked at from Canaan it lay on this side, not on the other side of the "flood". Had Woolley been too hasty in his conclusions? What reliable evidence had the expedition produced? What proof was there that Terah and his son Abraham lived actually in the city of Ur?

"The earlier journey from Ur of the Chaldees to Haran has, apart from the discovery of the city itself, no archaeological foundation," declares Professor W. F. Albright of Johns Hopkins University. This scholar, who has himself conducted successful excavations and is the foremost authority on the archaeology of Palestine and the Middle East, goes further. "The remarkable fact that the Greek translations [of the Bible] nowhere mention Ur but read instead the more natural

'Land [of the Chaldees]' might mean that the removal of Abraham's native place to Ur is possibly secondary and was not generally known in the third century B.C."

Ur emerged from the shadowy past as the capital city of the Sumerians, one of the oldest civilisations in Mesopotamia. As we know, the Sumerians were not Semites like the Hebrews. When the great invasion of Semitic nomads streamed out of the Arabian desert about 2000 B.C. its first encounter in the south was with the extensive plantations of Ur, its houses and its canals. It is possible that some recollection of that great journey through the lands of the "Fertile Crescent", in which Ur was involved, has resulted in its being mentioned in the Bible. Painstaking research, particularly excavations in the last two decades, make it almost certain that Abraham cannot ever have been a citizen of the Sumerian metropolis. It would conflict with all the descriptions which the Old Testament gives of the kind of life lived by the patriarch: Abraham is a tent dweller, he moves with his flocks from pasture to pasture and from well to well. He does not live like a citizen of a great city—he lives the life of a typical nomad.

As we shall see, it was much farther to the north of the "Fertile Crescent" that the stories of the Biblical patriarchs emerged out of their mystical obscurity on to the plane of history.

CHAPTER 3

DIGGING UP THE FLOOD

The graves of the Sumerian kings—A puzzling layer of clay—Traces of the Flood under desert sands—A catastrophic flood about 4000 B.C.

"And the Lord said unto Noah, Come thou and all thy house into the ark. For yet seven days and I will cause it to rain upon the earth, forty days and forty nights: and every living substance that I have made will I destroy from off the face of the earth.

"And it came to pass after seven days that the waters of the flood were upon the earth" (Gen. 7$^{1, 4, 10}$).

WHEN we hear the word Flood, almost immediately we think of the Bible and the story of Noah's Ark. This wonderful Old Testament story has travelled round the world with Christianity. But although this is the best known tradition of the Flood it is by no means the only one. Among people of all races there is a variety of traditions of a gigantic and catastrophic Flood. The Greeks told the Flood story and connected it with Deucalion: long before Columbus many stories told among the natives of the continent of America kept the memory of a great Flood alive: in Australia, India, Polynesia, Tibet, Kashmir and Lithuania tales of a Flood have been handed down from generation to generation up to the present day. Are they all fairy tales and legends, are they all inventions?

It is highly probable that they all reflect the same world wide catastrophe. This frightful occurrence must, however, have taken place at a time when there were human beings on earth who could experience it, survive it, and then pass on an account of it. Geologists thought that they could solve this ancient mystery by pointing to the warm periods in the earth's history, between the Ice Ages. They suggested that when the huge ice-caps covering the continents, some of them many thousand feet high, gradually began to melt, the level of the sea rose to four times its normal height all over the world. This great additional volume of water altered land contours, flooded low lying coastal areas and plains, and annihilated their population, their animals, and their vegetation. But all these attempts at explanation ended in speculation and theory. Possible hypotheses satisfy the historian least of all. He constantly demands unambiguous factual evidence. But there was none: no scientist, whatever his line, could produce any. Actually it was by a coincidence—during research into something quite different—that

43

unmistakable evidence of the Flood appeared, as it were, of its own accord. And that happened at a place we have already got to know: at the excavations at Ur.

For six years American and British archaeologists had been examining the ground at Tel al-Muqayyar, which by that time looked like one vast building site. When the Bagdad train stopped there for a moment, travellers looked with amazement at the soaring sandhills which had resulted from the diggings. Waggon loads of soil were removed, carefully searched, and put through the riddle. Rubbish thousands of years old was treated like precious cargo. Perseverance, conscientiousness, and painstaking effort had in six years yielded a handsome dividend. The Sumerian temples with their warehouses, workshops and law courts and the villa-type dwelling houses were followed, between 1926 and 1928, by discoveries of such magnificence and splendour that everything else so far paled into insignificance.

"The graves of the kings of Ur"—so Woolley, in the exuberance of his delight at discovering them, had dubbed the tombs of Sumerian nobles whose truly regal splendour had been exposed when the spades of the archaeologists attacked a 50 foot mound south of the temple and found a long row of superimposed graves. The stone vaults were veritable treasure chests, for they were filled with all the costly things that Ur in its heyday possessed. Golden drinking cups and goblets, wonderfully shaped jugs and vases, bronze tableware, mother of pearl mosaics, lapis lazuli and silver surrounded these bodies which had mouldered into dust. Harps and lyres rested against the walls. A young man, "Hero of the land of God" as an inscription described him, wore a golden helmet. A golden comb decorated with blossom in lapis lazuli adorned the hair of the beautiful Sumerian "Lady Puabi". Even the famous tombs of Nofretete and Tutankhamun contained no more beautiful objects. "The graves of the kings of Ur" are moreover 1,000 years older at least.

The graves of the kings had as well as these precious contents another more grisly and depressing experience in store for us, enough to send a slight shiver down the spine. In the vaults were found teams of oxen with the skeletons still in harness and each of the great waggons was laden with artistic household furniture. The whole retinue had clearly accompanied the noblemen in death, as could be gathered from the richly clad and ornamented skeletons with which they were surrounded. The tomb of the beautiful Puabi had twenty such skeletons, other vaults had as many as seventy.

What can have happened here so long ago? There was not the slightest indication that they were victims of a violent death. In solemn procession, it would seem, the attendants with the ox-drawn treasure-waggons accompanied the body to the tomb. And while the grave was being sealed outside they composed their dead master for his last rest within. Then they took some drug, gathered round him for the last time and died of their own free will—in order to be able to serve him in his future existence.

For two centuries the citizens of Ur had buried their eminent men in these tombs. When they came to open the lowest and last tomb the archaeologists of the 20th century A.D. found themselves transported into the world of 2800 B.C.

As the summer of 1929 approached the sixth season of digging at Tell al-Muqayyar was drawing to a close. Woolley had put his native diggers once more on to the hill of "the graves of the kings". It left him no peace. He wanted to be certain whether the ground under the deepest royal grave had fresh discoveries in store for the next season's excavation.

After the foundations of the tomb had been removed, a few hundred thrusts of the spade made it quite plain that further layers of rubble lay below. How far into the past could these silent chronometers take them?

When had the very first human settlement arisen on virgin soil under this mound? Woolley had to know. To make certain he very slowly and carefully sank shafts and stood over them to examine the soil which came up from the underlying strata. "Almost at once," he wrote later in his diary, "discoveries were made which confirmed our suspicions. Directly under the floor of one of the tombs of the kings we found in a layer of charred wood ash numerous clay tablets, which were covered with characters of a much older type than the inscriptions on the graves. Judging by the nature of the writing the tablets could be assigned to about 3000 B.C. They were therefore two or three centuries earlier than the tombs."

FIG. 3.—Traces of flood-clay about 4000 B.C.

(a) River bed (Euphrates).
(b) Layer of flood-clay.
(c) Hills which projected above the flood.

The shafts went deeper and deeper. New strata with fragments of jars, pots and bowls kept coming up. The experts noticed that the pottery remained surprisingly enough unchanged. It looked exactly like what had been found in the graves of the kings. Therefore it seemed as if for centuries Sumerian civilisation had undergone no radical change. They must, according to this conclusion, have reached a high level of development astonishingly early.

When after several days some of Woolley's workmen called out to him "We are on ground level" he let himself down on to the floor of the shaft to satisfy himself. Traces of any kind of settlement did in fact abruptly break off in the shaft. The last fragments of household utensils lay on the smooth flat surface of the base of the pit. Here and there were charred remains. Woolley's first thought was: "This is it at last." He carefully prodded the ground on the floor of the shaft and stopped short: it was clay, pure clay of a kind that could only have been deposited by water! Clay in a place like that? Woolley tried to find an explanation: it must be the accumulated silt of the Euphrates in bygone days. This stratum must have come into existence when the great river thrust its delta far out into the Persian Gulf, just as it still does, creating new land out of the sea at the river mouth at the rate of 75 feet a year. When Ur was in its heyday, the Euphrates flowed so close to it that the great staged tower was reflected in its waters and the Gulf was visible from the temple on its summit. The first buildings must therefore have sprung up on the mud flats of the delta.

Measurements of the adjacent area and more careful calculations brought Woolley eventually however to quite a different conclusion.

"I saw that we were much too high up. It was most unlikely that the island on which the first settlement was built stood up so far out of the marsh."

Fig. 4—Pit showing flood-stratum at Ur.

1. Graves of the kings.   2. Sherds and vessels.
3. Band of clay (10 feet).   4. Antediluvian vessels.

The foot of the shaft, where the layer of clay began, was several yards above the river level. It could not therefore be river deposit. What was the meaning then of this remarkable stratum? Where did it come from? None of his associates could give him a satisfactory answer. They decided to dig on and make the shaft deeper. Woolley gazed intently as once more basket after basket came out of the trench and their contents were examined. Deeper and deeper went the spades into the ground, 3 feet, 6 feet—still pure clay. Suddenly at nearly 10 feet the layer of clay stopped as abruptly as it had started. What would come now?

The next baskets that came to the surface gave an answer that none of the expedition would have dreamt of. They could hardly believe their eyes. They had expected pure virgin soil. But what now emerged into the glaring sunshine was rubble and more rubble, ancient rubbish and countless potsherds. Under this clay deposit almost 10 feet thick they had struck fresh evidence of human habitation. The appearance and quality of the pottery had noticeably altered. Above the clay-stratum were jars and bowls which had obviously been turned on the potter's wheel, here on the contrary they were hand-made. No matter how carefully they sifted the contents of the baskets, amid increasing excitement, metal remains were nowhere to be found, the primitive implement that did emerge was made of hewn flint. It must belong to the Stone Age!

That day a telegram from Mesopotamia flashed what was perhaps the most extraordinary message that had ever stirred men's imaginations "We have found the Flood". The incredible discovery at Ur made headline news in the United States and in Britain.

The Flood—that was the only possible explanation of this great clay deposit beneath the hill at Ur, which quite clearly separated two epochs of settlement. The sea had left its unmistakable traces in the shape of remains of little marine organisms embedded in the clay. Woolley had to confirm his conclusions without delay: a chance coincidence—although the odds were against it—might conceivably have been making fools of them. Three hundred yards from the first shaft he sank a second one.

The spades produced the same result: sherds—clay—fragments of hand-made pottery.

Finally to remove all doubt, Woolley made them dig a shaft through the rubble where the old settlement lay on a natural hill, that is to say, on a considerably higher level than the stratum of clay.

Just at about the same level as in the two other shafts the sherds of wheel-turned vessels stopped suddenly. Immediately beneath them came hand-made clay pots. It was exactly as Woolley had supposed and expected. Naturally the intermediate layer of clay was missing. "About sixteen feet below a brick pavement," noted Woolley, "which we could with reasonable certainty date about 2700 B.C. we were among the ruins of that Ur which had existed before the Flood."

How far did the layer of clay extend? What area was affected by the disaster? A proper hunt now started for traces of the Flood in other parts of Mesopotamia. Other archaeologists discovered a further important check-point near Kish, south-east of Babylon, where the Euphrates and the Tigris flow in a great bend towards each other. There they found a similar band of clay, but only 18 inches thick. Gradually by a variety of tests the limits of the Flood waters could be established. According to Woolley the disaster engulfed an area north-west of the Persian Gulf amounting to 400 miles long and 100 miles wide, looking at the map we should call it today "a local occurrence"—for the inhabitants of the river plains it was however in those days their whole world.

FIG. 5.—The extent of the Flood in Mesopotamia.

After endless enquiry and attempts at some explanation, without achieving any concrete results, any hope of solving the great riddle of the Flood had long since been given up. It seemed to lie in a dark and distant region of time which we could never hope to penetrate. Now Woolley and his associates had through their tireless and patient efforts made a discovery which shattered even the experts: a vast catastrophic inundation, resembling the Biblical Flood which had regularly been described by sceptics as either a fairy tale or a legend, had not only taken place but was moreover an event within the compass of history.

At the foot of the old staged tower of the Sumerians, at Ur on the lower Euphrates, anyone could climb down a ladder into a narrow shaft and see and touch the remains of a gigantic and catastrophic Flood which had deposited a layer of clay almost 10 feet thick. Reckoning by the age of the strata containing traces of human habitation, and in this respect they are as reliable as a calendar, it could also be ascertained when the great Flood took place. It happened about 4000 B.C.

Clearly people in Woolley's day tended to give dramatic interpretations to the results of excavations more readily than they do nowadays, for shortly after Woolley, another excavator, Stephen Langdon, claimed, "with strong support from the press", that he in turn had found in Kish, that is to say, in Babylon, "material traces of the Flood". It was Langdon's, but also Woolley's bad luck that the datings of these two flood catastrophes did not agree. Which flood was the right one, the genuine, Biblical Flood? Woolley protested vigorously against Langdon's claim to have discovered it and a vehement argument followed which, however, did not in the least disturb a number of writers, among them, for example, Sir Charles Marston, who asserted that both Woolley and Langdon had discovered "simultaneously the deposits left by the Flood".

Since then the excitement has somewhat subsided and given place to more sober consideration. The following four main points emerge from the pronouncements of the experts:-

Of Woolley's five shafts only two revealed any deposits at all from an inundation.

The inundation in Ur did not lead to the abandonment of the settlement. In fact, it did not even lead to an interruption in the occupation.

Traces of inundation were indeed discovered in other places in Mesopotamia, in Kish, as well as in Fara (Shuruppak), Nineveh and Uruk (Erech) but on the other hand, they are not found where they ought to be present if the whole of Mesopotamia was flooded.

The traces left by the inundations at the various excavation sites also vary, in some cases quite appreciably, in their chronological sequence. They belong to quite different periods; centuries separate them.

In other words, Woolley's "Flood" was obviously not of sufficient magnitude for the Biblical "Flood", unless we assume that one of the flood catastrophes shown by archaeology to have occurred in Mesopotamia had nevertheless had such a lasting effect on the inhabitants of those days that—with a considerable amount of exaggeration—the tradition of a catastrophe to humanity could arise from it. Naturally, however, this is mere supposition and the Biblical Flood, at any rate a flood of the unimaginable extent described in the Bible, still remains "archaeologically not demonstrated". The question consequently remains: do all the various "flood" reports, which occur in practically all parts of the world, describe merely mankind's earliest experience of the phenomenon "flood catastrophe" and were all the traditional, relevant accounts of floods simply compressed or exaggerated to form a number of stories of the "great flood of all floods" or are they the vestiges of much older traditions going back hundreds of years *before* Woolley's flood at Ur, to the time of the melting of the gigantic glaciers of the Ice Age when the ocean rose some two hundred metres and the limits of today's land and sea were formed? That event had world-wide consequences which could explain why the traditions of a flood have persisted among so many peoples. The following pages will discuss one of the flood traditions, parallel to that in the Bible, although it derives to a large extent also from "Biblical lands".

CHAPTER 4

A FLOOD-STORY FROM OLD BABYLONIA

The Epic of Gilgamesh and the Bible—Twelve clay tablets from Nineveh—An ancient epic from the Library of Ashurbanipal—Utnapishtim, a Sumerian Noah?—The secret of Mt. Ararat—A gigantic ship in a museum of ice—Expeditions in quest of the Ark.

"And God said unto Noah . . . Make thee an ark of gopherwood: rooms shalt thou make in the ark and shalt pitch it within and without with pitch" (Gen. 6^{13-14}).

ABOUT the turn of the century, long before Woolley discovered Ur, another find had aroused great interest and given rise to lively discussions about the nature of Holy Scripture.

From the dim recesses of the Ancient East an old mysterious story came to light: a heroic epic, of 300 quatrains, inscribed on twelve large clay tablets, which told of the wonderful experiences of the legendary king Gilgamesh.

The text was astonishing: Gilgamesh told a tale exactly like the Bible—of a man who was said to have lived before and after a mighty and disastrous Flood.

Where did this splendid and remarkable epic come from?

During excavations in the fifties of last century British archaeologists had found these twelve clay tablets, together with about 20,000 others, all in a good state of preservation, among the ruins of the library at Nineveh, which was reckoned to be the most famous in the ancient world. King Ashurbanipal had it built in the 7th century B.C. high above the banks of the Tigris in old Nineveh. Today on the other side of the river the oil-derricks of Mosul tower into the sky.

A priceless treasure in packing cases started out on its long journey from Nineveh to the British Museum.

But it was not for several decades that the true value of these texts was revealed when they could finally be deciphered. At the time there was no one in the world who could read them. Despite every effort the tablets held their peace. Shortly before 1900 in the modest laboratories of the British Museum the old texts began, after an interval of twenty-five centuries, to unfold anew one of the finest narratives of the Ancient East. Assyriologists heard for the first time the Epic of Gilgamesh. It is written in Akkadian, the language of the court and of diplomacy in the time of king Ashurbanipal. Its form, however, dates not from the time when it was placed in the library at Nineveh but from 1,000 years earlier. It goes back as far as Hammurabi, the great king of Babylon, for soon a second copy was discovered in his capital on the Euphrates. Further finds confirmed the view that the Gilgamesh Epic belonged to the rich heritage of all the great nations of the Ancient East. Hittites and Egyptians translated it into their own tongues, and cuneiform tablets discovered by the Nile still show clearly the marks in red ink opposite those parts which the Egyptian scribes found difficulty in translating.

At last a little clay fragment gave the clue to the origin of the Epic of Gilgamesh. The world owes its original composition to the Sumerians, the people whose capital stood on the site of Ur.

Gilgamesh, as the cuneiform writing on the eleventh tablet from the library at Nineveh tells us, decided to ensure his immortality and set out on a long adventurous journey to find his ancestor Utnapishtim, from whom he hoped to learn the secret of everlasting life which the gods had bestowed upon him. When he reached the island on which Utnapishtim lived, Gilgamesh asked of him the "Secret of Life". Utnapishtim related that he had once lived in Shuruppak and had been a true worshipper of the god Ea. When the gods decided to destroy mankind by a Flood Ea warned his devotee Utnapishtim and issued this command: "O man of Shuruppak, son of Ubar-Tutu, tear down thy house, build a ship; abandon wealth, seek after life; scorn possessions, save thy life. Bring up the seed of all kinds of living things into the ship: the ship which thou shalt build. Let its dimensions be well measured."

We all know the wonderful story which follows. For what the Sumerian Utnapishtim is said to have experienced, the Bible tells us about Noah.

> "And God said unto Noah ... Make thee an ark of gopher wood.... And of every living thing of all flesh, two of every sort shalt thou bring into the ark, to keep them alive with thee; they shall be male and female" (Gen. 6^{13ff}).

To make the comparison easier let us set side by side what Utnapishtim says of his great experience and what the Bible tells us of Noah and the Flood.

In accordance with the command of the god Ea, Utnapishtim builds the ship and says:

On the fifth day I decided upon its plan.	The length of the ark shall be 300 cubits the breadth of it 50 cubits and the height of it thirty cubits (Gen.6^{15}).
The floor was 200 ft. square.	

The walls were 200 ft. high.

I gave it six stories and divided the breadth seven times.	With lower, second, and third stories shalt thou make it (Gen. 6¹⁶).

With lower, second, and third stories shalt thou make it (Gen. 6^{16}).

Its interior I divided into nine.

... Rooms shalt thou make in the ark (Gen. 6^{14}),

6 sar of bitumen I poured into the kiln.

... and shalt pitch it within and without with pitch (Gen. 6^{14}).

When Utnapishtim had finished building his ship he arranged a sumptuous banquet. He provided venison and mutton for those who had helped with the work of building and dispensed "cider, beer, oil and wine to the people as if it were running water". Then he continues:

All that I had I loaded, of the seed of all living things.

And Noah went in, and his sons, and his wife, and his sons' wives, into the ark because of the waters of the flood.

Of clean beasts, and of beasts that are not clean, and of fowls, and of everything that creepeth upon the earth,

I brought into the ship my whole family and kinsfolk.

There went in two and two unto Noah into the ark, the male and the female, as God had commanded Noah (Gen. 7$^{7\text{-}9}$).

The cattle of the field, the beasts of the field, all craftsmen—I made them go up into it.

I went into the ship and closed my door.

And the Lord shut him in (Gen. 7^{16}).

As soon as a gleam of dawn shone in the sky, came a black cloud from the foundation of heaven. Inside it Adad thundered.

And it came to pass, after seven days, that the waters of the flood were upon the earth.
... the same day were all the fountains of the great deep broken up, and the windows of heaven were opened (Gen. 7$^{10\text{-}11}$).

Adad's rage reached to the
heavens: turning all light to darkness.

The gods of Mesopotamia are terrified by the Flood and flee to the
upper reaches of heaven where the god Anu has his abode. Before they
enter "they crouch and cower like dogs". They are grieved and shattered by what is happening and tearfully and in utter dejection lodge
their complaint.

A description worthy of Homer!

But the Flood rages on unceasing, as Gilgamesh learns:

Six days and nights	And the flood was forty days upon the earth and the waters increased. And the waters prevailed exceedingly upon the earth,
Raged the wind, the flood, the cyclone devastated the land.	and all the high hills, that were under the whole heaven, were covered (Gen. 7$^{17\text{-}19}$).
When the seventh day came, the cyclone, the flood, the battle was over,	And God remembered Noah ... and God made a wind to pass over the earth and the waters assuaged (Gen. 8^1).
Which had battled like an army. The sea became calm, the cyclone died away, the flood ceased.	The fountains of the deep and the windows of heaven were stopped; and the rain from heaven was restrained. And the waters returned from off the earth continually, and after the end of the hundred and fifty days the waters were abated (Gen. 8$^{2,\,3}$).
And all mankind had turned to clay. The ground was flat like a roof.	And all flesh died that moved upon the earth ... and every man (Gen. 7^{21}).

"And all mankind had turned to clay." Utnapishtim, the Sumerian
Noah, is recording what he himself claimed to have lived through.
Babylonians, Assyrians, Hittites and Egyptians who translated or read
aloud or narrated these words had no more notion that they were
describing something that actually happened, than did the modern

Assyriologists who painfully deciphered them from the cuneiform tablets.

Today we know that line 134 on the eleventh tablet of the Epic of Gilgamesh must depend on an eye-witness account. Only someone who had himself seen the desolation caused by the catastrophe, could have described it with such striking force.

The great layer of mud, which covered every living thing like a shroud and levelled the ground until it was as "flat as a roof", must have been seen with his own eyes by someone who had had a marvellous escape. The exact description of the great storm argues for this assumption. Utnapishtim expressly mentions a southern gale, which corresponds closely with the geographical situation. The Persian Gulf, whose waters were flung over the flat country by the gale, lies south of the estuary of the Tigris and Euphrates. To the last detail the weather conditions which he describes are characteristic of an unusual atmospheric disturbance. The appearance of black clouds and a roaring noise—sudden darkness in broad daylight—the howling of the southern gale as it drives the water in front of it. Any meteorologist recognises at once that this is a description of a cyclone. Modern weather experts recognise that, in tropical regions, coastal areas, islands, but above all alluvial river flats are subject to a spiral type of tidal wave which leaves devastation and destruction in its wake, and which is often caused by cyclones, accompanied by earthquakes and torrential rain.

All along the coast of Florida, in the Gulf of Mexico, and on the Pacific there is today an up-to-date alarm system with all the latest equipment. But for southern Mesopotamia in 4000 B.C. even a modern alarm system would not have been of much use. Sometimes cyclones produce an effect which takes the shape of the Flood. There is an example in recent times.

In 1876 a cyclone of this nature, accompanied by tremendous thunderstorms, swept across the Bay of Bengal and headed for the coast at the mouth of the Ganges. Up to 200 miles from its centre ships at sea had their masts splintered. It was ebb-tide along the coast. The receding water was seized by the broad high sweep of the cyclone and a gigantic tidal wave reared itself up. It burst into the Ganges area and sea water 50 feet high swept inland—141 square miles were buried and 215,100 people died.

Utnapishtim tells a horrified Gilgamesh what happened when the disaster was over:

I opened the window and the light fell on my face.	And it came to pass at the end of forty days, that Noah opened the window of the ark which he had made (Gen. 8[6]).

The ship lay upon Mt. Nisir.	And the ark rested in the seventh month, on the seventeenth day of the month, upon the mountains of Ararat (Gen. 8⁴).

Mount Nisir held the ship and allowed it not to move.

Old Babylonian cuneiform texts describe with care where Mt. Nisir is to be found. It lies between the Tigris and the lower reaches of the river Zab, where the wild and rugged mountain ranges of Kurdistan rise sharply from the flat country bordering the Tigris. The alleged resting place corresponds perfectly with the last lap of the great catastrophe which burst inland from the south. We are told that Utnapishtim's home was in Shuruppak. It lay near the present day Fara in the middle of the flat fenland where Tigris and Euphrates part company. A tidal wave from the Persian Gulf must have carried a ship from here right to the Kurdistan mountains.

Despite the precise descriptions in the Epic of Gilgamesh, Mt. Nisir has never tempted the curious to search for the remains of this giant ship. Instead, Mt. Ararat, which belongs to the Biblical tradition, has been the goal chosen by a series of expeditions.

FIG. 6.—Mt. Ararat—where three countries meet: Turkey, Iran and U.S.S.R.

Mt. Ararat lies in Eastern Turkey, near the borders of Russia and Iran. Its snow capped summit is over 16,000 feet high.

Last century, many years before any archaeologist turned a spadeful of Mesopotamian soil, the first expeditions were making their way to Mt. Ararat. A shepherd's story had started them off.

At the foot of Ararat lies the little Armenian village of Bayzit, whose inhabitants have for generations recounted the remarkable experience of a mountain shepherd who was said to have seen one day on Ararat a great wooden ship. A report from a Turkish expedition in 1833 seemed to confirm the shepherd's story since it mentioned a wooden prow of a ship which in the summer season stuck out of the south glacier.

The next person to claim to have seen it was Dr. Nouri, Archdeacon of Jerusalem and Babylon. This agile ecclesiastical dignitary undertook a journey in 1892 to discover the sources of the Euphrates. On his return he told of the wreckage of a ship in the eternal ice: "The interior was full of snow: the outer wall was of a dark red colour." In the First World War a Russian flying officer, by name Roskowitzki, announced that he had spotted from his plane "the remains of wreckage of a fair-sized ship" on the south flank of Ararat. Although it was the middle of the war, Czar Nicholas II despatched a search party without delay. It is supposed not only to have seen the ship but even to have photographed it. All proof of this however perished, presumably in the Revolution.

From the Second World War there are likewise several cases of aerial observation. They come from a Russian pilot and four American fliers.

These latter reports brought into the field the American historian and missionary Dr. Aaron Smith of Greensborough, an expert on the Flood. As a result of years of labour he has collected a complete history of the literature on Noah's Ark. There are 80,000 works in seventy-two languages about the Flood, of which 70,000 mention the legendary wreckage of the Ark.

In 1951 Dr. Smith spent twelve days with forty companions to no purpose on the ice-cap of Ararat. "Although we found no trace of Noah's Ark," he declared later, "my confidence in the Biblical description of the Flood is no whit the less. We shall go back."

Encouraged by Dr. Smith the young French Greenland explorer Jean de Riquer climbed the volcanic peak in 1952. He too came back without accomplishing anything. Despite this, fresh expeditions are always getting ready for a further attempt on Mt. Ararat.

In 1955, in the early morning of July 6th, Fernand Navarra from France, searching for the most famous ship in history, succeeded to his great surprise in salvaging three fragments of a wooden beam embedded in solid ice on top of the mountain. The timber was at least 5,000 years old, although whether this was actually a relic of Noah's Ark it is of course impossible to say.

No tradition of the early days of Mesopotamia is in such close agreement with the Bible as the Flood story in the Epic of Gilgamesh. In some places we find almost verbal correspondence. Yet there is a significant and essential difference. The familiar story in Genesis knows of one God only. The oddly amusing and primitive conception has disappeared of a heaven overcrowded with gods, many of whom bear all too human characteristics.

In all the flood traditions which have been mentioned, problems arise from mankind's unfortunate tendency to believe what it wants to believe. This is shown especially in the search for the ark on the 5,165 metre-high Ağri Daği which lies on the frontier between Turkey and the Soviet Union. According to the account in the Bible (Gen. 8⁴), that is where Noah's ark is supposed to have landed. When considered closely, however, the matter is by no means so unambiguous, for the Bible refers only to the "mountains of Ararat". Ararat is simply the name given to the old land of Urartu, which corresponds, roughly speaking, to present day Armenia. The Gilgamesh epic adds the "mountain Nisir" as the place where the ark came to rest, while Berossus, a Babylonian priest who lived in Hellenic times and who in his work *Babylonian Antiquities* also relates the Babylonian flood story, introduces a "Kordye mountain range" into the debate. Another claim for the honour of being regarded as the landing place of the ark is made for a mountain in Phrygia in Asia Minor, not far from the town of Kelainai, the centre of many legends in olden days, while the Mahometans prefer to situate the ark's landing place a good distance south of Ağri Daği on the mountain of Judi, which offers a view far across the Mesopotamian plain. One way and another there are in any case too many mountains figuring as landing places for the ark.

What has been done and is still being done on the mountain where according to Christian tradition the ark came to rest is, however, not yet sufficiently documented. André Parrot is of the opinion that silence is the only appropriate attitude to be adopted by scientific journals towards the periodically recurring attempts, usually accompanied by lively activity in the daily press, to discover remains of the Biblical ark high up amid the snow and ice. In fact, not a single specialist in archaeology has so far taken part in any of the attempts to recover the ark. The consequence is that we have no reliable account of methods used in the searches or of the circumstances in which finds have been made, not to mention photographic evidence providing proof of claims that have been put forward. This is not because professional archaeologists consider themselves too grand to undertake the strenuous exertions involved in climbing up Mount Ararat (or rather Ağri Daği), but because systematic archaeological investigations, particularly in such difficult terrain, involve enormous expenditure.

The necessary finance is granted, however, only when discoveries of great scientific and general interest are to be expected. Such finds are improbable on Mount Ararat, and so we are provisionally obliged to say that ever since the 5165 metre peak has been in existence and men have inhabited the earth, no scientifically recorded inundation in the world has risen high enough to carry up to such an altitude any kind of floating construction of the nature of the ark. The terrain around Mount Ararat during this period has not undergone such spectacular changes that the ark could have been deposited there at a time when perhaps the summit was lower than it is today. From the outset, the search for the ark on Ağri Daği must be considered a failure and as André Parrot has so well expressed it, expeditions with Mount Ararat as their goal have more to do with mountain-climbing than with archaeology.

But does there not exist wood from Ararat "at least five thousand years old"? Certainly wood has been produced for examination which, it is claimed, has come from Ararat, but again there is a difficulty about the dating, which we are told is based on "estimates by a forestry institute in Madrid", while "a laboratory" in Paris is reported to have arrived at 4,484 years as the age of the wood. On the other hand, a "Research Institute in Pre-History" in Bordeaux is said to have been content with vague general statements about the "great age" of the material. Even if these institutes were shown on closer examination to be reputable, however, and their reports proved to be unassailable, we must take into account that the samples extracted by non-specialists and brought long distances to the above mentioned places must have been exposed to a considerable degree to the effects of dirt. This obscures the measurements obtained, so that there can scarcely be any question of the determination of that wood's age which is not open to objection. A subsequent Ararat expedition did not even locate the original spot where the wood had been found. On the other hand, it claimed to have discovered wood elsewhere on Ağri Daği, but its age has been assessed at only something between 1300 and 1700 years. This result coincides very nicely with the conjecture by a number of scholars that as a possible consequence of being traditionally linked with the account of the Flood, Ağri Daği was regarded as "holy" and so already in the early Christian era a few huts for pilgrims or hermits' dwellings may have been built there.

CHAPTER 5

ABRAHAM LIVED IN THE KINGDOM OF MARI

A stone corpse—Lieut. Cabane reports a find—A Syrian Tell has important visitors—King Lamgi-Mari introduces himself—Professor Parrot discovers an unknown empire—A royal palace with 260 apartments and courtyards—23,600 clay tablets have survived for 4,000 years—Desert police report the "Benjamites"—Rebecca's home—A flourishing city—And Nuzi . . .?

"Now the Lord had said unto Abram, Get thee out of thy country, and from thy kindred, and from thy father's house, unto a land that I will show thee" (Gen. 12¹).

THE country of which the Bible is speaking in this case is Haran. Terah, his son Abram, his daughter-in-law Sarai, and his grandson Lot lived there (Gen. 11³¹).

What was actually meant by Haran was until recently quite unknown. We knew nothing of its early history. All the old Babylonian documents are silent about the middle reaches of the Euphrates —Mesopotamia, the land between the rivers—where Haran once stood.

A chance find led to excavations in 1933, which here also gave rise to a great and exciting discovery and added considerably to our knowledge. They brought the Haran of the Bible and the kind of life lived by the patriarchs quite unexpectedly into a historical context.

On the line between Damascus and Mosul, where it cuts the Euphrates, lies the small obscure town of Abu Kemal. Since, as a result of the First World War, Syria was placed under a French mandate, there was a French garrison in the place.

Over the broad Euphrates plain in midsummer 1933 lay a brooding, paralysing heat. Lieut. Cabane, the station-commander, expected, when he was called into the orderly room, that it was merely another of these quarrels among the Arabs that he was supposed to settle. He had had more than enough of that already. But this time the excitement in the office seemed to be about something different. Eventually he managed to extract through the interpreter the following story: These people had been burying one of their relatives. They were digging the grave on a remote hillside, by name Tell Hariri, when out popped a stone corpse!

Perhaps, thought Lieut. Cabane, this might be something that would interest the museum at Aleppo. At any rate it was a pleasant change from the endless monotony of this God-forsaken post.

In the cool of the evening he drove out to Tell Hariri, which lay about 7 miles to the north of Abu Kemal near the Euphrates. The Arabs led him up the slope to the broken statue in a flat earthen trough which had so upset them the day before. Cabane was no expert, but he knew at once that the stone figure must be very old. Next day it was taken by French soldiers to Abu Kemal. The lights were on till long after midnight in the little command-post. Cabane was writing a detailed report on the find to the competent authorities, to Henry Seyrig, Director of Antiquities in Beirut, and to the Museum at Aleppo.

Months went past and nothing happened. The whole thing seemed to be either unimportant or forgotten. Then at the end of November came a telegram from Paris, from the Louvre. Cabane could hardly believe his eyes and read the message again and again. In a few days important visitors from Paris would be arriving: Professor Parrot, the well known archaeologist, accompanied by scientists, architects, assistants and draughtsmen.

On the 14th of December Tell Hariri was buzzing like a bee-hive. The archaeologists had begun their detective-work. First of all the whole mound was carefully measured and photographed in detail. Soundings were taken for echoes, specimens of soil were removed and submitted to expert opinion. December went by and the first weeks of the New Year. The 23rd of January 1934 was the decisive day.

As they were digging carefully through the outer crust of the Tell there appeared out of the rubble a neat little figure which had some writing pricked out on the right shoulder. Everyone bent over it, fascinated. "I am Lamgi-Mari ... king ... of Mari ... the great ... Issakkv ... who worships his statue ... of Ishtar."

Slowly, word by word, this sentence rings in the ears of the silent circle as Professor Parrot translates it from the cuneiform. This is an unforgettable moment for him and his companions. An almost uncanny scene and probably unique in the history of archaeology with its surprises and adventures!

The monarch had solemnly welcomed the strangers from distant Paris and introduced himself to them. It was as if he wanted politely to show them the road into his kingdom of long ago which lay in a deep sleep beneath him, and of whose pomp and power the Parisian scholars had as yet no conception.

Carved in stone, a marvellous piece of sculpture, King Lamgi-Mari stood before Parrot: a commanding broad-shouldered figure upon its base. But the face lacks that incredible arrogance which is so typical of the portraits of other conquerors from the ancient East, the Assyrians, who without exception look fierce and bad-tempered. The king of Mari is smiling. He carries no weapons, his hands are folded in an attitude of worship. His robe, which leaves one shoulder bare, like a toga, is richly decorated with fringes.

Hardly ever has an excavation been so crowned with success from the word "go", and the first groping efforts. Mari, the royal city, must be lying slumbering under this mound.

Scholars had for a long time been familiar with the royal city of Mari which features in many old inscriptions from Babylonia and Assyria. One text maintained that Mari was the tenth city to be founded after the Flood. The great spade-offensive against Tell Hariri began.

With considerable intervals the digging went on from 1933 to 1939. For the greater part of the year the tropical heat made any activity impossible. Only in the cooler months of the rainy season, from the middle of December to the end of March, could anything be done.

The excavations at Tell Hariri brought a wealth of new discoveries to a chapter of the history of the Ancient East which is still unwritten.

No one knew as yet how close a connection the finds at Mari would prove to have with quite familiar passages in the Bible.

Year by year reports of the expedition provided fresh surprises.

In the winter of 1933–34 a temple of Ishtar the goddess of fertility was exposed. Three of Ishtar's royal devotees have immortalised themselves as statues in the shrine which is inlaid with a mosaic of gleaming shells: Lamgi-Mari, Ebin-il, and Idi-Narum.

In the second season of digging the spades came upon the houses of a city. Mari had been found! However great was the satisfaction with their success, far more interest, indeed astonishment was aroused by the walls of a palace which must have been unusually large. Parrot reported: "We have unearthed 69 rooms and courts, and there are still more to come." One thousand six hundred cuneiform tablets, carefully stacked in one of the rooms, contained details of household management.

The record of the third campaign in 1935–36 noted that so far 138 rooms and courtyards had been found but that they had not yet reached the outer walls of the palace. Thirteen thousand clay tablets awaited deciphering. In the fourth winter a temple of the god Dagon was dug up and also a Ziggurat, the typical Mesopotamian staged tower. Two hundred and twenty rooms and courtyards were now visible in the palace and another 8,000 clay tablets had been added to the existing collection.

At last in the fifth season, when a further forty rooms had been cleared of rubble, the palace of the kings of Mari lay in all its vast extent before Parrot and his assistants. This mammoth building of the third millennium B.C. covered almost ten acres. Never before during any excavations had such an enormous building with such vast ramifications come to light.

Columns of lorries had to be commissioned to remove the cuneiform tablets from the palace archives alone. There were almost 24,000 documents. The great find of the tablets at Nineveh was put in the shade, since the famous library of the Assyrian king, Ashurbanipal, amounted to a "mere" 22,000 clay texts.

To get a proper picture of Mari palace aerial photographs were taken. These pictures taken from a low altitude over Tell Hariri gave rise to almost incredulous amazement when they were published in France. This palace at Mari was, around 2000 B.C., one of the greatest sights of the world, the architectural gem of the Ancient East. Travellers came from far and near to see it. "I have seen Mari," wrote an enthusiastic merchant from the Phoenician seaport of Ugarit.

The last king to live there was Zimri-Lim. The armies of the famous Hammurabi of Babylon subjugated the kingdom of Mari on the central reaches of the Euphrates and destroyed its mighty capital about 1700 B.C.

Under the wreckage of roofs and walls were found the fire-pans of the Babylonian warriors, the incendiary squad who set fire to the palace.

But they were not able to destroy it completely. The walls were left standing to a height of 15 feet. "The installations in the palace kitchens and bathrooms," wrote Professor Parrot, "could still be put into commission without the need of any repair, four thousand years after its destruction." In the bathrooms they found the tubs, cake-moulds in the kitchens, even charcoal in the ovens.

The sight of these majestic ruins is an overwhelming experience. A single gate on the north side ensured easier control and better defence. Passing through a medley of courts and passages one reaches the great inner courtyard and broad daylight. This was the centre both of official life and the administration of the kingdom. The monarch received his officials as well as couriers and ambassadors in the neighbouring audience-chamber, large enough to hold hundreds of people. Broad corridors led to the king's private apartments.

One wing of the palace was used exclusively for religious ceremonies. It contained also a throne-room, approached by a marvellous staircase. A long processional way passed through several rooms to the palace chapel in which stood the image of the mother-goddess of fertility. From a vessel in her hands flowed perpetually "the water of everlasting life".

The entire court lived under the king's roof. Ministers, administrators, secretaries and scribes had their own roomy quarters.

There was a Foreign Office and a Board of Trade in the great administrative palace of the kingdom of Mari. More than 100 officials were involved in dealing with the incoming and outgoing mail, which amounted to thousands of tablets alone.

Wonderful great frescoes added a decorative effect to the palace. Even to this day the colours have hardly lost any of their brilliance. They seem to have been laid on only yesterday but in fact they are the oldest paintings in Mesopotamia—1,000 years older than the renowned coloured frescoes in the splendid edifices of the Assyrian rulers at Khorsabad, Nineveh and Nimrud.

The size and grandeur of this unique palace corresponded to the land that was governed from it. Through these many thousands of years the palace archives have preserved the record.

Notices, public papers, decrees, accounts, scratched out on clay by the busy styli of well-paid scribes 4,000 years ago, had to be brought to life again with tireless industry. In Paris, Professor George Dossin, of the University of Liège, and a host of Assyriologists wrestled with the problem of deciphering and translating them. It would be years before all the 23,600 documents were translated and published.

Each of them contains a little piece of the mosaic which makes up the true facts about the kingdom of Mari.

Numerous orders for the construction of canals, locks, dams, and embankments make it plain that the prosperity of the country largely depended on the widespread system of irrigation, which was constantly under the supervision of government engineers, who saw to its care and maintenance.

Two tablets contain a list of 2,000 craftsmen, giving their full names and the names of their guilds.

The news service in Mari functioned so quickly and successfully that it would bear comparison with modern telegraphy. Important

Fig. 7.—This picture from Room 106 in the palace of Mari shows the investiture of Zimri-Lim by the goddess Ishtar.

messages were sent by means of fire signals from the frontier of Babylon right up to present day Turkey in a matter of a few hours, a distance of more than 300 miles.

Mari lay at the intersection of the great caravan route from West to East and North to South. It is not surprising therefore that the traffic in goods, which extended from Cyprus and Crete to Asia Minor and Mesopotamia, necessitated a lively correspondence on clay concerning imports and exports. But the tablets do not merely record everyday matters. They also give an impressive account of religious life, of New Year Festivals in honour of Ishtar, auguries with the entrails of animals, and interpretation of dreams. Twenty-five gods made up the Mari pantheon. A list of sacrificial lambs, which Zimri-Lim presented, refers to these occupants of heaven by name.

From countless individual bits of evidence on these tablets we can form a picture of this masterpiece of organisation and administration which the kingdom of Mari constituted in the 18th century B.C. What is astonishing is that neither in their sculptures nor in their paintings is there any indication of warlike activity.

The inhabitants of Mari were Amorites who had been settled there for a long time, and who preferred peace. Their interests lay in religion and ceremonial, in trade and commerce. Conquest, heroism, and the clash of battle meant little to them. As we can still see from statues and pictures, their faces radiate a cheerful serenity.

That did not mean, however, that they were absolved from the necessity of defending and safeguarding their territory by force of arms. On their frontiers lived tribes of Semitic nomads, who found the lush pastures, market gardens and cornfields of Mari a constant temptation. They were always crossing the border, grazing their cattle over wide stretches of the countryside, and disturbing the population. They had to be watched. Frontier posts were therefore established as a check on this danger, and any incident was immediately reported to Mari.

In Paris the Assyriologists were deciphering a clay tablet from the archives of Mari. They read with astonishment a report from Bannum, an officer of the desert police:

"Say to my lord: This from Bannum, thy servant. Yesterday I left Mari and spent the night at Zuruban. All the Benjamites were sending fire-signals. From Samanum to Ilum-Muluk, from Ilum-Muluk to Mishlan, all the Benjamite villages in the Terqa district replied with fire-signals. I am not yet certain what these signals meant. I am trying to find out. I shall write to my lord whether or not I succeed. The city guards should be strengthened and my lord should not leave the gate."

In this police report from the central reaches of the Euphrates in the 19th century B.C. there appears the name of one of the tribes known to us from the Bible. It literally calls them Benjamites.

There is frequent mention of these Benjamites. They seem to have given the ruler of Mari so many headaches and caused so much trouble that periods of a king's reign were even called after them.

In the Mari dynasties the years of each reign were not numbered but were identified with some notable event, for example the building and consecration of new temples, the erection of great dams to improve irrigation, the strengthening of the banks of the Euphrates or a national census. Three times the chronological tables mention the Benjamites:

"The year in which Iahdulim went to Hen and laid hands upon the territory of the Benjamites", is referred to in the reign of King Iahdulim of Mari and

"The year that Zimri-Lim killed the dâvidum of the Benjamites"

"The year after Zimri-Lim killed the dâvidum of the Benjamites ..." in the reign of the last monarch of Mari, Zimri-Lim.

An elaborate correspondence between governors, district commissioners, and administrators takes place over the single question: Dare we take a census of the Benjamites?

In the kingdom of Mari a census of the people was not uncommon. It provided a basis for taxation and for enlistment for military service. The population was summoned by districts and a nominal roll was made of every man liable for call-up.

The proceedings lasted several days, during which free beer and bread were distributed by government officials. The administration in the palace of Mari would fain have included the Benjamites in this but the district officers had their doubts. They advised against it since they understood only too well the temper of these roaming and rebellious tribes.

"Reference the proposal to take a census of the Benjamites, about which you have written me," begins a letter from Samsi-Addu to Iasmah-Addu in Mari. "The Benjamites are not well-disposed to the idea of a census. If you carry it out, their kinsmen the Ra-ab-ay-yi, who live on the other bank of the river, will hear of it. They will be annoyed with them and will not return to their country. On no account should this census be taken!"

Thus the Benjamites lost their free beer and bread and also escaped paying taxes and military service.

Later the children of Israel were to experience a census of this sort many times, conducted exactly on the Mari-pattern. The first time was on the command of Yahweh after Moses had led them out of Egypt. All men over twenty who were fit to fight were registered according to their families (Num. 1–4). A generation later, after their sojourn in the desert, Moses took a second census with a view to dividing up the land of Canaan (Num. 26). During the monarchy David ordered a national census. What he had in mind on that occasion was the building up of an army and his commander in chief, Joab, was entrusted with the arrangements (2 Sam. 24). As the Bible depicts the incident, Yahweh had put the idea into the king's mind in order to punish the people. The Israelites loved their freedom above all else. Registration and the prospect of being called up were equally hateful to them. Even in the year A.D. 6 the census carried out by Governor Cyrenius almost led to open revolt.

It is worth noting that it is to peace-loving Mari that the world owes the original pattern of all recruiting campaigns. It was later followed by Babylonians and Assyrians, by Greeks and Romans, in exactly the same way, as indeed in later days by the nations of modern times. Thus Mari has given the lead to the whole world in this matter of taking a census for purposes of taxation and conscription for military service.

In Paris the mention of Benjamites gave rise to conjecture and anticipation along a particular line. Not without reason.

On other clay tablets the Assyriologists dealing with these reports of governors and district commissioners of the Mari empire came across one after another a whole series of familiar sounding names from Biblical history—names like Peleg, and Serug, Nahor and Terah and—Haran.

"These are the generations of Shem," says Gen. 11. "... Peleg lived 30 years and begat Reu: And Reu lived two and thirty years and begat Serug: And Serug lived thirty years and begat Nahor: And Nahor lived nine and twenty years and begat Terah: And Terah lived seventy years and begat Abram, Nahor, and Haran."

Names of Abraham's forefathers emerge from these dark ages as names of cities in north-west Mesopotamia. They lie in Padan-Aram, the plain of Aram. In the centre of it lies Haran, which, according to its description, must have been a flourishing city in the 19th and 18th centuries B.C. Haran, the home of Abraham, father of the patriarchs, the birthplace of the Hebrew people, is here for the first time historically attested, for contemporary texts refer to it. Further up the same Balikh valley lay the city with an equally well-known Biblical name, Nahor, the home of Rebecca, wife of Isaac.

> "And Abraham was old and well stricken in age, and the Lord had blessed Abraham in all things. And Abraham said unto his eldest servant of his house, that ruled over all that he had: Put, I pray thee, thy hand under my thigh; And I will make thee swear by the Lord, the God of heaven, and the God of the earth, that thou shalt not take a wife unto my son of the daughters of the Canaanites, among whom I dwell; But thou shalt go unto my country, and to my kindred and take a wife unto my son Isaac.... And the servant took ... of all the goods of his master ... and he arose and went to Mesopotamia, unto the city of Nahor" (Gen. 24$^{1-4, 10}$).

The Biblical city of Nahor is unexpectedly drawn into a recognisable historical setting. Abraham's servant set out for the land of the kings of Mari. The instructions of his master, according to the Biblical tradition, clearly indicate that Abraham must have known Northern Mesopotamia, including Nahor, extremely well. How else could he have spoken of the city of Nahor?

If we follow the dates given in the Bible we find that Abraham left his native place, Haran, 645 years before the exodus of the people of Israel from Egypt. They wandered through the desert towards the Promised Land under the leadership of Moses in the 13th century B.C. This date is, as we shall see, assured by archaeology. Abraham must therefore have lived about 1900 B.C. The finds at Mari confirm the accuracy of the Biblical account. About 1900 B.C., according to the evidence of the palace archives, Haran and Nahor were both flourishing cities.

The documents from the kingdom of Mari produce startling proof that the stories of the patriarchs in the Bible are not "pious legends"—as is often too readily assumed—but things that are described as happening in a historical period which can be precisely dated.

The fact that the Bible contains genuine early Western Semitic names found surprising confirmation in written sources from the Ancient East. Not only did personal names from the Biblical story of the patriarchs occur as placenames, but they also proved to be the names of individual persons and it is not at all rare or unusual for clay tablets to be found bearing the name of the patriarch Abraham. Yet has Abraham actually been brought nearer to us? The excavation of written sources at "Fennel Cape", Ras Shamra (ancient Ugarit), has revealed that there were even an Egyptian and a Cypriot among those bearing this name. The distinguished Bible archaeologist Father Roland de Vaux considered this "unusual and disturbing". Quite understandably so, for this being the case, Abraham, instead of drawing closer to us, is in danger of disappearing in the crowd of his numerous namesakes who appear during the various epochs of the history of the Near and Middle East.

Unfortunately the "Benjamites" of Mari have also disappeared. The conviction has established itself that the name in the texts from Mari which was interpreted as "Benjamites" really means simply "sons of the right (sc. hand)", that is to say, "sons of the south". It appears to have been a purely geographical designation rather than the name of a tribe, for in the Mari documents *banu rabbājā* and *banu šam'al* are contrasted with the "sons of the south". Moreover, the name of the territory Yemen in Southern Arabia has preserved the old Mari word across the millennia, for Yemen merely means south!

But Bible scholars have also learnt other things. A phrase such as "the year in which Zimri-Lim killed the *dâvidum* of the Benjamites" is

now translated as "the year in which Zimri-Lim inflicted an annihilat-
ing defeat on the 'sons of the south'", for dâvidum does not mean
"commander", as was previously thought, but "defeat".

Of course, the beginnings of Mari around 1800 B.C. agree extremely
well with the traditional dating of the Biblical patriarchs, somewhere
around or shortly after 2000 B.C. Paradoxically it was the astonishing
confirmation of statements in the Bible connecting the time of the
patriarchs with a period of the history of the Ancient East some 500
years later which thus raised doubts concerning the customary dating.
This confirmation comes from the archives of Nuzi in Yorgan Tepe,
fifteen kilometres south west of Kirkuk. The written documents from
this Horite city of the kingdom of Mitanni (c. 1500 B.C.) cast a light not
only on the ancient laws of the Horites, but also on the legal practices of
the Biblical patriarchs which agree to an amazing degree with the
Biblical texts. Three examples will suffice as illustrations:

1) Abraham laments the fact that he will die without a son and
   that a certain Eliezer will inherit from him (Gen. 15[2]). From the
   Nuzi tablets we know that it was customary for a childless
   couple to adopt a "son" who looked after his foster-parents and
   in return inherited from them. This arrangement could be
   reversed to a certain degree if an heir was subsequently born.
2) If a marriage remained childless, the wife had to provide a
   "substitute wife". This is what Sarah did when she presented
   Hagar to Abraham (1. Gen. 16[2]) and in the same way Rachel at
   a later time gave her husband Jacob her maid Bilhah (1. Gen.
   30[3]). The custom was precisely the same in Nuzi.
3) Jacob's wife Rachel stole the "images" of her father Laban (1.
   Gen. 31, [3] ff) and Laban moved heaven and earth to get these
   "images" back. The Nuzi tablets tell us why. The person who
   was in possession of these domestic images (teraphim) also had
   the rights to the inheritance.

Taken together there is a striking conformity between the Bible and
the Nuzi texts. Yet there is a bitter conclusion to be drawn, for if the
patriarchs followed the legal customs of the Horites of the fifteen
century before the birth of Christ, how could they have lived in the 18th,
19th or even the 20th century before Christ? In other words, did
Abraham really live in the "kingdom of Mari"? Or ought we to look for
him centuries later in the kingdom of Mitanni? In fact, we shall see that
certain concepts of the "patriarchal period", in the religious sphere this
time, are matched by ideas contained in texts from the coastal town of
Ugarit (Ras Shamra) whose "classical" period came still later, in the
15th to 14th centuries before Christ. Do we have, in consequence, to put
Israel's Biblical ancestors even later? The questions still facing us today
are innumerable!

If it seems that science is abandoning us to ourselves with a large number of new problems and if it seems that it is consequently so much more difficult for us to connect the above mentioned names and facts with definite and familiar individuals, this very same science has amazingly confirmed other Biblical statements as will become apparent later. And as our knowledge is continually advancing, it is by no means impossible that Biblical archaeology will one day provide us with further sensational discoveries.

CHAPTER 6

THE LONG JOURNEY TO CANAAN

Six hundred miles by the caravan route—Nowadays four visas are required—The land of purple—Punitive expeditions against "Sanddwellers"—Proud seaports with a troublesome hinterland—An Egyptian best-seller about Canaan—Sinuhe praises the Good Land—Jerusalem on magic vases—Strongholds—Sellin finds Shechem—Abraham chooses the high road.

"And Abram took Sarai his wife, and Lot his brother's son, and all their substance that they had gathered, and the souls that they had gotten in Haran: and they went forth to go into the land of Canaan" (Gen. 12⁵).

THE road from Haran, the home of the patriarchs, to the land of Canaan runs south for more than 600 miles. It follows the river Balikh as far as the Euphrates, thence by a caravan route thousands of years old via the oasis of Palmyra, the Tadmor of the Bible, to Damascus, and from there in a south-westerly direction to the Lake of Galilee. It is one of the great trade routes that have always led from Euphrates to Jordan, from the kingdom of Mesopotamia to the Phoenician seaports on the Mediterranean and the distant Nile lands in Egypt.

Anyone nowadays wanting to follow Abraham's route requires four visas: one for Turkey, in which the site of Haran lies, one for Syria to cover the section from the Euphrates via Damascus to the Jordan, and one each for the states of Jordan and Israel, which occupy what was once Canaan. In the time of the father of the patriarchs all this was much easier. For on his long trek he had only to pass through one large stretch of national territory, the kingdom of Mari, which he was in fact quitting. The smaller city states between the Euphrates and the Nile could be by-passed. The road to Canaan lay open.

The first city of any size that Abraham must have struck on his journey is still standing today: Damascus.

To go by car from Damascus to Palestine is, particularly in springtime, an unforgettable experience.

The ancient city with its narrow streets and dark bazaar-alleys, with its mosques and its Roman remains, lies in the centre of a wide and fertile plain. When the Arabs speak of Paradise they think of Damascus. What other Mediterranean city can compare with this place, which every spring is decked with an incredible mantle of gay blossom? In all the gardens and in the hedgerows beyond the city walls apricots and almonds are a riot of pink. Flowering trees line the road which climbs gently as it heads for the south-west. Tilled fields alternate with olive groves and large mulberry plantings. High above, to the right of the road, rises the El Barada river, to which the land owes its fertility. Here mighty Hermon thrusts its steep slopes 10,000 feet into the heavens above the flat and verdant plain. From the side of this famous mountain ridge, to the south, gushes the source of the Jordan. Towering over both Syria and Palestine and visible from afar it seems to have been placed there by Nature as a gigantic boundary stone between them. Even in the blazing heat of summer its peak remains covered in snow. The effect becomes even more impressive as on the left of the road the green fields disappear. Monotonous grey-brown hills, streaked with dried up river beds, pile up towards the distant shimmering horizon where the scorching Syrian Desert begins—the home of the Bedouins. The road climbs gradually for an hour and a half. Fields and groves become rarer. The green is more and more swallowed up by the sandy grey of the desert. Then suddenly an enormous pipeline crosses the road. The oil that flows through it has already come quite a way.

Fig. 8.—The route taken by the father of the patriarchs from the kingdom of Mari to Canaan.

Its journey began in the oil wells of Saudi Arabia, over a thousand miles away, and will end in the port of Saida on the Mediterranean. Saida is the old Sidon of the Bible.

Behind a ridge suddenly appear the hills of Galilee. A few minutes later comes the frontier. Syria lies behind. The road crosses a small bridge. Under the arch a fast moving narrow current hurries on its way. It is the Jordan: we are in Palestine, in the young state of Israel.

After a few miles between dark basalt rocks the bright blue of the Lake of Galilee sparkles up 'at us from far beneath. It was on this lake, where time seems to have stood still, that Jesus preached from a boat off Capernaum. Here he told Peter to cast his nets and raise the great draught of fishes. Two thousand years before that the flocks of Abraham grazed on its shores. For the road from Mesopotamia to Canaan went past the Lake of Galilee.

Canaan is the narrow mountainous strip of land between the shores of the Mediterranean and the borders of the desert, from Gaza in the south right up to Hamath on the banks of the Orontes in the north.

Canaan was the "Land of Purple". It owed its name to a product of the country which was highly prized in the olden days. From earliest times the inhabitants had extracted from a shellfish (Murex), which was native to these parts, the most famous dye in the ancient world, purple. It was so uncommon, so difficult to obtain and therefore so expensive, that only the wealthy could afford it. Purple robes were throughout the Ancient East a mark of high rank. The Greeks called the manufacturers of purple and the purple-dyers of the Mediterranean Phoenicians. The country they called Phoenicia, which meant "purple" in their language.

The land of Canaan is also the birthplace of two things which have radically affected the whole world: the word "Bible" and our alphabet. A Phoenician city was godparent to the Greek word for "book": from Byblos, the Canaanite seaport, comes "Biblion" and hence, later, "Bible". In the 9th century B.C. the Greeks took over from Canaan the letters of our alphabet.

The part of the country which was to become the home of the Israelite people was named by the Romans after Israel's worst enemies: Palestine comes from Pelishtim, as the Philistines are called in the Old Testament. They lived in the southernmost part of the coast of Canaan. "All Israel, from Dan even to Beersheba" (1 Sam. 3^{20}) is how the Bible describes the extent of the Promised Land, that is, from the sources of Jordan at the foot of Hermon to the hills west of the Dead Sea, and the Negev in the south.

If we look at a globe of the world, Palestine is only a tiny spot on the earth's surface, a narrow streak. It is possible to drive comfortably in a single day round the borders of the old kingdom of Israel: 150 miles from north to south, 25 miles across at its narrowest point, 9,500 square miles in all, its size was about that of the island of Sicily. Only for a few decades in its turbulent history was it any bigger. Under its renowned kings David and Solomon its territory reached to the arm of the Red Sea at Ezion-Geber in the south, and far beyond Damascus into Syria on the north. The present state of Israel with its 8,000 square miles is smaller by a fifth than the old kingdom.

There never flourished here crafts and industries whose products were sought after by the world at large. Traversed by hills and mountain chains, whose summits rose to over 3,000 feet, surrounded in the south and east by scrub and desert, in the north by the mountains of the Lebanon and Hermon, in the west by a flat coast with no natural harbours, it lay like a poverty stricken island between the great kingdoms on the Nile and the Euphrates, on the frontier between two continents. East of the Nile delta Africa stops. After a desolate stretch of 100 miles of desert Asia begins, and at its threshold lies Palestine.

When in the course of its eventful history it was constantly being dragged into the affairs of the wider world, it had its position to thank for it. Canaan is the link between Egypt and Asia. The most important trade route of the ancient world passes through this country. Merchants and caravans, migratory tribes and peoples, followed this road which the armies of the great conquerors were later to make use of. Egyptians, Assyrians, Babylonians, Persians, Greeks and Romans one after another made the land and its people the plaything of their economic, strategic and political concerns.

It was in the interests of trade that the giant on the Nile in the third millennium B.C. was the first great power to stretch out its tentacles towards Canaan.

"We brought 40 ships, laden with cedar trunks. We built ships of cedarwood: One 'Pride of Two Lands'—ship of 150 feet: And of meru-wood, two ships 150 feet long: We made the doors of the king's palace of cedarwood." That is the substance of the world's oldest advice note from a timber importer about 2700 B.C. The details of this cargo of timber in the reign of Pharaoh Snefru are scratched on a tablet of hard black diorite, which is carefully preserved in the museum at Palermo. Dense woods covered the slopes of Lebanon then. The excellent wood from its cedars and meru, a kind of conifer, were just what the Pharaohs needed for their building schemes.

Five hundred years before Abraham's day there was a flourishing import and export trade on the Canaanite coast. Egypt exchanged gold and spices from Nubia, copper and turquoise from the mines at Sinai, linen and ivory, for silver from the Taurus, leather goods from Byblos, painted vases from Crete. In the great Phoenician dye-works well-to-do Egyptians had their robes dyed purple. For their society women they bought a wonderful lapis-lazuli blue—eyelids dyed blue were all the rage—and stibium, a cosmetic which was highly thought of by the ladies for touching up their eyelashes.

In the sea-ports of Ugarit (now Ras Shamra) and Tyre there were Egyptian consuls; the coastal fortress of Byblos became an Egyptian colony; monuments were erected to the Pharaohs and Phoenician princes adopted Egyptian names.

If the coastal cities presented a picture of cosmopolitan life which was busy, prosperous and even luxurious, a few miles inland lay a world which provided a glaring contrast. The Jordan mountains have always been a trouble-spot. Bedouin attacks on the native population, insurrection and feuds between towns were unending. Since they also endangered the caravan route along the Mediterranean coast, Egyptian punitive expeditions had to bring the unruly elements to heel. The inscription on the tomb of the Egyptian Uni gives us a clear picture of how one of these expeditions was organised about 2350 B.C. Uni, an army commander, received orders from Pharaoh Phiops I to assemble a striking force against Bedouins from Asia who were attacking Canaan. His report on the campaign reads as follows:

"His Majesty made war on the desert peoples and His Majesty gathered an army: in the south beyond Elephantine ... all over the north ... and among the Jertet-, Mazoi-, and Jenam Nubians. I was entrusted with the whole campaign." The morale of this multi-coloured fighting force comes in for high praise, and in the course of it we learn what sort of attractions Canaan offered in those days in the way of loot: "None of them stole the sandals off anyone who came their way.... None of them stole food from any of the cities.... None of them stole any goats." Uni's war-diary proudly announces a great victory and in passing gives us valuable information about the country: "The king's army returned in good order, after laying waste the country of the desert peoples, ... after destroying their fortresses.... after cutting down their fig-trees and vines ... and carrying off a large number into captivity. His Majesty sent me five times to ravage the land of the desert peoples with these troops every time they revolted."

Semites thus made their first entry into the land of the Pharaohs as P.O.W.'s where they were contemptuously described as "Sand-dwellers". Chu-Sebek, adjutant to king Sesostris III of Egypt, wrote in his war-diary 500 years later the following account which had been preserved at Abydos on the Upper Nile, where it was chiselled out on a monument: "His Majesty proceeded northwards to crush the Asiatic Bedouins.... His Majesty went as far as a place called Sekmem.... Sekmem collapsed together with the whole miserable country of Retenu."

The Egyptians called Palestine and Syria together "Retenu". "Sek-mem" is the Biblical town of Shechem, the first town which Abraham struck on entering Canaan (Gen. 12⁶).

With the campaign of Sesostris III about 1850 B.C. we are right in the middle of the patriarchal period. Meantime Egypt had taken posses-sion of the whole of Canaan: the country now lay under the suzerainty of the Pharaohs. Thanks to the archaeologists we possess a unique document from this epoch, a gem of ancient literature. The author: a certain Sinuhe of Egypt. Scene: Canaan. Time: between 1971 and 1928 B.C. under Pharaoh Sesostris I.

Sinuhe, a nobleman in attendance at court, becomes involved in a political intrigue. He fears for his life and emigrates to Canaan:

"As I headed north I came to the Princes' Wall, which was built to keep out the Bedouins and crush the Sandramblers.[1] I hid in a thicket in case the guard on the wall, who was on patrol at the time, would see me. I did not move out of it till the evening. When daylight came ... and I had reached the Bitter Lake[2] I collapsed. I was parched with thirst, my

---

[1] "Sandramblers" and "Wilderness-Wanderers" were the favourite nicknames which the Egyptians gave to their eastern and north-eastern neighbours, the nomads. This also included the tribes in Canaan and Syria which had no fixed location.

[2] Still known as the "Bitter Lakes" on the Isthmus of Suez.

throat was red hot. I said to myself: This is the taste of death! But as I made another effort and pulled myself on to my feet, I heard the bleating of sheep and some Bedouins came in sight. Their leader, who had been in Egypt, recognised me. He gave me some water and boiled some milk, and I went with him to his tribe. They were very kind to me."

Sinuhe's escape had been successful. He had been able to slip unseen past the great barrier wall on the frontier of the kingdom of the Pharaohs which ran exactly along the line which is followed by the Suez Canal today. This "Princes' Wall" was even then several hundred years old. A priest mentions it as far back as 2650 B.C.: "The Princes' Walls are being built to prevent the Asiatics forcing their way into Egypt. They want water ... to give to their cattle." Later on the children of Israel were to pass this wall many times: there was no other way into Egypt. Abraham must have been the first of them to see it when he emigrated to the land of the Nile during a famine (Gen. 12[10]).

Sinuhe continues: "Each territory passed me on to the next. I went to Byblos,[1] and farther on reached Kedme[2] where I spent eighteen months. Ammi-Enschi,[3] the chief of Upper Retenu[4] made me welcome. He said to me: 'You will be well treated and you can speak your own language here.' He said this of course because he knew who I was. Egyptians[5] who lived there had told him about me."

We are told in great detail of the day to day experiences of this Egyptian fugitive in North Palestine. "Ammi-Enschi said to me: 'Certainly, Egypt is a fine country, but you ought to stay here with me and what I shall do for you will be fine too.'

"He gave me precedence over all his own family and gave me his eldest daughter in marriage. He let me select from among his choicest estates and I selected one which lay along the border of a neighbouring territory. It was a fine place with the name of Jaa. There were figs and vines and more wine than water. There was plenty of honey and oil; every kind of fruit hung on its trees. It had corn and barley and all kinds of sheep and cattle. My popularity with the ruler was extremely profitable. He made me a chief of his tribe in the choicest part of his domains. I had bread and wine as my daily fare, boiled meat and roast goose. There were also desert animals which they caught in traps and brought to me, apart from what my hunting dogs collected.... There was milk in every shape and form. Thus many years went by. My children grew into strong men, each of them able to dominate his tribe.

"Any courier coming from Egypt or heading south to the royal court

---

[1] Phoenician seaport north of present-day Beirut.
[2] Desert country east of Damascus.
[3] A western Semitic name, an Amorite.
[4] Name given to the hill country in the north of Palestine.
[5] Pharaoh's commissioners were at that time stationed all over Palestine and Syria.

lived with me.[1] I gave hospitality to everyone. I gave water to the thirsty, put the wanderer on the right way, and protected the bereaved.

"When the Bedouins sallied forth to attack neighbouring chiefs I drew up the plan of campaign. For the prince of Retenu for many years put me in command of his warriors and whichever country I marched into I made . . . and . . . of its pastures and its wells. I plundered its sheep and cattle, led its people captive and took over their stores. I killed its people with my sword and my bow[2] thanks to my leadership and my clever plans."

Out of his many experiences among the "Asiatics" a life and death duel, which he describes in detail, seems to have made the deepest impression on Sinuhe. A "Strong man of Retenu" had jeered at him one day in his tent and called him out. He was sure he could kill Sinuhe and appropriate his flocks and herds and properties. But Sinuhe, like all Egyptians, was a practised bowman from his earliest days, and killed the "strong man", who was armed with shield, spear and dagger, by putting an arrow through his throat. The spoils that came to him as a result of this combat made him even richer and more powerful.

At length in his old age he began to yearn for his homeland. A letter from his Pharaoh Sesostris I summoned him to return: ". . . Make ready to return to Egypt, that you may see once more the Court where you grew up, and kiss the ground at the two great gates. . . . Remember the day when you will have to be buried and men will do you honour. You will be anointed with oil before daybreak and wrapped in linen blessed by the goddess Tait.[3] You will be given an escort on the day of the funeral. The coffin will be of gold adorned with lapis-lazuli, and you will be placed upon a bier. Oxen will pull it and a choir will precede you. They will dance the Dance of the Dwarfs at the mouth of your tomb. The sacrificial prayers will be recited for you and animals will be offered on your altar. The pillars of your tomb will be built of limestone among those of the royal family. You must not lie in a foreign land, with Asiatics to bury you, and wrap you in sheepskin."

Sinuhe's heart leapt for joy. He decided to return at once, made over his property to his children and installed his eldest son as "Chief of his tribe". This was customary with these Semitic nomads, as it was with Abraham and his progeny. It was the tribal law of the patriarchs, which later became the law of Israel. "My tribe and all my goods belonged to him only, my people and all my flocks, my fruit and all my sweet trees.[4] Then I headed for the south."

He was accompanied right to the frontier posts of Egypt by Bedouins, thence by representatives of Pharaoh to the capital south of Memphis. The second stage was by boat.

[1] This points to a considerable traffic between Egypt and Palestine.
[2] The bow was the typical Egyptian weapon.
[3] Embalming.   [4] Date-palms.

What a contrast! From a tent to a royal palace, from a simple if dangerous life back to the security and luxury of a highly civilised metropolis. "I found his Majesty on the great throne in the Hall of Silver and Gold. The king's family were brought in. His Majesty said to the Queen: 'See, here is Sinuhe, who returns as an Asiatic and has become a Bedouin.' She gave a loud shriek and all the royal children screamed in chorus. They said to his Majesty: 'Surely this is not really he, my lord King.' His Majesty replied: 'It is really he.'

"I was taken to a princely mansion," writes Sinuhe enthusiastically, "in which there were wonderful things and also a bathroom ... there were things from the royal treasure house, clothes of royal linen, myrrh and finest oil; favourite servants of the king were in every room, and every cook did his duty. The years that were past slipped from my body. I was shaved and my hair was combed. I shed my load of foreign soil[1] and the coarse clothing of the Sandramblers. I was swathed in fine linen and anointed with the finest oil the country could provide. I slept once more in a bed. Thus I lived, honoured by the king, until the time came for me to depart this life."

The Sinuhe story does not exist in one copy only. An astonishing number of them has been found. It must have been a highly popular work and must have gone through several "editions". Not only in the Middle Kingdom but in the New Kingdom of Egypt it was read with pleasure, as the copies found indicate. One might call it a "best-seller", the first in the world, and about Canaan, of all places.

The scholars who came across it again at the turn of the century were as delighted with it as Sinuhe's contemporaries had been 4,000 years before. They regarded it however as a well-told story, exaggerated like all Egyptian writings and completely without foundation. The Tale of Sinuhe became a mine of information for learned Egyptologists, but not for historians. They were so busy disputing about the clarification of the text, the letters, the construction and connection of the sentences that the contents were forgotten.

Meantime Sinuhe came into his own. For we now know that the Egyptian had written a factual account of Canaan at about the time that Abraham migrated there. It is to hieroglyphic texts dealing with Egyptian campaigns that we owe the first evidence we possess about Canaan. They agree with Sinuhe's description. Similarly, the Egyptian nobleman's story shows in some places almost literal correspondence with verses of the Bible which are often quoted. "For the lord thy God bringeth thee into a good land" says Deut. 8[7]—"It was a fine country" says Sinuhe. "A land" continues the Bible "of wheat and barley and vines and fig trees...." "Barley and wheat, figs and vines were there" Sinuhe tells us. And where the Bible says: "A land of oil, olive and honey, a land wherein thou shalt eat bread without scarceness",

[1] i.e. the dirt that came off him.

the Egyptian text reads: "There was plenty of honey and oil. I had bread as my daily fare."

The description which Sinuhe gives of his way of life among the Amorites, living in a tent, surrounded by his flocks and herds, and involved in conflict with presumptuous Bedouins whom he has to drive away from his pastures and his wells, corresponds with the Biblical picture of life in patriarchal times. Abraham and his son Isaac have also to fight for their wells (Gen. 21^{25}, 26$^{15, 20}$).

The care and accuracy with which Biblical tradition depicts the actual living conditions of those days is best seen when we examine the results of sober investigation. For the variety of recently discovered documents and monuments makes it possible for us to reconstruct a true picture of the conditions of life in Canaan at the time when the patriarchs entered it.

About 1900 B.C. Canaan was but thinly populated. Properly speaking it was no-man's land. Here and there in the midst of ploughed fields a fortified keep could be seen. Neighbouring slopes would be planted with vines or with fig trees and date palms. The inhabitants lived in a state of constant readiness. For these widely scattered little townships, like veritable islands, were the object of daring attacks by the desert nomads. Suddenly, and when least expected, these nomads were upon them, with indiscriminate butchery, carrying off their cattle and their crops. Just as suddenly they would disappear again into the vast recess of the desert plains to the south and east. There was endless war between the settled farmers and cattle breeders and these plundering hordes who had no fixed abode, whose home was a goatshair tent somewhere out under the open skies of the desert. It was into this restless country that Abraham made his way with his wife Sarah, his nephew Lot, his kinsfolk and his flocks.

> "And into the land of Canaan they came. And Abram passed through the land unto the place of Sichem, unto the plain of Moreh.... And the Lord appeared unto Abram and said: Unto thy seed will I give this land; and there builded he an altar unto the Lord, who appeared unto him. And he removed from thence unto a mountain on the east of Bethel, and pitched his tent having Bethel on the west, and Hai on the east: and there he builded an altar unto the Lord, and called upon the name of the Lord. And Abram journeyed, going on still toward the south" (Gen. 12$^{5-9}$).

In the twenties, remarkable sherds were found on the Nile, the chief finds at Thebes and Saqqara. Archaeologists in Berlin obtained some of them, others went to Brussels, and the rest went to the great museum at Cairo. Under the careful hands of experts the fragments were reassembled into vases and statuettes, but the most astonishing thing about them was the inscriptions.

The writing is full of menacing curses and maledictions like: "Death strike you at every wicked word and thought, every plot, angry quarrel and plan". These and other unpleasant wishes were generally addressed to Egyptian court officials and other eminent people, but also to rulers in Canaan and Syria.

In accordance with an old superstition it was believed that at the moment the vase or statuette was smashed the power of the person cursed would be broken. It was common to include within the spell the family, relatives, even the home town of the victim of the curse. The magical texts include names of cities like Jerusalem (Gen. 14^{19}), Askelon (Jud. 1^{18}), Tyre (Josh. 19^{29}), Hazor (Josh. 11^{1}), Bethshemesh (Josh. 15^{10}), Aphek (Josh. 12^{18}), Achshaph (Josh. 11^{1}) and Shechem (Sichem). Here is a convincing proof that these places mentioned in the Bible existed already in the 19th and 18th centuries B.C., since the vases and statuettes date from that time. Two of these towns were visited by Abraham. He calls on Melchizedek "King of Salem" (Gen. 14^{18}) at Jerusalem. Jerusalem is well enough known, but where was Sichem?

In the heart of Samaria lies a broad flat valley, dominated by the high peaks of Gerizim and Ebal. Well cultivated fields surround Ashkar, a small village in Jordan. Nearby at the foot of Gerizim in Tell el Balata the ruins of Sichem were discovered.

It was due to the German theologian and archaeologist Professor Ernst Sellin that during excavations in 1913–14 strata from very early times came to light.

Sellin came across remains of walls dating back to the 19th century B.C. Bit by bit the picture emerged of a mighty surrounding wall with strong foundations, entirely built of rough boulders, some of them 6 feet in diameter. Archaeologists call this type a "cyclops-wall". The wall was further strengthened by an escarpment. The builders of Sichem fortified the 6 feet thick wall with small turrets and provided an earth wall in addition.

The remains of a palace also emerged out of the ruins. The square cramped courtyard, surrounded by a few rooms with solid walls, hardly deserved the name of palace. All the Canaanite towns whose names are so familiar, and which the Israelites feared so greatly in the early days, looked like Sichem. With few exceptions the notable building projects of that period are now known. Most of them have been excavated within the last sixty years. For thousands of years they have been buried deep in the ground, now they stand clearly before us. Among them are many towns whose walls the patriarchs had seen: Bethel and Mizpah, Gerar and Lachish, Gezer and Gath, Askelon and Jericho. Anyone who wanted to write the history of the building of fortresses and cities in Canaan, would have no great difficulty in doing so in view of the wealth of material going back to the third millennium B.C.

The Canaanite towns were fortresses, places of refuge in time of danger, whether it was from sudden attack by nomadic tribes or civil war among the Canaanites themselves. Towering perimeter walls built of these great boulders invariably enclose a small area, not much bigger than St. Peter's Square in Rome. Each of these town-forts had a water supply, but they were not towns in which a large population could have made a permanent home. Compared with the palaces and great cities in Mesopotamia or on the Nile they look tiny. Most of the towns in Canaan could have gone into the palace of the kings of Mari comfortably.

In Tell el-Hesi, probably the Eglon of the Bible, the ancient fortifications enclosed an area of just over an acre. In Tell es-Safi—formerly Gath—twelve acres; in Tell el-Mutesellim—formerly Megiddo—about the same amount; in Tell el-Zakariyah—the Biblical Azekah—less than ten acres; Gezer, on the road from Jerusalem to Jaffa, occupied just over twenty acres. Even in the more built-up area of Jericho, the inner fortified wall, the Acropolis proper, enclosed a space of little more than five acres. Yet Jericho was one of the strongest fortresses in the country.

Bitter feuds between the tribal chiefs were the order of the day. There was no supreme authority. Every chieftain was master in his own territory. No one gave him orders and he did what he pleased. The Bible calls the tribal chieftains "kings". As far as power and independence were concerned that is what they were.

Between the tribal chiefs and their subjects the relationship was patriarchal. Inside the wall lived only the chief, the aristocracy, Pharaoh's representatives, and wealthy merchants. Moreover they alone lived in strong, solid, mostly one-story houses with four to six rooms built round an open courtyard. Upper class homes with a second story were comparatively rare. The rest of the inhabitants—vassals, servants, and serfs—lived in simple mud or wattle huts outside the walls. They must have had a miserable life.

Since the days of the patriarchs two roads meet in the plain of Shechem. One goes down into the rich valley of the Jordan. The other climbs over the lonely hills southwards to Bethel, on past Jerusalem and down to the Negev, or the Land of the South as the Bible calls it. Anyone following this road would encounter only a few inhabited areas in the central highlands of Samaria and Judah: Shechem, Bethel, Jerusalem and Hebron. Anyone choosing the more comfortable road would find the larger towns and more important fortresses of the Canaanites in the lush valleys of the Plain of Jezreel, on the fertile coast of Judah and amid the luxuriant vegetation of the Jordan valley.

Abraham, as the Bible tells us, chose for his first exploration of

Palestine the lonely and difficult road that points over the hills towards the south. For here the wooded hillsides offered refuge and concealment to a stranger in a foreign land, while the clearings provided pasture in plenty for his flocks and herds. Later on he and his tribe and the other patriarchs as well went back and forth along this same wretched mountain track. However tempting were the fertile valleys of the plain Abraham preferred to establish himself at first up in the hill country. For with his bows and slings he was in no condition to risk a clash with the Canaanites, whose swords and spears were more than a match for him. Abraham was not yet ready to venture out of the highlands.

CHAPTER 7

ABRAHAM AND LOT IN THE LAND OF PURPLE

Famine in Canaan—A Family Portrait of the patriarchal age—Permit of access to the Nile grazings—The mystery of Sodom and Gomorrah—Mr. Lynch investigates the Dead Sea—The great fissure—Did the Vale of Siddim take a headlong plunge?—Pillars of salt at Jebel Usdum.

"And there was a famine in the land: and Abram went down into Egypt to sojourn there; for the famine was grievous in the land" (Gen. 12^{10}).

WE have to thank the dryness of the sands of the Egyptian desert for preserving a considerable variety of hieroglyphic texts, among which is to be found a wealth of written evidence of the immigration of Semitic families into the Nile valley. The best and clearest proof is however a picture.

Halfway between the old cities of the Pharaohs, Memphis and Thebes, 200 miles south of Cairo, there lies on the banks of the Nile amid green fields and palm groves the little settlement of Beni-Hasan. Here in 1890 a British expert, Percy A. Newberry, was given an assignment by the Cairo authorities to investigate some old tombs. The expedition was financed by the Egyptian Exploration Fund.

The tombs were located at the outer end of a desert wadi, where the remains of old quarries and a large temple also lay in peaceful seclusion. Week after week nothing but debris, rubble and the remnants of broken stone pillars streamed out of the rock-face behind which the last resting place of the Egyptian nobleman Khnum-hotpe was concealed. Hieroglyphs in a small entrance hall indicated the name of the occupant. He was the ruler of this district of the Nile, which at one time was called Gazelle Province. Khnum-hotpe lived under Pharaoh Sesostris II about 1900 B.C.

After a great deal of time and effort had been expended Newberry eventually reached a huge rock chamber. By the light of numerous torches he was able to see that there were three vaults and that the stumps of two rows of pillars protruded from the ground. The walls were bright with gorgeous coloured paintings on a thin lime-washed plaster. These depicted scenes from the life of the nobleman telling of harvest, hunting, dancing and sport. In one of the pictures on the north wall, immediately next to an over life-size portrait of the nobleman, Newberry discovered foreign looking figures. They were wearing a different type of clothing from the ordinary Egyptians, they were fairer-skinned and had sharper features. Two Egyptian officials in the foreground were obviously introducing this group of foreigners to the nobleman. What sort of people were they?

Hieroglyphs on a written document in the hand of one of the Egyptians gave the explanation: they were "Sanddwellers", Semites. Their leader was called Abishai. With thirty six men, women and children of his tribe Abishai had come to Egypt. He had brought gifts for the nobleman, among which special mention was made of some costly stibium[1] for the nobleman's wife.

Abishai is a genuine Semitic name. After the conquest of Canaan by Joshua the name occurs in the Bible during the reign of the second king of Israel: "Then answered David and said to ... Abishai the son of Zeruiah" (1 Sam. 26[6]). The Abishai of the Bible was the brother of king David's unpopular commander-in-chief Joab about 1000 B.C., when Israel was a large kingdom.

The artist whom Prince Khnum-hotpe entrusted with the decoration of his tomb has depicted the "Sanddwellers" with such care that the smallest detail is faithfully noted. This lifelike and unusually striking picture looks more like a coloured photograph. It gives the impression that this family of Semites had just stopped for a second, and that suddenly men, women and children would start off again and continue their journey. Abishai at the head of the column makes a slight obeisance and salutes the nobleman with his right hand, while his left hand holds a short cord to which a tame horned goat is attached, carrying between its horns a bent stick which is a shepherd's crook.

The shepherd's crook was so characteristic of the nomads that the Egyptians in their picture-writing used it for the name of these foreigners.

The style and colour of their clothing are faithfully reproduced. Square woollen blankets, reaching in the case of the men to the knee, in the case of the women to the calf, are caught up on one shoulder. They consist of highly coloured striped material and serve as cloaks. Does that not remind us of the famous "coat of many colours" which Jacob, much to the annoyance of his other sons, bestowed upon his favourite son Joseph? (Gen. 37[3]). The men's hair is trimmed into a pointed beard. The women's hair falls loosely over breast and shoulders. It is fastened by a narrow white ribbon round the forehead. The little curls in front of the ears seem to have been a concession to fashion. The men are wearing sandals, the women have dark brown half-length boots. They carry their water ration in artistically embroidered containers made of animal skins. Bows and arrows, heavy throw-sticks and spears

[1] Colouring for eyelashes.

serve as their weapons. Even their favourite instrument has been brought with them on their long journey. One of the men is playing the eight-stringed lyre. According to the instructions given in the Bible some of the Psalms of David were to be accompanied on this instrument: "To be sung to eight strings" is the heading of Psalms 6 and 12.

Since this picture dates from about 1900 B.C., which was the period of the patriarchs, we may imagine that Abraham and his family looked something like this. When he reached the Egyptian frontier a similar scene must have taken place. For the procedure for admitting foreign visitors was exactly the same at all the other frontier posts as in the case of the lord Khnum-hotpe.

It was thus no different long ago from what it is now to travel in a foreign country. Certainly there were no passports but formalities and officialdom made life difficult for foreign visitors even then. Anyone entering Egypt had to state the number in his party, the reason for his journey and the probable length of his stay. All the particulars were carefully noted down on papyrus by a scribe using red ink and then sent by messenger to the frontier officer who decided whether an entrance permit should be granted. This was however not left to his own judgment. Administrative officers at the court of Pharaoh issued from time to time precise directives, even to the point of specifying which grazings were to be put at the disposal of immigrant nomads.

In times of famine Egypt was for Canaanite nomads their place of refuge and often their only salvation. When the ground dried up in their own country, the land of the Pharaohs always afforded sufficient juicy pastures. The Nile with its regular annual flooding took care of that.

On the other hand the proverbial wealth of Egypt was often a temptation to thieving bands of daring nomads who were not interested in finding pasture but were much more concerned with the bursting granaries and sumptuous palaces. Often they could only be got rid of by force of arms. As a protection against these unwelcome invaders and to

FIG. 9.—A Semitic family at the time of the Patriarchs:

keep a closer check on the frontier, the erection of the great "Princes' Wall" was begun in the third millennium B.C. It consisted of a chain of forts, watchtowers and strongpoints. It was only under cover of darkness that the Egyptian Sinuhe with his local knowledge was able to slip through unobserved. Six hundred and fifty years later, at the time of the exodus from Egypt, the frontier was also strongly guarded. Moses knew only too well that escape from the country in defiance of Pharaoh's orders was impossible. The sentries would at once have sounded the alarm and summoned the guards. Any attempt to break through would have been nipped in the bud by sharpshooters and commandos in armoured chariots and would have ended in bloodshed. That was the reason why the prophet knowing the country chose another quite unusual route. Moses led the children of Israel southwards, as far as the Red Sea, where there was no longer any wall.

After their return from Egypt Abraham and Lot separated: "For their substance was great," says the Bible, "so that they could not dwell together. And there was a strife between the herdmen of Abram's cattle, and the herdmen of Lot's cattle.... And Abram said unto Lot, Let there be no strife I pray thee, between me and thee, and between my herdmen and thy herdmen: for we be brethren. Is not the whole land before thee? Separate thyself I pray thee from me: if thou wilt take the left hand, then I will go to the right: or if thou depart to the right hand, then I will go to the left" (Gen. 13$^{6-9}$).

Abraham left the choice to Lot. Lot, taking everything for granted, like so many young people, chose the best part, in the neighbourhood of the Jordan. It was "well-watered everywhere ... as thou comest into Zoar" (Gen. 13^{10}) and blessed with luxuriant tropical vegetation "even as the garden of the Lord, like the land of Egypt" (Gen. 13^{10}).

From the wooded mountain chain in the heart of Palestine Lot made his way downhill to the east, wandered with his family and his flocks southwards along the Jordan valley and finally pitched his tent in Sodom. South of the Dead Sea lay an extremely fertile plain, the "Vale

from a wall-painting in the prince's tomb at Beni-Hasan on the Nile.

of Siddim, which is the salt sea"[1] (Gen. 14³). The Bible lists five towns in this valley, "Sodom, Gomorrah, Admah, Zeboiim, and Zoar" (Gen. 14²). It also knows of a warlike incident in the history of these five towns: "And it came to pass" that four kings "made war with Bera king of Sodom, and with Birsha king of Gomorrah, and with Shinab king of Admah, and Shemeber king of Zeboiim, and the king of Bela, which is Zoar" (Gen. 14²). For twelve years the kings of the Vale of Siddim had paid tribute to king Chedorlaomer. In the thirteenth year they rebelled. Chedorlaomer sought help from three royal allies. A punitive expedition would bring the rebels to their senses. In the battle of the nine kings, the kings of the five towns in the Vale of Siddim were defeated, their lands were ravaged and plundered.

Among the captives of the foreign kings was Lot. He was set free again by his uncle Abraham (Gen. 14¹²⁻¹⁶), who with his followers dogged the withdrawal of the army of the victorious four kings like a shadow. He watches it unobserved from safe cover, makes accurate reconnaissance and bides his time. Not until they reach Dan, on the northern frontier of Palestine does the opportunity arise for which he has been waiting. Like lightning, under cover of darkness, Abraham and his men fall on the rearguard and in the confusion that follows Lot is set free.—Only those who do not know the tactics of the Bedouins will consider this an unlikely story.

Among the inhabitants of that stretch of country the memory of that punitive expedition has remained alive to this day. It is reflected in the name of a road which runs eastward of the Dead Sea and parallel with it, traversing what was in ancient times the land of Moab and leading to the north. The nomads of Jordan know it very well. Among the natives it is called, remarkably enough, the "King's Way". We come across it in the Bible, where it is called "the king's high way" or "the high way". It was the road that the children of Israel wished to follow on their journey through Edom to the "Promised Land" (Num. 20¹⁷, ¹⁹). In the Christian era the Romans used the "King's Way" and improved it. Parts of it now belong to the network of roads in the state of Jordan. Clearly visible from the air the ancient track shows up as a dark streak across the country.

"And the Lord said, Because the cry of Sodom and Gomorrah is great, and because their sin is very grievous.... Then the Lord rained upon Sodom and upon Gomorrah, brimstone and fire from the Lord out of heaven; And he overthrew those cities, and all the plain, and all the inhabitants of the cities, and that which grew upon the ground. But his [Lot's] wife looked back from behind

---

[1] Dead Sea.

him, and she became a pillar of salt. . . . And lo the smoke of the country went up as the smoke of a furnace" (Gen. 18^{20}; 19$^{24-26, 28}$).

The calamity which is the subject of this powerful Biblical story of divine punishment for incorrigible sin has probably in all ages made a deep impression on men's minds. Sodom and Gomorrah have become synonymous with vice and godlessness. When men have talked in terms of utter annihilation, again the fate of these cities has always sprung to their minds. Their imaginations have constantly been kindled by this inexplicable and frightful disaster, as can well be seen from the many allusions to it in ancient times. Remarkable and quite incredible things are said to have happened there by the Dead Sea, the "Sea of Salt", where according to the Bible the catastrophe must have happened.

During the siege of Jerusalem in A.D. 70 it is said that the Roman army commander Titus sentenced certain slaves to death. He gave them short shrift, had them bound together by chains and thrown into the sea at the foot of the mountains of Moab. But the condemned men did not drown. No matter how often they were thrown into the sea they always drifted back to the shore like corks. This inexplicable occurrence made such a deep impression upon Titus that he pardoned the unfortunate offenders. Flavius Josephus, the Jewish historian who lived latterly in Rome, repeatedly mentions a "Lake of Asphalt". Greeks lay stress on the presence of poisonous gases, which are reported as rising from all parts of this sea. The Arabs say that in olden times no bird was able to reach the opposite side. The creatures, as they flew across the water, would suddenly drop dead into it.

These and similar traditional stories were well enough known, but until a century ago we had no first hand knowledge of this odd mysterious sea in Palestine. No scientist had investigated it or even seen it. In 1848 the United States took the initiative and equipped an expedition to solve the riddle of the Dead Sea. One autumn day in that year the beach of the little coastal town of Akka, less than 10 miles from present-day Haifa, was black with spectators who were engrossed in an unusual manoeuvre.

W. F. Lynch, a geologist and leader of the expedition, had brought ashore from the ship which was lying at anchor two metal boats which he was now fastening on to large-wheeled carts. Pulled by a long team of horses, the trek began. Three weeks later after indescribable difficulties they had succeeded in getting the waggons over the hills of Southern Galilee. The two boats took to the water again at Tiberias. When Lynch set up his theodolite at the Lake of Galilee, the result produced the first big surprise of the expedition. To begin with he thought he had made an error of calculation, but a cross check confirmed the result. The surface of the lake, which played so notable a part in the life of Jesus, is 676 feet below the level of the Mediterranean. What then could be the height of the source of the Jordan, which flows through the Lake?

Some days later W. F. Lynch stood on the slopes of snow-capped Hermon. Among remains of broken columns and gateways lies the little village of Baniya. Local Arabs led him through a thick clump of oleanders to a cave, half choked with rubble, on the steep limestone flank of Hermon. Out of its darkness gushed a stream of pure water. This is one of the sources of the Jordan. The Arabs call the Jordan Sheri'at el Kebire, the "Great River". This was the site of Panium where

Fig. 10.—Diagram of the Jordan-drop.

Herod built a temple of Pan in honour of Augustus. Shell-shaped niches are hewn out of the rock beside the Jordan cave. "Priest of Pan" is still clearly legible in Greek characters. In the time of Jesus the Greek pastoral god was worshipped at the source of the Jordan. There the goat-footed Pan raised his flute to his lips as if he wanted to send the Jordan on its way with a tune. Only 3 miles west of this source lay Dan, which is frequently mentioned in the Bible as the most northerly point in the country. There too is another source of the Jordan where its clear waters spring out of the southern slopes of Hermon. A third stream rushes out of a wadi higher up. The bottom of the wadi just above Dan is 1,500 feet above sea level.

When the Jordan on its way south reaches little Lake Huleh 12 miles away, the river bed is only 6 feet above sea level. Then the river rushes down the next 6 miles to the Lake of Galilee. In the course of its descent from the slopes of Hermon to this point, a distance of only 25 miles, it has dropped 2,275 feet.

From Tiberias the members of the American expedition in their two metal boats followed the endless windings of the Jordan downstream. Gradually the vegetation became sparser and the thick undergrowth extended no farther than the banks. Under the tropical sun an oasis came into view on their right—Jericho. Soon afterwards they reached their goal. There before them, embedded between almost vertical precipices, lay the vast surface of the Dead Sea.

The first thing to do was to have a swim. But when they jumped in they felt as if they were being thrown out again. It was like wearing life-jackets. The old stories were therefore true. In this sea it is impossible to drown. The scorching sun dried the men's skins almost at once. The thin crust of salt which the water had deposited on their bodies made them look quite white. No shellfish, no fish, no seaweed, no coral—no fishing boat had ever rocked on this sea. Here was neither a harvest from the sea nor from the land. For the banks were equally bare and desolate. Huge deposits of coagulated salt made the beach and the rockface above it sparkle in the sun like diamonds. The air was filled with sharp acrid odours, a mixture of petroleum and sulphur. Oily patches of asphalt—the Bible calls it "slime" (Gen. 14^{10})—float on the waves. Even the bright blue sky and the all powerful sun could not breathe any life into this forbidding looking landscape.

FIG. 11.—Mediterranean and Jordan-Basin.

For twenty-two days the American boats went back and forth across the Dead Sea. They tested the water and analysed it, they took innumerable soundings. The mouth of the Jordan, at the Dead Sea, lies 1,280 feet below sea level. If there were any connection with the Mediterranean, the Jordan and the Lake of Galilee, 65 miles away, would disappear. A vast inland sea would stretch almost up to the shores of Lake Huleh.

"When a storm sweeps up through this rocky basin," observed Lynch, "the waves strike the sides of the boats like blows from a hammer. But the weight of the water is such that a short time after the wind has died down the sea is calm again."

The world learned for the first time from the report of the expedition two astonishing facts. The Dead Sea is over 1,200 feet in depth. The bottom of the sea is therefore about 2,500 feet below the level of the Mediterranean. The water of the Dead Sea contains approximately 30% of solid ingredients, most sodium chloride, i.e. cooking salt. The normal ocean has only 3·3 to 4% salt. The Jordan and many smaller rivers empty themselves into this basin of approximately 50 × 10 miles which has not a solitary outlet. Evaporation under the broiling sun takes place on the surface of the sea at a rate of over 230 million cubic feet per day. What its tributaries bring to it in the way of chemical substances remains deposited in this great basin's 500 square miles.

It was only after the turn of the century that, keeping pace with excavations in other parts of Palestine, interest was also awakened in Sodom and Gomorrah. Archaeologists began their quest for the vanished cities that were said to have existed in the Vale of Siddim in Biblical times. At the furthermost south-east point of the Dead Sea remains of a large settlement were found. The place is still called Zoar by the Arabs. The scientists were delighted, for Zoar was one of the five wealthy cities in the Vale of Siddim, which had refused to pay tribute to the four foreign kings. But exploratory digging which was immediately undertaken proved a disappointment. It remains uncertain, however, whether Zoar is identical with the place called Zoar in the Bible.

The date of the ruins that came to light showed it to be a town which had flourished there in the Middle Ages. There was no trace of the ancient Zoar of the king of Bela (Gen. 14^2) or of its neighbours. Nevertheless there were plentiful indications in the environs of mediaeval Zoar that there had been a numerous population in the country in very early times.

On the eastern shore of the Dead Sea the peninsula of el-Lisan protrudes like a tongue far into the water. El-Lisan means "the tongue" in Arabic. The Bible expressly mentions it when the country is being divided up after the conquest. The frontiers of the tribe of Judah are being carefully outlined. In the course of this Joshua gives an unusually illuminating description of their southern limits: "And their south border was from the shore of the Salt Sea, from the bay [lit. 'tongue'] that looketh southward" (Josh. 15^2).

Roman history has a story to tell of this tongue of land, which has always been wrongly regarded with considerable scepticism. Two deserters had fled to the peninsula. The legionaries in pursuit combed the ground for a long time in vain. When they eventually caught sight of the men who had given them the slip it was too late. The deserters were clambering up the rocks on the other side of the water—they had waded straight across the sea. Obviously the sea was more shallow at this spot in those days than it is today.

Unseen from the land the ground falls away here under the surface of the water at a prodigious angle, dividing the sea into two parts. To the right of the peninsula the ground slopes sharply down to a depth of 1,200 feet. Left of the peninsula the water remains remarkably shallow. Soundings taken in the last few years established depths of only 50–60 feet.

Geologists added to these discoveries and observations a fresh explanation which might clarify the occasion and the result of the Biblical story of the annihilation of Sodom and Gomorrah.

The American expedition under Lynch in 1848 produced the first information about the prodigious drop of the Jordan on its short course through Palestine. This plunging of the river bed until it is far below sea level is, as later investigation established, a unique geological phenomenon. "There may be something on the surface of another planet which is similar to the Jordan Valley, but on our planet there certainly is nothing," wrote George Adam Smith, the Scottish Old Testament scholar, in his "Historical Geography of the Holy Land". "No other part of the globe, which is not under water, lies deeper than 300 feet below sea level."

The Jordan Valley is only part of a huge fracture in the earth's crust. The path of this crack has meantime been accurately traced. It begins far north, several hundred miles beyond the borders of Palestine, at the foot of the Taurus mountains in Asia Minor. In the south it runs from the south shore of the Dead Sea through the Wadi el-Arabah to the Gulf of Aqabah and only comes to an end beyond the Red Sea in Africa. At many points in this vast depression signs of earlier volcanic activity are obvious. In the Galilean mountains, in the highlands of Transjordan, on the banks of the Jabbok, a tributary of the Jordan, and on the Gulf of Aqabah are black basalt and lava.

The subsidence released volcanic forces that had been lying

FIG. 12.—THE DEAD SEA (a) in 2000 B.C. before the end of Sodom and Gomorrah; (b) in 1900 B.C. after the disaster.

dormant deep down along the whole length of the fracture. In the upper valleys of the Jordan near Bashan there are still the towering craters of extinct volcanoes; great stretches of lava and deep layers of basalt have been deposited on the limestone surface. From time immemorial the area around this depression has been subject to earthquakes. There is repeated evidence of them and the Bible itself records them. Did Sodom and Gomorrah sink when perhaps a part of the base of this huge fissure collapsed still further to the accompaniment of earthquakes and volcanic eruptions? And did the Dead Sea then take on a further extension towards the south as shown in Fig. 12?

And Lot's wife—"looked back from behind him and she became a pillar of salt" (Gen. 19^{26}).

The nearer one gets to the south end of the Dead Sea the more wild and desolate it becomes. Landscape and mountain grow eerier and more forbidding. The hills stand there silent and everlasting. Their scarred slopes fall sheer and steep down to the sea, their lower reaches are crystal white. The unparalleled disaster which once took place here has left an imperishable and oppressive mark. Only occasionally is a band of nomads to be seen heading inland along one of the steep and rugged wadis.

Where the heavy oily water comes to an end in the south the harsh rock-face on either side breaks off abruptly and gives place to a salt-sodden swamp. The reddish soil is pierced by innumerable channels and can easily become dangerous for the unwary traveller. Sweeping southwards the bogland merges into the desert Wadi el-Arabah, which continues down to the Red Sea.

To the west of the southern shore and in the direction of the Biblical "Land of the South", the Negev, stretches a ridge of hills about 150 feet high and 10 miles from north to south. Their slopes sparkle and glitter in the sunshine like diamonds. It is an odd phenomenon of nature. For the most part this little range of hills consists of pure rock salt. The Arabs call it Jebel Usdum, an ancient name, which preserves in it the word Sodom. Many blocks of salt have been worn away by the rain and have crashed downhill. They have odd shapes and some of them stand on end, looking like statues. It is easy to imagine them suddenly seeming to come to life.

These strange statues in salt remind us vividly of the Biblical description of Lot's wife who was turned into a pillar of salt. And everything in the neighbourhood of the Salt Sea is even to this day quickly covered with a crust of salt.

The question of Abraham's journeyings has not allowed scholars any peace of mind even in recent times. Abraham's sojourn in Egypt, it has been pointed out, cannot be confirmed from non-Biblical sources and even in the Bible it is merely indicated incidentally in connection with a trick to which Abraham resorted because he feared he might be killed on account of his beautiful wife.

The story in question is one of those repetitions to which we refer in the appendix to the present revised edition. It also occurs in *two* places in the Bible (1 Gen. 12, 9ff and 1 Gen. 20, 1ff), except that in the second case there is no mention at all of Egypt, but of "south country" and of Gerar which lies between Gaza and Beersheba.

In whatever way we are to interpret all this, we can scarcely be encouraged to regard the story as historical. Furthermore, the wall paintings in the grave of Khnum-hotpe at Beni-Hasan, in the light of our most recent knowledge, do not fit into the framework of the Biblical account of the patriarchs. And what is the explanation of this? As one would expect of caravan people around 1900 B.C., the caravan people depicted in the Khnum-hotpe grave had donkeys, whereas the Bible says that Abraham and his people, who according to the traditional interpretation are supposed to have lived at the same period, already possessed camels. There is a vast difference between the two animals, whether used for riding or as beasts of burden, in the distance they can travel, their cost, their mobility and consequently also in the safety of caravans equipped with one or the other of these species.

The introduction of the camel as a mount and a bearer of burdens was equal to a revolution in the organisation of transport in the Ancient East. We shall have occasion to refer to the question again.

But when did this "revolution" take place? Zoologists and Orientalists specialising in the study of domestic animals have continued to puzzle over the question, but the famous camels of the patriarchs as well as the camels belonging to those merchants who took Joseph to Egypt (we shall return to this point at the end of the next chapter) quite definitely remain problematical.

Almost more problematical than Abraham's camels, however, is the tradition concerning Sodom and Gomorrah. In particular, we must remember there can be no question that the Jordan fissure was formed before about 4000 B.C. Indeed, according to the most recent presentation of the facts, the origin of the fissure dates back to the Oligocene, the third oldest stage of the Tertiary Period. We thus have to think in terms not of thousands, but of millions of years. Violent volcanic activity connected with the Jordan fissure has been shown to have occurred since then, but even so we do not get any further than the Pleistocene which came to an end approximately ten thousand years ago. Certainly we do not come anywhere near to the third, still less the second millennium before Christ, the period that is to say, in which the patriarchs are traditionally placed.

In addition, it is precisely to the south of the Lisan peninsula, where Sodom and Gomorrah are reported to have been annihilated, that the traces of former volcanic activity cease. In short, the proof in this area of a quite recent catastrophe which wiped out towns and was accompanied by violent volcanic activity is not provided by the findings of the geologists.

But what are we to think of the incursions of the Dead Sea into the more flat area of the southern basin? During the course of its chequered history the Dead Sea or its predecessors in the Pleistocene frequently extended far across today's southern basin into Wadi el Arabah. At times its surface lay as much as 623 feet higher than it does today. The vast sea which had collected there in those days completely filled the whole Jordan rift from Wadi el Arabah as far as the Lake of Galilee. Then the lake diminished in size, no less than 28 ancient shore terraces bearing witness to the process. It is even possible that it dried up completely. Only at a later date did the formation of the Dead Sea of today occur, accompanied probably by violent earth tremors. This, too, took place in the Late Pleistocene when man already existed, but when there could be no question of towns. There is nevertheless the very vague possibility that the experiences of Stone Age man in this region, transmitted from generation to generation, finally took shape as the traditions of "towns" which had disappeared or even gave rise to such a tradition. This tradition appears to be very old, much older than has so far been assumed. We shall refer to it again.

Certainly earthquakes occurred in the Dead Sea area at a later date. Flavius Josephus describes the destruction caused by one which took place in 31 B.C. and there was another in Khirbet-Qumran, where the famous Dead Sea scrolls were found, which left impressive traces behind it, although there are no indications of any catastrophe which might have destroyed towns during the early part of the second millennium before Christ.

Today's placenames such as Bahr-el-hut (sea of lead, which is the Arabic name for the Dead Sea), Jebel Usdum (Mount Sodom) and Zoar do not necessarily derive from genuine, independent, direct, primary traditions parallel to the Bible. It is quite possible that they were applied to these localities subsequently and so linked to the Bible story. If so, they would merely represent a secondary tradition. We have a similar state of affairs with "Joseph's Canal" (Arabic Bahr Yusuf) in Faiyûm in Egypt to which reference will be made in the next chapter. The "Egyptian Joseph" of the Bible also makes his appearance in Islamic tradition and the name of the waterway in question could, and in all probability does, merely refer to that tradition.

It is only very recently that a great stir was caused by the excavation of Tell-el-Mardikh south of Aleppo. It was here that the Italian scholars Paolo Matthiae and Giovanni Pettinato discovered Ebla, a town dating from the third millennium before Christ. The first sensational discovery was that in almost prehistoric times a high degree of culture had existed there with what was for those days an enormously differentiated social structure. The second sensation was that Ebla possessed rich archives of clay tablets. As always with archives of this nature, we are justified in having high hopes, but must be prepared to accept that opinions hitherto considered unassailable may be shown to have been built on insecure foundations. "When the texts have been studied, we shall perhaps have to forget the results of a whole century of research in the Ancient East," is how a German colleague of the Italian scholars expressed it. The third sensation and the most important in connection with the question of names is that the texts from Ebla dating from the third millennium before Christ contain names which are familiar to us from the Bible. The name of Abraham was encountered as well as those of the sinful towns of Sodom and Gomorrah, Admah and Zeboiim on the Dead Sea which were all destroyed by fire. At this point a number of fellow specialists expressed their scepticism. Had Pettinato read the texts correctly, they asked. Of course, they agreed that patriarchs' names have been found in other sources, as has already been mentioned, but did the names of Sodom and Gomorrah really occur in archives of the third millennium before Christ in Syria? Had these towns really existed as the archives said? Or do traditions concerning them go back to such early times, even earlier than the customary date accepted for the beginning of the period of the patriarchs?

A considerable period of time will elapse before all these questions are answered. In the normal way, scholars are not interested in sensations and a vast amount of work has to be done before it can be established beyond a doubt how sensational the finds at Tell-el-Mardikh really are.

II

In the Realm of the Pharaohs
From Joseph to Moses

CHAPTER 8

JOSEPH IN EGYPT

Had Potiphar a prototype?—The Orbiney Papyrus—Hyksos rulers on the Nile—Joseph, official of an occupying power—Corn silos, an Egyptian patent—Evidence of seven years famine—Assignments to Goshen—"Bahr Yusuf": Joseph's Canal?—"Jacob-Her" on scarabs.

"And Joseph was brought down to Egypt: and Potiphar, an officer of Pharaoh, captain of the guard, an Egyptian, bought him of the hands of the Ishmaelites, which had brought him down thither" (Gen. 39¹).

THE tale of Joseph, who was sold by his brothers to Egypt and later as grand vizier became reconciled to them, is undoubtedly one of the finest stories in the world's literature.

"And it came to pass after these things, that his master's [Potiphar's] wife cast her eyes upon Joseph; and she said, Lie with me. But he refused, and ..." (Gen. 39⁷⁻⁸). When her husband came home, she said: "The Hebrew servant, which thou hast brought unto us, came in unto me to mock me" (Gen. 39¹⁷).

Nothing new under the sun—smirked the Egyptologists whenever they started work on the translation of the "Orbiney Papyrus". What they were deciphering from hieroglyphics was a popular story about the time of the XIX Dynasty which bore the discreet title: "The Tale of the Two Brothers". "Once upon a time there were two brothers.... The name of the elder one was Anubis, the younger was called Bata. Anubis owned a house and a wife and his younger brother lived with him as if he were his own son. He drove the cattle out to the fields and brought them home at night and slept with them in the cowshed. When ploughing time came round the two brothers were ploughing the land together. They had been a few days in the field when they ran out of corn. The elder brother therefore sent the younger one off: 'Hurry and bring us corn from the city.' The younger brother found his elder brother's wife having a hair-do. 'Up', he said, 'and give me some corn, for I have to hurry back to the field. My brother said: "Quick, don't waste any time."' He loaded up with corn and wheat and went out with his burden.... Then said she to him: 'You have so much energy! Every day I see how strong you are.... Come! Let us lie down for an hour!—It

97

might give you pleasure, and I shall also make you fine clothes.' Then the young man was as angry as a southern panther at this wicked suggestion that had been made to him. He said to her: 'What a disgraceful proposal you have just made.... Never do it again and I shall say nothing to anyone.' So saying he slung his load on his back and went out to the fields. The wife began to be frightened about what she had said. She got hold of some grease paint and made herself up to look like someone who had been violently assaulted. Her husband ... found his wife lying prostrate as a result of the outrage. Her husband said to her: 'Who has been with you?' She replied: 'No one ... apart from your young brother. When he came to fetch the corn he found me sitting alone and said to me: "Come, let us lie down for an hour! Do up your hair." But I paid no attention to him. "Am I not your mother! and is your elder brother not like a father to you!" I said to him. But he was afraid and struck me to stop me telling you about it. If you leave him alive now I shall die.' Then his brother grew as wild as a southern panther. He sharpened his knife ... to kill his younger brother...."

We can almost see Pharaoh's courtiers whispering over it. They liked this story. Sex problems and the psychology of women interested people even then, thousands of years before Kinsey.

The story of an adulteress, in the heart of an Egyptian tale, as the prototype of the Biblical story of Joseph? Scholars argued the pros and cons based on the text of the "Orbiney Papyrus" long after the turn of the century. On the debit side, there was not the slightest trace of Israel's sojourn in Egypt apart from the Bible itself. Historians and professors of theology alike spoke of the "Legend of Joseph". Egypt was just the kind of country from which one might hope for and even expect contemporary documentation about the events recorded in the Bible. At any rate this ought to be true as far as Joseph was concerned, for he was Pharaoh's grand vizier and therefore a most powerful man in Egyptian eyes.

No country in the Ancient East has handed down its history so faithfully as Egypt. Right back to about 3000 B.C. we can trace the names of the Pharaohs practically without a break. We know the succession of dynasties in the Old, Middle and New Kingdoms. No other people have recorded so meticulously their important events, the activities of their rulers, their campaigns, their erection of temples and palaces, as well as their literature and poetry.

But this time Egypt gave the scholars no answer. As if it were not enough that they found nothing about Joseph, they discovered neither documents nor monuments out of this whole period. The records which showed hardly a break for centuries suddenly stopped about 1730 B.C. From then on for a long time impenetrable darkness lay over Egypt. Not before 1580 B.C. did contemporary evidence appear once again. How could this absence of any information whatever over so long a period be explained, especially from such a highly developed people and civilisation?

Something incredible and frightful befell the Nile country about 1730 B.C. Suddenly, like a bolt from the blue, warriors in chariots drove into the country like arrows shot from a bow, endless columns of them in clouds of dust. Day and night horses' hooves thundered past the frontier posts, rang through city streets, temple squares and the majestic courts of Pharaoh's palaces. Even before the Egyptians realised it, it had happened: their country was taken by surprise, overrun and vanquished. The giant of the Nile who never before in his history had seen foreign conquerors, lay bound and prostrate.

The rule of the victors began with a bloodbath. The Hyksos, Semitic tribes from Canaan and Syria, knew no pity. With the fateful year 1730 B.C. the thirteen hundred year rule of the dynasties came to an abrupt end. The Middle Kingdom of the Pharaohs was shattered under the onslaught of these Asian peoples, the "rulers of foreign lands". That is the meaning of the name Hyksos. The memory of this political disaster remained alive among the Nile people, as a striking description by the Egyptian historian Manetho testified:

FIG. 13.

"We had a king called Tutimaeus. In his reign, it happened. I do not know why God was displeased with us. Unexpectedly from the regions of the East, came men of unknown race. Confident of victory they marched against our land. By force they took it, easily, without a single battle. Having overpowered our rulers they burned our cities without compassion, and destroyed the temples of the gods. All the natives were treated with great cruelty for they slew some and carried off the wives and children of others into slavery. Finally they appointed one of themselves as king. His name was Salitis and he lived in Memphis and made Upper and Lower Egypt pay tribute to him, and set up garrisons in places which would be most useful to him ... and when he found a city in the province of Saïs which suited his purpose (it lay east of the Bubastite branch of the Nile and was called Avaris) he rebuilt it and made it very strong by erecting walls and installing a force of 240,000 men to hold it. Salitis went there every summer partly to collect his corn and pay his men their wages, and partly to train his armed troops and terrify foreigners."

Avaris is the town which under another name plays an important role in Biblical history. Avaris, later called Per-Ramesses, is one of the bond cities of Israel in Egypt (Ex. 1¹¹).

The Biblical story of Joseph and the sojourn of the children of Israel in Egypt probably come into this period of turbulent conditions on the Nile under the rule of the foreign Hyksos. It is therefore not surprising that no contemporary Egyptian information has come down to us. Nevertheless there is indirect proof of the authenticity of the Joseph story. The Biblical description of the historical background is authentic. Equally genuine is the colourful Egyptian detail. Egyptology confirms this from countless finds.

Fig. 14.—Installation of an Egyptian Vizier.

Spices and aromatic products are brought to Egypt by the Ishmaelites, the Arabian merchants who sell Joseph there (Gen. 37²⁵). There was a heavy demand for these things in the Nile country. They were used in religious services, where the wonderfully fragrant herbs were burned as incense in the temples. The doctors found them indispensable for healing the sick, and priests required them for embalming the bodies of the nobility.

Potiphar was the name of the Egyptian to whom Joseph was sold (Gen. 37³⁶). It is a thoroughly characteristic native name. In Egyptian it is "Pa-di-pa-rê", "the gift of the god Rê".

Joseph's elevation to be viceroy of Egypt is reproduced in the Bible exactly according to protocol. He is invested with the insignia of his high office, he receives the ring, Pharaoh's seal, a costly linen vestment, and a golden chain (Gen. 41[42]). This is exactly how Egyptian artists depict this solemn ceremony on murals and reliefs.

As viceroy Joseph rides in Pharaoh's "second chariot" (Gen. 41[43]). That could indicate the "period of Hyksos" at the earliest, for it is only during the period of the "rulers of foreign lands", or even presumably only before their expulsion and before the commencement of the "New Kingdom", that the fast war chariot reached Egypt in consequence of its being adopted by one people after another according to our most recent knowledge. The luxury model of it is the ostentatious chariot which was later used by the rulers of the "New Kingdom". Before their day this had not been the practice on the Nile. The ceremonial chariot harnessed to thoroughbred horses was in those days the Rolls Royce of the governors. The first chariot belonged to the ruler, the "second chariot" was occupied by his chief minister.

Fig. 15.—Ceremonial chariot from Thebes.

Joseph in accordance with his rank married Asenath (Gen. 41[45]) and thereby became the son-in-law of an influential man Potipherah, the priest of Heliopolis. Heliopolis is the On of the Bible and it lay on the right bank of the Nile a little to the north of present-day Cairo.

Joseph was thirty years of age when he "went out over all the land of Egypt" (Gen. 41[45]). The Bible says no more about this but there is a spot by the Nile which still bears his name.

The town of Medinet-el-Faiyûm, lying 80 miles south of Cairo in the middle of the fertile Faiyûm, is extolled as the "Venice of Egypt". In the lush gardens of this huge flourishing oasis grow oranges, mandarines, peaches, olives, pomegranates and grapes. Faiyûm owes these delicious fruits to the artificial canal, over 200 miles long, which conveys the water of the Nile and turns this district, which would otherwise be desert, into a paradise. The ancient waterway is not only to this day called "Bahr Yusuf", "Joseph's Canal", by the fellahin, but is known by this name throughout Egypt. People say that it was the Joseph of the Bible, Pharaoh's "Grand Vizier" as Arab legends would describe him, who planned it.

The Bible depicts Joseph as an able administrator who as grand vizier guides the Egyptian people through difficult times by his counsel and actions, making provision in years of plenty for years of want. Thus he gathers in corn and lays it up in granaries against times of need.

> "And the seven years of plenteousness that was in the land of Egypt were ended. And the seven years of dearth began to come ... and the dearth was in all lands" (Gen. 41[53, 54]).

Years of drought, bad harvests and famine are well attested in the lands of the Nile. In very early times, for example at the beginning of the third millennium, there is said to have been a seven year famine according to a rock inscription of the Ptolemies. King Zoser sent the following message to the governor of the great cataracts of the Nile at Elephantine: "I am very concerned about the people in the palace. My heart is heavy over the calamitous failure of the Nile floods for the past seven years. There is little fruit; vegetables are in short supply; there is a shortage of food generally. Everybody robs his neighbour.... Children weep, young folk slouch around. The aged are depressed, they have no power in their legs, they sit on the ground. The court is at its wits' end. The storehouses have been opened but everything that was in them has been consumed." Traces have been found of the granaries which existed even in the Old Kingdom. In many tombs there were little clay models of them. Apparently they were making provision for possible years of famine among the dead.

> "Now when Jacob saw that there was corn in Egypt, Jacob said unto his sons, Why do ye look upon one another? And he said, Behold I have heard that there is corn in Egypt: get you down thither and buy for us from thence: that we may live and not die. And Joseph's ten brethren went down to buy corn in Egypt" (Gen. 42[1-3]).

This is the reason for the great journey which led to the reunion with the brother who had been sold as a slave and to the migration of the

Israelites into Egypt. The viceroy brought his father, brothers and other relatives into the country: "... all the souls of the house of Jacob, which came into Egypt, were there three score and ten ... and they came into the land of Goshen" (Gen. 46²⁷⁻⁸). The viceroy had obtained permission from the highest authority for his family to cross the frontier, and what the Bible records corresponds perfectly with the administrative procedure of the government.

"And Pharaoh spake unto Joseph, saying, Thy father and thy brethren are come unto thee: The land of Egypt is before thee, in the best of the land make thy father and brethren to dwell: in the land of Goshen let them dwell" (Gen. 47⁵⁻⁶).

A frontier official writes to his superior on papyrus: "I have another matter to bring to the attention of my lord and it is this: We have permitted the transit of the Bedouin tribes from Edom via the Menephta fort in Zeku, to the fen-lands of the city of Per-Atum ... so that they may preserve their own lives and the lives of their flocks on the estate of the king, the good Sun of every land...."

FIG. 16.—Selling corn to Semites from Canaan.

Per-Atum, that crops up here in a hieroglyphic text, is the Biblical Pithom in the land of Goshen, later one of the bond-cities of Israel in Egypt (Ex. 1¹¹).

In cases of this sort the Egyptian frontier police, like the higher officials, were carefully graded in a chain of command right up to the court. The procedure to be followed was of a standard pattern: petitioners for pasture land, refugees from famine stricken countries, were accepted and almost always directed into the same area. It lay on the delta, on the right bank of the Nile in the Biblical "Land of Goshen". The seat of government of the Hyksos rulers was also in the delta.

The children of Israel must have appreciated life in the Land of Goshen. It was—exactly as the Bible describes it (Gen. 45¹⁸; 46³²; 47³)—extremely fertile and quite ideal for cattle breeding. When Jacob died at a ripe old age something happened to him which was quite as unknown and uncommon in Canaan and Mesopotamia as among his own family, who considered it a very remarkable proceeding. His body was embalmed.

"And Joseph commanded his servants, the physicians, to embalm his father, and the physicians embalmed Israel.[1] And forty days were fulfilled for him: for so are fulfilled the days of those which are embalmed" (Gen. 50$^{2-3}$).

We can read in Herodotus, the globetrotter of the ancient world and travel-diarist Number One, how closely this description corresponds with Egyptian practice. Later on Joseph was buried in the same way.

Under the Egyptian Pharaohs a "Sanddweller" could never have become viceroy. Nomads bred asses, sheep and goats and the Egyptians despised none so much as breeders of small cattle. "For every shepherd is an abomination unto the Egyptians" (Gen. 46^{34}). Only under the foreign overlords, the Hyksos, would an "Asiatic" have the chance to rise to the highest office in the state. Under the Hyksos we repeatedly find officials with Semitic names. On scarabs dating from the Hyksos period the name "Jacob-Her" has been clearly deciphered. "And it is not impossible," concludes the great American Egyptologist James Henry Breasted, "that a leader of the Israelite tribe of Jacob gained control for a time in the Nile valley in this obscure period. Such an occurrence would fit in surprisingly well with the migration to Egypt of Israelite tribes which in any case must have taken place about this time."

Like so much of what the Bible relates, the story of Joseph in Egypt has received astonishing confirmation, but this confirmation, as on so many occasions, runs into difficulties.

The confirmation

It is a fact that there were important officials in Egypt who came from Asia Minor. One of their number indeed ruled so independently that an ancient Egyptian source, referring presumably to this individual, even speaks of the "foreign rule of a Syrian".

Egypt's Pharaoh sees in a dream "well favoured kine and fatfleshed" (Gen. 41^{2ff} and ^{18ff}). Joseph interprets these kine as years (Gen. 41^{26f}). Egyptian inscriptions using the hieroglyphic symbol of the cow as a cryptogram, a kind of secret sign, with the meaning "years", have actually been encountered.

Joseph's "agrarian reform" did not affect the land owned by the Egyptian priests (Gen. 47^{22}). At least during one phase of the history of Ancient Egypt there were indeed tax reliefs for Egyptian priests. Herodotus of Halikarnassos, the Greek historian from Asia Minor, the "father of history", (c. 480–post 430 B.C.) is one of those who report this. Parallels to the official installation of Joseph (Gen. 41^{42}) have also been found. Paintings from the time of the New Kingdom at first led people

---

[1] Jacob received from Yahweh the name Israel (Gen. 32^{28}). The nation was later called the "Children of Israel" after him.

to see correspondences, but these would not quite take us back to the time of the Hyksos, although fairly close to their period.

The difficulty

All four confirmations of the Joseph story have nothing to do with the time of the Hyksos (*c.* 1650–1544/41 according to von Beckerath), the time to which the Joseph episode was generally ascribed, but all, without exception, concern later phases of ancient Egyptian history.

The influential Asiatics at the Egyptian court first appear in the time of the Ramessid dynasty (13–12th century B.C.). The case of the Syrian "foreign ruler", to whom reference is made in an ancient Egyptian source, is probably that of Biya or Bai, the powerful chancellor of Queen Tewosre (*c.* 1200 B.C.). This source is the great Harris papyrus, which presumably, if not quite certainly, makes reference to Bai. The Harris papyrus, the statement of accounts of the reign of Ramesses III, dates from the time of Ramesses IV (12th century B.C.).

The symbol of the cow in the meaning of "year" is found only at the time of the Ptolemies (305–30 B.C.) and not earlier. It is consequently a millennium and a few centuries younger than the period of the Hyksos.

The property and tax privileges of the Egyptian priests refer only to the time of the period of the Saïtes (664–525 B.C.).

The description in the Bible of the quite special form of Joseph's installation in office with seal ring, official robe and chain has no precise correspondence, when we examine it closely, to the ancient Egyptian representations from the New Kingdom of the "investiture" and the "conferring of the gold of honour", as was first thought. The closest parallels are found at the time of Sargon II of Ashur (722–705 B.C.). This special form of investiture presumably first came to Egypt through Ashurbanipal (669/8 to about 630 B.C.) who conquered Egypt in 667–666 and in 665 B.C. made Necho, prince of Saïs, Viceroy of Egypt with appropriate ceremony. Here, too, we find express mention of the threefold investiture with ring or rings, official robe and chain.

Two questions have to be asked.

1) If the Bible story of Joseph contains elements dating from such a late period, can it then be as ancient as has been thought until now or must it not have originated much later than has hitherto been assumed?

2) If the period is not right, however, what about the authenticity of the story? And what about the genuineness of its Egyptian atmosphere?

Scholars in all parts of the world had, in fact, been more or less convinced until now of the genuine nature of the "Ancient Egyptian background" of this Biblical story. The impressive list of the reputable scholars who were not averse to regarding Joseph as a Grand Vizier during the Hyksos period almost looks like a "Who's Who" of Egyptology according to a statement made about ten years ago by Donald

B. Redford who published a comprehensive study of the Joseph story in 1970.

Redford and others have scrutinised the Joseph story very closely since that time, however, with the result that considerable doubts have arisen regarding the connection it had hitherto been thought to have with the Hyksos period.

The merchants who bore Joseph away to Egypt had camels to carry their wares (Gen. 37^{25}). These camels are just as much a problem as the "camels of the patriarchs" which were discussed in an earlier chapter in connection with Abraham. For many a Biblical scholar they represent a stumbling-block. In short, they are the source of argument and indicate a later period rather than that of the Hyksos.

Let us proceed with the discussion of the various means of transport. Many have considered the mention of the "chariot" in the Biblical Joseph story as typical of the Hyksos period (Gen. 41^{43}). In this story what is in accordance with fact is that the single-axled, two-wheeled chariot really reached Egypt only during the Hyksos period. On the other hand, the chariot was not abolished at a later date, and indeed the Ancient Egyptian pictures of chariots began only in the time of the New Kingdom. In the famous grave of Tutankhamun, for example, Howard Carter even found war chariots and ceremonial chariots which had been placed in the grave with the dead king. The mention of the chariot can consequently indicate any later period of history.

The Biblical story of Joseph obviously presupposes the knowledge and use of coins (Gen 42^{25} and elsewhere). Principally, however, the word for "bundle of money" (Authorised Version), "moneybag" (Gen. 42^{35}) occurs at a time when coinage already existed. In Egypt and Palestine, this will scarcely have been the case until the sixth century B.C.

Potiphar's title, which is usually translated as "chamberlain" or "court official" and which in the Authorised Version appears as "an officer of Pharaoh, captain of the guard" (Gen. 39^1),[1] really means "eunuch". There was no such title as Potiphar's in Egypt until the time of the Persians (525–332 B.C.).

And so it goes on. Redford enumerates no less than 23 points which all testify against a date assigning the Joseph episode to the Hyksos period, but indicate rather that it belongs to the later period of Ancient Egypt. Even a Biblical scholar like George Ernest Wright, who was so convinced of the genuineness of the Ancient Egyptian atmosphere of the Joseph story, was obliged to admit in 1957 that the Egyptian names occurring in the story, and not least the name Potiphar (Pa-di-pa-Rê), had come into general use only in the time of David. The oldest

---

[1] Translator's note: The Authorised Version of the Bible gives "an officer of Pharaoh, captain of the guard". Luther's German translation says "Pharaoh's chamberlain and captain". I have added the precise words of the Authorised Version.

Egyptian mention of the name Pa-di-pa-Rê (Potiphar) could date only from the 21st Dynasty at the earliest in the opinion of another scholar much inclined towards the "Egyptian Joseph", the Frenchman Pierre Montet. The 21st Dynasty is situated by Jürgen von Beckerath in the period 1080–946 B.C., which would, after all, be the era of David and Solomon. Yet we are still about five hundred years removed from the Hyksos period!

Whatever the question under discussion, the indications always point to phases of Ancient Egyptian history later than the Hyksos period to which scholars have hitherto thought it proper to assign them. Even the pretence made by Joseph of accusing his brothers of being spies (Gen, 42[9] and [15]) has meaning only when levelled against men from Canaan, after Ashur's threat to the eastern frontier of Egypt.

And so the question remains more open today than ever whether the "Egyptian Joseph" of the Bible could be conceived as a historical personality. As things are at present, we can not accept him as the vizier of a Hyksos Pharaoh. We now have to proceed from the concept that the story about him, which reflects conditions in a later period of Ancient Egypt, comes into being very much later than many scholars have thought hitherto, unless we wish to have recourse to the idea that what is shown by direct evidence to have existed in the late period *might* naturally have existed also at an earlier time (and have been recorded exclusively in the Bible).

CHAPTER 9

FOUR HUNDRED YEARS' SILENCE

Reawakening on the Nile—Thebes instigates revolt—Rout of the Hyksos—Egypt becomes a world power—Indian civilisation in Mitanni—The "Sons of Heth" on the Halys—Pharaoh's widow in quest of a mate—The first non-aggression pact in the world—Hittite bridal procession through Canaan.

"And Israel dwelt in the land of Egypt in the country of Goshen: and they had possessions therein, and grew and multiplied exceedingly" (Gen. 47²⁷).

FOR a space of 400 years, during which, politically, the face of the "Fertile Crescent" was completely altered, the Bible is silent. In these four centuries there took place a vast rearrangement of the disposition of national groups. They interrupted the history of the Semitic kingdoms that for 1,000 years had maintained their sway on the Euphrates and the Tigris. The great island of civilisation in the Middle East was rudely dragged from its self-sufficient existence. Foreign peoples with foreign ways surged in from distant and hitherto unknown lands. For the first time it felt the clash with the outside world.

For 150 years there is also silence in Egypt. The prelude to the reawakening of the giant of the Nile opens with a remarkable motif: the roaring of hippopotami.

A papyrus fragment[1] tells how the ambassador of the Hyksos king Apophis went from Avaris to the prince of the City of the South. The City of the South was Thebes and its prince was the Egyptian Sekenenrê, who paid tribute to the foreign overlords on the upper delta. The prince in astonishment asked the emissary of the Asiatic occupying power: "Why have you been sent to the City of the South? Why have you made this journey?" The messenger replied: "King Apophis—may he have long life, health and prosperity!—bids me say to you: Get rid of the hippopotamus pool in the east end of your city. I cannot sleep for them. Night and day the noise of them rings in my ears." The prince of the City of the South was thunderstruck because he did not know what answer to give to the ambassador of king Apophis—may he have long life, health and prosperity! At last he said: "Very well, your master—may he have long life, health and prosperity!—will hear about this pool in the east end of the City of the South." The ambassa-

[1] Papyrus Sallier I (British Museum).

dor however was not to be so easily put off. He spoke more plainly:
"This matter about which I have been sent must be dealt with." The
prince of the City of the South then tried in his own way to get round the
determined ambassador. He was well aware of the ancient equivalent of
the present day slap-up lunch as a means of creating a friendly atmosphere and goodwill. Accordingly he saw to it that the Hyksos commissioner was "supplied with good things, with meat and cakes". But his
luck was out. For when the ambassador departed he had a promise
from the prince in his saddle-bag, written on papyrus. "All that you
have told me to do I shall do. Tell him that." Then the prince of the City
of the South summoned his highest officials and his leading officers and
repeated to them the message that king Apophis—may he have long
life, health and prosperity!—had sent him. "Then one and all remained
silent for quite a while...." At this point the papyrus text breaks off.
The end of the story is unfortunately missing, but we can reconstruct
the sequel from other contemporary evidence.

In the Cairo Museum lies the mummy of Sekenenrê. When it was
discovered at Deir-el-Bahri near Thebes, it attracted special attention
from medical men, for there were five deep sword cuts in the head.
Sekenenrê had lost his life in battle.

It sounds like a fairy tale, yet it is an attractive possibility that the
roaring of hippopotami at Thebes should have unseated the Hyksos
rulers up in the delta. The roaring of a hippopotamus is probably the
most extraordinary casus belli in world history.[1]

Beginning at Thebes the rebellion against the hated oppressors
spread like wildfire throughout the country. Egyptian battalions
marched once more down the Nile. They were accompanied by a
well-equipped fleet of galleys which headed north down the sacred
river. In 1580 B.C., after years of furious attacks, Avaris, the chief
fortress of the Hyksos in the delta, fell amid bloody and savage fighting.
Ahmose I, son of Sekenenrê, was the glorious liberator of Egypt. A
namesake of his, Ahmose, an officer in the new Royal Egyptian Navy,
has left us a record of this decisive battle on the walls of his tomb at
El-Kab. After a detailed description of his education he adds laconi-
cally: "Avaris was taken: I captured one man and three women, four
people in all. His Majesty gave them to me as slaves."

This naval officer had also something to say about the military side of
things: "Sharuhen was besieged for three years before his Majesty
captured it." This was also a profitable occasion for Ahmose: "I
collected two women and one labourer as my booty. I was given gold for
my bravery, as well as the prisoners for my slaves."

Sharuhen was, on account of its commanding position in the Negev,
an important strategic point south of the brown mountain chains of

[1] Apart from this literary tradition an unpublished historical text from Karnak
describes the beginning of the rebellion.

Judah. The small mound of rubble, Tell Far'a, is all that remains of it. Flinders Petrie, the famous British archaeologist, brought to light a thick wall here in 1928.

The multi-coloured army of mercenaries which the Egyptians controlled, consisting of Negroes, Asiatics, and Nubians, marched on northwards through Canaan. The new Pharaohs had learned a lesson from the bitter experience of the past. Never again would their country be taken by a surprise attack. Egypt lost no time in creating a buffer-state far in advance of its frontier posts. The remainder of the Hyksos empire was crushed and Palestine became an Egyptian province. What had once been consular stations, trading posts, and messengers' quarters in Canaan and on the Phoenician coast became permanent garrisons, fortified strong points and Egyptian fortresses in a subjugated land.

After a history of more than 2,000 years the giant of the Nile stepped out of the shadows of his Pyramids and Sphinxes and claimed the right to take an active part in affairs beyond his own border and to have some say in the outside world. Egypt matured more and more into a world-power. Previously, everyone who lived outside of the Nile valley was contemptuously described as "Asiatics", "Sandramblers", cattle-breeders—people not worthy of the attention of a Pharaoh. Now however the Egyptians became more affable. They began communications with other countries. Hitherto that had been unthinkable. Among the diplomatic correspondence in the archives of the palace of Mari there is not one single item from the Nile. *Tempora mutantur*—times change.

Their advance brought them eventually to Syria, indeed to the banks of the Euphrates. There, to their astonishment, they came up against people of whose existence they had no idea. The priests searched in vain through the ancient papyrus rolls in the temple archives, and studied without result the records of the campaigns of earlier Pharaohs. Nowhere could they find even a hint about the unknown kingdom of Mitanni. Its foundation is attributed to an extremely active and creative people, the Hurrians, named as Horites in the Bible about the time of Abraham (Gen. 14[6], etc.).

In the neighbourhood of the oil-wells of Kirkuk in Iraq, where now derricks draw immeasurable wealth from the earth, archaeologists from U.S.A. and Iraq came across a large settlement, the old Hurrian city of Nuzi. Stacks of tablets which have been salvaged, and among these principally marriage contracts and wills, contained extremely interesting information: the Biblical Horites were not a Semitic people. Their home was among the mountains round Lake Van. The names on many Hurrian documents indicate that at least the princely caste must be reckoned as Indo-Aryan. It is even certain that as far as their outward appearance was concerned they belonged to the brachycephalous type like present day Armenians.

In the north of Mesopotamia they had built up the powerful kingdom of Mitanni between the upper reaches of the Euphrates and the Tigris. Their kings had collected round them an aristocracy of warlike charioteers and they bore Indo-Aryan names. The aristocracy of the country was called Marya, which is the equivalent of "Young Warriors". Marya is an old Indian word and their temples were dedicated to old Indian gods. Magic incantations from the Rigveda were intoned in front of the images of Mithras, the victorious champion of Light against Darkness, of Indra, who ruled the storms, and of Varuna, who governed the eternal order of the universe. The old gods of the Semites had crashed from their pedestals.

The Mitanni were completely devoted to their horses, they were "horse-daft". They held the first Derbys in the world along the banks of their great rivers. Advice on the breeding and care of stud animals, directions for the training of cavalry horses, instructions on breaking-in young horses, regulations for feeding and training in racing stables fill veritable libraries of clay tablets. These are works on equitation which can bear comparison with any modern textbook on horse-breeding. As far as the Marya, these aristocratic charioteers, were concerned, horses were of more account than human beings.

It was with this state of Mitanni that Egypt had now a common frontier, nevertheless one on which there was to be no peace. Local feuds were unending. Raids on one side or the other constantly involved Egyptian archers in angry passages with the charioteers. In the course of these expeditions sometimes it was Egyptian striking forces, sometimes columns of Mitanni, who struck deep into the enemy's territory. The valleys of the Lebanon, the banks of the Orontes and the Euphrates were the scenes of endless battles and bloody mêlées. For almost a century the two great kingdoms were at each other's throats.

Shortly before 1400 B.C. the warlike Mitanni proposed a peaceful settlement with the Egyptians. The enemy became a friend.

What was the reason for the unexpected desire for peace on the part of the warlike Mitanni?

The impulse came from outside. Their kingdom was suddenly threatened with war on two fronts. A second powerful opponent began to storm the frontiers with his armies from Asia Minor in the northwest. This was a nation about which scholars until this century knew hardly anything, but which plays a considerable part in the Old Testament—the Hittites.

It was among the "Sons of Heth" that Abraham pitched his tent near Hebron, south of the hills of Judah, and it was from them that he bought the land where he laid his wife Sarah to rest (Gen. 23³³). Esau, much to the distress of his parents Isaac and Rebecca, married two Hittite women (Gen. 26³⁴), and king David himself took "the wife of Uriah, the Hittite" (2 Sam. 11). We are told by the prophet Ezekiel that Hittites

FIG. 17.

were partly responsible for founding Jerusalem: "Thy birth and thy nativity is of the land of Canaan: thy father was an Amorite, and thy mother a Hittite" (Ezek. 16[3, 45]).

The rediscovery of the Hittite people who had sunk into complete oblivion took place in the heart of Turkey shortly after the turn of the century.

In the highlands east of Ankara, the capital, the river Halys makes a huge bend on its way to the Black Sea. Almost exactly in the middle lies Boghaz-Keui: "Boghas" in Turkish means a gorge and "Keui" is a village. Near this "Village in the gorge" the German Assyriologist Professor Hugo Winckler discovered in 1905 a number of cuneiform texts, among which was also a peculiar type of hieroglyphics. They aroused tremendous interest and not only among scholars. The general public learned with amazement just what kind of people these Biblical "sons of Heth" were. The translations of the cuneiform writings brought to the notice of the world at large the hitherto unknown Indo-Germanic Hittites and their vanished empire.

Two years later a fresh expedition set out from Berlin for Boghaz-Keui. This time it was under the direction of the President of the Archaeological Institute of Berlin, Otto Puchstein. The great pile of ruins above the village was carefully examined. This was the site of royal Chattusas, the proud capital of the Hittite empire. What remained of it was a vast ruin of walls, temples, fortified gateways—the remnants of a great city. Its walls enclosed an area of 425 acres. Chattusas was almost as big as mediaeval Nuremberg. At the city gates were life-size reliefs. It is to these effigies, carved out of black basalt as hard as iron, that we are indebted for our knowledge of the appearance of Hittite kings and warriors: their long hair hung over their shoulders like a full-bottomed wig. On top sat a high dented cap. Their short aprons were fastened with a wide belt and their shoes had pointed toes.

When Shuppiluliuma, king of the Hittites, marched south-east with a powerful army about 1370 B.C. the days of the kingdom of Mitanni were already numbered despite all their clever dynastic politics. Shuppiluliuma crushed the kingdom of the warlike charioteers, compelled it to pay tribute, and then pressed on farther to the mountains of the Lebanon in the north of Canaan. Overnight, as it were, Egypt had a new equally powerful neighbour in Syria, thirsting for victory.

A delightful document has come down to us from this period. Prince Mursilis, son of Shuppiluliuma, tells in his autobiography of an episode at the Hittite Court, which must have made such a lasting impression on him that he had it recorded.

Anches-en-Amun, the wife of Pharaoh Tutankhamun, had become a widow. She had very famous parents, Akhnaten and Nofretete. We know her from wonderful Egyptian representations as a slight young thing. But she must have been a woman who knew what she wanted and used all her natural charm to further the aims of her people in the realm of high politics. Using the inviting bed and throne of the Pharaohs as a bait—and what an attractive one—she tried to take the wind out of the sails of her powerful new neighbours by discouraging their warlike intentions. Hittite warriors had just made an attack on Amqa, the fertile country between Lebanon and Anti-Lebanon.

Mursilis dictated: "When the Egyptians heard of the attack on Amqa they were alarmed. To make matters worse, her husband, Tutankhamun, having just died, his widow, the Egyptian queen, sent an ambassador to my father and wrote him the following letter: 'My husband is dead and I have no son. I am told that you have many sons. If you send me one of your sons he could become my husband. I do not wish to take one of my servants and make a husband of him.' When my father heard this he summoned his nobles to a council and said: 'I have never in all my life come across anything like this.' He despatched his chamberlain Hattu-Zitis: 'Go and find out if this is true. Perhaps they are trying to deceive me. There may in fact be a prince. Bring me back reliable information.' The Egyptian ambassador, the honourable Hanis, came to my father. Since my father had instructed Hattu-Zitis before he left for Egypt: 'Perhaps they have a prince of their own: They may be trying to deceive us. They may not need one of my sons at all to occupy the throne', the queen of Egypt now replied to my father in a letter: 'Why do you say, they may be trying to deceive me? If I had a son would I write to a foreign country in a manner that is humiliating both for me and my people? You do not trust me, otherwise you would not say such a thing. He who was my husband is dead and I have no sons. Am I to take one of my servants and make him into my husband? I have written to no other country, I have only written to you. They tell me you have so many sons. Give me one of your sons and he shall be my husband and king over the land of Egypt.' Since my father was so fine a king, he complied with the lady's request and sent her the son she asked for.''

Fate prevented the successful conclusion of this unusual offer of marriage. The royal throne and the bed of Anches-en-Amun both remained empty, since the candidate for both was murdered on his way to Egypt.

Seventy-five years later another offer of marriage on this same Halys-Nile axis had a happy ending, although the prelude to it, which was the din of battle and the clash of weapons, pointed to a different conclusion. Ramesses II, who was called the "Great", set out with his army for Palestine and Syria. He intended to deal with the hated Hittites once and for all.

In the valley of the Orontes, where today fields of cotton stretch far and wide and the old Crusader castle "Krak des Chevaliers" keeps an eye on the fertile plain of Bukea, there lay in those days the city of Kadesh, a little to the south of the dark green of Lake Homs. Before its walls four Egyptian armies threw themselves on the swift war-chariots and infantry of the Hittites. The battle did not, as it happened, bring Ramesses II the victory he had hoped for—he came in fact within an ace of being captured himself—but it put an end to these endless military incidents. In 1280 B.C. the Hittites and the Egyptians concluded the first non-aggression and mutual defence pact in world history. The good understanding was cemented at top level by the marriage of Ramesses II to a Hittite princess. Many lengthy inscriptions give in full and vivid detail the colourful background of what was in the circumstances an international event of the first order. Whether they are found on the walls of the temples at Karnak, Elephantine or Abu Simbel, or on the numerous monuments, they all tell the same story.

As far as self-advertisement and self-praise were concerned, Ramesses II put all his predecessors in the shade. "Then came a messenger to inform His Majesty. He said: 'Behold, even the great Prince of Hatti!

Prince of the Hittites. His eldest daughter is on her way and she brings untold tribute of all kinds. . . . They have reached His Majesty's frontiers. Let the army and the dignitaries come to receive her! Then His Majesty was greatly delighted, and the palace was glad to hear these unusual tidings which were quite unheard of in Egypt. He therefore sent forth the army and the dignitaries to receive her.'"

A large delegation was despatched to the north of Palestine to bring back the bride. Yesterday's enemies became brothers: "So the daughter of the great Prince of Hatti came to Egypt. Whilst the infantry, charioteers and dignitaries of His Majesty accompanied them, they mingled with the infantry and charioteers from Hatti. The whole populace from the country of the Hittites was mixed up with the Egyptians. They ate and drank together, they were like blood-brothers. . . ."

The great bridal train proceeded from Palestine to the city of Per-Ramesses-Meri-Imen in the Nile delta: "Then they brought the daughter of the Great Prince of Hatti . . . before His Majesty. And His Majesty saw that she was fair of countenance like a goddess. . . . And he loved her more than anything else. . . ."

Any of the children of Israel, or their ancestors who were in Egypt at that time, could have been eye-witnesses of the ceremonial arrival of the bridal procession in the city of Per-Ramesses-Meri-Imen, which means "The House of Ramses the Beloved of Amun". As the Biblical description indicates however their presence in this city was by no means of their own accord. It is at this point also that the Bible resumes its narrative. Four hundred years which the Children of Israel had spent as immigrants in the land of the Nile have been passed over in silence. A new and significant chapter of the history of the Biblical people now begins.

To assert that the Bible remains silent concerning a period of four hundred years is correct only if the period of the patriarchs really occurred between 2000 B.C. and approximately 1800 B.C. It is precisely this, however, which recent discoveries have already obliged us to express doubts about. For example, if the legal practices of the Biblical "patriarchs" were to correspond so very exactly to those of the Hurrian town of Nuzi in Mitanni, as we noted in Book I, Chapter 5, the beginning of the patriarchal period at around 1900 B.C. becomes extraordinarily problematical.

The places, too, where the Bible speaks of Hittites appear to consign Abraham and consequently all the Biblical "patriarchs" as well to a later period. Allegedly Abraham acquired the burial-place in Hebron of his wife Sarah from Hittites (Gen. 23[1ff]).

It is a fact that the negotiations for the sale, which are described in detail in the Bible, become clear to us today only by comparison with Hittite documents. Obviously Abraham wanted nothing but the cave and not the whole plot. Hittite documents tell us why. In accordance with Hittite customs, the plot would otherwise have been free for utilisation by the previous owner! In the end, however, agreement was reached and Abraham took not only the cave but also the field and all the trees. This, too, reminds us of Hittite documents dealing with such transactions which always state with scrupulous exactness the number of trees! This is undoubtedly another example of the surprising confirmation of details found in the Bible.

And yet we must ask what Hittites these were with whom Abraham was negotiating. Where did they come from if Abraham, as is alleged, lived at such an early date that the Hittite Empire, which according to Hittite sources was not founded until about the sixteenth century B.C., was not even in existence? And how did Hittites get to Hebron? In other words, to Southern Palestine, between the Dead Sea and the Mediterranean, and, what is more, how does it come about that the Bible (Gen. 23⁷) refers to them as "the people of the land", although the southern border of the Hittite Empire at the time of its greatest extension ran very much farther to the north, somewhat south of the modern town of Aleppo, at any rate "right up on the edge" of the maps of Palestine in current use today? And nothing else is known about any further advance southwards by Hittite settlers.

The Hittite Uriah, whom King David first cuckolded and then sent to his death (2 Sam.11) perhaps came from one of the small early or late Hittite lands which continued to exist in Northern Syria even after the collapse of the Hittite Empire around 1200 B.C. When the Hittites are mentioned as the founders or co-founders of Jerusalem, however, this is perhaps one of those Biblical statements, according to which the "children of Heth" must have been more probably a Canaanite mountain tribe (cf. Numbers 13²⁹⁻³⁰). "The Amalekites dwell in the land of the south; and the *Hittites*, and the Jebusites (i.e. the original inhabitants of Jerusalem) and the Amorites dwell in the mountains; and the Canaanites dwell by the sea, and by the coast of Jordan." These inhabitants of Canaan cannot have had much to do with the Indo-European Hittites of history.

One thing is certain. The problems raised by the references to the Hittites in the Bible have not been cleared up by the discovery of the Hittite Empire in Asia Minor. On the contrary, we now have two categories of Hittites, those in the Bible and the others whose presence in Asia Minor has been proved by archaeology. The statements about the two kinds do not coincide in all respects. The difficulties have not been removed, they are just beginning! It is only the future, as we now know, that can show whether the Bible is correct in what it has to say about the Hittites.

It is necessary to add a "late news item" regarding the Hittites. Mention has already been made of the young widow of a Pharaoh who

requested the Hittite King Shuppiluliuma to send her one of his sons to
be her husband. Until quite recently indeed the conviction was general
that this must refer to Anches-en-Amun, the widow of Tutankhamun.
It is only recently that a dissenting view has been expressed, which is
not yet accepted by all but appears nevertheless to be well founded, to
the effect that the petitioner was not Anches-en-Amun but her elder
sister Meritaton who after the death, or was it the repudiation, of her
mother Nofretete, was made queen and was perhaps the last wife of her
own father, Akhnaten. This deduction has been made because of the
connection between the request for a bridegroom and the Egyptian-
Hittite war, which took place in the time of Akhnaten and not of
Tutankhamun.

CHAPTER 10

FORCED LABOUR IN PITHOM AND RAAMSES

Joseph had died a long time ago—A story in pictures from a prince's tomb—Pithom labour camp in Egyptian texts—The royal seat is transferred to the delta—Ramesses II—A builder's enthusiasm and vanity lead to a fraud—Montet unearths the bond-city of Raamses—Moses wrote his name "MS"—A Mesopotamian story about a baby in the bulrushes—Moses emigrates to Midian—Plagues are no strangers to Egypt.

"Now there arose up a new king over Egypt, which knew not Joseph. Therefore they did set over them taskmasters, to afflict them with their burdens. And they built for Pharaoh treasure-cities [R. V. Store-cities], Pithom and Raamses" (Ex. 1$^{8-11}$).

THE new king who "knew not Joseph" was most likely Ramesses II or one of his predecessors. His ignorance is understandable if Joseph lived centuries before him in the days of the Hyksos. The names of these Hyksos rulers who were so cordially detested by Egyptians have hardly been recorded, far less the names of their dignitaries and officials. Even if this pharaoh of the new dynasty, whether it was Ramesses II or a predecessor, had known of Joseph, that is as far as he would have wanted it to go. Joseph was bound to be an object of contempt to any nationally conscious Egyptian for two reasons. One, that he was an "Asiatic" and a miserable "Sandrambler", and, two, that he was the highest official of the hated occupying power. From the latter point of view any appeal to Joseph would hardly have been a recommendation for Israel in the eyes of a pharaoh.

What forced labour meant in ancient Egypt, and what the Children of Israel experienced at the great building projects on the Nile, can be gathered from a very old painting that Percy A. Newberry, the discoverer of the portrayal of the people who comprise the caravan at Beni-Hasan, found in a rock tomb west of the royal city of Thebes.

On the walls of a spacious vault there is a series of paintings from the life of a great dignitary, the vizier Rekhmirê, showing what he had done for the benefit of his country. One scene shows him in charge of public works. The detail shows the manufacture of Egyptian bricks, the most notable feature being the light-skinned workmen, who are clad only in linen aprons. A comparison with the dark-skinned overseers shows that the fair-skinned men are probably Semites, but

FIG. 18.—Bricklaying with foreign labour in Egypt.

certainly not Egyptians. "He provides us with bread, beer and every good thing." Yet despite these words of praise about the quality of the diet, there is no doubt about the fact that they are not working voluntarily but compulsorily. "The rod is in my hand," one of the Egyptian overseers is saying, according to the hieroglyphic inscription. "Be not idle."

The picture is an impressive illustration of the Biblical words: "And the Egyptians made the children of Israel to serve with rigour, and they made their lives bitter with hard bondage in mortar and in bricks" (Ex. I[13,14]). Israel was of shepherd stock, unused to work of any other kind, which was therefore twice as hard for them. Building and brick making were forced labour.

The painting in the rock-tomb shows a scene from the building of the Temple of Amun in Thebes. The "classical" bond-cities of the children of Israel were however Pithom and Raamses. Both names appear in slightly different form in Egyptian inventories. "Per-Itum", "House of the god Atum", is the name of a town which does not date back further than the time of Ramesses II. Per-Ramesses-Meri-Imen, which has already been mentioned, is the Biblical Raamses. An inscription of the time of Ramesses II speaks of "'PR", "who hauled the stones for the great fortress of the city of Per-Ramesses-Meri-Imen". "'Pr" is Egyptian hieroglyphics for Semites.

The question of where these bond-cities were situated remained a problem. It was known that the rulers of the New Kingdom had moved their seat from ancient Thebes northward to Avaris, which was the place from which the Hyksos had also ruled the country. The new type of international power-politics made it seem advisable to be nearer the centre of things than was the case with Thebes, which lay much farther south. From the delta they could much more easily keep an eye on turbulent "Asia", their dominions in Canaan and Syria. Pharaoh Ramesses II gave his name to the new capital. Avaris became the city of Per-Ramesses-Meri-Imen.

After a fair amount of guesswork and supposition archaeologists' picks put an end to all differences of opinion about the site of one of the bond-cities. Anyone who goes to Egypt can include a trip round its ruins in his programme. It is 60 miles by car from Cairo. About half way down the Suez Canal, where it goes through what was the Lake of Crocodiles,[1] a dried up watercourse known as Wadi Tumilat stretches westward till it strikes the easternmost arm of the Nile. There two mounds of rubble lie about 9 miles apart. One is Tell er-Retabe, which was perhaps the Biblical Pithom, the other is Tell el-Maskhuta, which many scholars consider to be Pithom, whereas others consider it to be the Biblical Succoth (Ex. 12[37]; 13[20]). Apart from remains of granaries, inscriptions have also been found which refer to storehouses.

If there had been patent laws 4,000 years ago, the Egyptians could have claimed exclusive rights over granaries. The silos on Canadian and American wheat farms are still built on the same principle. Admittedly Egyptian silos did not reach the same gigantic proportions, but granaries, circular buildings about 25 feet in diameter with ramps leading up to the feeder, were not uncommon on the Nile. As grand vizier Joseph built granaries (Gen. 41[48ff]) and as slave labourers his descendants built granaries in the land of Goshen.

FIG. 19.—Corn silos in Egypt.

The search for the other bond-city, Raamses,[2] went on for a long time without success. Then nearly thirty years after the discovery of Pithom it was eventually found in 1930.

Ramesses II, the "Great", has given the archaeologists many a hard nut to crack. Apparently his vanity was even greater than his passion for building. He never hesitated to deck himself in borrowed plumes: posterity would marvel at the great builder Ramesses II! And indeed it did. The experts could hardly grasp at first how it came about that on so many temples, public buildings and in other places they came upon the cipher "Ramesses II". But when they examined the buildings a little more closely the explanation was plain. Many of these buildings must have been built centuries before Ramesses II. To pander to his own vanity however Ramesses II decided to have his monogram carved on them all.

In the delta the search for the city of Per-Ramesses-Meri-Imen led from one mound to another. One excavated site after another, throughout the Nile delta, was thought to be the one they were looking for: Pithom, Heliopolis, Pelusium and others. Guesswork came to an end

---

[1] Lake Timsah.
[2] Per-Ramesses-Meri-Imen, probably the earlier Tanis/Avaris or Qantir, eleven miles to the south.

only when the spade of Professor Pierre Montet of Strasbourg struck the ground near the present day fishing village of San in 1929. Thirty miles south-west of Port Said, Montet unearthed between 1929 and 1932 an unusual number of statues, sphinxes, columns, and fragments of buildings, all of them stamped with the crest of Ramesses II. This time there was scarcely any doubt that it was the remains of Per-Ramesses-Meri-Imen, the Biblical bond-city of Raamses. Just as in Pithom they found here ruins of granaries and storehouses.

The Israelites became the victims, in the truest sense of the word, of Pharaoh's lust for building. The position of their immigration area made it easier for them to be dragooned into forced labour. The Goshen of the Bible with its rich grazings began just a few miles south of the new capital and went as far as Pithom. Nothing could be simpler than to drag these foreigners who lived, so to speak, on the doorstep of these great building projects, away from their flocks and tents and force them into servitude.

The ruins at San no longer give any indication of the splendour of the former metropolis. What the columns of Israelite levies saw on their daily march to the building sites we can only gather from a contemporary papyrus letter. It is written by a schoolboy Pai-Bes to his teacher Amen-em-Opet: "I have come to Per-Ramesses of the Beloved of Amun and find it wonderful. A splendid city without a rival. Rê, the same god who founded Thebes, founded this according to the same plan. To live here is to have a glorious life. The countryside provides a wealth of good things. Every day they get fresh provisions and meat. Their pools are full of fish, their lagoons are thick with birds, their meadows are covered with green grass, the fruit from their well tilled fields has the taste of honey. Their storehouses are full of barley and corn and tower up to the sky. There are onions and chives to season the food, also pomegranates, apples, olives and figs from the orchards. Sweet wine from Kenkeme, which tastes nicer than honey. The Shi-Hor branch of the Nile produces salt and saltpetre. Their ships come and go. Everyday here there are fresh victuals and meat. People are glad to be able to live there and nobody cries: God help me! Simple folk live like great folk. Come! Let us celebrate there the festivals of heaven and the beginning of the seasons."

Years later life in the barren wilderness had blotted out the recollection of their forced labour from the minds of the children of Israel. All they remembered was the plentiful food of the delta: "Would to God we had died by the hand of the Lord in the land of Egypt, when we sat by the flesh pots and when we did eat bread to the full" (Ex. 16³). "Who shall give us flesh to eat? We remember the fish which we did eat in Egypt freely: the cucumbers, and the melons, and the leeks, and the onions and the garlic." "Who shall give us flesh to eat for it was well with us in Egypt" (Num. 11 ⁴⁻⁵,¹⁸).

Discoveries during excavations, and contemporary texts, sometimes providing almost literal correspondence, confirm the Biblical picture. We must not think however that the academic dispute over the historicity of these events in the life of Israel is thereby settled.

Professor William Foxwell Albright of America has some sharp words to say on this subject. Since he is one of the few scholars with almost universal qualifications—as theologian, historian, philosopher, orientalist, archaeologist, and comparative philologist—they may well be cited as conclusive. "According to our present knowledge of the topography of the eastern delta the account of the start of the Exodus, which is given in Ex. 12^{37} and Ex. 13^{20}, is topographically absolutely correct." Further proofs of the essentially historical nature of the Exodus story and of the journey in the area of Sinai, Midian and Kadesh can be supplied without great difficulty thanks to our growing knowledge of topography and archaeology.

We must content ourselves here with the assurance that the hypercritical attitude which previously obtained in respect of the earlier historical traditions of Israel has no longer any justification. Even the long-disputed date of the Exodus can now be fixed within reasonable limits.... If we put it at about 1290 B.C. we cannot go far wrong, since the first years of the reign of Ramesses II (1301–1234) were to a large extent occupied with building activities in the city to which he has given his name—the Raamses of Israelite tradition. The striking correspondence between this date and the length of their stay given by Ex. 12^{40} as 430 years—"Now the sojourning of the children of Israel, who dwelt in Egypt, was 430 years" (Ex. 12^{40})—may be purely coincidental but it is very remarkable. According to this the migration must have taken place about 1720 B.C.

The reign of Ramesses II is the time of the oppression and forced labour of Israel, but also the time at which Moses the great liberator of his people appears.

> "And it came to pass in those days, when Moses was grown, that he went out unto his brethren, and looked on their burdens: and he spied an Egyptian smiting an Hebrew, one of his brethren. And he looked this way and that way, and, when he saw that there was no man he slew the Egyptian and hid him in the sand. Now when Pharaoh heard this thing, he sought to slay Moses. But Moses fled from the face of Pharaoh, and dwelt in the land of Midian: and he sat down by a well" (Ex. 2$^{11, 12, 15}$).

Moses is a Hebrew who was born in Egypt, brought up by Egyptians, whose name can be connected with a Semitic root meaning "bring or take out, remove, extract", but can also be interpreted as Egyptian. "Moses" means simply "boy, son". A number of Pharaohs are called Ahmose, Amasis, Thutmose. And Thutmose was the name of the famous sculptor, among whose masterpieces the incomparably beautiful head of Nofretete is still the admiration of the world.

These are facts. Egyptologists know that. But the general public picks on the famous Biblical story of Moses in the bulrushes, and it is not difficult for the eternal sceptic to produce it as an apparently valid argument against the credibility of Moses himself. "It is simply the birth-legend of Sargon"—they say. But they add mentally: "Plagiarism".

Cuneiform texts have this to say of King Sargon, the founder of the Semitic dynasty of Akkad in 2360 B.C.: "I am Sargon, the powerful king, the king of Akkad. My mother was an Enitu priestess, I did not know any father. . . . My mother conceived me and bore me in secret. She put me in a little box made of reeds, sealing its lid with pitch. She put me in the river. . . . The river carried me away and brought me to Akki the drawer of water. Akki the drawer of water adopted me and brought me up as his son. . . ."

The similarity with the Biblical story of Moses is in fact astounding: "And when she could no longer hide him, she took for him an ark of bulrushes, and daubed it with slime and with pitch and put the child therein: and she laid it in the flags by the river's brink" (Ex. 2³ᶠᶠ).

The basket-story is a very old Semitic folk-tale. It was handed down by word of mouth for many centuries. The Sargon legend of the third millennium B.C. is found on Neo-Babylonian cuneiform tablets of the first millennium B.C. It is nothing more than the frills with which posterity has always loved to adorn the lives of great men. Who would dream of doubting the historicity of the Emperor Barbarossa, simply because he is said to be still sleeping under Kyffhäuser?

Officials everywhere and all the time enjoy the protection of the state. So it was in the time of the Pharaohs. So it is today. It was for this reason that Moses had no choice but to flee from certain punishment after he had in righteous indignation killed the guard in charge of the labour gangs.

Moses does what Sinuhe had done before him. He flees eastward to get out of Egyptian territory. Since Canaan is occupied by Egypt, Moses chooses for his exile the mountains of Midian east of the Gulf of Aqabah, with which he had a remote connection. Ketura had been Abraham's second wife, after Sarah's death (Gen. 25¹). One of her sons was called Midian. The tribe of Midian is often called Kenites in the Old Testament (Num. 24²¹). The name means "belonging to the coppersmiths"—Qain in Arabic, Qinâya in Aramaic = a smith. This designation connects up with the presence of metal in the neighbourhood of the tribal territory. The mountain ranges east of the Gulf of Aqabah are rich in copper, as the investigations of Nelson Glueck of America have indicated.

No country will willingly part with a cheap supply of forced foreign labour. Israel had to learn that too. Eventually we are told that it was the occurrence of plagues that compelled the Egyptians to give way. Whether they raged exactly at the time of Moses can so far neither be affirmed nor denied since no contemporary evidence on the subject has so far been found. But plagues are neither improbable nor unusual. Indeed they are part of Egypt's local colour. The water of the Nile "was turned to blood". "And the frogs came up and covered the land of Egypt". "Flies" appear, "lice", a "cattle murrain" and "boils"—finally "hail", "locusts" and "darkness" (Ex. 7–10). These things which the Bible describes are still experienced by the Egyptians, as, for example, the "red Nile".

Deposits from the Abyssinian lakes often colour the flood waters a dark reddish-brown, especially in the Upper Nile. That might well be said to look like "blood".—At the time of the floods "frogs" and also "flies" sometimes multiply so rapidly that they become regular plagues on the land.—Under the heading of "lice" would come undoubtedly the dog-fly. These often attack whole areas in swarms, affect eyes, nose and ears, and can be very painful.

Cattle pest is known all over the world.—The "boils" which attack human beings as well as animals may be the so-called "Nile-heat" or "Nile-itch". This is an irritating and stinging rash which often develops into spreading ulcers. This horrible skin disease is also used as a threatened punishment by Moses in the course of the journey through the desert: "The Lord will smite thee with the botch of Egypt, and with the emerods and with the scab and with the itch whereof thou canst not be healed" (Deut. 28[27]).

"Hailstorms" are extremely rare on the Nile, but they are not unknown. The season for them is January or February.—"Swarms of locusts" on the other hand are a typical and disastrous phenomenon in the countries of the Orient.—The same is true of sudden "darkness". The Khamsin, also called the Simoon, is a blistering hot wind which whirls up vast masses of sand and drives them before it. They obscure the sun, give it a dull yellowish appearance and turn daylight into darkness.—Only the death of the "first-born" is a plague for which there is no parallel (Ex. 12) and the statement in the Bible that the plague of "darkness in all the land of Egypt" affected only the Egyptians, but not the Israelites living in Egypt is, of course, incapable of any scientific explanation. . . .

Forty Years in the Wilderness
From the Nile to the Jordan

CHAPTER 11

ON THE ROAD TO SINAI

Departure from Raamses—Two possible sites for the "Miracle of the Sea"—Traces of fords beside the Suez Canal—Three days without water—Swarms of quails at the migration season—An expedition clears up the mystery of manna—Egyptian mining centre in Sinai—The alphabet at the Temple of Hathor.

"And the children of Israel journeyed from Rameses to Succoth (Ex. 12^{37}). But God led the people about through the way of the wilderness of the Red Sea (Ex. 13^{18}). And they took their journey from Succoth and encamped in Etham, in the edge of the wilderness (Ex. 13^{20}). But the Egyptians pursued after them, all the horses and chariots of Pharaoh, and his horsemen and his army, and overtook them encamping by the sea, beside Pi-Hahiroth before Baal-Zephon" (Ex. 14^{9}).

THE first section of the route followed by the fugitives can easily be followed on the map. It is expressly noted that they did not travel in the direction of the "Way of the Land of Philistines" (Ex. 13^{17}), which was the AI route from Egypt to Asia via Palestine. This main highway for caravans and military expeditions ran almost parallel with the Mediterranean coast and was the shortest and best route, but the one which was most closely guarded. An army of soldiers and officials in the frontier posts kept a sharp watch on all traffic in both directions.

The main road was too risky. The Israelites therefore head southwards. From Per-Ramesses on the eastern branch of the delta the first stage is Succoth in Wadi Tumilat. After Etham the next stage is Pi-Hahiroth. According to the Bible this place lay "between Migdol and the sea, over against Baal-Zephon" (Ex. 14^{2}) "Miktol" appears also in Egyptian texts, it means a "tower". A fort which stood there guarded the caravan route to the Sinai area. All that remains of it has been excavated at Abu Hasan, 15 miles north of Suez.

"And Moses stretched out his hand over the sea: and the Lord caused the sea to go back by a strong east wind all that night and made the sea dry land, and the waters were divided. And the children of Israel went into the midst of the sea upon the dry ground: and the waters were a wall unto them on their right hand and on their left" (Ex. 14²¹⁻²²).

... a detachment of Egyptian chariots, which was attempting to recapture the Israelites, was swallowed up by the sea, the horses and their riders were drowned.

This "Miracle of the Sea" has perpetually exercised men's minds. The difficulty which faced science and research for a long time was not to shed light on the escape itself, for which there were several real possibilities. The only dispute was about the scene of the event, and on this point it is barely possible even yet to get a clear picture.

The first difficulty is one of translation. The Hebrew words "Yam Suph" are sometimes translated as the "Red Sea", at other times as the "Reed Sea". The "Reed Sea" is frequently mentioned: "For we have heard how the Eternal dried up the water of the Reed Sea before you when you left Egypt" (Josh. 2¹⁰: Moffatt's Translation). In the Old Testament up to Jeremiah it is called the "Reed Sea". The New Testament speaks only of the "Red Sea" (Acts 7³⁶; Hebrews 11²⁹).[1]

On the shores of the Red Sea there are no reeds. The Reed Sea proper lay farther north. A reliable reconstruction of the situation that existed then is hardly possible, and that is the second difficulty. The building of the Suez Canal last century has altered the appearance of the landscape to an extraordinary degree. According to those calculations which seem to have most probability, the so called "Miracle of the Sea" must have taken place in that area. What was once Lake Balah, for example, which lay south of the "Way of the Land of the Philistines", disappeared when the canal was constructed and became marshland. In the time of Ramesses II the Gulf of Suez, in the south, was connected to the Bitter Lakes. Probably the connection extended up to Lake Timsah, the Lake of Crocodiles. In this area there was at one time a Sea of Reeds. The waterway to the Bitter Lakes could be forded at several points. Fords can actually be traced there. The flight from Egypt by way of the Sea of Reeds is therefore perfectly credible.

In early Christian times pilgrims surmised that the flight of Israel led them through the Red Sea. At that time they thought in terms of the northern end of the Gulf near the town of Es-Suwez, present-day Suez. The crossing could have taken place here too. Occasionally strong north-west winds drive the water at the northern extremity of the Gulf back so far that it is possible to wade across. In Egypt the prevailing wind is from the west. The east wind mentioned in the Bible is on the other hand typical of Palestine.

[1] Translator's Note: The German Bible uses two expressions: Ried-Meer = Reed Sea and Rotes Meer = Red Sea. The English Bible makes no distinction and uses "Red Sea" throughout. The Hebrew words Yam Suph mean Reed Sea or Papyrus Marsh as modern translations recognise.

"So Moses brought Israel from the Red Sea: and they went out into the wilderness of Shur: and they went three days in the wilderness and found no water. And when they came to Marah they could not drink of the waters of Marah, for they were bitter" (Ex. 15$^{22-23}$).

"And they came to Elim where were twelve wells of water and three-score and ten palm trees" (Ex. 15^{27}).

"And they took their journey from Elim and all the congregation of the children of Israel came unto the wilderness of Sin, which is between Elim and Sinai...." (Ex. 16^1).

The laborious journey began—a nomadic existence in a barren scrub land that was to last for forty years.

With donkeys, goats and sheep only short stretches of about 12 miles a day could be covered. The goal each day was invariably the next water-hole.

Forty long years the children of Israel wandered round the edge of the desert from well to well, from water-hole to water-hole. From the stopping places which the Bible mentions the most important stages of the journey can be marked out.

The route is realistically and convincingly described in Numbers ch. 33. As we should expect with a mixed company of human beings and animals, they never moved far from the oases and pastures of the Sinai peninsula and the Negev.

From the Nile to the mountains of the Sinai peninsula stretches an ancient beaten track. It was the road followed by the countless labour gangs and slave gangs who had been digging for copper and turquoise in the Sinai mountains since 3000 B.C. More than once in the course of these millennia the mines had been forsaken and lapsed for centuries into oblivion. Ramesses II remembered the treasure that was lying dormant and started up the mines once more.

It was along this road to the mines that Moses led his people. It begins at Memphis, crosses the top of the Gulf, at what is now Suez, and then bends south along a waterless stretch of 45 miles, without a single oasis or spring. The Bible expressly mentions that at the beginning of their journey they wandered for three days in the desert without water, then came to a well of undrinkable water, after which they soon reached a particularly rich oasis with "twelve wells and seventy palm trees". This very exact Biblical description helped the experts to find the historical route of the Exodus.

A 45-mile trek with herds of cattle and a large contingent of people would take three days. Nomads can cope with the problem of thirst for a period of this length. They have always their "iron rations" for such an emergency, water in goatskin containers, like the patriarchal family in the mural painting at Beni-Hasan. Forty-five miles from the northern tip of the Red Sea there is still a spring called "Ain Hawarah" by the Bedouins. Nomads are very reluctant to stop here with their cattle. The water is not inviting for a long stay. It is salty and sulphurous, or "bitter" as the Bible calls it. This is Marah of olden times.

Fifteen miles farther on to the south, exactly a day's march, lies Wadi Gharandel. A fine oasis with shady palms and plenty of water-holes. That is the Biblical Elim, the second stopping place. After Elim begins the Wilderness of Sin, on the shore of the Red Sea, now known as the Plain of El Kaa. The children of Israel have come no great distance, but they are untrained and unused to privation after what was despite its rigours a well fed and well ordered life in Egypt. It is no wonder that they gave tongue to their disappointment and complaints. However they were able to augment their scanty diet with two unexpected but most welcome items.

> "And it came to pass that at even the quails came up and covered the camp: and in the morning ... when the dew that lay was gone up, behold upon the face of the wilderness there lay a small round thing, as small as the hoar frost on the ground. And when the children of Israel saw it, they said one to another, it is manna [i.e. What is this?], for they wist not what it was. And Moses said unto them, This is the bread which the Lord hath given you to eat" (Ex. 16$^{13-15}$).

Time and again more or less profound discussions have taken place over this question of the quails and the manna. What a vast amount of disbelief they have occasioned. The Bible is telling us about things that are miraculous and inexplicable! On the contrary quails and manna are perfectly matter of fact occurrences. We need only ask a naturalist or natives of these parts who can see the same thing happening today.

The Exodus of the Israelites began in the spring, the time of the great bird migrations. From Africa, which in summer becomes unbearably hot and dry, the birds have from time immemorial migrated to Europe along two routes. One route goes via the west coast of Africa to Spain, the other via the Eastern Mediterranean to the Balkans. In the early months of the year, quails, together with other birds, fly across the Red Sea, which they must cross on the eastern route. Exhausted by their long flight, they alight on its flat shores to gather fresh strength for the next stage of their journey over the high mountains to the Mediterranean. Josephus (*Antiquities*, III, 1, 5) describes an experience of this kind, and even today the Bedouins of this area catch the exhausted quails in spring and autumn by hand.

As far as the famous manna is concerned, we have reliable information from the botanist. To anticipate: anyone who is interested in manna will find it on the list of exports from the Sinai peninsula.

Further, its supplier is registered in every botanical index of the Middle East, it is the Tamarix Mannifera, Ehr.

There is no lack of fully authenticated descriptions of its occurrence. The following eye-witness account is almost five hundred years old.

"In every valley throughout the whole region of Mt. Sinai there can still be found Bread of Heaven, which the monks and the Arabs gather, preserve and sell to pilgrims and strangers who pass that way." These words were written in 1483 by Breitenbach, Dean of Mainz, in an account of his pilgrimage to Sinai. "This same Bread of Heaven", he continues, "falls

FIG. 20.—Catching quails on the Nile.

about daybreak like dew or hoarfrost and hangs in beads on grass, stones, and twigs. It is sweet like honey and sticks to the teeth. We bought a lot of it."

In 1823 the German botanist G. Ehrenberg published a paper[1] which even his colleagues received with incredulity. His explanation seemed indeed to ask people to believe too much, namely that this notorious manna is nothing more than a secretion exuded by tamarisk trees and bushes when they are pierced by a certain type of plant-louse which is found in Sinai.

A hundred years later an organised manna expedition was under way. Friedrich Simon Bodenheimer and Oskar Theodor, botanical experts from the Hebrew University at Jerusalem, set out for the Sinai Peninsula, to clear up the disputed question of the existence of manna once and for all. For several months the two scientists investigated the dry water-courses and oases in the whole area of Mt. Sinai. Their report caused a sensation. They not only brought back the first photographs of manna and fully confirmed the findings of Breitenbach and Ehrenberg, but also established the factual truth of the Biblical description of the desert migration of the people of Israel.

Without the plant-louse mentioned first by Ehrenberg there would in fact be no manna at all. These little insects live primarily off tamar-isks which are a type of tree indigenous to Sinai. They exude a peculiar resinous secretion, which according to Bodenheimer is about the same shape and size as a coriander seed. When it falls to the ground it is white in colour, but after lying for some time it becomes yellowish-brown. Naturally the two scientists did not fail to taste the manna.

[1] "Symbolae Physicae".

Bodenheimer's verdict was: "The taste of these crystallised grains of manna is peculiarly sweet. It is most of all like honey when it has been left for a long time to solidify." "And it was like coriander seed, white: and the taste of it was like wafers made with honey", says the Bible (Ex. 16[31]).

The findings of the expedition likewise confirmed the other features of the Biblical description of manna. "And they gathered it every morning, every man according to his eating: and when the sun waxed hot, it melted" (Ex. 16[21]). Exactly in the same way today the Bedouins of the Sinai peninsula hasten to gather up their "Mann es-Samâ", the "Manna from Heaven", as early as possible in the morning, for the ants are keen competitors. "They begin gathering when the ground temperature reaches 21 degrees centigrade," says the report of the expedition, "which is about 8.30 a.m. Until then the insects are inert." As soon as the ants become lively, the manna disappears. That must have been what the Biblical narrator meant when he said that it melted. The Bedouins prudently do not forget to seal the manna they have collected carefully in a pot, otherwise the ants pounce on it. It was just the same in Moses' day during the sojourn in the desert: "But some of them left of it until the morning: and it bred worms. . . ." (Ex. 16[20]).

The incidence of the manna depends on favourable winter rains and is different from year to year. In good years the Bedouins of Sinai can collect 4 pounds per head in a morning,—a considerable quantity which is quite sufficient to satisfy a grown man. Thus Moses was able to order the children of Israel to "gather of it every man according to his eating" (Ex. 16[16]).

The Bedouins knead the globules of manna into a purée which they consume as a welcome and nourishing addition to their often monotonous diet. Manna is indeed an exportable commodity, and if it is carefully preserved, forms an ideal "iron ration" since it keeps indefinitely.—"And Moses said unto Aaron: Take a pot and put an omer full of manna therein, and lay it up before the Lord, to be kept for your generations" (Ex. 16[33]).

"And the children of Israel did eat manna forty years, until they came to a land inhabited: they did eat manna until they came unto the borders of the land of Canaan" (Ex. 16[35]). Tamarisks with manna still grow in Sinai and along the Wadi el Arabah right up to the Dead Sea.

So far we have listened to science. But the question that has to be asked is whether we have not at this point crossed the frontiers of science and entered the territory of the unknown, the sphere of the miraculous? For it is clear beyond all possible doubt that the Bible does not intend us to think of this as something that happened in the normal course of events but as an act of God. The same thing is true of the quails.

"And they took their journey out of the wilderness of Sin, and encamped in Dophkah" (Num. 33^{12}).

Several hundred metres above the waters of the Red Sea lies the monotonous expanse of the Wilderness of Sin. On this torrid plateau the only things that break the bright yellow flatness of the sand are camel-thorns and sparse brushwood. Not a breath of wind or a breeze fans the traveller's brow. Anyone following the ancient beaten track to the south-east encounters an unforgettable sight: directly ahead on the horizon a jagged mountain range rises abruptly from the plateau—the Sinai massif. At closer quarters geological formations of unusual and rare ranges of colour meet the eye. Precipitous cliffs of pink and mauve granite thrust their way upwards to the blue sky. Between them sparkle slopes and gorges of pale amber and fiery red, streaked with lead-coloured veins of porphyry and dark-green bands of felspar. It is as if all the colour and beauty of a garden had been poured into this wild serrated symphony in stone. At the margin of the Wilderness of Sin the beaten track ends abruptly and is lost in a wadi.

No one knew where to look for Dophkah until the turn of the century. The only clue was contained in the name of the place itself. "Dophkah", so the subtleties of philology inform us, is related in Hebrew to the word for "smelting operations". Smelting operations take place where there are mineral deposits.

In the spring of 1904 Flinders Petrie, who had made a name for himself in England as a pioneer of Biblical archaeology, set out from Suez with a long camel caravan. A veritable mass-formation of scholars, thirty surveyors, Egyptologists and assistants accompanied him. From the banks of the Suez Canal the expedition followed the line of the Egyptian beaten track into the wilds of Sinai. Through the Wilderness of Sin as far as the mountains it followed the same route as Israel.

Slowly the caravan made its way along a wadi and round a sharp bend in the hills—suddenly time seemed to rush back three or four thousand years. The caravan was transported straight back into the world of the Pharaohs. Petrie ordered a halt. From a terrace in the rock face a temple projected into the valley. From the square columns at the gateway stared the face of a goddess with great cow's ears. A jumble of pillars with one very tall one seemed to be growing out of the ground. The yellow sand round a number of little stone altars showed unmistakable evidence of the ashes of burnt offerings. Dark caverns yawned round the cliff-face and high above the wadi towered the solid massif of Sinai.

The cries of the drivers were silenced. The caravan stood motionless as if overpowered by the almost ghostly sight.

In the ruined temple Petrie found the name of the great Ramesses II carved on the walls. The expedition had reached Serabit el-Khadem, the ancient Egyptian mining and manufacturing centre for copper and turquoise. In all probability this is where we should look for the Dophkah of the Bible.

For two long years a camp in front of the old temple brought new life into the valley. Representations of cultic acts and pictures of sacrifices on the walls of the temple indicate that this had been a centre of worship of the goddess Hathor. An almost endless confusion of half choked galleries in the neighbouring wadis bore witness to the search for copper and turquoise. The marks of the workmen's tools were unmistakable. Tumbledown settlements which housed the workers lie in the immediate neighbourhood.

The pitiless sun beat down on this cauldron of a valley, filling it with unbearable heat and making the work of the expedition doubly difficult. A worker's life in these mines in the desert must have been, above all in summer, pure hell. An inscription from the reign of Amenemhet III about 1800 B.C. told the party what it had been like.

Hor-Ur-Re, bearer of the royal seal and "Minister of Labour" under Pharaoh, is addressing the miners and slaves. He tries to cheer them on and encourage them: "Anyone should think himself lucky to work in this area". But the reply is: "Turquoise will always be in the mountain. But it is our skins we have to think about at this time of the year. We have already heard that ore has been quarried at this season. But really, our skin is not made for that sort of thing at this time of the year." Hor-Ur-Re assures them: "Whenever I have brought men out to these mines my one consideration has always been the honour of His Majesty.... I never lost heart at the sight of work.... There was no talk of: 'O for a tough skin'. On the contrary, eyes sparkled...."

While the excavations in the old mines, the dwelling houses, and the temple precincts were in full swing, only a few paces from the sanctuary of the goddess fragments of stone tablets were dug out of the sand together with a statue of a crouching figure. On both the tablets and the sculpture there were unusual markings. Neither Flinders Petrie nor the Egyptologists in the party could make anything of them. They were obviously written characters of a type never seen before. Although the inscriptions give a pictographic impression—they are reminiscent of Egyptian hieroglyphics—they can hardly be said to be a picture language. There are too few different signs for that.

When all the circumstances of the find had been carefully gone into Flinders Petrie came to the following daring conclusion: "Workmen from Retenu, who were employed by the Egyptians and are often mentioned, had this system of linear writing. The inference that follows from that is extremely significant, namely that about 1500 B.C. these simple workmen from Canaan were able to write and that the type of writing is independent both of hieroglyphics and cuneiform. Further, it invalidates once and for all the hypothesis that the Israelites who came through this area from Egypt, were at that stage still illiterate."

This explanation aroused considerable attention among anti-quarians, palaeographers, and historians. All existing theories about the origin and first use of writing in Canaan were at once out of date. It seemed incredible that the inhabitants of Canaan could have had their own type of script as far back as the middle of the second millennium B.C. Only from the text of the Sinai tablets could it be proved whether Petrie was actually right. Immediately on his return to England Petrie had the tablets copied.

Palaeographers from all countries pounced upon these awkward-looking scratched-out characters. No one was able to make any sense of them. It was not till ten years later that Sir Alan Gardiner, the brilliant and tireless translator of Egyptian texts, lifted the veil. He it was who first succeeded in deciphering parts of the inscriptions.

The repeated appearance of the notched "shepherd's crook" helped him along. Eventually Gardiner conjectured that a combination of four or five signs which occurred several times represented ancient Hebrew words. The five characters l-B-'-l-t he interpreted as "(dedicated) to (the goddess) Baalath".

In the second millennium B.C. a female deity with the name of Baalath was venerated in the seaport of Byblos. It was to this same goddess that the temple at Serabit el-Khadem had been erected by the Egyptians. Only the Egyptians called her Hathor. Workmen from Canaan had dug for copper and turquoise beside her temple.

The chain of evidence was complete. The significance of the discov-ery at Sinai did not fully emerge until six years after Flinders Petrie's death, by which time it had had further exhaustive research and study.

Gardiner had only been able to decipher part of the strange charac-ters. Thirty years later, in 1948, a team of archaeologists from the University of Los Angeles found the key which made it possible to give a literal translation of all the characters on the Sinai tablets. Without a doubt the inscriptions had their origin about 1500 B.C. and are written in a Canaanite dialect.

What Flinders Petrie wrested from the burning sands of Sinai in 1905 nowadays meets the eye everywhere in a different form in newspapers, magazines, books—and the keys of a typewriter. For these stones in Serabit el-Khadem provided the ancestor of our alphabet. The two primary modes of expression in the "Fertile Crescent", namely hiero-glyphics and cuneiform, were already quite ancient when a third fundamental way of expressing men's thoughts was born in the second millennium B.C.—namely the alphabet. Possibly stimulated by the picture language of their Egyptian comrades, these Semitic workmen in Sinai devised their own peculiar and quite different type of script.

	SINAI 1500 B.C.	CANAAN 1000 B.C.	PHOENICIAN 750 B.C.	OLD GREEK	PRESENT DAY
OX-HEAD					A
FENCE					H
WATER					M
MAN'S HEAD					R
BOW					S

Fig. 21.—Development of our alphabet.

The famous Sinai inscriptions are the first stage of the North Semitic alphabet, which is the direct ancestor of our present alphabet. It was used in Palestine, in Canaan, in the Phoenician Republics on the coast. About the end of the 9th century B.C. the Greeks adopted it. From Greece it spread to Rome and from there went round the globe.

"And the Lord said unto Moses, Write this for a memorial in a book...." (Ex. 17[14]). The first time that the word "write" is mentioned in the Old Testament is when Israel reaches the next stopping place after Dophkah. Previously the word is never used. The deciphering of the Sinai tablets shows up this Biblical passage in a completely new light as a historical statement. Because we now know that three hundred years before Moses led his people out of Egypt to Sinai, men from Canaan had already been "writing" in this area, in a language which was closely related to that of Israel.

CHAPTER 12

AT THE MOUNTAIN OF MOSES

The "Pearl of Sinai"—Israel was 6,000 strong—Striking water from rock—Practical experience in desert life—Was the Burning Bush a gasplant?—The valley of the monks and hermits—The great miracle.

"And all the congregation of the children of Israel journeyed from the wilderness of Sin, after their journeys, according to the commandment of the Lord, and pitched in Rephidim (Ex. 17^1). Then came Amalek and fought with Israel in Rephidim (Ex. 17^8)."

REPHIDIM is now Feiran, extolled by the Arabs as the "Pearl of Sinai". Protected by the lonely but colourful rock barrier which surrounds it, this miniature paradise has presented the same appearance for thousands of years. A small grove of palm trees provides welcome shade. As they have always done since the days of their remote ancestors, the nomads bring their flocks here to drink and rest on the tiny grass carpet.

From the main camp Flinders Petrie organised parties to investigate the neighbouring territory. By dint of exhausting and difficult journeys he got to know the wadis and mountains right down to the shores of the Red Sea. He established that Feiran is the only oasis in the whole southern part of the massif. For the nomads who lived, and still live here it is essential for existence and is their most precious possession. "The Amalekites must have been trying to defend Wadi Feiran from the foreign invaders," reflected Flinders Petrie. His next thought was: "If the climate has not changed—and the proof of that lies in the fact that the sandstone pillars in Serabit-el-Khadem show no sign of erosion despite the thousands of years of their existence—the population must also be numerically the same. Today at a rough estimate 5,000 to 7,000 nomads live with their flocks on the Sinai peninsula. Israel must therefore have been about 6,000 strong since the battle with the Amalekites appears to have been indecisive." "And it came to pass, when Moses held up his hand, that Israel prevailed: and when he let down his hand Amalek prevailed" (Ex. 17^{11}).

Bitter fighting continued all day "until the going down of the sun", when at length Joshua won a decisive victory for Israel. Thereafter the way was open to the water supply in the oasis of Rephidim. Before that "there was no water for the people to drink" (Ex. 17^1). In this emergency Moses is said to have taken his rod and produced water by striking a rock (Ex. 17⁶), an action which has been regarded, and not only by sceptics, as quite incomprehensible, although the Bible is merely once more recording a perfectly natural occurrence.

Major C. S. Jarvis, who was British Governor of Sinai in the thirties, has seen it happen himself. "Moses striking the rock at Rephidim and the water gushing out sounds like a genuine miracle, but the writer has actually seen this happen. Several men of the Sinai Camel Corps had halted in a dry wadi and were in process of digging about in the rough sand that had accumulated at the foot of a rock-face. They were trying to get at the water that was trickling slowly out of the limestone rock. The men were taking their time about it and Bash Shawish, the coloured sergeant, said: 'Here, give it to me!' He took the spade of one of the men and began digging furiously in the manner of N.C.O.'s the world over who want to show their men how to do things but have no intention of keeping it up for more than a couple of minutes. One of his violent blows hit the rock by mistake. The smooth hard crust which always forms on weathered limestone split open and fell away. The soft stone underneath was thereby exposed and out of its apertures shot a powerful stream of water. The Sudanese, who are well up in the activities of the prophets but do not treat them with a vast amount of respect overwhelmed their sergeant with cries of: 'Look at him! The prophet Moses!' This is a very illuminating explanation of what happened when Moses struck the rock at Rephidim."

C. S. Jarvis had witnessed a pure coincidence. For the men of the Camel Corps were Sudanese and not in any sense natives of Sinai, who might be expected to be familiar with the technique of producing water in this way. On the journey from Kadesh to Edom Moses employed this method of striking water once more. "And Moses lifted up his hand and with his rod he smote the rock twice," as we are told in Num. 20¹¹. "And the water came out abundantly and the congregation drank and their beasts also." He had obviously got to know this highly unusual method of finding water during his exile among the Midianites.

At the beginning of the Christian era many monks and hermits settled in Feiran, where Israel had had to cope with its first hostile attack under Moses. In the gullies and on the cliffs they built their tiny cells. A church was founded in Feiran and 25 miles south of the oasis a little chapel was erected at the foot of Jebel Musa.

The barbaric tribes of nomads however gave the hermits and monks of Sinai no peace. Many of them lost their lives in these repeated attacks. St. Helena, eighty year old mother of Constantine, the first Christian emperor, during a visit to Jerusalem in A.D. 327, learned of the plight of the monks of Sinai and founded a tower of refuge which was erected at the foot of the mountain of Moses.

In A.D. 530 the Byzantine emperor Justinian caused a strong defensive wall to be built round the little chapel at the mountain of Moses. Right up to the Middle Ages this fortified church at Jebel Musa was the goal of devout pilgrims who came to Sinai from every land. A legend tells how this notable spot came to be called "St. Catherine's Monastery", which is the name it bears still.

Napoleon was instrumental in saving the masonry of this isolated early Christian fortress from collapse.

In 1859 the German theologian Constantine von Tischendorf discovered in the monastery at Sinai in a good state of preservation one of the most precious parchment manuscripts of the Bible, the famous "Codex Sinaiticus". It dates from the 4th century A.D. and contains the New Testament and parts of the Old Testament.

The Czar accepted it as a gift, giving the monastery 9,000 roubles for it. Then this priceless possession found its way into the library at St. Petersburg. Finally in 1933 the British Museum bought the "Codex Sinaiticus" from the Soviet Government for £100,000.

The little chapel at the foot of Jebel Musa was built on the site where Moses according to the Bible encountered the Burning Bush: "And he looked and behold the bush burned with fire, and the bush was not consumed" (Ex. 3²).

Different attempts have been made to find a scientific explanation of this remarkable phenomenon. An expert on the botany of the Bible, Dr. Harold N. Moldenke, director and curator of the Botanical Garden in New York, has this to say: ". . . Among the commentators who think that a natural explanation can be found, some think that the phenomenon of the bush that 'burned with fire' and yet 'was not consumed' can be explained as a variety of the gas-plant or Fraxinella, the Dietamnus Albus L. This is a plant with a strong growth about three feet in height with clusters of purple blossom. The whole bush is covered with tiny oil-glands. This oil is so volatile that it is constantly escaping and if approached with a naked light bursts suddenly into flames. . . . The most logical explanation seems to be that suggested by Smith. He puts forward the theory that the 'flames' may have been the crimson blossoms of mistletoe twigs (Loranthus Acaciae) which grow on various prickly acacia bushes and acacia trees throughout the Holy Land and in Sinai. When this mistletoe is in full bloom the bush becomes a mass of brilliant flaming colour and looks as if it is on fire."

"For they were departed from Rephidim, and were come to the desert of Sinai, and had pitched in the wilderness: and there Israel camped before the mount. And Moses went up unto God" (Ex. 19²⁻³).

"So Moses went down unto the people and spake unto them. And God spake all these words saying, I am the Lord thy God. . . . Thou shalt have no other gods before me" (Ex. 19²⁵; 20¹⁻³).

At Sinai something happened which is unique in the history of mankind. Here lie both the roots and the greatness of a faith which was strong enough to conquer the globe.

Moses, this child of a world which believed in a host of deities and in gods of all shapes and forms, proclaimed his faith in one God alone. Moses was the herald of monotheism—that is the true greatness of this incomprehensible miracle of Sinai. Moses—this unknown son and grandson of desert nomads, brought up in a foreign land, "went down unto the people and spake unto them". Nomads in their goatshair tents, camping in the desert under the open sky, are the first to hear this astounding message, to accept it and transmit it. First of all for thirty-nine years, in the solitude of the desert, by gurgling springs, beside the still waters of shady oases, and facing the biting wind which sweeps across the sullen landscape, as they feed their sheep, their goats and their donkeys, they speak among themselves of the one great God, YHWH.

So begins the wonderful story of this world embracing faith. Simple shepherds, inured to hardship, carried the great new idea, the new faith, to their homeland, whence the message was one day to go out into the whole world and to all the peoples of the earth. The great nations and mighty empires of these far off days have long since disappeared into the dark recesses of the past. But the descendants of those shepherds who were the first to pledge their faith in one sole omnipotent God, are still alive today.

"I am the Lord thy God. Thou shalt have no other gods before me." That was a word heard for the first time since man inhabited this planet. There was no pattern for this faith, no hint of it from other nations.

We can make this assertion with confidence thanks to archaeological discoveries in Egypt, the land in which Moses grew up and received his education, as well as in other lands of the ancient East. Both the sun-worship of Akhnaten and the appearance in Mesopotamia of a blending of many deities into one sole god, Ninurta, god of war, are but vague preludes to monotheism. In all these conceptions what is lacking is the concentrated power and redemptive moral purpose rooted in the Ten Commandments, which Moses brought down from the lonely heights of Mt. Sinai into the hearts and minds of men.

It is only among the people of Israel out of the whole of the "Fertile Crescent" that there is this awakening of the new idea of God in all its clarity and purity, untainted by magic, free from a variegated and grotesque imagery, and conceived as something other than a materialistic preparation for perpetuating the self beyond the grave. Without precedent and prototype seems likewise the clear imperative of the Ten Commandments. The Israelites are bidden not to sin because they are under the obedience of Yahweh!

It was certainly possible to be quite convinced that the God-given moral law of Israel was without precedent in the Ancient East until parallels became known which show quite clearly that the Bible is certainly not alone, as seemed to be the case, in one of its most essential passages, the Ten Commandments together with Israel's other statutes. On the contrary, the Bible now proves to be completely penetrated by the spirit of the Ancient East. The Ten Commandments are thus a kind of "treaty of alliance", the "fundamental constitutional law" between Israel and its God. It is not to be wondered at, therefore, if they are in complete accordance with the treaties made with vassals in the Ancient East defining the relations between a ruler and the vassal kings he appointed to govern the peoples he had subjugated.

Such treaties began with the enumeration of the names, titles and services of the "great king". "I am the Lord thy God which have brought thee out of the land of Egypt, out of the house of bondage" (Exodus, 20^2). Here, too, we have the name (the word "Lord" according to Biblical usage in place of the real name of God, Yahweh, which it was not permitted to pronounce), the title, "God", and the essential service rendered ("which have brought you out of the land of Egypt") by the "great king", except that in this case it was Israel's heavenly "great king", the God of the Covenant. Vassals were forbidden, moreover, to enter into any relationships with foreign rulers and the commandment "Thou shalt have no other gods but me" (Ex. 20^3) corresponds to this. The imperious "thou shalt" and "thou shalt not" continually occur in the treaties with vassals. These words are consequently not by any means restricted to the Biblical Ten Commandments as many scholars have thought. One treaty with a vassal, for example, prescribes that "thou shalt not covet any territory of the land of the Hatti". Similarly the Bible prescribes that "thou shalt not covet thy neighbour's house ..." (Ex. 20^{17}).

Other correspondences have also been noted and even include not only the safe-keeping of the tables of the law in the Ark of the Covenant in the same way that treaties with vassals were deposited in holy shrines, but also the sealing of the treaties on the one hand and the pronouncement of blessings and curses on the other. In the words of Moses (Deut. 11$^{26-28}$): "Behold, I set before you this day a blessing and a curse; a blessing, if ye obey the commandments of the Lord your God, which I command you this day: and a curse, if you will not obey the commandments of the Lord your God ..."

The well-known Catholic Bible scholar Roland de Vaux, of whom mention has already been made, discovered in a number of Hittite treaties with vassals the injunction that the text of the treaty was to be read out regularly in the presence of the vassal king and his people. And similarly with the Biblical code of laws for we read (Deut. 31^{10ff}): "And Moses commanded them saying, At the end of every seven years ...

thou shalt read this law before all Israel in their hearing ... that they may hear, and that they may learn, ... and observe to do all the words of this law."

All this concerns merely the outer form of the Ten Commandments. What about the spirit? Again there is no lack of parallels. In Assyria, for example, a priest who was driving the "demons" out of a sick person, had to ask: "Has he (i.e. the sick person) offended a god? Or slighted a goddess? ... Has he shown contempt to his father and mother? Or set little store by his elder sister? ... Has he said 'It is' instead of 'It is not' (and vice versa)? ... Has he given wrong weight? Has he broken into his neighbour's house? Has he approached too near to his neighbour's wife? Has he shed his neighbour's blood?"

Finally, two examples from Ancient Egypt where we find in "the Teachings of Amenemope" the injunction:

> Remove not the boundary stone on the boundaries of the fields and displace not the measuring cord, be not covetous of a yard of ploughland and tear not down the widow's boundary.
>
> Be not covetous of the poor man's goods and hunger not for his bread.
>
> Set not the balance wrongly, tamper not with the weights, reduce not the portions of the corn measure.
>
> Bring nobody into misfortune before the judges and warp not justice.
>
> Ridicule not the blind man nor be scornful of any dwarf, render not vain the intentions of the lame.

The perfect example customarily quoted nowadays by specialists of Biblical antiquity is, however, what is known as the "negative confession" in the introduction to chapter 125 of the "Book of the Dead". According to ancient Egyptian belief, deceased persons had to make the following confession before 42 judges of the dead in a "court room".

> I have not made any man sick
> I have not made any man weep
> I have not killed
> I have not commanded any man to kill
> I have not done harm to any man
> I have not diminished the amount of the foodstuffs in the temples
> I have not damaged the loaves offered to the gods
> I have not stolen the loaves offered to the dead
> I have not had any (illicit) sexual relations
> I have not engaged in any unnatural lewdness

And so on....

Elsewhere we shall see that according to our most recent knowledge the contrast between sublime monotheism on the one side and a bizarre crowd of gods on the other no longer appears so striking. At one time a "crowd of gods" certainly existed in Israel, at least in the religion of the *people* during the *early period*, but the concept of the sublime nature of royal gods was not by any means foreign to the religions of other peoples living near to the "Holy Land". So we are bound to conclude that restraint was also practised elsewhere. Responsibility, morality, law, order and ethics were all practised beyond the frontiers of Israel while the accepted norms of human behaviour which in both letter and spirit were in accordance with Israel's divine code of laws were also current elsewhere. Once again the Bible is proved right, that is to say insofar as it transmits in its legal texts, the essence of which consists of the Ten Commandments, a striking piece of cultural and moral history from the Ancient East which can be substantiated by parallels. The consequence of this renders it difficult for us today to maintain the earlier claim that the Biblical code of laws was unique. This fact may well shake the confidence of many people. We cannot remove this feeling of uncertainty. On the other hand, in consequence of confirmation from non-Biblical sources of the relevant Bible texts, Israel's relationship to the cultural and historical world around it as well as to the precepts of its neighbours now appears to us in a much clearer light.

CHAPTER 13

UNDER DESERT SKIES

Sinai—150 miles to Kadesh—Two springs at the chief halting-place—Scouts sent out to Hebron—The bunch of grapes was a vine—Foreign races—Peasant woman finds the Amarna Tablets—Letters from Indo-Aryan Canaanite princes—Scouts' report leads to a new decision—The "wilderness" of the Bible was steppe.

"And the children of Israel took their journeys out of the wilderness of Sinai" (Num. 10^{12}).

ISRAEL had pledged itself to believe in one God and his laws. The portable palladium that they had constructed for him—the Ark of the Covenant—had been made out of acacia wood (Ex. 25^{10}), which is still indigenous to Sinai and widely used.

For almost a year they had lingered at Mt. Sinai. Now they set out again, heading north for Canaan. Kadesh, the next stage, which is a landmark in the long desert wanderings of the children of Israel, lies 150 miles from Sinai as the crow flies.

This stretch too can be accurately traced on the basis of the very precise topographical details given in the Bible. The route lies along the west side of the Gulf of Aqabah to the "Wilderness of Paran" (Num. 12^{16})—now Bàdiet et-Tin, i.e. "Wilderness of Loneliness"—and then continues along its eastern edge. Among the halts made on this journey (Num. 33$^{16-36}$) Hazeroth and Ezion-Geber can be identified with certainty. Hazeroth is the present-day Ain Huderah, which lies near the

FIG. 22.—The Ark of the Covenant with Cherubim and carrying-poles. (Reconstruction.)

142

Gulf. Ezion-Geber lies at the topmost point of the Gulf of Aqabah and is the place which was later to become a centre for shipping and industry in the days of King Solomon (1 Kings 9[26]).

As they made their way along the shores of the Gulf the "miracle" of the quails was repeated. Once more it was springtime, the time of bird migration, and again the description is true to nature: "And there went forth a wind from the Lord, and brought quails from the sea, and let them fall by the camp" (Num. 11[31]).

"And they removed from Ezion-Geber, and pitched in the wilderness of Zin which is Kadesh" (Num. 33[36]).

Below Hebron the hill country of Judah falls away into a fairly flat plain, the southern part of which, towards the frequently mentioned "Brook of Egypt", which is a ramification of wadis, is always very poorly supplied with water (Num. 34[5]; Josh. 15[4]; 1 Kings 8[65]). This is the Negev, the Biblical "Land of the South" (Num. 13[17]). Amid innumerable wadis—dried-up river beds which only run with water in the rainy season during the winter months—lies Kadesh. The old name Kadesh is preserved in the name of the little spring "Ain Qedeis", from which passing Bedouins water their cattle. But this trickle of spring water can hardly have been sufficient to provide for 6,000 Israelites and their flocks for any length of time. Only about 5 miles to the north-west of Kadesh, however, lies the most ample supply of water in the whole area, "Ain el-Qudeirât". Wadi Qudeirât has this to thank for its fertility. It was from here that the children of Israel saw in the distance the land that had been promised to them, of which as yet they had been able to form no clear picture. It may be that their hasty departure from Egypt had prevented them from finding out about it before they left. Palestine was so well known to the inhabitants of the Nile country that anyone who was lacking in detailed knowledge of it was reckoned to be lacking in proper education. Aman-Appa, a "commissioned scribe of the army" under Ramesses II, was even ridiculed for his ignorance about Palestine. Hori, an officer of the royal stables, replies to a letter from him in an extremely satirical vein and puts his geographical knowledge to the test: "Your letter is overloaded with big words. You have asked for it and you shall have it—and more than you bargained for. What we say is: If what you say is true, come and let us test you. We shall harness a horse for you which will bring you as fast as any jackal can run. Let us see what you can do. Have you not seen the country of Upe near Damascus? Don't you know its peculiarities, or those of its river? Have you not been to Kadesh? Have you never found your way to the Lebanon where the sky is dark in broad daylight? It is overgrown with cypresses, oaks and cedars which rise sky-high. I shall also mention a mysterious city, Byblos by name. What does it look like? Tell me too about Sidon and Sarepta. They talk about another city that lies in the sea, the port of Tyre is its name. Water is carried to it by ship. If you go to Jaffa you will find that the fields are green. Go ... and look for the pretty girl who is in charge of the vineyards. She will accept you as her mate and grant you her favours.... You will be drowsy and indolent. They will steal ... your bow, your knife, your quiver. Your reins will be slashed in the darkness ... your chariot will be smashed to pieces. But you will say: Bring me food and drink, I am happy here! They will pretend they are deaf and pay no attention. Come with me south to the region of Akka. Where is the hill of Shechem? Can this clever scribe tell me how to get to Hazor? What is special about its river? Now let me ask you about some other towns. Tell me what Kjn near Megiddo looks like, describe Rehob to me, give me a picture of Bethshan and Kiriath-El. Let me know how to get past Megiddo. How does one cross the Jordan? You see," concludes Hori, officer of the royal stables, "I have taken you through the whole of Palestine ... have a good look at it, so that in future you will be able to describe it properly, and ... you will ... be made a councillor." Government officials, soldiers, merchants had at least some clear notion of Palestine. Moses, who belonged to a poor shepherd folk, had first to find out about this country. He sent out scouts.

> "And Moses sent them to spy out the land of Canaan, and said unto them, Get you up this way southward, and go up into the mountain: and see the land, what it is; and the people that dwelleth therein, whether they be strong or weak, few or many" (Num. 13[17-18]).

Among the twelve scouts was Joshua, a man with great gifts as a strategist, as later became plain during the conquest of Canaan. They chose as the best spot to spy out the land the country round Hebron in the south of Judah. Forty days later the men reported back to Moses. As proof that they had done their job they brought fruit from the area they had scrutinised: figs and pomegranates. Incredulous astonishment greeted one gigantic bunch of grapes, cut at the "Brook of Eshcol", for "they bare it between two upon a staff" (Num. 13[23]). Posterity is equally sceptical because the narrative speaks of only one cluster. Surely it must have been a whole vine with all its fruit. The spies would cut it down with the grapes on it to keep them fresher. At all events the place of their origin according to the Bible is reliable. "Brook of Eshcol" means "Valley of Grapes"; it lies south-west of Hebron and even today this district is rich in vines. Fine heavy bunches of from 10–12 pounds are no rarity. The scouts made their report and described Canaan, like Sinuhe 650 years earlier, as a land that "floweth with milk and honey", only "the people be strong that dwell in the land, and the cities are walled and very great" (Num. 13[27, 28]; Deut. 1[28]).

In their recital of the different inhabitants of the country they mention some we already know, Hittites, Amorites, Jebusites in and around Jerusalem, Canaanites and Amalekites with whom Israel had already come into conflict in Sinai. They also mention the "children of Anak", which is supposed to mean the "children of the giants" (Num. 13[22, 28, 33]), "Anak" might mean "long necked", and that is as much as the experts can tell us. It has been surmised that these "giants" are possibly survivals of ancient pre-Semitic elements in the population but there is no certainty in the matter.

Actually there were people from other countries living in Canaan at that time who must have been quite unknown to Israelites coming from Egypt. Whose "children" they were, they intimated to posterity themselves on clay tablets which were accidentally discovered by a peasant woman at Tell el-Amarna[1] in 1887. Further investigation produced eventually a collection of 377 documents in all. These are cuneiform letters from the royal archives of Amenophis III and his son Akhnaten who built himself a new capital at El-Amarna on the Nile. The tablets contain correspondence from the princes of Palestine, Phoenicia and Southern Syria to the Foreign Office of both Pharaohs. They are written in Akkadian, the diplomatic language of the second millennium B.C. Most of the writings are full of typically Canaanite words, some of them are in fact written almost exclusively in this dialect. This priceless find threw light for the first time on conditions in Palestine in the 15th and 14th centuries B.C.

One of the letters runs: "To the King, my Lord, my Sun, my God, say: Thus (says) Suwardata, thy servant, the servant of the King and the dust under his feet, the ground on which thou dost tread: At the feet of the King, my Lord, the Sun of Heaven, seven times, seven times I prostrated myself, on my belly and on my back. . . ."

This is only the introduction. Nor is it in any way extravagant. On the contrary it is extremely formal, in accordance with contemporary protocol. Suwardata then comes to the matter in hand: "The King, my Lord, should know that the Habiru have risen in the lands which the God of the King, my Lord, has given me, and that I have beaten them, and the King, my Lord, should know that all my brothers have left me; and that I and Abdi-Kheba alone are left to fight against the leader of the Habiru. And Zurata, prince of Acco (Jud. 1[31]) and Indaruta, prince of Achshaph (Josh. 11[1]) were the ones who hastened to my help in return for 50 chariots of which I have now been deprived. But behold, [now] they have been fighting against me and may it please the King, my Lord, to send the Janhamu, so that we can wage a proper war and restore the land of the King, my Lord, to its old frontiers. . . ."

This letter from a prince of Canaan paints a picture which faithfully reflects the times. In these few sentences we can recognise unmistakably the intrigues and endless feuds both among the princes themselves

[1] Middle Egypt.

and with the warlike nomadic tribes. The most interesting point about the letter, apart from the style and contents, is its author, Prince Suwardata. His name shows clearly that he was of Indo-Aryan descent. Prince Indaruta whom he mentions is also an Indo-Aryan. Though it may sound extraordinary, a third of these princely correspondents from Canaan have Indo-Aryan ancestry. Biryawaza of Damascus, Biridiya of Megiddo, Widia of Askelon, Birashshena of Shechem in Samaria have all Indo-Aryan names. Indaruta, the name of the prince of Achshaph, is in fact identical with names from the Vedas and other early Sanskrit writings. Abdi-Kheba of Jerusalem, who has been mentioned, belongs to the Hurrite people often referred to in the Bible as Horites.

The reliability of this tradition has recently been illuminated by the discovery of Egyptian papyri of the 15th century B.C., in which the land of Canaan is repeatedly called "Khuru" after the Hurrites, the Horites of the Bible. According to this the Hurrites must for a time at least have been widespread throughout the whole country.

> "And all the congregation lifted up their voice, and cried: and the people wept that night ... wherefore hath the Lord brought us into this land, to fall by the sword, that our wives and our children should be a prey?" (Num. 14$^{1-3}$).

The reports that the spies brought back telling of the strongly fortified cities of Canaan, "great and walled up to heaven" (Deut. 1^{28}), and of their superbly armed inhabitants, were not exaggerated. Turreted fortresses built of "Cyclops-walls" were to the children of Israel an unaccustomed and menacing sight. In the land of Goshen, which for many generations had been their home, there was only one fortified town, Raamses. In Canaan the fortresses were practically cheek by jowl. The country was plastered with them. Numerous strongpoints stared down from hilltops and mountain peaks, which made them look even more powerful and terrifying. Little wonder that the report of the scouts was shattering in its effect.

Israel was quite unskilled in the use and manufacture of implements of war. They had at their disposal nothing but the most primitive weapons—bows, javelins, swords, knives—to say nothing of horse-drawn chariots which the Canaanites possessed in vast numbers. Israel was still spoilt by the "fleshpots of Egypt", for which especially the older people among them were continually sighing and bemoaning their lot. Despite their new faith and the experiences of the Exodus which they had shared together, they were not yet welded into a community which would be prepared to risk a clash with superior forces.

In view of these facts Moses wisely resolved not to carry out his original intention of marching upon Canaan from the south. Neither the time nor the people was ripe for the great moment. They must begin their roaming afresh, the time of testing and proving their mettle must be prolonged in order to allow these refugees and land-hungry wanderers to develop into a tough and compact national group schooled to bear any privation. A new generation must first emerge.

We know very little about the obscure period which now follows. Thirty-eight years—almost a generation, and time enough to mould a nation. This was the duration of their sojourn in the "wilderness". Frequently associated with the "miracles" of the quails and the manna, this section of Biblical chronology and topography sounds highly improbable. And with good reason, as would appear from systematic investigations, though on different grounds from those generally supposed. Actually there never was a "sojourn in the wilderness" in the proper sense of the words.

Although the Biblical data for this period are very scanty, we can obtain a sufficiently clear picture from the few places that can be scientifically established. According to this the children of Israel with their flocks spent a long time in the Negev, near the two sources of water at Kadesh. Once they went back again to the Gulf of Aqabah into the area of Midian and the Sinai peninsula. Compared with the deadly stretches of African sand-dunes in the Sahara, this tract of land has never been a proper desert. Examination of the terrain has established the fact that since neither the irrigation nor the rainfall has altered greatly, the "wilderness" must have had at least the character of steppe country with possibilities for grazing and waterholes.

The archaeological activities of Nelson Glueck of the U.S.A. have enhanced our knowledge of the general conditions of that period. According to him these regions were inhabited about the 13th century B.C. by semi-nomadic tribes who had brisk and flourishing trading and commercial relations with both Canaan and Egypt. Among them we should include the Midianites with whom Moses lived during his exile and one of whom, Zipporah, he married (Ex. 2[21]).

The latest Bible research proceeds somewhat differently and is not content with the demonstration that places named in the Bible really existed and with showing that certain events related in the Bible such as the way in which Moses smote the rock causing the water to flow (Ex. 17[1-7]), Num. 20[2-13]; Deut. 32[51]) or the episode of the burning bush (Ex. 3[2]) might well have had a basis in fact. Such occurrences, however striking they may be, might after all provide nothing but the framework for a story which is mere invention. To give an example from the present day—it would be perfectly conceivable to write a story in which the progress of the intrigue is completely fictional although all the details, beginning with the going off of the alarm clock in the morning and proceeding with the nerve-shattering ringing of the telephone, squealing brakes, noisy tramcars, fast tube trains and so on are correct in every respect. Whether such details are described correctly or wrongly is not, therefore, fundamentally a safe indication of the truth or falseness of the story itself. And so the account of the migration of the Israelites from Egypt has been subjected to closer examination than ever before without pausing unduly to consider details.

Rather have people asked what really lies behind this story *as a whole*, the account of a migration through the desert or steppe which lasted for a generation and after which the Israelites reached their goal only by very strange detours. The result of this examination was not a world shaking discovery, nothing sensational for the press. On the contrary, it was the common and for the scientist quite unsensational realisation that things are somewhat more complicated than they appear to be at the outset. We, too, should have become accustomed by now to this fact. Thus, for example, the Bible mentions Succoth and Migdol (Ex. 13^{20} and 14^2) as places where the Israelites halted on their way out of Egypt. Obviously these places lay on a well-known escape route used by Egyptian slaves, for an Ancient Egyptian reader, which was used for instruction purposes in schools and deals with the pursuit of runaway slaves (*Papyrus Anastasi* V, XIX 2–XX 6), mentions the same placenames.

Certainly it was not "the whole of Israel" which left Egypt, but only a number of groups of people who—themselves or their descendants—were later absorbed in the greatness that was Israel. The Bible itself lets us glimpse the fact that it was not "the whole of Israel" which was then migrating, for an "Israelite" was plainly not exclusively the person who arrived in the Promised Land at the end of the journey. On the contrary, there were Israelites resident there already when the migrants arrived. Thus it came about that Joshua assembled "the whole of Israel" between the mountains of Ebal and Gerizim near Shechem and quite explicitly we are told "as well the stranger as he that was born among them" (Joshua 8^{33}). In other words, at the time when the Israelites took possession of the land, there must have been others who had already been living there for some time. We are left to ponder whether these people had arrived with a previous migration, or, if not, what this all indicates. . . .

Perhaps the various incidents of the migration which took place in Egypt, on the Sinai Peninsula and finally in the land on the banks of the Jordan, simply reflect different traditions of these various regions which have merely been brought into harmony with one another in the Bible and linked together to form a continuous narrative thus providing a mixture of traditions. Such a mixture is usually indicated by the repetitions which occur. And such repetitions do indeed occur here. The most obvious example is the repetition of the miracle of the sea (Ex. 14) when the Israelites cross the Jordan (Joshua 3$^{4-17}$). For the second time Israel is reported to have passed dry-shod across a body of water whose waves "failed and were cut off" on the one side whereas they rose up "upon an heap" on the other. In whatever way attempts have been made to render plausible the earlier crossing of the Red Sea or rather the Reed Sea, the repetition with the crossing of the Jordan must leave us sceptical. Is it after all only fiction and not history that the writers of the Bible books are serving up to us when they relate Israel's journeyings from Egypt to the Promised Land?

Surprisingly enough quite recently we have had archaeological confirmation of two occurrences in the Biblical account of the journey through the desert which nobody would have expected in this connection. In spite of all the planning and systematic work, chance nevertheless has its part to play in archaeology and chance does not always pay any attention to what the scholars expect! In this case it enabled the Israeli archaeologist Benno Rothenberg to discover a "serpent of brass" and a tabernacle in the copper mine area of Timna (Wadi Arabah).

The "serpent of brass" is a serpent idol to which magical powers were attributed (Num. 21[9]). It is reported that there was a similar idol in the temple at Jerusalem which was not removed until it was broken in pieces by King Hiskia (Hezekiah) of Judah, who reigned around 700 B.C. (2 Kings 18[4]). The serpent idol naturally reminds us of the Sumerian serpent staff on a vase dedicated to the god of life Ningizidda. It reminds us, too, of the Aesculapius's staff of a later phase of Classical Antiquity as well as of the numerous serpents of Ancient Egypt. Already at the beginning of this century a German scholar, H. Gressmann, had asserted that the "brazen serpent" in the Bible must have been taken over from the Midianites with whom the Israelites were in contact during the journey through the desert.

According to the Bible, the Midianites were descended from Abraham's wife Keturah (Gen. 25[2-6]) and Reuel (or Jethro), a priest of the Midianites, who was the father-in-law, adviser and co-celebrant "before the Lord" (Ex. 2[16]; 3[1]; 18[1ff]) of Moses. The Israelites are supposed to owe the strange cult of the brazen serpent to Reuel. It is not without a touch of dramatic effect that we note that it was at an archaeological site showing signs of Midianite occupation that Benno Rothenberg found an idol in the form of a brazen serpent five inches in length and partly decorated with gold. As though this sensational confirmation of an important part of the Biblical accounts of the journey through the desert, which have been the object of so much discussion, were not enough, this small bronze serpent was found in the Holy of Holies of a tabernacle! That really was the crowning point of Rothenberg's discoveries, for the unearthing of a tabernacle was something of extraordinary importance, as ever since the nineteenth century Biblical scholars of the most varied persuasions had expressed doubts concerning the existence of the tabernacle about which the Bible has so much to say (Ex. 25–31 and 35–39). It is true that some critics had fallen silent when a very small, transportable tabernacle was discovered on a relief on the Bel Temple at Palmyra (Tadmor). At any rate the possibility of the existence of a tabernacle was no longer completely excluded, although the details of the Biblical descriptions of tabernacles were still considered to be a back projection on to the period of the wandering in the desert of conditions in the Temple at Jerusalem. In any case, the nomads' shrine on the relief at Palmyra was extremely small and strictly speaking it is rather a representation of the Ark of the Covenant than of the Tabernacle which contained the Holy Ark.

The Midianite tabernacle unearthed by Rothenberg is quite different. Its measurements bring it much closer to the tabernacle described in the Bible. It was found on the site of an older, Egyptian place of worship dedicated to the goddess Hathor. The Midianites who, following the Egyptians, were mining copper on their own account at Timna, converted this place of worship into a shrine of their own religion and covered it with an awning of which Rothenberg found not only the holes into which the posts had been rammed at an angle but even some remnants of material.

Of course, details of the interior lay-out and arrangement of the Biblical tabernacles still remain to be clarified. Thus, for example, the altar for burnt offerings is supposed to have been equipped with brass fittings and "a grate of network of brass" (Ex. 27$^{1-8}$), but at a very much later date not even King Solomon had at his disposal craftsmen who could carry out such work. He was obliged to request them from King Hiram of Tyre (2 Chron. 2^6 and ^{12f}). The horns of this altar in the tabernacle, as they are called (Ex. 27^2; 30^{2f}) did not appear, according to the archaeological find in Israel, until the beginning of the time of the kings, that is to say not until the Temple had been built. It is only in connection with the time of the kings (cf. 1 Kings 1^{50f}; Ps. 118 (117); Jer. 17^1; Amos 3^{14}) that the Bible mentions them again. Whatever the truth of the matter, after Rothenberg's discovery, there is now *in principle* nothing to prevent us from supposing that at quite an early date Israel possessed a tabernacle and that it was more or less like that described in the Bible.

CHAPTER 14

ON THE THRESHOLD OF THE PROMISED LAND

Rise of a new generation—Change of plan—Transit permit through Edom requested—Pressing on through Transjordan—King Og's "iron bedstead"—Dolmen discovered near Amman—Moab sends its daughters—Baal worship in Canaan—Moses sees the Promised Land—Camping opposite Jericho.

"And he made them wander in the wilderness forty years, until all the generation that had done evil in the sight of the Lord was consumed" (Num. 32^{13}).

NOT until the long years of their wanderings are approaching an end does the Bible take up the thread again of the story of the children of Israel. A new generation has sprung up and is ready to cross the threshold of the Promised Land. None of the men who led the Exodus out of Egypt will, according to the Bible, set foot in the land of promise—not even Moses himself.

The new plan of campaign is to conquer Canaan from the east, i.e. the territory east of the Jordan. Nevertheless the road to Upper Transjordan from Kadesh is blocked by five kingdoms, which occupy the broad strip of land between the Jordan valley and the Arabian desert: in the north, beginning at the spurs of Hermon is the kingdom of Bashan, then the Amorite kingdom of Sihon, next, the kingdom of Ammon, then the kingdom of Moab, on the east side of the Dead Sea, and, right in the south, Edom.

Edom is therefore the first kingdom that has to be negotiated on the way to Upper Transjordan. The children of Israel ask permission to pass through:

"And Moses sent messengers from Kadesh unto the king of Edom.... Let us pass, I pray thee, through thy country" (Num. 20$^{14, 17}$).

Main roads are the quickest roads to anywhere. In those days what corresponded to our trunk roads and motorways in the 20th century was a road that ran right through the middle of Edom. This was the old "King's Highway" which dated back to Abraham's time. "Let us pass, I pray thee, through thy country", they asked; "We will go by the king's highway" (Num. 20^{17}).

The settled population of the East always distrusts nomads,

nowadays as much as long ago, even though Israel's emissaries declare expressly: "We will not pass through the fields, or through the vineyards ... we will not turn to the right hand nor to the left, until we have passed thy borders.... And if I and my cattle drink of thy water, then I will pay for it" (Num. 20[17, 19]).

In the course of an expedition which lasted several years Nelson Glueck confirmed the aptness of the Biblical description of Edom. In the southern part of Transjordan, in the territories that had once belonged to Edom and Moab, he came across numerous traces of a settlement which dated from the beginning of the 13th century. Signs of cultivated ground, which were also discovered, suggested well stocked fields. It is therefore understandable that in spite of all assurances Edom refused the children of Israel permission to use the road and pass through their country.

Their hostility compelled Israel to go a long way round. They trek northwards along the western edge of Edom towards the Dead Sea. Punon, now called Kirbet-Feinan, an old copper-mine, and Oboth, are visited for the sake of their water supplies. Then the Israelites follow the little river Sered, which marks the frontier between Edom and Moab, and reach Transjordan. They make a wide circle round Moab on the south-east side of the Dead Sea. By this time they have reached the river Arnon and the southern frontier of the kingdom of the Amorites (Num. 21[13]). Once more the Israelites ask for permission to use the "King's Highway" (Num. 21[22]). Once more it is refused, this time by Sihon, king of the Amorites. A battle begins and the process of conquest by force of arms has started.

By defeating the Amorites the Israelites collect their first laurels. Conscious of their strength they push northwards over the river Jabbok and conquer the kingdom of Bashan in addition. Thus by their first determined attack they have become masters of Transjordan from the river Arnon to the banks of the Lake of Galilee.

Into the matter-of-fact description of this military offensive in Transjordan there has crept a reference to the "iron bed" of a giant, king Og of Bashan (Deut. 3[11]), which may have puzzled many people. This mysterious and improbable sounding passage in the Bible, has, however, a very natural and at the same time striking explanation. The Bible is preserving here in all faithfulness a memory which takes us back to Canaan's dim and distant past.

When the scholars were searching the Jordan country for evidence which would tie up with Biblical history, they came upon remarkable structures such as archaeologists had already encountered in other countries as well. These consisted of tall stones, built in oval formation and every now and then roofed over with a heavy transverse block—the famous Great Stone Graves. They are also called megalithic graves or dolmens, and were once used for burying the dead. In Europe—they are found in North Germany, Denmark, England and North-west France—they are called locally "Giants' Beds". Since these massive monuments are also found in India, East Asia and even the South Sea Islands, they are ascribed to a great mass migration in early times.

In 1918 Gustav Dalman, the German scholar, discovered in the neighbourhood of Amman, the modern capital of Jordan, a dolmen which aroused unusual interest because it seemed to shed light on a factual Biblical reference in quite an astonishing way. Amman stands precisely on the old site of Rabbath-Ammon. The Bible says about this giant king Og: "Behold his bedstead was a bedstead of iron; is it not in Rabbath of the children of Ammon [Rabbath-Ammon]? nine cubits was the length thereof, and four cubits the breadth of it, after the cubit of a man" (Deut. 3[11]). The size of the dolmen discovered by Dalman corresponded approximately to these measurements. The "bed" consists of basalt, an extremely hard grey-black stone. The appearance of such a burying-place may have given rise to the Biblical description of the "iron bed" of the giant king. Further investigations have proved that dolmens are common in Palestine, principally in Transjordan above the river Jabbok, that is, in present day Ajlun. Well over a thousand of these ancient monuments are to be found among the coarse grass of the highlands. The country above the Jabbok, so the Bible tells us, is the kingdom over which king Og of Bashan is said to have reigned, Og who alone "remained of the remnant of giants" (Deut. 3[11]). Bashan, which was conquered by Israel, was also called "the land of giants" (Deut. 3[13]).

West of the Jordan the only dolmens to be found are in the neighbourhood of Hebron. The scouts, whom Moses sent out from Kadesh, "ascended by the south, and came unto Hebron ... and there we saw the giants, the sons of Anak" (Num. 13[22, 33]). They must have seen the stone graves which have now been discovered at Hebron in the vicinity of the Valley of Grapes.

Who the "giants" really were is still quite unknown. Possibly they were a people who were much taller than the old established population around the Jordan. Clearly there was some racial memory of a taller type of man, which was enough to make a deep impression, and perhaps this is the reason why it appears in the Bible too.

These huge stone graves and the stories about giants once again bear witness to the colourful and varied history of the Land of Canaan, that narrow strip of land on the Mediterranean coast, into which from earliest times waves of alien peoples surged incessantly and left their mark behind them.

The news that Israel had conquered the whole of Jordan put king Balak of Moab into a panic. He was afraid that his own people too would be no match in physique or military skill for these tough sons of the desert. He convenes "the elders of Midian" and incites them against the children of Israel (Num. 22⁴). They resolve to employ other than military measures. They will attempt to impose a check on Israel by means of magic. Incantations and curses, in the efficacy of which the peoples of the Ancient East firmly believed, will assuredly smash Israel's power. Balaam is summoned in haste from Pethor in Babylonia, where these black arts flourish. But Balaam, the great sorcerer and magician, fails. As soon as Balaam tries to utter a curse, a blessing upon Israel comes out instead (Num. 23). Then the king of Moab throws the most dangerous trump card in existence into the balance, a wicked card that is to have a lasting effect on the lives of the children of Israel.

The Bible passage which contains a description of the abominable stratagem of King Balak is felt by theologians to be embarrassing and therefore they prefer to gloss it over. The real question is, however, why such a scandalous affair appears in the Bible at all. The answer is simple: the event was one which was of the deepest and most fateful significance for the people of Israel. That is the reason why the narrator does not maintain a modest silence but gives a frank and candid account of what actually happened.

It was in the thirties that French archaeologists, working at the Mediterranean port of Ras Shamra—the "White Haven" on the coast of Phoenicia—under the direction of Professor Claude Schaeffer of Strasbourg brought to light some evidence of Canaanite religious practices. Only then was it possible to estimate and understand what is recorded in Num. 25.

> "And Israel abode in Shittim, and the people began to commit whoredom with the daughters of Moab. And they called the people unto the sacrifices of their gods" (Num. 25¹⁻²).

It is not the attractions of vice that the children of Israel are faced with. That is something that is and always had been universal. It was not professional prostitutes who led Israel astray. It was the daughters of the Moabites and the Midianites, their own wives and sweethearts. They enticed and seduced the men of Israel to take part in the rites of Baal, the fertility cult of Canaan. What Israel encountered, while still on the other side of Jordan, was the voluptuous worship of the Phoenician gods. The leaders of Israel struck swiftly and struck hard. They did not even spare their own men. Offenders were slaughtered and hanged. Phinehas, grand-nephew of Moses, who saw an Israelite taking a Midianite woman into his tent, took a javelin "and thrust both of them through, the man of Israel, and the woman through her belly" (Num. 25⁸). The people of Moab were spared since they were related to Israel—Lot, Abraham's nephew, was regarded as their ancestor (Gen. 19³⁷). But against the Midianites a war of extermination was let loose, the classical "herem" or ban, as it is laid down in the Law (Deut. 7²ᶠᶠ;

20¹³ᶠᶠ). "Now therefore kill every male among the little ones and kill every woman that hath known man by lying with him," ordered Moses. Only the young girls were spared, everyone else was killed (Num. 31 ⁷, ¹⁷, ¹⁸).

"And Moses went up from the plains of Moab unto the mountain of Nebo, to the top of Pisgah, that is over against Jericho. And the Lord showed him all the land" (Deut. 34¹).

Moses had now fulfilled his heavy task. From the bond-cities of Egypt, through the years of hardship and privation in the steppes right up to that moment he had had to travel a long and bitterly hard road. He had nominated as his successor Joshua, a tried and trusted man and an unusually gifted strategist, which was what Israel was most in need of. Moses had finished the course and could take his leave of the world. He was not allowed to set foot himself on the soil of the Promised Land. But he was allowed to glimpse it from afar, from Mt. Nebo.

To visit this Biblical mountain means a journey of about 18 miles from Amman, centre and seat of government of the present kingdom of Jordan. The trip takes rather more than half an hour in a Land-Rover, crossing the hill-country on the edge of the Arabian desert, through wadis and sometimes past ploughed fields, heading straight for the south-east in the direction of the Dead Sea.

After a short climb over bare rocks we reach a broad barren plateau, 2,500 feet above sea level. On the western edge the cliffs drop sharply down to the Jordan basin. A fresh breeze blows on the summit. Under the clear blue skies there stretches into the distance in front of the enchanted visitor a unique panorama.

To the south lie the broad waters of the Salt Sea with their silvery sheen. On the far bank rises a dreary desolate scene of stone humps and hillocks. Behind it towers the long chain of brownish white limestone mountains of the Land of Judah. Just where it begins, rising sharply out of the Negev, lies Hebron. In the west, towards the Mediterranean, two tiny dots can be distinguished with the naked eye from the mountain range that stands out against the horizon—the towers of Bethlehem and Jerusalem. The eye wanders northward over the highlands of Samaria, past Galilee to the snow capped peaks of Hermon in the shimmering distance.

At the foot of Nebo narrow gorges slope downwards, brilliant with the green of their pomegranate trees and their orange coloured fruit. Then the ground sinks abruptly into the desolate steppe of the Jordan basin. A landscape of dazzling white chalk hills, almost as ghostly as the mountains of the moon and without a single blade of grass, flanks the mere 30 foot width of the river Jordan. The only comfort to the eye is a small green patch in front of the mountains that rise steeply on the west side of the Jordan—the oasis of Jericho.

This view from Nebo into Palestine was the last thing that Moses saw.

But beneath him on the broad steppe of Moab thin columns of smoke are rising heavenwards. Day and night campfires are burning among the mass of black goatshair tents. Joined to the hum of voices of all these men, women and children, the wind also carries over to the Jordan valley the bleating of grazing flocks. It is a peaceful scene. But it is only a moment of respite before the long yearned for day, the great calm before the storm which is decisively to affect the destiny of Israel and that of the land of Canaan.

IV

The Battle for the Promised Land
From Joshua to Saul

CHAPTER 15

ISRAEL INVADES

The world about 1200 B.C.—The weakness of Canaan—The first iron merchants—The ford across the Jordan—The stronghold of Jericho, the oldest city in the world—Scholars quarrel over broken walls—A trail of fire—Pharaoh mentions "Israel" by name for the first time—Excavations at Hazor—Graves at the Village of Joshua.

"Now after the death of Moses the servant of the Lord it came to pass, that the Lord spake unto Joshua, the son of Nun, Moses' minister, saying: Moses my servant is dead; now therefore arise, go over this Jordan, thou, and all this people, unto the land which I do give to them, even to the children of Israel" (Josh. 1$^{1-2}$).

ABOUT the same time as Israel was standing by the Jordan ready to march into the Promised Land, fate was advancing upon Mediterranean Troy and the days of the proud stronghold of King Priam were numbered. Soon the Homeric heroes of Greece, Achilles, Agamemnon and Odysseus would be arming for the fray—the hands of the timepiece of history were moving towards 1200 B.C. Israel could have chosen no better time for invasion. No danger threatened them from Egypt. Under Ramesses II Egypt had indeed known a last period of glory during which it had consolidated its power in Palestine, but even the might of Egypt crumbled in the political upheavals which marked the transition between the Bronze and the Iron Ages. Its influence in Canaan declined rapidly.

Torn by internal feuds between the innumerable petty kingdoms and principalities of its city-states, and sucked dry by the corrupt politics of Egyptian occupation, Canaan itself had shot its bolt.

Ever since the expulsion of the Hyksos about 1550 B.C. Palestine had been an Egyptian province. Under the Hyksos a feudal system had broken up the old patriarchal social structure as it had existed in the towns of Abraham's day. Under an aristocratic ruling class, which was self-centred and despotic, the people were reduced to the level of subjects without rights, and became mere plebeians. Egypt left this feudal system in Palestine unaltered. Native princes could do as they pleased: they had their own armies, which consisted of patrician charioteers and plebeian infantry. Bloody warfare between the city-states did not worry the

Egyptians. All they were interested in was the payment of tribute, which was supervised by strict and inflexible Egyptian inspectors. Garrisons and defence posts tacitly lent their activities the necessary weight. Gaza and Joppa housed the most important Egyptian administrative centres. By means of labour levies—supplied by the feudal lords—roads were built and maintained, the royal estates on the fertile plain of Jezreel south of Nazareth were managed and the glorious cedar forests of Lebanon were felled to the ground. The commissioners of the Pharaohs were corrupt. Often the troops' pay and rations were misappropriated. Whereupon they took the law into their own hands, and mercenaries from Egypt and Crete, Bedouins and Nubians plundered defenceless villages.

Under Egyptian rule the land of Canaan bled to death. The population shrank. Patrician houses of the 13th century B.C. are more primitive than they had been in earlier times, as is shown by excavations. Objets d'art and jewellery of any value are rarer, and gifts deposited with the dead in their tombs are of poorer quality. Fortress walls have lost their old solidity.

Only on the coast of Syria, protected on the landward side by the mountain ridges of the Lebanon and less affected by the quarrels of the princes, life in the maritime republics pursued its untroubled way. Whatever else happens seaports are always places where men can exchange what they have for what they want. About 1200 B.C. an entirely new metal—as valuable to begin with as gold or silver—appeared on the price lists: iron. Since it came from the Hittite country, the Phoenicians were the first to deal in this metal, which was to give its name to one of the ages of man's history. The Egyptians had known about iron for nearly 2,000 years and valued it as an extremely unusual and rare commodity. The iron they knew however did not come from our planet at all but from meteors. And the few expensive weapons that they managed to produce in this way were very properly called "Daggers from Heaven".

With the appearance of this new metal a new epoch, the Iron Age, was announced. The Bronze Age with its unique civilising achievements died away and a great epoch of the ancient world came to an end.

At the end of the 13th century B.C. a great new wave of foreign peoples surged down from the northern Aegean. By land and water these "Sea Peoples" flowed over Asia Minor. They were the fringes of a great movement of population to which the Dorian migration to Greece also belonged. The impetus of these foreigners—they were Indo-Germanic—was directed to Canaan and Egypt. For the time being Israel, waiting poised by the Jordan, had nothing to fear from them. And the Canaanites were divided and weak. Israel's hour had come. The Biblical trumpets of Jericho gave the signal.

"... and they removed from Shittim and came to Jordan ... and all the Israelites passed over on dry ground, until all the people were passed clear over Jordan ... and encamped in Gilgal, in the east border of Jericho" (Josh. 3[1,17]; 4[19]).

Today there is a bridge over the river at this point: the Jordan is very narrow and has always been fordable in many places. The natives know exactly where these fords are. In the dry season the dirty yellow water at Jericho is only about 30 feet wide.

When Israel reached the Jordan they found it in full spate, "for Jordan overfloweth all his banks all the time of harvest" (Josh. 3[15]). As happened every year, the snow on Hermon had begun to melt. "... the waters which came down from above stood and rose up upon an heap" (i.e. were dammed) "very far from the city Adam ... and all the Israelites passed over on dry ground, until all the people were passed clear over Jordan" (Josh. 3[16,17]). A much frequented ford on the middle reaches of the Jordan, el-Damiyah, recalls the "city Adam". Should there be a sudden spate it can quite easily be dammed at such a place for a short time, and while it is blocked the lower part of the river is almost dried up. (An alternative explanation is offered on pp. 148–9.)

Considerable damming of the Jordan has however often been attested as a result of earthquake. The last thing of this kind happened in 1927. As a result of a severe quake the river banks caved in, tons of soil crashed down into the river bed from the low hills that follow the Jordan's winding course. The flow of water was completely stopped for twenty-one hours. In 1924 the same thing happened. In 1906 the Jordan became so choked up with debris as the result of an earthquake that the river bed on the lower reaches near Jericho was completely dry for twenty-four hours. Arab records mention a similar occurrence in A.D. 1267.

It is easy to see from the air why this part of the Jordan valley was so important thousands of years ago. To the east, between the river and the Arabian desert, stretches the hilly plateau of Jordan, which has always been the home of countless tribes of nomads and from which they have always been able to look across to the fertile pastures and ploughed fields of Canaan. It is a natural line of attack—the principal ford across the Jordan, easily negotiated by man and beast. But anyone trying to force his way in from the east had to face the first serious obstacle soon after crossing the river—Jericho, the strategic key to the conquest of Canaan.

"And it came to pass, when the people heard the sound of the trumpet, and the people shouted with a great shout, that the wall fell down flat, so that the people went up into the city, every man straight before him, and they took the city.... And they burnt the city with fire and all that was therein" (Josh. 6[20,24]).

Joshua's battle for this city has made it famous. Today a battle rages round it, but it is between experts armed with spades, picks and chronological tables. According to the Bible it took Joshua seven days to subdue Jericho. The battle of the archaeologists over what is left of it has lasted—with intervals—for more than seventy years now and is by no means settled.

The exciting and dramatic excavations at Jericho are rife with remarkable finds and unexpected discoveries, with surprises and disappointments, with assertions and counter-assertions, with disputes over interpretation and chronology.

The Jordan basin has a tropical climate. The village of Eriha, the modern successor of Jericho, gives the impression of being an oasis on the edge of a barren waste of chalk. Even palm-trees grow here although they are seldom found anywhere else in Palestine, except to the south of Gaza. The Bible too calls Jericho "the city of palm trees" (Jud. 3[13]). Golden red clusters of dates shimmer among the green foliage. From ancient times the spring called "Ain es-Sultan" has produced as if by magic this lush patch of vegetation. North of present day Jericho a mound of ruins is named after it, Tell es-Sultan. This is the battle ground of the archaeologists. Anyone wanting to examine it must buy a ticket. The site of the excavations lies behind a barbed wire fence.

The remains of Jericho have made Tell es-Sultan one of the most extraordinary scenes of discovery in the world, for it has long since been not merely a matter of investigating the fortress of Biblical times. In this mound, under the strata of the Bronze Age, lie traces of the Stone Age, which take us back to the earliest times of all, to the days when man first built himself settled habitations. The oldest of Jericho's houses are 7,000 years old and, with their round walls, resemble Bedouins' tents. But the art of pottery was as yet unknown among their inhabitants. In 1953 a British expedition conducted excavations here, and the director of the enterprise, Dr. Kathleen M. Kenyon declared: "Jericho can lay claim to being by far the oldest city in the world."

Shortly after the turn of the century archaeologists directed their attention to this lonely mound of Tell es-Sultan. From 1907 to 1909 picks and spades carefully felt their way through layer after layer of this massive mound of ruins. When the two leaders of the German–Austrian expedition, Professor Ernst Sellin and Professor Karl Watzinger, made known what they had discovered, they caused genuine amazement. Two concentric rings of fortification were exposed, the inner ring surrounding the ridge of the hill. It is a masterpiece of military defence made of sun-dried bricks in the form of two parallel walls about 10 or 12 feet apart. The inner wall, which is particularly massive, is about 12 feet thick throughout. The outer ring of fortification runs along the foot of the hill and consists of a 6 foot thick wall, about 25–30 feet high, with strong foundations. These are the famous walls of Jericho. The two lines of fortification, their exact historical placing, the dates of their erection and destruction have given rise to a vehement dispute among the experts who advance the pros and cons in a welter of opinions, hypotheses and arguments. It began with the first announcement by Sellin and Watzinger and has continued ever since.

Both discoverers arrived themselves at what they called a "considerable modification" of their first conclusion. They issued a joint statement in which they maintained that the outer wall "fell about 1200 B.C., and therefore must be the city wall which Joshua destroyed". To shed

FIG. 23.—The walls of the old Canaanite fortress of Jericho. (Reconstructed.)

new light on the whole business a British expedition set out for Tell es-Sultan in 1930. After six years' digging further portions of the fortifications were exposed. Professor John Garstang as leader of the expedition noted every detail with the utmost precision. He described graphically the violence with which the inner circle of parallel fortifications had been destroyed: "The space between the two walls is filled with fragments and rubble. There are clear traces of a tremendous fire, compact masses of blackened bricks, cracked stones, charred wood and ashes. Along the walls the houses have been burned to the ground and their roofs have crashed on top of them."

After Garstang had consulted the most knowledgeable experts, the outcome of the second archaeological battle was that the inner ring was the more recent, therefore the one which must have been destroyed by the Israelites. But that did not settle the matter. The wrangle about the Walls of Jericho continues. Garstang dates the destruction of the inner ring about 1400 B.C. Father Hugues Vincent, a leading archaeologist and one of the most successful investigators into Jerusalem's ancient past, also studied the evidence and dated the destruction of the walls between 1250 and 1200 B.C.

Today we know that both experts were mistaken. Since their day, archaeologists have developed methods which allow us to understand excavation sites much better than was the case a few decades ago. Professor Garstang and Father Hugues Vincent both thought that walls from the *early* Bronze Age belonged to the *late* Bronze Age. Today we know that this is not so. The mistake occurred because wind and weather had largely carried away the more recent layers which covered the earliest remains. It is in one area only, at the highest place on Tell es-Sultan, on the northwest of the heap of ruins, that the remains of middle Bronze Age defence works, built on top of what is left of early Bronze Age walls, have been preserved at their full height. Scanty vestiges of late Bronze Age dwellings have been found only on the lower eastern slopes of the hill. We owe all this information to the great British archaeologist Kathleen M. Kenyon who by her extensive and success-ful excavations in Jericho during the fifties of the present century laid the foundations of our present-day knowledge. It was Kathleen M. Kenyon, too, who convincingly interpreted the very small amount of pottery found at Jericho. She was also able to interpret the informa-tion provided by the graves which constitute the only evidence concern-ing the late period of ancient Jericho.

According to her findings the walls of Jericho had to be rebuilt during the Bronze Age no less than seventeen times. The walls were repeatedly destroyed either by earthquakes or by erosion. Perhaps this weakness of the walls of Jericho found expression in the Bible account of how the children of Israel, in order to conquer Jericho, merely had to shout their war cry when the priests blew the trumpets. The middle Bronze Age city dated from the time of the Hyksos and came to an end at the same time as they, around 1550 B.C. Thereafter Jericho remained uninha-bited for about a century and a half. It is only about the year 1400 B.C., as is shown by pottery, objects found in graves and the few late Bronze Age remains of dwellings on the eastern slope of the hill, that people began to settle there once more. This late Bronze Age town, of whose existence we have only such sparse evidence, was again deserted by its inhabitants, however, around 1325 B.C. Did they become the victims of conquerors of some kind who were subsequently absorbed in the melting-pot of "Israel" and whose conquests were ultimately incorpo-rated in the Biblical account of the settlement of the land? For if it is the case that Israelites did not come to Jericho until the time of the occupation, i.e. about the middle or towards the end of the 13th century B.C., they did not need to conquer the city for they found it uninhabited! Jericho was not rebuilt until the 9th century before Christ, in the days of King Ahab (1 Kings, 16[34]). As the Bible tells us (Joshua, 6[26]), it was as though a curse had lain on the place for centuries.

Jericho was the first strong point to be overcome on the way to the Promised Land. Archaeologists have been able on other sites to follow the further progress of the children of Israel towards their conquest of Canaan.

About 12 miles southwest of Hebron lay the Debir of the Bible. Defended by a strong enclosing wall it dominated the Negev. Excavations by W. F. Albright and M. G. Kyle of the U.S.A. in Tell Beit Mirsim since 1926 disclosed a layer of ashes and considerable destruction. The stratum of ashes contained sherds which undoubtedly date from the end of the 13th century B.C. Immediately above the burnt layer are traces of a new settlement by Israel. "And Joshua returned, and all Israel with him, to Debir, and fought against it" (Josh. 10[38]).

Thirty miles south-west of Jerusalem the Lachish of the Bible can be identified. It must have been an extraordinarily strong fortress for Canaan. In the thirties at Tell ed-Duweir a British expedition under James Lesley Starkey measured out an area of twenty-four acres which had at one time been built up and surrounded by a strong wall. This city also fell a victim to a conflagration which destroyed everything. A bowl which was salvaged from the ruins bears an inscription giving

Fig. 24.

its date as the fourth year of Pharaoh Merenptah. That corresponds to the year 1230 B.C. "And the Lord delivered Lachish into the hand of Israel" (Josh. 10[32]).

In the Cairo Museum there is a monument from a mortuary temple near Thebes, on which the victory of Pharaoh Merenptah[1] over the

[1] Acceded to the throne in 1234 B.C.

Libyans is commemorated and celebrated. In order to augment his triumph, other notable victories which this ruler is said to have achieved are also mentioned. The end of the hymn of praise runs as follows: "Canaan is despoiled and all its evil with it. Askelon is taken captive, Gezer is conquered, Yanoam is blotted out. The people of Israel is desolate, it has no offspring: Palestine has become a widow for Egypt."

This triumphal hymn, written in 1229 B.C., is in more than one respect valuable and illuminating. Here for the first time in human history the name "Israel" is immortalised, and that by a foreigner and a contemporary. Israel is expressly described as a "people" and moreover in connection with Palestinian placenames—surely a proof for the most hardened sceptic that Israel was already properly settled in Canaan in 1229 B.C. and no longer completely unknown.

Shortly before 1200 B.C. Israel had reached the goal which had for so long been the object of its aspirations. It is now in Canaan, but it is not yet in full control of the country. A trail of burnt out cities marks its path and indicates an extremely shrewd strategic plan. Joshua avoided the strongest fortresses like Gezer and Jerusalem. Obviously he followed the line of least resistance. The fertile plains and river valleys are likewise still in the hands of the Canaanites and will remain so for many generations to come. Israel has neither the armour to resist the dreaded chariots, nor the technique and experience required to war against strongly fortified cities. But it has secured a foothold in the more sparsely populated areas, the hill country on both sides of the Jordan is in its hands.

About ten miles north of the Lake of Galilee lay the mighty stronghold of Hazor, which was still quite powerful, although it had had to suffer, about 1300 B.C., at the hands of conquerors, probably the Egyptians under the Pharaoh Sethos I; Joshua "took Hazor, and smote the king thereof with the sword: for Hazor beforetime was the head of all those kingdoms" (Joshua 11[10]). The word "beforetime" provides us with cause for reflection. The town, devastated probably by Sethos I, before its destruction by the Israelites, had indeed been richer and more flourishing than the Hazor they found. The more crucial event and the one which had the gravest consequences in the town's history was undoubtedly this destruction by Israel towards the end of the 13th century B.C.

The rediscovery of this royal city can be counted as one of the most surprising pieces of good fortune in recent Biblical archaeology. John Garstang, the English archaeologist, had already identified as the site of old Hazor the extensive mound of rubble Tell el-Qedah, which stands out prominently to the west of the Jordan between Lake Huleh and the Lake of Galilee. But it was not until excavations, begun in 1953 under the auspices of the Hebrew University of Jerusalem and directed by Yigael Yadin of the James A. de Rothschild expedition, had continued over several seasons that the hitherto undisturbed Tell could be awakened from its dreams and induced to part with its closely guarded secrets. Bit by bit its layers began to tell the experts the long and exciting story of the chequered fortunes of Hazor.

No fewer than twenty-one stages of development can be distinguished: twenty-one cities growing up on top of one another, each built on the rubble of past generations and each in its turn levelled to the ground, destroyed by war or fire or the force of nature. Surmounted by its citadel and fortified area the city spread its lower reaches far out into the plain. An ingenious drainage system consisting of clay pipes looked after public sanitation.

What has been discovered confirms in a striking way what the Bible has to say about the powerful role that Hazor played in Canaan at the time of the Israelite conquest. Hazor was in fact not only one of the largest settlements of the country but also one of the strongest fortresses. In the 13th century B.C. it was destroyed, as the Book of Joshua records. A layer of burnt rubble indicates a great conflagration about that time. Many scholars do not hesitate to attribute this burnt rubble to Joshua and his hosts.

With these victories and the promised occupation of Canaan, Joshua's great assignment has been fulfilled. At a ripe old age he dies and is buried, "in Timnath-Serah which is in mount Ephraim, on the north side of the hill of Gaash" (Josh. 24[30]). The Greek text (LXX 24[30b]) adds a very significant remark: "There they put with him into the tomb in which they buried him, the knives of stone with which he circumcised the children of Israel in Gilgal." In Gilgal, on the way from the Jordan to Jericho, the rite of circumcision was carried out on the men of Israel according to tradition "with stone knives". "Now all the people that came out were circumcised: but all the people that were born in the wilderness by the way as they came forth out of Egypt, them they had not circumcised" (Josh. 5[5]). Ten miles north-west of Bethel lies Kefr Ishu'a, the "Village of Joshua". In the neighbouring hillside are some rock tombs. In 1870 in one of these sepulchres a number of stone knives was found. . . .

The Biblical account of what appears in the history books as Israel's occupation of the land and the confirmation by archaeological finds of what the Bible says once again provide excellent examples of the fact that new knowledge gives rise to new problems. Hazor is a prime example. With its burnt rubble, its layer of ashes and its broken idols, it seems to support the following passage: "But the Lord thy God shall deliver them (the Canaanites) unto thee, and shall destroy them with a mighty destruction, until they be destroyed. And he shall deliver their kings into thine hand, and thou shalt destroy their name from under heaven: there shall no man be able to stand before thee, until thou have destroyed them. The graven images of their gods shall ye burn with fire..." (Deuteronomy 7$^{23-25}$). Hazor's late Bronze Age layer of rubble does indeed fit in chronologically very well with the beginning of Joshua's conquest towards the end of the 13th century B.C. Hazor nevertheless presents us with a problem for the king of Hazor was Jabin whom Joshua defeated "by the waters of Merom" (Joshua 11^{5ff}). According to the Book of Judges (Judges 4^2) which deals with a later phase of Israel's history, Jabin was still ruler over the same town and Israel had been "sold into the hand of Jabin king of Canaan, that reigned in Hazor" (Judges 4^2). It was only subsequently that Jabin was "subdued" (Judges 4^{23}) by Barak, the commander of the Israelites, although it is not clear whether the decisive battle took place on the banks of the River Kishon (Judges 5^{21}) or on Mount Tabor. What are we to think of this duplication? Archaeology here comes to our aid for after the catastrophe towards the end of the 13th century Hazor was by no means such an important town that it could have been considered as the residence of a "king of Canaan" into whose hands Israel was "sold". After an interlude of occupation by semi-nomads and sparse early Israelite settlement (12th–11th century B.C.), it was not until the days of King Solomon (10th century B.C.) that Hazor again became a fortified place. It seems, in consequence, that King Jabin from the period of the Judges probably never existed. He is presumably merely a literary reflection of that earlier king of Hazor of the same name during the period of the occupation of the country, that is to say, of the late Bronze Age, except that in the traditions which attached themselves to his person, late Bronze and early Iron Age elements became mingled.

Hazor is situated fairly far to the north, quite a distance north of the Lake of Galilee. Yet the Biblical accounts of a number of other sites which have been excavated in the south of the Promised Land reveal a similar mingling of Iron Age and Bronze Age traditions. Thus the town of Ai is of considerable importance among the Canaanite towns conquered by Joshua (Joshua 7^{2ff} as well as 8$^{1-24}$). According to the Bible (Joshua 12^{16}) the neighbouring Beth-el is of subsidiary importance. In point of fact, a thick layer of ash and soot-covered brick rubble which covered the late Bronze Age stratum has been found in Beth-el, just as was to be expected. But what happened at Ai? Judith Marquet-Krause, who excavated there, was unable to find any stratum providing evidence of destruction in Joshua's time, the late Bronze Age. In his day Ai had long since lain in ruins and had been deserted ever since the early Bronze Age—thus justifying its name, which in Hebrew merely means "ruin", but not the detailed description of its conquest in the eighteenth chapter of the Book of Joshua! It was not until the beginning of the Iron Age that new settlers arrived, but their village was also destroyed in the end. Had Judith Marquet-Krause been mistaken? Fresh excavations directed by J. A. Callaway were intended to investigate the question.

Callaway could do no more, however, than confirm that there had not been any settlement in Ai during the late Bronze Age. The Israelites, therefore, had never been able to conquer the town.

The experts racked their brains. Could the Bible have been in error to this extent? Or had the writers of the Bible confused something? Did the Biblical account of the capture of Ai really refer to the neighbouring place Beth-el which had indeed fallen into ruins at the end of the Bronze Age? Finally the idea occurred to them that all that was needed was not to cling slavishly to the hypothesis that all the events related in the Bible in connection with the occupation of the country really took place towards the end of the Bronze Age. Could the Bible perhaps be referring to the Ai of the early Iron Age? In that case, it was not only the results of excavations at Ai and the Biblical account which would correspond with one another, but a number of other sites as well such as Arad, Dibon and Gibeon which also had not yielded any traces of occupation during the late Bronze Age except for one grave in Gibeon. Even the statement that Gibeon was greater than Ai (Joshua 10[2]) is correct in regard to the Iron Age settlements. Once more the Bible is right if we accept that the traditions concerning the occupation of the country mingle facts from the Bronze Age and the Iron Age.

It was in consequence of these and similar inaccuracies, however, that the specialists found themselves able to look upon the Biblical account of the occupation of the country as the condensed description of an extremely complicated and lengthy process which lasted for several centuries, but which the Bible presents to us in compressed form concentrating it all on the person of Joshua. In doing so, the Bible selects specific events and combines them to form a story in which the episodes do not always agree. Some specialists even claim that an occupation, such as is described in the Bible, never occurred and surprisingly this can be substantiated in the Bible. After his first victories in the land of the Canaanites, Joshua assembled "all Israel" by Mount Gerizim and Mount Ebal which rise above the old town of Shechem now known as Nablus. In connection with this event, the Bible expressly uses the words "all Israel . . . as well the stranger, as he that was born among them" (Joshua, 8[33]). How could that be the case? Had not "all Israel" only just arrived in the Promised Land? What did this mention of those "born among them" signify? Many scholars are of the opinion that the subsequent influx of Israelites occurred in several waves. That might be the explanation—when the newcomers arrived, the others were already there. They were already residents.

There are other theories finding support in the scholarly discussions on the settlement of the land. One of them claims that what the Bible describes as an occupation was really a series of clashes between residents of the towns and the nomads or semi-nomadic inhabitants of the steppes which were brought about by social and religious motives.

Still another theory advances the idea that the occupation was really a mostly peaceful infiltration of foreign immigrants only now and then leading to tensions which worked themselves out in warlike conflicts.

CHAPTER 16

UNDER DEBORAH AND GIDEON

Israel settles down—Pioneering in the mountains—Peasants' huts instead of palaces—Deborah incites to revolt—Clash in the plain of Jezreel—Victory over the "chariots of iron"—Israelite crockery at Megiddo—Marauders from the desert—Traces of Abimelech's destruction of Shechem—Gideon's successful tactics—First battle in history against a camel-corps—A new breed of long-distance carriers.

"And the Lord gave unto Israel all the land which he sware to give unto their fathers: and they possessed it and dwelt therein" (Josh. 21[43]).

IMMEDIATELY after the conquest an astonishing thing happened: the tribes of Israel dug their toes into the ground they had won. They can therefore no longer have been a typical nomadic people. Canaan had experienced invasions of nomads from time immemorial but they had always been merely episodes. The tribes would graze their flocks and then one day they would disappear as suddenly as they had come. Israel on the other hand became static, cultivating fields and clearing forests ... "if thou be a great people, then get thee up to the wood country and cut down for thyself there" (Josh. 17[15]). They gave up their tents and built themselves huts: they settled down among the ruins of the houses in the towns they had conquered. In Debir, Bethshemesh and Bethel remains of their primitive and poverty-stricken furnishings were found on top of the strata which were deposited when the towns were burned down.

FIG. 25.—Israelite Storing-jar.

This break with the past is clearly recognisable from the excavations. Where previously patrician houses and palaces of the long established feudal barons had been standing, there now arose peasants' huts and fences. The massive defence walls show signs of having had necessary repairs done to them. But what the men of Israel replaced was of the thinnest masonry. The construction of a new system of strong defensive walls would have entailed forced labour and there was nothing the Israelites hated more. They regarded themselves as freemen, as independent farmers. "But every man did that which was right in his own eyes" (Jud. 17[6]). Even the word generally used in

Canaan meaning a bondsman, was used by the Israelites in exactly the opposite sense to mean a freeman. In the feudal system under the princes of the city-states all the drudgery was done by slaves. In the case of Israel the work of the farm was done by the freeborn sons of the family. At their head stood the father, the patriarch. Countless new settlements sprang into being. Archaeologists have found traces of them throughout the highlands. But there is very little of them left. For the first building material they used was sun-dried mud bricks, and the buildings they put up in this way did not last.

Real pioneer work was done by the Israelites in the mountains. Uninhabitable areas, districts without springs or streams were opened up. Although it sounds unbelievable, what remains of a new technique used by their ancestors has been partly taken over and put into commission again by the state of Israel today. They dug cisterns in the ground to collect the rainfall, and lined the insides with a type of limestone plaster which was hitherto unknown. These fixtures were so solidly built that they have been able to withstand the ravages of time for thousands of years.

As the Book of Judges tells us, and investigation confirms, the Israelites struck roots in their new home as settlers and farmers. In continuous fighting with their neighbours and feuds among themselves they gradually gained in military power and experience. The Bible mentions disputes with Moabites, Ammonites and Aramaean tribes from the Syrian desert. It speaks of bloody civil war, when the tribes fought against Benjamin (Jud. 20). Bethel lay in the territory of Benjamin, and Albright, digging there, found strata which showed that the place had been destroyed four times between 1200 and 1000 B.C.

It was around this time too that "Abimelech fought against the city all that day: and he took the city and slew the people that was therein, and beat down the city, and sowed it with salt" (Jud. 9[45]). So runs the description in the Book of Judges of the conquest of Shechem by Abimelech, the ambitious and vindictive son of Gideon who murdered all his brothers.

In 1959 at Tell el Balata, on the site of this Biblical city which had been the first place Abraham encountered on his arrival in Canaan, excavations by American archaeologists from Drew University and McCormick Theological Seminary led by Professor G. Ernest Wright, who was following the earlier investigations of Professor Ernst Sellin of Germany, were able to confirm what the Bible has to say about the fate of Shechem. Fragments of clay jars which were scattered about among the ruins and could be identified as typical Israelite pottery put the date of the destruction of Shechem towards the end of the 12th century B.C., that is, about the period of Abimelech. At the same time the remains of the "tower of Shechem" were identified, as well as the "hold of the house of the god Berith" and the "house of Millo" which are mentioned in Jud. 9[20, 46]. It does seem however that all of these were part of a single building which towered above the city wall and which had been built upon the ruins of an earlier Hyksos temple.

FIG. 26.—Canaanite Prince from Megiddo seen on his throne, with harpist and war-chariot (1200 B.C.).

These troubled years of the first colonists have found an imperishable memorial in three narratives of the Book of Judges: in the Song of Deborah, in the story of Gideon and in the doughty deeds of Samson.

The background of these "pious tales" is made up of facts, contemporary events which as a result of recent research can be dated with considerable accuracy. When Israel entered Canaan about 1230 B.C. it had to be content with the mountains ... for it "could not drive out the inhabitants of the valley, because they had chariots of iron" (Jud. 1[19]). It was not until a century later that the tide turned. It would seem that among the mountains of Galilee tribes which had settled there had to render bond-service to the Canaanites. Among them was the tribe of Issachar which is ridiculed in the Bible as "a strong ass". It is accused of "couching down between two burdens" and of becoming a "servant unto tribute" (Gen. 49[14, 15]).

Revolt broke out in Galilee in protest against this oppression. The impetus was supplied by a woman, Deborah. She summoned the tribes of Israel to fight for their freedom. It is from her that that wonderful song, which she sang to the assembled throng, has come down to us.

Barak, one of the tribe of Issachar, became the leader. Other tribes joined in and a great army was formed. Then Barak took a decisive step. He dared to do what Israel had never previously risked, he came to grips with the dreaded enemy on the plain: "So Barak went down from mount Tabor, and ten thousand men after him" (Jud. 4[14]). The scene of the encounter was the broad and fertile plain of Jezreel between the mountains of Galilee in the north and Samaria in the south—absolute and sovereign domain of the Canaanite city princes and feudal barons. Here they awaited the dangerous fighting forces of the Canaanites.... "then fought the kings of Canaan in Taanach by the waters of Megiddo" (Jud. 5[19]). The incredible happened—Israel won. For the first time they had succeeded in smashing and routing a force of chariots in open battle. The spell was broken: Israel had shown that it had the measure of the military technique of the Canaanites and could beat them at their own game.

Two mounds of rubble in the plain of Jezreel preserve all that is left of Taanach and Megiddo, lying about 5 miles apart. Both cities changed places several times in order of importance. About 1450 B.C. Taanach was a large city-state while Megiddo was only a small Egyptian garrison. About 1150 B.C. Megiddo was destroyed and deserted by its inhabitants. For a long time it lay in ruins, and was not rebuilt and inhabited until 1100 B.C. The pottery of the new settlers there is striking. It consists of large clay preserving jars of exactly the same type as were used at this time by the Israelites. Archaeologists found them in all the other settlements in the mountains of Samaria and Judaea. Taanach is specifically mentioned in the Song of Deborah as the site of the battle. The reference to its being "by the waters of Megiddo" is presumably a more precise description of its situation. Megiddo itself, whose "water" is the river Kishon, cannot at that time have been in existence.

Archaeological discoveries and Biblical references make it possible to date the first battle against the Canaanite chariots in the period between the destruction and rebuilding of Megiddo, about 1125 B.C.

The Gideon story tells of the second triumph of Israel. Suddenly out of the East came a new, unfamiliar and sinister threat to Israel's safety. Hordes of Midianite nomads, mounted on camels, attacked the country, plundering, burning and massacring ... "for both they and their camels were without number: and they entered into the land to destroy it" (Jud. 6[5]). For years Israel was at the mercy of these Midianite attacks. Then Gideon appeared as their deliverer. He adopted successfully, as the Bible describes in detail (Jud. 7[20ff]), a new kind of surprise tactics which routed the Midianites and apparently persuaded them to leave the Israelites in peace from then on.

It is often the lot of peaceful inventions to be used first of all in time of war. The new "invention" which made it possible for the Midianites to terrorise Israel was the taming of the camel!

Tame camels are likely to have been something quite new in the ancient world. The people of the Bronze Age probably knew nothing of them. Egyptian texts never mention them. Even in Mari, next door to the great Arabian desert, there is no single reference to them in any of that vast collection of documents. We must eliminate the camel from our conception of life in the ancient world of the orient. References to them in the book of Genesis must have crept in at a later date. The attractive scene, for example, where we meet Rebecca for the first time in her native city of Nahor, must make do with a change of stage props. The "camels" belonging to her future father-in-law Abraham which she watered at the well were donkeys (Gen. 24[10ff]). Similarly it was donkeys that for thousands of years carried on their backs all kinds of burdens and costly merchandise along the great trade routes of the ancient world until the tame camel saved them.

It is not quite certain when exactly the taming of the camel took place but there are some facts which point to a general conclusion. In the 11th century B.C. the camel appears in cuneiform texts and reliefs and from then on is more and more frequently mentioned. This must be about the time of the Gideon story. Doubtless such marauding attacks with animals that had until then been regarded as wild must have come as a frightful shock.

The third challenge held the greatest and deadliest danger for Israel and threatened its very existence: the clash with the Philistines.

CHAPTER 17

THE WARRIORS FROM CAPHTOR

Krethi and Plethi—Invasion by the "Sea Peoples"—The great trek from the Aegean—Triumphal progress with ox-waggons and ships—The Hittite empire disappears—Seaports in flames on the coast of Canaan—General mobilisation on the Nile—Pharaoh Ramesses III saves Egypt—The great land and sea engagement—Interrogation in P.O.W. camps—Life size portraits of the Philistines.

"Have not I brought up Israel out of the land of Egypt? and the Philistines from Caphtor ...?" (Amos 9⁷).

THE fabulous tales of the redoubtable Samson, that great bear of a man full of pranks and derring-do, herald the beginning of the great tussle.

Philistines!—This name has become common currency in so many ways. We talk of someone being "a proper Philistine", or of someone else as a veritable "Goliath". He also was one of them. We speak disparagingly of the "Cherithites and Pelethites" without realising that these terms designate "Cretans and Philistines". Who does not know the tragic love story of Samson and Delilah, the woman who betrayed him to the Philistines? Who does not remember the superhuman strength of Samson, who could strangle lions with his bare hands, who slew 1,000 Philistines with the jawbone of an ass, and in the end, blind and deserted by the woman he loved, brought a Philistine temple crashing down about his head in the fury of his anger? Yet very few of us ever really think how little we know of these Philistines whom we talk so much about.

The Philistine people, who played a decisive role in the life of Israel, were for a long time wrapped in mystery. It is only quite recently that it

FIG. 27.—Examination of Philistine

174

has been possible to find out something about them. Bit by bit, as a result of careful examination of the fruits of scientific research, the picture has become clearer. Fragments of pottery, inscriptions in temples and traces of burnt-out cities give us a mosaic depicting the first appearance of these Philistines, which is unrivalled in its dramatic effect.

Terrifying reports heralded the approach of these alien people. Messengers brought evil tidings of these unknown strangers who appeared on the edge of the civilised ancient world, on the coast of Greece. Ox-waggons, heavy carts with solid wheels, drawn by hump-backed bullocks, piled high with household utensils and furniture, accompanied by women and children, made their steady advance. In front marched armed men. They carried round shields and bronze swords. A thick cloud of dust enveloped them, for there were masses of them. Nobody knew where they came from. The enormous trek was first sighted at the Sea of Marmora. From there it made its way southwards along the Mediterranean coast. On its green waters sailed a proud fleet in the same direction, a host of ships with high prows and a cargo of armed men.

Wherever this terrifying procession halted it left behind a trail of burning houses, ruined cities and devastated crops. No man could stop these foreigners; they smashed all resistance. In Asia Minor towns and settlements fell before them. The mighty fortress of Chattusas on the Halys was destroyed. The magnificent stud horses of Cilicia were seized as plunder. The treasures of the silver mines of Tarsus were looted. The carefully guarded secret of the manufacture of iron, the most valuable metal of the times, was wrested from the foundries beside the ore deposits. Under the impact of these shocks one of the three great powers of the second millennium B.C. collapsed. The Hittite Empire was obliterated.

A fleet of the foreign conquerors arrived off Cyprus and occupied the island. By land the trek continued, pressed on into northern Syria, reached Carchemish on the Euphrates and moved on up the valley of

prisoners by Egyptian officers.

the Orontes. Caught in a pincer movement from sea and land the rich seaports of the Phoenicians fell before them. First Ugarit, then Byblos, Tyre and Sidon. Flames leapt from the cities of the fertile coastal plain of Palestine. The Israelites must have seen this wave of destruction, as they looked down from their highland fields and pastures, although the Bible tells us nothing about that. For Israel was not affected. What went up in flames down there in the plains were the strongholds of the hated Canaanites.

On and on rolled this human avalanche by sea and by land, forcing its way all the time towards the Nile, towards Egypt....

In Medinet Habu west of Thebes on the Nile stands the imposing ruin of the splendid temple of Amun, dating from the reign of Ramesses III (1195–1164 B.C.). Its turreted gateway, its lofty columns, and the walls of its halls and courts are crammed with carved reliefs and inscriptions. Thousands upon thousands of square feet filled with historical documents carved in stone. The temple is one vast literary and pictorial record of the campaigns of the Pharaohs and is the principal witness to events on the Nile at that time.

It is more than plain from these records that Egypt was then in a state of acute panic and only too conscious of the danger in which it stood. One of the texts rings with a note of anxious foreboding: "In the eighth year of the reign of Ramesses III.... No country has been able to withstand their might. The land of the Hittites, Kode,[1] Carchemish ... and Cyprus have been destroyed at one stroke.... They have crushed their peoples, and their lands are as if they had never been. They marched against Egypt.... They laid hands on every land to the farthest ends of the earth. Their hearts were high and their confidence in themselves was supreme: 'Our plans will succeed'."

FIG. 28.—The battle between Pharaoh Ramesses III and the Philistines.

Ramesses III made feverish preparations for battle and decreed a general mobilisation: "I manned my borders ... and drew up my armies before them: princes, garrison commanders and warriors. I

[1] The coastal area of Cilicia and Northern Syria.

turned the river mouths into a strong defensive wall, with warships, galleys and coastal vessels ... fully manned from stem to stern with brave warriors armed to the teeth. The troops were the best that Egypt could muster. They were as ready for battle as lions roaring on the mountains. The chariot detachments consisted of the swiftest runners, and every first class charioteer available. The horses flew like the wind ready to crush foreign lands under their feet...."

With an enormous fighting force and every able bodied warrior that Egypt could call on, Ramesses III advanced to engage in a great battle on land against the foreign hordes. The inscriptions have nothing very definite to say about this battle. As usual, the Egyptian war reports confine themselves in this case to singing the praises of the victor. "His troops", it is recorded of Ramesses III, "were like bulls ready for battle: his horses were like falcons amid a flock of tiny birds...." But a huge relief still portrays this terrible battle after 3,000 years: the Egyptian commandos have scurried in among the armed enemy trekkers. Fearful slaughter rages among the ponderous ox-waggons carrying the women and children. Under the hooves of the bullocks and horses the bodies of the slain lie in heaps. Victory seems to have been won already, since Egyptian soldiers are seen plundering the ox-waggons.

Egypt had won a battle of prime significance in world history. The enemy land forces had been annihilated. Ramesses III hastened to the coast in a swift chariot, since "they had entered the mouths of the river" with their ships.

This great naval battle is likewise perpetuated on a stone relief in the temple at Medinet Habu: the fleets of the two opposing forces have approached each other. Shortly before their encounter the wind must have suddenly died down, since the sails are reefed. That meant a severe handicap for the foreigners. Their ships could no longer be manoeuvred. The warriors are standing there, ready for the fray but helpless. Their swords and spears were useless except in hand to hand fighting when the ships were close enough together. The calm let the Egyptians have it all their own way. Their vessels, manned by oarsmen, approach the enemy ships at a safe distance, then the archers are given the order to fire. A murderous hail of arrows pour down upon the foreigners who provide a mass target and fall overboard in vast numbers. The bodies of badly wounded and dead men cover the water. When the enemy had been decimated and was in complete disorder, the Egyptians rowed towards them and capsized their boats. Those who escaped death by the hail of arrows or by drowning were killed or captured by Egyptian soldiers on the nearby shore.

Ramesses III had been able to ward off this deadly threat to Egypt on land and sea in these two decisive battles. There had been no victory like it in all the past history of the Nile.

After the victory a gruesome reckoning was made of dead and wounded by hacking off their hands and piling them in heaps. This was the method of counting the numbers of a defeated enemy. About what happened to the women and children of the foreigners the inscriptions tell us nothing. The reliefs show the first P.O.W. camps in history. The defeated soldiers are herded together.

The treatment which the mass of prisoners received was in principle the same as happens today. Drawn up in rank and file they squat on the ground awaiting checking. Even the much maligned questionnaire was included: Egyptian officers dictate to scribes the statements made by the prisoners. Only one matter was differently dealt with in those days. Nowadays prisoners of war have P.O.W. or K.G. painted on their tunics; the Egyptians branded Pharaoh's name on their prisoners' skins. It lasted longer.

It is to the hieroglyphics of these oldest questionnaires in the world that we owe the first historical information about the famous Philistines in the Bible.

Among these "Sea Peoples" as the Egyptians called the foreign conquerors, one racial group assumed special importance, the Peleste or PRST. These are the Philistines of the Old Testament.

Egyptian artists were masters at depicting the physiognomy of foreign races and had an extraordinary ability to distinguish characteristic features. The reliefs at Medinet Habu indicate with this wonted accuracy the faces of the Biblical Philistines. They look like photographs carved in stone 3,000 years ago. The tall slim figures are about a head higher than the Egyptians. We can recognise the special type of dress, and weapons, and their tactics in battle. If we substitute the men of Israel for the Egyptian mercenaries we have a true-to-life picture of the battles which took place years later in Palestine and which reached the height of their fury in the reigns of Saul and David about 1000 B.C.

CHAPTER 18

UNDER THE YOKE OF THE PHILISTINES

Philistines on the coast—Swan pattern pottery—Beer mugs with filters—Carefully guarded iron monopoly—Philistines occupy the highlands—Traces of the burning of Shiloh—Choosing a king from dire necessity—Allenby successfully uses Saul's tactics—Surprising the Turks—Albright finds Saul's castle—Two temples in Beth-Shan—The end of Saul.

"And the children of Israel did evil in the sight of the Lord and the Lord delivered them into the hand of the Philistines forty years" (Jud. 13^1).

It was in 1188 B.C. that the Philistines suffered their severe defeat at the hands of Ramesses III. Thirteen years later they were firmly settled on the coastal plain of southern Canaan, the fertile brown plain between the mountains of Judah and the sea. The Bible lists the five cities which they possessed: Askelon, Ashdod, Ekron, Gaza and Gath (1 Sam. 6^{17}). Each of these cities, and the land adjoining, which was cultivated by soldiers under the command of paid leaders, was ruled over by a "lord" who was independent and free. For all political and military purposes however the five city rulers always worked hand in hand. In contrast to the tribes of Israel the Philistines acted as a unit in all matters of importance. That was what made them so strong.

The Biblical narrator tells of other groups of these "Peoples of the Sea" who had arrived with the Philistines and had settled down on the coast of Canaan: "Behold I will stretch out mine hand upon the Philistines, and I will cut off the Cherethims (Cretans) and destroy the remnant of the sea coast" (Ezek. 25^{16}). Crete is an island in the Mediterranean which lies far removed from Israel. Since we have learned of the historical attack of the "Sea Peoples" on Canaan the otherwise obscure meaning of these words has become clear. They fit exactly the situation at that time.

When the Philistines appeared in Canaan a new and distinctive type of pottery also made its appearance. It is easily recognisable as different from the pottery which had previously been in use both in the cities of the Canaanites and in the hill settlements of the Israelites. Throughout the area occupied by the five Philistine cities—and only there—excavations have unearthed this type of ceramic ware. The Philistines must therefore have produced their own pottery.

179

The first find of this Philistine crockery astonished the archaeologists. They had seen these shapes and colours and patterns before. The leather coloured drinking cups and jars, with red and black geometrical designs and swans cleaning their feathers, were already known as coming from Mycenae. From 1400 B.C. onwards the wonderful pottery made by Mycenaean manufacturers was greatly sought after in the ancient world and their export trade had flooded

FIG. 29.—Philistine jar with swan pattern.

every country with them. Shortly before 1200 B.C. with the destruction of Mycenae this import from Greece suddenly stopped. The Philistines must have come by way of Mycenae, and must have started up in Canaan the manufacture of this type of ware with which they were familiar. "Have not I brought up Israel out of the land of Egypt? and the Philistines from Caphtor?" (Amos 9⁷). Caphtor is Crete, the great island that lies close to Greece.

But Philistine pottery illustrates another interesting fact, which is also hinted at in the Bible. Many of their handsome mugs are fitted with a filter, and there can be no doubt what it was used for. They are typical beer mugs. The filter served to keep back the barley husks: they floated about in the home-brewed ale and would tend to lodge in the throat. Large numbers of wine cups and beer mugs have been found in the Philistine settlements. They must have been powerful drinkers. Carouses are mentioned in the Samson stories (Jud. 14¹⁰; 16²⁵), where the fact is emphasised that the strong man himself drank no alcohol.

Beer is however no Philistine invention. The first great breweries flourished in the Ancient East. In the hostelries of Babylon there were in fact five kinds of beer: mild, bitter, fresh, lager, and a special mixed beer for export and carrying, which was also called honey beer. This was a condensed extract of roots which would keep for a long time. All that had to be done was to mix it with water and the beer was ready—an ancient prototype of our modern dry beer for use in tropical countries.

But another discovery was much more important. The Philistines were the first people in Canaan to process iron and they made the most of it. Their graves contain armour, implements and ornaments made of this rare and costly metal, as it then was. As in the case of the Mycenaean jars they manufactured their own iron. The first iron foundries in Canaan must have been built in Philistine territory. The secret of smelting iron was brought back as part of their booty as they drove through Asia Minor, where the Hittites had been the first iron-founders in the world until 1200 B.C.

This formula which they had acquired was guarded by the Philistine princes like the apple of their eye. It was their monopoly and they traded in it. Israel during this first period of settlement up on the mountains, was far too poor to be able to afford iron. The lack of iron farm implements, of iron nails for building houses and of iron weapons was a severe handicap. When the Philistines had occupied the mountains as well as the plains, they tried to prevent the making of new weapons by prohibiting the trade of smiths. "Now there was no smith found throughout all the land of Israel: for the Philistines said, Lest the Hebrews make them swords or spears. But all the Israelites went down to the Philistines, to sharpen every man his share and his coulter and his axe and his mattock" (1 Sam. 13$^{19-20}$).

Equipped with the most up to date weapons, tested and tried in their long experience of military campaigns, organised into a first class political system, there stood the Philistines about 1200 B.C. on the west coast hungry for conquest. They had their eye on the same goal as Israel: Canaan.

Samson's mighty deeds and his pranks are legendary tales (Jud. 14–16). But there are hard facts behind them. The Philistines were beginning to push forward and extend their territory eastwards.

Separated from each other by long valleys, lines of hills sweep up from the coastal plain to the mountains of Judah. One of these long valleys is the valley of Sorek. Samson lived in Zorah (Jud. 13^{2}) and in Timnath, not far from it, he married a "daughter of the Philistines" (Jud. 14^{1}). Delilah too lived there (Jud. 16^{4}). It was along this valley that the Philistines later on sent back the Ark of the Covenant which they had captured (1 Sam. 6^{12ff}). This penetration of the Philistines into the hill country below the mountains of Judah was only the prelude to the great clash with Israel which followed years later.

> "Now Israel went out against the Philistines to battle, and pitched beside Eben-Ezer; and the Philistines pitched in Aphek" (1 Sam. 4^{1}).

Aphek lay on the northern rim of the Philistine domains. A mound of ruins, Tell el-Muchmar, conceals all that is left of this place which lay on the upper reaches of a river which flows into the sea to the north of Jaffa. From a strategic point of view Aphek was extremely favourably situated. Eastward lay the road to the mountains of central Palestine where Israel had settled. On the edge of the mountain range lay Eben-Ezer where the opposing forces met. At the first encounter the Philistines were victorious. The Israelites in dire straits sent to Shiloh for the Ark of the Covenant, their sacred talisman. In a second encounter they were completely beaten by the vastly superior force of the Philistines. The Israelite army was routed and the victors carried off the sacred Ark as the spoils of war (1 Sam. 4$^{2-11}$).

The hill country was occupied, Israel was disarmed, and garrisons were located in the tribal territories. At their first assault the Philistines had achieved their purpose, central Palestine was in their hands.

This advance of the Philistines must have gone hard with Israel, as can be judged from the contemporary evidence which has been discovered. The temple at Shiloh which Israel had built for the Ark of the Covenant was burnt to the ground. Fifteen miles south of Shechem lies Seilun which was once the flourishing town of Shiloh. On a neighbouring hill lay the sacred precincts, Israel's sanctuary and place of pilgrimage (Josh. 18¹; Jud. 21¹⁹ff; 1 Sam. 3²¹). After the Old Testament period early Christian and Mohammedan memorials were erected on the site.

Between 1926 and 1929 a Danish expedition carried out excavations at this spot, under the direction of H. Kjaers. The remains of Shiloh clearly indicate that the city was destroyed about 1050 B.C. at the time of the Philistine victory over Israel. Shiloh must have stood in ruins for a long time. For 400 years after its fall the prophet Jeremiah refers to it: "But go ye now unto my place which was in Shiloh, where I set my name at the first, and see what I did to it for the wickedness of my people Israel" (Jer. 7¹²). Other places in the mountains of Judah shared the same fate as Shiloh. Archaeologists found tell-tale traces of ashes in Tell Beit Mirsim near Hebron, the Debir of the Bible, and in Beth-zur, south of Jerusalem.

About 1050 B.C. Israel's very existence was threatened. It saw itself to be on the point of losing all the fruits of its conquests and all its work of colonisation lasting almost 200 years. It was on the verge of falling under the yoke of the Philistines and facing an existence of hopeless slavery. The only way to meet this frightful peril would be to amalgamate the loosely federated tribes and form a solid united front. It was in face of this pressure from without that Israel became a nation. In those days there was only one possible form of government, a monarchy. The choice fell upon Saul, a Benjamite, a man renowned for his bravery and his great height (1 Sam 9²). It was a wise choice, for Saul belonged to the weakest tribe (1 Sam. 9²¹) and the remaining tribes would therefore have no cause to be jealous.

Saul constituted his native town Gibeah as the capital (1 Sam. 10²⁶; 11⁴), collected round him a small standing army and began guerrilla warfare (1 Sam. 13¹ff). By surprise attacks he hunted the Philistine occupation troops out of the tribal territory.

That Saul was a tactician of a high order has recently, after 3,000 years, been demonstrated anew. One example, unique in its way, shows how accurate the Bible can be even in the smallest details and how reliable its dates and information.

We owe to Major Vivian Gilbert, a British army officer, this description of a truly remarkable occurrence. Writing in his reminiscences[1] he

[1] "The Romance of the last Crusade."

says: "In the First World War a brigade major in Allenby's army in Palestine was on one occasion searching his Bible with the light of a candle, looking for a certain name. His brigade had received orders to take a village that stood on a rocky prominence on the other side of a deep valley. It was called Michmash and the name seemed somehow familiar. Eventually he found it in 1 Sam. 13 and read there: "And Saul, and Jonathan his son, and the people that were present with them, abode in Gibeah of Benjamin but the Philistines encamped in Michmash." It then went on to tell how Jonathan and his armour-bearer crossed over during the night "to the Philistines' garrison" on the other side, and how they passed two sharp rocks: "there was a sharp rock on the one side, and a sharp rock on the other side: and the name of the one was Bozez and the name of the other Seneh" (1 Sam. 14[4]). They clambered up the cliff and overpowered the garrison, "within as it were an half acre of land, which a yoke of oxen might plough". The main body of the enemy awakened by the mêlée thought they were surrounded by Saul's troops and "melted away and they went on beating down one another" (1 Sam. 14[14-16]).

Thereupon Saul attacked with his whole force and beat the enemy. "So the Lord saved Israel that day."

The brigade major reflected that there must still be this narrow passage through the rocks, between the two spurs, and at the end of it the "half acre of land". He woke the commander and they read the passage through together once more. Patrols were sent out. They found the pass, which was thinly held by the Turks, and which led past two jagged rocks—obviously Bozez and Seneh. Up on top, beside Michmash, they could see by the light of the moon a small flat field. The brigadier altered his plan of attack. Instead of deploying the whole brigade he sent one company through the pass under cover of darkness. The few Turks whom they met were overpowered without a sound, the cliffs were scaled, and shortly before daybreak the company had taken up a position on "the half acre of land".

The Turks woke up and took to their heels in disorder since they thought that they were being surrounded by Allenby's army. They were all killed or taken prisoner.

"And so", concludes Major Gilbert, "after thousands of years British troops successfully copied the tactics of Saul and Jonathan."

Saul's successes gave Israel new heart. The pressure of the occupying power on the highlands had certainly been eased, but it was only a short respite. In the following spring the Philistines launched their counter attack.

Towards the end of the winter rainy season they gathered their fighting forces once again in Aphek (1 Sam. 29[1]). But this time they had a different plan of action. They avoided an engagement in the mountains since Israel knew that country far too well. The Philistine princes chose rather to advance northwards across the coastal plain to the Plain of Jezreel (1 Sam. 29[11]), the scene of Deborah's battle "at Taanach by the waters of Megiddo", and then eastwards almost to the banks of the Jordan.

"By a fountain which is in Jezreel" (1 Sam. 29[1])—the spring of Harod at the foot of the mountains of Gilboa—king Saul and his army ventured to meet the Philistines on the plain. The result was fatal. At the very first attack the army was scattered, the retreating troops were pursued and struck down. Saul himself committed suicide, after his own sons had been killed.

The triumph of the Philistines was complete. The whole of Israel was now occupied—the central uplands, Galilee and Transjordan (1 Sam. 31[7]). Saul's body and the bodies of his sons were impaled and exposed on the city walls of Beth-Shan not far from the battlefield. "And they put his armour in the house of Ashtaroth" (1 Sam. 31[10]), the goddess of fertility. Israel's last hour appeared to have struck. It seemed doomed to extinction. The first kingdom which began so hopefully had come to a fearful end. A free people had sunk into slavery and its Promised Land had fallen into the hands of foreigners.

The spades of the archaeologists have unearthed from among the masses of heavy black rubble silent evidence of this fateful period. The wind sweeps over the broken and crumbling masonry of the walls which saw the success and the tragedy of Israel. Ruins which witnessed Saul's happiest hours as a young king and also his shameful end.

A few miles north of Jerusalem, near the ancient road which leads to Samaria, lies Tell el-Ful, which means, literally, "hill of beans". This was once Gibeah.

In 1922 a team from the American Schools of Oriental Research began digging there. Professor W. F. Albright, who promoted the expedition, directed the operations. Remnants of walls came to light. After a long interval Albright continued his work at Tell el-Ful in 1933. A log-shaped corner turret was exposed, and then three more. They are joined by a double wall. An open courtyard forms the interior. The total area is about 40×25 yards. The uncouth looking structure of dressed stone gives an impression of rustic defiance.

Albright examined the clay sherds which were scattered among the ruins. They came from jars which had been in use about 1020 to 1000 B.C. Albright had discovered Saul's citadel, the first royal castle in Israel, where "the king sat upon his seat, as at other times, even upon a seat by the wall" (1 Sam. 20[25]). It was here that Saul reigned as king, surrounded by his closest friends, with Jonathan his son, with Abner, his cousin and commander of the army, and with David, his young armour-bearer. Here he forged his plan to set Israel free and from here he led his partisans against the hated Philistines.

The other place where king Saul's destiny was fulfilled and which research has brought once more to the light of day lies about 45 miles farther north.

On the edge of the Plain of Jezreel rises the great mound of rubble called Tell el-Husn, which is visible far beyond the Jordan valley. This is the site of the ancient Beth-Shan. On the north and south slopes the strong foundation walls of two temple buildings emerge out of the piles of cleared debris.

Archaeologists of the University of Pennsylvania, led by Clarence S. Fisher, Alan Rowe, and G. M. Fitzgerald excavated them in 1921 and 1933 almost at the same time as king Saul's castle was rediscovered at Gibeah.

Religious objects found among the ruins, principally medallions and little shrines with a serpent motif, indicate that these temples were dedicated to Astarte, the Canaanite goddess of fertility, and to Dagon the chief god of the Philistines, who was half fish half human. Their walls witnessed what the Philistines did to Saul, as the Bible records: "And they put his armour in the house of Ashtaroth; and they fastened his body to the wall of Beth-Shan" (1 Sam. 31[10]). The house of Ashtaroth is the temple ruins on the south side. "... and [they] fastened his head in the temple of Dagon" (1 Chron. 10[10]). That is the temple which has been excavated on the north slope.

V

When Israel was an Empire
From David to Solomon

CHAPTER 19

DAVID, A GREAT KING

A man of genius—From armour-bearer to monarch—Unintentional military aid for Assyria—From the Orontes to Ezion-Geber—Revenge at Beth-Shan—New buildings with casemated walls—Finding of the Pool of Gibeon—Jerusalem fell by a stratagem—Warren discovers a shaft leading to the city—The Sopher kept the "Imperial Annals"—Was David called David?—Ink as a novelty—Palestine's climate is unpropitious for keeping records.

"So all the elders of Israel came to the king to Hebron: and king David made a league with them in Hebron before the Lord. And they anointed David king over Israel ... and he reigned forty years"(2 Sam. 5^{3,4}).

THE new king was so versatile that it is difficult to decide which of his qualities deserves most admiration. It would be just as difficult to find as gifted and rounded a personality within the last few centuries of our own times. Where is the man who could claim equal fame as soldier, statesman, poet and musician?

Certain it is, in any case, that no people were more devoted to music than the inhabitants of Canaan. Palestine and Syria were renowned for their music as we learn from Egyptian and Mediterranean sources. Part of the essential goods and chattels which the group of members of the caravan, depicted in the wall painting at Beni-Hasan, took with them on their journey to Egypt, were musical instruments. The ordinary household instrument was the eight-stringed lyre.

The lyre travelled from Canaan to Egypt and Greece.

In the New Kingdom of Egypt (1580–1085 B.C.) inscriptions and reliefs deal with a series of themes connected with Canaanite musicians and instruments. Canaan was an inexhaustible treasure house of musicians, from which court chamberlains and seneschals obtained singers and even orchestras to provide entertainment for their masters on the Nile, the Euphrates and the Tigris. Above all ladies' bands and ballerinas were in great demand. Artists with international engagements were by no means a rarity. And king Hezekiah of Judah knew very well what he was doing in 701 B.C. when he sent men and women singers to Sennacherib the formidable king of Assyria.

FIG. 30.—Captive musicians from Judah.

From the depths of despair, from their hopeless situation under the yoke of the Philistines, Israel climbed within a few decades to a position of power, esteem and greatness. All of that was the work of David. He first appears, completely unknown, as Saul's armour-bearer, becomes a condottiere, then a fierce maquis fighter at war with the Philistines and ends up as an old man seated on the throne of a people that had become a great power.

As happened a few centuries earlier at the time of the conquest of Canaan, David's efforts were assisted by favourable external circumstances. Just after the beginning of the last millennium B.C. there was no state in Mesopotamia or Asia Minor, Syria or Egypt, which was in a position to stop an expansion of Canaanite territory.

After the death of Ramesses XI, the last of the Ramessid dynasty, about 1080 B.C. Egypt fell into the greedy hands of a priestly clique who ruled the land from Thebes. Vast wealth had come into the possession of the Temple.

A hundred years earlier, as the Harris Papyrus informs us, 2 per cent of the population was employed as temple slaves and 15 per cent of agricultural land was temple property. Their herds of cattle amounted to half a million head. The priests had at their disposal a fleet of eighty-eight vessels, fifty-three workshops and wharves, 169 villages and towns. The pomp with which the daily ritual of the great deities was carried out beggared all description. To make the temple scales alone, on which the sacrifices at Heliopolis were weighed, 212 pounds of gold and 461 pounds of silver were used. To look after the luxury gardens of Amun in the old royal city of Per-Ramesses in the delta 8,000 slaves were employed.

We get some idea of Egypt's status in the eyes of the outside world during this priestly regime from a unique document, the travel diary of Wen-Amun, an Egyptian envoy, dating from 1080 B.C. Wen-Amun's mission was to get cedar wood from Phoenicia for the sacred barge of the god Amun in Thebes. Herihor, the high priest, furnished him with only a small amount of gold and silver but with a picture of Amun, which he obviously expected to be more effective.

The frightful experiences which Wen-Amun had to go through on his journey have left their mark in his report. In the seaports he was treated like a beggar and an outlaw, robbed, insulted and almost murdered. He, an ambassador of Egypt, whose predecessors had always been received with the greatest pomp and the utmost deference.

At last Wen-Amun, having had his money stolen on the way, reached the end of his journey. "I came to the port of Byblos. The prince of Byblos sent to me to tell me: 'Get out of my harbour'."

This went on for nineteen days. Wen-Amun in desperation was on the point of returning to Egypt "when the harbour master came to me and said: 'The prince will see you tomorrow!' When tomorrow came he sent for me and I was brought into his presence. . . . I found him seated in his upper room, with his back leaning against a window. . . . He said to me: 'What have you come here for?' I replied: 'I have come to get timber for the splendid great barge of Amun-Re, the king of the gods. Your father gave it, your grandfather gave it, and you must also give it.' He said to me: 'It is true that they gave it. . . . Yes, my family supplied this material, but then Pharaoh sent six ships here laden with the produce of Egypt. . . . As far as I am concerned I am not your servant, nor the servant of him who sent you. . . . What kind of beggar's journey is this that you have been sent on!' I replied: 'Don't talk nonsense! This is no beggar's errand on which I have been sent.' "

In vain Wen-Amun insisted on Egypt's power and fame, and tried to beat down the prince's price for the timber. For lack of hard cash he had to bargain with oracles and a picture of the god which was supposed to guarantee long life and good health. It was only when a messenger sent by Wen-Amun arrived from Egypt with silver and gold vessels, fine linen, rolls of papyrus, cow hides, ropes, as well as twenty sacks of lentils and thirty baskets of fish, that the prince permitted the required quantity of cedars to be felled.

"In the third month of summer they dragged them down to the sea shore. The prince came out and said to me: 'Now, there is the last of your timber and it is all ready for you. Be so good as to get it loaded up and that will not really take very long. See that you get on your way and do not make the bad time of year an excuse for remaining here.' "

David had nothing to fear from a country whose ambassador had to put up with disrespect of this sort. He advanced far into the south and conquered the kingdom of Edom, which had once refused Moses permission to pass through it on the "King's Highway" (2 Sam. 8¹⁴). This meant for David an accession of territory of considerable economic significance. The Arabah desert, which stretches from the south end of the Dead Sea to the Gulf of Aqabah, is rich in copper and iron, and what David needed most of all was iron ore. His most dangerous opponents, the Philistines, had a monopoly of iron in their clutches (1 Sam. 13¹⁹⁻²⁰). Whoever controlled Edom could break the Philistine monopoly. David wasted no time: "And David prepared iron in abundance for the nails for the doors of the gates, and for the joinings: and brass in abundance without weight" (1 Chron. 22³).

The most important caravan route from South Arabia, the famous "Incense Road", likewise terminated in the south of Edom. By pressing forward to the shores of the Gulf of Aqabah the sea route lay open to him across the Red Sea to the remote shores of South Arabia and East Africa.

The situation was also favourable for a northward advance.

In the broad plains at the foot of Hermon and in the fertile valleys which lay in front of Antilebanon, Arab desert tribes had settled down and become static. They belonged to a race which was destined to play an important role in Israel's life, the Aramaeans, called simply Syrians in our Bible. They had founded city-states and smallish kingdoms as far down as the river Yarmuk, south of the Lake of Galilee over in Transjordan.

About 1000 B.C. they were in the process of reaching out eastward into Mesopotamia. In the course of it they came up against the Assyrians, who were within the next few centuries to become the strongest power in the ancient world. After the downfall of Babylonia, the Assyrians had subjugated Mesopotamia as far as the upper reaches of the Euphrates. Cuneiform texts recovered from palaces on the Tigris and dating from this period, mention Assyria as being threatened by danger from the west. These were the Aramaeans whose thrusting attacks were made with ever increasing force.

In face of this situation David pushed north through Transjordan right up to the Orontes. The Bible says: "And David smote Hadarezer king of Zobah unto Hamath, as he went to stablish his dominion by the river Euphrates" (1 Chron. 18³). Reference to contemporary Assyrian texts shows how accurately these words in the Bible describe the historical situation. King David attacked the Aramaean king as he was on his way to conquer Assyrian territory on the Euphrates.

Without being aware of it David was aiding those same Assyrians who later wiped out the kingdom of Israel.

The frontier posts of Israel were moved forward by David to the fertile valley of the Orontes. His most northerly sentries patrolled Lake Homs at the foot of the Lebanon, where now petroleum gurgles through the great pipelines from distant Kirkuk. From this point it was 400 miles as the crow flies to Ezion-Geber on the Red Sea, the most southerly point in the kingdom.

Excavations have revealed plenty of traces of the acquisitions and expansion of the kingdom under David. There is a clear trail of evidence which accompanies his advance, including the burning of the cities of the Plain of Jezreel. Not much later than 1000 B.C. Beth-Shan, together with its pagan sanctuaries, was levelled to the ground. Archaeologists from the University of Pennsylvania dug up on these sites of ruthless fighting, shattered temples, deep layers of ashes on top of ruined walls, ritual objects and pottery belonging to the Philistines. David's vengeance administered a crushing blow to the city which had compassed the shameful end of the first king of Israel, a blow from which it did not recover for many years to come. There is no indication above the layer of ashes which points to any habitation having existed there during the centuries immediately following.

Various building projects dating from the earlier years of David's reign remain in some state of preservation, principally fortresses in Judah which had been erected for defence against the Philistines. The structures clearly reflect the pattern of Saul's stronghold in Gibeah. They have the same rough-hewn casemated walls.

Seven miles north of Jerusalem, American excavations in 1956 brought to light not only traces of the walls of the town of Gibeah, which is so frequently mentioned in the Bible, but also uncovered the scene of a bloody encounter in these olden days. As we are told in II Samuel, once upon a time on this spot there took place a murderous hand-to-hand combat between supporters of the rival generals Joab and Abner—twelve on each side, the one lot on the side of David, the other owing allegiance to the surviving son of Saul. According to 2 Sam. 2[13], they "met together by the pool of Gibeon". Beneath a field of tomatoes in el-Jib, as the place is now called, Professor J. B. Pritchard, of Columbia University, discovered the "Pool of Gibeon", apparently in its day a well known spot. He found a circular shaft, over thirty feet in diameter and thirty feet deep, which had been driven vertically into bed rock. A spiral path led down a ramp cut into the inside wall. Below that a winding staircase, with two openings for light and air, descended for a further forty-five feet to the reservoir itself, chiselled out of solid limestone. When the rubble which covered the whole lay-out had been cleared away, the great cistern began to fill slowly again with water from the fissures in the rock as it had done 3,000 years ago. This Biblical "Pool of Gibeon" had also provided the town with an ample supply of fresh drinking water during an emergency or in time of siege.

Valuable evidence as to the celebrated wealth of the

place—"because Gibeon was a great city, as one of the royal cities" (Josh. 10²)—was collected by the American scholars from among the rubble of the vast cistern. It is now clear that the source of Gibeon's prosperity was a flourishing and well organised wine trade. Sixty handles belonging to clay wine-pitchers, together with the appropriate clay stoppers and fillers, were stamped in ancient Hebrew characters with firms' trade marks—among them vinters with genuine Biblical names. Repeatedly the stamp of "Gibeon" cropped up and a word that probably means "walled vineyard" and might indicate a wine of special quality. Other handles again bore the names of towns in Judah, like Jericho, Succoth and Ziph (Josh. 15²⁴) to which the various consignments were to be delivered.

Quite near the reservoir, further diggings in the winter season of 1959–60 led to the discovery of extensive wine cellars. Sixty-six almost circular cavities about six feet deep and the same in diameter had been carved out of the rock and sealed with round stone bungs. Some of these cellars had obviously been used as wine presses for trampling out the grapes; other cavities, protected by a waterproof cover, could be identified as fermentation vats. The total storage capacity so far discovered approaches 50,000 gallons.

In view of this new evidence of what was at one time a flourishing wine industry at Gibeon, a hitherto apparently insignificant point in the Biblical narrative acquires fresh significance. It concerns an incident which took place while the Israelites were bent on the conquest of Canaan. We are told in Josh. 9³⁻⁵ that "when the inhabitants of Gibeon heard what Joshua had done unto Jericho and to Ai they did work wilily ... and took ... wine bottles, old and rent and bound up ... and old garments upon them". In this guise they appeared before Joshua and succeeded in hiding from him both where they came from and what a prosperous place it was.

Finally, in Jerusalem, later David's capital, the foundations of a tower and large sections of the revetment certainly point to David as the builder. "So David dwelt in the fort and called it the city of David. And David built round about...."

The romantic manner in which the stoutly guarded stronghold of Jerusalem fell into David's hands was brought to light last century partly by chance and partly by the scouting proclivities of a British army captain.

On the east side of Jerusalem where the rock slopes down into the Kidron valley lies the "Ain Sitti Maryam", the "Fountain of the Virgin Mary". In the Old Testament it is called "Gihon", "bubbler", and it has always been the main water supply for the inhabitants of the city. The road to it goes past the remains of a small mosque and into a vault. Thirty steps lead down to a little basin in which the pure water from the heart of the rock is gathered.

In 1867 Captain Warren, in company with a crowd of pilgrims, visited the famous spring, which, according to the legend, is the place where Mary washed the swaddling clothes of her little Son. Despite the semi-darkness Warren noticed on this visit a dark cavity in the roof, a few yards above the spot where the water flowed out of the rock. Apparently no one had ever noticed this before because when Warren asked about it nobody could tell him anything.

Filled with curiosity he went back to the Virgin Fountain next day equipped with a ladder and a long rope. He had no idea that an adventurous and somewhat perilous quest lay ahead of him.

Behind the spring a narrow shaft led off at first horizontally and then straight up into the rock. Warren was an alpine expert and well acquainted with this type of chimney climbing. Carefully, hand over hand, he made his way upwards. After about 40 feet the shaft suddenly came to an end. Feeling his way in the darkness Warren eventually found a narrow passage. Crawling on all fours he followed it. A number of steps had been cut in the rock. After some time he saw ahead of him a glimmering of light. He reached a vaulted chamber which contained nothing but old jars and glass bottles covered in dust. He forced himself through a chink in the rock and found himself in broad daylight in the middle of the city, with the Fountain of the Virgin lying far below him.

Closer investigation by Parker, who in 1918 went from the United Kingdom under the auspices of the Palestine Exploration Fund, showed that this remarkable arrangement dated from the second millennium B.C. The inhabitants of old Jerusalem had been at pains to cut a corridor through the rock in order that in time of siege they could reach in safety the spring that meant life or death to them.

Warren's curiosity had discovered the way which 3,000 years earlier David had used to take the fortress of Jerusalem by surprise. David's scouts must have known about this secret passage, as we can now see from a Biblical reference which was previously obscure. David says: "Whosoever getteth up to the gutter and smiteth the Jebusites..." (2 Sam. 5[8]). The Authorised Version translated as "gutter" the Hebrew word "sinnor", which means a "shaft" or a "channel".

Warren solved only half the problem, however, for the opening of the shaft lay outside the walls which in his day were thought to be those of the old Jebusite Jerusalem dating from before David's time. Anybody who had climbed through the shaft would still have found himself facing the Jebusite wall. It was not until the sixties of this century that the extensive excavations of Kathleen M. Kenyon cleared the matter up. The wall of what had been considered the most ancient Jerusalem was, in fact, not so old as had been thought. A much older wall was revealed which dated from before David's day and this wall ran along the slope below the opening to the entrance to the spring. David's men, who had climbed through the shaft, consequently emerged not *in front of* but a good distance *behind* what was actually Jerusalem's oldest wall; they were *right inside* the town which they were aiming to capture. This confirms the second Book of Samuel 5[8] and thus removes much of the puzzling nature of this passage.

It was in David's reign that the exact recording of Old Testament history began. "We must regard the David narratives as largely historical," writes Martin Noth, who is an extremely critical German theologian.

The increasing clarity and lucidity of contemporary records is closely associated with the gradual creation of a political system which was David's great achievement and something new for Israel. A loose federation of clans had become a nation: a settlers' colony grew into an empire which filled Palestine and Syria.

For this extensive territory David created a Civil Service, at the head of which, next to the Chancellor, stood the Sopher. "Sopher" means "writer of chronicles" (2 Sam. 8[16,17]). A writer in the second highest position in the state!

In face of the millions of secretaries and typists in the modern world, and the thousands of tons of paper that they put into their machines and cover with type every day, the legendary glory of the "scribe" has long since departed. Not even the enviable post of chief secretary to an oil magnate can be compared with that of her ancient colleague either in salary or still less in influence. It was only on the stage of the ancient orient that the scribes played the role of their profession incomparably and uniquely. And little wonder, considering how much depended on them. Mighty conquerors and rulers of great empires were their employers and they could neither read nor write!

This can clearly be seen from the style of the letters. It is not the person to whom the letter or message is sent who is addressed in the first instance. Greetings and good wishes from scribe to scribe take precedence. There is also a request to read out the contents of the letter distinctly, and, most important, correctly and under no circumstances to suppress any of it. How things were managed within this scribal sphere of authority is indicated by a vivid scene in the Foreign Office of Pharaoh Merenptah. The scribes' department is divided into three sections. In each of the two side aisles about ten secretaries sit tightly packed together. Some of them have one foot on a stool, great rolls of papyrus lie across their knees. The spacious middle section is reserved for the chief. A zealous slave keeps the troublesome flies off him with a fan. At the entrance stand two commissionaires. One is telling the other "Spray some water and keep the office cool. The chief is busy writing."

No doubt the administrative office at the court of Jerusalem was considerably less impressive. The young state of Israel was still too rustic and too poor for that. Yet David's "recorder" must have been an important and awe-inspiring official. It was his job to compile the "Imperial Annals", which doubtless were the basis of all the factual Biblical references to the administrative system and social structure under David. Among these are the great national census conducted on the approved Mari-plan (2 Sam. 24) as well as the information about his bodyguard of "Cherethites and Pelethites", a kind of Swiss guard, which consisted of Cretans and Philistines (2 Sam. 8[18]; 15[18]; 20[7]).

FIG. 31.—A Government office on the Nile.

Undoubtedly the "Sopher" would also be the first to write down the new name of his sovereign.

This name has presented a problem to the specialists, for they repeatedly came across a very similar word in texts from the Ancient East, texts from Mari; the word "dâvidum". Did this puzzling word mean "commander of an army", "supreme commander", "chief", and was David's name consequently no name at all but a title which had become a name when he mounted the throne? In addition, the Bible more than once mentions a certain Baal-hanan, the son of an Edomite king Saul (Gen. 36[38] and 1 Chron. 1[49]). On the other hand, a certain Elhanan is reported as having vanquished David's adversary Goliath and on another occasion Goliath's brother (2 Sam. 21[19] and 1 Chron. 20[5]). The names Baal-hanan and Elhanan obviously contain the names of the Canaanite gods Baal and El.

Was David's name then originally Baal-hanan or Elhanan and did he first take the name David after his accession to the throne? Thirty years ago a number of scholars were convinced of this, but since then greater caution has been shown, at least concerning the linguistic connection between the words "David" and "dâvidum", for it has become apparent that "dâvidum" does not mean "commander of an army" or anything similar, but "defeat". And nobody has ever thought of deriving the title of a commander from that word! Nor can it be accepted that personal names like Baal-hanan or Elhanan, elements of which are the names of Canaanite gods, would have met with the approval of the Biblical writers. The problem of David's name still remains unsolved.

This question of "writing" conjures up one of the arguments levelled by critics of the Bible. In Egypt waggon loads of papyrus have been found, similarly in Babylonia and Assyria mountains of cuneiform tablets—where then are the literary documents of Palestine?

Archaeologists and meteorologists may be permitted to answer this question.

About the beginning of the last millennium B.C. Canaan deserted its angular cuneiform script and the use of clumsy clay tablets in favour of a less cumbersome method of writing. Until then the text of the document had to be scratched in soft clay with a stylus. The clay had then to be baked or dried in the sun, a time-wasting procedure, before the bulk letters were ready for despatch. A new type of writing, with wavy lines, became more and more fashionable. This was the alphabet which we have already encountered in the attempts at writing made by the Semitic miners at Sinai. Stylus and clay were clearly unsuited for these new smoothly rounded letters. So they looked for new writing utensils and found them in their baked clay tablets, inkpot and ink. Archaeologists call these little tablets with their flowing script "Ostraca". They were replaced in special cases by papyrus, the most elegant writing material of the ancient world. The Wen-Amun report shows how greatly this Egyptian export was in demand. The prince of Byblos received in return for his cedars 500 rolls of it: well over a mile of writing paper!

Palestine has a damp climate in winter on account of its rainfall. In such a climate ink is very quickly washed off hard clay, and papyrus soon disintegrates. Greatly to the distress of archaeologists, scientists and historians, all of them thirsting for knowledge, practically the sum total of Canaan's records and documents has been lost to posterity for this reason. The fact that the archaeologists were able to produce such an impressive haul from Egypt is simply the result of its proximity to the desert and the unusually dry climate.

CHAPTER 20

WAS SOLOMON A "COPPER-KING"?

Expedition to the Gulf of Aqabah—Iron ore and malachite—Glueck discovers Ezion-Geber—Desert storms used as bellows—The Pittsburgh of old Israel—Shipyards on the Red Sea—Hiram brought the timber—Ships' captains from Tyre—The mysterious land of Ophir—An Egyptian portrait of the queen of Punt—U.S. archaeologists buy a Tell—A model dig at Megiddo—The fateful plain of Jezreel—Royal stables with 450 stalls?

"So king Solomon was king over all Israel (1 Kings 4[1]) and Solomon had 40,000 stalls of horses for his chariots, and 12,000 horsemen" (1 Kings 4[26]).

"And Solomon built . . . all the cities of store . . . and cities for his chariots and cities for his horsemen" (1 Kings 9[17, 19]).

"And king Solomon made a navy of ships in Ezion-Geber which is beside Eloth . . . and they came to Ophir" (1 Kings 9[26, 28]).

"And all king Solomon's drinking vessels were of gold . . . none were of silver: it was nothing accounted of in the days of Solomon. For the king had at sea a navy . . . bringing gold and silver, ivory and apes, and peacocks" (1 Kings 10[2, 22]).

"And the house which king Solomon built for the Lord . . . was . . . overlaid with gold" (1 Kings 6[2, 22]).

"And Solomon had horses brought out of Egypt and linen yarn . . . and so for all the kings of the Hittites, and for the kings of Syria, did they bring them out by their means" (1 Kings 10[28, 29]).

"Now the weight of gold that came to Solomon in one year was six hundred threescore and six talents of gold" (1 Kings 10[14]).

DOESN'T it sound like a fairy-tale?

Any man, even a king, about whom so much is told, is hard put to it to escape the charge of boasting. And any chronicler, telling such a story, easily gets a reputation for exaggeration. There are certainly stories in the Bible which are regarded by scholars as legends, such as the tale of Balaam the sorcerer and his talking ass (Num. 22) or the tale of Samson whose long hair gave him strength (Jud. 13–16). But this most fabulous of all stories is really no fairy tale at all.

The archaeologists dug their way to the heart of the trustworthiness of these Solomon stories—and lo and behold Solomon became their unique showpiece.

197

When the "fairy-tale" of king Solomon—as many still believe it to be—has been stripped of its frills, there remains a framework of sober historical facts. That is one of the most exciting discoveries of recent times. It was only in 1937 that a wealth of surprising finds during excavations by two American expeditions produced proof of the truth of this Biblical story.

Packed high with the latest equipment, with drills, spades and picks and accompanied by geologists, historians, architects, excavators and the photographer who

is now indispensable on a modern expedition, a caravan of camels is leaving Jerusalem. Its leader is Nelson Glueck, who like the others is a member of the famous American Schools of Oriental Research.

Soon they have left the brown mountains of Judah behind. They head south through the dreary Negev. Then the caravan enters Wadi el-Arabah, the "Valley of the Desert". The men feel as if they had been transported into some scene from a primeval world,

FIG. 32.—Life in a harem. "Solomon had 700 wives..." (1 Kings 11³).

where some Titanic power out of the depths had left its mark when it formed the earth. The "Valley of the Desert" is part of the mighty fissure which begins in Asia Minor and ends in Africa.

The scientists pay their respects to this impressive vista and then turn to the task which awaits them. Their questing eyes roam over the steep rock-face. Light and shade vary with the sun, and here and there the stone is hacked away and dented. They find that it consists of muddy yellow felspar, silvery white mica, and, where the stone shows up reddish black, iron ore and a green mineral—malachite, copper spar.

Along the whole length of the wadi the American scientists come upon deposits of iron ore and copper. Wherever their tests indicate the presence of ore they find galleries let into the rock, all that remains of mines long since deserted.

At last the caravan reaches the shores of the Gulf. However invitingly the white houses of Aqabah, the Eloth of the Bible, seem to beckon them in the glaring sun, however tempting are the sounds of this busy eastern seaport after their trek through the desolate wadi, nevertheless the scientists turn their backs on this intersection of three worlds.[1]

[1] Africa, Arabia and Palestine/Syria.

Their goal is "Tell el-Kheleifeh". This lonely mound, which seems no more than a pile of rubble, rises inland out of the shadeless plain.

Careful probing with spades prefaces the first stage of the excavation and produces unexpectedly quick results. Fish hooks come out; they are made of copper. Then tiles and remnants of walls. Some coarse looking lumps of some material in the vicinity of the Tell show traces of green. They turn out to be slag. Everywhere around them the scientists meet this sandstone with the distinctive green colour.

In his tent one evening Glueck reflects on the results of the work up to date. It has produced nothing remarkable. Meantime the whole of Transjordan is still on the programme. Glueck wants to track down the past in Edom, Moab, Ammon, even as far as Damascus. Looking through his notes, he stops and ponders. Iron-ore and malachite in the Arabah—and, in this mound of debris in front of his tent, remains of walls, slag, and copper fish-hooks—and all of it in' the immediate neighbourhood of the Gulf which the Bible calls the "Red Sea". Thoughtfully Glueck turns up the Bible passage which mentions the Red Sea in connection with a great king: "And king Solomon made a navy of ships in Ezion-Geber, which is beside Eloth, on the shore of the Red Sea, in the land of Edom" (1 Kings 9[26]). In Biblical times Edom came right down to the gulf of the Red Sea. Could this mound be . . . ?

It is decided to make a thorough investigation of Tell el-Kheleifeh next day. As they dig up the material from the test-shafts they find that at several points they come upon wall foundations at the same level. Below that is virgin soil. Sherds give them an indication of the date of construction of the masonry. It is within the period of Solomon's reign, after 1000 B.C.

The time factor compelled Glueck to stop operations. This particular expedition had other tasks ahead. But in the following years the Americans continued the excavations in three stages, which ended in 1940 and confirmed Glueck's theory. It appeared that the first ruins that came to light had once been workers' dwellings. Then came ramparts of the casemated type, the unmistakable building style of the first Iron Age. After that remains of an extensive settlement were excavated. The most interesting things were casting-moulds and a vast quantity of copper slag.

Casting-moulds and copper slag in the middle of the scorching pitilessly hot plain?

Glueck tried to find an explanation for this strange fact. Why did the workshops have to be located right in the path of the sand-storms which almost incessantly sweep down the wadi from the North? Why were they not a few hundred yards farther on in the shelter of the hills, where there were also fresh water springs? The astonishing answer to these questions was not forthcoming until the last excavation period.

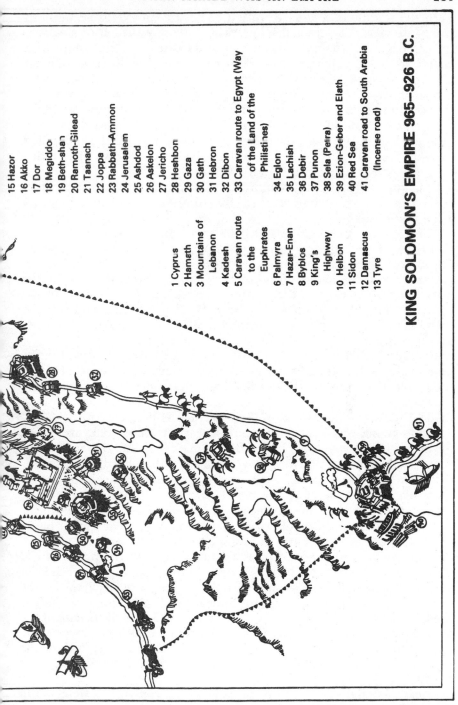

KING SOLOMON'S EMPIRE 965–926 B.C.

1 Cyprus
2 Hamath
3 Mountains of
   Lebanon
4 Kedesh
5 Caravan route
   to the
   Euphrates
6 Palmyra
7 Hazar-Enan
8 Byblos
9 King's
   Highway
10 Helbon
11 Sidon
12 Damascus
13 Tyre

15 Hazor
16 Akko
17 Dor
18 Megiddo
19 Beth-shan
20 Ramoth-Gilead
21 Taanach
22 Joppa
23 Rabbath-Ammon
24 Jerusalem
25 Ashdod
26 Askelon
27 Jericho
28 Heshbon
29 Gaza
30 Gath
31 Hebron
32 Dibon
33 Caravan route to Egypt (Way
   of the Land of the
   Philistines)
34 Eglon
35 Lachish
36 Debir
37 Punon
38 Sela (Petra)
39 Ezion-Geber and Elath
40 Red Sea
41 Caravan road to South Arabia
   (Incense road)

In the middle of a square walled enclosure an extensive building came into view. The green discolouration on the walls left no doubt as to the purpose of the building: it was a blast furnace. The mud-brick walls had two rows of openings. They were flues: a skilful system of air passages was included in the construction. The whole thing was a proper up-to-date blast furnace, built in accordance with a principle that celebrated its resurrection in modern industry a century ago as the Bessemer system. Flues and chimneys both lay along a north to south axis. For the incessant winds and storms from the Wadi el-Arabah had to take over the role of bellows. That was 3,000 years ago: today compressed air is forced through the forge.

One question alone still remained unanswered: how was the copper refined in this ancient apparatus? Smelting experts of today cannot solve the mystery.

Earthenware smelting-pots still lie about in the vicinity: many of them have the remarkable capacity of 14 cubic feet. In the surrounding hill-slopes the multiplicity of caves hewn out of the rock indicate the entrances to the galleries. Fragments of copper sulphate testify to the busy hands that worked these mines thousands of years ago. In the course of fact-finding excursions into the surrounding country the members of the expedition succeeded in identifying numerous copper and iron mines in the wadis of the Arabah desert.

Eventually Nelson Glueck discovered in the casemated wall of the mound of rubble a stout gateway with a triple lockfast entrance. He was no longer in any doubt. Tell el-Kheleifeh was once Ezion-Geber, the long-sought vanished seaport of king Solomon: "And king Solomon made a navy of ships in Ezion-Geber which is beside Eloth...."

Ezion-Geber was however not only a seaport. In its dockyards ships for ocean travel were also built. But above all Ezion-Geber was the centre of the copper-industry. Nowhere else in the "Fertile Crescent", neither in Babylonia nor in Egypt, was such a great furnace to be found. Ezion-Geber had therefore the best smelting facilities in the ancient orient. It produced the metal for the ritual furnishings of the Temple at Jerusalem—for the "altar of brass", the "sea", as a great copper basin was called, for the "ten bases of brass", for the "pots, shovels, basins" and for the two great pillars "Jachin and Boaz" in the porch of the Temple (1 Kings 7[15ff]; 2 Chron. 4). For "in the plain of Jordan did the king cast them in the clay ground between Succoth and Zarthan...." (1 Kings 7[46]). One of the most recent finds in Biblical archaeology fell to the lot of a Dutch expedition which has now established the site of the former of these two places. At Tell deir Alla in Transjordan, where the river Jabbok leaves the hills six miles before it joins the Jordan, the expedition discovered traces of Succoth, the Israelite city dating from the days of Joshua.

Glueck's delight at these unparalleled finds can still be detected in the official report which gathered together the results of the researches at the Gulf of Aqabah: "Ezion-Geber was the result of careful planning and was built as a model installation with remarkable architectural and technical skill. In fact practically the whole town of Ezion-Geber, taking into consideration place and time, was a phenomenal industrial

FIG. 33.—Brass laver from Solomon's Temple (1 Kings 7^{27ff}; 2 Chron. 4^6). (Reconstruction.)

site, without anything to compare with it in the entire history of the ancient orient. Ezion-Geber was the Pittsburgh of old Palestine and at the same time its most important seaport."

King Solomon, whom Glueck describes as the "great copper-king", was on this basis reckoned among the greatest exporters of copper in the ancient world. Research on other sites completed this picture of Palestine's economy under king Solomon. South of the old Philistine city of Gaza, Flinders Petrie dug up iron-smelting installations in Wadi Ghazze. The furnaces are like those at Tell el-Kheleifeh but smaller. David had disputed the Philistines' right to their monopoly of iron and he had extracted their secret smelting process as one of the prices of their defeat. Then under Solomon the iron and copper deposits were apparently mined on a large scale and smelted.

Twenty years after Professor Glueck's first discovery of the presence of copper and slag heaps, an archaeologist, Benno Rothenberg, made a striking find in the same Wadi el-Arabah of a large copper mine dating from the same time. In the spring of 1959, twenty miles north of Ezion-Geber in Wadi Timna, Rothenberg's expedition came across extensive workings where the stone had been cut out of the rocks in thick slices and then subjected to the first process of removing the slag in basalt smelting vats.

> "For the Lord thy God bringeth thee into a good land ... a land whose stones are iron and out of whose hills thou mayest dig brass" (Deut. 8[7-9]).

So runs part of the detailed description of the Promised Land which Moses gives the children of Israel. Copper and iron in Palestine? The work of the archaeologists has now produced evidence showing how true is this description which the Bible gives, and introduces a new factor into our picture of Old Palestine which we shall in future have to take into account, namely its remarkable industrial development.

Solomon was a thoroughly progressive ruler. He had a flair for exploiting foreign brains and foreign skill and turning them to his own advantage. That was the secret, otherwise scarcely understandable, of how the simple peasant regime of his father David developed by leaps and bounds into a first class economic organism. Here also was to be found the secret of his wealth which the Bible emphasises. Solomon imported smelting technicians from Phoenicia. Huram-Abhi,[1] a craftsman from Tyre, was entrusted with the casting of the Temple furnishings (1 Kings 7[13, 14]). In Ezion-Geber Solomon founded an important enterprise for overseas trade. The Israelites had never been sailors and knew nothing about shipbuilding. But the Phoenicians had behind them practical experience accumulated over many centuries. Solomon therefore sent to Tyre for specialists for his dockyards and sailors for his ships: "And Hiram[2] sent in the navy his servants, shipmen that had knowledge of the sea...." (1 Kings 9[27]).

Ezion-Geber was the well-equipped and heavily defended export centre for the new foreign trade. From Ezion-Geber the ships set sail on their mysterious voyages to distant and unfamiliar shores. Ophir?—where was the legendary land of Ophir, the "warehouse" in which the ancient orient purchased the costliest and choicest commodities?

Many a scholarly quarrel has broken out about Ophir. Someone was always claiming to have found it. In 1871 Carl Mauch of Germany came across a large area covered with ruins in Rhodesia. Fifteen years

---

[1] A.V.=Hiram.   [2] The king of Tyre.

later Steinberg of South Africa dug up, a few miles to the south, pre-Christian mining installations which were thought to be connected with the temple city. Rock-tests were supposed to show that gold and silver had at one time been quarried there. In 1910 the famous African explorer, Dr. Karl Peters of Germany, photographed carvings on this site in which experts claimed that they detected odd Phoenician characteristics.

This mysterious land of Ophir has however so far eluded the grasp of the scientists. Many indications nevertheless point to East Africa. Experts like Prof. Albright suggest that it was located in Somaliland. That would tie up very well with what the Bible says about the length of time it took to get there.

"Once in three years came the navy..." (1 Kings 10[22]). "The fleet may have sailed from Ezion-Geber in November or December of the first year," suggested Albright, "and returned in May or June of the third year. In this way the hot weather in summer would be avoided as much as possible. The journey in this case need have taken no more than eighteen months." Further, the nature of the merchandise "gold, silver, ivory and apes" (1 Kings 10[22]) points to Africa as the obvious place of origin.

The Egyptians were well informed about "Punt", which may be identifiable with Ophir. They must have been on the spot and kept their eyes open. How otherwise could these impressive pictorial representations of "Punt" have originated, which light up the walls of the terraced temple of Deir el-Bahri? Wonderful coloured reliefs adorn this temple on the west side of Thebes, lending splendour and charm to a dusky lady—the queen of Punt—and her retinue. As usual the Egyptians have here too lavished devoted attention to the details of the costumes, the round huts, the animals and plants of "Punt". Anyone looking at

FIG. 34.—One of Queen Hatshepsut's ships returning from Punt (Ophir) with a cargo of myrrh and apes.

them has a clear picture in his mind's eye of what this legendary Ophir looked like.

Inscriptions adjoining the reliefs give an account of the sensational expedition which a woman ordered to be equipped and to set out for "Punt" in 1500 B.C. On the throne of the Pharaohs at that time, as co-regent of Tutmose III, sat the famous Queen Hatshepsut, "the first great woman in history" as Breasted the Egyptologist calls her. In response to an oracle of the god Amun, which enjoined that the routes to "Punt" should be explored and that trade relations with the Red Sea ports which had been interrupted by the Hyksos wars should be resumed, the queen sent out a flotilla of five sea-going vessels in the ninth year of her reign. They were to bring back myrrh trees for the temple terraces. The fleet sailed from the Nile along a canal in the eastern part of the delta into the Red Sea and "arrived safely in Punt", where it exchanged Egyptian produce for a precious cargo of myrrh trees, ebony, gold, as well as all sorts of sweet smelling wood and other exotic articles like sandalwood, panther skins, and apes.

A display such as they had never seen before met the gaze of the Thebans as at the close of a successful trip the strange collection of dark-skinned natives of Punt made their way to the queen's palace with the marvellous products of their country. "I have made his garden into another Punt, as he commanded me . . ." says Hatshepsut exultingly, referring to the myrrh trees on the temple terraces. Egyptologists found dried up roots of myrrh in the hot yellow sand in front of the temple of Deir el-Bahri.

Like the Thebans, men and women of Israel must also have stood in wonder and amazement on the quayside of Ezion-Geber when their king Solomon's fleet returned from distant Ophir and discharged its cargo of sandalwood "and precious stones, gold, silver, ivory, apes and peacocks" (1 Kings 10[11, 22]).

Archaeological work can normally only be started when permission to excavate has been given by the landowner or by the government of the country. This is not always easy to obtain, quite apart from the fact that in the course of the operations protests or restrictions can make life difficult for the investigators. In 1925 the Americans hit upon an unusual way of ensuring that they would be left in peace to get on with the work. They bought without a moment's hesitation the mound of rubble called Tell el-Mutesellim in the Plain of Jezreel from ninety native proprietors, peasants and shepherds, lock, stock and barrel. For the Oriental Institute of the University of Chicago had in mind a model excavation for the whole of the Middle East, the most comprehensive, most painstaking, and most accurate investigation that had ever been started in Palestine.

Tell el-Mutesellim covers the site of the Megiddo of the Bible. This discovery is based on the first large-scale excavation which was undertaken on this spot by the German Oriental Society under Dr. J. Schumacher between 1903 and 1905.

Like a small edition of Table Mountain, Tell el-Mutesellim lies in the heart of a unique scenic setting. Looking down from the plateau is like looking down on a vast green lake. Into the far distance stretches the great plain, the "valley of Jezreel" (Jos. 17^{16}), in which the green meadows of the fenland and well-stocked fields of grain alternate with one another. Flocks of cranes and storks frequent the spot. Where the plain ends, the wooded hump of Carmel stands guard over the Mediterranean shore. To the north the hills of Galilee with the little village of Nazareth sweep upwards, tinted a delicate blue, and far to the right the sombre summit of Mt. Tabor bars the view into the deep cleft of the Jordan valley.

Nothing in this fertile triangle, this friendly countryside girt with gentle lines of hills, suggests that this tiny bit of land was for many thousands of years the scene of mighty battles and of momentous and decisive history.

About 1500 B.C. Pharaoh Thutmose III, riding in a "golden chariot", led his army through a narrow pass into the plain and attacked the Canaanites, who fled in terror and complete disorder to Megiddo. On the same plain the Israelites, incited by the heroic Deborah, smashed the supremacy of the Canaanite charioteers, Gideon surprised the plundering camel-borne nomads from Midian, Saul lost the battle against the Philistines, and king Josiah of Judah died about 600 B.C. as he and his men threw themselves in vain against the armed might of Egypt under Pharaoh Necho. Ruins mark the site of the Frankish castle of Faba, which the knights of St. John and the Templars occupied during the Crusades, until Saladin drove them off the plain after a frightful massacre. On the 16th April 1799 there was a battle here between the Turks and the French. With only 1,500 men Kleber, the French general, held 25,000 of the enemy at bay. The French fought like heroes from sunrise till noon. Then over a ridge to the rescue charged a troop of 600 mounted men. The officer at their head was called Napoleon Bonaparte. After the victorious "Battle of Tabor" Napoleon rode up into the hills of Galilee and ate his supper in Nazareth. In 1918 British cavalry under Lord Allenby swept through the same pass as Thutmose III and destroyed the Turkish army which was encamped on the plain.

A silent witness of all these events was Tell el-Mutesellim, where Clarence S. Fisher began operations on the model excavation in the spring of 1925.

The hill was literally cut into slices inch by inch—like cutting a cake except that the slices were horizontal ones. The centuries flashed past like a kaleidoscope. Every layer that was removed signified a chapter of world history from the 4th to the 10th century B.C.

Of the four top layers Stratum I contained ruins from the time of the Persian and Babylonian empires. Cyrus, king of Persia, destroyed the power of Babylon in 539 B.C. King Nebuchadnezzar of Babylon had conquered Syria and Palestine fifty years earlier in 597 B.C. The walls of an unusually solidly built palace still remain from that period. Stratum II provided evidence of Assyrian rule with ruins of a palace dating from the 8th century B.C. Tiglath-Pileser III subdued Palestine in 733 B.C. Stratum III and Stratum IV incorporated the Israelite period.

The most important find in this case was two seals with old Hebrew letters on them. One of them bore the inscription, "Shema, servant of Jeroboam". Jeroboam I was the first ruler of Israel after the kingdom had been divided (926–907 B.C.). A stone preserved another familiar name: Pharaoh Sheshonk I, of Egypt. The Bible calls him Pharaoh Shishak. In 922 B.C., the fifth year of king Jeroboam's reign, he attacked Palestine.

After almost ten years of toil, picks and spades had reached the layers dating from the time of king Solomon, who had died four years before the attack of Sheshonk in 926 B.C. The lowest level of rubble in Stratum IV then produced sensational surprises from king Solomon's time for the archaeologists, Gordon Loud and P. L. O. Guy, as well as for posterity.

In Solomon's day a new method of construction was adopted in the case of public buildings, defence walls, etc. Instead of the previous style of building this new type involved the introduction of smooth dressed stones at the corners and at intervals along the walls. On the lowest level of the rubble of Stratum IV ruins of a palace were exposed which displayed this characteristic feature. They are enclosed by a square wall whose sides are about 60 yards long. Additional protection was afforded by the handsome entrance gateway flanked by three pairs of close-set pillars. Archaeologists came across similar town gates with this threefold security in Ezion-Geber and in Lachish. A building with massive walls that was excavated almost at the same time turned out to be a granary, one of the "cities of store that Solomon had" (1 Kings 9[19]). Storehouses of this kind were also found at Beth-Shan and Lachish. Megiddo was the administrative centre of the 5th District in the Israel of Solomon's day. Solomon's representative in the palace, who was also responsible for the deliveries of taxes in kind to the "city of store" was "Baana, the son of Ahilud, to him pertained Taanach and Megiddo" (1 Kings 4[12]).

Although these finds were remarkable they were not sensational. The sensation was still lying untouched in the heart of Tell el-Mutesellim as if the old mound had been keeping the best to the last. In the course of the excavations there appeared among the rubble on the edge of the Tell a flat stone surface, studded with stone stumps, ranged one behind the other in long rows and square in shape.

Loud and Guy had at first no idea what it could have been. There seemed to be no end to this remarkable series of flat surfaces which emerged yard by yard out of the rubble. It occurred to Guy that they might be the remains of stables. Did the Bible not speak of the untold horses of king Solomon?

Amid the generally monotonous sameness of a dig that had lasted several years with its daily stint of carrying away, emptying out, sifting and arranging every fragment worth considering, Guy's idea gave at once a new fillip to the excavations, which even the digging gangs shared.

The archaeologists' astonishment grew with every new structure which came to light. They found that several large stables were always grouped round a courtyard, which was laid with beaten limestone mortar. A 10-foot wide passage ran down the middle of each stable. It was roughly paved to prevent the horses from slipping. On each side, behind the stone stumps, lay roomy stalls, each of which was exactly 10 feet wide. Many of them had still remains of feeding troughs and parts of the watering arrangements were still recognisable. Even for present day circumstances they were veritable luxury stables. Judging by the extraordinary care which had been lavished on buildings and services, horses in those days were at a premium. At all events they were better looked after than were human beings.

When the whole establishment was uncovered, Guy counted single stalls for at least 450 horses and sheds for 150 chariots. A gigantic royal stable indeed. "And this is the reason of the levy which king Solomon raised: for to build ... the wall of Jerusalem and Hazor and Megiddo..." (1 Kings 9[15]). "And Solomon gathered together chariots and horsemen: and he had a thousand and four hundred chariots and twelve thousand horsemen, whom he bestowed in the cities for chariots..." (1 Kings 10[26]). In view of the size of the royal stable at Megiddo and the stables and chariot sheds of similar type which have been found at Tell el-Hesi, at Taanach and also at Jerusalem, the Biblical references must be regarded as mere hints at the reality. These tremendous results of the excavations give us a clear conception of the lavishness to which old Israel was accustomed in its imperial days.

Megiddo was after all only one of the garrisons for Solomon's new chariot corps, which formed part of the king's standing army.

In one of the ancient stable buildings which were cut deep into the rock under the high walls of the city of Jerusalem the Crusaders tethered their horses after the conquest of the Holy City by Godfrey of Boulogne almost 2,000 years after Solomon.

Horses and chariots alike were considered in Solomon's day to be worth-while trading commodities. Israel had indeed in this matter a complete monopoly (1 Kings 10[28, 29]).

FIG. 35.—"And a chariot came ... out of Egypt for six hundred shekels of silver" (1 Kings 10²⁹).

All the important caravan routes between Egypt, Syria and Asia Minor went through Solomon's kingdom. Egypt was the chief exporter of war-chariots ". . . the king's merchants received the linen yarn at a price. And a chariot came up and went out of Egypt for six hundred shekels of silver." Egyptian wheelwrights were unsurpassed craftsmen in building swift two-wheeled chariots for war and hunting. The hardwood for them had to be imported from Syria. This explains the high rate of exchange. According to the Bible one chariot was worth four horses (1 Kings 10²⁹). In this connection it will not be necessary to insist on the fact that the "shekels of silver" mentioned by the Bible are an anachronism since minted coins were still unknown in King Solomon's day.

The horses came from Egypt, "and from Koa" as another tradition tells us. "Koa" was the name of a state in Cilicia which lay in the fertile plain between the Taurus Mountains and the Mediterranean. After the destruction of the kingdom of Mitanni by the Hittites, Cilicia became the land of horse breeders and the livery stables of the ancient world. Herodotus mentions that later on the Persians fetched the best horses for their Imperial Messenger Service from Cilicia.

Israel's trading partners in the north were the "Kings of Syria and the Kings of the Hittites" (1 Kings 10²⁹). This too is historically accurate. The kingdom of the Hittites had long been extinct by Solomon's day but some smaller successor states had taken its place. One of them was discovered in 1945 by Professor H. T. Bossart of Germany, although it is a century younger than Solomon. This was the royal castle in the forest of Mt. Karatepe, not far from Adana in the southeast of Turkey. Asitawanda, who built it in the 9th century B.C., was one of these "Kings of the Hittites".

The most recent researches have thrown light on Solomon, the "copper king", providing not only confirmation of statements in the Bible but also the refutation of views previously held. The Israeli professor of archaeology, Benno Rothenberg (Tel Aviv), who was born at Frankfurt am Main, has made very important contributions in this field. Mention has already been made on several occasions of his investigations at Timna in the Wadi Arabah area. What Rothenberg discovered there contradicts, however, the opinion held by Nelson Glueck: between the 12th century B.C. and the time of the Romans there was no extraction of copper in the "Biblical" mines at Timna. In other words, King Solomon's mines were not producing in Solomon's day, in the 10th century B.C. In fact, the Bible gives us no cause to regard Solomon as a "copper king" for there is no mention of copper exploitation at his time. On the contrary, the Bible tells us expressly that Solomon obtained the metal he required from plunder as well as from the store of his father David (1 Chron. 18[8]; 22[3, 14]). Once again the Bible is right. It does not refer to copper mining in Solomon's time and it has not been possible so far to prove that any took place.

Where then does the persistent tradition about "Solomon's mines" originate? Today light has also been thrown on this question. It has nothing to do with the Bible, but a great deal with Sir Rider Haggard's novel *King Solomon's Mines* which appeared at the end of last century. Even the great Bible archaeologist Nelson Glueck, without doubt one of the most prominent figures in this field, was deceived by this pseudo-Biblical tradition of recent date.

Perhaps even greater caution than with "Solomon's mines" is required in the attempt to localise Ophir, which continues to defeat all attempts by specialists to identify it. What the German geologist Carl Mauch found in Rhodesia—and to a large extent destroyed by inexpert excavations—was Zimbabwe which was not built until some 2,000 or 2,500 years after Solomon's day, some time, therefore, between the 11th and the 15th century A.D. Zimbabwe has nothing in common with the building practices of the Phoenicians or the Arabs, nor has it any connection with the Awwam Temple of the moon god Ilumquh or Almaqah near distant Marib in Southern Arabia, a temple which, by the way, also does not date from Solomon's time but probably from the 8th or 7th century B.C. No, Zimbabwe is definitely a product of indigenous architecture, however unpleasant this fact may be for the present government of Rhodesia. The expert who made this discovery and published it, Peter S. Garlake, was deprived of his post as Curator of the Commission for Historic Monuments in Southern Rhodesia and was obliged to emigrate to a black African country. Obviously a certain amount of courage is required even today in the exercise of the archaeologist's profession and discoveries are not always followed by fame alone!

Just as it was with Solomon's copper mines, of which the Bible makes no mention, so it is with the no less famous "Solomon's stables" in Megiddo. The opinion has become more widely accepted that they date not from Solomon's time but from that of King Ahab of Israel (c. 875 to 852 B.C.), who according to the Assyrian account of the Battle of Qarqar (c. 854 B.C.) assembled 2,000 chariots, the largest force of war-chariots in the anti-Assyrian alliance. And so, basically the Biblical story has once more been confirmed, for we read (1 Kings 9[15]) merely that Solomon *fortified* Megiddo and not that he built stables there and that, speaking generally, he *had* "chariots and horsemen" (1 Kings 10[26]), but not that they were garrisoned in Megiddo.

It remains merely to add that in the view of a number of experts, among them the Israeli specialist in Biblical archaeology, Professor Yohanan Aharoni of Tel Aviv, what are reputed to be "Solomon's stables" not only date from the time of Ahab but also are not stables. It seems they are storehouses for supplies. Similar buildings destined for the same purpose have been excavated by Yohanan Aharoni in Beersheba.

Fairly long and quite detailed passages of the Bible, chapters 6 and 7 of 1 Kings, chapters 3 and 4 of 2 Chronicles and chapters 40 to 43 of the prophet Ezekiel have received striking confirmation. These passages all refer to King Solomon's most famous building, the Temple in Jerusalem.

As excavations are impossible within the Temple area, we do not know what remains today of Solomon's construction beneath the stones of Herod the Great's temple pavement and the rock dome (Qubbet es-Sachra) built by the Omayyads, one of the most magnificent examples of Islamic architecture. Yet we know from the descriptions in the Bible as well as from parallel finds from the Canaanite-Phoenician region that this temple was a model construction such as was continually encountered in Semitic temples from the early Stone Age onwards. It consists of three connecting halls, access to each of which is possible only through the preceding one. The "small temple" of *Tell Tainat* (9th century B.C.), the late Bronze Age Canaanite temple from Layer XV in excavation section H at Hazor (13th century B.C.), and the Iron Age temple on the northwest corner of the citadel of *Tell Arad* show the closest contacts with the Biblical accounts. The latter is of particular interest as this is an Israelite sanctuary and is chronologically closest to Solomon's temple.

Connected to these three temple rooms there is first a porch (*ulam*) to which a "hall" was attached (*hekal*). The Authorised Version also refers to the *hekal* as the "greater house" or simply as the "Temple", although strictly speaking only a part of the temple complex is meant. It was this "greater house" that gave admittance to the actual sanctuary, the Holy of Holies (*debir*). The entrance to the *hekal* was flanked by two pillars,

Jachin and *Boaz*. In fact, two stone slabs were found on *Tell Arad*, one on each side of the entrance to the *hekal*, which might well have served as the bases of pillars. The entrance to the middle room in the late Bronze Age temple of Hazor is also flanked by the bases of pillars.

Although it dates from the century *after* Solomon, the temple of *Tell Tainat* still belongs architecturally as it were to Solomon's time. It confirms the statements in the Bible concerning certain constructional details which are made mainly in connection with the building of Solomon's palace (1 Kings 7^{1-12}).

According to 1 Kings 6^{10} and 6^{33}, it appears that wood was used to cover the building both inside and out, and that wood was also used for beams and posts. Exactly the same thing occurred at *Tell Tainat*. The walls of this temple were built of bricks on a stone foundation—brick walls which were supported by wooden posts!

The temple at *Tell Tainat* was Phoenician and Solomon obtained Phoenician workmen for the construction of his Temple at Jerusalem from King Hiram of *Tyre* (1 Kings 5^{32}; 2 Chron. 2^{6}; 2^{12f}). The interior appointments of the temple were in part Phoenician or at least influenced by the Phoenicians. In particular, this was probably so with the *cherubim* which watched over the ark in the Holy of Holies (Ex. 25^{18-22}; 37^{7-9}; 1 Kings 6^{23-25}; 2 Chron. 3^{7}; 3^{10-14}). Similar carved statues providing us with an idea of the appearance of this strange creature of dual nature have been discovered in the Phoenician cultural region. The same assertion can be made regarding the ritual vessels described in the Bible which have been encountered in the Canaanite-Phoenician region and even as far away as Cyprus, which lay within the Phoenician orbit. The archaeologist can be compared to a tracker, who fits one indication in with another like a mosaic as soon as he has begun to follow a trail. In the search for models of Solomon's Temple in Jerusalem it seems that all the indications point to Canaan and Phoenicia.

CHAPTER 21

THE QUEEN OF SHEBA AS A BUSINESS PARTNER

"Arabia Felix", the mysterious land—Death-march of 10,000 Romans—Number One exporter of spices—First news of Marib—Halévy and Glaser have a dangerous adventure—When the great dam burst—American expedition to Yemen—The temple of the moon in Sheba—Camels –the new long distance transport—Export talks with Solomon.

"And when the queen of Sheba heard of the fame of Solomon, she came to prove Solomon with hard questions at Jerusalem, with a very great company, and camels that bare spices, and gold in abundance and precious stones" (2 Chron. 9[1]).

FOR thousands of years richly laden caravans have made their way from "fortunate Arabia" to the north. They were well-known in Egypt, in Greece and in the Roman Empire. With them came tales of fabulous cities, of tombs filled with gold, tales which persisted through the centuries. The Roman Emperor Augustus determined to find out the truth about what camel drivers continually extolled in their remote country. He instructed Aelius Gallus to fit out a military expedition and to satisfy himself on the spot as to the truth of these incredible tales about south Arabia. With an army of 10,000 Roman soldiers Gallus marched south from Egypt and proceeded along the desolate shores of the Red Sea. Marib, the legendary capital city, was his goal. But he was never to reach it. For in the pitiless heat of the desert, after endless clashes with wild tribes, decimated by treacherous diseases, his army went to pieces. The few survivors who reached their native land again had no reliable factual details to add to the legendary stories of "Arabia Felix".

"In fortunate Arabia", writes Dionysius the Greek in A.D. 90, "you can always smell the sweet perfume of marvellous spices, whether it be incense or wonderful myrrh. Its inhabitants have great flocks of sheep in the meadows, and birds fly in from distant isles bringing leaves of pure cinnamon."

South Arabia was even in the ancient world export country Number One for spices and it is still so today. Yet it seemed to be shrouded in dark mystery. No man had ever seen it with his own eyes. "Arabia Felix" remained a book with seven seals. The first man in recent times to embark upon this dangerous adventure was Carsten Niebuhr, a

German, who led a Danish expedition to south Arabia in the 18th century. Even he only got as far as Sana. He was still 60 miles from the ruined city of Marib when he had to turn back.

A Frenchman, J. Halévy, and an Austrian, Dr. Eduard Glaser, were the first white men actually to reach this ancient goal about a century ago. Since no foreigner, far less a European, was allowed to cross the frontier of the Yemen, and no permit could be obtained, Halévy and Glaser embarked on an enterprise which might have cost them their lives. They chartered a sailing boat and landed secretly in the Gulf of Aden disguised as Orientals. After an arduous journey of over 200 miles through parched and desolate mountain country they eventually reached Marib. Greatly impressed by what they saw they threw caution to the winds and clambered around the ruins.

Suspicious natives came towards them. The two scholars knew that it would cost them their lives if their disguise was discovered and took to their heels. At last after many adventures they reached Aden by a circuitous route. However they had been able to smuggle out copies and rubbings of inscriptions, concealed under their burnous, on the strength of which they were able to prove that Marib really existed.

Travelling merchants likewise brought inscriptions with them later on. Up to the present day their number reaches the sizeable total of 4,000. Scholars have examined and sifted the material. The script is alphabetic and therefore originated in Palestine. Dedicatory inscriptions give us information about gods, tribes and cities of a million inhabitants. And the names of four countries—"The Spice Kingdoms"—which are mentioned are: Minaea, Kataban, Hadhramaut and—Sheba.

The kingdom of Minaea lay in the northern part of Yemen and is referred up to the 12th century B.C. Writings of the 9th century B.C. mention its southern neighbour, the land of the Shebans. Assyrian documents of the 8th century B.C. likewise speak of Sheba and of close trade relations with this country whose kings were called "Mukarrib", "priest-princes".

Gradually, with the discovery of documentary evidence, this fairy-tale country of Sheba began to take definite shape.

A gigantic dam blocked the river Adhanat in Sheba, collecting the rainfall from a wide area. The water was then led off in canals for irrigation purposes, which was what gave the land its fertility. Remains of this technical marvel in the shape of walls over 60 feet high still defy the sand-dunes of the desert. Just as Holland is in modern times the Land of Tulips, so Sheba was then the Land of Spices, one vast fairy-like scented garden of the costliest spices in the world. In the midst of it lay the capital, which was called Marib. For 1,500 years this garden of spices bloomed around Marib. That was until 542 B.C.—then the dam burst. The importunate desert crept over the fertile lands and destroyed them. "The people of Sheba", says the Koran, "had beautiful gardens in which the most costly fruits ripened." But then the people turned their backs upon God, wherefore he punished them by causing the dam to burst. Thereafter nothing but bitter fruit grew in the gardens of Sheba.

In 1928 the German scholars Carl Rathjens and H. von Wissmann uncovered the site of a temple near Sana which had been first seen by their countryman Niebuhr. It was a significant start but almost another quarter of a century was to elapse before the greatest team of experts so far set out on an expedition at the end of 1951 to solve the archaeological riddle of Sheba. "The American Foundation for the Study of Man" provided the expedition with unusually large financial resources. The organiser of the enterprise was an extremely versatile palaeontologist from the University of California, Wendell Phillips, then only twenty-nine years old. After long drawn-out negotiations they succeeded in getting permission from King Imam Achmed to excavate at Marib. Marib lies at the southern tip of the Arabian peninsula about 6,000 feet up on the eastern spurs of the mountain range that skirts the Red Sea. The archaeologists started with high expectations.

A long column of jeeps and trucks rolled northwards in a cloud of dust through barren mountain country with neither roads nor paths. Suddenly like a phantom out of the shimmering yellow sand dunes there appeared before them massive ruins and columns—"Haram Bilqis". It was the ancient Ilumquh temple of Awwam, a centre of worship wrapped in legend, in the neighbourhood of Marib, the capital of the old Arabian kingdom of Sheba. Although partly covered by sand dunes as high as houses the lines of this oval-shaped temple over 300 feet long were clearly recognisable. A cursory examination of the sanctuary reveals a circular shape similar to that of the Zimbabwe ruins in Rhodesia where at one time the search for the Biblical Ophir was made. Closer investigation has shown, however, that the conformities are purely superficial. Zimbabwe, moreover, which was built between the 11th and the 15th centuries A.D., is around two thousand years younger than the old moon god sanctuary at Marib.

According to an inscription on the wall, Ilumquh, god of the moon, was worshipped in "Haram Bilqis". Masses of sand covered the temple which stood in the middle of the oval. Digging therefore began on the entrance to the great circle. The archaeologists wanted to try to approach the temple gradually from that point.

Under a boiling sun a gatehouse of surprising splendour and beauty was exposed amid understandable excitement. Wide steps covered with bronze led inside. The inner court was surrounded by a pillared hall. Stone columns 15 feet high once bore a roof which shielded it from the sun. Flanked by pillars on each side the processional way led from this point to the sanctuary of the moon god. An unusual ornamental fixture caused astonishment. From a height of 15 feet glittering fountains of water must in those days have played into this quiet courtyard. As it descended the water was caught in a narrow channel which then wound its way through the whole pillared court.

What must have been the feelings of pilgrims who made their way past these splashing sparkling fountains, fanned by the drowsy fragrance of incense and myrrh, through the pillared courts of this most marvellous edifice in old Arabia.

The digging went steadily forward until they were within a few yards of the temple. The archaeologists could see in front of them the wonderful temple gate, flanked by two slender columns—but at this point the excavation had to be precipitately abandoned. The chicanery of the governor of Marib which had been going on for weeks had now reached a dangerous point and the members of the expedition were no longer sure of their safety. They had to rise and run, leaving everything behind them. Fortunately they had some

FIG. 36.—In Marib a U.S. expedition discovered the Temple of the Moon in the Kingdom of Sheba in 1951.

photographs among the few things they had been able to salvage on their hasty escape to Yemen.

Nearby in the Hadhramaut three digs were carried out in the following few years which were crowned with more success.

Soon after the experts had begun to evaluate the results of these four brief and somewhat dramatic expeditions, Professor W. F. Albright could say: "They are in process of revolutionising our knowledge of Southern Arabia's cultural history and chronology. Up to now the results to hand demonstrate the political and cultural primacy of Sheba in the first centuries after 1000 B.C."

Just as king Solomon's ships made long sea voyages through the Red Sea to Arabia and Africa, so long distance travel began on the Red Sea coast route through the southern Sea of Sand. The new form of transport called, not unjustly, "Ships of the Desert", consisted of camels. They were able to compass distances which were hitherto reckoned impossible. An unsuspected development both in trade and transport through these vast desolate territories took place about 1000 B.C. thanks to the taming and training of these desert animals. South Arabia, which had for so long been almost as far away as the clouds, was suddenly brought into the Mediterranean world and into closer contact with the other kingdoms of the Old World. Just as with the introduction of stratosphere aircraft America was suddenly brought closer to Europe in transatlantic services, so was it also, even if on a different scale, with south Arabia and the Old World.

Previously it was by the employment of donkeys, plodding endlessly and painfully month after month, each short day's journey governed by the distance from water hole to water hole, and always in danger of attack, that the treasures of Arabia trickled northwards along the ancient Incense Road through 1,250 miles of desert. With the arrival of the new type of long-distance transport, however, a wide range of goods began to flow out of "fortunate Arabia". The new method was quicker,

FIG. 37.

almost independent of water holes and therefore not tied to the old traffic routes which zig-zagged from well to well. It had also a greater capacity. The camel could carry many times the burden which an ass could carry.

The terminus of the Incense Road was Israel. Solomon's official agents, the "king's merchants" took delivery of the costly wares.It also depended on them whether the caravans would be allowed to proceed on their journey through Solomon's kingdom to Egypt, Phoenicia and Syria.

No wonder that "the fame of Solomon" came to the knowledge of the queen of Sheba (1 Kings 10¹). Bearing all this in mind, if we read carefully the tenth chapter of the First Book of Kings, we shall think of it no longer in terms of a "pious story" or of the queen of Sheba as a character in a fairy tale. On the contrary the whole passage rings true and is completely intelligible. "And she [i.e. the queen of Sheba] came to Jerusalem . . . and when she was come to Solomon, she communed with him of all that was in her heart" (1 Kings 10²). The queen of Sheba had assuredly quite a number of things she wanted to talk about. The head of a state whose chief export trade could only be with and through Israel, and that for unavoidable geographical reasons, would certainly have plenty to discuss with the king of that country. We should nowadays describe the affair more concretely as trade talks and should send experts minus crowns to other countries for discussions. They too would carry with them in their diplomatic bags presents which would show the respect due to the head of the state, like the queen of Sheba.

Admittedly, however vividly we are able to imagine all this, and however colourfully popular Oriental tradition embellishes the relationship between Solomon and the Queen of Sheba—throughout the East they became one of the "classical" pairs of lovers of popular tradition—the Queen of Sheba nevertheless retained a certain majestic distance.

It is a fact that popular tradition once more does indeed connect the Sheban *Awwam* temple at Marib with this "queen", but there is no doubt that this temple does not date from the time of Solomon (10th century B.C.). It was probably not built until the 8th or even the 7th century B.C. and consequently is considerably more recent than Solomon. But there are other considerations—although women such as Queen Hatshepsut and Queen Tewosre had ruled in Ancient Egypt centuries before Solomon, any non-Biblical indication of a scientifically reliable nature of a ruling princess during the time of Solomon has been denied us in southern Arabia. The Queen of Sheba, to whom we seemed already to have drawn so near, thus once again becomes inaccessible.

CHAPTER 22

ISRAEL'S COLOURFUL DAILY LIFE

Israel's love of ornamentation—Secrets of the boudoirs of Palestine—Sleeping with myrrh and aloes—The Balsam gardens of Jericho—Mastic, a favourite chewing gum—Perfumes of Canaan—Did the Egyptians invent the bed?—An ostracon describes a cloak being taken in pledge—Noisy flour-mills.

AMID these revelations of Egyptian, Babylonian or Assyrian splendour to which archaeology has borne witness, we have been inclined to forget until now the grey and apparently monotonous daily life of Israel. Certainly there has been nothing to record which could compare with the golden treasure of Troy, no Tutankhamun, no charming Nofretete. But was the daily life of Israel really so drab, with no colour and no sparkle?

The Israelites loved bright colours. They coloured their dress, the walls of their houses and the faces of their women. Even in the days of their patriarchs their delight in colour was apparent: "Now Israel loved Joseph more than all his children and he made him a coat of many colours" (Gen. 37³). One of the pictures in the tomb at Beni-Hasan shows this type of coat with a wonderful red and blue pattern. Red and blue were the colours for men's wear, green seems to have been reserved for women. During the desert days mention is made of "blue and purple and scarlet" (Ex. 25⁴). "Ye daughters of Israel, weep over Saul, who clothed you in scarlet . . ." (2 Sam. 1²⁴), cries David in his grief after the death of the first king. "And she had a garment of divers colours upon her," it is recorded of Tamar, daughter of David, "for with such robes were the king's daughters that were virgins apparelled" (2 Sam. 13¹⁸).

Nature had given the land of Canaan one of the most wonderful painters' palettes. The children of Israel only needed to stretch out their hands. Pomegranates and saffron yielded a lovely yellow, madder-root and safflower a fiery red, woad a heavenly blue: there was also ochre and red chalk. The sea donated the queen of all dye merchants, the murex snail. Its soft colourless body turned purple in the sunlight. That was its undoing. Vast mountains of empty snail shells have been found at Tyre and Sidon, which leads us to the conclusion that this was the centre for the extraction of purple. The Phoenicians were the first to create a proper industry for the extraction of purple in their seaports, but later Palestine too devoted itself to the profitable business of snail catching.

The textile town of Beth-Asbea in south Judah was famous for byssus, the finest kind of bleached linen. "10 shirts of byssus" are actually mentioned in an inscription of Esarhaddon, the mighty king of Assyria. Hebron and Kirjath-Sepher had the reputation of being important centres of the dye industry. Great stone basins and things like cauldrons with inflow and outflow pipes, which were dug up in these places turned out to be dyeing vats. In Tell Beit Mirsim, the ancient Debir, they were au fait even with the technique of cold dyes. "That saith, I will build me a wide house," says Jeremiah (22[14]), "... and it is cieled with cedar and painted with vermilion." Walls were varnished, mosaic chips and fabrics, leather and wood were dyed, as also were the lips, cheeks, and eyelids of beautiful women.

"Thy lips are like a thread of scarlet ... thy temples are like a piece of pomegranate ...", "... the hair of thy head like purple ...", "... how much better ... the smell of thine ointments than all spices" (Song of Songs 4[3]; 7[6]; 4[10]), sings king Solomon himself in his Song of Songs, one of the most beautiful love songs in the world.

Fig. 38.—Stone dyeing plant in ancient Israel.

In highly poetic language it refers to Israel's delight in adornment and discreetly deals with the secrets of the beauty-parlour. These perfumes and paints, ointments and hair dyes, choice and expensive, manufactured with the best ingredients that the world could provide would still do credit to the much lauded cosmetics industry of Europe and overseas.

Sweet smelling perfumes have always been highly prized; aromatic resins were not only primarily esteemed as incense in the ritual of the temple, but they had also their place in everyday life, in the home, in clothing, on the hair and in divans and beds.

"I have decked my bed with coverings of tapestry ... of Egypt. I have perfumed my bed with myrrh, aloes and cinnamon" (Prov. 7[16]) runs the warning against the artful wiles of the adulteress. "All thy garments smell of myrrh, and aloes and cassia, out of the ivory palaces, whereby they have made thee glad" is the song of praise in Ps. 45[8].

Botanists have investigated these stories that often sound like fairy tales, and have hunted up the ingredients of perfumes and the suppliers of dyes. They found them among delicate flowers and herbs, in the sap of shrubs and blossoms. Many came from foreign lands, but many still grow in Palestine today.

From India came cassia (Cinnamomum Cassia), a tree with a cinnamon-like bark, and calamus (Andropogon Aromaticus), also called ginger-grass. They came across the Indian Ocean in the course of foreign trade to the packing stations for spices in South Arabia and made their way from there by caravan to the Mediterranean countries.

Cinnamon had a world tour behind it. Originally it came from China, then on to Persia, thence to India, where it became indigenous and was exported to Arabia.

Incense was obtained from the Boswellia bush. Its home is in Arabia and Somaliland, like the Commiphora Myrrha, the myrrh tree. The cradle of the aloe is the island of Socotra at the lower end of the Red Sea, whence comes its name Aloe Succotrina.

There was many a dispute about the origin of balsam. The Bible seemed to be really in error, for botanists know very well that the balsam bush (Commiphora Opobalsamum) grows only in Arabia. How could Ezekiel (27[17]) claim that Judah and Israel had sent to Tyre "wax, honey, oil and balsam" (Moffatt)?

The botanists and Ezekiel are both right. The botanists had merely forgotten to look up Josephus, the great Jewish historian, where he tells us that there has been balsam in Palestine since the time of Solomon. The bushes were cultivated principally in the neighbourhood of Jericho. Josephus also answers the question as to how they got there. They were reared from seeds which had been found among the spices which the queen of Sheba brought as gifts.

That seems a daring assertion.

But there is a further bit of evidence. When the Romans entered Palestine, they actually found balsam plantations in the plain of Jericho. The conquerors prized the rare shrub so highly that they sent twigs of it to Rome as a sign of their victory over the Jews. In A.D. 70 Titus Vespasian put an imperial guard in charge of the plantings to protect them from destruction. A thousand years later the Crusaders found no trace of the precious bushes. The Turks had neglected them and allowed them to die.

Mastic, which Ezekiel also mentions, is still found in Palestine. These are the yellowish-white transparent globules from a pistachio-bush (Pistacia Lentiscus). They are greatly valued for their perfume and are used medicinally. Children gladly surrender their last baksheesh for a few drops of this native chewing-gum, which was wisely extolled in ancient times as being good for teeth and gums.

In the Promised Land the following aromatic resins are indigenous: Galbanum from a parsley-shaped plant (Ex. 30[34]), Stacte from the Storax bush (Ex. 30[34]), Ladanum from the rock-rose and Tragacanth (Gen. 37[25]) from a shrub of the clover family. Botanists found all the Biblical spices.

The receptacles for these often expensive items have been found by archaeologists under the debris of walls, among the ruins of patrician houses, and in royal palaces. Bowls of limestone, of ivory and sometimes of costly alabaster, with little pestles, were used for mixing the aromatic ingredients of the finest unguents. The recipes of experts in ointments were greatly sought after. Tiny bottles of burnt clay were used for keeping perfumes. In larger jars and jugs the scented spices were replaced with olive oil. Oil was well known for keeping hair and skin in good condition. Even poor folk rubbed it into their hair and skin, without the scented and generally very expensive ingredients. They got plenty of oil from their olive groves.

Washing in water was a daily necessity and was done as a matter of course. They washed before and after meals, washed the feet of their guests and washed themselves each evening.

FIG. 39.—Stone footbath, with heel-rest, handles and waste-pipe.

Stone basins, foot baths and clay bowls found throughout the whole country during excavations, confirm the numerous Biblical references to this practice. (Gen. 18⁴; 19²; 24³²; Song of Songs 5³; Job 9³⁰; Luke 7⁴⁴; Mark 7³ etc.) Lyes from plants and minerals provided lotions and soap (Jer. 2²²; Job 9³⁰).

"A bundle of myrrh is my well beloved unto me: he shall lie all night betwixt my breasts" (Song of Songs 1¹³). This is a transference of ideas referring to the discreet practice whereby women carried a small bag containing myrrh under their dresses. Neither curling pins, nor hair pins, nor mirrors—brightly polished metal discs—failed to find a place on the dressing table. These important items of beauty culture counted as luxury imports from the Nile, where they had been regarded as indispensable by the wives of the Pharaohs for many dynasties.

However much the prophets railed against it they were never able to drive the ancient equivalents of rouge and mascara completely out of the boudoirs of the wealthy.

Women were fond of decorating their hair with delicate yellow sprays of the lovely Loosestrife bush. But they were even more fond of a yellowish red powder which was extracted from the bark and from the leaves of the same shrub. The Arabs call it Henna. With this henna they dyed their hair, their toe nails and their finger nails. Astonished archaeologists found nail varnish of this bright red hue on the hands and feet of Egyptian mummies. Cosmetic laboratories and factories still use henna despite all recent developments. Eyebrows and eyelashes were tinted with Galena, powdered Lapis-lazuli gave the desired shadows on the eyelids. Dried insects provided, as in the modern lipstick, the necessary carmine for a seductive mouth.

In view of the dainty perfume flasks, the ivory ointment boxes, the mixing jars and rouge pots, which have been salvaged from the ruins of Israelite cities, we can well imagine how harsh the threats of the prophet Isaiah sounded in this world which cared so much for colour, cosmetics and perfume: "And it shall come to pass, that instead of sweet smell there shall be stink; and instead of a girdle, a rent; and instead of well-set hair baldness; and instead of a stomacher a girding of sackcloth; and burning instead of beauty" (Is. 3²⁴).

In the Old Testament there is certainly mention of sitting at table on couches but no one goes to bed in our sense. The bed is a rare de luxe item of furniture.

The question whether the bed was invented in the Nile region is one that we cannot answer with certainty. Naturally beds were to be found in all the countries of the Ancient East and one has even been found in a middle Bronze Age grave (grave H 18) at Jericho. Together with other items this grave also contained a table. It can nevertheless be stated without fear of contradiction that beds were more common in Egypt than elsewhere. With

FIG. 40.—Spice-mill (left) and stone grater for grinding corn.

great delight Sinuhe on his return observes: "I slept on a bed once more." But even 500 years later a bed was still a novelty. For when the Princess of Mitanni, Taduchepa, presumably afterwards Queen Nofretete, was married into the Egyptian royal family, she brought bedspreads as her dowry, admittedly expensively woven, but only bedspreads. The royal palace in her home country did not know what a bed was—everybody slept on the floor.

FIG. 41.—Simple oil lamp and seven-pointed candlestick.

In Israel too only court circles and the well-to-do possessed so expensive an item. The plain man's bed was his cloak. At night he wrapped himself in it (Ex. 22²⁷). The law made allowance for this in that while it declared that a man's "bed" could be taken in pledge, that was only permissible during the day. At night he had to have it back again (Ex. 22²⁶). A lucky chance led to the discovery in 1959 among the ruins of Yavne Yam, eight miles south of Tel Aviv, of a unique document which records an actual case of a cloak being taken in pledge. In a letter of the 7th century B.C., the text of which is clearly written in ink on a fragment of pottery, an "ostracon", a peasant from whom such a cloak had been taken in pledge, defends himself against the charge of being in debt. The archaeologists could make out distinctly . . . "And he took thy servant's cloak after I had brought in the harvest . . . and all my brothers will testify truthfully on my behalf that I am not in his debt." The "cloak" was in reality only a woollen cover and seems to have been designed for any emergency. As well as keeping out the cold in our sense and serving as a bed it was also used as a carpet (2 Kings 9[13]; Matt. 21[7,8]).

The bed was never regarded as the ideal place to rest either in Israel or in the Ancient East in general. It was a rare luxury and always remained so. Its cousin the divan, however, likewise a product of the "Fertile Crescent", became famous for its comfort and its cushions. With its arrangement of pillows during the day which were spread out at night, it was the prototype of our modern variety. What even bombed-out Central Europe and the smallest 20th-century households have been able to afford was the last word in furniture 3,000 years ago. The divan was also known in Israel. "And satest upon a stately bed, and table prepared before it ..." (Ezek. 23[41]).

We are prone to thunder against the nerve shattering noise of our machine age and often wish the good old days of peace and quiet would come back again. Was Israel any better off?

Instead of the blaring of loudspeakers, from daybreak onwards houses and tents echoed to the sound of stone hand-mills. At crack of dawn began the grinding of the corn and pounding it into flour. This was as much the woman's job as grinding coffee today. Only grinding flour was incomparably harder and heavier work. It often took two of them to turn the heavy stone.

The threat of a thorough going anti-noise campaign which is often talked about nowadays would have meant something frightful in those circumstances. If the noise of the mill stopped, hunger crept over the land. Jeremiah had a vision of this as he foretold what would happen during the Exile in Babylon: "Moreover I will take from thee the voice of mirth ... the sound of the millstones and the light of the candle, and this whole land shall be a desolation...." (Jer. 25[10,11]).

VI

Two Kings—Two Kingdoms
From Rehoboam to Jehoiachin

CHAPTER 23

THE SHADOW OF A NEW WORLD POWER

The Empire splits—Frontier posts between Israel and Judah—Napoleon reads Shishak's report on Palestine—Samaria, the northern capital—Traces of Ahab's "ivory palace"—A mysterious "third man"—Arabs blow up victory monument in Moab—Mesha the mutton-king's song of triumph—Assyria steps in—The black obelisk from Nimrud—King Jehu's portrait in Assyria—Consignments of wine for Jeroboam II—Uzziah's palace—The prophet Amos warns in vain—The walls of Samaria are strengthened to 30 feet.

"So Israel rebelled against the house of David unto this day . . . there was none that followed the house of David, but the tribe of Judah only" (1 Kings 12^{19,20}).

SOLOMON the Great died in 926 B.C. The dream of Israel as a great power was buried with him for ever. Under the leadership of two unusually gifted men—David and Solomon—this ambitious dream had been built up stone by stone for two generations. But at the very moment of Solomon's passing, the old tribal dissensions broke out again and the empire of Syria and Palestine was shattered as the inevitable end of the quarrel. Two kingdoms took its place—the kingdom of Israel in the north, the kingdom of Judah in the south. A new chapter in the history of the people of the Bible had begun.

It was the Israelite people themselves that gnawed away their own foundations and destroyed their empire. It became only too plain what road they proposed to follow slowly until the bitter end when the inhabitants of Israel fell a prey to the Assyrians, and the inhabitants of Judah a prey to the Babylonians. Divided among themselves, what happened to them was worse than simply sinking back into obscurity. They were caught between the millstones of the great powers which were in the following centuries to dominate the world stage. Israel and Judah collapsed amid a welter of dispute and barely 340 years after Solomon's death both kingdoms were no more.

Solomon's last wish was certainly carried out: his son Rehoboam sat on the throne at Jerusalem for a short spell as ruler of all the tribes. The endless quarrelling of the tribes among themselves hastened the end of the empire, since this resulted in civil war. Ten tribes in the north seceded. Jeroboam, who had lost no time in returning from exile in

Egypt, assumed the crown in 926 B.C. and became king of Israel in the north. The remainder stayed faithful to Rehoboam, and formed Judah in the south with its capital Jerusalem (1 Kings 12^{19,20}).

There was no harmony between Judah and Israel. They shed each other's blood in feud after feud. Time and again fighting broke out on the question of frontiers. "And there was war between Rehoboam and Jeroboam all their days" (1 Kings 14^{30}). It was no different under their successors. "And there was war between Asa and Baasha king of Israel all their days" (1 Kings 15^{16}). Judah built the fortress of Mizpah on the

Fig. 42.—Border stronghold of Mizpah between Judah and Israel.
(Reconstruction.)

main strategic route from Jerusalem to the north, farther to the east they strengthened Geba "... and king Asa built with them Geba of Benjamin and Mizpah" (1 Kings 15^{22}). That was the final frontier.

From 1927–35 an American expedition from the Pacific School of Religion, under the direction of William Frederick Bade, excavated abnormally massive stonework at Tell en-Nasbe, 7 miles north of Jerusalem. It was the remains of the old frontier fortress of Mizpah. The enclosing wall was 26 feet thick. This tremendous defensive wall shows how hard and bitter was the civil war that raged between north and south.

Israel was hemmed in on both sides: by Judah on the south, who even summoned the hated Philistines to help to keep Israel in check, and in the north by the kingdom of the Aramaeans, whose powerful aid had been secured by Judah through an alliance (1 Kings 15^{18ff}).

Centuries passed, centuries of endless conflict with this vastly superior power which was the deadly enemy. The continuous sequence of wars did not end until the new world power Assyria had crushed the Aramaeans. But with the emergence of Assyria Israel's days, indeed the days of both kingdoms, were numbered.

Over and above all this, just after the civil war had started the country suffered unexpectedly the first foreign invasion for generations.

Shishak[1] of Egypt attacked with his armies and marched through the country, plundering as he went. His greatest haul was from the old capital Jerusalem, "... and he took away the treasures of the house of the Lord, and the treasures of the king's house; he even took away all: and he took away all the shields of gold which Solomon had made" (1 Kings 14[25, 26]). The Temple and the House of Lebanon, as the Bible calls the royal palace, had hardly been standing twenty years, and already these proud tokens of Solomon's greatness were robbed of their glory. Instead of the golden shields which had been plundered "king Rehoboam made in their stead brazen shields" (1 Kings 14[27]). It was an ill-omened act.

The first European of note to stand in front of a large document of the Pharaoh whom the Bible calls Shishak was Napoleon Bonaparte. He was not aware of it however since at that time no one had as yet deciphered hieroglyphics. It was in 1799 that he wandered, deeply impressed, with a company of French scholars, through a vast Egyptian temple area at Karnak on the east side of Thebes. In the middle of this, the greatest temple area ever constructed by human hands, 134 columns up to 75 feet high support the roof of a colossal court. On the outer wall, on the south side, an imposing relief

FIG. 43.—Victory relief of Pharaoh Sheshonk I (the "Shishak" of the Bible) in the Temple at Karnak.

which perpetuates the marauding expedition of this Pharaoh stands out boldly in the bright sunshine of the Nile.

The god Amun, holding in his right hand a sickle-shaped sword, brings to Pharaoh Sheshonk I 156 manacled Palestinian prisoners who are attached by cords to his left hand. Every prisoner represents a city or a village. Some of them have Biblical names such as "the Father of Arad" (Josh. 12[14]; Jud. 1[16]) and "the Field of Abraham". The fortified city of Megiddo is among those represented, and in the ruins of Megiddo the name of Sheshonk I has been found.

[1] Pharaoh Sheshonk I.

Sheshonk's campaign was for a long time the last. Not for more than 300 years was Egypt again in a position to enforce its ancient claim to the suzerainty of the Syrian–Palestine territories.

The deadly danger that faced Israel came from the north—Assyria. During the reign of King Omri (882–871 B.C.) Assyria prepared to pounce. As if in a practice manœuvre for the real thing it tried a thrust westwards from Mesopotamia.

"From Aleppo I launched the attack and crossed the Orontes." This sentence from a cuneiform inscription of Ashurnasirpal II rings out like an opening fanfare of trumpets. It had taken Assyria over 200 years to dispose of its enemies inside and outside Mesopotamia. From the ancient city of Ashur on the Tigris, which bore the name of their chief god, the Semitic race of Assyrians, eager for conquest and skilled in administration, had extended their dominion over all the peoples of Mesopotamia. Now their eyes were fixed on the conquest of the world. The prelude to that had to be the possession of the narrow coastal strip of Syria and Palestine which barred the way to the Mediterranean, as well as the occupation of the important seaports, the control of the chief caravan routes and of the only military road into Egypt.

When Assyria set itself this target the fate of Syria and Palestine was sealed.

The report of Ashurnasirpal indicates briefly what was also in store for Israel and Judah. "I marched from the Orontes . . . I conquered the cities . . . I caused great slaughter, I destroyed, I demolished, I burned. I took their warriors prisoner and impaled them on stakes before their cities. I settled Assyrians in their place. . . . I washed my weapons in the Great Sea."

As unexpectedly as the Assyrians had appeared, so with equal abruptness they departed, laden with "silver, gold, lead, copper", the tribute of the Phoenician cities of Tyre, Sidon and Byblos.

King Omri of Israel heard of all this with dark foreboding. This former army officer however still showed his outstanding flair for soldiering now that he had become king. In the heart of the Samarian highlands he bought a hill on which he built a new capital for Israel, the stronghold of Samaria (1 Kings 16^{24}). He was certain that Israel would need it, and need it badly.

The choice of a site revealed the expert who was guided by strategic considerations. Samaria lies on a solitary hill, about 300 feet high, which rises gently out of a broad and fertile valley and is surrounded by a semi-circle of higher mountains. A local spring makes the place ideal for defence. The view westwards from the summit extends as far as the Mediterranean.

King Omri made an impression on the Assyrians. A century after his dynasty had crashed Israel was still officially called "The House of Omri" in cuneiform texts.

Eighteen years after Omri's death what they had dreaded actually happened. Shalmaneser III fell upon Carchemish on the Euphrates and was on his way to Palestine.[1]

Ahab, Omri's son who succeeded him on the throne, guessed what a violent clash with the rising world-power of Assyria would mean and did the only proper thing in the circumstances. He had recently beaten his old enemy Benhadad of Damascus, king of the Aramaeans. Instead of letting him taste to the full the victor's power, he handled him with unwonted magnanimity, he "caused him to come up into the chariot", called him "my brother", made "a covenant with him and sent him away" (1 Kings 20[33, 32, 34]). So he made an ally out of an enemy. His people misunderstood his policy and one of the prophets took him to task. Only the future would show how well he had known what he was doing. War on two fronts had been avoided.

"In sheepskin boats I crossed the Euphrates in flood," runs the cuneiform report of Shalmaneser III, king of Assyria. His sappers knew how to make a pontoon bridge out of inflated animal skins.

In Syria he was met by an opposing coalition from Syria and Palestine, and he took careful note of how the army was made up. Apart from the troops of the Biblical Benhadad of Damascus and another Syrian prince, there were "2,000 chariots and 10,000 horses belonging to Ahabbu the Sirilaean". Ahabbu the Sirilaean, who provided the third strongest army, was king of Israel.

The alliance between Israel and Damascus did not last long. Hardly had the Assyrians left the country when the old enmities broke out again and Ahab lost his life fighting the Aramaeans (1 Kings 22[34-38]).

The Bible devotes six chapters to the life of this king. Much of it has been dismissed as legend, such as "the ivory house which he made" (1 Kings 22[39]), or his marriage to a Phoenician princess, who brought with her a strange religion, "... he took to wife Jezebel the daughter of Ethbaal king of the Zidonians, and went and served Baal and worshipped him ... and made the Asherah ..." (1 Kings 16[31, 33] —R.V.) or the great drought in the land, "And Elijah ... said unto Ahab: As the Lord, the God of Israel liveth, before whom I stand, there shall not be dew nor rain these years, but according to my word" (1 Kings 17[1]).

None the less they are historical facts.

Two great assaults have been made on the old ruined mound of Samaria. The first campaign was led by George A. Reisner, Clarence S. Fisher, and D. G. Lyon of the University of Harvard from 1908–10, the second excavation by an Anglo-American team under the British archaeologist J. W. Crowfoot from 1931–35.

The foundations of Israel's capital rest on virgin soil. Omri had in fact acquired new land.

[1] 853 B.C.

During the six years when he reigned there this otherwise peaceful and lonely hill must have been one great bustling building site. The huge blocks of the strong fortifications make the strategic intention of the builder plain. The walls are 15 feet thick. On the acropolis on the west side of the hill foundations and walls of a building were exposed.

This enclosed a wide courtyard and was the royal palace of the northern kingdom of Israel.

After Omri, Ahab his son, the new king, lived here. He continued building in accordance with his father's plans. The construction was carried out with remarkable skill, nothing but these huge carefully dressed limestone blocks being used.

As the rubble was being carted off the diggers very quickly noticed the innumerable splinters of ivory that it contained. Finds of ivory itself are nothing unusual in Palestinian excavation. On almost every site this expensive material is encountered, but always in isolated pieces, yet in Samaria the ground is literally covered with them. At every step, every square yard, they came across these yellowish brown chips and flakes, as well as fragments which still showed the marvellous craftsmanship of these elegant reliefs carved by Phoenician masters.

FIG. 44.

1. "Cyclops" wall at Jericho (patriarchal age).
2. Wall of Saul's royal castle at Gibeah (1020 B.C.).
3. Wall of Solomon's "chariot city" of Megiddo (950 B.C.).
4. Wall of King Ahab's palace in Samaria (850 B.C.).

There was only one explanation of these finds: this palace was the famous "ivory house" of king Ahab (1 Kings 22[39]).

Obviously this monarch did not build his entire palace of ivory. Since this has however generally been assumed, the veracity of the Biblical passage has been questioned. It is now quite clear what happened: Ahab had the rooms of the palace decorated with this wonderful material and filled them with ivory furniture.

The proofs of the historical basis for the drought and for Ahab's father-in-law Ethbaal of Sidon were provided by Menander of Ephesus, a Phoenician historian. The Ethbaal of the Bible was called Ittobaal by the Phoenicians and in Ahab's day he was king of the port of Tyre.[1]

[1] The Biblical historians often used the term Sidonian to mean Phoenicians generally.

Menander records the catastrophic drought which set in throughout Palestine and Syria during the reign of Ittobaal and lasted a whole year.

Under king Jehoram, Ahab's son, Israel suffered an invasion which had terrible consequences and resulted in a considerable loss of territory.

The Aramaeans attacked them and besieged Samaria. A frightful famine racked the inhabitants. Jehoram, who held the prophet Elisha responsible for it, wanted to have him put to death. Elisha however prophesied that the famine would end on the following day. As the Bible records, "a lord, on whose hand the king leaned" (2 Kings 7[2]), doubted this prophecy.

This "lord" has given rise to great discussions. His function appeared to be extremely mysterious. Nothing was known of any office of this sort. Biblical commentators sought in vain for some explanation. Eventually philologists found a slight clue. The Hebrew word "shalish", which has been translated as "lord", comes from the word for "three". But there was never a third-class officer. When Assyrian reliefs were examined more closely the true explanation was found.

Every chariot was manned by three men: the driver, the fighter, and a man who stood behind them. With outstretched arms he held on to two short straps which were fastened to the right and left sides of the chariot. In this way he protected the warrior and the driver in the rear and prevented them from being thrown out during those furious sallies in battle when the open car passed over dead and wounded men. This then was the "third man". The inexplicable "lord, on whose hand the king leaned" was the strap-hanger in king Jehoram's chariot.

Under Jehoram Israel lost a large slice of territory east of the Jordan. Moab in Transjordan was a tributary of Israel. There is a detailed account of a campaign against Mesha, the rebellious "Mutton-King": "And Mesha, king of Moab, was a sheepmaster, and rendered unto the king of Israel a hundred thousand lambs, and a hundred thousand rams, with the wool. But it came to pass, when Ahab was dead, that the king of Moab rebelled against the king of Israel" (2 Kings 3[4, 5]). Israel summoned to her aid the southern kingdom, Judah, and the land of Edom.

They decided to make a joint attack on Moab from the south. This meant going round the Dead Sea. Relying on the prophecy: "Ye shall not see wind, neither shall ye see rain: yet that valley shall be filled with water, that ye may drink, both ye, and your cattle and your beasts" (2 Kings 3[17]), the allies venture to march through that desolate country. "And they fetched a compass of seven days' journey: and there was no water for the host, and for the cattle that followed them." On the advice of the prophet Elisha they made the valley "full of ditches". "And it came to pass in the morning ... behold there came water by the way of Edom, and the country was filled with water." This was seen by spies from Moab, who "saw the water on the other side as red as blood" (2 Kings 3[9, 16, 20, 22]) and thought that the enemy were fighting among themselves.

The allied forces were successful in Moab, they laid waste the land, "they beat down the cities, and on every good piece of land cast every man his stone, and filled it: and they stopped all the wells of water, and felled all the good trees: only in Kir-Haraseth left they the stones thereof" (2 Kings 3[25]).

FIG. 45.

Oddly enough the end of this successful campaign was "that they departed from him and returned to their own land" (2 Kings 3[27]).

It seemed impossible to check up on the accuracy of this Biblical story.

In 1868, F. A. Klein, a missionary from Alsace, was visiting Biblical sites in Palestine. The route he followed took him through Transjordan, through Edom and eventually to Moab. As he was riding in the neighbourhood of Diban, the ancient Dibon on the middle reaches of the Arnon, his attention was particularly aroused by a large smooth stone. The yellow sand had almost completely drifted over it. Klein jumped from his horse and bent over the stone curiously. It bore unmistakably ancient Hebrew writing. He could hardly believe his eyes. It was as much as he could do in the heat of the mid-day sun to stand the heavy basalt stone upright. It was three feet high and rounded on top. Klein cleaned it carefully with a knife and a handkerchief. Thirty-four lines of writing appeared.

He would have preferred to take the stone document away with him there and then, but it was far too heavy. Besides, in no time a mob of armed Arabs was on the spot. With wild gesticulations they surrounded the missionary, maintaining that the stone was their property and demanding from him a fantastic price for it.

Klein guessed that his discovery was an important one and was in despair. Missionaries never have much money. He tried in vain to make the natives change their minds. There was nothing for it but to mark the site carefully on his map. He then gave up the idea of continuing his journey, hurried back to Jerusalem and from there straight home to Germany to try to collect the necessary money for the Arabs.

But in the meantime other people got busy, which was a good thing. Otherwise an extremely valuable piece of evidence for Biblical history might well have been lost for ever.

A French scholar, Clermont-Ganneau, who was working in Jerusalem, had heard of the German missionary's discovery and had at once set out for Diban. It needed all his powers of persuasion to get the suspicious Arabs even to allow him to examine the writing on the basalt stone. Surrounded by the hostile eyes of the natives, Clermont-Ganneau took a squeeze of the surface. Months later, when Parisian scholars had translated the text, the French government sanctioned the purchase without hesitation. But judge the Frenchman's disappointment when he reached Diban, equipped with a caravan and the necessary sum of money, and found that the stone had disappeared. Only a patch of soot indicated the spot where it had been. The Arabs had blown it to pieces with gunpowder—from avarice. They hoped to do a more profitable trade with Europeans whose obsession with antiquity would make them willing to buy individual pieces.

What could Clermont-Ganneau do but set out on the trail of the individual pieces of the valuable document. After a great deal of trouble and searching, and after endless haggling, he was successful in retrieving some of the broken fragments. Two larger blocks and eighteen smaller pieces were reassembled and completed in accordance with the squeeze, and before Klein had even collected the necessary money, the impressive stone from Diban was standing among the valuable recent acquisitions in the Louvre in Paris.

This is what it says: "I am Mesha, son of Chamosh, king of Moab.... My father was king of Moab for thirty years and I became king after my father: and I built this sanctuary to Chamosh[1] in Qerihoh,[2] a sanctuary of refuge: for he saved me from all my oppressors and gave me dominion over all my enemies. Omri was king of Israel and oppressed Moab many days, for Chamosh was angry with his land. And his son succeeded him and he also said, I will oppress Moab. In my days he said

[1] God of Moab, worshipped also in Jerusalem among other foreign deities in the time of Solomon.
[2] The capital of Moab: the Kir-Haraseth of the Bible (2 Kings 3[25]).

this: but I got the upper-hand of him and his house: and Israel perished for ever.... I have had the ditches of Qerihoh dug by Israelite prisoners...."

This Moabite victory message aroused considerable interest in learned circles. Many scholars did not conceal their suspicion that it was a forgery. International experts scrutinised the stone and its inscription. All the tests made it plain beyond doubt that this was in fact a historical document, a contemporary record of the King Mesha of Moab who is mentioned in the Bible.

It is also Palestine's oldest written document, dating from about 840 B.C. in Moabite dialect, which is closely related to Biblical Hebrew. That caused a real sensation.

Audiatur et altera pars—There are always two sides to a story!

If we want an objective picture it is always advisable to study the war-diaries of both opponents. There is more likelihood of getting a clearer picture of the real situation. In this particular case, as it happens, the Biblical description and the Moabite text supplement each other admirably. The Mesha-stele[1] adds the necessary colour to the Biblical narrative and illumines its obscurity. The stele and the Bible agree on the decisive point, namely that the campaign ended with the defeat of the Israelite king. The Bible describes at length the initial success of Israel, which king Mesha passes over in silence. The unfortunate outcome of the campaign is only briefly hinted at in the Bible, whereas the Moabite king revels in his victory. Both are telling the truth.

As far as the "bloody water" is concerned, which saved the allies from dying of thirst on their march through this barren country, a geologist found a natural explanation. If trenches are dug in the tufa beside the Dead Sea, they fill up with water at once, which seeps through from the high plateau and owes its reddish colour to the character of the soil. To this day shepherds in Transjordan often manufacture water-holes in exactly the same manner.

"And Israel perished for ever," says the Mesha stele triumphantly. By this is meant the bloody extirpation of the dynasty of Omri from the throne of Israel. Jehoram was killed. Not one member was spared of the ruling house which had propagated the hated worship of Baal in Israel through king Ahab's marriage to the Phoenician princess Jezebel (2 Kings 9[24ff]; 10[11ff]).

Information about king Jehu's reign is scanty: "In those days the Lord began to cut Israel short: and Hazael smote them in all the coasts of Israel" (2 Kings 10[32]). The total extent of the losses in men and material first becomes plain in a passage about the reign of Jehoahaz, son of Jehu:[2] "Neither did he leave of the people to Jehoahaz but fifty

---

[1] A "stele" in archaeology is an independent upright column or pillar, also tombstone.

[2] 818–802 B.C.

horsemen, and ten chariots, and ten thousand footmen: for the king of Syria had destroyed them and had made them like the dust by threshing" (2 Kings 13⁷). Ahab's proud chariot-corps was reduced from 2,000 to ten. How could that have happened?

A young Englishman, Henry Layard, a lawyer by profession and attaché-elect at Constantinople, had an incredible stroke of luck as a novice in archaeology in 1845. With literally only £50 in his pocket he had set out to excavate an old mound on the Tigris, Tell Nimrud. On the third day he came upon remains of a palace. He dug a trench, but nothing but masses and masses of sand came out of it. When the trench was 20 feet deep Layard had to stop work, to his great disappointment, as his money had run out.

He was feeling depressed as he loaded his few tools on to the pack-mules, when excited cries from the natives make him pause. One of them ran up to him and got him to go and look at the end of the trench where something dark was showing up against the golden yellow sand. Digging was hastily resumed and produced a huge pure black stone in the shape of an obelisk. Layard tenderly cleaned the ancient dust and dirt off his find. And now he could see reliefs, pictures and inscriptions in cuneiform writing on all four sides.

Well wrapped up and guarded like the apple of his eye the black stone sailed up the Tigris in one of the fragile river-boats to be presented to the more than somewhat astonished officials of the British Embassy in Constantinople. A meagre £50 had produced unexpected dividends indeed. Never again in the history of archaeology would such a valuable find result from such a small investment.

Proudly the technicians cleared a fitting site for the stone in the British Museum. Thousands of Londoners and European scholars marvelled at this ancient piece of evidence from the distant east. The tip of the 6 foot obelisk of black basalt is in the shape of a three-tiered temple tower. Visitors gazed in astonishment at the wonderful reliefs displayed in five rows round the column.

Magnificently attired royal personages are chiselled out as in real life: some of them prostrate themselves with their faces to the ground in front of a commanding figure. Long columns of bearers are laden with costly treasures, such as ivory tusks, bales of fringed fabrics borne on poles, pitchers and baskets full to the brim. Among the animals included can be observed an elephant with remarkably small ears: there are camels with two humps, apes, antelopes, even a wild bull and a mysterious unicorn.

Anyone trying to interpret the meaning of the reliefs was thrown back on pure conjecture. For at that time no one in the world could read cuneiform script. The stone remained dumb. Even the scholars learned no more about the Assyrians than the Bible told them. At the beginning of the 19th century even the names Sumerian and Akkadian meant nothing. "One box, not more than three feet square," wrote Layard, "fitted with little inscribed cylinders, seals and textual fragments, which could not even be systematically arranged, were at that time all that London knew of the early period of Mesopotamian history."

It was only later, when the text had been translated, that it transpired that the black obelisk was a victory monument by the Assyrian king, Shalmaneser III,[1] contemporary and adversary of king Ahab of Israel. It celebrates an endless succession of bloody campaigns.

The enumeration of them contains an extremely interesting cross-reference to the Biblical tradition dealing with the period.

FIG. 46.—Tribute of King Jehu to Shalmaneser III.

Three times, in the sixth, eleventh, and fourteenth year of his reign, the Assyrian came up against a coalition of kings of Syria and Palestine during his victorious incursions into the West. In the campaign in the eighteenth year of his reign however only one king opposed him in this territory. The Assyrian texts name as the adversary only king Hazael of Damascus, whom the Bible also mentions.

But the victory monument gives ample information about the former ally of the king of Damascus, Jehu of Israel.

The second row of the relief shows a long queue of heavily laden envoys in richly ornamented tunics and peaked caps. The relevant text reads: "Tribute of Jaua of Bit-Humri: Silver, gold, a golden bowl, golden goblets, a golden beaker, pitchers of gold, lead, sceptres for the king and balsam-wood I received from him."

"Jaua of Bit-Humri" is none other than King Jehu of Israel. The Assyrians called Israel "Bit-Humri", which means "House of Omri".

This hint from the royal palace on the Tigris provides the key to our understanding of the losses which the northern kingdom of Israel sustained during the reign of Jehu.

Tribute is only paid by those who voluntarily surrender: a van-

[1] 858–824 B.C.

quished enemy supplies loot. Jehu had been disloyal to Damascus and had brought gifts to the Assyrians. For his faithlessness towards his old ally, for deserting Damascus, Jehu and his son Jehoahaz and most of all the people of Israel had to pay a bitter price. Hardly had the Assyrians turned their backs on Syria than Hazael of Damascus began to make a destructive onslaught on Israel in revenge. The result of it is described in the Bible: "In those days the Lord began to cut Israel short: and Hazael smote them in all the coasts of Israel . . . and made them like the dust by threshing" (2 Kings 10³²).

"That lie upon beds of ivory, and stretch themselves upon their couches, and eat the lambs out of the flock, and the calves out of the midst of the stall: that chant to the sound of the viol, and invent to themselves instruments of music, like David; that drink wine in bowls and anoint themselves with the chief ointments. . . ." (Amos 6⁴⁻⁶).

The fact that Assyria had, after Shalmaneser III, a succession of weak kings, allowed both kingdoms, Israel and Judah, another respite, which, however meant only a postponement. Since Assyria was occupied with unrest in its own territory, Israel and Judah were able to enjoy a spell of peace from 825 to 745 B.C.

For forty years Uzziah, the leper, reigned as king of Judah. Israel was governed by Jeroboam II.[1] Under his long rule Israel flourished again, became rich, wallowed in luxury, and the aristocracy lived for themselves and for the moment, effete, corrupt and vicious. The prophet Amos raised his voice in warning. He lashed out at their unbridled love of pleasure.

Archaeological reports and dry accounts of expeditions shed a powerful light upon these prophetic warnings. In Israel, in and around the old mound of ruins that represented ancient Samaria, evidence was lying dormant which would indicate this materialism and luxury in the soil strata from the decades following 800 B.C. in the reign of Jeroboam II. The royal palace of Samaria contained a considerable number of elegant clay tablets inscribed with ink and paint. On sixty-three of these invoices for wine and oil which had been delivered at the Court the senders are the managers of the crown lands of Jeroboam II, farmers and their employees, whose handwriting is extremely good.

From the same period comes a number of beautifully carved ivories, some of which are expensively embellished with gold and semi-precious stones and ornamented with colourful powdered glass. They show mythological motifs borrowed from Egypt, like Harpocrates on the lotus flower or figures of gods like Isis and Horus or cherubs. At that time all over Israel granaries and storehouses were being built to hold goods of all descriptions whose supply exceeded demand.

What was the reason for this sudden change? To what did they owe their new found riches?

[1] 787–747 B.C.

A few decades previously things had looked black for Israel. A sentence from the record of the forty-one-year reign of Jeroboam II contains the clue to the problem: "He restored the coast of Israel

from the entering of Hamath unto the sea of the plain" (2 Kings 14^{25}). The "sea of the plain" is the Dead Sea. Once again the kingdom stretched into Transjordan and—as in David's and Solomon's time—up to Syria.

About 800 B.C. the conquest of Damascus by the Assyrians had broken the power of the Aramaeans and thereby—it sounds as if fate were being ironical—cleared Israel's arch-enemy out of the way. Israel seized the opportunity to reconquer long-lost territory, exploited the situation to its own advantage and the tribute exacted from Transjordan proved a source of new wealth for Israel.

FIG. 47.—Nobleman's house at Megiddo during the monarchy. (Reconstruction.)

Evidence of a similar period of peace and prosperity in the southern kingdom of Judah has since come to hand. Professor Michael Evenari, vice-president of the Hebrew University, discovered in 1958 traces of several Judaean farms equipped with cisterns, irrigation systems, and fortifications, far south in the arid Negev near Mizpeh Ramon. The finds date from the reign of Uzziah, king of Judah. We are specifically told in 2 Chron. 26^{10} that this king "built towers in the desert and digged many wells; for he had much cattle...."

In 1959 Professor Aharoni of the Hebrew University was the first to discover a Judaean palace two miles south of Jerusalem. On Rachel's hill on the road to Bethlehem, at the spot where, according to tradition, Mary and Joseph on their way to Bethlehem "to be taxed" refreshed themselves at the spring, the site of a large castle was excavated, 250 feet by 150 feet square, and dating from the 8th century B.C. It had been surrounded by a casemated wall like that of King Ahab in Samaria and had a triple gate in the style of Solomon's day. Three sides of the courtyard were surrounded by buildings, two sides residential and the third for stores. When the excavators asked themselves the question as to who could have been the builder and first tenant of this lordly rural demesne they were given only one hint: "And Uzziah the king was a leper unto the day of his death, and dwelt in a several house, being a leper; for he was cut off from the house of the Lord" (2 Chron. 26^{21}).

Individual items removed from the palace rubble indicate how right the prophets were in their condemnation. Several symbols of Astarte witness to the "idolatry" that went on in this princely home (2 Kings 15[4]).

Harsh and full of foreboding in these days of pseudo-prosperity ring out the prophetic words of Amos: "Woe ... to them, that trust in the mountain of Samaria ... ye that put far away the evil day and cause the seat of violence to come near.... Therefore now shall they go captive with the first that go captive and the banquet of them that stretched themselves shall be removed" (Amos 6[1, 3, 7]). But in vain—they fall upon deaf ears. Only king Jeroboam cannot have had much faith in the peace, perhaps because the words of the prophet found an echo in his heart. At all events he feverishly set about strengthening the defences of the royal city of Samaria, which were in any case sufficiently forbidding.

J. W. Crowfoot, the English archaeologist, found what Jeroboam in his wisdom and foresight had achieved. Samaria had been surrounded with a double wall and the existing walls which were already massive had been further strengthened. In the northern section of the acropolis, where Samaria must have been most vulnerable, Crowfoot exposed a titanesque bastion. He measured it and was certain he must have made a mistake. He measured it carefully once more. No doubt about it, the wall—solid stone through and through—was 30 feet thick.

CHAPTER 24

THE END OF THE NORTHERN KINGDOM

Pul the soldier becomes Tiglath-Pileser III—King Pekah mentioned at Hazor—Assyrian governors over Israel—Samaria's three-year defiance—Consul Botta looks for Nineveh—The bourgeois king opens the first Assyrian museum—Searching for evidence by moonlight—The library of Ashurbanipal—Deportation of a people.

"And Pul the king of Assyria came against the land" (2 Kings 15[19]).

CONCISE, sober and dispassionate, these words announce the end of the northern kingdom. The death of Jeroboam II introduced the last act. In the same year 747 B.C. the leprous king Uzziah of Judah also died. In the short intervening period during which anarchy reigned Menahem made himself king at Samaria. In 745 B.C. a former soldier by name Pulu had ascended the throne of Assyria, and from then on was known as Tiglath-Pileser III.[1] He was the first of a succession of brutal tyrants who conquered what was so far the greatest empire of the Ancient East. Their goal was Syria, Palestine, and the last cornerstone of the old world, Egypt. That meant that both Israel and Judah were caught between the pitiless millstones of a military state, for which the word peace had a contemptible sound, whose despots and cohorts had only three values: marching, conquering, oppressing.

From North Syria Tiglath-Pileser III swept through the Mediterranean countries, and forced independent peoples to become provinces and tributaries of the Assyrian Empire. Israel at first submitted voluntarily: "And Menahem gave Pul[2] 1,000 talents of silver, that his hand might be with him, to confirm the kingdom in his hand. And Menahem exacted the money of Israel, even of all the mighty men of wealth, of each man fifty shekels of silver, to give to the king of Assyria. So the king of Assyria turned back, and stayed not there in the land" (2 Kings 15[19, 20]). "I received tribute from Menahem of Samaria," notes Tiglath-Pileser III in his annals.

One thousand talents correspond to 6 million gold sovereigns, 50 shekels per head from the "men of wealth" amounted to 100 gold sovereigns each. Economists and statisticians will gather that there must have been 60,000 well to do people in Israel.

King Menahem entertained the illusion that a pact with the tyrant

[1] 745–727 B.C.   [2] Tiglath-Pileser III.

and voluntary tribute would be the lesser of two evils. But the result was bad blood among his own people. Anger at the Assyrian taxes found an outlet in conspiracy and murder. Pekah, an army officer, murdered Menahem's son and heir and ascended the throne. From then on the anti-Assyrian party was the determining factor in the policy of the Northern Kingdom.

FIG. 48.—Tiglath-Pileser III (with bow and sword) besieging a fortress. Battering-rams pound the walls. Impaled victims in background.

Rezin, king of Damascus, powerfully grasped the initiative. Under his leadership the defensive league of the Aramaean states against Assyria came to life again. Phoenician and Arab states, Philistine cities and Edomites joined the alliance. Israel too took its place in the federation. Only king Ahaz of Judah remained obstinately outside. Rezin and Pekah tried to force Judah into the league violently. "Then Rezin, king of Syria, and Pekah son of Remaliah king of Israel, came up to Jerusalem to war: and they besieged Ahaz, but could not overcome him" (2 Kings 16⁵).

In dire straits the king of Judah sent out an S.O.S. "So Ahaz sent messengers to Tiglath-Pileser king of Assyria, saying, I am thy servant, and thy son: come up and save me out of the hand of the king of Syria, and out of the hand of the king of Israel, which rise up against me. And Ahaz took the silver and gold that was found in the house of the Lord, and in the treasures of the king's house, and sent it for a present to the king of Assyria" (2 Kings 16⁷,⁸).

"I received tribute from Jauhazi [Ahaz] of Judah," observes the Assyrian once more.

Now events took their disastrous course. For our knowledge of further developments we are indebted to two great historical records. Firstly, the Bible and secondly the cuneiform tablets of stone and clay, on which—over 600 miles from where the terrible events took place—the military developments were officially recorded. For more than two and a half millennia these documents lay in the magnificent palaces on the Tigris until scholars ran them to earth and translated them into our tongue. They make it plain once more in quite a unique way how true to history are the contents of these Biblical stories.

The Bible and the Assyrian monuments are in entire agreement in their description of these events which were fatal for the Northern Kingdom. The Old Testament historian notes down the facts soberly, the Assyrian chronicler records every brutal detail:

Second Book of Kings	*Cuneiform Text of Tiglath-Pileser III*
"The king of Assyria went up against Damascus, and took it, and carried the people of it captive to Kir, and slew Rezin" (2 Kings 16[9])	"His noblemen I impaled alive and displayed this exhibition to his land. All his gardens and fruit orchards I destroyed. I besieged and captured the native city of Reson (Rezin) of Damascus. 800 people with their belongings I led away. Towns in 16 districts of Damascus I laid waste like mounds after the Flood." (From: Western Campaign 734–733 B.C.)

Second Book of Kings	*Cuneiform Text of Tiglath-Pileser III*
"In the days of Pekah king of Israel came Tiglath-Pileser king of Assyria and took ... Hazor and Gilead and Galilee, all the land of Naphtali, and carried them captive to Assyria" (2 Kings 15[29])	"Bet-Omri (Israel) all of whose cities I had added to my territories on my former campaigns, and had left out only the city of Samaria. ... The whole of Naphtali I took for Assyria. I put my officials over them as governors. The land of Bet-Omri, all its people and their possessions I took away to Assyria." (From: Western Campaign and Gaza/Damascus campaign 734–733 B.C.)

"And Hoshea ... made a conspiracy against Pekah ... and slew him and reigned in his stead" (2 Kings 15³⁰)

"They overthrew Pekah their king and I made Hoshea to be king over them." (From: Gaza/Damascus campaign.)

Sombre evidence of the capture of Hazor by Tiglath-Pileser III, king of Assyria (2 Kings 15²⁹), has been supplied by a layer of rubble at Tell el-Qedah in Israel. In the course of more recent excavations by archaeologists from the Hebrew University, traces came to light of the shattered Israelite fortress which had been rebuilt during the monarchy for defence purposes by Solomon and Ahab on the site of the old Canaanite fort which had been conquered by Joshua. The strength of the keep with its six-foot thick walls was such that it was only surpassed by the famous royal palace at Samaria, now likewise rediscovered.

The apartments in the castle at Hazor were covered by a layer of ashes three feet thick, the stones were blackened with smoke, charred beams and fragments of what had been at one time panelled ceilings lay scattered about the ground. By exercising the utmost care the archaeologists were able to salvage from the piles of rubble some precious examples of the arts and crafts of northern Israel: a statuette of a well-groomed young woman and a marble incense-spoon. The greatest thrill was to find among the fragments of broken pottery the name of king Pekah himself, written in old Semitic script. This was the first written evidence of an Israelite king in Galilee.

When the armed hordes of Assyrians withdrew from Palestine they left Israel mortally wounded, smashed to the ground, decimated by deportation, beaten back into a tiny corner of the northern kingdom. With the exception of Samaria all its cities had been annexed and the country had been divided into provinces over which Assyrian governors and officials exercised strict control.

All that was left of Israel was a dwarf state, a tiny pinpoint on the map: the mountain of Ephraim with the royal city of Samaria. There lived king Hoshea.

The southern kingdom of Judah still remained free from foreign domination—for the time being. But it had to pay tribute to Tiglath-Pileser III.

The warlike Assyrian colossus had enclosed in his mighty grip the whole of the "Fertile Crescent" from the shores of the Persian Gulf, from the mountains of Persia to Asia Minor, from the Mesopotamian plain through Lebanon and Antilebanon as far as Palestine. Alone, away to the south-west, the 20 acre royal city of Samaria with its few square miles of hinterland, providing it with corn and barley, was unsubdued.

From this corner a gauntlet of defiance flew through the air to land at Assyria's feet.

After the death of Tiglath-Pileser III Hoshea conspired with Egypt. He refused to pay his annual tribute to Assyria. Shalmaneser V[1] the successor of Tiglath-Pileser III at once struck back. For when he "found conspiracy in Hoshea: for he had sent messengers to So[2] king of Egypt, and brought no present to the king of Assyria, as he had done year by year: therefore the king of Assyria shut him up and bound him in prison" (2 Kings 17⁴). Part of the organisation of the hated reign of terror—even in those days—was a widespread net of informers and spies.

With the fall of Samaria the last remnant of the Northern Kingdom of Israel suffered the fate of Damascus, ". . . in the ninth year of Hoshea the king of Assyria took Samaria and carried Israel away into Assyria" (2 Kings 17⁶).

For three years the little mountain fortress withstood the deadly pressure of superior forces with the courage of a lion (2 Kings 17⁵).

Cuneiform texts record that Shalmaneser V died unexpectedly during the siege of Samaria. His successor Sargon II[3] nevertheless continued the attack. "In the first year of my reign," boasts Sargon in his annals, "I besieged and conquered Samaria. . . . I led away into captivity 27,290 people who lived there."

The discovery of the Sargon inscriptions over 100 years ago is like a romantic tale from the fabulous land of the caliphs. None the less it is a milestone in our knowledge of the ancient world. For it marked the birth of Assyriology, which by its sensational discoveries has for the first time given many Biblical narratives a genuine historical content.

The motor car had not been invented: electric light was still unknown: no steel frames of derricks towered out of the sandflats by the Tigris: Mosul still wore the colourful variegated garb of a city from the Arabian Nights. Bazaars, harems, and a real live caliph were all there. It was the heart of the ancient orient and the year was 1840.

Summer lay like a red-hot breath over the city with its elegant white minarets and its narrow dirty muddy alleyways.

For a European the heat was enervating and unbearable. Paul Emile Botta, the new French consular agent, escaped from the incubator as often as he could to take a ride by the Tigris and breathe fresher air. But soon certain desolate mounds on the other side of the river began to fascinate him more. Admittedly they had nothing to do with the routine duties of a consular agent, but M. Botta was a scholar. He had been carefully following an academic dispute which had broken out over the Biblical name Nineveh. No one could say with any certainty where this city lay in olden times. It was a case of one surmise being as good as another. One suggestion pointed in the direction of Mosul. In the course of his wanderings among the yellow brown sandhills on the far

[1] 727–722 B.C.   [2] So=Sewe, ruler of Egypt, called Sib'e by the Assyrians.
[3] 721–705 B.C.

side of the river Botta had repeatedly noticed fragments of bricks. They were only plain looking uncommunicative fragments. Nevertheless he mentioned them in a letter to Paris. In reply came a letter from M. Mohl, secretary of the Société Asiatique. It encouraged him to examine the terrain a little more closely.

Botta hired a bunch of natives out of his own pocket. In the typical round Tigris-boats they headed up river towards the mounds and prepared to excavate.

This first attempt of a modern European to come to grips with ancient Nineveh and wrest its secrets from it, failed to achieve the desired result. Botta ordered digging to begin on several slopes. Some weeks flashed past as the work went busily on. But the result was precisely nothing. Botta saw his money being expended to no purpose and brought his private expedition which had been started with such enthusiasm to a disappointing end.

Perhaps he might have kept his hands off any further researches in this area except that he heard something which spurred him to new activity. In the village of Khorsabad, 7 miles to the north, Arabs working in the fields were said to have found great pillars.

In the early part of March 1842 Botta and his workers were on the spot. They began to excavate, and on the same day they struck stonework, apparently the inner wall of a large building.

Botta was highly delighted although at that moment he had no idea that he was responsible for a historic event of the greatest importance for scholarship. The stonework was part of the first of the gigantic Assyrian palaces which after lying dormant for thousands of years were now to come to light. It was the birth of Assyriology. And the first thing that this new science got itself involved in was—as we shall see in a moment—an erroneous idea.

Once again French scholarship displayed in this case sound judgement. The Académie des Inscriptions, which Botta informed at once, saw to it that the government placed funds at his disposal. It was to begin with no vast amount of money but gold francs were still worth something in the East. The sultan gave the required permission for excavation.

But on the site itself Botta had to endure unimaginable difficulties due to the extremely underhand dealings of the local authorities in Mosul. At one moment the trenches came under suspicion as being military defences; at another the primitive shelters of the members of the excavations were suspected of being army bivouacs. It seemed that by every possible means the great excavation was to be thwarted. More than once Botta had to send an S.O.S. to Paris and invoke the aid of the French diplomatic service.

Despite all this, sections of a huge palace were liberated from the sand at Khorsabad.

Eugène N. Flandin, a well-known Paris artist, who had specialised in antiquities, had been given the assignment by the Louvre which nowadays falls on the official photographer of any expedition. His pencil reproduced accurately on paper all that the ground yielded up. The drawings were collected into a handsome folio and the large volume was adorned with the proud title "Le Monument de Ninive". For Botta was convinced that he had found the Biblical city of Nineveh at Khorsabad. And that was where he was wrong.

If he had only dug a few inches deeper into the mounds opposite Mosul, where two years earlier he had given up the apparently hopeless task in disgust, he would in fact have made the discovery of his life. As it happened the credit for discovering Nineveh went to Henry Layard, who at the instigation of the British Government commenced digging in 1845 at the very spot where Botta had given up.

At the first spadeful, so to speak, he came upon the walls of one of the great palaces of Nineveh.

What Botta had excavated at Khorsabad was the great castle of Sargon, the home of Sargon II, king of Assyria. But that did not emerge until later. If Botta had been able to read the tablets which were salvaged at Khorsabad he would never have made his mistake. "Dur-Sharrukin", Castle of Sargon, was written there in cuneiform, which at that time, 1842, had not yet been completely deciphered. The key to its translation was not agreed on until fifteen years later.

FIG. 49.—Ruins of the royal homes of Assyrian monarchs on the Tigris.

In 1857 Rawlinson and Hincks in England and Oppert in France independently of each other produced translations of a piece of text which corresponded exactly. With that the correct interpretation of Assyrian script was assured.

In October 1844 the tablets salvaged by Botta containing reliefs and historical texts, as well as statues and sections of pillars started out on an adventurous journey. From Khorsabad the precious cargo rocked its way down the Tigris on skiffs and rafts. At Basra on the Persian Gulf the valuable freight was transferred to the "Cormoran", which conveyed it to Europe. It made a great sensation in Paris and evoked as lively an interest among the general public as among the scholars.

On 1st May 1847 in the splendid galleries of the Louvre designed by Percier and Fontaine, Louis Philippe, the bourgeois king, handed over to the public with impressive ceremony this collection, which contained the earliest evidence from the realm of Biblical story. With that the first Assyrian museum in the world had been founded.

The mounds of old Nineveh provided the new world with its most extensive collection of information about ancient times.

The story of the discovery of this left a bitter taste in French mouths. When the British began their diggings, the French had also staked a claim on a section of the mounds.

In the British excavation area a vast palace had come to light which had been identified as the historic Nineveh of the Bible. But what might still be lying hidden over there in the French sector? Rassam, one of the members of the British party, decided to take time by the forelock. He took advantage of the absence of his chief, Rawlinson, leader of the expedition, and of the presence of a full moon to make a purposeful excursion into the French reservation. At the first stroke he came upon the palace of Ashurbanipal with the famous library belonging to that monarch, which was indeed the most famous in the whole of the ancient orient. Twenty-two thousand cuneiform tablets found their way into the British Museum.

They contained the essential material for understanding the historical and intellectual background of Mesopotamia, its peoples, its kingdoms with their arts and crafts, cultures and religions. Among them were the Sumerian flood story and the epic of Gilgamesh.

What had been until then a mysterious sealed chapter of our world's history was suddenly opened and page after page was turned over. Rulers, cities, wars and stories which people had only heard about through the Old Testament revealed themselves as real facts.

We must include among these the city of Erech which is described in the tenth chapter of Genesis as part of the kingdom of Nimrod, the "mighty hunter before the Lord". About fifty miles to the north-west of Ur of the Chaldees, Professor H. J. Lenzen was the director of excavations which from 1928 onwards provided valuable information. From a pile of ruins, which the Arabs call Warka, he would produce impressive evidence of the ancient city of Uruk, as Erech is styled in the cuneiform texts, including written tablets which go back to the fourth and third millennium B.C. In the course of his investigations the German archaeologist came across the remains of walls which could be credited to the legendary king Gilgamesh. Over five miles in length they afforded their protection to this ancient Biblical city.

Meantime the original starting point of all these exciting investigations and discoveries had long been forgotten. But if it had not been for the Bible perhaps the quest would never have begun.

About the middle of last century, Nineveh, Sargon's castle, and, at Tell Nimrud, the Calah of Genesis which Nimrod built (Gen. 10¹¹) were all discovered. But it was several decades before the enormous quantity of cuneiform texts was deciphered, translated, and made available to a wider circle. It was not until the turn of the century that several comprehensive scholarly works appeared, containing translations of some of the texts, including the annals of Assyrian rulers well known to readers of the Old Testament, Tiglath-Pileser or Pul, Sargon, Sennacherib, and Esarhaddon.

Since then they have become essential features of all national libraries, as well as of universities and colleges. A unique mine of information eagerly studied and used by historians, Assyriologists and theological students—all of them people with a professional interest. But who else reads them or knows about them? Yet they could easily, even taking the reliefs alone, provide a large clear illustrated commentary on the Bible.

The Assyrian documents contain a wealth of interesting and informative details which corroborate the historical truth of the Bible.

Botta found in Sargon's castle at Khorsabad his reports on his campaigns in Syria and Palestine, and his capture of Samaria in Israel.

". . . in the first year of my reign I besieged and conquered Samaria." Sargon II reigned from 721 to 705 B.C. According to that the northern kingdom of Israel collapsed in 721 B.C. (2 Kings 17⁶).

"People of the lands, prisoners my hand had captured, I settled there. My officials I placed over them as governors. I imposed tribute and tax upon them, as upon the Assyrians." So reads the account of the conquest of Samaria in the annals. The Old Testament describes the uprooting tactics employed in this case too by ruthless dictators, the first large scale experiment of its kind in the world made by the Assyrians: "And the king of Assyria brought men from Babylon, and from Cuthah, and from Ava, and from Hamath, and from Sepharvaim, and placed them in the cities of Samaria, instead of the children of Israel: and they possessed Samaria, and dwelt in the cities thereof" (2 Kings 17²⁴).

Tens of thousands of human beings were violently driven from their homeland, deported to foreign lands, and their places filled by others dragged from different areas.

The aim of this was clear: national consciousness, and with it the will to resist, was to be broken. The "Fertile Crescent" was ploughed up, its peoples tossed about hither and thither. Instead of a varied range of races and religions existing side by side the result was a jumble.

Samaria shared this fate. Its motley collection of inhabitants became known as "Samaritans". "Samaritans" became a term of abuse, an expression of abhorrence. They were despised not only on religious grounds but also as individuals: "For the Jews have no dealings with the Samaritans" (John 4⁹). It was only when Jesus told the story of the

"Good Samaritan" that he turned this term of abuse into a byword for practical Christian charity (Luke 10^{3ff}).

The people of the Northern Kingdom and their kings with them disappeared, were absorbed into the population of these foreign lands, and never emerged again in history. All investigation into what became of the ten tribes who had their home there has so far come to nothing.

CHAPTER 25

JUDAH UNDER THE YOKE OF ASSYRIA

Hopes aroused by Sargon's death—A fig poultice cures king Hezekiah—A well-tried Ancient Eastern remedy—Merodach-Baladan: gardener and rebel—Secret armaments in Judah—Aqueduct through the rocks of Jerusalem—Inscription describes Hezekiah's tunnel—The fate of Lachish in stone relief—Traces of Assyrian battering-rams in the ruins—A puzzling retreat—Herodotus' story of the king with the mouse—Starkey finds a plague-grave—Sennacherib describes the siege of Jerusalem.

"Therefore I will wail and howl, I will go stripped and naked: I will make a wailing like the dragons, and mourning as the owls. For her (i.e. Samaria's) wound is incurable: for it is come unto Judah: he is come unto the gate of my people, even to Jerusalem" (Micah 1⁸⁻⁹).

IN Judah there may have been some who rejoiced at the downfall of their hostile brother. The prophet Micah however was overwhelmed with grief and filled with deep anxiety at the news. He guessed that the blow that had crushed Samaria would one day strike the people of Judah and the city of Jerusalem. At that time Hezekiah was king of Judah,[1] "and he did that which was right in the sight of the Lord" (2 Kings 18³). Since the father of Hezekiah had voluntarily submitted to Tiglath-Pileser III in 733 B.C., Judah had been a dependent vassal-state, whose deliveries of tributes were carefully noted in Nineveh. Hezekiah was not prepared to follow in his father's footsteps. The reaction set in when he came to the throne. "He rebelled against the king of Assyria" (2 Kings 18⁷).

Hezekiah was no hothead, but a clever, cool, calculating and far-sighted man. He knew very well that what he was about was a highly dangerous and risky business for himself and his people. Only 30 miles from Jerusalem the Assyrian governor of Samaria was sitting eyeing him with suspicion. One careless step, a nod to Nineveh, and Hezekiah would find himself off his throne and clapped in irons. He merely held the throne in fee. Hezekiah proceeded with the utmost caution, "and he prospered, whithersoever he went forth" (2 Kings 18⁷).

In the Philistine city-state of Ashdod, which was oppressed in the

[1] 725–697 B.C.

252

same way, anti-Assyrian riots broke out. That brought into being a league against the tyrant on the Tigris.[1] Hezekiah saw a chance to further his plan. He showed his sympathy but remained officially aloof, and intrigued behind the scenes.

Jerusalem had at this time visitors from overseas, tall personages from "beyond the rivers of Ethiopia" (Is. 18[1]). These were Ethiopian envoys. The king of Egypt at that point was Shabaka, a Pharaoh from Ethiopia. The Assyrians replied to the riots in Ashdod with armed force. A "turtanu", a field-marshal, appeared on the scene with an army. "In the year that Tartan came unto Ashdod [when Sargon the king of Assyria sent him] and fought against Ashdod and took it. ..." (Is. 20[1]).

On the walls of Sargon's castle the court chroniclers describe the carrying out of this punitive expedition as follows: "Ashdod ... I besieged and conquered ... its gods, its women, its sons, its daughters, its goods and chattels, the treasures of its palace, and all the people of its territory I counted as plunder. I settled those cities anew...."

The anti-Assyrian league had gone to pieces on the approach of the Assyrians. Ashdod's territory became an Assyrian province.

FIG. 50.

Nothing happened to Hezekiah, although his name was on the black list. Assyrian informers had seen through his game and had given Sargon II full details of Hezekiah's secret dealings with Egypt, as can be seen from the text of a fragment of a prism:

"Philistia, Judah, Edom and Moab, who planned hostilities, infamies without number ... who, in order to prejudice him against me and make him my enemy, brought gifts in homage to Pharaoh, king of the land of Egypt ... and begged him to form an alliance...."

In 705 B.C. news spread like wildfire, raising at once fresh hopes of liberation from the Assyrian yoke: Sargon had been murdered! All over the "Fertile Crescent", in the Assyrian provinces and in the vassal states, conspiracies, discussions and intrigues began.

[1] 713 B.C.

"In those days was Hezekiah sick unto death" (2 Kings 20[1]).

Happening precisely at this moment of feverish political activity it was a grave handicap. For many states in Syria and Palestine were looking expectantly to the able king of Judah.

How could Hezekiah be cured of his serious illness? "And Isaiah said, Take a lump of figs, And they took and laid it on the boil, and he recovered" (2 Kings 20[7]).

The course of history is often rich in remarkable parallels and associations. So it is in the case of this Biblical therapy.

In the north Syrian harbour of Ras Shamra, French excavators in 1939, digging among the ruins of the Phoenician seaport of Ugarit,

came upon fragments of an old book of veterinary science, which contained prescriptions for the treatment of sick and ailing horses. The captain of the household cavalry of the king of Ugarit had, about 1500 B.C., entered in it tried remedies of this sort: "If a horse has a swollen head or a sore nose, prepare a salve from figs and raisins, mixed with oatmeal and liquid. The mixture should be poured into the horse's nostrils."

FIG. 51.—King Sargon II of Assyria with his Tartan (relief from Khorsabad).

For every kind of sickness there is a very detailed prescription. The chief medicaments are plants and fruit, like mustard and liquorice juice. Advice is even given on how to deal with horses that bite and neigh too much. Does any modern breeder or owner of horses know how to cure that? In those days a neighing horse could in certain circumstances be fatal. Horses were used exclusively for fighting and hunting. A troop of chariots, however well hidden in an ambush, could be betrayed by a sudden loud neighing. It was the same with hunting.

These recognised cures have been tried out successfully from time immemorial by the peoples of the ancient orient. They are nature's remedies which can also be profitably used in the case of human beings. One of them, which is particularly commended in the veterinary manual, is "Debelah", a sort of poultice of compressed figs. It was a "Debelah" that the prophet prescribed for Hezekiah's abscess. It worked, and he was all right again in three days.

Many of these tried remedies dating back to Biblical times, and largely consisting of ingredients supplied by Mother Nature, have been either lost or forgotten in the whirligig of time. Many of them on the other hand have been quietly passed on from generation to generation. This prescription for figs is one of them. Swiss doctors still prescribe finely chopped up figs steamed in milk, for certain kinds of abscesses. An Arabic remedy reminds us of the "Debelah". A thick sticky liquid made from grape-juice is called "Dibis" in the native tongue.

"At that time Berodach-Baladan,[1] the son of Baladan king of Babylon, sent letters and a present unto Hezekiah: for he had heard that Hezekiah had been sick" (2 Kings 20[12]).

This was the traditional practice in court circles and was part of the royal etiquette in the ancient East. Presents were sent and enquiries made about the health of "our brother". The clay tablets of El-Amarna mention the habit frequently.

Merodach-Baladan[2] however found Hezekiah's illness a convenient pretext for making contact with him. The real reason for his polite courtesies lay in the field of high level politics.

"Merodach-Baladan, king of Babylon", was for a long time a mysterious personage both to readers of the Bible and to scholars. It is now quite certain that he was in his own day an extremely important person. We even know something about his private habits. He was for example a great gardener, not in the sense of being keen to lay out handsome royal parks, but with a real down to earth interest in the vegetables and fruit of Mesopotamia, whether it was endives, beetroot, cucumbers, thyme, coriander, saffron, peaches or medlars. He described the various types of plants and how to cultivate them, and was in fact the author of a practical handbook on vegetable gardens, as archaeologists discovered with no little astonishment.

Apart from his private hobby of gardening, Merodach-Baladan both as a king and as a Babylonian was the most bitter and determined opponent of Nineveh. No other monarch in the "Fertile Crescent" attacked the Assyrians so vigorously over many years, engaged them in so many heated battles, or intrigued so unremittingly against the tyrants of the Tigris, as he did.

The assassination of Sargon brought Merodach-Baladan into the field. It was at this point that his ambassadors visited Hezekiah. What was in fact discussed on the occasion of the official visit during the convalescence of Hezekiah, can be read between the lines: "And Hezekiah hearkened unto them, and showed them all the house of his precious things ... and all the house of his armour" (2 Kings 20[13]), Judah's arsenal. Secret armaments and feverish preparations for D-day, the great show-down with Assyria which they saw to be imminent, were in full swing. "Also ... he built up all the wall that was

---

[1] Here wrongly spelt Berodach-Baladan. Isaiah (39[1]) spells it correctly Merodach-Baladan.

[2] = Marduk-Aplaiddin in Babylonian.

broken, and raised it up to the towers, and another wall without, and
repaired Millo in the city of David, and made darts and shields in
abundance" (2 Chron. 32⁵).

Jerusalem's defences were overhauled and strengthened for a long
siege, the old perimeter wall was renewed, breaches repaired, and
turrets erected. On the north side of the city, its most vulnerable point,
a second outer wall was added. Hezekiah even pulled down houses to
make room for it (Isa. 22¹⁰). But that did not exhaust his precautions.
"And the rest of the acts of Hezekiah, and all his might, and how he
made a pool, and a conduit, and brought water into the city, are they
not written in the book of the Chronicles of the kings of Judah?" (2
Kings 20²⁰).

The Chronicler completes the story: "This same Hezekiah also
stopped the upper water course of Gihon, and brought it straight down
to the west side of the city of David...." (2 Chron. 32³⁰).

Jerusalem, the old city of David, has many mysterious corners.
Pilgrims from all over the world, travellers of three faiths, Christians,
Jews, Mohammedans, come to pay homage at its holy places. Seldom
does one of these endless visitors stumble upon the dark depressing spot
outside the walls, far below the noisy streets of the city, which bears
eloquent testimony to one of the most
dire moments in its ancient story, to a
time fraught with fear and menace.
This spot had sunk into oblivion. In
1880 it was discovered by a fluke. It
still bears as plain as day all the marks
of feverish haste.

Outside the city, where its south-
eastern slopes sweep gently down to
the Valley of the Kidron, lies a small
still sheet of water, enclosed by walls,
the Pool of Siloam. Two Arab boys
were playing there—one of them fell
in. Paddling for all he was worth, he
landed on the other side, where a rock
wall rose above the pool. Suddenly it
was pitch black all round him. He
groped about anxiously and discovered a small passage.

Fig. 52.—King Hezekiah's great
Tunnel of Siloam in Jerusalem.

The name of the Arab boy was forgotten but not his story. It was
followed up and a long underground tunnel was discovered.

A narrow passage about 2 feet wide and barely 5 feet high had been
cut through the limestone. It can only be negotiated with rubber boots
and a slight stoop. For about 500 yards the passage winds imperceptibly uphill. It ends at the Virgin's Fountain, Jerusalem's water supply

since ancient times. In Biblical days it was called the Fountain of Gihon.

As experts were examining the passage they noticed by the light of their torches old Hebrew letters on the wall.

The inscription, which was scratched on the rock only a few paces from the entrance at the Pool of Siloam, reads as follows: "The boring through is completed. And this is the story of the boring: while yet they plied the pick, each toward his fellow, and while yet there were three cubits to be bored through, there was heard the voice of one calling to the other that there was a hole in the rock on the right hand and on the left hand. And on the day of the boring through the workers in the tunnel struck each to meet his fellow, pick upon pick. Then the water poured from the source to the pool twelve hundred cubits, and a hundred cubits was the height of the rock above the heads of the workers in the tunnel."

FIG. 53.—"The boring through is completed. And this is the story of the boring: while yet ..." (Beginning of the Siloam inscription.)

The Turkish government had the inscription prized out before the First World War. It is now exhibited in the museum at Istanbul.

It was Hezekiah's aqueduct.

During a siege the Number One problem is that of providing drinking water. The founders of Jerusalem, the Jebusites, had sunk a shaft down through the rock to the Fountain of Gihon. Hezekiah directed its water, which would otherwise have flowed into the Kidron valley, through the mountain to the west side of the city. The Pool of Siloam lies inside the second perimeter wall which he constructed.

There was no time to lose. Assyrian troops could be at the gates of Jerusalem overnight. The workmen therefore tackled the tunnel from both ends. The marks of the pickaxes point towards each other, as the inscription describes.

Oddly enough the canal takes an S-shaped course through the rock. Why did the workmen not dig this underground tunnel the shortest way to meet each other, that is, in a straight line? The wretched job would have been finished quicker. Seven hundred feet of hard work would have been saved out of the total 1,700 feet.

Locally, there is an old story which has been handed down which claims to explain why they had to go the long way round. Deep in the rock, between the spring and the pool, are supposed to lie the graves of David and Solomon.

Archaeologists took this remarkable piece of folk-lore seriously and systematically tapped the walls of the narrow damp tunnel. They sank shafts into the rock from the summit and R. Weill actually came across cavities cut in the rock, which were perhaps graves, but which had obviously been despoiled in early times. Were these perhaps the graves of David's line? Kathleen M. Kenyon, one of the most prominent Biblical archaeologists of recent years, does not think so. Others, however, are of a different opinion. We shall probably never know what these "royal graves" really were. . . .

"Now in the fourteenth[1] year of king Hezekiah did Sennacherib king of Assyria come up against all the fenced cities of Judah and took them" (2 Kings 18[13]).

The states of Syria and Palestine had four years left in which to take defensive measures. The Assyrian governors were expelled. A strong league was formed. The kings of Askelon and Ekron joined up with Hezekiah, and Egypt promised help in case of military developments.

Naturally the new Assyrian ruler Sennacherib[2] was not unaware of all this. But his hands were tied. After the assassination of his predecessor Sargon, the eastern part of his empire revolted. The leading spirit in this was Merodach-Baladan. As soon as Sennacherib was once more in control of the situation in Mesopotamia, by the end of the year 702 B.C., he set out for the west and smashed the rebellious little countries in one single campaign. A similar fate overtook the Egyptian army which pharaoh Shabaka had sent under the command of his nephew Taharka against the Assyrians. The Second Book of Kings and the Book of Isaiah confer upon the latter, a future pharaoh, who was also related to the Ethiopian dynasty, distinction which was still to come, in that they described him even in those troubled times as "Tirhakah, king of Ethiopia" (2 Kings 19[9]; Isa. 37[9]). The whole of Judah was occupied by Sennacherib's troops, Hezekiah was shut up in Jerusalem. Among the frontier fortresses Lachish alone still offered resistance. Sennacherib deployed his storm-troopers against this unusually strong fortified city.

Anyone who wishes to re-live the frightful battle of Lachish, vividly and dramatically to the smallest detail, must pay a visit to the British Museum. It is here that the massive relief, which eye-witnesses created on the orders of Sennacherib 2,650 years ago, have found a resting place. Sir Henry Layard salvaged this precious object from the ruins of Nineveh.

On the turrets and breastwork of the stronghold of Lachish with its stout high walls the Judahite defenders fought with clenched teeth. They showered a hail of arrows on the attackers, hurled stones down upon them, threw burning torches—the fire-bombs of the ancient world—among the enemy. The faces, curly hair, and short beards are easily recognisable. Only a few wear any protection for head or body.

[1] Biblical chronology is out here by ten years. It was the twenty-fourth year.
[2] 705–681 B.C.

FIG. 54.—Assyrians storming Lachish 701 B.C.

At the foot of the wall the Assyrians are attacking with the utmost violence and with every type of weapon. Sennacherib had deployed the whole range of approved assault-tactics. Every Assyrian is armed to the teeth: each one wears shield and helmet. Their engineers have built sloping ramps of earth, stones and felled trees. Siege-engines, the first tanks in history, push forward up the ramps against the walls. They are equipped in front with a battering ram which sticks out like the barrel of a cannon. The crew consists of three men. The archer shoots his arrows from behind a sheltering canopy. A warrior guides the ram, and under its violent blows stones and bricks crash down from the walls. The third man douses the tanks with ladlefuls of water, extinguishing the smouldering fire-bombs. Several tanks are attacking at the same time. Tunnels are being driven into the rock beneath the foundations of the walls. Behind the tanks come the infantry, bowmen, some of them kneeling, some stooping, protected by a shield-bearer. The first captives, men and women, are being led off. Lifeless bodies are hanging on pointed stakes—impaled.

James Lesley Starkey, a British archaeologist, dug up the ruins of the walls of the fortress of Lachish. The holes and breaches made by the Assyrian tanks can be seen to this day.

Amid the confusion of the battle and the din of the siege around the frontier fortress of Judah an order went out from Sennacherib: "And the king of Assyria sent Tartan, and Rabsaris and Rab-Shakeh from Lachish to king Hezekiah with a great host against Jerusalem" (2 Kings 18[17]).

That meant attack on Jerusalem.

The historians of the Assyrian king have preserved a record of what happened next. A hexagonal prism from the rubble heaps of Nineveh says: "And Hezekiah of Judah who had not submitted to my yoke ... him I shut up in Jerusalem his royal city like a caged bird. Earthworks I threw up against him, and anyone coming out of his city gate I made to pay for his crime. His cities which I had plundered I cut off from his land...."

Surely now must come the announcement of the fall of Jerusalem and the seizing of the capital. But the text continues: "As for Hezekiah, the splendour of my majesty overwhelmed him ... 30 gold talents ... valuable treasures as well as his daughters, the women of his harem, singers both men and women, he caused to be brought after me to Nineveh. To pay his tribute and to do me homage he sent his envoys."

It is simply a bragging account of the payment of tribute—nothing more.

> "And the king of Assyria appointed unto Hezekiah king of Judah three hundred talents of silver and thirty talents of gold" (2 Kings 18[14]).

The Assyrian texts pass on immediately from the description of the battle of Jerusalem to the payment of Hezekiah's tribute. Just at the moment when the whole country had been subjugated and the siege of Jerusalem, the last point of resistance, was in full swing, the unexpected happened: Sennacherib broke off the attack at five minutes to twelve. Only something quite extraordinary could have induced him to stop the fighting. What might it have been?

Whilst the Assyrian records are enveloped in a veil of silence, the Bible says: "And it came to pass that night, that the angel of the Lord went out, and smote in the camp of the Assyrians an hundred fourscore and five thousand: and when they arose early in the morning, behold, they were all dead corpses. So Sennacherib, king of Assyria departed, and went and returned, and dwelt at Nineveh" (2 Kings 19[35,36]).

Herodotus of Halicarnassus, the most famous traveller in the ancient world, historian and author of an early Baedeker, helped to solve the puzzle. This friend of Pericles and Sophocles, who was born about 500 B.C., had a definite flair for finding out strange facts about people and nations. Like a personified questionnaire he extracted from his contemporaries on his travels through the Ancient East information on all sorts of things which he thought were worth knowing or were unknown to him. In Egypt he had a long conversation with a temple priest who imparted a strange story to the inquisitive Greek.

It happened that at the very time that Sennacherib the Assyrian marched against Egypt with a large armed force, there was a priest-king on the throne of Egypt who treated the army as a contemptible profession. The Egyptian warriors, who had been so disdainfully dealt with, refused to take the field. Thereupon the priest-king hurried to the temple in deep despair. There he was told that the god would help him. Relying upon this, the king, who had actually no soldiers behind him but only shopkeepers, trades-men and market folk, went to meet Sen-nacherib. At the narrow entrances into the country "an army of field-mice swarmed over their opponents in the night ... gnawed through their quivers and their bows, and the handles of their shields, so that on the following day they fled minus their arms and a great number of them fell. Hence," con-cludes Herodotus' story, "this king still stands in Hephaistos' temple with a mouse in his hand, and with the following inscrip-tion: 'Look on me and live in safety'."

However obscure the meaning of this religious legend may be its core is historical.

For the peoples of the ancient world—as also for the Bible (1 Sam. 6[4])—the mouse was what the rat was for the people of the Middle Ages. It was the symbol of plague.

On the edge of the city of Lachish, Star-key, the archaeologist, found possible confirmation of the story in 1948: a mass grave in the rock with 2,000 human skele-tons, unmistakably thrown in with the

FIG. 55.—King Sennacherib seated on his throne in front of the vanquished city of Lachish. (Detail of a cam-paign relief.)

utmost haste. If these were the remains of the victims of an epidemic, then its effects must have been devastating.

The drama of the campaign had been unfolded and once more Jerusalem had escaped. But all round it the land of Judah presented a pitiable spectacle: "The daughter of Zion is left as a cottage in a vineyard," laments the prophet Isaiah, "as a lodge in a garden of cucumbers." The "country is desolate", the "cities are burned with fire ... and it is desolate as overthrown by strangers" (Isa. 1[8,7]).

Only the thought of the marvellous deliverance of the city of David gives the sorely tried people new hope and courage. Undaunted, they bend all their energies to rebuilding, which, without interference from

Nineveh, goes quickly forward. Sennacherib never came back. For the next twenty years the tyrant devoted himself to campaigns and battles in Mesopotamia. Then Sennacherib, like his father Sargon, fell by an

FIG. 56.—Assyrian encampment in Sennacherib's day—a relief from Nineveh.

assassin's hand. "And it came to pass, as he was worshipping in the house of Nisroch his god, that Adrammelech and Sharezer his sons smote him with the sword: and they escaped into the land of Armenia. And Esarhaddon his son reigned in his stead" (2 Kings 19[37]). So runs the brief account of the event in the Bible.

Esarhaddon himself, the successor to the throne, describes in vivid detail these turbulent days in Nineveh: "Disloyal thoughts inspired my brothers.... They rebelled. In order to exercise royal authority they killed Sennacherib. I became a raging lion, my mind was in a fury...."

Despite the intense cold and amid snow and ice he set out without delay to destroy his enemies in the eleventh month of the year 681 B.C. "These usurpers ... fled to an unknown land. I reached the quay on the Tigris, sent my troops across the broad river as if it were a canal. In Addar[1] ... I reached Nineveh well pleased. I ascended my father's throne with joy. The south wind was blowing ... whose breezes are propitious for royal authority.... I am Esarhaddon king of the world, king of Assyria ... son of Sennacherib."

[1] Twelfth month.

CHAPTER 26

THE SEDUCTIVE RELIGIONS OF CANAAN

The "abominations of the heathen"—Harsh words from the prophets—Philo of Byblos: a witness—Eusebius, the Christian Father, finds no one to believe him—Ploughman stumbles upon Ugarit—A powerful seaport disappears—Schaeffer digs at the "Head of Fennel"—The library in the priest's house—Three scholars decipher an unknown alphabet.

"Manasseh was twelve years old when he began to reign, and reigned fifty and five years in Jerusalem.... And he did that which was evil in the sight of the Lord, after the abominations of the heathen, whom the Lord cast out before the children of Israel" (2 Kings 21[1,2]).

"Abominations of the heathen," says the official report. Isaiah, the great prophet who was contemporary with king Manasseh,[1] puts it more plainly when he complains bitterly: "How is the faithful city become a harlot" (Isa. 1[21]).

All the other prophets through the centuries constantly utter the same harsh and unambiguous accusation, which seems so monstrous to readers of the Bible.

The charge runs like a red thread through many books of the Old Testament, accompanying the chances and changes of Israel's history.

It rings out from the time when Israel after its long desert wanderings reached the Jordan about 1230 B.C. (Num. 25[1,3]). We hear it in the time of the Judges (1 Sam. 2[22]). It echoes through the two kingdoms, Judah (1 Kings 14[23,24]) as well as Israel (Hosea 4[13,14]). Even in the years of captivity by the waters of Babylon in the 6th century B.C. it is not silent (Ezek. 16[15ff]).

For 1,500 years after the books of the Bible had made their way into Europe, their contents were communicated to the people exclusively by priests and monks. For they were written in Greek, Latin and Hebrew. It was only at the Reformation, when the first translations had been printed and could be obtained by everyone, that as more and more people came to read the Bible for themselves they came across passages which startled them. The Bible spoke about harlots. It is understandable that people whose houses and dwellings lay close in the shadow and protection of cathedrals and churches which pointed them heavenwards, found difficulty in comprehending this fact.

[1] 696–642 B.C.

What did the European, for whom God was "a safe stronghold", know about the religions of the land in which the Bible was first written?

The prophets and chroniclers tended to be thought of as men who, in their zeal for Yahweh and their anger against foreign religions, had probably gone too far. This objection was levelled at the Bible right up to the present day.

There is secular evidence for what the Bible calls "the abominations of the heathen". Philo of Byblos, a Phoenician scholar, who lived 100 years before Christ, had collected abundant material from his native land and had written a history of Phoenicia, the "Phoinikika". It deals with historical events in the seaports and maritime republics of Canaan from earliest times, and describes the Phoenician gods, mythologies and religious practices. As a reliable source for his work Philo of Byblos cites the Phoenician priest Sanchuniathon, who has been already referred to, and who lived in the 6th or 7th century B.C. When, as the result of an earthquake, the inscribed pillars in the temple of Melkart at Tyre crashed to the ground, Sanchuniathon is said to have copied the ancient inscriptions.

Bishop Eusebius of Caesarea in Palestine discovered the writings of Philo of Byblos in A.D. 314 and gave an account of them. Much of what they recorded, particularly as regards mythology and religion, seemed quite incomprehensible.

At the head of the baals of Canaan was the god El. His wife was Asherah, a goddess who is also mentioned in the Bible. El married his three sisters, one of whom was Astarte. She is frequently referred to in the Old Testament as Ashtaroth (Judges 10[6] etc.). El not only kills his brother but also his own son: he cuts off his daughter's head, castrates his father, castrates himself and compels his confederates to do the same.

Little wonder that people in the Christian era were not prepared to believe stories of enormities of this sort.

With us it is accepted as a matter of course that every half civilised community controls the morality of its citizens. But in Canaan in those days the cult of sensuality was regarded as the worship of the gods, men and women prostitutes ranked as "sacred" to the followers of the religion, the rewards for their "services" went into the temple treasuries as "offerings for the god".

The last thing the prophets and chroniclers did was to exaggerate. How well founded their harsh words were has only become fully understood since the great discoveries of Ras Shamra.

On the north coast of Syria exactly opposite the east tip of Cyprus lies Mînet El-Beidâ, the "White Haven". The Mediterranean waves break here on dazzling snow white limestone rocks in a wonderful display of colour, changing from light green to deep violet. Inland, great banks of clouds surrounded the lonely mountain top of "Jebel Aqra". The natives say that long ago it was the dwelling-place of the gods of their ancestors.

Near the sea in 1928 a peasant who was ploughing discovered a long underground passage. Initial investigation showed that it led to a tomb. It was a sepulchral vault in the style of Mycenae.

When the discovery was announced France, which as mandatory power was in control of Syria, reacted with its customary alacrity. M. Dussaud, curator of oriental antiquities in the Louvre, despatched Professor Claude F. A. Schaeffer with some other experts to the "White Haven". Exciting discoveries awaited them.

Half a mile from the shore and the old Mycenae grave rose an artificial hill. Round its base flowed a pleasant rippling brook. It had always been called by the natives Ras es Shamra, "Head of Fennel". Fennel was actually growing on the old heap of ruins which concealed the remains of the Phoenician royal city of Ugarit. More than 3,000 years ago it had been wiped out for good by the onslaught of the Sea Peoples.

Schaeffer had incredible luck with his excavations on the "Head of Fennel". For here at last the long-sought information about the religions of Canaan came to light. Between two temples, one of them dedicated to the god Baal and the other to the god Dagon, he found among the houses of rich merchants the house of the High Priest of Ugarit, who owned a handsome library, as is clear from the large number of inscribed tablets which were found there. Schaeffer's trained eye recognised at once that the writer must have been using a hitherto unknown Phoenician alphabet. It was surprisingly quickly deciphered in 1930 by three scholars—Professor H. Bauer, of the University of Halle, Germany, and C. Virolleaud and E. Dhorme of France. The bilingual documents—one of the languages is an ancient Canaanite dialect, which is something like pre-Mosaic Hebrew—are exclusively concerned with the gods and religions of old Canaan, with which Israel on entering the Promised Land had its first fateful encounter.

FIG. 57.—Phoenician merchantman.

The myths and practices described in this unique collection of documents abounding in barbaric activities of gods and demigods, indicate the particular significance which was attached to the rites of the goddesses of fertility in Canaan.

The forms of worship which Canaan connected with fertility extended to everyday life. Under each of the houses which were excavated was found a burial vault in which the inhabitants of Ugarit buried their dead. Oddly shaped clay funnels were sunk into the ground through which water, wine, oil and the flesh and blood of animal sacrifices were offered to the dead. The fertility cults did not hesitate to penetrate even the world beyond death. The feeding-funnels leave us in no doubt about that. They are decorated with the appropriate symbols.

Mandrakes played a large part in the ritual of the living. Ancient Canaanites and Phoenicians ascribed aphrodisiac properties to these fleshy roots. They were supposed to be able to stimulate passion and cure barrenness.

Gruesome and ferocious are Astarte and Anath, goddesses of fertility and of war alike. The Baal-epic of Ugarit depicts the goddess Anath: "With her might she mowed down the dwellers in the cities, she struck down the people of the sea-coasts, she destroyed the men of the east." She drove the men into her temple and closed the doors so that no one could escape. "She hurled chairs at the youths, tables at the warriors, footstools at the mighty men." "She waded up to the knees, up to the neck in blood. Human heads lay at her feet, human hands flew over her like locusts. She tied the heads of her victims as ornaments upon her back, their hands she tied upon her belt." "Her liver was swollen with laughing, her heart was full of joy, the liver of Anath was full of exultation." "When she was satisfied she washed her hands in streams of human blood before turning again to other things."

Anath is the sister and wife of Baal, the god of storm and rain. His symbol is a bull's head. Baal fertilises the cattle in the meadows with

rain to make them fat. He is also concerned with their propagation. When he dies at the turn of the seasons, overpowered "like the bull under the knife of the sacrificer", his son takes over his duties. "And the children of Israel did evil in the sight of the Lord and served Baalim" (Jud. 2[11]). Quite recently an image of one of these gods was recovered on Israeli territory at Hazor. It was found in one of the heathen shrines which according to the Bible the Israelites erected in many places for the worship of strange gods. In the centre of an area encircled with flat stones, with two altars for burnt offerings dating from the days before the monarchy, stood some weapons and a clay jar. It contained, together with other bronze votive figures, an image of a seated god—a "baal".

Fig.   58.—
Gold   pla-
quette of a
naked goddess
of fertility.

Professor Schaeffer also found in Ugarit small images and amulets of Astarte. They are made of clay and gold and the goddess is naked. Snakes and pigeons, renowned in the Ancient East for their fertility, are her symbols.

The goddesses of fertility were worshipped principally on hills and knolls. There their votaries erected for them Asherim, set out "sacred pillars", trees, under which the rites were practised, as the Bible repeatedly points out: "For they also built them high places and pillars, and Asherim on every high hill and under every green tree" (1 Kings 14[23]—R.V.).

It is only since the results of scientific investigation into Canaanite gods and Phoenician religions have come to light that we can properly gauge the intensity of the moral struggle that the people of Israel had to face.

What temptation for a simple shepherd folk, what perilous enticement! More than once the Baal religions got a firm foothold and penetrated right into the temple of Yahweh, into the Holy of Holies.

Without its stern moral law, without its faith in one God, without the commanding figures of its prophets, Israel would never have been able to survive this struggle with the Baals, with the religions of the fertility goddesses, with the Asherim and the high places.

That was the reason for the "objectionable passages". In the interests of truth the matter could not be passed over in silence.

If we look at these things with "Biblical eyes", as it were, then such is undoubtedly the impression we receive. Intensive study of the archaeological finds at Ugarit, particularly of the clay tablets, has revealed not only contrasts but also remarkable correspondences between Biblical and old Canaanite religious conceptions.

The Bible continually gives us glimpses of a state of affairs which presumably was quite different from what it appears to have been at first glance. For example, the authentic people's religion of the "children of Israel" as it was actually practised over wide areas must have been very different from what the authors of the Biblical writings would have liked to see.

The prophets continually found cause for anger and the Bible authors complained increasingly about "the worship of idols" and "golden calves". Such statements are in themselves of necessity an indication that cults must have been practised to which a part of the population obviously clung, but which were not in accordance with the norm regarded as valid by the Biblical authors and were consequently condemned.

A few examples will show what the real state of affairs must have been. Mention has already been made in another connection of the way in which Rachel, the wife of the Biblical "patriarch" Jacob, stole the "images" (*teraphim*) of her father, Laban (Gen. 31[19ff]). A brazen serpent idol from the early nomadic period (Numbers 21[9]) was worshipped in the Temple at Jerusalem until the time of King Hezekiah of Judah, around 700 B.C. (2 Kings 18[4]). Even Solomon, the builder of the Temple, incurred the wholehearted disapproval of the Biblical writers by allowing the ladies of his harem to adhere to gods and cults with which they considered it a grave mistake to have contact.

He not only allowed "high places" to these gods to be built on the Mount of Olives (1 Kings 11[1-8]; 2 Kings 23[13]) but himself took part in such cults. Almost all the Israelite and Jewish rulers after him acted in the same way. Even a fanatic like the cruel Jehu of Israel (842/1–815/4 B.C.) who was responsible for the dreadful slaughter of the worshippers of Baal (2 Kings 10$^{18-28}$) was said to have taken part in unorthodox cults (2 Kings 10^{29}). Among the "children of Israel" naked figures of "Astarte" were quite common. Even "in the shadow of the Temple", so to speak, of Solomon's Temple in Jerusalem, the British archaeologist Kathleen M. Kenyon excavated a room which pillars for the cult showed to be a heathen place of worship. Popular religion as practised by the "children of Israel", then, was in reality rather different from what the Bible would have us believe. The Bible itself allows us far too many glimpses of this.

Whilst on the one hand things were occurring in the "Holy Land" which were not all in accordance with the Biblical conception of worship, there was no lack on the other hand, among Israel's neighbours, who are often under such heavy attack in the Bible, of divine personifications of moral principles. The Canaanites were also acquainted with the "Biblical" concept of the kinghood of God, which was consequently not confined to the Bible. Now that texts from Ugarit have made us better acquainted with ancient Canaanite gods like El and Baal, we can only be amazed at the extent to which these gods gave expression to religious concepts which we later encounter in the Bible. This goes so far that even the God of the Bible is the "King above all Gods" (Psalms 95^3; 96^4; 97^{7,9}), which naturally only means anything if people believe in other gods as well. Like the Ugaritic Baal, the Biblical King of Gods has his "mountain of holiness" in the north (Psalm 48^3). It is thanks to the Biblical scholar Otto Eissfeldt of Halle that we know which mountain was meant—the 1,770 metre-high Zaphon or Mons Casius which, visible from afar and frequently shrouded by rain clouds, is today known as Jebel al-Agra, and lies 30 kilometres north of Ras Shamra on the Mediterranean coast of northern Syria. And just as Baal, the storm god, rides on the clouds, so the God of the Bible rides on the clouds and winds (Psalm 104^3).

In spite of all the continual disapproval of the prophets, El and Baal personified moral values. El was "holy" and Baal, like the God of the Covenant, acted as "judge" and ensured justice. The Bible has thus received confirmation and elucidation from a quarter from which it was least to be expected. The despised and accursed religion of ancient Canaan has helped us to reach a new understanding of Biblical statements about the "religion of the fathers". And when the Biblical fathers called upon El-Elyon (the "all highest"), El-Olam (the "ancient of ancients", "the eternal"), El-Roy ("he who appears", "he who sees me") and El-Shaddai ("the highest" or "almighty"), their prayers were directed, as many scholars believe, to the chief Canaanite god El in one of his local variants.

El and Baal were the divine kings of the Canaanite Pantheon. They were later replaced by Yahweh, the god of the "chosen people" of the Bible. Yet there were certain differences. El was static, at rest, unapproachable, while Baal, in contrast, was dynamic, active, actual.

One thing is clear—a royal god such as the God of the Bible, beside whom there was no place for other gods even in a subservient rôle, was naturally incompatible with a myth which included other gods—the exuberant growth of a myth of this kind endowed the ancient gods of Canaan with features which we find bizarre—for such a myth would have implied adherence to the belief in other gods....

CHAPTER 27

THE END OF NINEVEH AS A WORLD POWER

Ashurbanipal plunders Thebes—An empire stretching from the Nile to the Persian Gulf—The "great and noble Asnapper"—Big game hunting with bow and arrow—Assyria's strength is exhausted—Crushed between two powers—Medes and Chaldeans arm—Scythian hordes in Palestine—Nineveh sinks in ruins—The "Fertile Crescent" breathes again—A Biblical slip of the pen—Gadd's discovery in London—Nebuchadnezzar, crown prince of Babylon.

"Art thou better than populous No, that was situate among the rivers, that had the waters round about it.... Ethiopia and Egypt were her strength and it was infinite.... Yet was she carried away, she went into captivity: her young children also were dashed in pieces at the top of all the streets ..." (Nahum 3⁸⁻¹⁰).

In 663 B.C. the Assyrians celebrated the greatest triumph in their whole history. King Ashurbanipal conquered the capital of Upper Egypt No-Amun, which the Greeks called Thebes. According to Homer it had 100 gates and until then it had been regarded as impregnable. It was an event which caused an enormous stir in the world of the ancient orient, in the "Fertile Crescent" itself and as far as Greece. The Assyrians plundered the metropolis, whose temples contained boundless wealth. "I conquered the whole city ... silver, gold, precious stones, the whole contents of its palace, coloured vestments, linen, magnificent horses, slaves, both men and women, two great obelisks of shining bronze weighing 2,500 talents; I took the temple gates from their place and brought them to Assyria. Enormous spoils of priceless worth did I take with me from Thebes," exulted Ashurbanipal.

The Assyrian war machine had made a tabula rasa of the far famed temple-city on the Nile. Excavations fully confirm the description of the catastrophe given by the prophet Nahum and by the victor himself. The capital of Upper Egypt never again recovered from this blow.

After this victorious expedition the world of those days lay at Assyria's feet. From the upper reaches of the Nile to the mountains of Armenia and the mouth of the Euphrates the nations were under its yoke, their peoples reduced to vassals.

But scarcely had Assyria reached the pinnacle of its might when the power of the empire began to wane. Ashurbanipal was not a conqueror

270

FIG. 59.

or war lord of the calibre of his father Esarhaddon, to say nothing of his prodigious grandfather Sennacherib. Ashurbanipal, the "great and noble Asnapper" (Ezra 4[10]), had already developed other interests.

After the long succession of bloodstained tyrants this one Assyrian did the world an inestimable service. He ordered the transcription of the masterpieces of Akkadian literature, including the Babylonian Creation story: he commissioned the production of dictionaries and grammars of the various languages which were spoken in his colossal empire. The library which he built up in Nineveh was by far the largest and most important in the Ancient East. Without this precious collection mankind would have been infinitely poorer in its knowledge of the thought and literature of the "Fertile Crescent" from earliest times.

Nevertheless the wild streak in this last important scion of the race of Assyrian rulers was not completely tamed. As well as being a lover of art and literature he loved hunting. Ashurbanipal was a big game hunter in the proper sense of the word, and his successors in this pursuit can hardly compete with him. It was not with planes and armour-plated jeeps at 60 miles an hour, not with elephant-howdahs equipped with telescopic sights which enable the fatal shot to be fired from a safe distance where there is no threat of slashing paws or snapping teeth, that this big game hunter of the ancient world set out to attack his prey. On these wonderfully vivid large reliefs which were found in his palaces on the Tigris he hunts in a light two-wheeled hunting car or on horseback—with bow and arrow or javelin. "30 elephants, 257 wild beasts, 370 lions," according to the cuneiform texts, made up the splendid total of Ashurbanipal's bag.

> "Woe to the bloody city! ... There is a multitude of slain and a
> great number of carcases, and there is none end of their
> corpses...." (Nahum 3[1,3]).

So the prophet Nahum announces the end of Nineveh, the end of its world empire and centuries of bloody tyranny.

With the death of Ashurbanipal[1] the sudden and rapid collapse began. The new great powers of Indo-Aryans and Semites gripped the gigantic structure between them like a vice, crushed it and divided the colossal spoil between them.

To the north-east the kingdom of the Medes in the mountains of Iran had come into being. Then "Cyaxares came to power," writes Herodotus, "and united all Asia beyond the Halys under him. Then he gathered together all his peoples and marched against Nineveh to take the city."

In the south-east of Mesopotamia a second adversary had sprung up whom the Assyrians had to take seriously. From the fringe of civilisation south of the estuary of the Euphrates, where "Ur of the Chaldees" was also situated, Semitic tribes had pushed their way inland and had imported new vigour into the old kingdom of Babylon. They called themselves "Chaldeans". Merodach-Baladan, who a century before had made a name for himself and had plagued Assyria for many years, was one of them.

Meantime his countrymen had succeeded in penetrating the whole country in a series of waves of invasion. In 625 B.C. a Chaldean assumed control over South Mesopotamia. Nabopolassar became king and founder of the Neo-Babylonian Empire. The Chaldeans likewise had only one end in view, the destruction of Assyria.

At the same time as the two powers, north and south, were lying in wait to administer the death blow to Assyria, a wild horde burst out of the Caucasus into the "Fertile Crescent", penetrated into Media and inundated the Assyrian empire. These were the Scythians. Looting and burning, they forced their way from Mesopotamia through Palestine to the very frontiers of Egypt.

Through the maritime plain by the Mediterranean stormed this unruly mob of Scythian horsemen. Fearful and frightening rumours

[1] 626 B.C.

heralded their approach. The inhabitants of Judah must have seen them as they looked down from the mountains; the prophet Zephaniah foresees with horror what will happen. "For Gaza shall be forsaken, and Ashkelon a desolation: they shall drive out Ashdod at the noonday and Ekron shall be rooted up. . . . In the houses of Ashkelon shall they lie down in the evening. . . ." (Zeph. 2[4,7]).

"They headed for Egypt," Herodotus relates, "and while they were in Palestinian Syria, Psammitichus,[1] king of Egypt, went to meet them and persuaded them with gifts and pleas to go no further. And while the Scythians on their way back were in the Syrian city of Ashkelon a few of them remained behind and plundered the temple of Aphrodite Urania. Those Scythians who had plundered the temple in Ashkelon together with their descendants for ever were smitten by the goddess with a gynaecological ailment."

Within ten years the Asiatic horsemen had disappeared again like an evil apparition.

In Palestine the name of a city kept the memory of the Scythians green. Beth-Shan was re-named Scythopolis. It is not known, however, how the town acquired this name. There are no traces of occupation by the Scythians nor of occupation by a garrison of Scythian mercenaries which would also be conceivable as the origin of the placename. Scythopolis thus remains one of the many points of disagreement among experts who have specialised in the archaeology of the Holy Land.

Then the Medes and the Neo-Babylonians bore down upon the Assyrians on two fronts. They attacked from north and south at the same time. Ashur, the great city and fortress on the Tigris, was the first to fall in 614 B.C. "The king of Babylon and his army, which had set out to assist the Medes, did not arrive in time for the battle. The king of Babylon and Cyaxares[2] met each other among the ruins of the city," says a Neo-Babylonian chronicle, "and pledged themselves to friendship and a confederacy. . . . They took vast quanties of booty in the city and reduced it to a heap of rubble and ruins."

In 612 B.C. the alliance of Medes and Neo-Babylonians achieved its aim. After a "violent battle the city was taken": Nineveh was destroyed. "And he will stretch out his hand against the north and destroy Assyria: and will make Nineveh a desolation, and dry like a wilderness." Zephaniah had prophesied this (Zeph. 2[13]) and now it had happened:—the nerve-centre of Assyrian power destroyed and reduced to ashes, the Nineveh which for centuries with its armies of conquest and occupation, with torture, terror and mass deportations had brought nothing but blood and tears to the ancient world.

The "Fertile Crescent" breathed again. Jubilation filled its afflicted peoples—new hope began to spring up, in which Judah shared.

[1] Psamtik I 663–609 B.C.   [2] King of the Medes.

After the death of Ashurbanipal, when the hated Assyrian colossus was shaken by the first signs of ultimate collapse, king Josiah[1] had without hesitation banned the practice of foreign religions in Jerusalem. There was more to that than merely religious objections. It clearly signified the termination of the state of vassalage, of which the gods of Nineveh, imported by compulsion, were symbolic. Together with these compulsory deities, Josiah expelled all the Mesopotamian "workers with familiar spirits, and the wizards, and the images and the idols" (2 Kings 23[24]). He also cleared out all the Canaanite religious practices (2 Kings 23[7]).

Josiah's reforms paved the way for a renewed religious and national vitality which developed into a regular frenzy when news of the fall of Nineveh confirmed their freedom.

Meantime something quite unexpected happened which threatened to ruin everything.... "Pharaoh-Nechoh king of Egypt went up against the king of Assyria to the river Euphrates: and king Josiah went against him, and he slew him at Megiddo, when he had seen him" (2 Kings 23[29]). This passage from the Bible is a perfect example of how a single word can completely change the meaning of a narrative. In this case the wrong use of the little word "against" brands Josiah as the accomplice of the hated tyrant. At some point or other the word translated "against" has been wrongly copied. In reality Pharaoh Necho went to the aid of Assyria, i.e. "towards". It was only through a chance discovery that the Assyriologist C. I. Gadd found out this historical slip of the pen.

The place of discovery was quite outside the normal archaeological pattern—it was a museum. In 1923 Gadd was translating a badly damaged fragment of cuneiform text in the British Museum which had been dug up in Mesopotamia many years previously.

It read as follows: "In the month of Du'uz [June-July][2] the king of Assyria procured a large Egyptian army and marched against Harran to conquer it.... Till the month of Ulul [August-September] he fought against the city but accomplished nothing."

The "large Egyptian army" was the forces of Pharaoh Necho.

After the fall of Nineveh what remained of the Assyrian forces had retreated to Northern Mesopotamia. Their king embarked upon the forlorn hope of reconquering from there what he had lost. It was for this purpose that Pharaoh Necho had hastened to his aid. But when after two months of fighting not even the town of Harran had been recaptured, Necho retired.

It was the appearance of Egyptian troops in Palestine that decided Josiah to prevent the Egyptians at all costs from rendering military aid to the hated Assyrians. So it came about that the little army of Judah marched against the far superior Egyptian force, with the tragic ending

[1] 639–609 B.C.   [2] 609 B.C.

at Megiddo. "Neko," writes Herodotus, "also defeated the Syrians[1] in a land engagement at Magdolus."[2]

On the way back to Egypt Pharaoh Necho assumed the role of overlord of Syria and Palestine. He made an example of Judah, so as to leave it in no doubt on whom the country now depended. Jehoahaz, Josiah's son and successor, was stripped of his royal dignities and taken as a prisoner to the Nile (2 Kings 23[31-34]). In his stead Necho placed another son of Josiah upon the throne, Eliakim, whose name he changed to Jehoiakim (2 Kings 23[34]).

Egyptologists have not been able so far to produce any hymns of triumph of Pharaoh Necho. Herodotus learned from Egyptian priests a century and a half later that he had presented to the temple of Apollo in Miletus "the garb in which he had accomplished these deeds" in thankoffering for the participation of Greek mercenaries in his expedition. In the land he conquered he left nothing but a stele. It bears his name in hieroglyphic script. Its fragments were left lying in Sidon.

Four years later—605 B.C.—Necho's dream of suzerainty over "Asia", as his predecessors had always called it, was at an end.

Even while he was collecting tribute in Palestine, decisions were being taken about his "conquest" elsewhere. After their joint victory the Medes and the Neo-Babylonians had divided the empire of Assyria between them. The Medes annexed the north and north-east; Babylon the south and south-west. Syria and Palestine thus fell to king Nabopolassar. But in the meantime he had grown old and was no longer fit for the fray. He therefore sent the crown prince of Chaldea, his son Nebuchadnezzar, to take possession of the new territories.

Necho made an attempt to repulse him but failed miserably. Near Carchemish, in the same region where four years previously he had endeavoured to assist the last king of Assyria, he suffered total defeat at the famous passage across the Euphrates from Mesopotamia to North Syria (Jer. 46[2]).

Necho fled through Palestine followed by the jeers of the prophet Jeremiah: "Pharaoh king of Egypt is but a noise: he hath let the appointed time pass by.... The sound thereof shall go like the serpent...." (Jer. 46[17, 22]—R.V.).

After this shameful flight Judah saw no more of Necho. "And the king of Egypt came not again any more out of his land: for the king of Babylon had taken, from the river of Egypt unto the river Euphrates, all that pertained to the king of Egypt" (2 Kings 24[7]). The crown prince of Chaldea was not able to exploit his victory at Carchemish. In the course of the battle news of the death of his father overtook him, and he had perforce to return to Babylon. After Nebuchadnezzar[3] had acceded to the throne more important affairs of state kept him in his own country

[1] Judah   [2] Megiddo.   [3] 605–562 B.C.

for the next few years. Judah was spared a fresh occupation for a time and was left to itself.

There are no contemporary records giving us the details of what happened in Judah around the turn of the 6th century. The Bible gives no clear picture of when, for example, the Chaldeans made their first appearance in the country, or of when they started to demand tribute. The Neo-Babylonian kings, unlike their predecessors the Assyrians, left no informative annals behind them. Inscriptions on buildings which have been preserved merely indicate historical events.

CHAPTER 28

THE LAST DAYS OF JUDAH

First deportation—King Jehoiachin in Babylonian court records—Discovery in the basement of the Berlin Museum—Nebuchadnezzar on the conquest of Jerusalem—Second punitive campaign—Despatches on clay—Starkey's tragic death—Incendiary technique of Babylonian engineers—A clean slate for the archaeologists.

"In his days Nebuchadnezzar king of Babylon came up, and Jehoiakim became his servant three years" (2 Kings 24[1]).

ABOUT the turn of the 6th century there took place the calamitous event which in a few years was to blot out Judah for ever as a nation with a place in the history of the ancient orient. Events now began to close in with frightening speed upon the tiny vassal state on the Jordan and its inhabitants, which were to result in Judah's most grievous hour of affliction. They ended with the road to exile and forcible removal to Babylon.

It began with refusal to pay tribute, and rebellion against the new feudal lord. In 598 B.C. open revolt broke out in Judah. King Jehoiakim "... turned and rebelled against him" (2 Kings 24[1]).

At first Nebuchadnezzar did not intervene in person. Perhaps he did not think it sufficiently important: in a great empire local rebellions are no rare occurrence. He was content to leave it, to begin with, to troops from Moab, Ammon and Syria, strengthened by Chaldean regulars. They do not appear to have taken control of the situation however, whereupon Nebuchadnezzar himself hurried to Judah.

He was already on his way to Palestine with a considerable force when Jehoiakim unexpectedly died. It appears that so far he is the only king of Judah of whom we have a portrait. In Ramath-Rahel near Jerusalem, where a royal citadel from the time of Jehoiakim was found, a sherd with a line drawing on it was recently unearthed. This is thought to represent Jehoiakim. His son followed him upon the throne: "Jehoiachin was eighteen years old when he began to reign, and he reigned in Jerusalem three months.... And Nebuchadnezzar king of Babylon came against the city and his servants did besiege it.... And he carried away all Jerusalem.... And he carried away Jehoiachin to Babylon" (2 Kings 24[8-15]).

In 597 B.C., as the Bible says, king Jehoiachin and his family were deported to Babylon as prisoners. But after 2,500 years who could hope to check up on the reliability of this factual statement? Nevertheless, shortly before the beginning of the 20th century an opportunity came the way of the archaeologists to find out something definite about the destination of the royal family of Judah.

In 1899 the German Oriental Society equipped a large expedition under the direction of Professor Robert Koldewey, the architect, to examine the famous ruined mound of "Babil" on the Euphrates. The excavations, as it turned out, took longer than anywhere else. In eighteen years the most famous metropolis of the ancient world, the royal seat of Nebuchadnezzar, was brought to light, and at the same time, one of the Seven Wonders of the World, the "Hanging Gardens", loudly extolled by Greek travellers of a later day, and "E-temen-an-ki", the legendary Tower of Babel. In the palace of Nebuchadnezzar and on the Ishtar-Gate, which was situated beside it, countless inscriptions were discovered.

Nevertheless the scholars were conscious of a certain disappointment. In contrast to the detailed records of Assyrian rulers, in which the names and fortunes of the kings of Israel and Judah were frequently given a historical setting, the Neo-Babylonian records hardly mentioned anything apart from the religious and architectural events of their day. They contained for example no corroboration of the fate of Judah.

Thirty years later, when the great finds at "Babil" had long since found their way into archives and museums, there emerged a number of unique documents from the immediate neighbourhood of the Ishtar Gate—in Berlin!

On Museum Island, in the middle of the Spree in the heart of the German capital, the wonderful Ishtar Gate from Babylon had been reconstructed in the great Central Court of the Kaiser-Friedrich Museum. Menacing and sinister, the bright yellow bodies of the long row of lions stood out against the deep blue of the glazed tiles on the Processional Way of Marduk.[1] As it had done by the Euphrates, so now it led astonished citizens of the 20th century to the splendid gate dedicated to the goddess Ishtar, with its dragons and wild oxen.

While deeply impressed visitors from all over the world stood in the Central Court upstairs in front of the lofty and brilliantly coloured twin-gate, and, as Nebuchadnezzar had done long ago, turned under its arch on to the Processional Way, 300 cuneiform tablets lying in the basement rooms of the museum were waiting to be deciphered.

Koldewey's team had rescued them from the outbuildings of Nebuchadnezzar's palace near the Ishtar Gate, had numbered them and packed them in boxes. Together with masses of brightly glazed tiles, bearing reliefs of lions, dragons and wild oxen, they had made the long journey to Berlin, where, as luck would have it, the old tablets were

[1] Babylonian god.

lying in their packing-cases by the Spree, almost exactly as they had been in Babylon, only a few yards under the Ishtar Gate.

After 1933 E. F. Weidner, the Assyriologist, took in hand to look through the tablets and sherds in the basement rooms of the Kaiser-Friedrich Museum. He then translated them one by one. They contained nothing but court inventories, receipted accounts from the royal commisariat, book-entries of ancient bureaucrats, nothing but ordinary everyday matters.

Despite that, Weidner stuck it out manfully day after day in the basement under the Ishtar Gate and worked at his translations tirelessly.

Then all of a sudden his monotonous job came unexpectedly to life. Among this dull administrative rubbish Weidner suddenly found some priceless relics of red tape in the ancient world.

On four different receipts for stores issued, among them best quality sesame oil, he came upon a familiar Biblical name: "Ja'-u-kinu"—Jehoiachin!

There was no possibility of his being mistaken, because Jehoiachin was given his full title: "King of the [land of] Judah". The Babylonian clay receipts moreover bear the date of the thirteenth year of the reign of king Nebuchadnezzar. That means 592 B.C., five years after the fall of Jerusalem and the deportation. In addition the Babylonian steward of the commissariat has mentioned in three cases five of the king's sons, who were in charge of a servant with the Jewish name of "Kenaiah".

Other personnel on the ration-strength of Nebuchadnezzar's stores are noted as "eight persons from the land of Judah", who possibly belonged to the retinue of king Jehoiachin, among them a gardener by the name of "Salam-ja-a-ma".

Jehoiachin, the deposed king of Judah, lived with his family and his retinue in the palace of Nebuchadnezzar in Babylon. We may conclude from Weidner's discovery that the Biblical account in the Second Book of Kings may be thus supplemented: "And for his diet, there was a continual diet given him of the king of Babylon, every day a portion, until the day of his death, all the days of his life" (Jer. 52[34]).

A sensational addition to the account of these events was made in 1955 through the examination of 2,500-year-old cuneiform tablets which had long lain in peaceful oblivion in the British Museum. D. J. Wiseman was engaged in deciphering these tablets when to his great surprise he came across the following entry in the official records of the Babylonian royal house:

"In the seventh year, in the month Chislev, the king assembled his army and advanced on Hatti-land [Syria]. He encamped over against the city of the Judaeans and conquered it on the second day of Adar [16th March 597]. He took the king [Jehoiachin] prisoner, and appointed in his stead a king after his own heart [Zedekiah]. He exacted heavy tribute and had it brought to Babylon."

Here we have the original account in Babylonian chronicles of the first conquest of Jerusalem by Nebuchadnezzar as it has been preserved for us in the Bible in the 24th chapter of the Second Book of Kings.

> "And it came to pass in the ninth year of his reign, in the tenth month, in the tenth day of the month, that Nebuchadnezzar, king of Babylon, came, he and all his host, against Jerusalem.... And the city was besieged unto the eleventh year of king Zedekiah" (2 Kings 25^{1,2}).

Eleven years had gone by since the capture of Jehoiachin and the first deportation to Babylon. The time had now come for Judah's fate to be sealed.

The last scene in the tragedy of this tiny nation provides a classic example of how Biblical narratives and archaeological discoveries illuminate the same event from different points of view, and how accurate are the statements of the prophet alongside the official account in the Second Book of Kings and in Chronicles. Jeremiah sketches with swift strokes of his brush scenes taken from the exciting and anxious events of the last days, which through discoveries in Palestine in our own day are confirmed as being startling in their accuracy and historically genuine.

After the first conquest in 597 B.C. Nebuchadnezzar allowed Judah to continue its existence as a vassal state. The successor to the throne, after Jehoiachin had been led off into captivity, was his uncle Mattaniah, who was renamed Zedekiah by the Chaldean king. As we may conclude from Jer. 13^{19} the territory of Judah was reduced: "The cities of the south shall be shut up and none shall open them" (Jer. 13^{19}).

The deportation of their kinsmen before their very eyes, the bitter experiences of a century and a half, the miserable fate of the northern kingdom, still only too fresh in their memories, nevertheless did not extinguish the will to resist.

Soon indeed voices were being raised, denouncing Babylon, and demanding the recovery of all that had been lost (Jer. 28$^{1-4}$). The prophet Jeremiah raised his voice in warning but it was the anti-Babylonian group which was more and more heeded. They egged the people on and eventually got the upper hand of the spineless and vacillating king. Alliances were struck with the bordering vassal states. There was a meeting of "messengers" from Edom, Moab, and Ammon as well as from the seaports of Tyre and Sidon in the presence of king Zedekiah in Jerusalem (Jer. 27^3).

The fact that in 588 B.C. a new Pharaoh, Apries,[1] ascended the throne had clearly a decisive influence on the decision to revolt (Jer. 44^{30}). The

[1] 558–568 B.C. Jeremiah calls him "Hophra".

new ruler of Egypt must have given Judah assurances of armed help, for "Zedekiah rebelled against the king of Babylon" (2 Kings 24[20]).

In the "tenth month" (2 Kings 25[1]) of the same year 588 B.C.—it was "the ninth year" of king Zedekiah—Nebuchadnezzar arrived with a strong army from Babylon. With the speed of lightning the punitive campaign against rebellious Judah was unfolded.

The Chaldean divisions of infantry, fast cavalry and charioteers smashed all resistance and conquered city after city. Except for the capital, Jerusalem, and the frontier fortresses of Lachish and Azekah in the south, the whole land was finally subdued.

Jerusalem, Lachish and Azekah were determined to fight to the end: "When the king of Babylon's army fought against Jerusalem and against all the cities of Judah that were left, against Lachish and against Azekah: for these defenced cities remained of the cities of Judah" (Jer. 34[7]).

Impressive and enduring evidence of the last phase of this hopeless struggle lies before us.

Twenty miles south-west of Jerusalem the green valley of Elah pushes its way far into the mountains of Judah. This was the scene of the duel between young David and Goliath the Philistine giant (1 Sam. 17[19f]).

FIG. 60.—Fortress of Lachish in Judah with double walls and triple gate.
(Reconstruction.)

The little brook out of which David gathered "five smooth stones" for his sling still runs and burbles between its oak trees (1 Sam. 17[40]).

From the river bed the hill slopes gently upwards to a height of 1,000 feet. From the top the cornfields and olive groves of the old plain of Philistia can be seen stretching away to the far horizon where they meet the silvery sparkle of the Mediterranean. On this spot Dr. Frederick J. Bliss, the British archaeologist, identified a fort with eight stout towers as ancient Azekah, one of the frontier fortresses which, as we have seen, remained unconquered. Just about 12 miles to the south the ruins of Lachish were found to contain valuable evidence. J. L. Starkey, the archaeologist, disinterred them in the thirties when the Well-come–Marston expedition from the U.K. investigated the ruins of the great city gate, where the battle was fiercest. Eighteen ostraca, inscribed clay sherds, contained information about forward posts, observation posts and strong points held by Judahite troops which had not yet been overwhelmed. These despatches on clay had been sent to "Jaosh", the "commandant of the fort of Lachish", during that fateful "tenth month" of the year 558 B.C. The messages, scratched out in haste, indicate with every line the frightful tension that existed just before the collapse. One of the last of these eye-witness reports reads: "May Yahweh grant that my lord should hear good tidings ... we are watching for the signal stations of Lachish, according to the signals which my lord has given ... we are no longer receiving signals from Azekah." This message told Jaosh, the commanding officer at Lachish, that Azekah had fallen. Nebuchadnezzar could now withdraw his engineers for the attack on the last fortress but one.

British archaeologists with the Wellcome–Marston expedition obtained information about the terrible end of Lachish in 1938 after six strenuous seasons of excavating.

It was the last success that was to crown the career of James Lesley Starkey, the famous excavator of Lachish. During the Palestinian troubles which had broken out he was shot by Arabs at the age of forty-three in the neighbourhood of Hebron on the road from Lachish to Jerusalem. His death was a tragic case of mistaken identity. In the course of the protracted excavations he had grown a beard and the Arabs took him for a Jew.

In 701 B.C. the storm troops of Sennacherib, king of Assyria, had rushed the walls of Lachish with "tanks" fitted with battering rams. Nebuchadnezzar's special detachments adopted an entirely different technique to force the city to surrender.

Investigation of the stratum which marked the Babylonian work of destruction produced, to Starkey's astonishment, ashes. Ashes in incredible quantities. Many of the layers are several yards thick and are still—after 2,500 years—higher than the remains of the solid walls of the fortress. Nebuchadnezzar's engineers were specialists in the art of incendiarism, past masters at starting conflagrations.

Whatever wood they could lay hands on they dragged to the spot, stripped the whole area around Lachish of its forests and thickets, cleared the hills of timber for miles around, piled the firewood as high as a house outside the walls and set it alight. Countless olive-groves were hacked down for this purpose: the layer of ashes contains masses of charred olive stones.

Day and night sheets of flame leapt sky high, a ring of fire licked the walls from top to bottom. The besieging force piled on more and more wood until the white-hot stones burst and the walls caved in.

So Lachish likewise fell and only Jerusalem still offered resistance. The whole weight of the Babylonian war machine could now be directed against it. It was impossible to use the new incendiary technique in this case, for the forests around Jerusalem had, since the time of the patriarchs and of Joshua's conquest, been reduced to miserable little plantings and undergrowth (Josh. 17[15,18]). They therefore preferred to storm Jerusalem with the approved technique of battering rams and siege engines. For eighteen months Jerusalem was besieged and heroically defended: "And the city was besieged unto the eleventh year of king Zedekiah" (2 Kings 25[2]).

What made the defenders hold out, despite the fact that famine had long been raging in the city and was taking a heavy toll, was a desperate hope that Egypt might come to their assistance.

It seemed that this hope was to be fulfilled, for the Babylonians suddenly withdrew. "Then Pharaoh's army was come forth out of Egypt: and when the Chaldeans that besieged Jerusalem heard tidings of them, they departed from Jerusalem" (Jer. 37[5]). An army did in fact at that time come up from the Nile under Pharaoh Apries, as Herodotus also mentions. Its destination was however not Jerusalem. Apries was making an attack by land and sea against the Phoenician ports.

Archaeologists have found evidence on fragments of Egyptian monuments of Pharaoh's presence in Tyre and Sidon at that time.

So it came about as Jeremiah had prophesied: "Behold, Pharaoh's army, which is come forth to help you, shall return to Egypt unto their own land" (Jer. 37[7]). After a few days the enemy was back in front of Jerusalem, the siege continued with the utmost fury, and the end could no longer be delayed.

> "And the city was broken up, and all the men of war fled by night, by the way of the gate between two walls which is by the king's garden" (2 Kings 25[4]).

Thanks to the result of excavations, the route taken by the defenders in their flight can now be reconstructed without difficulty.

King Hezekiah had strengthened the old fortifications of the city of David by a second wall on the south side (2 Chron. 32[5]). There is still no certainty as to the line it followed.

The moment the enemy entered the city through a breach in the walls the defenders retreated in the first instance behind the double walled southern part of the fortifications and only with the onset of darkness did they escape through an outer gate into freedom and then over the hills to Jericho. In the process King Zedekiah was taken. His children were "slaughtered" before his eyes, he himself had his eyes put out (2 Kings 25[7])—the harsh Babylonian martial law for traitors. This cruel punishment by blinding is frequently attested on pictorial reliefs.

Jerusalem was given over to plundering: the royal palace and the temple were set on fire, the city walls and fortifications were razed to the ground. The order to destroy was given to "Nebuzar-Adan, captain of the guard" (2 Kings 25[8]), a grand vizier who appears in the Babylonian list of court officials as "Nabu-Seri-Idinnam". Once more in 587 B.C. part of the population was deported (2 Kings 25[11]). Nebuchadnezzar erased the royal house of David, which had reigned without interruption for 400 years. The land of Judah became a Babylonian province. Those who were left waged a maquis type of war from their hide-outs in the mountains and claimed as their victim Gedaliah, who had been appointed governor by the Babylonians. There are those who believe that the third and last deportation was in reprisal for this (Jer. 52[30]). Little groups of Judahites were able to escape it by fleeing to Egypt (2 Kings 25[26]; Jer. 43[7]). The curtain of history was lowered on an empty land. The tribes of Israel were scattered to the four winds.

Scholars like S. A. Cook and C. C. Torrey have denied the truth of the Biblical tradition of this carrying off into exile. In their view there was never a mass deportation from Judah, at the most some of the nobility were imprisoned in Babylon.

FIG. 61.

On the other hand, Professor Albright in his writings never tires of emphasising the severity and the extent of the devastations in Judah, so that one is more inclined to believe that the Babylonians made a clean sweep in Judah as the Bible indicates. What was the real state of affairs? One year after the first edition of the present work, a publication appeared which earned a doctorate for Enno Janssen, a Protestant theologian, at the University of Kiel. With great diligence he had assembled all the available results of the investigations of modern research and all the views expressed by experts on the situation in the devastated kingdom of Judah at the time of the Babylonian exile. Janssen did not by any means demolish what Albright insisted upon so emphatically. Systematically, painstakingly, almost pedantically, he listed the towns which had been worst hit, he assembled the information on how extensive the destruction had been in the towns which had been less affected—insofar as that can be ascertained today—and the places which continued to be inhabited during the period of exile. His results may surprise many who find it difficult to free themselves from the idea that the towns of Judah had been completely laid waste.

Certainly the destruction was great and the human losses through war, deportations and executions were not small, yet there were still people, including priests, even in Jerusalem, who lamented the destruction of the Temple and went about earning their living. Land was distributed among people of the poorer classes by the Babylonians and those who were better off were not completely liquidated or deported.

It can be deduced from certain statements in the Bible that there apparently still were comparatively well-to-do people who had managed to survive the catastrophe in their "wainscotted houses", or at least had once again been able to acquire "wainscotted houses" in Judah during the period of exile. The governor, appointed by the Babylonians, was a Jew named Gedaliah and the Bible mentions his father as a friend and protector of the prophet Jeremiah. When Jeremiah escaped the deportation, he went to Gedaliah in Mizpa where the remnants of the Jewish upper classes had assembled. As has already been mentioned, Gedaliah was finally assassinated by a Jewish nationalist, but the mere fact that there was a governor indicates that something was left to administer, or to put it in other words, that people were still living in Judah. The fact that Gedaliah lived in Mizpa, which is situated to the north of Jerusalem, tells us that Mizpa was still functioning tolerably well as a community.

Certainly we do not wish to minimise what had happened to Judah. Perhaps we may refer to the experience of towns and cities throughout the world which in our own day have been reduced to rubble, which despite devastation, despite all the horrors of war, despite the deportation of their inhabitants and all the risks and uncertainties brought about by warfare, were far from being completely depopulated. Moreover, our interpretation of the past depends at least as much on how we experience the present as on what actually happened in the past. In 1945 nobody would have raised any objections if a writer had described cities such as Coventry, Hiroshima, Stalingrad, Dresden or Berlin as "completely destroyed". When we read in Jeremiah 34[22]: "Behold ..." saith the Lord, "... I will make the cities of Judah a desolation without an inhabitant", these words may well express what Judah's inhabitants felt but perhaps even more what was felt by those people carried off into Babylonian exile, for they probably thought all hope lost of ever seeing Ancient Israel rise again to its former greatness. The end of the Kingdom of Judah marked the end of the history of Ancient Israel; the history of the Jews now began.

VII

From the Exile to the Maccabean Kingdom
From Ezekiel to John Hyrcanus

CHAPTER 29

EDUCATION THROUGH EXILE

Good advice from the prophet Jeremiah—The firm of Murashu and Sons, Nippur—Interest 20 per cent—Farmers and shepherds turned traders—Koldewey excavates Babylon—A town plan like New York—The greatest city in the ancient world—Tower of Babel 300 feet high—Chamber of Commerce on the Euphrates.

"Build ye houses, and dwell in them: and plant gardens, and eat the fruit of them ... that ye may be increased there and not diminished. And seek the peace of the city whither I have caused you to be carried away captives" (Jer. 29⁵⁻⁷).

So wrote the prophet Jeremiah from Jerusalem to the elders, priests, prophets and to the whole nation that at Nebuchadnezzar's bidding had been carried off to Babylon. Following his well-considered advice, they sought and found "the peace of the city", and did not fare at all badly. The Exile in Babylon was not to be compared with the harsh existence of the children of Israel on the Nile, in Pithom and Raamses in the days of Moses. Apart from a few exceptions (Is. 47⁶) there was no heavy forced labour. Nowhere is there any mention of their having to make bricks by the Euphrates. Yet Babylon ran what was probably the greatest brick-making industry in the world at that time. For never was there so much building going on in Mesopotamia as under Nebuchadnezzar.

Anyone who took Jeremiah's advice as his guide got on well, some indeed very well. One family which had made the grade has left to posterity its dust-covered business documents on clay. "Murashu and Sons"—International Bank—Insurance, Conveyancing, Loans—Personal and real estate—Head office: Nippur—Branches everywhere—a firm with a reputation throughout the world, the "Lloyd's" of Mesopotamia.

The Murashus—displaced persons from Jerusalem—had done well for themselves in Nippur since 587 B.C. They were an old established office. Their firm still stood for something in Mesopotamia even in the Persian era. The "books" of "Murashu and Sons" are full of detailed information about the life of the exiles, such as their names, their occupations, their property.

Scholars from the University of Pennsylvania discovered some of the

Jewish firm's deeds stored in its former business premises in Nippur. They were in great clay jars, which, in accordance with security precautions in those days, had been carefully sealed with asphalt. It was not only Assyriologists who read the translations of these documents with delight.

The offices of Murashu and Sons were a hive of activity. For 150 years they enjoyed the confidence of their clients, whether it was a matter of conveyance of large estates and sections of the canals or of slaves. Anyone who could not write, when he came eventually to add his signature, put, instead of his name, the print of his finger-nail on the documents. It corresponded to putting a cross, in the presence of witnesses, as in the case of illiterates today.

One day three jewellers called on Murashu and Sons ... "Elil-aha-idinna and Belsunu and Hatin said to Elil-nadin-sum, son of Murashu: In the case of this emerald ring, we give a twenty-years guarantee that the stone will not fall out of the gold. If the emerald falls out of the ring before the expiry of twenty years, Elil-aha-idinna, Belsunu and Hatin undertake to pay damages to Elil-nadin-sum amounting to 10 Minas of silver." The document is signed by seven people. Before the lawyer's name the clay bears the imprint of three finger-nails. These are the signatures of the three jewellers who were unable to write.

An exiled Jew, Mannudannijama, came to Murashu and Sons, because he wanted to arrange a deed of conveyance with a Babylonian concerning an important herd of cattle: "13 old rams, 27 two year old rams, 152 lambing ewes, 40 year old rams, 40 year old ewe-lambs, an old he-goat, a two year old he-goat ... a total of 276 white and black, large and small sheep and goats ... cash on delivery. ... Mannudanni-jama to be responsible for pasture, feeding, and safe custody. ... Nippur, the 25th of Ulul ... Signed: Fingernail of Mannudannijama."

Securities for those imprisoned for debt were deposited with the bank. There were special departments for all eventualities of life.

The rate of interest was 20 per cent, not introduced by Murashu, let it be said. That was the normal rate in those days.

"Murashu and Sons" may serve as an example of the profession, which since the days of the Exile has been associated with the children of Israel. It became for them the profession par excellence and has remained so until now: that of merchant and trader. In their homeland they had only been peasants, settlers, cattle breeders and tradesmen. The law of Israel had made no provision for commerce: it was an alien occupation. The word "Canaanite" was for them synonymous with "shopkeeper", "merchant", people whom the prophets had vigorously castigated for their sins. "He is a merchant, the balances of deceit are in his hand: he loveth to oppress" (Hos. 12[7]; Amos 8[5,6]).

The switchover to this hitherto forbidden profession was extremely clever—a fact that is seldom properly understood. For it proved to be in the last resort, when added to a tenacious attachment to their old faith, the best guarantee of the continuance of Israel as a people. As farmers and settlers scattered throughout a foreign land they would have inter-married and interbred with people of other races and in a few genera-tions would have been absorbed and disappeared. This new profession demanded that their houses should be in more or less large societies, within which they could build themselves into a community and devote themselves to their religious practices. It gave them cohesion and continuity.

The Israelites could have chosen no better training college. Babylon as an international centre of trade, industry and commerce, was the great school for the cities and capitals of the whole world, which from then on were to become the home of the homeless. The metropolis, whose ruins after 2,500 years still betray its ancient power and glory, had no equal in the ancient world.

Sixty miles south of busy Bagdad the desert is churned up, scarred and furrowed. As far as the eye can see, there stretches a maze of trenches, rubble heaps, and pits which bear witness to the efforts of German archaeologists, over a period of eighteen years. As a result of this prolonged campaign[1] Professor Robert Koldewey has been able to bring to light the fabulous Babylon of the Bible.

Scarcely forty years after the excavations the site presented a dismal and chaotic appearance. Wind and desert sand were slowly but relent-lessly covering up again the gigantic skeleton of the old metropolis. Only on one side a few block-like towers stood out with sharply defined silhouette against the sky. Their brick walls, once brightly tiled, were bleak and bare. Here at the Ishtar Gate began the long Processional Way. Where it ended, a massive hump on the other side of the city proclaimed the presence of one of the greatest edifices of the ancient world, the Tower of Babel .

The pomp and glory, the power and might of the city which "sinned against the Lord" (Jer. 50[14]) were all destroyed and disappeared. It was never again inhabited. Could the oracle of the prophet Isaiah have been more completely fulfilled?

> "And Babylon, the glory of kingdoms, the beauty of the Chal-deans' pride shall be as when God overthrew Sodom and Gomor-rah. It shall never be inhabited, neither shall it be dwelt in from generation to generation. . . . But wild beasts of the desert shall lie there: and their houses shall be full of doleful creatures: and ostriches shall dwell there. . . . And wolves shall cry in their castles and jackals in the pleasant palaces" (Is. 13[19-23]—R.V.).

It is a long time now since the site was deserted by jackals and owls

[1] 1899–1917.

and more so by ostriches. Even the mighty Euphrates has turned its back on it and has chosen a new bed. Once upon a time the arrogant walls of the city and the lofty Tower were reflected in its waters. Now a silhouette of palm trees in the distance indicates its new course. The little Arab settlement of "Babil" preserves in its name the memory of the proud city: but it lies some miles north of the ruins.

"Babylon Halt" is written in Arabic and English on the signboard of the station on the Bagdad railway which lies a few hundred yards from the mounds and allows the visitor, a rare occasion these days, to make a tour of the desolate yellowish-brown ruins. Here he is surrounded by the silent stillness of utter solitude.

The ruins preserved as their most precious treasure documents of incomparable value: it is thanks to them that we are able today to reconstruct an accurate picture of the time of the Jewish exile which was also the period of Babylon's greatest prosperity.

"Is not this great Babylon, that I have built for the house of the kingdom, by the might of my power, and for the honour of my majesty" (Dan. 4^{30}). These words which Daniel puts into the mouth of King Nebuchadnezzar do not exaggerate. Hardly any other monarch in the past was such an assiduous builder. There is scarcely any mention of warlike activities, conquests and campaigns. In the forefront there is the constant building activity of Nebuchadnezzar. Hundreds of thousands of bricks bear his name, and the plans of many of the buildings have been preserved. Babylon in fact surpassed all the cities of the ancient orient: it was greater than Thebes, Memphis and Ur, greater even than Nineveh.

"The centre of the city, which is full of three and four-storied buildings, is traversed by dead straight streets not only those that run parallel to the river but also the cross streets which lead down to the water side." So Herodotus described what he himself had seen. The town plan of Babylon is reminiscent of the blueprints for large American cities.

Coming from Palestine, even from proud Jerusalem, the exiles had only known narrow twisting streets, little better than alleys. In Babylon however they made the acquaintance of streets as broad as avenues and as straight as if they had been drawn with a ruler. Every one of them bore the name of one of the gods in the Babylonian pantheon. There was a Marduk street and a Zababa street on the left bank of the river. In the right-hand corner of the city they crossed the streets of the moon-god Sin and of Enlil, the "Lord of the World". On the right bank Adad street ran from east to west, and intersected the street of the sun-god Shamash.

Babylon was not only a commercial but a religious metropolis as can be seen from an inscription: "Altogether there are in Babylon 53 temples of the chief gods, 55 chapels of Marduk, 300 chapels for the

earthly deities, 600 for the heavenly deities, 180 altars for the goddess
Ishtar, 180 for the gods Nergal and Adad and 12 other altars for
different gods."

Polytheism of this kind with worship and ritual which extended to
public prostitution must have given the city, in terms of the present day,
the appearance of an annual fair.

"But the most vicious practice of the Babylonians is the following,"
writes Herodotus in shocked astonishment (I, 199). "Every woman in
the country must take her seat in the shrine of Aphrodite, and once in
her life consort with a stranger. ... And only when she has been with
him, and done her service to the goddess, is she allowed to go home: and
from then on no gift is great enough to tempt her. All the women who
are tall and beautiful are quickly released: but the unattractive ones
have to wait for a long time before they can fulfil the law: some of them
have to wait three or four years."

The abominable temptations and enticements which were part of
everyday life in Babylon remained indelibly fixed in the minds of the
exiled Jews. Through the centuries until the time of Christ the brilliant
metropolis was for them: "Babylon the Great, the mother of harlots and
abominations of the earth" (Rev. 17[5]). The idea of Babylon as a
cesspool of vice is rooted in the vocabulary of every modern language.

The German archaeologists had to clear away over a million cubic
feet of rubble before they had exposed part of the temple of Marduk on
the Euphrates, which had been rebuilt under Nebuchadnezzar. The
structure, including its out-buildings, measured approximately 1,500
feet by 1,800 feet. Opposite the temple rose the Ziggurat, the tower of
Marduk's sanctuary.

> "Go to, let us make brick, and burn them thoroughly. And they
> had brick for stone, and slime had they for mortar. And they said,
> Go to, let us build us a city, and a tower whose top may reach unto
> heaven: and let us make us a name. ..." (Gen. 11[3,4]).

The bricklaying technique described in the Bible at the building of
the Tower of Babel corresponds with the findings of the archaeologists.
As the investigations confirmed, actually only asphalted bricks were
used in the construction, especially in the foundations. That was clearly
necessary for the security of the structure in accordance with building
regulations. In the neighbourhood of the river the regular rise in the
level of the water and the constant dampness of the ground had to be
borne in mind. Foundations and stonework were therefore made
waterproof and damp-proof with "slime", i.e. asphalt.

The beginning of the building of the Tower of Babel is described in
the book of Genesis and comes before the days of the patriarchs.
Abraham lived, as we can gather from what has been discovered at
Mari, in the 19th century B.C. Is this a contradiction? The history of the

tower, "whose top may reach unto heaven", points back into the dim past. More than once it had been destroyed and rebuilt. After the death of Hammurabi the Hittites tried to raze the mighty structure to the ground. Nebuchadnezzar merely had it restored.

Seven stages, "seven squares", rose one above the other. A little tablet belonging to an architect which was found in the temple expressly mentions that length, breadth and height were equal and that only the terraces had different measurements. The length of the sides at the base is given as being rather more than 290 feet. The archaeologists measured it as 295 feet. According to that the tower must have been almost 300 feet high.

The Tower of Babel was also involved in dubious religious rites. Herodotus describes them: "On the topmost tower there is a spacious temple, and inside the temple stands a couch of unusual size richly adorned, with a golden table by its side. There is no statue of any kind set up in the place, nor is the chamber occupied at nights by anyone but a single native woman, who, as the Chaldeans, the priests of this god, affirm, is chosen for himself by the deity out of all the women of the land. They also declare—but I for my part do not believe it—that the god himself comes down into the temple and sleeps upon the couch. This is like the story told by the Egyptians of what takes place in Thebes, where a woman always sleeps in the temple of the Theban Zeus...."

On the streets and squares between the temples, the chapels and the altars, trade and commerce flourished. Solemn processions, heavily laden caravans, traders' barrows, priests, pilgrims, merchants surged to and fro, colourful and noisy. Religious life and business life were so closely associated in Babylon's everyday affairs that they often dovetailed into each other, as they did in the temples. What else could the priests do with all the sacrificial animals, all the "tithes" that were presented daily on the altars, many of them quickly perishable, apart from turning them into money as soon as possible? Just as in Ur, the temple authorities in Babylon ran their own department stores and warehouses. They also ran their own banks to invest their revenues to the best advantage.

Outside the double walls of the city, which were broad enough "to allow a four-horse chariot to turn on them",[1] lay the "Chambers of Commerce". It was on the river-bank that prices were fixed and exchange rates established for the commodities that arrived by boat. "Karum", "quay", was the name the Babylonians gave to what we now call the Exchange. As well as taking over the Quay, or Exchange, from the Babylonians the old world has also taken over its system of weights and measurements.

However much the Jews may have sought "the peace of the city" and found it; however much they may have learned in the cities of

[1] Herodotus.

Babylonia which would profit future generations, broaden their own outlook and raise their standard of living, all of which would benefit future generations in many ways—nevertheless their heart-yearnings for their distant little homeland on the Jordan left them no inward peace. They could not forget the city of David, their beloved Jerusalem. "By the rivers of Babylon, there we sat down; yea, we wept, when we remembered Zion" (Ps. 137). These were no empty words. For thousands of them set out on the difficult journey home. They rebuilt their shattered city and the temple of Yahweh. Without a passionate longing for the homeland they had lost, that would never have happened.

CHAPTER 30

SUNSET IN THE ANCIENT ORIENT

The old world about 500 B.C.—Last spasms before the end—Escape into the past—Nabonidus restores ancient buildings—First museum in the world at Ur—Semitic empires make their exit—The birth of the west.

> "Behold evil shall go forth from nation to nation and a great whirlwind shall be raised up from the coasts of the earth" (Jer. 25[32]).

THE hands of the cosmic clock are approaching 500 B.C. The ancient orient carries more than 3,000 years on its shoulders. The nations in the "Fertile Crescent" and on the Nile have grown old, their creative impulse is exhausted, they have fulfilled their task, and the time is drawing near for them to step off the stage of history.

The sun of the ancient orient is setting and its peoples are vaguely conscious of the approaching night.

Yet there is to be a last flicker of life among these weary nations: they summon up enough strength for one last effort. From Egypt to the lands on the Euphrates and the Tigris it is as if there is to be one final attempt to rise before sinking into insignificance. Were they looking back and thinking of the leading role they had played on the world's stage? It would almost seem as if they were. Their monarchs look back to the great symbols of their glorious past. They believe that with a new display of strength they can delay the inevitable.

Pharaoh Necho and Pharaoh Apries made great efforts to reconquer Syria and Palestine. The Old Kingdom with its "campaigns against Asia" became the ideal of the 26th dynasty.[1] Large navies were built and an attempt was made to restore the old canal between the Nile and the Red Sea.

Even if the new manifestations of strength bore no fruit, and success eluded their military exploits, nevertheless the example of the great days of the builders of the Pyramids lent vitality in other directions. Painters and sculptors copied the works of their great predecessors. Names of Pharaohs of the third millennium were engraved on new scarabs. Ancient official titles and court titles were revived, the civil service was, as it were, antiquarianised.

The same thing happened on the Mediterranean coast in Phoenicia. In 814 B.C. according to tradition, but somewhat later according to the

[1] 663–525 B.C.

results of archaeological research, Carthage was founded as a North African colony of the city of Tyre. By this time the power of these Phoenician merchant sailors had reached its limit. From the Black Sea to the Straits of Gibraltar they had trading posts and bases along the shores of the Mediterranean. A century later the Greeks had inherited their world trade. Sanchuniathon, the priest, wrote the history of Phoenicia. He was commissioned by a king to copy old inscriptions and texts which Philo of Byblos was to use much later as the source for his history.

With Ashurbanipal[1] the Assyrian Empire reached the zenith of its power. It stretched from the Persian Gulf to Upper Egypt. The tiger of the ancient orient had eaten his fill, and the ruler of the most powerful of all conquering nations allowed himself to be painted in an arbour of grape-vines, reclining on soft cushions and being handed a goblet of wine. Collecting old books was his hobby and he had the biggest library in the ancient world. On his instructions the repositories of old temples were ransacked in a search for lost documents. His scribes made copies of thousands of tablets from the reign of the great Sargon I (2350 B.C.). The hobby of his brother Shamash-Shumukin of Babylonia went even further. He had the events of his day written up in the ancient language of Sumeria.

Nebuchadnezzar too,[2] the last great ruler on the throne of Babylon, was afflicted with this longing for old forgotten far-off things. His court chroniclers had to compose inscriptions in Old Babylonian, which nobody could either speak or read. Architecture and literature flourished once again among the Chaldeans.

Observing the sky in the interests of astrology led to undreamt of advances. They were able to predict eclipses of the sun and moon. In the Babylonian School of Astronomy about 750 B.C. observations of heavenly bodies were recorded and continued without interruption for over 350 years, the longest series of astronomical observations ever made. The accuracy of their reckoning exceeded that of European astronomers until well into the 18th century.

Nabonidus[3] may well have been the first archaeologist in the world. This monarch, the last of the Babylonian rulers, caused ruined shrines and temples to be excavated, old inscriptions to be deciphered and translated. He restored the staged tower at Ur which had been weakened by age, as was shown by the finds at Tell al Muqayyar.

Princess Bel-Shalti-Nannar, sister of the Belshazzar in the Bible, had the same interests as her father Nabonidus. Woolley discovered in an annexe to the temple in Ur, where she had been priestess, a regular museum with objects which had been found in the southern states of Mesopotamia—probably the earliest museum in the world. She had actually carefully catalogued her collection piece by piece on a clay

[1] 669–626 B.C.   [2] 605–562 B.C.   [3] 555–538 B.C.

cylinder. This is, in Woolley's words, the "oldest museum catalogue known".

One people alone—broken up into many parts and at that time scattered far and wide throughout the "Fertile Crescent"—did not succumb to surfeit or slackness: the children of Israel, descendants of the patriarchs, were filled with eager hope and had a definite end in view. They did not disappear: they found the strength to preserve themselves for new millennia—up to the present day.

For 1,500 years mankind's biggest light had come from the "Fertile Crescent," the oldest centre of civilisation since the Stone Age. About 500 B.C. darkness fell, imperceptibly but irresistibly, over the lands and peoples who had within them the seed of all that would come after them—but in other lands.

A new light was already shining from the mountains of Iran: the Persians were coming. The great Semitic states and Egypt had fulfilled their assignment in history: the most significant and decisive part of man's early existence had helped to prepare the ground for the Indo-Germanic kingdoms which gave birth to Europe.

From the extreme south-eastern tip of the continent the light travelled farther and farther west. From Greece to Rome, across the barrier of the Alps, across Western Europe and up to Scandinavia and the British Isles. Light from the East!

On its way, within a few centuries, new civilisations would appear, art would reach unimagined heights of beauty and harmony, the human mind in the philosophy and science of the Greeks would soar to pinnacles denied to the ancient orient.

On its way the light would also bring the varied colourful legacy of the ancient orient, from a practical system of weights and measures to astronomy, it would bring writing, the alphabet and—the Bible.

CHAPTER 31

CYRUS, KING OF PERSIA

Two famous dreams—Cyrus unites Media and Persia—The Writing on the Wall—Belshazzar was merely crown prince—Peaceful entry into Babylon—Persian toleration.

"Thus saith the Lord to his anointed, to Cyrus, whose right hand I have holden, to subdue nations before him; and I will loose the loins of kings, to open before him the two leaved gates; and the gates shall not be shut" (Is. 45^1).

SEVEN years after Nebuchadnezzar's death, Nabonidus, the "first archaeologist", ascended the throne of Babylon in 555 B.C. He was to be the last ruler from Mesopotamia. For events in the highlands of Iran suggested that world history was quickly heading for a great revolution.

Five years after the accession of Nabonidus the new era began with the Persians' rise to power.

The Medes—who since the fall of Nineveh in 612 B.C. had shared the stricken Assyrian empire with the Babylonians—were unexpectedly overcome by their neighbours and vassals, the Persians. Astyages, king of the Medes, was beaten by his own grandson, Cyrus.

In the ancient world great men were wont to herald their arrival in extraordinary ways; often the remarkable circumstances of their birth took them outside the normal framework of the lives of their contemporaries. Two unusual dreams are said to have decided the destiny of Cyrus. They were gossiped around the whole of the ancient orient and in this way came to the ears of Herodotus, who recounts them:

"Astyages . . . had a daughter who was named Mandane. He dreamt that from her such a stream of water flowed forth as not only to fill his capital but to flood the whole of Asia. This vision he laid before such of the Magi as had the gift of interpreting dreams, who expounded its meaning to him in full, whereat he was greatly terrified. On this account, when his daughter was of marriageable age, he would not give her to any of the Medes lest the dream should be accomplished, but married her to a Persian by name Cambyses. . . .

"When Mandane was living with Cambyses, Astyages in the very first year saw another vision. He fancied that a vine grew from the womb of his daughter and overshadowed the whole of Asia. After this dream, which he submitted also to the interpreters, he sent to Persia and fetched away Mandane, who was now with child, and was not far from her time. On her arrival he set a watch over her, intending to destroy the child to which she should give birth: for the Magian interpreters had expounded the vision to foreshow that the offspring of his daughter would reign over Asia in his stead. To guard against this, Astyages, as soon as Cyrus was born, sent for Harpagus, a man of his own house and the most faithful of the Medes ... and addressed him thus: '... Take the child born of Mandane: carry him with thee to thy home and slay him there....'"

Harpagus found that he had no heart to carry out this murderous command of the child's grandfather. No more had a shepherd to whom he deputed the task. So Cyrus remained alive.

It was not only the birth and boyhood of Cyrus that were wrapped in legend. This Persian king's son, descended from the royal race of Achaemenes, has, more than any other prince of the ancient world, caught the imagination and evoked the admiration of all nations. Xenophon, the Greek, celebrated the foundation of his empire in a complete romance, the "Cyropaedia".

The Bible remembers him as an enlightened monarch. His unparalleled, swift and brilliant rise to power was marred by no deed of violence. His able and humane policy made him one of the most attractive figures in the ancient orient. The most repugnant feature of oriental monarchs before him, despotic cruelty, was foreign to this Persian.

The figure of Cyrus became a hard fact of history in 553 B.C. In that year he captured Ecbatana, capital of the kingdom of Media. His royal grandfather Astyages was banished. Cyrus amalgamated Media with the Persian kingdom. Babylonia, Lydia in Asia Minor and Sparta formed an alliance against the conqueror. Croesus king of Lydia—his name is still proverbial for great riches—attacked the Persians. Cyrus took Sardis,[1] his capital, and defeated him.

The way to Babylonia was open and Babylon lay invitingly before him. Against the background of such a situation a strange and mysterious story got about which, since it has been recorded in the Bible, has gripped the imagination of the western world:

"Belshazzar the king made a great feast to a thousand of his lords, and drank wine before the thousand. ... They drank wine, and praised the gods of gold, and of silver, of brass, of iron, of wood and of stone. In the same hour came forth fingers of a man's hand, and wrote over against the candlestick upon the plaister of the wall of the king's palace. ... Then the king's countenance was changed, and his thoughts troubled him, so that the joints of his loins were loosed, and his knees smote one against another. ... And the king spake and said to the wise men of Babylon, Whosoever shall read this writing, and shew me the interpretation thereof, shall be clothed with scarlet, and have a chain of

[1] Fifty miles east of Izmir.

gold about his neck, and shall be the third ruler in the kingdom" (Daniel 5$^{1,4-7}$). "Mene, Mene, Tekel, Upharsin" were the words on the wall which have become famous. They mean: "God hath numbered thy kingdom". "Thou art weighed in the balances and art found wanting". "Thy kingdom is divided and given to the Medes and Persians" (Dan. 5$^{25-28}$).

When Joseph in Egypt was able to interpret Pharaoh's dreams of the seven fat kine and the seven lean kine and of the ears of corn, he was made second man in the kingdom, grand vizier.

What was the meaning of the promised reward for guessing the meaning of the mysterious writing to be "the third ruler in the kingdom"?

This Biblical statement was unintelligible and was only explained with the help of archaeology.

Who Belshazzar was has now been established by cuneiform texts from his own father. He was not, in fact, as the book of Daniel says (5^{2}), the son of Nebuchadnezzar, but of Nabonidus, who says in an inscription: "And put into the heart of Belshazzar, my first born son, the fruit of my loins, fear of thy sublime divinity, that he commit no sin, and that he may have fulness of life."

Thus it is clear that Belshazzar was crown prince, therefore the second man in Babylonia. He could only therefore hold out a promise of third highest place in the kingdom.

The story of Belshazzar's Feast and the Writing on the Wall reflects through the eyes of the prophets a contemporary political situation. In 539 B.C. Cyrus turned his attack against Nabonidus, and the Babylonian army was defeated. With that the hours of the last great Mesopotamian empire were numbered.

"Come down, and sit in the dust, O virgin daughter of Babylon: there is no throne, O daughter of the Chaldeans" (Is. 47^{1}).

A year after the battle Cyrus, king of Persia, made his triumphal entry into conquered Babylon.

Hittites, Kassites, Assyrians had at various times threatened the great city with the same fate. This conquest however did not follow the normal pattern: it was without a parallel in the military practice of the ancient orient. For this time there were no columns of smoke rising from behind shattered walls, no temples or palaces razed to the ground, no house plundered, no man was butchered or impaled. The clay cylinder of Cyrus narrates in Babylonian script what took place:

"As I entered Babylon in peace, and established my royal residence in the palace of the princes amid jubilation and rejoicing, Marduk, the great lord, warmed the hearts of the Babylonians towards me, while I for my part devoted myself daily to do him reverence. My troops wandered peacefully widespread throughout Babylon. In all Sumer and Akkad I let no man be afraid. I concerned myself with the internal affairs of Babylon and all its cities. The dwellers in Babylon. ... I freed from the yoke that ill became them. I repaired their houses, I healed their afflictions ... I am Cyrus, king of all, the great king, the mighty king, king of Babylon, king of Sumer and Akkad, king of the four corners of the earth...."

The last sentences almost suggest that the Biblical Chronicler had known the text of the clay cylinder. "Thus saith Cyrus, king of Persia, All the kingdoms of the earth hath the Lord God of heaven given me...." (2 Chron. 36²³).

That rulers should make tolerance, including religious tolerance, their motto was uncommon, and marked the Persian king out from the first.

After his entry into Babylon Cyrus at once had the images and shrines of the local gods set up again. He was concerned with "the daily worship of the chief god of the city Marduk". In the city of Ur he did the same. On a broken cylinder which was preserved among the ruins Cyrus himself says: "Sin, the light of heaven and earth, with his favourable omens gave into my hands the four corners of the earth. I brought the gods back into their sanctuaries."

His tolerance was also to the advantage of the Jews. After these many years of exile their dearest wish was now to find fulfilment.

CHAPTER 32

RETURN TO JERUSALEM

The edict of Cyrus—The trek of the 42,000—A caravan of fateful significance—Starting work on the ruins—A lonely grave in Pasargadae—Rebuilding the Temple—The Persian Empire: from the Nile to India—Duncan finds Nehemiah's work—The secret of the "thick water"—A theocratic state—Judah coins stamped with the Athenian owl—A Persian province for two centuries.

"In the first year of Cyrus the king, the same Cyrus the king made a decree concerning the house of God at Jerusalem, Let the house be builded, the place where they offered sacrifices, and let the foundations thereof be strongly laid: the height thereof threescore cubits, and the breadth thereof threescore cubits" (Ezra 6³).

THIS meant permission for them to return to Jerusalem. The text of the royal decree is in imperial Aramaic, the new official language of the Persian government. Archaeology has been able to establish the authenticity of this permit, which has been incorporated in chapter six of the Book of Ezra.

It was a matter of reparation. It is clear from the terms of the enactment that the Persians regarded themselves as successors of the Babylonians: ". . . let the expenses be given out of the king's house. And also let the golden and silver vessels of the house of God, which Nebuchadnezzar took forth out of the temple which is at Jerusalem, and brought into Babylon, be restored and brought again unto the temple, which is at Jerusalem, every one to his place, and place them in the house of God" (Ezra 6⁴,⁵).

The carrying out of the order was entrusted by Cyrus to Sheshbazzar,[1] the governor (Ezra 5¹⁴), a prince of Judah, and probably a member of the house of David.

It is understandable that fifty years after the deportation not everyone would take advantage of this permission to return to the land of their fathers. In any case it was a risky business to leave this wealthy country of Babylon where they had established themselves and where most of them had grown up and to set out on the difficult road back to the ruins of a ravaged land. Despite this, in the spring of 537 B.C., after long preparations a lengthy caravan set out on the trail towards the old

[1] It is thought that Sheshbazzar is the same as Shenazar, the fourth son of king Jehoiachin (1 Chron. 3¹⁸).

homeland. "The whole congregation together was forty and two thousand three hundred and threescore. Besides their servants and their maids, of whom there were seven thousand three hundred thirty and seven, and there were among them two hundred singing men and singing women. Their horses were seven hundred thirty and six: their mules two hundred forty and five, their camels four hundred thirty and five, their asses six thousand seven hundred and twenty" (Ezra 2[64-67]).

Whether this list of people returning to their homeland really is that of the members of a mighty trek from the Euphrates to Judah is debatable. It is all repeated in Nehemiah almost word for word except that the number of singing men and singing women is not quite the same as there is a difference of 45. In this instance, however, the list is of a population census, a register of the Persian satrapy which Judah had become under Persian rule. However this may be and whatever the number of people who did, in fact, return to Judah after the long years in exile, we can vividly imagine their journey into the land west of the Jordan.

Almost 800 miles have to be covered between Babylon and distant Jerusalem, with the clouds of dust churned up by the caravan as a faithful companion throughout the whole journey. One day they would pass the site of old Mari. They would reach the spot where, on the opposite side of the river, the Balikh, on whose lower reaches Haran was situated, enters the Euphrates.

From then on the returning exiles were following the same track which had been taken by Abraham 1,400 years earlier, when he left the land of his fathers to go to Canaan, via Damascus and along the foot of Hermon to the Lake of Galilee. Then came the day when from among the brown peaks of the mountains of Judah the desolate ruins of the city of Zion rose before their eyes—it was Jerusalem.

What fateful significance this journey had for the generations that were still to come!

"The future of the world lay in this procession to Jerusalem," says the American scholar and educationist Mary Ellen Chase, who lectured in universities on "The Bible as Literature" from 1926 onwards. "It rested with it whether we should have a Bible at all as we know it—the Bible, the Jewish faith, Christianity and many centuries of western culture. If there had been no return to Jerusalem, Judah would assuredly have shared by and large the fate of Israel, become intermingled with the east and eventually been lost as a united people."

Soon after their arrival in Jerusalem the foundations of the new Temple were laid amid great enthusiasm. But then the work slackened off (Ezra 5[16]). The great enthusiasm of the returned settlers quickly waned: life was too hard and barren in this depopulated land, where dilapidated houses provided the scantiest of shelter. Added to this was the problem of making a living, as Haggai said "ye run every man unto his own house" (Haggai 1⁹). Everyone was too concerned with his own problems.

The rebuilding advanced but slowly. The first settlers were poor, and as the remains of their household belongings indicate, few in number. The objects which have been discovered clearly reflect the harshness of that first early stage.

Cyrus, the liberator, died on an expedition to the east in 530 B.C. and was buried in the royal palace of Pasargadae near Persepolis.[1] His palace was built in the form of individual pavilions: each one lay in the centre of a magnificent garden: the whole area was enclosed by a high wall.

On the southern slopes of a long range of hills there still stands among the rough grass of the highlands a small unpretentious stone building dating from the time of Cyrus. Six square blocks form the steps which lead up to a small chamber, above the entrance to which there could at one time be read the following plea: "O man, whoever you are and whenever you come, for I know that you will come—I am

FIG. 62.—Mausoleum of Cyrus.

Cyrus, who gave the Persians their empire. Do not grudge me this patch of earth that covers my body." Alas, the small stone chamber in which a golden sarcophagus enclosed the mortal remains of the great Persian is now as empty as the place above the entrance which bore the inscription. Occasionally shepherds with their flocks pass unconcernedly by this forgotten spot, as they did in olden times, across the wide plateau where the lion is still lord of the chase.

Cyrus was followed by his son Cambyses II.[2] With the conquest of Egypt Persia became under him the greatest empire that the world had ever seen: it stretched from India to the Nile.

It was not until the reign of his successor Darius I[3] that the rebuilding of the Temple in Jerusalem was finally taken in hand. Almost twenty years had passed since the foundations had been laid. At the request of the official responsible for the administration of Judah, the Satrap of Transeuphrates, Darius I expressly confirmed the permit issued by Cyrus. The official exchange of letters with the Persian court on this matter can be found in the Book of Ezra (5⁶–6¹²).

Many experts are convinced of the historicity of these documents although others are doubtful. If they are not genuine, however, they are very clever imitations both as to form and content. The Bible here even uses the Aramaic of the empire, the commercial language of the

[1] Thirty miles north-east of Shiraz in Southern Iran, famous in modern times as a centre of carpet weaving.

[2] 530–522 B.C.   [3] 522–486 B.C.

FIG. 63.

Achaemenide Empire. Numerous other contemporary texts confirm, moreover, the extent to which Darius fostered the indigenous cults of the peoples incorporated in his empire, not only in Palestine, but also in Asia Minor and Egypt.

For example the inscription of Usahor, an Egyptian doctor, runs as follows: "King Darius—may he live for ever—commanded me to go to Egypt ... and make up once more the number of the holy scribes of the temple and bring new life into what had fallen into decay...."

Darius wrote to Gadata, the steward of his demesnes, in no uncertain manner. He took him sharply to task for his attitude to the priesthood of the temple of Apollo in Magnesia: "I hear that you are not carrying out my instructions properly. Admittedly you are taking trouble over my estates, in that you are transferring trees and plants from beyond the Euphrates to Asia Minor. I commend this project and the Court will show its gratitude. But in disregarding my attitude to the gods you have provoked my displeasure and unless you change your tactics you will feel its weight. For you have taken away the gardeners who are sacred to Apollo and used them for other gardening jobs of a secular character, thereby showing a lack of appreciation of the sentiments of my ancestors towards the god who has spoken to the Persians...."

The efforts of the returned exiles were for many years confined exclusively to rebuilding the Temple at Jerusalem. Building operations started in October–November 520 B.C. and by 12 March 515 B.C. they were completed.[1]

[1] Zech. 1[1]—the eighth month of the second year of Darius=Oct.–Nov. 520 B.C. (Start of building operations).

Ezra 6[15]—the third day of the month of Adar, (Babylonian: Addaru) in the sixth year of Darius=12 March 515 B.C. (Completion of Temple).

They had to wait for the city wall until the next century. It was not until the time of Nehemiah, who was installed as independent governor of Judah by king Artaxerxes I[1] of Persia in 444 B.C., that they began work on the wall, which was finished in record time. "So the wall was finished ... in fifty and two days" (Neh. 6[15]). A new wall in fifty-two days—impossible! Nehemiah himself tells us of "the walls of Jerusalem which were broken down, and the gates thereof were consumed with fire" (Neh. 2[13]). The walls were thus merely repaired. And that must have happened in a hurry. For the neighbouring tribes, above all the Samaritans, wanted to stop the refortification of Jerusalem by every means in their power. The Jews had to be constantly on the look out: "everyone with one of his hands wrought in the work, and with the other hand held a weapon" (Neh. 4[17]).

It is no different today in the case of the building operations of farmers, workers and shepherds in the modern state of Israel.

The speedy filling up of holes and patching up of gaps in the walls reflect the pressure of the time factor and the feverish anxiety with which the work went forward. The British archaeologist J. Garrow Duncan dug up parts of the wall on the little hill to the south-east above the Gihon spring. In his report he says: "The stones are small, rough, irregular and unequal. Some of them are unusually small and seem to be merely chips broken off from bigger stones, just as if they were using any kind of material that came to hand. The large holes and hollow spaces are filled up with a haphazard mixture of clay plaster mixed with tiny chips of stone...."

Fig 64.— Stamp on J u d a h i t e pitcher bearing the inscription "Jerusalem".

During the time that Nehemiah was governor of Jerusalem we are told how the holy fire of the Temple was rediscovered. The first two chapters of 2 Maccabees tell how Nehemiah "sent in quest of the fire the descendants of the priests that hid it". They "had found no fire but thick water". When at Nehemiah's command they poured this thick water over "the wood and the things laid thereupon" "There was kindled a great blaze so that all men marvelled" (2 Macc. 1[21-22]). Nobody paid much attention to the observation that followed: "And Nehemiah and they that were with him called this thing Nephthar" (2 Macc. 1[36]). Yet this passage in the Bible contains a very clear hint regarding a quite specific mineral product which must have been well known to the Israelites, and it is only very recently that this was recognised. In the new state of Israel petroleum, or naphtha—the word is of Babylonian derivation—has in fact been found. Since 1953, drilling near the Dead Sea, in the Negev and in the neighbourhood of Askelon has led to the successful opening of Israeli oil-wells.

[1] 465–424 B.C.

The rebuilding of the Temple and of the old city of David after the return from exile in Babylon make it abundantly clear that Israel knew full well that the days of the monarchy had gone for ever and that only the inward solidarity of a religious community could guarantee the further existence of the tiny state in face of what political developments might be in store for them. With this end in view they made the holy city the centre of Jewry, both for those Jews who lived in the homeland of Judah and for those who were scattered throughout the world. The High Priest of the new Temple at Jerusalem became head over all Israel. The little theocracy in Palestine took no noteworthy part in the affairs of the world during the subsequent centuries. Israel turned its back on politics.

With Persian approval the Law of God became the law of Israel, indeed of Jews everywhere, as the Book of Ezra clearly indicates (Ezra 7[23-26]).

The Biblical passage is convincingly borne out by another document from the same period.

In 1905 three papyrus documents were discovered on the palm-covered island of Elephantine, which lies beside the first cataract of the Nile near the Aswan dam. They are written in imperial Aramaic and date from the year 419 B.C. One of them is an Easter message from king Darius II of Persia containing instructions as to how the Feast of the Passover is to be celebrated. The recipients of the letter were the Jewish military colony in Elephantine. The sender signs himself Hananiah, "agent for Jewish affairs at the court of the Persian governor of Egypt".

Fig. 65.—Coin from Judah with Zeus and the Athenian owl (Persian period).

For two centuries the Persians were liege lords of Jerusalem. The history of Israel during this period seems to have been subjected to no violent variations. The Bible makes no mention of it, nor have the layers of rubble anything significant to tell us of this long space of time. At all events there is a complete absence of large buildings, or objects of art and craft, among the archaeological trophies recovered from the appropriate layer. Fragments of simple household utensils prove how miserably poor life in Judah must have been at that time.

Coins certainly occur in the course of the fourth century B.C. They bear the proud legend "Yehud", "Judah". Apparently the Persians had granted the high priest the right to mint silver coins. Following the example of the Attic drachma, they are decorated with the portrait of Zeus and the owl of Athens, testimony to the way in which Greek trade and influence had been able to penetrate everywhere in the Orient long before the days of Alexander the Great.

CHAPTER 33

UNDER GREEK INFLUENCE

Alexander the Great in Palestine—Causeway forces capitulation of Tyre—Siege towers 160 feet high—Alexandria: the new metropolis—Ptolemies occupy Judah—Seventy-two scholars translate the Bible—Pentateuch in Greek—The Septuagint came from Pharos—A stadium below the Temple—High Priest in "gaming house"—Jewish athletes give offence.

"And it came to pass, after that Alexander the Macedonian, the son of Philip, who came out of the land of Chittim,[1] and smote Darius king of the Persians and Medes, it came to pass, after he had smitten him, that he reigned in his stead, in former time, over Greece. And he fought many battles, and won many strongholds. ..." (1 Maccabees 1[1]—R.V.).

IN the 4th century B.C. the centre of political power gradually shifted from the "Fertile Crescent" to the West. The prelude to this development, which was of decisive importance for the whole world, had been two famous battles in the previous century, in both of which the Greeks called a halt to any further Persian advance. At Marathon in 491 B.C. they defeated the Persian armies of Darius I. At Salamis, off Athens, they smashed the Persian fleet eleven years later in 480 B.C.

With the victory of Alexander the Great[2] over Darius III,[3] king of Persia, in 333 B.C. at Issus, near the present day seaport of Alexandria in North Syria, the Macedonians arrogated to themselves the leading role among the nations of the world.

Alexander's first target was Egypt. With a picked force of 32,000 infantry and 5,000 cavalry he marched south at the age of twenty-four, accompanied off shore by a fleet of 160 ships. Twice he was held up on the coast of Syria and Palestine.

The first occasion was at Tyre. This Phoenician city, heavily fortified and protected by stout high walls, was built on a small island which guarded the coastline. Alexander performed here a miracle of military ingenuity by building a 2,000 foot mole in the sea out to the island city. To safeguard the operations, mobile protective shields, so-called "tortoises" had to be employed. Despite this the construction of the causeway was greatly hindered by an incessant hail of missiles. Meantime his engineers were on shore building veritable monsters: "Helepoleis". These were mobile protective towers many stories high, which held the

[1] Greece.   [2] 336–323 B.C.   [3] 336–331 B.C.

detachments of bowmen and light artillery. A drawbridge on the front of the towers enabled a surprise attack to be made on the enemy's walls. They were the highest siege towers ever used in the history of war.

FIG. 66.—Alexander the Great built a 650 yard causeway across to Tyre.

Each of them had twenty stories and the topmost platform towered at a height of over 160 feet far above the highest city walls.

When after seven months preparation these monsters, bristling with weapons, slowly and clumsily rolled towards Tyre, the fate of the maritime stronghold, which was considered to be impregnable, was sealed.

"And Tyrus did build herself a stronghold and heaped up silver as the dust and fine gold as the mire of the streets. Behold, the Lord will cast her out and he will smite her power in the sea; and she shall be devoured with fire." (Zechariah 9³⁻⁴). This is the Bible's comment on Alexander's conquest. It was incorporated in the Book of Zechariah, in the later, second part. Today nobody has any doubts about

FIG. 67.—Alexander's mobile siege-towers were 160 feet high.

the authenticity of these words as a genuine commentary by the Jewish community of Alexander's day on the events of the year 332 B.C.

"... Gaza shall ... be very sorrowful" we read in the following verse (Zechariah 9⁵) which deals with this year in Alexander's life. It was indeed the old Philistine town of Gaza which brought the Macedonian king to a halt for the second time. But this siege lasted only two months, and then the road to the Nile lay open.

The siege of Gaza in southwest Palestine especially must have made some impact on the Jews. The noise of troops marching down the coast below them and camping there must have been heard on their hills above. Yet the Bible has as little to say about these events as indeed about the whole period of Greek supremacy for almost 150 years. Its historians do not take us beyond the end of the kingdoms of Israel and Judah and the creation of the theocracy under Persian sovereignty. It is only with the beginning of the Maccabean wars that it embarks once more upon detailed history.

But Flavius Josephus, the Jewish historian, gives an account which is not found in the Bible of the campaign of the victorious Greek through Syria and Palestine at this time. After the capture of the fortress of Gaza, he says, Alexander the Great came to Jerusalem. The people and Jaddua the High Priest received him with great ceremony. Alexander offered sacrifices in the Temple and granted the people favours.

Alexander can hardly have found time for a trip to Jerusalem, since he had already been held up for nine months by the resistance of Tyre and Gaza. After the fall of Gaza he hurried on by the quickest road to Egypt, leaving the conquest of the territory inland to his general Parmenion, who had no difficulty in subduing the country. Only Samaria, the seat of the governor of the province, had to be forcibly brought to heel. As a punishment it had a colony of Macedonians settled in it.

Jerusalem and the province of Judah seems to have submitted to their new masters without more ado. At all events no contemporary source has so far suggested that there was any resistance from the theocracy.

The visit of Alexander to Jerusalem is probably only a legend which nevertheless contains a grain of truth. It bears eloquent witness to the fact that the Greek conqueror too tolerated the way of life of the theocracy of Judah. It was left unmolested as a religious community.

This is quite in accord with what archaeology has been able to establish. There are no traces of either a Greek conquest or a Greek occupation of Judah at that time.

Only in the neighbouring city of Samaria a strong Greek fortress came into existence about 322 B.C. Excavations disclosed a whole series of round towers. They lean against the old casemated wall which was built in the days when Samaria was still the capital of the kingdom of Israel.

Alexander remained in Egypt, which welcomed him as a liberator, during the winter of 332–331 B.C. On the outermost tip of the Nile delta he founded the city of Alexandria, which was destined for the role of the metropolis of the new age. It quickly blossomed into the centre of a new intellectual life which attracted the best minds of the Greek and oriental world within its orbit.

At its foundation Alexander issued instructions which were to be of the highest significance in future days. He guaranteed to the Jews—descendants of the refugees in the Babylonian era—the same rights as were accorded to his own countrymen. This provision, carried on by the successors of the great Macedonian, led to Alexandria becoming subsequently one of the great reservoirs of Jewish life and culture.

The name of the city founded by Alexander does not appear in the Bible earlier than the Book of Acts: "And a certain Jew named Apollos, born at Alexandria, an eloquent man and mighty in the scriptures, came to Ephesus" (Acts 18[24]).

On the way to one of the greatest and most successful military expeditions known to history, Alexander marched once more through Palestine. Every country in the Ancient East fell before him. He pressed on to the Indus, almost to the foot of the Himalayas. On the way back he was attacked by a fever. Alexander died in Babylon at the age of 33 on the 13th of June 323 B.C.

In view of the fact that, long before Alexander, the Greeks had been stretching out their feelers in a thousand ways in the direction of Mesopotamia and Egypt, we can only shake our heads in amazement at Jewish ignorance of the ways of the world. Time seems to have been standing still in the little theocracy and the life of its tiny religious community appears to have been influenced only by the Torah, the Law of God.

A long way back there had been Greek mercenaries in the armies of Pharaoh Psamtik II and Nebuchadnezzar, king of the Chaldeans. It was also a long time since the first Greek forts and trading stations had started to spread along the coast of Syria and Palestine. In the 5th century B.C. there were already highly educated Greeks travelling and studying in all countries of the ancient orient: Herodotus and Xenophon, Hecataeus and Ctesias.

FIG. 68

Were these men in their theocratic community no longer able to recognise or understand the signs of the times? Or did they intentionally shut their eyes and blindly hope to keep the future at bay?

If so they must have had all the ruder awakening when they came face to face with Greece but a few steps from the sanctuary of the Temple and could disguise from themselves no longer that Jewish youth had fallen completely for the sport of throwing the discus, which had been imported from Greece. Athletic contests on the Greek pattern quickly found an enthusiastic response among the young people.

Greece was not a danger to the Jews by reason of its growing ascendancy, or militarism, or seductive temptations. The danger lay far more in the freer atmosphere of a fabulous modern world. Hellas, with its Pericles, Aeschylus, Sophocles, Euripides, with its Phidias and Polygnotus, its Plato and its Aristotle, had climbed up to a new stage in human development.

Undisturbed by the new era of mankind the tiny theocracy went on obstinately in its own way, held tenaciously and inflexibly to its traditions and to the past. Despite all this it was forced to join issue with the new ideas. But there was still time enough before the 2nd century B.C.

> "So Alexander . . . died. And his servants bore rule every one in his place. And after his death they all put crowns upon themselves: so did their sons after them many years: and evils were multiplied in the earth" (1 Macc. 1$^{7-9}$).

The idea behind the struggle for power of Alexander's captains—the Diadochi—is not unknown even in 20th century politics. In its original form it was no more of an advertisement for the profession of army commanders. Alexander's generals had no scruples about getting rid of his whole family by murdering them: Philip Arrhidaeus his half brother, his mother Olympia, his widow Roxana and his posthumous son. The conflict came to a head in the division of the empire into three kingdoms.

The kingdom of Macedonia in Northern Greece.

The kingdom of the Seleucids, which extended from Thrace through Asia Minor and Syria to the border of India. Antioch, in the north of Syria, situated on the lower reaches of the Orontes, was founded as capital of this second and by far the largest of the successor states. Thereafter almost all the Seleucid monarchs added to their own names the name of this city: Antiochus.

The third was the Ptolemaic kingdom on the Nile with Alexandria as its capital. It was ruled by a dynasty whose last representative, Cleopatra, has ever since enjoyed a certain amount of fame for having so successfully turned the heads of her distinguished contemporaries Julius Caesar and Mark Antony.

Ptolemy I was the first ruler of this dynasty.

Two unusually far-sighted rulers, Ptolemy I and his son Ptolemy II Philadelphus, developed their capital city of Alexandria into a nursery of Hellenistic culture and learning, whose fame extended far beyond the borders of their own kingdom and made it a radiant centre of attraction for emigrants from Judah among others. In this crucible they steeped themselves in the beauty of the Greek language, the only means of tasting the delights of the prodigious advances of the human mind and the human spirit. It was the international language of learning and of commerce, the language of tens of thousands of Israelites who knew no other home.

The rising generation no longer knew Hebrew as their mother tongue. They could no longer follow the sacred text in the services of the synagogue. Thus it came about that the Jews in Egypt decided to translate the Hebrew scriptures. About 250 B.C. the Torah was translated into Greek, a fact of immeasurable import for Western civilisation.

The translation of the Bible into the Greek tongue was for the Jews in Egypt such an incredible step forward that legend took hold of it. The story is told in an apocryphal letter of Aristeas of Alexandria.

Philadelphus,[1] the second of the Ptolemaic dynasty, took great pride in the fact that he possessed a collection of the finest books in the world. One day the librarian said to the monarch that he had brought together in his 995 books the best literature of all nations. But, he added, the greatest books of all, the five books of Moses, were not included among them. Therefore Ptolemy II Philadelphus sent envoys to the High Priest to ask for a copy of these books. At the same time he asked for men to be sent who could translate them into Greek. The High Priest granted his request and sent together with the copy of the Torah 72 learned and wise scribes. Great celebrations were organised in honour of the visitors from Jerusalem, at whose wisdom and knowledge the king and his courtiers were greatly astonished. After the festivities they betook themselves to the extremely difficult task which had been assigned to them, and for which there was neither prototype nor dictionary. They set to work out at sea, on the island of Pharos off Alexandria, at the foot of one of the seven wonders of the world—the 300 feet high lighthouse which Ptolemy II had erected as a warning for shipping far and near. Each of them worked in a cell by himself. When the scholars had completed their work and the translations were compared with one another all seventy-two are said to have corresponded exactly, word for word. Accordingly the Greek translation of the Bible was called the "Septuagint", meaning "the Seventy".

[1] 285–246 B.C.

What had previously been made known only in the sanctuary, only in the old tongue, and only to the one nation was now all at once available and intelligible for people of other tongues and other races. The hitherto carefully guarded door was thrown wide open.

Judah's attachment to the kingdom of the Ptolemies lasted for more than 100 years. Then the Seleucids of Antioch forced their way southwards, an expansion for which they had long been striving. After a victorious battle against Ptolemy V at the sources of the Jordan, Antiochus III, called the Great, took over Palestine in 195 B.C., and Judah thereby once more came under a new sovereignty.

Gradually the foreign seed began to sprout even in the theocracy. The manifold and enduring influence of the Greek attitude of mind, which had been infiltrating since Alexander's victorious campaigns, became more and more apparent.

When "Antiochus surnamed Epiphanes ... reigned in the hundred and thirty and seventh year of the kingdom of the Greeks" (1 Macc. 1[10]) and "Jason ... laboured underhand to be high priest ... he forthwith brought his own nation to the Greekish fashion. ... For he built gladly a place of exercise under the tower itself, and brought the chief young men under his subjection.... Now such was the height of Greek fashions, and increase in heathenish manners through the exceeding profaneness of Jason, that ungodly wretch and no high priest; that the priests had no courage to serve any more at the altar, but despising the temple, and neglecting the sacrifices, hastened to be partakers of the unlawful allowance in the place of exercise, after the game of Discus called them forth" (2 Macc. 4[7-14]).

This "place of exercise"—Luther even translated it as a "gaming-house"—was nothing more or less than a stadium. Why then so much excitement over a sports ground? Gymnastics in Jerusalem—discus throwers and sprinters in the holy city—it sounds perhaps unusually progressive, but why should Yahweh be displeased at it, how could a High Priest be denounced as ungodly on that account?

Between the method of playing games today and playing games in those days there is a slight but very essential difference. It has nothing to do with the exercises themselves, which have remained practically the same for over 2,000 years. The difference lies in dress. True to the Olympic pattern, games were played completely naked. The body could only be "covered" with a thin coat of oil!

Nakedness itself must have been regarded by all orthodox believers in Judah as a challenge. They firmly believed in the corruption of human nature from youth onwards and in the sinfulness of the body. It is impossible that athletics in full view of the Temple, only a few steps from the Holy of Holies, should not have been regarded as an outrageous insult or that it should not have given rise to vigorous opposition. According to contemporary sources the High Priest, Jason, had located the stadium in the heart of Jerusalem, in the valley[1] which bordered the Temple hill.

But that was not the end of the scandal. It was not long before Jewish athletes were guilty of a serious crime against the Law, they "made themselves uncircumcised" (1 Macc. 1[15]).

The Greek conception of beauty and the circumcision of Jewish athletes displayed in full view of the public eye were two irreconcilable things. Jewish teams—not in Jerusalem among their own people naturally—met with scorn and ridicule, and even aversion, as soon as they appeared in contests away from home. The Bible speaks of "the game that ... every fifth year was kept at Tyrus" (2 Macc. 4[18]), although this does not refer to a Jewish team but to a ceremonial delegation whose duty was confined to the presentation of gifts.

Many of them must have suffered so much from the disgust which they encountered that they sought a remedy. Other translations refer to a surgical operation which restored the natural state (see Kautzsch on 1 Macc. 1[15]).

Nakedness had come for a second time to be Judah's great temptation. Nakedness had been the outstanding characteristic of the fertility goddesses of Canaan, nakedness was now paraded by the athletes in the sports grounds which had sprung up all over the country. In those days a much deeper significance was attached to athletics than to sport in the modern sense. They were religious exercises, dedicated to the foreign Greek gods Zeus and Apollo. The reaction of orthodox Judaism to this revival of a real threat to their religion could only be uncompromising.

Their new overlords, the Seleucids, gave them all too soon every reason to be so.

[1] Josephus calls it the "Tyropoeon"—"(Valley) of the cheesemakers".

CHAPTER 34

THE BATTLE FOR RELIGIOUS LIBERTY

Tax official plunders Jerusalem—Worship of Zeus in the Temple—The revolt of the Maccabees—The Battle of the Elephants at Bethlehem—Americans find Beth-Zur—Coins from Antioch among the rubble—Canteen supplies from Rhodes—Pompey storms Jerusalem—Judah becomes a Roman province.

> "And taking the holy vessels with polluted hands, and with profane hands putting down the things that were dedicated by other kings to the augmentation and glory and honour of the place he gave them away" (2 Macc. 5¹⁶).

KING ANTIOCHUS IV,[1] called Epiphanes, plundered and desecrated the Temple in Jerusalem in 168 B.C. Plundering temples was his speciality, so his contemporaries tell us. Polybius, the Greek historian, observed in his forty-volume "History of the World" that Antiochus IV had "despoiled most sanctuaries".

However, the treasures of the Temple were not enough for the Seleucid king. He sent in addition his chief tax collector Apollonius with an armed force to Jerusalem. This man, "when he had taken the spoils of the city, [he] set it on fire, and pulled down the houses and walls thereof on every side. But the women and children took they captive, and possessed the cattle" (1 Macc. 1²⁹⁻³²; 2 Macc. 5²⁴ᶠᶠ).

Throughout the chances and changes of its history Israel had been spared none of the horror and ignominy which could befall a nation. But never before, neither under the Assyrians nor under the Babylonians, had it received such a blow as the edict issued by Antiochus Epiphanes by which he hoped to crush and destroy the faith of Israel.

> "And the king sent letters by the hand of messengers unto Jerusalem and the cities of Judah, that they should follow laws strange to the land" (1 Macc. 1⁴⁴).

The worship of Olympian Zeus was set up in the Temple of Yahweh. For taking part in any Jewish religious ceremonies, the traditional sacrifices, the sabbath or circumcision, the penalty was death. The holy scriptures were destroyed. This was the first thoroughgoing religious persecution in history.

But Israel gave the world an example of how a nation that refuses to

[1] 175–163 B.C.

be untrue to itself can and must react to a violation of its conscience of this kind.

There were of course even in those days weak characters who chose the way of least resistance. Nevertheless many "... chose rather to die, that they might not be defiled ..." (1 Macc. 1[63]). But it was the resolute and fervent faith of an old man which first kindled the torch of revolt in the land.

Modin was the name of a small village, 20 miles from Jerusalem on the western fringe of the highlands of Judah. Today it is the market town of el-Medieh. Here lived the priest Mattathias with his five sons. When Antiochus' officers came to Modin to force the inhabitants to "forsake the law", to offer sacrifices and to burn incense, Mattathias steadfastly refused to obey the order, and when he saw one of his countrymen offering a sacrifice he could not "forbear to show his anger according to judgement: wherefore he ran and slew him upon the altar. Also the king's commissioner, who compelled men to sacrifice, he killed at that time, and the altar he pulled down" (1 Macc. 2[1-25]). This act was the signal for open resistance, for a life and death struggle for religious freedom—the "Wars of the Maccabees".

Mattathias and his sons escaped. In their secret haunts in the mountains and in caves they gathered round them a band of those who shared their beliefs and with their assistance waged bitter guerrilla warfare against the occupying power. After the death of the old priest his son Judas, whose surname was Maccabaeus,[1] became the leader.

It was in the highlands of Judah that the rebels achieved their first successes. Their achievements were indeed remarkable. This small untrained and badly equipped band mastered the well-drilled and numerically superior occupation troops. Beth-Horon, Emmaus and Beth-Zur were captured. The Seleucids had to retreat until reinforcements arrived from Antioch. Judas Maccabaeus liberated Jerusalem in 164 B.C. and restored the old order in the Temple. The altar was rebuilt and sacrifices to Yahweh were offered as in former times (1 Macc. 4[36ff]).

In the course of military expeditions which took him more and more across the frontiers of the province of Judah, Judas Maccabaeus entered Galilee and Transjordan and wherever there were Israelites who remained true to the old faith. On the way to Idumaea, the old town of Hebron in Southern Judah was besieged and destroyed. This continuing good fortune of Judas Maccabaeus in battle compelled king Antiochus V Eupator,[2] son of Epiphanes, to intervene with a large armed force. In the decisive battle, which took place a few miles south-west of Bethlehem near Beth-Zachariah,[3] the Seleucids employed elephants, flanked by detachments of cavalry. The Maccabeans were unable to cope with this colossal superiority and were

---

[1] i.e. "Hammer". [2] 163–162 B.C. [3] Now Bet-Iskarje.

defeated. Dissension amongst themselves drove the victors to make peace with surprisingly favourable terms for the vanquished. The decrees of Antiochus IV Epiphanes of 167 B.C. were rescinded, liberty of worship was guaranteed and the religious community at Jerusalem was once more recognised (1 Macc. [30ff,58ff]).

The aims of the Jewish rebellion had been achieved.

Not content with that, the Maccabees wanted political independence as well as freedom of religion. The successors of Judas Maccabaeus, his brothers Jonathan and Simon, began the struggle anew. It ended in 142 B.C. under Simon, with Syria granting them also political freedom (1 Macc. 15[1ff]).

A fortress which was in the midst of the struggle and changed hands several times was Beth-Zur.[1] The results of excavation correspond to the historical circumstances described in the first book of the Maccabees.

"Khirbet et-Tubeka" is the modern name of this once hotly contested spot. It controls the old road from Jerusalem to Hebron on the frontier between Judah and Idumaea which lies to the south of it. In 1931 the American archaeologist W. F. Albright and O. P. Sellers found here a large collection of coins. One hundred and twenty-six out of a total of over 300 were stamped with the names of Antiochus Epiphanes and Antiochus Eupator.

FIG. 69

The hill still bears the foundations of a powerful fortress in which three stages of construction can be clearly distinguished. Only fragments remain of the lowest and oldest. They date from Persian times. The next stage above it is of oriental character. This is the work of Judas Maccabaeus dating from the first period of his successful revolt. "And they set there a garrison to keep it, and fortified Bethsura to preserve it: that the people might have a defence against Idumaea" (1 Macc. 4[61]).

After the Battle of the Elephants near Beth-Zachariah, Antiochus V

[1] Or Beth-Sur.

Eupator occupied this border fortress: "So the king took Bethsura, and set a garrison there to keep it" (1 Macc. 6⁵⁰).

The troops of the Seleucids likewise have left unmistakable traces of their stay. As the archaeologists were able to establish, these consisted of relics of their catering arrangements, which were found among the ruins of the walls erected by Judas Maccabaeus. Part of the rations of these soldiers was wine of excellent quality from the hills of Greece. From the handles of the jars, which lay about among the mass of broken earthenware, Albright and Sellers were even able to tell where the wine came from. A wine merchant in Rhodes must have been the army's principal supplier.

That was in 162 B.C. A year later the Seleucids fortified Beth-Zur anew. A new citadel, with characteristic Hellenistic masonry, arose upon the ruined Maccabean walls. Their general Bacchides "repaired the strong cities in Judah. . . . He fortified also the city Bethsura . . . and put forces in them and provision of victuals" (1 Macc. 9⁵⁰,⁵²).

The Biblical record ends with the murder of Simon, brother of Judas Maccabaeus. The spiritual and political leadership of Judas was transferred, with the office of High Priest, to Simon's son John. He was called John Hyrcanus. "John, the High Priest, and the Jewish people" and "John the High Priest, Head of the Jewish people" are the inscriptions on coins which he had minted and which have since been found.

We are indebted to Flavius Josephus' careful account of the history of the period for accurate information about this Maccabean and his successors.[1] By dint of incessant and purposeful fighting the frontiers of Judah were extended farther and farther. Under Alexander Jannaeus[2] they enlarged their territories until they almost covered the area previously occupied by the kingdoms of Israel and Judah.

As time went on the Seleucids became less and less serious adversaries. They lacked the strength to cope with the Maccabeans when Rome—now, having overthrown Hannibal of Carthage,[3] undisputed mistress of the Western Mediterranean—had expanded its sovereignty beyond Greece into Asia Minor.

Pompey, the Roman general, marched through the kingdom of the Seleucids into Palestine. After a three months' siege Roman legions entered Jerusalem in 63 B.C. Judah became a Roman province.

With this event the political independence of Israel came to an abrupt end.

---

[1] Josephus calls them "Hasmoneans" from the name of their ancestor the father of Mattathias ("Wars of the Jews", I, 1. 3).
[2] 103–76 B.C.   [3] At the battle of Zama in 202 B.C.

DIGGING UP THE NEW TESTAMENT

I
Jesus of Nazareth

CHAPTER 35

PALESTINE ON MARE NOSTRUM

A Province of the Roman Empire—Greek cities on the Jordan—The New Testament—The governor appears in history—A census every fourteen years.

"But when the fulness of the time was come God sent forth his son...." (Gal. 4[4]).

In the wide circle of countries which surround Mare Nostrum,[1] from North Africa and Spain to the shores of Asia Minor, the will of Rome, now mistress of the world, reigned supreme. After the disappearance of the great Semitic empires of the "Fertile Crescent", Palestine was drawn into the new world and shared its destinies. Roman occupation troops enforced the will of Rome in a land which was ruled and exploited by men who were likewise nominees of Rome.

Life in the Roman Empire took on more and more the stamp of Greece: Roman civilisation was to a large extent Greek civilisation: Greek was the world language which united all the subject peoples of the East.

Anyone wandering through Palestine at the turn of the eras might have imagined he was in Greece. Across the Jordan lay out and out Greek cities. The "Ten Cities"[2] of the gospels (Matt. 4[25]; Mk. 5[20]) took Athens as their model: they had temples which were sacred to Zeus and Artemis, they had their theatre, their pillared forum, their stadium, their gymnasium and their baths. Greek in architecture as well as in the habits of their citizens were likewise Caesarea, the seat of Pilate's government, which lay on the Mediterranean south of Carmel, Sepphoris and Tiberias, which lay a few miles north of Nazareth on the Lake of Galilee, Caesarea Philippi, built at the foot of Hermon, and likewise Jericho. Only the many small towns and villages in Galilee, as in Judah, had retained their Jewish style of architecture. It was in these genuine Jewish communities that Jesus lived and worked, and nowhere do the Gospel writers speak of his ever having lived *in* one of the Greek cities but only in their neighbourhood (Mark 7[31]).

Nevertheless Greek dress and much of the Greek way of life had long before Jesus' day penetrated into the purely Jewish communities.

[1] The Roman name for the Mediterranean.   [2] Greek: Dekapolis.

Natives of Galilee and Judah wore the same sort of clothes as were worn in Alexandria, Rome or Athens. These consisted of tunic and cloak, shoes or sandals, with a hat or a cap as head covering. Furniture included a bed and the Greek habit of reclining at meals was generally adopted.

The Old Testament covers a period of nearly 1,200 years if we reckon from the Exodus from Egypt under Moses, or nearly 2,000 years if we reckon from the time of the patriarchs. The New Testament on the other hand covers a period of less than 100 years. From the beginning of the ministry of Jesus to the end of the Acts of the Apostles is only a little more than thirty years. The Old Testament largely reflects the varied history of the people of Israel; the New Testament is concerned with the life and sayings of a few individuals: it revolves exclusively round the teaching of Jesus, round his disciples and the apostles.

Archaeology cannot produce extensive evidence from the world of the New Testament. For the life of Christ offers nothing that would leave any material traces on this earth: neither royal palaces nor temples, neither victorious campaigns nor burnt cities and country-sides. Jesus was essentially a man of peace, he taught the Word of God. Archaeologists have recognised their task to be that of reconstructing his environment and rediscovering the villages and cities where he lived, worked and died. Yet for this purpose they have been given a unique guide. No event out of the whole of Graeco-Roman history, no manuscript of any classical author has come down to posterity in anything like so many ancient copies as the scriptures of the New Testament. They can be numbered in thousands, and the oldest and most venerable among them are only a few decades removed from the time of Christ.

A manuscript containing part of St. John's Gospel, for example, the famous Papyrus Bodmer II, comes from the time of Trajan, the Roman emperor who reigned from A.D. 98–117. This precious document in Greek script, so far probably the oldest New Testament writing, was discovered by a lucky chance in Egypt in 1935.

> "And it came to pass in those days that there went out a decree from Caesar Augustus that all the world should be taxed. (And this taxing was first made when Cyrenius was governor of Syria.) And all went to be taxed every one into his own city. And Joseph also went up from Galilee, out of the city of Nazareth, into Judaea, unto the city of David, which is called Bethlehem (because he was of the house and lineage of David) to be taxed with Mary his espoused wife ..." (Luke 2$^{1-5}$).

The census is by no means the invention of modern statisticians. Practised in ancient times, it fulfilled then as now two extremely reasonable purposes. It provided the relevant information firstly for calling up men for military service and secondly for taxation purposes. In subject countries it was the second of these that mostly concerned the Romans.

Without exacting tribute from its foreign possessions, Rome would never have been able on the strength of its own resources to afford the luxury of its much admired magnificent buildings and pleasances, its extravagant way of living, or its expensive system of administering its empire. Roman emperors were able to guarantee their people "Panem et Circenses", "bread and circuses", on a grand scale at no cost to themselves. Egypt had to provide the corn for the free bread. And the great arenas for the games were built by slaves with money derived from tribute.

The census, which was its official name in Rome, was originally held every five years. This five year period even entered the literature of Rome as the "lustrum" and this word enjoyed great favour among Roman writers and in formal speech. Changes in the economy as well as in the constitution, the introduction of immunity from taxation for Roman citizens and the troubles of the later Republican period led to the gradual abandonment of the census. Especially in the later Republican period there was no longer any question of a regular five yearly census. It is true that Augustus revived the census, particularly in the provinces, but even he did not reintroduce it on the old five year basis. It is important to remember this for the dating of the birth of Jesus depends upon it to some extent.

"Cyrenius the governor" was the senator P. Sulpicius Quirinius, who is otherwise known to us from Roman documents. The Emperor Augustus rated highly the outstanding ability of this social climber both as soldier and administrator. He was born in modest circumstances near Tusculum in the Alban hills, a place which was reckoned among the favourite resorts of the noble Roman families.

In A.D. 6 Quirinius went as legate to Syria. Coponius was sent with him from Rome to be the first Procurator of Judaea. Between A.D. 6 and 7 they carried out a census. Can this refer, however, to the census mentioned by St. Luke? In the first place, Luke speaks of an Imperial decree "that all the world should be taxed", i.e. the whole Roman empire. But the census taken in the years 6 and 7 A.D. was merely a provincial one and, secondly, Jesus would then have been born around 7 or 6 B.C. as many believe. According to the Biblical account, the census decreed by Caesar Augustus took place about the year Christ was born. There is no record of a general census throughout the empire in the years 7 and 6 B.C.

Is it possible that St. Luke made a mistake?

For a long time it seemed as if he had. It was only when a fragment of a Roman inscription was discovered at Antioch that the surprising fact emerged that Quirinius had been in Syria once before on a mission from the Emperor Augustus in the days of Saturninus the pro-consul.

At that time his assignment had been purely military. He led a campaign against the Homonadenses, a tribe in the Taurus mountains in Asia Minor. Quirinius established his seat of government as well as his headquarters in Syria between 10 and 7 B.C.

CHAPTER 36

THE STAR OF BETHLEHEM

A suggestion by Origen—Halley's comet over China—Kepler's observations in Prague—Astronomical tablets found at Sippar—Babylonian astronomers' records—Modern astronomical calculations—December frost in Bethlehem.

"Now when Jesus was born in Bethlehem of Judaea, in the days of Herod the king, behold, there came wise men from the east to Jerusalem, saying, Where is he that is born king of the Jews? for we have seen his star in the east, and are come to worship him" (Matt. 2[1,2]).

INTERNATIONAL expeditions of astronomers have been regarded as a matter of course for a long time now. Scientists from all countries, laden with special instruments and measuring apparatus, stream into every corner of the globe when there is a total eclipse or some other important astronomical phenomenon to be observed.

For centuries St. Matthew's story of the Messianic star has exercised men's imaginations. Laymen and experts alike have aired their views on the subject and these have found expression in a considerable volume of literature. Anything that has ever moved across the canopy of heaven, as well as much that has only existed in men's imaginations, has been dubbed the "Star of Bethlehem".

That this is a case of a phenomenon in the sky of quite an unusual type is indicated by the Bible in unmistakable terms. Astronomers are the experts in these matters of heavenly phenomena and we should therefore expect from them an explanation which would fit in with modern scientific knowledge.

If we think of a sudden bright light in the sky, we can only reckon with two types, apart from shooting stars: either a comet or an exploding star, technically known as a "nova".

Conjectures of this kind were expressed in early times. Origen, one of the Christian Fathers, who lived in Alexandria about A.D. 200, wrote as follows: "I am of the opinion that the star which appeared to the Wise Men in the east was a new star which had nothing in common with those stars which appear either in the firmament or in the lower levels of the atmosphere. Presumably it belonged to the category of these heavenly fires which appear from time to time and have been given names by the Greeks depending on their shape, either comets, or fiery beams, or starry hosts, or starry tails, or vessels or some such name." Bright comets, with tails often stretching half across the sky, have always made a deep impression on men's minds. They were held to portend special events. Is it surprising that this most magnificent of all stellar spectacles should be associated with the idea of the star of the Wise Men of the East? Artists seized upon this attractive motif: in many popular representations of the crib in pictures of the birth of Christ a radiant comet shines over the manger bed of Bethlehem.

Excavations and ancient writings which have come to light have produced astonishingly detailed information about astronomical occurrences stretching back over thousands of years. We now possess notes and observations from Greek, Roman, Babylonian, Egyptian and Chinese sources.

After the assassination of Caesar, shortly after the Ides of March in 44 B.C., a brilliant comet was seen. Seventeen years before the turn of the eras, another extremely bright comet appeared suddenly, and was observed for a whole night in Mediterranean countries. The next dazzling comet to be reported was in the year A.D. 66, shortly before Nero committed suicide.

Between these two there is another account with most precise details, this time from Chinese astronomers. Their observations are recorded in the Wen-hien-thung-khao encyclopaedia of the Chinese scholar Ma Tuan-lin: "In the first year of [the Emperor] Yuen-yen, in the 7th month, on the day Sin-ouei [25 August] a comet was seen in the region of the sky known as Toung-tsing [beside the Mu of the Gemini]. It passed over the Ou-tschoui-heou [Gemini], proceeded from the Ho-su [Castor and Pollux] in a northerly direction and then into the group of Hien-youen [the head of Leo] and into the house of Thaiouei [tail of Leo].... On the 56th day it disappeared with the Blue Dragon [Scorpio]. Altogether the comet was observed for 63 days."

This very full account from ancient Chinese sources contains the first description of the famous Halley's comet, that great trailing star which always reappears close to the sun after an interval of seventy-six years. The last time it was seen was between 1909 and 1911. The strange display will be seen again in 1986. For the comet keeps to a strict time schedule on its tremendous elliptical course through space. But it is not always visible and not equally visible everywhere. Thus in the year 12 B.C in China it was an astral phenomenon which could be accurately observed in all its phases. Whereas in the Mediterranean countries, in Mesopotamia and Egypt, there is no mention whatever at that time of a heavenly body of such striking and impressive brilliance.

The same is true of "new stars". These "Novae" are constellations in space which suddenly burst asunder in an atomic explosion of colossal magnitude. Their radiance, which outshines the light of all other stars, is so noticeable and so unusual that it is always remarked upon. About the turn of the eras the blazing light of a new star is only twice mentioned, in 134 B.C. and A.D. 173. None of the old sources and traditions says anything about a bright comet or a new star in the Mediterranean world about the year A.D. I.

Shortly before Christmas 1603, on December 17th, the Imperial Mathematician and Astronomer Royal Johannes Kepler was sitting through the night high above the Moldava in the Hradçyn in Prague, observing with his modest telescope the approach of two planets. "Conjunction" is the technical name for the position of two celestial bodies on the same degree of longitude. Sometimes two planets move so close to one another that they have the appearance of a single larger and more brilliant star. That night Saturn and Jupiter had a rendezvous in space within the constellation of Pisces.

Looking through his notes later Kepler suddenly remembered something he had read in the rab-
binic writer Abarbanel, referring to an unusual influence which Jewish astrologers were said to

FIG. 70.—Conjunction of Mercury, Jupiter and Saturn in December 1603 according to Kepler.

have ascribed to this same constellation. Messiah would appear when there was a conjunction of Saturn and Jupiter in the constellation of Pisces.

Could it have been the same conjunction at the time of the birth of Christ as Kepler had observed at Christmastide in 1603? Had it announced, as Kepler wrote later, the coming of the real "Star of Bethlehem"? Or was this constellation perhaps itself the "Christmas Star" as some people believed at a still later date with Kepler as their authority?

Kepler checked his calculations again and again. He was a mixture of scholar and quack, astronomer and astrologer, a disciple of those doctrines which had been put in the same class as mixing poisons as far back as the Code of Justinian. The result was a three-fold conjunction within the space of a year. Astronomical calculations gave the year as 7 B.C. According to astrological tables it must have been 6 B.C. Kepler decided in favour of 6 B.C. and dated the conception of Mary consequently 7 B.C.

His fascinating discovery was published in a number of books, but this enlightened genius who established the planetary laws named after him eventually steeped himself overmuch in the realm of mysticism. Consequently Kepler's hypotheses were for a long time rejected and finally disregarded. It was not until the 19th century that astronomers remembered them again.

Finally in 1925 the German scholar P. Schnabel deciphered the "papers" in Neo-Babylonian cuneiform of a famous professional institute in the ancient world, the School of Astrology at Sippar in Babylonia. Among endless series of prosaic dates of observations he came across a note about the position of the planets in the constellation of Pisces. Jupiter and Saturn are carefully marked in over a period of five months. Reckoned in our calendar the year was 7 B.C.!

Archaeologists and historians have to reconstruct their picture of a bygone age with enormous effort, from monuments and documents, from individual discoveries and broken fragments. It is simpler for the modern astronomer. He can turn back the cosmic clock at will. In his planetarium he can arrange the starry sky exactly as it was thousands of years ago for any given year, any month, even any day. The position of the stars can be calculated backwards with equal precision.

In the year 7 B.C. Jupiter and Saturn did in fact meet in Pisces and, as Kepler had already discovered, they met three times. Mathematical

FIG. 71.—Third conjunction of Jupiter and Saturn on December 4th in 7 B.C. in the constellation of Pisces.

calculations established further that this threefold conjunction of the planets was particularly clearly visible in the Mediterranean area.

The time-table of this planetary encounter when it is presented in the prosaic dating system of modern astronomical calculations looks something like this:

About the end of February in 7 B.C. the clustering began. Jupiter moved out of the constellation Aquarius towards Saturn in the constellation of Pisces. Since the sun at that time was also in the sign of Pisces its light covered the constellation. It was not until April 12th that both planets rose in Pisces heliacally with a difference of 8 degrees of longitude. "Heliacal" is the word used by astronomers to indicate the first visible rising of a star at daybreak.

On May 29th, visible for fully two hours in the morning sky, the first close encounter took place in the 21st degree of Pisces with a difference of 0 degrees of longitude and of 0·98 degrees of latitude.

The second conjunction took place on October 3rd in the 18th degree of the constellation of Pisces.

On December 4th for the third and last time a close encounter of the planets Jupiter and Saturn took place. This time it was in the 16th degree of Pisces. At the end of January in the year 6 B.C. the planet Jupiter moved out of Pisces into Aries.

"We have seen his star in the east" (Matt. 2²), said the Wise Men, according to the A.V. The translation is however incorrect, for the words "in the east" are in the original "En té anatolé"—the Greek singular—but elsewhere "the east" is represented by "anatolai" —the Greek plural. The singular form "anatolé" has, it is maintained, quite a special astronomical significance, in that it implies the observation of the early rising of the star, the so-called heliacal rising. The translators of the Authorised Version could not have known this.

When "en té anatolé" is translated properly, Matt. 2² reads as follows:

"We have seen his star appear in the first rays of dawn." That would have corresponded exactly with the astronomical facts, if the constellation under discussion, and this, of course, is the big question, was the Star of the Wise Men, the Star of Bethlehem, the Christmas Star. Perhaps the following considerations will help us.

But why this ancient learned expedition of the three Wise Men to Palestine when, as we know, they could see the occurrence just as well in Babylon?

The skygazers of the east in their capacity as astrologers attached a special significance to each star. According to the Chaldeans, Pisces was the sign of the West, the Mediterranean countries: in Jewish tradition it was the sign of Israel, the sign of the Messiah. The constellation of Pisces stood at the end of the sun's old course and at the beginning of its new one. What is more likely than that they saw in it the sign of the end of an old age and the start of a new one?

Jupiter was always thought of by all nations as a lucky star and a royal star. According to old Jewish tradition Saturn was supposed to protect Israel: Tacitus equates him with the god of the Jews. Babylonian astrology reckoned the ringed planet to be the special star of the neighbouring lands of Syria and Palestine.

Since Nebuchadnezzar's time many thousands of Jews had lived in Babylon. Many of them may have studied at the School of Astrology in Sippar. This wonderful encounter of Jupiter with Saturn, guardian of Israel, in the constellation of the "west country", of the Messiah, must have deeply moved the Jewish astrologers. For according to astrological ways of thinking it pointed to the appearance of a mighty king in the west country, the land of their fathers. To experience that in person, to see it with their own eyes, that was the reason for the journey of the wise astronomers from the East.

This is what may have happened: on May 29th in the year 7 B.C. they observed the first encounter of the two planets from the roof of the School of Astrology at Sippar. At that time of year the heat was already unbearable in Mesopotamia. Summer is no time for long and difficult journeys. Besides that, they knew about the second conjunction on October 3rd. They could predict this encounter in advance as accurately as future eclipses of the sun and moon. The fact that October 3rd was the Jewish Day of Atonement may have been taken as an admonition, and at that point they may have started out on their journey.

Travel on the caravan routes even on camels, the swiftest means of transport, was a leisurely affair. If we think in terms of a journey lasting about six weeks, the Wise Men would arrive in Jerusalem towards the end of November.

"Where is he that is born King of the Jews? for we have seen his star in the east, and are come to worship him." "When Herod the king had heard these things, he was troubled, and all Jerusalem with him" (Matt. 2$^{2-3}$). For these Eastern astronomers that must have been the first and obvious question, which would however arouse nothing but startled concern in Jerusalem. They knew nothing about schools of astrology in the Holy City.

Herod, the hated tyrant, was alarmed. The announcement of a new-born king brought his sovereignty into question. The people on the other hand were pleasurably startled, as appears from other historical sources. About a year after this conjunction of planets which has just been described, a strong Messianic movement came into being. Flavius Josephus, the Jewish historian, records that about this time a rumour went around that God had decided to bring the rule of the Roman foreigners to an end and that a sign from heaven had announced the coming of a Jewish king. Herod, who had been appointed by the Romans, was in fact not a Jew but an Idumaean.

Herod did not hesitate. He "gathered all the chief priests and scribes of the people together" and "demanded of them where Christ should be born". They searched through the ancient sacred scriptures of the nation and found the allusion which is contained in the book of the prophet Micah, who had lived 700 years before in the kingdom of Judah: "But thou, Bethlehem Ephratah, though thou be little among the thousands of Judah, yet out of thee shall he come forth unto me that is to be ruler in Israel ..." (Micah 5^2).

Herod therefore summoned the Wise Men and "sent them to Bethlehem" (Matt. 2$^{4-8}$). Since Jupiter and Saturn came together for the third time in the constellation of Pisces on the 4th December, "they rejoiced with exceeding great joy" and set out for Bethlehem "and lo, the star, which they saw in the east, went before them" (Matt. 2^{10,9}).

On the road to Hebron, 5 miles from Jerusalem, lies the village of "Bet Lahm", which was the old Bethlehem of Judah. The ancient highway, which Abraham had once passed along, lay almost due north and south. At their third conjunction the planets Jupiter and Saturn appeared to have dissolved into one great brilliant star. In the twilight of the evening they were visible in a southerly direction, so that the Wise Men of the East on their way from Jerusalem to Bethlehem had the bright star in front of their eyes all the time. As the gospel says, the star actually "went before them".

Every year millions of people all over the world hear the story of the Wise Men of the East. "Star of Bethlehem", a symbol which is always associated with Christmas, impinges on life in other ways. In biographical dictionaries and on tombstones it has its place beside the date of birth.

Christendom celebrates Christmas from December 24–25. Astronomers and historians, secular and ecclesiastical, are however unanimous that December 25 of the year one was not the authentic date of the birth of Christ, neither as regards the year nor the day. The responsibility for this lies at the door of the Scythian monk Dionysius Exiguus, who made several mistakes and miscalculations. He lived in Rome, and in the year 533 he was instructed to fix the beginning of the new era by working backwards. But he forgot the year zero which should have been inserted between 1 B.C. and A.D. 1. He also overlooked the four years when the Roman emperor Augustus had reigned under his own name Octavian.

The Biblical tradition gives us this clear indication: "Now when Jesus was born in Bethlehem of Judaea, in the days of Herod the king …" (Matt, 2¹). We know from numerous contemporary sources who Herod was and when he lived and reigned. In 40 B.C. Herod was designated king of Judaea by the Romans. His reign ended with his death in 4 B.C. Jesus must therefore have been born before 4 B.C. if Matthew's statement is correct.

December 25 is referred to in documents as Christmas Day in A.D. 354 for the first time. Under the Roman emperor Justinian[1] it was recognised as an official holiday. An old Roman festival played a major part in the choice of this particular day. December 25 in ancient Rome was the "Dies Natalis Invicti", "the birthday of the unconquered", the day of the winter solstice and at the same time, in Rome, the last day of the Saturnalia, which had long since degenerated into a week of unbridled carnival, and therefore a time when the Christians could feel most safe from persecution.

Meteorologists as well as historians and astronomers have something of importance to contribute to this question of fixing the date of the birth of Jesus. According to St. Luke: "And there were in the same country shepherds abiding in the field, keeping watch over their flock by night" (Luke 2⁸).

Meteorologists have made exact recordings of the temperature at Hebron. This spot in the southern part of the highlands of Judah exhibits the same climatic conditions as Bethlehem, which is not far distant. The temperature readings show over a period of three months that the incidence of frost is as follows: December—2·8°; January—1·6°; February—0·1°. The first two months have also the greatest rainfall in the year: approximately 6 inches in December, and nearly 8 inches in January. According to all existing information the climate of Palestine has not changed appreciably in the last 2,000 years,

[1] A.D. 527–565.

consequently modern accurate meteorological observations can be taken as a basis.

At Christmas-time Bethlehem is in the grip of frost, and in the Promised Land no cattle would have been in the fields in that temperature. This fact is borne out by a remark in the Talmud to the effect that in that neighbourhood the flocks were put out to grass in March and brought in again at the beginning of November. They remained out in the open for almost eight months.

Around Christmas-time nowadays both animals and shepherds are under cover in Palestine.

What St. Luke tells us points therefore to the birth of Jesus as having taken place before the onset of winter, and the description of the brilliant star in St. Matthew's gospel points to the year 7 B.C.

In recent years, several publications dealing with the life of Christ have appeared. They have attracted a good deal of attention although some of them are not from the pens of professional Biblical specialists. We cannot merely disregard them, as some of them provide us with thoroughly prepared collections of material while also presenting us with a reliable assessment of the opinions of the specialists. These publications have not actually produced any new facts, although they have sometimes shed new light on already published material. Yet, in fact, this new light is not really new, for these views have for long been under discussion among the experts. The public has been made aware of these questions, however, by these publications and this is a sufficient reason for not neglecting them.

It will probably not be generally realised that Johannes Kepler himself did not consider the conjunction of the planets Mercury, Jupiter and Saturn, which he had calculated, as the actual "Star of Bethlehem", the "Christmas Star", but merely as its forerunner. For his part he still remained convinced that Jesus was born *later* and not as early as 7 or 6 B.C. Of course, nobody can guarantee that in the days of Jesus people saw any connection between him and the heavenly phenomenon calculated by Kepler and observed in Babylon. Everything else that can be deduced and has actually been deduced from this heavenly phenomenon and from the fact that it was also noticed in Mesopotamia may indeed be very ingenious, but it remains mere speculation, however brilliant, which in itself lacks all conclusiveness and would require convincing proof in order to be unreservedly accepted as correct.

For the problem of the "assessment" mentioned in Luke 2$^{1-5}$ still remains. It is a historical fact that it was made in the year 6/7 *after* Christ's birth, although with the reservation that during the year in question no general census throughout the empire was made, as Luke asserts, but merely a limited provincial one.

In consequence of all these facts and considerations, the views expressed today in regard to the date of the birth of Jesus are much more restrained than was the case a few years ago. The period between the year 7 B.C. (if Kepler's conjunction of planets is to be connected in any way with the birth of Jesus) and the year A.D. 7 (on account of the population census by Quirinius) is the time span in question. Jesus must have been born during this period. It is not possible today to be more specific ...

One thing is remarkable. Towards the end of Herod's reign, about the year 6 B.C., a Messianic dispute between Herod, who regarded himself as a kind of Messiah, and the Pharisees who had other notions about the Messiah, became so acute that the Pharisees predicted Herod's early death, whereupon Herod had the ringleaders executed. This was about the time of Kepler's conjunction of the planets. We naturally do not know whether there were people who believed in the stars and who actually ascribed some Messianic interpretation to this conjunction and whether it was this, among other things, which inflamed people's minds and feelings. That would, however, be a possibility. It would also be possible that the action taken by Herod against his opponents in the Messianic quarrel was the reason why the Evangelist Matthew portrays Herod as a pitiless persecutor of the Messiah who did not even shrink from the Massacre of the Innocents at Bethlehem (Matthew 2[16]).

CHAPTER 37

NAZARETH IN GALILEE

Death of King Herod—"The most cruel tyrant"—Unrest in the land—Checking Jerusalem's finances—Sabinus steals the Temple treasures—Varus crucifies 2,000 Jews—"Nazarene" or "Nazarite"?

"But when Herod was dead, behold, an angel of the Lord appeareth in a dream to Joseph in Egypt, saying, Arise, and take the young child and his mother, and go into the land of Israel: for they are dead which sought the young child's life. . . . But when he heard that Archelaus did reign in Judaea in the room of his father Herod, he was afraid to go thither" (Matt. $2^{19, 20, 22}$).

HEROD died at the age of seventy in 4 B.C., thirty-six years after Rome had made him king. It is said that immediately after his death there occurred an eclipse of the moon which modern astronomers reckon to have happened on March 13th.

Flavius Josephus passes harsh judgement on him when he comes to write about Herod a few decades later: "He was no king but the most cruel tyrant who ever ascended the throne. He murdered a vast number of people and the lot of those he left alive was so miserable that the dead might count themselves fortunate. He not only tortured his subjects singly but ill treated whole communities. In order to beautify foreign cities he robbed his own, and made gifts to foreign nations which were paid for with Jewish blood. The result was that instead of their former prosperity and time honoured customs the people fell victim to utter poverty and demoralisation. Within a few years the Jews suffered more misery through Herod than their forefathers had done in the long period since they left Babylon and returned under Xerxes."

In thirty-six years hardly a day passed without someone being sentenced to death. Herod spared no one, neither his own family nor his closest friends, neither the priests nor least of all the people. On his list of victims stand the names of the two husbands of his sister Salome, his wife Mariamne and his sons Alexander and Aristobulus. He had his brother-in-law drowned in the Jordan and his mother-in-law Alexandra put out of the way. Two scholars who had torn down the golden Roman eagle from the gateway of the Temple were burned alive. Hyrcanus the last of the Hasmoneans was killed. Noble families were exterminated root and branch. Many of the Pharisees were done away with. Five days before his death the old man had his son Antipater assassinated. And that is only a fraction of the crimes of this man who "ruled like a wild beast".

The Massacre of the Innocents at Bethlehem, which the Bible lays at his door (Matt. 2^{16}), fits in perfectly with this revolting picture of his character.

After the murder of Antipater, Herod on his death bed made a will in which he nominated three of his younger sons as his successors. Archelaus was to succeed to the kingdom, Herod Antipas and Philip were to be tetrarchs, rulers of Galilee and Peraea, part of Transjordan, and the territory north-east of the Lake of Galilee. Archelaus was acknowledged as king by his family and was acclaimed by Herod's mercenaries—Germans, Gauls and Thracians. But throughout the country the news of the despot's death brought uprisings of a violence which had seldom been seen in Jewry. Their burning hatred of the house of Herod was mingled with their loathing of the Romans.

Instead of lamenting the death of Herod they proclaimed their grief over the deaths of his innocent victims. The people demanded that the learned Jehuda ben Saripha and Mattathias ben Margoloth, who had been burned like torches, should be atoned for. Archelaus replied by sending his troops to Jerusalem. Three thousand people were butchered on one day alone. The courts of the Temple were strewn with corpses. This first act of Archelaus revealed at one stroke the true character of the man—Herod's son yielded nothing to his father in cruelty and injustice.

However, the will had to be approved by the Emperor Augustus. Archelaus and Herod Antipas accordingly set out for Rome one after the other. At the same time fifty of the elders representing the people of Israel hastened to Augustus to beseech him to rid them of this "monarchy". In the absence of the Herodians the unrest assumed more serious proportions. As a security measure a Roman legion was despatched to Jerusalem. Right in the midst of this turmoil, as luck would have it, there arrived one of the hated Romans in the person of Sabinus, agent of the Imperial Treasury. Disregarding all warnings he took up his abode in Herod's palace and proceeded to audit the taxes and tribute of Judaea.

Masses of pilgrims were streaming into the Holy City for the Feast of Weeks. Bloody clashes ensued. Bitter fighting broke out in the Temple area. Stones were thrown at the Roman troops. They set fire to the arcades, then rushed into the Temple and pillaged all they could lay hands on. Sabinus himself relieved the Temple treasury of 400 talents. At which point he had to retreat precipitately to the palace and barricade himself in.

Revolt spread from Jerusalem through the country like wildfire. The royal palaces of Judaea were plundered and set ablaze. The governor of Syria hastened to the scene with a powerful Roman army strengthened with troops from Beirut and Arabia. As soon as the marching columns appeared in sight of Jerusalem the rebels fled. They were pursued and captured in droves.

Two thousand men were crucified.

The Roman governor of Syria who issued this order wrote his name in the history books through a decisive defeat which he suffered in A.D. 9. He was Quintilius Varus, who was posted from Syria to Germany, and lost the battle of the Teutoburgian Forest.

This was the terrifying situation when Joseph, on his way back from Egypt, "heard that Archelaus did reign in Judaea in the room of his father Herod". It was for this reason that "he was afraid to go thither".

King Herod is one of those figures in world history whom we know only from what their adversaries said about them. The impression created is correspondingly sinister. It is confirmed by the account of the Massacre of the Innocents at Bethlehem (Matthew 2[16]). At the same time, however, it must be remembered that we have here an example of the widespread literary motive of the chosen child, who for that very reason is exposed to danger—a motive that was attached to a number of prominent figures in antiquity, to Sargon of Akkad, Moses, Cyrus the Great and even to the Emperor Augustus as well as to such mythical characters as Oedipus whom his father Laius maimed and rejected.

We have consequently become much more cautious nowadays in regard to our views on the historicity of the Massacre of the Innocents at Bethlehem. Today we look upon the doubtful story rather as an attempt, prompted by the mentality of those days and using the methods current at the time, to emphasise the importance of Jesus. In so doing, matters such as the historicity of the measures taken by Herod in his quarrel with the Pharisees concerning the Messiah form an additional factor (cf. the end of the preceding chapter). Furthermore, the story of the Massacre of the Innocents linked Jesus with Moses who, as the Bible tells us, miraculously escaped from similar persecution by the Pharaoh of Egypt (Exodus 1[15]-2[10]). Herod's persecution of Jesus fits in very well with the flight of Joseph, Mary and the child to Egypt, for which the Evangelist gives as the real reason: ". . . that it might be fulfilled which was spoken of the Lord by the prophet, saying, Out of Egypt have I called my son (Matthew 2[15]. Cf. also Hosea 11[1]). This constitutes another reference to Moses whose name can mean "son" in Egyptian. On the other hand, there is absolutely no historical or archaeological proof of the flight to Egypt any more than there is for Jesus' stay in Nazareth.

Strictly speaking, the term "Nazarene" is capable of more than one interpretation. Although it means "man from Nazareth", there may also be a punning intention on the Hebrew word *nezer* which means "twig" or "rod" (cf. Isaiah 11[1]: ". . . a rod out of the stem of Jesse"). The word "Nazarene" occurs in Matthew in connection with a promise: "... that it might be fulfilled which was spoken by the prophets, He shall be called a Nazarene" (Matthew 2[23]). This does not make matters any easier, for to which words Matthew is referring, if not to the words quoted from Isaiah, is not clear. Perhaps a certain echo of the appellation *Nazarite* ("consecrated by or dedicated to God") is intended, although this presents certain philological difficulties. *Nazarite* is a descriptive term, earlier applied to Samson (Judges 13[5] and[7], also 16[17]) which demanded of him who claimed to be one, a certain asceticism, such as the observance of a number of taboos. Again there is uncertainty and it cannot be denied that more than one specialist considers the statements in the Gospels regarding the birth-place of Jesus as emanations from the fantasy of the Gospel writers who, not properly understanding the word, simply changed it to Nazarene. Mark Lidzbarski has even asserted that a place called Nazareth did not exist in the time of Jesus. It can be objected, however, even if we do not know what Nazareth was called in Jesus' day, that occupation of this spot, if by "occupation" we mean living in wretched caves, was continuous from about 900 B.C. to about A.D. 600, as has been shown by the unearthing of small objects among which are a number dating from the time of King Herod the Great (40 or 37–4 B.C.). The somewhat deprecatory words of Nathanael (John 1[46]): "Can there any good thing come out of Nazareth?" may well refer to the wretchedness of the place in those days, although the Bible calls it a "town". There is no reference to Jesus, Mary or Joseph. The spring in Nazareth where women still draw water in pitchers as they did in the time of Jesus is not on record under the name "Mary's spring or fountain" before the 11th century ...

CHAPTER 38

JOHN THE BAPTIST

The witness of Josephus—A forbidden marriage—Herod Antipas orders an arrest—The castle of Machaerus in Moab—The dungeon of death—Princess Salome—Capernaum "on the sea"—Ruins in a eucalyptus grove—The place where Jesus taught.

"Then cometh Jesus from Galilee to Jordan, unto John, to be baptised of him" (Matt. 3¹³).

THIS was the event which took Jesus for the first time from his Nazareth home. After the years of childhood and youth, about which we are told almost nothing, he stepped on to the stage for his public ministry. "And Jesus himself, when he began to teach, was about thirty years of age" (Luke 3²³—R.V.).

John preached and baptised in the Jordan valley south of Jericho, where the river is crossed by the well-known ford. He was therefore in the territory of Herod Antipas, the tetrarch appointed by Rome.

Apart from his baptism of Jesus, it is principally through his tragic end that John has become known throughout the world. He was beheaded.

Specialists are puzzled by many questions concerning him. What was his attitude towards the Essenes who left behind them the famous Dead Sea scrolls in Qumran? Was he perhaps a Nazarite, as the Old Testament calls the sort of person, like the hero Samson, who had dedicated himself entirely to God and as a sign of this observed certain taboos? And was he really the forerunner of Jesus as the New Testament describes him? What part did he play in the Messianic movements of his day? Did he consider himself, or did people consider him perhaps as a kind of Messiah? Was he perhaps, as has been suggested, a sort of rival to Jesus whom the Jesus tradition has appropriated and remodelled as the forerunner of Jesus?

Did the godly Baptist, who appears at the decisive turning point in Jesus' life, exist at all? His contemporary, Josephus, tells us that John was a high-minded man "who urged the Jews to strive towards perfection and exhorted them to deal justly with one another and walk humbly with God and to present themselves for baptism. As they flocked to him from all directions Herod Antipas began to be alarmed lest the influence of such a man might lead to disturbances. In conse-

338

quence of Herod's suspicions John was put in chains, sent to the castle of Machaerus and there beheaded."

"For Herod had laid hold on John, and bound him and put him in prison for Herodias' sake . . ." (Matt. 14[3]; Mark 6[17]; Luke 3[19]). According to the Gospels this was the reason for John's arrest. Josephus has some more background detail to offer:

In the course of a trip to Rome Herod Antipas, a son of Herod the Great got to know Herodias, his brother's wife, and was so much attracted by her that he ventured a proposal of marriage. Herodias agreed and brought with her into the marriage her daughter Salome.

According to Mosaic law marriage with a sister-in-law was forbidden and—according to the gospels—John the Baptist denounced it, an offence which in the eyes of the enraged Herodias could only be expiated by his death.

Josephus puts the event in a concrete historical setting, the castle of Machaerus, one of the numerous strongholds which Herod the Great had built in Palestine.

Machaerus, the place where John forfeited his life, lies in dark and rugged country on the east side of the Dead Sea. No road links this isolated spot with the outside world. Narrow paths lead up from the valley of the Jordan into the bare and desolate mountains of what was once Moab. In the deep wadis a few Bedouin families wander with their flocks over the scanty rough grass.

Not far from the river Arnon one lofty peak rises above the round humps of the other mountains. Its summit, which is swept by chill winds, is still crowned with ruins. "El Mashnaka", "The Hanging Palace", is what the Bedouins call this deserted place. This was the fortress of Machaerus. Far to the north can be seen with the naked eye the part of the Jordan valley where John baptised the people and where he was arrested.

So far no excavations have been carried out among the ruins of "El Mashnaka" and few have visited the lonely spot at all. Below the summit the rock-face is at one point hollowed out to a considerable depth. Narrow passages lead into a large vaulted chamber which from time to time provides shelter for nomads and their flocks when sudden storms take them by surprise among the mountains of Moab. From the carefully shaped walls it is obvious that this was once the castle dungeon. This gloomy vault sheltered John the Baptist after his arrest. It is probable that he was beheaded here, if the statement of Josephus is correct, for according to Mark 6[17ff] the execution evidently took place in Galilee, presumably in the new palace which had recently been constructed by Herod Antipas at Tiberias on the Lake of Galilee.

Anyone who has heard of the beheading of John associates automatically with it the name of Salome, and thinks at once of the daughter of Herodias who at her mother's behest is said to have asked for the head of John as a reward for her dancing. This Salome has taken her place in the literature of the world. Oscar Wilde wrote a play "Salome", Richard Strauss made the story of this Jewish princess the theme of his famous opera "Salome", even Hollywood has used the story of Salome as the subject of one of its epoch-making films.

But in the New Testament we may search in vain for the name of this princess. The Bible makes no mention of Salome. In the story of John the Baptist she is simply called the "daughter of Herodias" (Mark 6[22]).

It is Josephus who has told us the name of this "daughter of Herodias". A small coin has preserved her appearance for posterity. She is depicted on it with her husband Aristobulus. The coin bears the inscription "King Aristobulus–Queen Salome". Salome must have been still a girl when John the Baptist was beheaded—about nineteen years old.

> "Now when Jesus had heard that John was cast into prison he departed into Galilee: and leaving Nazareth, he came and dwelt in Capernaum, which is upon the sea coast, in the borders of Zabulon and Nephthalim" (Mat. 4[12, 13]).

During the short course of Jesus' ministry, which according to the evangelists Matthew, Mark and Luke cannot have lasted more than a year and a half, one place always takes priority. Matthew indeed on one occasion calls it "his own city" (Matt. 9[1]): Capernaum on the Lake of Galilee.

At the north end, not far from the spot where the fast running waters of the Jordan pour into the lake, the shore curves into a small bay. Out of the dark greenness of eucalyptus bushes comes a glint of white stone flags with four pillars rising out of them. Tufts of grass sprout from between the paving stones of the courtyard, shattered columns and blocks of basalt with carved ornamentation lie strewn around. All that remains of what was once the entrance are the broad steps of a staircase, the last remnants of a one-time splendid synagogue.

That is all that is left to bear witness to ancient Capernaum.

In 1916 the German archaeologists H. Kohl and C. Watzinger discovered hidden under rubble and overgrown with grass the fragmentary remains of this edifice. Franciscans rebuilt part of the old façade out of the ruins. The walls of the original building consisted of white limestone: on three sides it was surrounded by rows of tall pillars. The interior, measuring 80 × 50 feet, was decorated with sculptures of palms, vine branches, lions and centaurs. From there the view through a large window ranged southwards over the broad surface of the lake to where Jerusalem lay behind the pale blue outlines of distant hills.

Both archaeologists were convinced that they had found the synagogue of Capernaum dating from the time of Christ. But in the whole of Palestine there is not one synagogue left from those days.

When the Romans in two bloody wars razed Jerusalem to the ground and the inhabitants of the ancient country were scattered to the four winds, their sanctuaries also fell a prey to destruction.

This building came into being for the first time about A.D. 200 on top of the ruins and foundations of the synagogue in which Jesus often stood and taught on the Sabbath day: "And they went into Capernaum; and straightway on the sabbath day he entered into the synagogue and taught" (Mark 1²¹).

Most of the inhabitants of the little town of Capernaum lived on the natural riches of the lake: huts and houses in large numbers nestled quietly on the gentle slopes or surrounded the synagogue. On the day when Jesus came from Nazareth to Capernaum he took the first decisive step towards proclaiming his message: "Now as he walked by the sea of Galilee, he saw Simon and Andrew his brother, casting a net into the sea; for they were fishers. And Jesus said unto them: Come ye after me, and I will make you fishers of men" (Mark 1¹⁶⁻¹⁷). He met another pair of brothers, James and John, as they were mending their nets. The first people to listen to his words, to accept his teaching and to become his disciples, were simple men, fishermen of Galilee.

Jesus often wandered up from the lake into the Galilean hills, and preached in many of the towns and villages, but always returned to the little fishing town: it remained the main centre of his mission. And when one day he left Capernaum and set out with twelve disciples for Jerusalem, it was his last journey.

CHAPTER 39

THE LAST JOURNEY,
TRIAL AND CRUCIFIXION

Detour through Transjordan—The tax-collector of Jericho—View from the Mount of Olives—Arrest on the Mount of Olives—The "clubs" of the high priests—The Procurator Pontius Pilate—Vincent discovers the "Pavement"—Scourging in the courtyard of the Antonia—"The most cruel form of execution"—A crown of Syrian Christ-thorn—A drink to stupefy—Heart failure as the cause of death—Crurifragium hastens the end—A solitary tomb under the Church of the Holy Sepulchre—Tacitus mentions "Christus"—The evidence of Suetonius.

"Then he took unto him the twelve and said unto them, Behold we go up to Jerusalem, and all things that are written by the prophets concerning the Son of man shall be accomplished" (Luke 18³¹).

OUT of all the journeys that Jesus undertook in his lifetime, one can be traced without difficulty—his last journey through Palestine, the journey from Capernaum to Jerusalem.

He went a long way round to get there. The shortest route from Galilee to the Holy City lies directly south through the hills of Samaria. The path keeps to the hills, over the tops of Gerizim and Ebal, the site of ancient Shechem, and then on through Bethel into the heart of Judah, along the old high road which Abraham followed with his family and his flocks.

It took three days to make this journey on foot from Galilee to Jerusalem.

Jesus too would have chosen this road through Samaria (Luke 9⁵¹⁻⁵⁶). But since the anti-Jewish feeling among the Samaritans was well known it seemed doubtful to him whether they would permit his little company to pass through their territory. To make sure, he sent his disciples James and John in advance. And indeed the Samaritans refused permission.

Jesus and his disciples therefore went by way of "the borders of Judaea and beyond Jordan" (Mark 10¹—R.V.). The road goes downstream through the middle of the wide and torrid valley, where the banks alone are fringed with tropical growth, with little clumps of tamarisks and poplars, with castor oil and liquorice trees. There is solitude and stillness in the "pride of Jordan" (Zech. 11³; Jer. 12⁵). For

342

the valley, which for nine months of the year is as sultry as the tropics, is but thinly populated.

At the ancient ford, where once the children of Israel under Joshua's leadership had passed over in safety, Jesus crossed the Jordan and arrived in Jericho (Luke 19[1]). It was no longer the fortified city of old Canaan, entrenched behind its walls. On the south side of the hill lay a new up to date city, built by Herod the Great, a gem of Graeco–Roman architecture. At the foot of the citadel called Cyprus, a magnificent palace had arisen. A theatre, an amphitheatre, cut into the hillside, and a circus, all adorned with dazzling white pillars, sparkled in the sunlight. Magnificent fountains played in the luxuriant gardens with their massed banks of flowers. Outside the town stretched the balsam plantations—the most precious plants in the whole of the Mediterranean land—while deep palm groves offered coolness and shade.

Jesus spent the night in Jericho in the house of the Jewish tax-collector Zacchaeus (Luke 19[2ff]), far away from all this magnificence. He could not have avoided Jericho, which was a centre of Greek paganism. For the road to Jerusalem led through the city.

It is 23 miles from Jericho to Jerusalem. Twenty-three miles of dusty road winding and twisting between steep and almost barren cliffs nearly 4,000 feet high. Hardly anywhere else in the world can there be a stronger contrast than this short stretch of road affords. Straight from the wonderfully luxuriant growth and the sheer unbearable heat of a tropical sun by the Jordan's banks, one is whisked into the chill air of forbidding and barren mountain peaks.

This was the road, like a prelude to the end, which Jesus followed with his disciples a week before the Passover. This was the time when Jews from far and near flocked to celebrate the feast in the Holy City.

At the highest point on the road, which is almost at the end of the journey, the Holy City emerges from behind the top of the Mount of Olives as if some wizard had conjured it out of the hills. The view that Jerusalem presented to Jesus and the disciples can be imagined from a contemporary description:

"Anyone who has not seen Jerusalem in all its beauty has never beheld a great and lovely city in all his life: and anyone who has not seen the structure of the second Temple has never seen an impressive building in his life." This was the proud verdict of the Jewish rabbis of the time.

Research into the appearance of old Jerusalem has been summed up by Garstang in the following words: "At no point in their history can the Temple and the city have presented a more wonderful picture. The rhythm and harmony of Graeco–Roman art, which stood out so marvellously against the eastern sky, repressed the extravagant architectural tendencies of Herod, and brought order and good taste into the traditional chaos of the city."

The great walls towered 250 feet high above the valley. Behind their battlements rose the contours of mighty edifices from a constricted chequer-board of houses, streets and alleys.

Immediately opposite the Mount of Olives lay the Temple, right in the foreground, and outshining all other buildings in its magnificence. Its façade 150 feet high and of equal breadth, faced eastward and consisted entirely of light marble. Its decorations were of pure gold. Pillared colonnades hemmed in the spacious courts and vestibules. The crowning glory was however the Tabernacle in the centre, sparkling "like a snow capped mountain", to quote Josephus' words.

Directly on the north-west side of the Temple wall rose the Tower of Antonia, perched on a rocky eminence. Each of its four great corner turrets measured nearly 120 feet high. A viaduct led from the south side of the Temple area to the palace of the Hasmoneans in the upper city. At the highest point in the city stood Herod's palace by the west wall, likewise surmounted by three towers 130, 100 and 80 feet high. Herod had named them Hippicus, Phasael and Mariamne. From this point a thick wall ran through the sea of houses to the Temple area, thus dividing the heart of the city once more into two sections.

There is an indomitable air about this city with its multiplicity of fortifications, walls and towers surrounding its Temple. As the sight-seer looks over Jerusalem he almost feels that he is breathing in its obstinacy, rigidity and inflexibility. It was these very attributes of obstinacy, rigidity and inflexibility which helped Israel for more than 1,000 years to stand out against every world-power. Obstinacy, rigidity and inflexibility were also responsible for the eventual destruction of Jerusalem and the ejection of Israel from the land of their fathers.

Jesus predicted the future fate of Jerusalem. "And when he was come near, he beheld the city, and wept over it" (Luke 19[41]).

> "And straightway in the morning the chief priests held a consultation with the elders and scribes and the whole council, and bound Jesus, and carried him away, and delivered him to Pilate. ... And so Pilate willing to content the people ... delivered Jesus, when he had scourged him, to be crucified" (Mark 15[1,15]).

The descriptions of the trial, sentence and crucifixion in the four Gospels have been checked with scientific thoroughness by many scholars and have been found to be historically reliable accounts even to the last detail. The chief witnesses for the prosecution against Jesus have been indirectly attested and the place where sentence was pronounced has been accurately ascertained by excavations. The various incidents in the course of the trial can be verified from contemporary sources and modern research.

With the arrest the incomparable tragedy began to unfold. Jesus had gathered his disciples round him in the Garden of Gethsemane on the

Mount of Olives, "and immediately, while he yet spake, cometh Judas, one of the twelve, and with him a great multitude with swords and staves, from the chief priests and the scribes and the elders" (Mark 14^{43}).

A taunt-song in the Talmud reminds us of the "clubs" and "staves" of the Boethusian high priests who had been in control since Herod's day:

> "A plague on the house of Boethus: a plague on their clubs!
> A plague on the house of Annas: a plague on their spying!"

It ends: "For they are high priests and their sons are in the Treasury, and their sons-in-law in the Government and their servants beat the people with staves."

Among the high priests who are expressly named is one well known to us: the "Annas" in the gospels. "Then the band and the captain and officers of the Jews took Jesus, and bound him, and led him away to Annas first: for he was father-in-law to Caiaphas, which was the high priest that same year. Now Caiaphas was he, which gave counsel to the Jews, that it was expedient that one man should die for the people" (John 18$^{12-14}$).

Joseph ben Caiaphas had been appointed high priest by the Roman procurator Valerius Gratus. He remained in office[1] under his successor Pontius Pilate also.

After his arrest Jesus was brought before the High Council—the Sanhedrin—which at that time was the highest Jewish authority and combined within itself all spiritual and temporal power. At the same time it functioned as the highest judicial court of the Jews. It met below the Temple near the bridge which gave access to the upper city.

What were the grounds on which the council condemned Jesus to death?

"The expectation of the old Jewish prophets which centred on a future Messianic king," writes Professor Martin Noth, "had developed during the long period of foreign domination into hope of a political liberator; and the greater the resentment of the Roman government of the country the more this picture of a Messianic conqueror who would destroy the hateful foreign power filled their minds. Measured by these standards Jesus of Nazareth could not be the Messiah they were waiting for. ... But if Jesus of Nazareth was not the Messiah, 'the Christ', then he must be a fraud and an impostor. And if he was a fraud and an impostor then for the safety and peace of the religious life of Jerusalem he must be got rid of. ... The fact that Jesus during his trial claimed to be the Messiah and therefore, on the basis of Old Testament teaching, the Son of God was sufficient ground for condemning him to death on a charge of outrageous blasphemy."

[1] From A.D. 18–36.

According to the existing law the sentence had to be confirmed by the Roman procurator, to whom belonged the so-called ius gladii. Only he could authorise the death penalty. The procurator of Judaea was Pontius Pilate.[1]

Contemporaries like Josephus and Philo of Alexandria describe him as an extortioner, a tyrant, a blood sucker and a corruptible character: "He was cruel and his hard heart knew no compassion. His day in Judaea was a reign of bribery and violence, robbery, oppression, misery, executions without fair trial and infinite cruelty."[2] That Pilate hated and despised the Jews was made unmistakably plain to them again and again.

Pilate must have recognised at once that the accused man, Jesus, was the object of a hatred which had been stirred up by the Pharisees. That alone must have been sufficient reason for him to reject their demand and to acquit him. Indeed first of all and without hesitation he actually declared him to be innocent: "Then said Pilate to the chief priests and to the people, I find no fault in this man" (Luke 23[4]).

But the mob, incited and goaded by the councillors, tumultuously repeated their demand for the death penalty. Pontius Pilate gave in.

How was it that this tyrannical enemy of the Jews yielded to their request?

St. John's Gospel contains a cogent explanation: "But the Jews cried out, saying, if thou let this man go, thou art not Caesar's friend: whosoever maketh himself a king, speaketh against Caesar" (John 19[12]).

FIG. 72.—Coins of the Roman Procurator, Pontius Pilate.

This was a dangerous political threat which clearly implied reporting Pilate to Rome for neglect of duty in acquitting a rebel. "Making himself a king" meant treason against the Roman emperor. According to the Lex Juliana the penalty for that was death. Pilate was afraid of this unambiguous threat. He had not forgotten that the Jews had carried it out once before.

As Philo tells us, Pontius Pilate had brought to Jerusalem the golden shields bearing the emperor's name and had hung them up in Herod's palace in the middle of the city. That was a serious offence against the rights of the Jewish religious community which had been guaranteed by Rome. It was a challenge. He scornfully rejected their request to have the golden shields removed from the Holy City. Thereupon the Jews appealed to Rome and secured their rights. The Emperor Tiberius himself ordered the removal of the golden shields. Because of this and sundry other arbitrary actions, which ran counter to Roman colonial

---

[1] A.D. 26–36.　　[2] Philo of Alexandria A.D. 25–50.

policy, Pontius Pilate's reputation in Rome was at a low ebb at the time of the trial.

> "When Pilate therefore heard that saying, he brought Jesus forth, and sat down in the judgement seat, in a place that is called the Pavement, but in the Hebrew, Gabbatha. ... Then delivered he him therefore unto them to be crucified" (John 19[13,16]).

The Pavement in Pilate's court, where this scene took place, survived even the destruction of Jerusalem in A.D. 70. Its rediscovery was the result of years of work on the part of the archaeologist Father L. H. Vincent. His success was due to the exact description given in St. John's Gospel.

The Authorised Version has translated the word "Lithostroton" by "Pavement". It means a stone pavement. The Aramaic word "Gabbatha" means "raised ground".

Just beside the north-west perimeter wall of the Temple there lay in the time of Jesus the powerful Tower of Antonia. It stood upon a rocky eminence, therefore on "raised ground". Herod I had built it and called it after a friend. The Roman occupation troops had taken it over as a garrison. In A.D. 70, at the conquest of Jerusalem, Titus had the castle of Antonia demolished. Later buildings arose upon the ruins.

On the spot where the courtyard of the Antonia had been, Vincent was able to establish the existence of a large flat pavement nearly 3,000 square yards built in the Roman style and typical of the time of Jesus.

This was where Jesus stood before Pilate while the mob howled outside. It was on this Pavement too that the scourging took place (John 19[1]). This always preceded crucifixion, as Josephus expressly mentions twice. For this horrible punishment the body was stripped naked and flogged until the flesh hung down in bloody shreds.

Then Jesus was seized by Roman soldiers to complete the sentence of crucifixion. Cicero calls it "the most cruel and most frightful means of execution", Josephus recoils from it as "the most pitiable of all forms of death". This typically Roman death penalty was unknown in the Jewish penal code.

Still inside the court buildings the soldiers vented their wanton mischief on Jesus and "clothed him with purple and platted a crown of thorns and put it about his head" (Mark 15[17]).

So far, botanists have not been able to agree on what sort of plant this was. The only thing that is certain is that the "Christ's Crown of Thorns",[1] familiar to Europe and U.S.A. in the present day, has nothing to do with the Biblical crown of thorns. "It is a native of Madagascar and was completely unknown in Jesus' day," says the American botanist Dr. Harold Moldenke. Many other experts assume that the crown of thorns was woven from the Syrian Christ-thorn,[2]

---

[1] Euphorbia milii Desmoul.   [2] Sisyphus spina Christi.

hence its name. The Syrian Christ-thorn is a bush or small tree, 10 to 15 feet high, with pliant white twigs. Its stipulae have each two strong thorns which curve backwards. According to Dr. G. E. Post, who is an expert on these matters, this plant grows in the neighbourhood of old Jerusalem, especially in the area where Golgotha is said to have been.

The way from the courthouse to Golgotha was mercifully short: "for the place ... was nigh to the city" (John 19[20]), beside the main road which entered Jerusalem from the north-west. A pilgrim from Bordeaux who visited Jerusalem in the year 333 specifically mentioned "the little hill of Golgotha[1] where the Lord was crucified".

"And they gave him to drink wine mingled with myrrh: but he received it not" (Mark 15[23]). Similar acts of mercy are frequently recorded on other occasions. We read in an old Jewish Baraita: "Anyone who is led out to execution is given a small piece of incense in a beaker of wine to numb his senses. ... The good women of Jerusalem have a custom of dispensing this generously and bringing it to the victims." Moldenke, who has done much research into Biblical flora, has this to say: "Wine mixed with myrrh was given to Jesus just before the Crucifixion to lessen the pain, just as in the days before anaesthetics, intoxicating drinks were poured into the unfortunate patients on the eve of big operations." Jesus however declined the drink and endured with all his senses the torture of being nailed to the cross.

"And it was the third hour and they crucified him" (Mark 15[25]).

According to our division of time the "third hour" in the Ancient East is 9 a.m. "And at the ninth hour", in our reckoning three o'clock in the afternoon, the tragedy came to an end. "And Jesus cried with a loud voice, and gave up the ghost" (Mark 15[34,37]).

What was the cause of Jesus' death? Some years ago Dr. Hermann Mödder of Cologne carried out scientific tests in an attempt to answer the question from a medical point of view. In the case of a person suspended by his two hands the blood sinks very quickly into the lower half of the body. After six to twelve minutes blood pressure has dropped by 50% and the pulse rate has doubled. Too little blood reaches the heart, and fainting ensues. This leads to a speedy orthostatic collapse through insufficient blood circulating to the brain and the heart. Death by crucifixion is therefore due to heart failure.[2]

It is a well authenticated fact that victims of crucifixion did not usually die for two days or even longer. On the vertical beam there was often a small support attached called a "sedile" (seat) or a "cornu" (horn). If the victim hanging there eased his misery from time to time by supporting himself on this, the blood returned to the upper half of his body and the faintness passed. When the torture of the crucified man

[1] Monticulus Golgotha.   [2] Coronary insufficiency.

was finally to be brought to an end, the "crurifragium" was proceeded with: his legs were broken below the knee with blows from a club. That meant that he could no longer ease his weight on the footrests and heart failure quickly followed.

Jesus was spared the "crurifragium". "Then came the soldiers, and brake the legs of the first, and of the other which was crucified with him. But when they came to Jesus, and saw that he was dead already, they brake not his legs" (John 19[32-33]).

The Jews had asked Pilate for the "crurifragium", for it was "the day before the sabbath" (Mark 15[42]; Luke 23[54]) and also the day of preparation for the Passover. According to Jewish law the bodies of victims after crucifixion were not allowed to remain hanging overnight (Deut. 21[23]). And at 6 p.m. the Sabbath of Passover week began, when all kinds of normal activity were forbidden. The imminence of this important festival explains the precipitate haste of the events which preceded it, the arrest by night, the condemnation, execution and burial of Jesus all within a few hours.

It is barely 1,000 paces from the Ecce Homo arch, the site of Pilate's judgement seat, along the narrow Via Dolorosa to the Church of the Holy Sepulchre.

In 326 the Emperor Constantine erected a magnificent sepulchral tower over the tomb of Jesus, which had just then been rediscovered. Richly decorated pillars supported a roof of gilded beams, as can be seen from old books on pilgrimages and early Christian art. Today the Church of the Holy Sepulchre is a chaotic jumble of dim chapels. Every branch of the Christian Church has established for itself a little place of worship in this holiest of all the sites of Christendom.

In the Chapel of the Holy Sepulchre a well worn flight of steps leads down to a grotto where a 6 foot long tomb is hewn out of the rock. Is this the burial place of Jesus?

Over 1,000 graves have been found in Palestine dating from this period, but all of them were in cemeteries or family vaults. This tomb is however by itself. According to the Gospel tradition Jesus was the first to be laid in a great sepulchre: "And when Joseph had taken the body, he wrapped it in a clean

FIG. 73.—It was in a Palestinian tomb of this sort, with a millstone rolled across the entrance, that Christ was buried.

linen cloth, and laid it in his own new tomb, which he had hewn out in the rock: and he rolled a great stone to the door of the sepulchre, and departed" (Matt. 27[59-60]).

One question has always been pressing for an answer since early times: How is it possible that apart from the books of the New

Testament no contemporary records exist which deal with the events of those days? "World history at the time took no notice of him [Jesus of Nazareth]," writes Professor Martin Noth in his important *History of Israel*. "For one short moment his appearance stirred men's minds in Jerusalem: then it became an episode in past history and people had to concern themselves with what seemed more important things. And yet this was a final decisive crisis in the history of Israel. It was only when the numbers of his followers made them a force to be reckoned with in terms of world history that his name began to be mentioned at all."

Josephus in his *Antiquities of the Jews*, which he wrote in the last part of the 1st century A.D., in referring to the early Christian community in Jerusalem, speaks of "Jesus who was called Messiah".[1] Tacitus the Roman historian mentions Jesus specifically in his *Annals*,[2] while explaining the meaning of the word "Christians": "Christ, from whom they derive their name was condemned to death by the procurator Pontius Pilate in the reign of the Emperor Tiberius."

The most important comment comes however from the Roman Suetonius:[3] he is describing a messianic movement during the reign of Claudius, who was Roman emperor from A.D. 41 to 54. Suetonius says of him in his account of the life of the Emperor Claudius: "He drove the Jews out of Rome who were rioting because of Chrestus." The writer Orosius mentions that this expulsion took place in the ninth year of Claudius' reign, i.e. A.D. 49. That means that a Christian community is attested in Rome not more than fifteen to twenty years after the Crucifixion.

There is, in the Acts of the Apostles, an amazing corroboration of this Roman evidence. When Paul came from Athens to Corinth he found there "a certain Jew named Aquila, born in Pontus, lately come from Italy, with his wife Priscilla: because that Claudius had commanded all Jews to depart from Rome" (Acts 18[2]).

It cannot be denied, however, that the rare non-Biblical reports on Jesus are very problematical. Although there is a phonetic connection between Greek long "e" and "i", which is known as "itacism", so that *chrestos* meaning "capable", "skilful", "valuable", "good", could easily be confused with *christos*, which means "the anointed one" and is the Greek translation of the Hebrew word *Messias*, it is not at all certain whether the disturbances in Rome which were provoked by the question of the Messiah and which Suetonius mentions in his account of the life of the Emperor Claudius, really had anything to do with Jesus. The above quoted passage in Josephus must be considered a forgery. In its positive and approving tone it does not fit in either with Josephus' basic anti-Messianic attitude or with the surrounding

[1] Antiquities XX, 9, para. 200. [2] Annals, XV, 44—written A.D. 115–117.
[3] A.D. 65–135.

text which gives an account of the uprisings of Jewish nationalists which in the opinion of Joseph were abominable and to be condemned. Moreover, the internal structure of this passage is not typical of Josephus' way of writing. It is more like the preaching style of the Evangelist Luke. The statement made by Tacitus does not yield much either. It nevertheless confirms that there were Christians who derived from Christ their name "Christians"—Christ who had been crucified at the time of the Emperor Tiberius (A.D. 14–37) under the procurator Pontius Pilate. It is an open question whether Tacitus himself thought this true. The only safe deduction we can make is that during the reign of the Emperor Nero (A.D. 54–68), whose persecution of the Christians provides the opportunity for Tacitus to make his statement about them, a Christian community was in existence in Rome and that in certain respects their traditions coincided with points in the New Testament.

The year of Jesus' death, moreover, is no less debated than the date of his birth, concerning which we were able to say with any certainty only that it must have occurred somewhere and at some time between 7 B.C. and A.D. 7. The time span between the limits set by modern specialists for the year of Jesus' death is not so great, however, as that for his birth. Today the possibilities have been narrowed down to A.D. 29, 30, 32 and 33. If we wish to be very cautious, then we have at our disposal the ten years of the period that Pontius Pilate held his office (A.D. 26–36). Caiaphas, the High Priest, held office from A.D. 18–37.

Even the day of the trial and execution of Jesus is uncertain for if we work out the dates indicated by the Evangelists Matthew, Mark and Luke and compare them with those given by John, they show a difference of a day. There is even less uniformity concerning the hour of Jesus' death.

Moreover, the Evangelists linked the crucifixion of Jesus with so many passages from the Old Testament that it would almost be possible to have doubts about Jesus' crucifixion. Can all these terrible things have been imagined merely for the sake of cross references in the Bible? And it must not be forgotten that Jesus was by no means the first god to be crucified! He had been preceded by fertility gods who suffered and were put to death. In Berlin, for example, there is a small amulet with a crucified person, the Seven Sisters and the moon which bears the inscription ORPHEUS BAKKIKOS. It has a surprisingly Christian appearance. The same can be said of a representation of the hanging Marsyas in the Capitoline Museum in Rome.

On the other hand, we know that a crucifixion took place and we also know who ordered the crucifixion and who suffered this dreadful form of death. The Dead Sea Scrolls mention as outrageous a mass crucifixion ordered by Alexander Iannaios (103–76 B.C.). The Romans showed a preference for this manner of execution. It was inflicted on persons belonging to defeated peoples who had committed crimes against the Roman State as well as on slaves. But the question arises as to the actual cause of death of the crucified person as well as to the length of time he remained alive on the cross.

There was also disagreement concerning certain details of the way in which the cruel punishment was carried out. A macabre discovery on a hill named *Givat Hamivtar* on the eastern edge of Jerusalem helped solve the problem. Two Israeli specialists, the archaeologist Vassilios Tzaferis and the pathologist Nicu Haas, have published a report on it, while the American journalist and author Jerry M. Landay has written an account of it for the general public in his book on Biblical archaeology *Silent cities, sacred stones*.

It was in the summer of 1968. In the course of construction work a bulldozer cut into graves dating from the time between the accession of Herod the Great (37 B.C.) and the destruction of Herod's temple (A.D. 70). These graves lay on the hill of *Givat Hamivtar* so that the people buried in them must more or less have been contemporaries of Jesus. The name of one of the dead was *Johanan Ben Ha'galgol*. It was noticed with feelings of horror that his feet were separated from the smashed skeleton and were lying one on top of the other and joined together by a rusty nail which had been driven through both feet. Fragments of wood, the remains of a wooden slab, were attached to it. Behind Johanan's feet, the nail was bent obviously by having been driven into harder material. Johanan's fore-arms also showed signs of having had nails driven through them. In the course of Johanan's death struggles, his skin had suffered abrasions on the nails.

This discovery undeniably called for detailed investigation. Vassilios Tzaferis and Nicu Haas wondered whether any conclusions could be drawn from Johanan's injuries concerning the shape of the crucifix and the way in which the victim had been nailed to it. In fact, the nails had not been driven through the palms of the hands in the way usually depicted, but through the forearms near the wrist. Presumably this was the usual practice for this manner of execution, for the palms of the hands when pierced by nails would have torn under the weight of a body writhing in the agonised throes of death. This fact had already been established, moreover, in the gruesome experiments of Dr Barbet of Paris in connection with the "Turin Shroud" which will be discussed in the next chapter. The crucified person, whose imprint the shroud shows, contrary to all the artistic conventions of the usual manner of depicting a crucifixion, had not had the nails driven through his palms. There was one way, however, in which the case of Johanan Ben Ha'galgol obviously differed from the normal Roman method of execution. The question has been raised whether the *crurifragium*, the smashing of the shinbones with a blunt instrument, was an additional torture or perhaps in the end an act of mercy, a "coup de grâce", for the victim then collapsed and died more quickly. In Johanan Ben Ha'galgol's case, however, this "act of mercy" was not deemed sufficient. Together with the nail and the wooden slab his feet had been cut off his smashed legs. . . .

CHAPTER 40

THE TURIN SHROUD

Books from Constantinople—Discovery in the photographic negative—Tests by forensic medical experts—A scientific proof of authenticity?

"Then took they the body of Jesus, and wound it in linen clothes with the spices, as the manner of the Jews is to bury" (John 19[40]).

IN THE year 1204, during the course of the Fourth Crusade, the Crusaders captured Constantinople. In connection with this event the chronicler Robert de Clari reports that a Frenchman named Otto de la Roche came into the possession of a linen cloth as part of the spoils. This cloth, which measured 1.10 metres in width and 4.36 metres in length, had the peculiarity that it bore marks made by blood and sweat. On closer inspection the indistinct outlines of a human body, which must have measured about 1.80 metres in height, became apparent. Otto de la Roche took it with him back to France.

A century and a half later, the linen cloth reappeared in Besançon where it was worshipped as Christ's shroud. When a fire occurred, it was not consumed by the flames, it is true, but it did sustain slight damage. Its subsequent history can be followed in detail.

When the plague broke out in Milan, the devout Carlo Borromeo, bishop of the town, who was subsequently canonised, fulfilled his vow to make a pilgrimage to the shroud which had been brought for him from the south of France to Turin where it has since remained.

The linen cloth is said to have been in Jerusalem until the fifth or sixth century. Tradition has it that this is the linen cloth in which Joseph of Arimathea wrapped the body of Christ.

It is impossible to provide historical proof of these claims. There are, moreover, two pieces of linen in addition to that in Turin, for which the claim is also made that they came into contact with Christ's body.

The more important of these is the handkerchief of Saint Veronica. According to legend, the saint gave Christ her handkerchief as he was on the way to his crucifixion. When she received it back, it bore the imprint of his face.

The portrait of Christ in the possession of King Abgar V of Edessa, "Antiochia", was also considered authentic, but the French theologian and historian Chevalier came across proof to the contrary in the Papal archives in a document dated 1389 which states that an artist had painted such a cloth. When this became known, the Turin shroud was identified as a copy by that artist and consequently in the estimation of all those interested, it ceased to have any value as a contemporary document.

That might have been the end of the matter if interest in the legendary piece of linen had not been aroused anew in 1889. Technical progress had made possible the first photograph of the "Turin shroud". Something extraordinary was the result, for the photographic plate converted the impressions on the cloth into black and white. A face became clearly visible.

Specialists all over the world studied the sensational photograph. Art specialists, to whom it was submitted, noticed, moreover, that the negative was astonishingly natural and anatomically correct for, as with every human being, the features are not the same on both sides of the face. Artists in the early Middle Ages certainly did not pay any attention to this dissimilarity. Attempts made by painters showed that no artist was able, even when using a model, to convert a human face by the processes of the mind into a negative image and paint it.

The "Turin Shroud" could consequently not be a forgery insofar as it was the imprint of a human face. Even art specialists, who began by denying its authenticity, now admit that it cannot have been painted as a negative. Nobody can do that.

After this exciting discovery, scientists also began to take an interest in the shroud and a number of prominent specialists in various branches of science began their researches. Decades of study, experiments and investigations have brought certain conclusions. Concrete and very significant results have been obtained. A whole mosaic of infinitely painstaking studies exists which were undertaken to answer the question:

How did the shroud originate?

Professor Vignon of Paris was the first to concern himself experimentally with the impression of a body on linen. He placed a cloth sprinkled with aloes in contact with a corpse. The experiments were not satisfactory, however, as considerable distortions seemed unavoidable. Italian forensic medical specialists, Professors Judica of Milan and Professor Romanese of Turin, were more successful. In their experiments they adhered to the Biblical account which indicates the correct method: "And there came also Nicodemus ... and brought a mixture of myrrh and aloes, about an hundred weight. Then they took the body of Jesus, and wound it in linen clothes with the spices, as the manner of the Jews is to bury" (John 19[39-40]). A long series of experiments showed that the corpse must be powdered and the cloth moistened with aromatic oil. Impressions which do not show any distortion are obtained more particularly when the hair on the head prevents too close contact of the side of the face with the cloth. The results of the Italian tests provide the highest degree of correspondence.

The imprint on the "Turin shroud" shows swellings on the face. It is possible that they result from blows. "Then did they spit in his face, and buffeted him; and others smote him with the palm of their hands" (Matthew 26[67]). Patches of blood are clearly visible on the forehead and neck. "And the soldiers platted a crown of thorns, and put it on his head" (John 19[2]). Small swellings can also be seen on other parts of the body. They come from wounds on the hands and feet made by nails as well as from a wound on the right side of the chest "... one of the soldiers with a spear pierced his side, and forthwith came there out blood and water" (John 19[34]).

Dr Barbet of Paris has thoroughly investigated the nature of these wounds and here, too, the results were surprising. The wounds do not correspond to the customary manner of artistic depiction. The "Turin shroud" clearly shows the places where the nails were driven in. They were not driven through the palms of the hands, but through the wrists. From the physical and medical angle, the artistic depictions are wrong. And here, too, an unusual experiment led to a conclusion in the shroud's favour.

Dr Barbet nailed a corpse to a crucifix. The wound in the palm of the hand was torn when bearing a weight of 40 kilos. A wide tendon runs through the wrist, however, and is strong enough to support the weight of the human body.

Some medical men believed they were able to detect two kinds of blood in the traces left by the wounds. They distinguished between blood which must have flowed while the victim was still alive—such traces are found on the head, the hands and the feet—and blood after death from the wound in the side of the chest and also on the feet.

From what period does the linen of the famous shroud date? Because of the manner of weaving, specialists have repeatedly situated the shroud in the decades around the beginning of our era, although a precise determination of the time has not yet been attempted. It would be possible to undertake this, however, by using highly sensitive Geiger counters. The C_{14} method developed by Professor W. F. Libby of the Chicago Institution of Nuclear Physics would allow the date to be determined within a range of a few years. We should then know at least when the flax was grown from which the linen was made (cf. also p. 376).

These are the results which scientific investigation could achieve, but the question as to who the dead man was who lay in the shroud and when he lay there would still not have been answered.

II

In the days of the apostles

CHAPTER 41

IN THE STEPS OF ST. PAUL

The tentmaker from Tarsus—Triumphal arch in Antioch—Galatia, a Roman province—Wood digs in Ephesus—The temple of Artemis—The ruins of the gateway of Philippi—In ancient Corinth—A meat-market with a cooling system—"The Hebrew Synagogue"—A prisoner on the way to Rome.

"And ye shall be witness unto me, both in Jerusalem, and in all Judaea, and in Samaria, and unto the uttermost part of the earth" (Acts 1⁸).

"I AM a man which am a Jew of Tarsus, a city in Cilicia, a citizen of no mean city." Thus Paul, who was by trade a tentmaker (Acts 18³), describes himself in Acts 21³⁹. Tersoos, a little town of 20,000 inhabitants lying at the foot of the Taurus mountains in the south of Turkey, has preserved none of its former glory. Paul had every reason to laud his native city to the skies. An inscription calls Tarsus "the great and wondrous metropolis of Cilicia", and the Greek geographer Strabo[1] mentions that Tarsus had a university to match those of Athens and Alexandria. The famous teacher of the emperor Augustus, Athenodorus the philosopher, was one of its sons. All that remains from the past is its tentmaking. As in Paul's day, the material comes from flocks of goats who grow magnificent thick coats among the Taurus mountains where the snow lies right up to the month of May.

Long journeys by sea and land, such as Paul undertook, were in those days nothing out of the ordinary. Roman roads were in their way the finest that even Western Europe knew until the railways began to be built in the 19th century. An inscription on the tombstone of a Phrygian merchant in the heart of modern Turkey proudly proclaims that in his lifetime he made seventy-two journeys to Rome alone. The busy, well maintained Imperial roads were equipped with halts for changing chariots and horses. Inns and hostelries offered rest and refreshment to travellers. A special police force was responsible for the protection of the roads against the attacks of brigands.

The marvellous network of roads throughout the vast empire—a masterpiece of Roman skill and organisation—together with the Greek language which Paul could make use of on all his journeys contributed

[1] 63 B.C.–A.D. 20.

as much to the speedy spread of Christianity as the widely dispersed Jewish communities. "Jerusalem is not only the capital of Judaea," wrote king Herod Agrippa I[1] to the emperor Caligula, "but also of most countries in the world through the colonies which it established in neighbouring lands when it had the opportunity."

Even last century scholars had begun to search for the cities in Asia Minor whose names have become so.familiar to the Christian world through the Acts of the Apostles and the Epistles of St. Paul. Where were the places whose inhabitants received the famous Epistle to the Galatians?

In 1833, Francis V. J. Arundell, British chaplain in Smyrna, discovered the ancient "Antioch in Pisidia" (Acts 13[14]) near the Turkish town of Yalovach. North of the Taurus a great arched aqueduct sweeps down from the majestic scenery of the Sultandagh mountains into the valley. In the early twenties of this century scholars of the University of Michigan stood entranced before the remains of monuments of unique beauty. In the centre of the old city the archaeologists uncovered a broad flight of steps at the top of which stood three triumphal arches. Marvellous reliefs depicted the victories of the emperor Augustus on land, while a frieze with Poseidon, Tritons and dolphins commemorated the naval victory of Augustus at Actium. In the Roman quarters they found the gaming tables where the soldiery whiled away their leisure hours. The archaeologists were looking at the Antioch, so often mentioned, where Paul founded a church on his first missionary journey (Acts 14[21]).

And they "came unto Iconium ... unto Lystra and Derbe, ... and unto the region that lieth round about: and there they preached the gospel" (Acts 13[51]; 14[6,7]).

Konia, 60 miles south-east of Antioch and main station on the Anatolian railway, was the Iconium of Paul's missionary activity. In 1885 Professor J. R. Sitlington Sterrett discovered the remains of an altar in the mountains 25 miles farther south. A thick stone slab bore a Latin inscription to the effect that a Roman colony had existed on this site. He was able to decipher the name "Lustra".[2]

A day's journey farther on Sterrett also discovered the ancient Derbe. These four cities—Antioch, Iconium, Lystra and Derbe—belonged in Paul's day to the Roman province of Galatia, the home of the "Galatians".

On the island of Cyprus near the ancient town of Paphos a Roman inscription came to light. It made mention of Paulus, the proconsul who is described as "a prudent man" in the Book of Acts (13[7]), likewise the riot at Ephesus, as the New Testament depicts it, has become a living reality, thanks to the tireless efforts of the archaeologists.

"For a certain man named Demetrius, a silversmith, which made

[1] King Agrippa (A.D. 37–44): see Acts 12.   [2] i.e. Lystra.

silver shrines for Diana, brought no small gain unto the craftsmen: whom he called together with the workmen of like occupation, and said: Sirs, ye know that by this craft we have our wealth." He then went on to incite them: "not alone at Ephesus, but almost throughout all Asia, this Paul hath persuaded and turned away much people", and graphically described how they would all be reduced to starvation as a result. "Great is Diana of the Ephesians!" was the answering cry. "And the whole city was filled with confusion: and having caught.... Paul's companions in travel, they rushed with one accord into the theatre" (Acts 19[24-29]).

This story fired an English architect J. T. Wood with a desire to investigate the Temple of Artemis,[1] which was widely renowned in the ancient world. The British Museum put funds at his disposal for this enterprise, and in the beginning of May 1863 Wood landed on the coast opposite the island of Samos. If he had not been so incredibly persistent and obsessed with his purpose he might well never have achieved it. For six long years he dug down doggedly through layer after layer of what was left of the masonry of the old city—and found nothing. Eventually while digging in the old amphitheatre, the site of the riot, he found a signpost which put him on the right road.

An inscription listed several gold and silver images of Artemis from two to six pounds in weight which were to be offered as a gift to the goddess and placed in the temple. The vanity of that Roman donor showed Wood the way to the fulfilment of his dream without further ado. For in order to ensure that the greatest possible number of people would admire his gifts he had described in detail the exact route along which they were to be borne in solemn procession on the goddess' birthday, from the temple to the ceremony in the amphitheatre and back again.

They were to be carried in through the Magnesian Gate.... Wood searched for the gate and found it, followed the prescribed route and found himself a mile north-east of the city, at the finishing point of the procession which was also the end of his own indefatigable quest.

Under nearly 25 feet of soil and rubble he came upon a magnificent pavement, the bases of massive pillars, and great stone cylinders adorned with sculptures: the Temple of Artemis.

Dinocrates, the famous Alexandrian architect, had designed the shrine; Alexander the Great had been responsible for completing it in such splendour that in olden times the temple was admired as one of the Seven Wonders of the World.

The foundations measured 390 feet long by 260 feet broad, sheets of white marble covered the roof, and a hundred columns 65 feet high led the way into the interior of the temple, which was extravagantly decorated with sculptures, paintings and gold ornamentation.

[1] Artemis, the Greek goddess of hunting, was called Diana by the Romans.

Thirty-five years later one of Wood's countrymen, David G. Hogarth, found under the shattered altar a large collection of statues of the goddess made of bronze, gold, ivory and silver. They had been made by those craftsmen and workers who scented in Paul's preaching of the Gospel at Ephesus a threat to their livelihood and therefore responded to Demetrius with cries of: "Great is Diana of the Ephesians."

"Immediately we endeavoured to go into Macedonia, assuredly gathering that the Lord had called us for to preach the gospel unto them. Therefore loosing from Troas...." (Acts 16[10,11]).

Where once the proud stronghold of Priam's Troy held sway, St. Paul boarded a sailing ship for his first journey to Europe. Near the fishing village of Kavalla[1] he set foot on European soil and set out on the ancient Via Egnatia which climbed up into the wild mountains of Macedonia to Philippi.

Can anyone hear the name of this city without thinking of the ominous words: "Thou shalt see me at Philippi"? For it was here in 42 B.C. that the legions of Antony and young Octavian won a brilliant victory over Brutus and Cassius, who had assassinated Caesar in an attempt to save the republic of Rome from dictatorship. But who reflects that it was outside the walls of Philippi that St. Paul won for Christianity its first congregation on European soil?

French archaeologists on the strength of the concrete evidence in the Book of Acts excavated the Roman colony. They found the old forum, the temples and public buildings, the pillared arcades, the paved streets and squares with their rain-gutters still intact. At the western exit of the city a great colonial archway spanned the Via Egnatia which soon afterwards crossed the swift narrow river Gangites. "And on the sabbath day we went forth without the gate by a river side where we supposed there was a place of prayer" (Acts 16[13]—R.V.). On the banks of the Gangites Paul's first convert was Lydia, the seller of purple.

By way of Thessalonica[2] and Athens, where he preached only for a short time, St. Paul turned his steps towards Corinth.

In 1893 dredgers cut a narrow channel through the isthmus which joined the Peloponnese with the mainland and thus realised a plan which was already in the minds of notable figures in the ancient world, Alexander the Great and Julius Caesar. In A.D. 63 Nero had indeed begun to put the plan into effect. After a song in praise of Neptune in which he accompanied himself on the harp, he dug the first sod with a golden spade. Six thousand Jews had been commandeered from Pales-

---

[1] One of the many towns called *Neapolis* (new town) in Classical Antiquity.
[2] Now Salonika.

tine to cut the canal, which was however very quickly filled in again when the suspicion was voiced that a breach in the land might wash away the Peloponnese.

Three years after the first ship passed through the new canal the American School of Classical Studies began to search for the renowned and important trading and packing centre of Corinth, where the wares of the ancient orient met those of Europe. Here too the archaeologists followed the footsteps of St. Paul to the places which if they could only speak could tell so much about his activities.

The road from Lechaeum, the west harbour, led into the heart of the old city of Corinth. Through the great marble arch of the Propylaeum it debouched into the market place, the agora. In those days the business quarter lay to the west of Lechaeum street, and colonnades led past its shops and up to the steps of the Temple of Apollo. What aroused genuine admiration among the hygienically-minded Americans was the ingenious system of water mains which they found immediately under the houses which fronted the broad and handsomely paved market place. It obviously provided the shops with a constant supply of fresh mountain water to keep fresh such foodstuffs as were liable to perish quickly. An inscription at this place dating from the last years of the reign of Augustus actually mentioned a "meat-market". The Christians in Corinth were allowed to make their purchases in these shops without scruple. "Whatsoever is sold in the shambles, that eat", is Paul's advice to the church in 1 Cor. 10[25].

At the marble steps of the Propylaeum the excavators found a heavy stone lintel on which they were able to decipher the words "Hebrew Synagogue", clearly cut out in Greek letters. The house in which Paul proclaimed the new doctrine must have stood beyond the colonnade in the region of Lechaeum street. For "he reasoned in the synagogue every sabbath, and persuaded the Jews and the Greeks" (Acts 18[4]). Among the ruins of the numerous dwelling houses in the same quarter of the city must certainly be those of the house of the Justus with whom Paul lodged, "whose house joined hard to the synagogue" (Acts 18[7]).

Finally the archaeologists found in the market place a raised platform, on which a Latin inscription indicated that it had been the rostra, the judgement-seat. "And when Gallio was the deputy of Achaia, the Jews made insurrection with one accord against Paul, and brought him to the judgement-seat, saying, This fellow persuadeth men to worship God contrary to the law." Gallio however declined to intervene "and drave them from the judgement seat" (Acts 18[12-16]).

The detailed reproduction of the trial scene made it possible to establish the exact time that Paul spent in Corinth. Lucius Junius Annaeus Novatus Gallio—which was the governor's full name—was the worthy offspring of a highly respected family. His brother, Lucius Annaeus Seneca, the great Roman philosopher and tutor of Nero,

SPREAD OF CHRISTIANITY
IN THE ROMAN EMPIRE
■■ 45 A.D.
▥▥▥ 325 A.D. (Emperor Constantine)

FIG. 74

dedicated two books to him.[1] And the poet Statius called him the "beloved Gallio".

In old Delphi a letter of the emperor Claudius came to light from which it appeared that Gallio must have been in Corinth from A.D. 51–52. The letter contains the words: "As Lucius Junius Gallio, my friend the proconsul of Achaia,[2] wrote ..." and is dated at the beginning of the year 52. According to a decree of Claudius newly appointed officials had to leave Rome for their provinces on June 1. Gallio must therefore have arrived in Achaia about July 1, A.D. 51. Paul "continued there a year and six months, teaching the word of God among them" (Acts 18[11]) until the Jews became incensed and dragged him before the governor. Thus it is highly probable that the apostle went to Corinth at the beginning of A.D. 50.

Two years after the crucifixion of Christ the fanatical persecutor of the Christians, Saul of Tarsus, was converted to Christianity (Acts 6[3ff]). Almost exactly thirty years later the great missionary and evangelist embarked upon his last journey, this time as a prisoner. In Judaea Festus had been procurator since A.D. 61. He sent Paul to Rome to face a serious charge in the custody of the centurion Julius (Acts 27[1]). There Paul was allowed "to dwell by himself with a soldier that kept him" (Acts 28[16]).

"And Paul dwelt two whole years in his own hired house, and received all that came in unto him, preaching the kingdom of God, and teaching those things which concern the Lord Jesus Christ with all

[1] *De Ira* and *De Vita Beata*.
[2] The Peloponnese was in Roman times the province of Achaia.

confidence, no man forbidding him." With these words St. Luke concludes his narrative in the Book of Acts.

In the persecution of the Christians which took place under Nero, Paul died a martyr's death. As a Roman citizen he did not die on a cross like Peter but was beheaded.

CHAPTER 42

THE DESTRUCTION OF JERUSALEM

Rebellion—The Jewish War—Fighting in Galilee—General Titus—80,000 Romans advance—Order to attack—Parade outside the gates—500 crucifixions daily—Jerusalem sealed off—The spectre of famine—Castle of Antonia taken—The Temple in flames—The city is razed—Triumph in Rome.

> "And as some spake of the temple, how it was adorned with goodly stones and gifts, he said, As for these things which ye behold, the days will come, in the which there shall not be left one stone upon another, that shall not be thrown down. . . . And when ye shall see Jerusalem compassed with armies, then know that the desolation thereof is nigh. . . . For there shall be great distress upon the land and wrath upon this people. And they shall fall by the edge of the sword, and shall be led away captive into all nations: and Jerusalem shall be trodden down by the Gentiles. . . ." (Luke 21 [5, 6, 20, 23, 24]).

COUNTLESS royal palaces and castles, cities, mansions and temples, buildings whose foundations were laid in the first, second or even third millennium before Christ, have been wrested from the past. Archaeology has used its spades and the sharp wits of its experts to free them from the dust in which they have been buried at a cost of untold effort. But the city and Temple of Jerusalem, whose importance for posterity cannot be rated too highly, have eluded the endeavours of the archaeologists: they have been blotted out for ever from this earth. For barely within a generation after the crucifixion of Jesus they suffered in "the days of vengeance" (Luke 21 [22]) the fate that Jesus prophesied for them.

Old Israel, whose history no longer included the words and works of Jesus, the religious community of Jerusalem which condemned and crucified Jesus, was extinguished in an inferno which is almost unparalleled in history—the "Jewish War" of A.D. 66–70.

Louder and louder grew the protests against the hated Romans. In the party of the "Zealots" fanatics and rebels banded themselves together, demanding incessantly the removal of the foreign power. Every one of them carried a dagger concealed under his cloak. Their deeds of violence disturbed the country. Autocratic encroachment by the Roman procurator heightened the tension. More and more supporters flocked to the side of the radicals.

This mounting anger broke into open revolt in May 66, when the procurator, Florus, demanded 17 talents from the Temple treasury. The Roman garrison was overrun. Jerusalem fell into the hands of the rebels. The prohibition of the daily sacrifices to the emperor meant an open declaration of war against the Roman world empire. Tiny Jerusalem threw down the gauntlet at Rome's feet and challenged the great Imperium Romanum.

This was the signal for the whole country. Rebellion flared up everywhere. Florus was no longer in command of the situation. The governor of the province of Syria, C. Cestius Gallus, marched to the rescue with one legion and a large number of auxiliary troops, but was forced to retire with heavy losses. The rebels controlled the country.

Being certain that Rome would strike back with all its might, they hastened to fortify the cities. They repaired the old defence walls and appointed military commandants. Joseph, later known as Josephus the historian, was appointed commander-in-chief of Galilee. On the Roman side, the Emperor Nero entrusted the command to General Titus Flavius Vespasianus, who had proved himself a brilliant soldier and distinguished himself during the conquest of Britain.

Accompanied by his son Titus, three of the best legions in the army and numerous auxiliaries, he attacked Galilee from the north.

The villages on the Lake of Galilee, where but a few years earlier Jesus had been preaching to the fishermen, saw the first of the bloody butchery. The whole of Galilee was subdued by October 67. Among the crowds of prisoners marched Josephus, the commander-in-chief. He was put in chains and conveyed to headquarters at Vespasian's orders. From then on he saw the Jewish War from inside the enemy's camp. Six thousand Jews went as slaves to build the Corinth canal.

In the following spring the suppression of the rebels in Judaea was resumed. In the midst of the fighting news came which for the time being halted the campaign—Nero had committed suicide.

Civil war broke out in Rome. Vespasian awaited developments. One after another three insignificant emperors lost their thrones and their lives. At last the legions in the east stepped in. A year after Nero's death the cry went up in Egypt, in Syria, in Palestine, throughout the whole of the orient: "Vivat Caesar". Vespasian became master of the Roman empire. From Caesarea on the coast of Palestine, where the news reached him, he embarked without delay for Rome, leaving his son Titus to finish the last act of the Jewish War.

Shortly before the full moon in the spring of 70 Titus appeared with an enormous army outside Jerusalem. Marching columns filled the highways and byways leading to the city such as Judaea had never seen before. They were made up of the 5th, 10th, 12th and 15th Legions, accompanied by cavalry, engineers and other auxiliary troops, almost 80,000 men.

The Holy City was swarming with people: pilgrims had come from far and near to celebrate the Passover. Disputes between the extremists among the Zealots and the moderate party interrupted the devotions: the wounded and the dead remained untended.

Meantime the Romans moved into their camps in the environs of the city. A call to surrender was met with derisive laughter. Titus replied with the command to attack. The Roman artillery, "scorpiones", quick-firing siege engines and "ballistae", stone throwers, closed in. Every one of these heavy weapons could throw stones weighing a hundredweight a distance of 600 feet. On the north side the engineers were cracking open the Achilles heel of the fortress. On the south, east and west sharp precipices protected the ramparts. The north side was however unusually strongly fortified by three massive walls. Battering rams and siege engines began to crack and thunder as they attacked the foundations. Only when an incessant hail of great stones came hurtling into the city, and when night and day the heavy thud of the battering rams could be heard, did civil war end within the fortress. The rival factions came to terms. Simon bar Giora, leader of the moderates, took over the defence of the north side, John of Gischala, leader of the Zealots, took over the defence of the Temple area and the Tower of Antonia.

By the beginning of May the siege engines had in the space of two weeks made a gaping hole in the most northerly wall. In five more days the Romans were through the second wall. A determined counter-attack put the defenders once more in possession of the wall and it took the Romans several days before they could recapture it. With that the northern suburb was firmly in Roman hands.

FIG 75.—Roman siege technique during the conquest of Jerusalem.

Convinced that in view of this situation Jerusalem would surrender, Titus called off the attack. The grandiose spectacle of a great parade of his forces immediately under the eyes of the beleagured people would surely bring them to their senses.

The Romans doffed their battledress and polished their full-dress uniform until it shone. The legionaries put on their armour, their coats of mail and their helmets. The cavalry decked their horses with the richest caparisons, and amid loud blasts from the trumpets tens of thousands of warriors marched past Titus and received their pay and ample rations in full view of the garrison. For four days from early morn till dusk the sound of the tramping feet of these unbeaten Roman columns echoed in the air.

It achieved nothing. Packed tight along the old wall, on the north side of the Temple, on every roof, the people spat hatred down at the Romans. The demonstration had been useless—the beleagured garrison had no thought of surrender.

Titus made one last attempt to win them round. He sent their captive countryman Flavius Josephus, the Jewish commander-in-chief in Galilee, to harangue them under the fortress walls.

Josephus' voice hailed them from below: "O hard hearted men, throw away your weapons, have pity on your country that stands on the edge of the abyss. Look round and behold the beauty of all that you are ready to betray. What a city! What a Temple! What gifts from so many nations! Who would dare to let all of this be given to the flames? Is there one of you who can wish for all this to be no more? What more precious treasure could have been given to man to preserve—You obdurate creatures, more unfeeling than these very stones!"

In heartrending words, Josephus reminded them of the great deeds of the past, of their forefathers, of their history, of the mission of Israel—his exhortations and pleas fell on deaf ears.

The battle began anew from the second wall and surged against the castle of Antonia. The front was pushed forward through the streets of the suburbs to the Temple area and the upper part of the city. The engineers built ramps and auxiliaries dragged trees for this purpose from far and near. The Romans proceeded with all their tried methods of siege warfare. Their preparations were constantly being sorely hampered by the determined efforts of the defenders to upset them. Apart from wild sorties, no sooner were their wooden ramparts in position than they went up in flames. When darkness set in, the Roman camp was surrounded by swarms of figures who had crept out of their hiding places or through subterranean passages or over the walls.

Titus ordered reprisals to be made against these half starved ghostly figures and against deserters. Anyone caught outside—deserters, raiders or foragers—was to be crucified. Mercenaries nailed 500 of them every day to crosses just outside the city. Gradually a whole forest of crosses sprang up on the hillsides till the lack of wood called a halt to the frightful practice.

Tree after tree was sacrificed for crosses, siege ramps, scaling ladders and camp fires. The Romans had come into a flourishing countryside. Now the vineyards had disappeared as had the market gardens, the wealth of fig-trees and olive-trees; even the Mount of Olives no longer provided shade. An unbearable stench hung over the bare and desolate countryside. The corpses of those who had died of starvation and of those who had died in battle, thrown over the ramparts by the beleaguered garrison, were piled beneath the walls by the thousand. Who had the strength to bury them in the traditional way?

FIG. 76.—Jerusalem during the siege by Titus, A.D. 70.

"No stranger who had seen Judaea of old, and the lovely suburbs of its capital, and now saw this devastation," mourned Josephus, "could have restrained his tears and lamentations at the hideous change. For the war had turned all that beauty into a wilderness. And no man who knew these places of old and suddenly saw them again could possibly have recognised them."

To seal off the city hermetically Titus ordered the erection of a "circumvallatio". Working night and day they constructed a massive high wall of earthwork in a wide circle round Jerusalem, strengthened by thirteen fortified strong points and guarded by a close chain of pickets. If so far it had been possible to smuggle supplies and provisions into the city by night by way of secret paths through tunnels or ditches, the "circumvallatio" stopped even this last meagre reinforcement.

The spectre of famine haunted the city, which was filled to overflowing with pilgrims, and death mowed them down in a dread harvest. The craving for food, no matter of what sort, drove men beyond all bounds and killed all normal feeling.

"The terrible famine that increased in frightfulness daily annihilated whole families of the people. The terraces were full of women and children who had collapsed from hunger, the alleys were piled high with the bodies of the aged. Children and young people, swollen with lack of food, wandered around like ghosts until they fell. They were so far spent that they could no longer bury anyone, and if they did they fell dead upon the very corpses they were burying. The misery was unspeakable. For as soon as even the shadow of anything eatable appeared anywhere, a fight began over it, and the best of friends fought each other and tore from each other the most miserable trifles. No one would believe that the dying had no provisions stored away. Robbers threw themselves upon those who were drawing their last breath and ransacked their clothing. These robbers ran about reeling and staggering like mad dogs and hammered on the doors of houses like drunk men. In their despair they often plunged into the same house two or three times in the one day. Their hunger was so unbearable that they were forced to chew anything and everything. They laid hands on things that even the meanest of animals would not touch, far less eat. They had long since eaten their belts and shoes and even their leather jerkins were torn to shreds and chewed. Many of them fed on old hay and there were some who collected stalks of corn and sold a small quantity of it for four Attic drachmas.—But why should I describe the shame and indignity that famine brought upon men, making them eat such unnatural things?" asks Josephus in his history of the Wars of the Jews.

"Because I tell of things unknown to history, whether Greek or barbarian. It is frightful to speak of it and unbelievable to hear of it. I should gladly have passed over this disaster in silence, so that I might not get the reputation of recording something which must appear to posterity wholly degrading. But there were too many eye-witnesses in my time. Apart from that my country would have little cause to be grateful to me were I to be silent about the misery which it endured at this time."

Josephus, whose own family suffered with the defenders, was not afraid to describe an inhuman occurrence which proves that the raging famine had begun to cloud the brains of the blockaded citizens.

Zealots were foraging through the lanes of the city in quest of food. From one house came the smell of roast meat. The men plunged into the house at once and were confronted by Maria, daughter of the noble line of Beth-Ezob in Transjordan, an extremely wealthy family. She had come to Jerusalem on pilgrimage for the Passover. The Zealots threatened her with death unless she handed over the roast meat to them. With a wild look she gave them what they asked for. Aghast, they found themselves looking at a half consumed infant—Maria's own child.

Soon not only the whole city learned of this, but the news also seeped out through the walls to the Roman camp. Titus swore that he would bury this dreadful deed under the ruins of the whole city.

Many fled from death by starvation under cover of darkness and ran into the arms of an equally cruel fate. The story had got around among the Romans' auxiliaries that fugitives from within the walls always carried gold and jewels, which they had swallowed in the hope of preserving them from being seized by strangers. If any of these unsuspecting people were caught they were felled to the ground and their bodies slit open in the endless quest for plunder. In one night 2,000 alone lost their lives in this way. Titus was furious. Without mercy he got his cavalry to decimate an auxiliary unit. An order of the day made the crime punishable by death. But it was of little avail, the slaughter continued secretly.

Meantime day and night the battering rams were hammering on the suburbs of Jerusalem. New ramps were laid down. Titus was in a hurry. He wanted to end this frightful nightmare as quickly as possible.

At the beginning of July his soldiers stormed the Tower of Antonia. The castle, on whose "Pavement" Jesus of Nazareth had been sentenced to death, was razed to its foundations. Its walls abutted on the north wall of the Temple.

It was now the turn of the Temple, that powerful and extremely well fortified complex of galleries, balustrades and forecourts. The commander-in-chief discussed the situation with his officers. Many of them wanted to treat the Temple like a fortress. Titus opposed them. He wanted if possible to spare this famous sanctuary which was known throughout the empire. For the last time his heralds demanded that the rebels should surrender. Once more the answer was a refusal. Titus then finally embarked upon the attack against the sacred precincts.

An incessant hail of heavy stones and a rain of arrows showered down upon its courts. The Jews fought like men possessed and did not yield an inch. They relied on Yahweh hastening to their aid at the last moment and protecting his shrine. More than once legionaries on scaling ladders reached the perimeter wall. Every time they were thrown back. Rams and siege engines were powerless against these walls. It was impossible to shatter the vast stone blocks of which Herod had built the Temple. In order to force an entry Titus set fire to the wooden Temple gates.

Hardly were they consumed when he gave instructions to put out the flames and make a passage for the legionaries to attack. Titus' order of the day read "Spare the sanctuary". But during the night the fire had reached the inner court and the Romans had their hands full to put it out. The beleaguered rebels profited by this favourable opportunity to make a violent attack. With remorseless slaughter the legionaries drove the Jews back, and pursued them through the courts. In wild tumult the battle raged round the sanctuary. Carried away by excitement, "one of the soldiers, without waiting for orders and without any sense of the horror of his deed, or rather being driven by some evil spirit, seized a blazing torch and, hoisted on the shoulders of one of his comrades, flung it through the Golden Window that opened into the rooms which lay beside the Holy of Holics".

These rooms were panelled with old wood and contained, as well as highly inflammable materials for the sacrifices, jars of holy oil. The flaming torch found instantaneous and ample fodder. Titus saw the flames springing up and tried to check the spread of the fire.

"Caesar[1] then commanded that the fire should be put out, calling in a loud voice to the soldiers who were in the thick of the fighting and giving them a signal with his right hand. But they did not hear what he said for all his shouting.... And since Caesar was unable to restrain the hot rage of the soldiery, and since the flames were spreading further and further, he entered the Holy Place in the Temple together with his commander and viewed it and all its contents.... But since the flames had not yet reached the inner rooms, and were still devouring the rooms that surrounded the Tabernacle, Titus, assuming, as was indeed the case, that the Tabernacle itself could still be saved, hurried away and made every effort to get the soldiers to put out the fire, giving orders to Liberalius, the centurion and to one of his own body guard, to beat the soldiers with staves if they refused and by every means to restrain them. But however great their enthusiasm for Caesar and their dread of what he had forbidden them to do, their hatred of the Jews and their eagerness to fight them was equally great.

"In addition the hope of booty spurred many of them on. They had the impression that all these rooms within were full of gold, and they saw that all around them was made of pure gold.... Thus the Holy Place was burnt down without Caesar's approbation."

In August A.D. 70 Roman legionaries erected their banners in the sacred precincts and sacrificed before them. Although half of Jerusalem was in the hands of the enemy, although ominous black columns of smoke rose from the burning Temple, the Zealots would not surrender.

John of Gischala escaped with quite a large band from the Temple area into the upper part of the city on the western hill. Others fled into the strong towers of Herod's palace. Once again Titus had to deploy his engineers, artillery, siege engines and all his brilliant technical skill. In September these walls too were forced, and the last bastions conquered. Resistance was finally at an end.

Murdering and plundering, the victors took possession of the city

[1] Titus became Emperor in 79.

that had so fiercely and bitterly resisted them and cost them so much blood and time. "Caesar ordered the whole city and the Temple to be razed to the ground. He left standing only the towers of Phasael, Hippicus, and Mariamne and part of the city wall on the west side. This was to provide quarters for the garrison that was to remain behind."

The legion that occupied the garrison in this dreadful place for sixty long years bore the symbol "Leg XF", which meant "Tenth Fretensian Legion". Their home station was on the "Fretum Siciliense", the straits of Messina. They left behind them in and around Jerusalem thousands upon thousands of indications of their presence. Gardeners and peasants still find occasionally small tiles with the legion's number and its emblems of a galley and a boar.

The loss of life among the Jews was unimaginably high. During the siege, according to Tacitus, there were 600,000 people in the city. Josephus gives the number of prisoners as 97,000, not counting those crucified or ripped open, and adds that within a period of three months 115,800 corpses were taken out of one of the city gates alone by the Jews.

In the year 71 Titus paraded his great victory over Jerusalem in a gigantic triumphal procession through Rome. Among 700 Jewish prisoners John of Gischala and Simon bar Giora were marched past in chains. Amid great rejoicing two other costly trophies of pure gold were born in procession, the seven branched candlestick and the table of the shewbread from the Temple at Jerusalem. They found a new home in the Temple of Peace in Rome. Both these accessories of Jewish ritual can still be seen on the great arch of Titus which was erected to commemorate his successful campaign.

On top of these desolate and cheerless ruins, on which neither Jews nor Christians were allowed to set foot on pain of death, the emperor Hadrian[1] built a new Roman colony: Aelia Capitolina. The sight of a foreign settlement on this sacred Jewish soil provoked yet another open rebellion. Julius Severus was summoned to Judaea from his governorship in Britain and smashed the last desperate attempt of the Jews to regain their freedom. But it took him three years to do so. The emperor Hadrian then erected a race-course, two baths, and a large theatre. A statue of Jupiter was enthroned above the ruins of the Jewish Temple as if in derision, and on the site which Christian tradition believed to be that of the Holy Sepulchre, strangers climbed the terraced steps to do homage at a shrine of the pagan goddess Venus.

The greatest part of the population of the Promised Land, which was not massacred in the bloody Jewish War of 66–70 and in the Bar-Kokhba rebellion of 132–135, was sold into slavery: "And they shall fall by the edge of the sword and shall be led away captive into all nations."

Archaeologists have found no material evidence of Israel's existence

[1] A.D. 117–138.

in Palestine after the year 70, not even a tombstone with a Jewish inscription. The synagogues were destroyed, even the house of God in quiet Capernaum was reduced to ruins. The inexorable hand of destiny had drawn a line through Israel's part in the concert of nations.

But by then the teaching of Jesus was well started on its irresistible and victorious journey, uniting and giving new life to the nations.

THE DEAD SEA SCROLLS

A lost lamb—The Dead Sea Scrolls—Harding and de Vaux in Wadi Qumran—Archbishop Samuel goes to Chicago—Nuclear physicists assist with the dating—Testing linen in the "Atomic Clock"—A book of Isaiah 2,000 years old—A prophetic roll in Jesus' day—A mysterious flood of documents—In the valley of the pirate-diggers—A text that corresponds after 2,000 years.

"The grass withereth, the flower fadeth: but the word of our God shall stand for ever" (Is. 40⁸).

MOHAMMED DIB, a Bedouin shepherd of the tribe of Ta 'Amireh, shared the experience of young Saul, who set out to find his father's asses which were lost and acquired a kingdom (1 Sam. 9, 10).

One fine day in the spring of 1947 Mohammed was combing the rocky ravines on the north shore of the Dead Sea in quest of a lost lamb, when he unwittingly came upon a veritable royal treasure in the shape of Biblical material.

He had been clambering to no purpose for several hours up and down the clefts and gullies of the ridge, which had many a time served as a hideout for hermits and sectaries, to say nothing of bandits, when he spied a dark crevice above his head in the rock face of Wadi Qumran. Could his lost lamb have taken refuge there? A well aimed stone whistled through the air. But instead of the sharp crack which he expected in reply, a dull rumbling noise came from the cave instead. Mohammed Dib fled in terror and fetched two of his fellow tribesmen to the scene. They approached the cave with great caution and eventually squeezed their way through its narrow entrance. To their amazement they saw in the dim light of the little vault some clay jars. Treasure was their first thought and the three shepherds pounced on the jars and smashed them. But to their disappointment they contained neither jewels, nor gold, nor coins: nothing appeared but battered looking written scrolls of ancient leather and papyrus, wrapped in linen. In their annoyance they threw their finds carelessly aside, trampling on many of them, until it suddenly dawned on them that there might be money in them. At all events they took a few of the best looking scrolls to see if perhaps they had some cash value. With that the ancient documents set out on a remarkable journey.

They were smuggled into Bethlehem and came via the black market into the hands of antique dealers. Jewish and Arab collectors bought some of the scrolls, and a bundle of four came into the possession of the Orthodox archbishop of Jerusalem, Yeshue Samuel, for a handful of coins. The archbishop had no idea how precious was the treasure he had acquired, until experts from the American School of Oriental Research paid a visit to St. Mark's Monastery, where the documents were stored. A cursory examination convinced the archaeologists that they were dealing with Biblical documents of an uncommonly early date. A 23-foot-long scroll with the complete text of the book of Isaiah in Hebrew was among them. A short published report by the Americans on their find aroused incredulous astonishment among experts all over the world. The immediate question however as to the exact age of the leather and the papyrus could best be solved by examining the place where they were discovered.

With endless trouble and patience the origin of the documents was therefore traced back through the dealers and the black market in Bethlehem to the Arabs of the Ta 'Amireh tribe and so eventually to the cave in Wadi Qumran. But access to the cave was prohibited. For following on the establishment of the new state of Israel the Arab–Jewish war had broken out in 1948 and the whole of Palestine was a hotbed of unrest.

The persistence of a Belgian United Nations observer in Jerusalem finally helped to overcome all difficulties. Captain Philippe Lippens had studied papyrology at the ancient University of Louvain. At the end of 1948 he established contact with Gerald Lankester Harding, the British director of the Department of Antiquities in Amman, the capital of Jordan. Their united efforts succeeded in interesting officers of the Arab Legion in the cave where the discovery was made. Thirty miles in a jeep from Amman to Wadi Qumran presented no problems. After several fruitless quests among the numerous caves they eventually found the right one. The entrance to the cave was guarded by sentries until in February 1949 G. L. Harding and Father Roland de Vaux, Dominican director of the French Ecole Biblique et Archéologique at Jerusalem, arrived at the spot in person.

Their hopes were however disappointed. They found neither complete scrolls nor undamaged jars. Everything pointed to the fact that in the meantime others had rummaged through the mysterious cave on their own. With infinite patience and labour the two scholars examined the floor of the cave, literally with their finger-nails, in search of even the tiniest remains of manuscripts or of clay jars. What they collected in the way of fragments permitted them nevertheless to draw some important conclusions. The potsherds were uniformly Graeco-Roman, dating from 30 B.C. to A.D. 70. Six hundred tiny scraps of leather and papyrus made it possible to recognise Hebrew transcriptions from Genesis, Deuteronomy and the book of Judges. Pieces of linen fabric which had served to wrap up the scrolls completed the meagre spoils.

In response to an American invitation Archbishop Yeshue Samuel took his precious scrolls to the United States in the summer of 1949 and submitted them for examination to the Oriental Institute in Chicago. A violent dispute broke out among the experts on the question of the age and authenticity of the documents. To settle the matter, one of them proposed a course which was still unfamiliar to archaeologists, namely to invite the assistance of a nuclear physicist. This was all the easier since the Oriental Institute is next door to the University of Chicago, where nuclear physicists had begun to determine the age of organic substances with the aid of Geiger-counters.

Professor Willard F. Libby of the Chicago Institute of Nuclear Physics had already carried out his first astonishingly accurate calculations of age by the use of the so-called "atomic calendar" which he had evolved.

The idea behind this method is as follows: As a result of the bombardment of cosmic rays, which are constantly penetrating our atmosphere from outer space, nitrogen is transformed into the radioactive isotope of carbon C-14. Every living organism—men, animals, plants—absorbs this C-14 with its food and the air it breathes every day until it dies. In the course of 5,600 years this carbon loses half of its original radioactivity. In the case of any dead organic substance a highly sensitive Geiger-counter can establish how much radiation has been lost from its content of C-14. This makes it possible to calculate how many years ago it was since it absorbed carbon for the last time.

Professor Libby was asked to conduct an investigation. He took pieces of the linen, in which the Isaiah scroll had been wrapped, burned them to ashes, put them into a battery of Geiger-tubes, and came to an astonishing conclusion. The linen had been made from flax which had been harvested in the time of Christ. The documents which had been wrapped in it must therefore have been older still. After exhaustive and minute examination the papyrologists came to the same conclusion. The text of Isaiah from the cave of Qumran had actually been copied about 100 B.C., as Professor Albright once more had been first to recognise.

This discovery means more than simply a scientific sensation. To estimate the importance of the Dead Sea Scrolls it is necessary to remember that the oldest text of the Bible which we possess in the Hebrew language—the so called Massoretic Text (Massora = tradition), which is the work of rabbinical scribes—dates from no earlier than the 9th–10th century A.D. The chief sources for our version of the scriptures are the Septuagint, the Greek translation, and the Vulgate, the Latin translation of St. Jerome (4th century A.D.). Our knowledge of the text of the Bible rested for a long time on nothing but these two translations and the very late Hebrew manuscript. But with the discovery of the Dead Sea Scroll of Isaiah we have a Hebrew text of the Bible which is 1,000 years older. And the remarkable and wonderful fact is that that ancient scroll of Isaiah, just like the book of the prophet in any printed Bible, whether in Hebrew, Greek, Latin, German or any other language, has sixty-six chapters and agrees with our present day text.

Seventeen sheets of leather, sewn together into a length of almost 23 feet—this must have been what the roll of the prophet looked like as it was handed to Jesus in the synagogue at Nazareth so that he might read from it to the congregation. "And there was delivered unto him the book of the prophet Esaias" (Luke 4^{16,17}). "Every movement of Jesus' hands is brought closer to us," writes Professor André Parrot, "for we can still see on the reverse side of the leather the marks of the readers' fingers."

That first chance find made by a Bedouin in 1947 at Qumran was to lead to a whole series of most astonishing and highly significant discoveries. Soon after, for the first time a systematic investigation of the Judaean hills was undertaken with a view to finding more documents and further historical evidence. Expeditions were mounted both in Israel and Jordan. Hundreds upon hundreds of lonely gullies and hitherto unexplored caves in the Dead Sea area were searched. Many a time it was a race between the experts and unofficial explorers, because it had very quickly become clear to the natives that there was big money in these unlikely scraps of parchment and papyrus with any hint of writing on them. The result was that within ten years a whole host of documents and written records, including many Old Testament writings, came to light, providing a vast amount of new knowledge about Biblical and post-Biblical times.

In Khirbet Qumran, near the cave where the first discoveries were made, scholars came upon the ruins of a settlement and a cemetery of the Jewish sect of Essenes, of whose existence we had only previously known from the accounts given by ancient writers—Philo, Josephus, and Pliny. The Essenes—first mentioned in the time of Jonathan, brother of Judas Maccabaeus (160–143 B.C.)—were members of an ascetic order who lived strictly in accordance with the law. They formed communities which were completely self-supporting and refused to do military service. The particular group at Qumran survived up to the Roman invasion in A.D. 68. Presumably it was members of this group who were responsible for many of the copies of the books of the Old Testament which have been rescued from caves in the adjacent hills, since a proper scriptorium was discovered among the ruins of the settlement. This Jewish monastic order, as their records now disclose, recognised as their head a "Teacher of Righteousness" who had revealed to them a secret rule of life. Some scholars were at first inclined to say that Qumran had strongly influenced John the Baptist, Jesus, and the early Church. This view, which caused a stir at the time, has on closer investigation proved to be unfounded.

Almost at the same time as the Dead Sea Scrolls were discovered, a collection of manuscripts was found not far from Luxor in Egypt which was to prove highly significant for our understanding of early Christianity. Fellaheen had discovered at Nag Hammadi, near the ancient Chenoboskion, a clay jar containing thirteen leather-bound volumes with about 1,000 leaves. These papyrus manuscripts written in Coptic, dating from the 3rd and 4th centuries A.D., and including a collection of the Sayings of Jesus ascribed to the Apostle Thomas, "the Gospel according to Thomas", shed light on an early Christian Gnostic sect of which, apart from the writings of the early Christian Fathers, we hitherto knew little or nothing. The Fathers attacked the Gnostics as heretics since they tried to combine Egyptian, Babylonian, Greek, Persian, and Jewish mysticism with Christian doctrine. The Nag Hammadi manuscripts, apart altogether from what further research discloses as to the authenticity of the teaching of Jesus which they contain, give us some idea of the formidable opposition and competition which the early Christian teachers had to face.

Following on the finds at the Dead Sea which aroused worldwide interest, came the discovery in 1952 of two inscribed copper scrolls in a cave to the north of the ruined monastery of Qumran. When eventually in the winter of 1955–56, after careful chemical experiments, experts in the Manchester College of Technology succeeded in opening them, the contents about which everyone had been agog turned out to be a curious inventory of hidden treasure. While the experts are still far from clear as to the real significance of this list, a geographical reference in the text confirmed the reliability of a piece of topographical information contained in the Fourth Gospel. According to John 5[2] "there is at Jerusalem by the sheep market a pool, which is called in the Hebrew tongue Bethesda, having five porches ..." The accuracy of this description was questioned until quite recently, when Bethesda was cleared of the rubble of centuries and brought once more to the light of day: a vast double pool covering over 5,000 square yards to the north of the Temple area. It had in fact five colonnades. Four of these surrounded the whole place, but the fifth porch, in which the sick folk lay waiting to be healed, stood on a ridge of rock which divided the two pools. The text of the copper scroll makes it quite clear that the lay-out at Bethesda consisted of two pools, since one of the hiding places is given as the smaller of the two reservoirs.

In the ancient Jewish fortress of Massada on the Dead Sea, Israeli scholars in 1956 came upon armouries and storehouses of Herod the Great. A fragment of papyrus was discovered inscribed with Hebrew characters and written in black ink. According to Dr. Aharoni, the fort

and Herod's palace which crowned it were destroyed by the Romans in
A.D. 73 after the end of the Jewish War.

Other expeditions have made interesting discoveries which shed an
odd ray of light here and there on the Jewish rebellion under Simon
Bar-Kokhba, which took place after the Biblical period. Hitherto, all
that was known of this great revolt of the Jews against the emperor
Hadrian and their struggle against the legions of Julius Severus consisted of comments in later Jewish writings, in the works of the Greek
historian Dio Cassius, and the Christian Fathers Eusebius and Jerome.

In 1951 Professor Lankester Harding and Father de Vaux had
retrieved original letters of the leader of the revolt dating from A.D.
130—including several copies of a document proclaiming the liberation and issued by Bar-Kokhba—from caves to the south of Qumran in
Wadi Murabba'at, one of the most desolate spots in Palestine. Then in
1960 a group of archaeologists under the direction of Professor Yigael
Yadin of Jerusalem University found army orders from the leader to his
subordinates in caves in the Hever Ravine. The original letters deal
with arrests, confiscation of crops and removal of population from
Tekoa, the birthplace of the prophet Amos. A second expedition led by
Professor Yadin in 1961 found in the same place a bundle of
documents—papyri in Hebrew, Greek, and Aramaic. It is thought that
these are minutes dating from the year A.D. 134 from the archives of the
commandant of the stronghold at En-Gedi by the Dead Sea who had
been installed there by Bar-Kokhba. Together with coins of the "Son of
a Star"—which was Bar-Kokhba's title—and pieces of crockery, a
gruesome discovery awaited the archaeologists: skeletons of rebels
indicated the desperate last act of this historical tragedy. Women and
men who had taken refuge there had obviously died of starvation in
their hide-out.

With all these discoveries since the first finds in 1947, quite apart
from the recovery of numerous Biblical manuscripts, the period
immediately after Biblical times has for the first time been illuminated
in a way which no one a few years ago would have dared to hope.

So far the total number of manuscripts discovered at the Dead Sea
amounts to over 400, including 100 Biblical manuscripts. Apart from
the Book of Esther every book of the Old Testament is represented. The
best known is the complete scroll of the Book of Isaiah. The scrolls and
fragments which come from Qumran date from about 200 B.C. to A.D.
68; those from Wadi Murabba'at go up to A.D. 132–135.

These unexpected discoveries in the words of Professor Lankester
Harding are "perhaps the most sensational archaeological event of our
time. It will take a whole generation of Biblical scholars to assess the
value of these manuscripts."

In the summer of 1947 a sheer coincidence led to the discovery of the
oldest manuscripts of the Bible so far known. Among a collection of

writings on leather and payrus which Bedouin shepherds came across in a cave in Wadi Qumran on the north side of the Dead Sea was a 23-foot leather scroll containing the complete text of the book of Isaiah in Hebrew. Expert examination of the document revealed beyond doubt that the Isaiah text dated from 100 B.C. It is an original prophetic scroll of the type that Jesus held in his hands when he read the lesson in Nazareth on the sabbath (Luke 4[16ff]). This copy of Isaiah, over 2,000 years old, is a unique proof of the reliability of the holy scriptures that have been handed down to us, for the text agrees exactly with what we have in our present day Bible.

The oldest and most complete text of the Old and New Testaments were, until recently, the famous Codex Vaticanus and Codex Sinaiticus dating from the 4th century A.D., supplemented in 1931 by the Chester Beatty papyri dating from the 2nd and 3rd centuries A.D. Besides these, there were some fragments of the Old Testament from pre-Christian times (Fuad and Rylands Fragments). But all of these documents are in Greek, that is to say translations as far as the Old Testament is concerned. The oldest and fullest MS. in Hebrew was the Codex Petropolitanus, dating from A.D. 916. By the discovery of the leather scroll of Isaiah at the Dead Sea the Hebrew text has been carried back to almost exactly 1,000 years before. In 1935 a part of St. John's Gospel in Greek—the famous Bodmer papyrus—dating from the time of Trajan (98–117) was discovered. These old MSS. are the most convincing answer to all doubts as to the reliability of the text that we have in our Bibles today.

Much has been written about Qumran in the meantime. The Dead Sea Scrolls have been the subject of publications of a strictly specialised nature, but Qumran has also figured in literature intended for the general public. The time has certainly come to ask whether Qumran has actually proved to be the sensational find it seemed to be. The answer cannot be definitely either positive or negative. Once more we shall be obliged to record that the reply to this question is: partly "yes" and partly "no". The Dead Sea Scrolls have failed to provide the spectacular discoveries concerning the lives and activities of John the Baptist and Jesus the Nazarene, for which people had secretly hoped. Instead the "voice from the desert" of Qumran has made us aware of how little we really know about the historical John the Baptist and the historical Jesus. What a part of the scrolls does confirm, however, is the striking agreement between the Old Testament texts on which they are based and the Masoretic version of the Hebrew Old Testament of a full thousand years later. This fact is of the greatest importance in the textual history of the Old Testament.

The contents of the Qumran texts with their innumerable anticipations of Christian concepts, teachings, demands, rules and regulations were and still are grist to the mill of the sceptics and to those who doubt the originality of Jesus and his Church. After the Qumran discoveries, they are not willing to grant Christianity anything from the Beatitudes of the Sermon on the Mount to the white baptismal robe, from the Last Supper to the community organisation. Among the people belonging to the Qumran sect, the Essenes, there was a "community council" consisting of 12 men and 3 priests. The number twelve corresponds not merely to the 12 tribes of Israel but also to the 12 apostles of Jesus. The Qumran people had "elders" and the word "priest" comes ultimately from the term loaned from the Greek for an elder of the Christian community, "presbyter".[1] Even the office of bishop was not unknown to the people of Qumran. The word "bishop" has its origins in the Greek word "episkopos" which literally means "overseer". The dignity of "overseer", which in Aramaic is "mebagger", was not unknown to the Qumran sectarians.

In short, from the 12 apostles and the whole "community organisation" to the value concepts and beliefs as well as to the consciousness of guilt, the idea of redemption and the expectation of eternity, all these Christian fundamentals were already known to the Essenes.

Occasionally the correspondences verge on the grotesque. Thus we find in Paul the curious passage: "For this cause ought the woman to have power on her head because of the angels" (1 Corinthians 11[10]). As a last resort we can understand this to mean that women should wear a veil as a sign that they were in the power of the man. But what has this to do with the "angels"? The Qumran rule provides the explanation. The Essenes believed that at the sacral community meal there were "holy angels" who could be offended by the presence of certain persons or groups of persons. As far as women were concerned, the early Christians acted in the same way, even if they did not go so far as the Essenes and exclude women completely from their sacral community meal. They merely imposed on them certain restrictions such as the wearing of a veil. In the case of the sick, the lame, the blind, the deaf and the maimed, the Essene ordinance went beyond what they could accept. "Go out quickly into the streets and lanes of the city, and bring in hither the poor, and the maimed, and the halt and the blind" (Luke 14[21]). Some scholars consider these words to be a clear protest and a refusal to accept the regulation of the community of Qumran.

Here we reach the differences between Qumran and Christianity. Again we find in Luke something like a disagreement. He records the parable of the unjust steward and has Jesus say: "... for the children of this world are in their generation wiser than the children of light" (Luke 16[8]). The Essenes were "children of light". The members of the early Christian communities are here called upon not to imitate the Essenes who isolated themselves and withdrew into the desert and so lost

---

[1] The German text has been slightly adapted to bring it into line with facts of English rather than German.

contact with the world. Whilst the people of Qumran concealed themselves from the rest of the world, the Christian messengers went out into
"the streets and lanes" and what they preached was meant not only for
the chosen, but also for "the poor, and the maimed, and the halt, and
the blind". The message was not "justice", but "judge not, that ye be
not judged" (Matthew 7[1]) and also "... love one another, As I have
loved you" (John 15[12]). This was a new message which was unknown
to the "voice from the desert" of Qumran. In whatever way
Christianity subsequently developed and whatever cause for criticism
it has offered, even its sharpest critics cannot deny that it is *kindliness*
which made it different from Qumran with its strict ordinances.

REBUILDING WITH THE HELP OF THE BIBLE

Economic planning with the help of the Old Testament—The wells of the patriarchs provide for the settlers—"Honey out of the rock"—Stone walls to collect dew—Digging again in Solomon's mines—Pioneering on the Biblical pattern.

No one would dispute that the Old Testament is filled with that imponderable moral and spiritual power which outlasts time and loses nothing with its passing. But that its power should extend to the sober and prosaic business of remoulding the economy of a country is a sensational development.

Since 1948, the Book of Books, now more than 3,000 years old, has been playing the role of a trusted adviser in the rebuilding of the modern state of Israel. In the growth of both agriculture and industry the exact historical information given in the Bible has proved to be of the highest importance.

The territory of the new state covers about 8,000 square miles. In 1948 it was only in the Plain of Jezreel and the productive lowlands by the Lake of Galilee that there seemed to be even a remote reflection of the Biblical description of the Promised Land, flowing with milk and honey. Large areas in Galilee and almost the whole of the Judaean highlands presented an entirely different picture from Biblical times. Centuries of mismanagement had even destroyed the grass roots. Careless cultivation of olive and fig groves on the hillsides had dried them up. Increasing barrenness and considerable erosion were the sequel.

The inexperienced settlers, to whom the country was a completely unknown quantity, found the Old Testament of priceless assistance. It helped them to make many a decision in questions of cultivation, afforestation or industrial development. It is nothing unusual even for experts to consult it on doubtful problems.

"Fortunately," says Dr. Walter Clay Lowdermilk, an expert on agricultural economics, "the Bible tells us what plants can grow in particular places. We know from the book of Judges that the Philistines grew corn, for Samson tied foxes tails together, 'and put a firebrand in the midst between two tails' and 'let them go into the standing corn of the Philistines'. In the same manner he set fire to their olive groves and as he was on his way to visit his lady love he passed vineyards (Judges 15^5; 14^5). All these plants are now doing well there."

Every attempt to settle in the Negev must have seemed hopeless.

383

South of the mountains of Judah between Hebron and Egypt lay nothing but desert, interspersed with wadis and barren of any vegetation. Meteorological measurements showed an average annual rainfall of less than 6 inches. It was a discouraging prospect.

Nothing can grow with a rainfall as small as that. But had the stories of the days of the patriarchs nothing of value to contribute? "And Abraham journeyed from thence toward the south country, and dwelled between Kadesh, and Shur and sojourned in Gerar" (Gen. 20[1]). The father of the patriarchs was a shepherd, he kept close company with his large flock, and it needed pasture and water.

A reconnaissance party spent weeks with geologists scouring the desolate sand-dunes and rocky hills of the "south country".[1] They actually found what they were looking for. And the Israelis did exactly what Isaac had done. "And Isaac departed thence, and pitched his tent in the valley of Gerar, and dwelt there. And Isaac digged again the wells of water which they had digged in the days of Abraham his father" (Gen. 26[17,18]). Choked with sand, the ancient wells are still there and still as before at the foot of them runs clear pure water, "springing water", as Isaac's servants called it. They meant by that drinking water, for otherwise the underground water in the Negev—as was proved by testing the soil—is brackish and unpalatable. Once again tents stood on the same spots by the water-holes. The well beside which Abraham's rejected bondwoman Hagar rested with her son Ishmael (Gen. 21[14-19]) now supplies water for sixty families of settlers. Rumanian Jews have settled on a nearby hillside only a mile or two from the Beersheba of the Bible.

In the same area there is another remarkable feature. The settlers have planted seedlings, slender young trees which are coming along famously. "The first tree which Abraham planted in the soil of Beersheba was a tamarisk," declared Dr. Joseph Weitz, the Israeli forestry expert. "Following his example we have planted 2,000,000 of them in this area. Abraham did absolutely the right thing. For the tamarisk is one of the few trees, as we have proved, that will flourish at all in the south where the annual rainfall is under 6 inches." Here again the Bible pointed the way: "And Abraham planted a tamarisk tree in Beersheba" (Gen. 21[33]—R.V.).

Afforestation is an essential prerequisite in making a countryside which is short of water into a fertile land. Since the beginning of the return of the Jews to Palestine the settlers have been planting forests. In choosing the types of trees they could rely on the observations of their forefathers just as much as in the choice of suitable areas. A few years ago, when the question arose as to whether the bare mountain slopes in the northern part of the country could be afforested, the book of Joshua gave them the answer. "And Joshua spake unto the house of Joseph,

[1] Negev.

even to Ephraim and to Manasseh saying: 'Thou art a great people and hast great power: thou shalt not have one lot only: but the mountains shall be thine for it is a wood and thou shalt cut it down'" (Josh. 17[17-18]).

Both these tribes, it was known, settled north of Jerusalem from the mountain ridge of Bethel past Biblical Shechem at the foot of Mt. Gerizim right to the Plain of Jezreel. "Since trees are known to grow better in places where there have been trees before," argued Professor Zohary of the Hebrew University, "we are relying on the Book of Books."

Much discussion has centred round an extremely obscure reference which until a few years ago was understood by nobody: "He made him (Israel) . . . that he might eat the increase of the fields: and he made him to suck honey out of the rock, and oil out of the flinty rock" (Deut. 32[13]). The riddle was solved when in the Negev they came across thousands of little circular stone walls. There was no water in the neighbourhood, neither springs nor any pools of underground water worth speaking of. When the sand was shovelled out of them they found the remains of the roots of ancient olive trees and vines. The stone walls had served their ancestors as valuable collectors of dew.

Their construction indicated an astonishing practical knowledge of the process of condensation. The stones in the circles were loosely stacked to ensure that the wind could blow through them. In this way the moisture from the air was deposited inside. This moisture was enough to feed an olive or a vine. Inside each wall there was always one tree only. The sweet juice of the grapes was often extolled in ancient times as "honey". The olive tree produces oil. Honey and oil were sucked "out of the rock . . . out of the flinty rock". Present day Israelis set great store by these serviceable little dew-collectors in the redevelopment of their agriculture.

In the second half of 1953 for the first time in Israel 3,000 tons of copper were mined. Where the houses of Solomon's workmen and slaves stood 3,000 years ago, new miners' houses stand today. Copper mining still pays. Dr. Ben Tor, the geologist, had the ancient copper mines tested in 1949 as to their mineral resources and their possibilities as an economic proposition. Experts estimated that there was enough ore to provide 100,000 tons of copper. According to their calculations the ramifications of the mines could produce at least another 200,000 tons. Since then, "Ezion Geber, which is beside Eloth on the shores of the Red Sea" (1 Kings 9[26]), has been a hive of activity. Jeeps and trucks scurry around, churning up clouds of yellow dust, and gangs of sunburnt men ply pick and shovel. "Wherever the ore is particularly rich," maintains a mining engineer, "we come upon the slag and furnaces of Solomon's miners. It often seems as if they had just left the place."

In the company's main office there is a text hanging on the wall. It reads: "For the Lord thy God bringeth thee into a good land . . . a land whose stones are iron, and out of whose hills thou mayest dig brass" (Deut. 8[7,9]).

Iron is however not yet being mined. But the outcrops have already been recorded. Not far from Beersheba, exactly where the iron-smelting Philistines lived, Dr. Ben Tor noticed steep hillsides with reddish-black veins, the sign of iron ore deposits. Investigation showed that they amounted to 15,000,000 tons on a rough estimate. Most of this is ore of inferior quality but in the course of the survey excellent ores were discovered with between 60%–65% of pure iron.

Another very well known Biblical passage kept running in the mind of Xiel Federmann, a shrewd business man. It was the sentence in which the destruction of Sodom and Gomorrah is described, ". . . and lo, the smoke of the country went up as the smoke of a furnace" (Gen. 19[28]). He could get no peace. Did these conflagrations not indicate subterranean gas? And where there is underground gas there are also deposits of oil, as has long been recognised. A company was formed and the experts who were sent to the Dead Sea confirmed completely Federmann's guess. On November 3, 1953, the first Israeli oil well was drilled.

More than fifty farming communities have sprung up again between the sites of the Biblical settlements of Dan and Beersheba. Almost every one of them possesses a small modern pumping station above a spring or a well dating from ancient times. Gradually many parts of the country are coming to resemble once more the cheerful picture of Old Testament times.

It is a hard task that the state of Israel has set itself. But its people are fully convinced that they and their descendants will overcome all difficulties—not least thanks to the Bible—and that the prophecy of Ezekiel to the children of Israel will be fulfilled.

"And the desolate land shall be tilled, whereas it lay desolate in the sight of all that passed by. And they shall say, this land that was desolate is become like the garden of Eden" (Ezek. 36[34-35]).

POSTSCRIPT TO THE REVISED EDITION

Joachim Rehork

Is the "accuracy" of the Bible important?—Inaccuracies—Problematical patriarchs—The Bible: the most diligently researched work in world literature—Endless questions—Contact with the past—Is the Bible right after all?—Ancient Israel between the fronts—Reading between the lines—The Bible as a record of events.

MORE than twenty years have passed since the first appearance of this book. We have now come to the end of an attempt to incorporate new knowledge into it without disturbing the substance of the original text by tendentious criticism arising from the fresh discoveries. If we now ask ourselves again: "Well, is the Bible right after all?", some readers will reply with a definite "yes", while others will answer with a no less definite "no". Between these two answers there is room for a wide variety of opinion.

There is no lack of scholars—among them historians, theologians, philologists and archaeologists—who after conscientious examination of the Biblical tradition have come to the conclusion that fundamentally it is of secondary importance whether the facts reported in the Bible are correct or not. According to them, the Bible is primarily "prophecy". It is a religious message, made known with the means available at the time of its origin, or rather the different times of its origin, for the Bible is the extraordinarily complex product of numerous "growth strata" which in the course of centuries produced the "Bible" in its present form while leaving clear indications of the stages of its growth. It is more important in their view to shed light on the *origin*, the growth process of the collection of writings known as the "Bible" and to understand how the various elements of the Biblical tradition fit into the whole in order to obtain an idea, with the help of such knowledge, of what the authors of the individual books of the Bible wanted to tell their readers. In any case, the emphasis lay on getting the message across and not on the accuracy of historical details.

For the majority of Bible readers, on the other hand, as well as for a large number of Biblical scholars, a great deal still depends on the question whether statements in the Bible can be proved. The Dominican father, Roland de Vaux, for example, one of the most prominent figures in the history of Biblical antiquity, regarded the capacity to survive of the Jewish and Christian faith as dependent upon the agree-

387

ment between "religious" and "objective" history. He stated his opinion thus: "... if Israel's historical faith does not have its roots in history, then it is wrong and the same is true of our faith." The no less distinguished American Biblical archaeologist George Ernest Wright expressed the opinion that in Biblical belief everything depends on whether the main events actually took place. That is exactly the spirit in which the present work had its origin twenty years ago.

These two scholars, de Vaux and Wright, however, encountered active opposition in specialist circles. Not from less deeply religious colleagues, but from specialists who took their religion no less seriously than de Vaux and Wright, but who at the same time felt the desire to base their religious convictions on a more solid foundation than the confirmation of historical statements in the Bible. This is no cause for surprise since the Bible certainly does not make things easy for the researcher. It is full of problematical statements with the consequence that representatives of the most diverse disciplines, "schools" and opinions have racked their brains again and again over contradictions, repetitions and inconsistencies in the Biblical text—inconsistencies of which the following are a few examples.

In the Bible there are *two* accounts of the Creation (Genesis $1^{1-2,3}$ and Genesis 2^{4ff}).

In the first of these two accounts of the Creation, God created man *last*; in the second, however, God created him *first*, that is to say, before all other creatures.

In one case God created mankind from the beginning as "male and female"; then, however, only the man came into being from "the dust of the ground", while woman was formed subsequently from a rib of the man.

The second account of the Creation contains details not mentioned in the first.

The two accounts of the Creation also differ from one another in their literary form. The first is hymnal, of the nature of a litany, whilst the second is a simple narrative.

So far reference has been made only to repetitions. The name of Moses' father-in-law has been transmitted in *three* different forms, once as Jethro (Exodus 3^1; 4^{18}; 18^{1-12}), once as Reuel (Exodus 2^{18}) and finally as Hobab (Judges 4^{11}). Other passages in the Bible also make us wonder what their meaning is, for example:

What sort of darkness "over the land of Egypt" was it from which the Egyptians suffered whilst the Israelites in bondage in Egypt did not (Exodus 10^{22f})?

How could Moses describe his own death (Deuteronomy chap. 34)? Or to put the question in another way: can the first five books of the Bible really have been written by Moses when they tell us of his death?

These are only a few examples of inconsistencies in the Bible. These and similar incongruities have raised questions, however, which have led scholars to examine the Bible time and time again and to offer fresh interpretations. For generations the Bible has been the object of critical investigation and it can claim to be not only one of the most widely distributed and best selling books, but also the work of world literature which has been subjected to the most objective and thorough scholarly research. It has long been known that it contains elements belonging to the most varied literary genres, from the edifying treatise to the thriller, from the sermon to the legal text, from the liturgical hymn to the love song, from historiography to the novel, not to mention legends, anecdotes and folk-tales. A complete "national literature" is to be found in this collection known as the "Bible". In consequence, we also know that from the outset historians and archaeologists attach more historical weight to some books of the Bible than to others which have rather to be considered as "literary". In short, we know that the Bible is certainly not homogeneous and to a certain extent we are aware of the "joins".

It was indeed a matter of centuries before the various books of the Bible were brought together and codified, that is to say, given a final written form. Perhaps what we know as the song of Miriam (Exodus 15^{21}) is really a genuine example which has come down to us from the Late Bronze period (13th century B.C.), whilst the second Epistle of Saint Peter, which is probably the nearest to us in date of the Biblical works, may not have been composed until the second quarter of the second century A.D. The majority of the Biblical works were probably brought together to form the "Bible" between the sixth century B.C. and the first century A.D., although in indicating these dates a few centuries must be added at the beginning of the period for a number of books of the Bible and some source material as well as a few decades at the end for some of the books of the New Testament.

Yet however much we know about the Bible today, we still do not know nearly enough. There is no end to the problems. On the contrary, every new discovery raises new questions. And there is no lack of fresh discoveries, certainly not of those in the area of archaeology. A veritable boom in archaeology has occurred precisely in the principal region where the events of the Bible took place, in ancient and present day Israel. The results of archaeological work there achieve a publicity which it is unlikely they will ever receive here. This is no cause for surprise, since for the Israelis of today archaeology is "a handshake with the past". Archaeological finds are called "greetings from our forefathers". Archaeology is part of the search for the collective identity which is here being documented, a search for what binds together the immigrants to Israel from all over the world, whether they be religious orthodox or liberal. Each one of the "greetings from the forefathers", however, each one of the direct "handshakes with the past", is also more or less a contribution to Bible research and each of the discoveries helps not only to solve problems but also indicates fresh problems. The situation in Bible scholarship is no different from that in other branches of knowledge. This is also the reason why a book such as this was in need of revision after the passage of two decades.

The discovery of the tablets at Nuzi (Yorgan Tepe) can here be cited again as an example. It provided striking enlightenment concerning the legal customs of the patriarchs, whilst at the same time opening to question the generally accepted date for the beginning of the period of the patriarchs.

In view of such a host of questions and correspondences, can we really say that the Bible "is right"? Of course, there are quite different levels of "being right". There is the level of *belief*, of religious conviction and of subjective feeling that something is right. Such belief is not at all in question here and must remain a matter of belief. The Bible cannot be proved as a document of faith, nor for the believer can it be convincingly disproved, for belief begins where knowledge and proof have their limit. In any case, proofs such as we are seeking can only be produced for or against the Bible as a historical source.

Here we have to condemn a bad habit current these days. Recently the rather derogatory term "less than a history book" has become customary in referring to the Bible. Quite respectable writers today have adopted this bad habit. In so doing they forget that the Bible is intended to be a representation of history. This is true of at least a large number of its texts. It would be foolish to criticise these texts because their authors did not yet adhere to the standards which we are now accustomed to apply to the writing of history and which in their turn are not destined to be eternal. Let us not forget that the Bible speaks to us from the historical past! But the historical past is powerful. It has to do with the state of man, his moods, the trends of the period which affect him, the influences exerted by his environment, the spirit of the times, the fads to which he is exposed. It is only in the light, or the twilight, of all these things that we experience our environment and all these things determine what can enter our sphere of experience and thus become available to us as knowledge.

In other words, if we do not wish to subject it to force, we must not squeeze the Bible into the Procrustean bed of our demands for "historical truth" and "scientific objectivity", which are themselves sufficiently problematical. It is, or rather, it was an historical work, but not such as we understand the term. It is the account of a people and its god, whose powers his worshippers came to know in the course of history. The Bible does not attempt to be a neutral, objective account of the events it relates. It is far too committed for that, much too rooted in its own times, in the times of which it speaks the language. This, too, must not be forgotten—the Bible uses descriptive methods which are by no means always those we employ. Biblical language is naturally abstract, yet is much more rich in images than ours. What we reduce to a short, conceptual formulation, the Bible converts into a story and its descriptions are often puzzles whose ambiguity is quite often intentional.

The sacrifice of Isaac by Abraham commanded by God but not carried out just at the last moment (Genesis $22^{1\text{-}13}$) may serve as an example. It can be interpreted in three ways.

In the first place it may be the vestige of a primitive initiation rite, a kind of "blood baptism". Only he who wholly and unconditionally submits himself to his god becomes a full member of the community.

Secondly, the passage is a renunciation, in more or less allegorical form, of the custom of human sacrifice and more particularly of the sacrifice of boys which was widespread in the Ancient East.

Thirdly, it is a test of faith for Abraham. The author of this chapter in the Bible himself suggests this when he writes at the beginning of his account: "God did tempt Abraham."

As our time and patience have grown short, we usually feel extremely ill at ease when faced with the task of decoding these "linguistic allegorical puzzles".

In order to transport ourselves back into the thoughts of the Bible authors, we have simultaneously to turn back the wheel of history to that point in time which marks the beginning of the codification, the definitive text of the hitherto oral or written separate traditions of Ancient Israel, and thus of the growth of the complex structure known as the "Bible".

Is the Bible always right? We shall certainly be able to answer in the affirmative for those passages which have been confirmed by non-Biblical parallel sources or by archaeological discoveries. The Bible can claim another form of "rightness", however, insofar as it brings nearer to us its times and the people of its times with their ways of thought and behaviour so that we learn how better to understand their sermons, parables, allegories, visions, symbols, and allusions. Perhaps we shall some day be in a position to affirm, even of passages which are still unclear and puzzling to us today, that the Bible is right after all, as seen through the eyes of the people of its times!

CHRONOLOGICAL TABLE OF BIBLE DEVELOPMENT
(From: Claus Westermann: Abriss der Bibelkunde, p. 266 f.)

Epoch	Date	Parts of the Bible
Occupation of the land	13th century B.C.	Song of Miriam (Exodus 15[21]).
Period of the judges	c. 12th/11th century B.C.	Book of the Covenant (Exodus 20[22] to 23[33]).
David	c. 1000 B.C.	Beginning of the composition of the Psalms. Story of the Ark of the Covenant. (1 Samuel 4–6; 2 Samuel 6)
Period of the kings (Solomon and later the two kingdoms)	10th century to 722/721 B.C.	Origin of the written source by the Elohists and Jahvists[1].
Hezekiah of Judah	727 (721) to 698 (693) B.C.	The so-called "Proto-Isaiah" (=Isaiah 1–39), Micah.
The so-called "Deuteronomistic Reform"[2] (621 B.C.)	King Josiah of Judah (639/638 to 609 B.C.)	Deuteronomy (5th Book of Moses) Habakkuk, Nahum, Zephaniah.
First exile	597 B.C.	Jeremiah (original scroll). A small part of the Book of Ezekiel.
"Babylonian exile"	586 to 539/8 B.C.	Lamentations, the so-called "Deutero-Isaiah" (=Isaiah 40–55), the so-called "Deuteronomical historical work"[3] (Joshua, Judges, Samuel, Kings), the so-called "priestly writings".
Restoration until the consecration of the "Second Temple"	539/8 to 515 B.C.	The so-called "Trito-Isaiah" (=Isaiah 56–66), Haggai, Zechariah 1–8.
Persian period	539/8 B.C. until Alexander the Great (King 336 to 323 B.C.)	460 Malachi, around 450 probably Ezra and Nehemiah (Nehemiah was governor under Artaxerxes I, [465–424 B.C.]). Between 400 and 200 B.C.: Jonah, perhaps in the 4th century B.C.: Job, 4th or 3rd century B.C.: Joel and the so-called "chroniclers' history work".
Hellenism	From Alexander the Great until Rome's annexation of Egypt (30 B.C.)	Around 332: Zechariah 9–14. 3rd century: Proverbs and Song of Solomon. Around 250: Ecclesiastes. Beginning of the Septuagint (between 285 and 246 B.C.).
Maccabees	167/166 B.C. until the intervention of Pompey (63 B.C.) or until Herod the Great (37–4 B.C.)	Between 170 and 160 B.C.: Book of Esther, Book of Daniel. (Perhaps between 166 and 160 B.C.: first canon of the Bible [under Judas Maccabaeus]?) Qumran texts.

Epoch	Date	Parts of the Bible
Roman period	From A.D. 6 (A.D. 66: rebellion; A.D. 70: destruction of Herod's temple; A.D. 73: fall of Masada.	Middle of the first century A.D.: New Testament Epistles. About A.D. 70: Gospel of St. Mark. Between 75 and about A.D. 95.: Matthew and Luke. Probably after 90: John's apocalypse. End of the 1st century: Acts of the Apostles and Gospel of St. John. Also the establishment of the Hebrew Bible canon at Jabneh (Jamnia). Further New Testament Epistles. Middle of the 2nd century A.D.: Second Epistle of St. Peter.

[1] The written sources of the first five books of the Bible, known as the "Pentateuch", which are attributed to Moses. The source we owe to the Jahvists employs the name "Jahveh" for "God", whilst that due to the Elohists employs the name "Elohim". The work by the Jahvists originated in Southern Judaea probably during the 10th–9th century B.C., that of the Elohists probably in the 8th century B.C. in northern Israel. The two works were later merged with one another to begin with and subsequently together with the "Second Book of the Law" (*Deuteronomy* [7th century B.C.]) and the "priestly writings" (6th century [period of exile] or not until the 5th century B.C.) to form what are known as the "five books of Moses".

[2] The "Deuteronomistic Reform" is referred to in this way because this reform carried out by King Josiah of Judah (639/8–609 B.C.) in 621 B.C. attempts to put into practice the norms of the "Second Book of the Law" (*Deuteronomy* [the so-called fifth book of Moses]) which had only recently been codified (622 B.C.); efforts were made to lend importance to it by giving it the style of an address to the people by Moses at the end of the wanderings in the wilderness.

[3] The Biblical books Joshua, Judges, Samuel and Kings are called the "Deuteronomistic History" because, having originated probably in the 6th century B.C., they are composed entirely in the spirit of the "Second Book of the Law" (*Deuteronomy* [the so-called fifth book of Moses]), which was codified in the 7th century (622 B.C.), and of the "Deuteronomistic Reform" of King Josiah (621 B.C.). It has a connection with "Deuteronomy" only by reason of *content*, however, but not of chronology, for it originated, as stated, not before the 6th century B.C. and possibly later.

BIBLIOGRAPHY

Abel, F.-M.: Géographie de la Palestine I (1933), II (1938), Histoire de la Palestine depuis la conquête d'Alexandre jusqu'à l'invasion Arabe I/II (1952).
Adams, J. M. K.: Ancient Records and the Bible (1946).
Albright, W. F.: Archaeology and the Religion of Israel (1953), Recent Discoveries in Bible Lands (1936), Exploring Sinai with the University of California (1948), Archaeology of Palestine (1954), From the Stone Age to Christianity (1949).
Alt, A.: Die Herkunft der Hyksos in neuer Sicht (1954), Kleine Schriften zur Geschichte des Volkes Israel I/II (1953).
Andrae, W.: Das wiedererstandene Assur (1938).
Augstein, R.: Jesus Menschensohn (1972).
Avigad, N.: Bullae and seals from a post-exilic Judean archive (1976).

Bailey, A. E.: Daily life in Bible Times (1943).
Barrois, A. G., Manuel d'archéologie biblique I/II (1939/53).
Bauer, H.: Die alphabetischen Keilschrifttexte von Ras-Shamra (1936).
Begrich, J.: Die Chronologie der Könige von Israel und Juda (1929).
Ben-Chorin, Sch.: Bruder Jesus. Der Nazarener in jüdischer Sicht (1970).
Benzinger, I.: Hebräische Archäologie (1927).
Biblisches Nachschlagewerk, Stuttgarter (1955).
Bittel, K.: Die Ruinen von Bogazköy (1937).
Bittel, K., und R. Naumann: Bogazköy (1938).
Bodenheimer, Fr. S. u. O. Theodor: Ergebnisse der Sinai-Expedition 1927 (1929).
Boschke, F. L.: Die Schöpfung ist noch nicht zu Ende (Econ, 1962).
Bossert, H. Th.: Altanatolien (1942).
Breasted, J. H.: The Dawn of Conscience (1933), Ancient Records of Egypt I–V (1906/07), History of Egypt, 2nd Ed. 1954.
Budge, W. E. A.: The Babylonian Story of the Deluge and the Epic of Gilgamesh (1920) revised by C. J. Gadd (1929).
Burrows, M.: What mean these Stones? (1941).

Caiger, S. L.: Bible and Spade (1936).
Canyon, Fr.: Bible and Archaeology (1955).
Carleton, P.: Buried Empires (1939).
Chase, M. E.: The Bible and the Common Reader (1946).
Clay, A. T.: Business Documents of Murashu Sons (1898).
Clemen, C.: Die phönikische Religion nach Philo von Byblos (1939).
Clermont-Ganneau, C. S.: La Stèle de Mésa (1887).
Collart, Philippes ville de Macédoine.
Contenau, G.: La civilisation phénicienne (1949), La vie quoditienne à Babylone et en Assyrie (1953), Les civilisations anciennes du Proche Orient (1945), Manuel d'Archéologie orientale I–IV (1927/47).
Cornfeld, G., ed.: Pictorial Biblical encyclopedia; a visual guide to the Old and New Testaments. Edited by Gaalyahu Cornfeld assisted by Biblical scholars, historians and archaeologists (1964).
Craveri, M.: Das Leben des Jesus von Nazareth (1970).

Crowfoot, J. W., Kathleen M. Kenyon, E. L. Sukenik: The Buildings at Samaria (1942).
Cuneiform Texts: British Museum (Ed.).

Dalman, G.: Heilige Stätten und Wege (1935), Licht vom Osten (1923), Arbeit und Sitte in Palästina I–VII (1928/42).
Dalmas, G.: Die talmud. Texte über Jesu (1900).
Davis, J. D.: Dictionary of the Bible (1953).
Davis, J. D. and H. S. Gehman: The Westminster Dictionary of the Bible (1944).
Delitzsch, Fr.: Babel und Bibel (1903).
Deschner, K.: Jesusbilder in theologischer Sicht (1966).
Dobschütz, E. v.: Die Bibel im Leben der Völker (1954).
Dougherty, R. P.: Nabonitus and Belshazzar (1929).
Duncan, G.: Digging up Biblical History I/II (1931).
Dussaud, R.: Les Découvertes de Ras Shamra et l'Ancien Testament (1941).

Ebeling, E. u. B. Meissner: Reallexikon der Assyriologie I/II (1932/38).
Eberhard, E. G.: Bible-Thesaurus (1953).
Eissfeldt, O.: Philister und Phönizier, Der Alte Orient (1930), Baal Zephon, Zeus Kasios und der Durchzug der Israeliten durchs Meer (1932), Handbuch zum Alten Testament (1935).
Ellermeier, F.: Prophetie in Mari und Israel (1968).
Elliger, K.: Ein Zeugnis der judischen Gemeinde im Alexanderjahr 332 v. Chr., in: ZAW 62=Neue Folge 21 (1949/50), 63ff. Kleine Propheten (1975).
Ephesus, Forschungen in Veröffentl. V. Österr. Archäol. Inst. (1937).
Eusebius, Historica ecclesiastica, ed. by E. Schwartz (1914), The Life of Constantine.

Finegan, J.: Light from the Ancient Past (1954).
Frayzel, S.: A. History of the Jews (1952).
Fritz, V.: Israel in der Wüste (1970).

Gadd, E.: The Fall of Nineveh (1923).
Galling, K.: Biblisches Reallexikon (1937), Textbuch zur Geschichte Israels (1950).
Gardiner, A. H. and E. Peet: The Inscriptions of Sinai (1952).
Garis-Davies, N. de: The Tomb of Rekh-mi-re at Thebes (1943).
Garlake, P. S.: Great Zimbabwe (1973).
Garstang, J. B. E.: The Story of Jericho (1940).
Gerke, S.: Die Christ. Sarkophage d. vorkonstantin. Zeit (1940).
Gese, H. u.a.: Die Religion Altsyriens (1970).
Glueck, N.: The Other Side of the Jordan (1940), The River Jordan (1946).
Goldschmidt, L.: Der Babylonische Talmud (1935).
Gordon, C. H.: The Living Past (1941), Ugaritic Literature (1949).
Götze, A.: Hethiter, Churitter u. Assyrer (1936).
Gressmann, H.: Die älteste Gesichtsschreibung und Prophetie Israels (1921), Altorientalische Texte und Bilder zum Alten Testament (1927).
Gunkel, H., W. Stark u. a.: Die Schriften des Alten Testaments in Auswahl I–VII (1921/25).
Guthe, H.: Bibelatlas (1926), Palästina, Monographien zur Erdkunde 21 (1927).

Haag, H.: Bibellexikon (1968).
Haas, N.: Skeletal Remains from Givat ha-Mivtar (1970).
Harper: Bible Dictionary (1952).
Heidel, A.: The Gilgamesh-Epic and the Old Testament (1953).
Hengel, M.: Mors turpissima crucis. Die Kreuzigung in der antiken Welt und die »Torheit« des »Wortes vom Kreuz« (1976).
Herodotus: History. Herrmann, S.: Israels Aufenthalt in Ägypten (1970).

Hogarth, D. G.: Excavations in Ephesus (1908).
Honor, L. L.: Sennacherib's Invasion of Palestine (1926).

International Standard Bible Encyclopaedia (1952).

Jannsen, E.: Juda in der Exilheit (1956).
Jansen, H. L.: Die Politik Antiochus' IV (1943).
Jirku, A.: Die ägypt. Listen palästinens. u. syr. Ortsnamen (1937).
Josephus, Flavius: Antiquities, Wars of the Jews.
Junge, P. J.: Dareios I., König der Perser (1944).

Kaiser, O.: Altes Testament. Vorexilische Literatur (1973), Einleitung in das Alte
    Testament (1975), Der Prophet Jesaja (1977), Israel und Ägypten (1963), Zwischen
    den Fronten (1972).
Kapelrud, A. S.: The Ras Shamra Discoveries and the Old Testament (1965).
Kaufmann, C. M.: Handbuch der christl. Archäologie I–III (1922).
Kenyon, Sir F.: Bible and Archaeology (1940).
Kenyon, K. M.: Jerusalem; excavating 3000 years of history. (New Aspects of Anti-
    quity) Thames, London (1967), Archaeology in the Holy Land (1970), Royal Cities
    of the Old Testament (1971), Digging up Jerusalem (1974).
Klausner, J.: Jesus von Nazareth (1950), Von Jesus zu Paulus (1950).
Knopf, Lietzmann, Weinel: Einführung in das Neue Testament (1949).
Knudtzon, J. A.: Die El-Amarna-Tafeln I/II (1908/15).
Koeppel, P. R., Palästina (1930).
Kohl und Watzinger: Antike Synagogen in Galiläa (1916).
Koldewey, R.: Das wiedererstehende Babylon (1925).
Kraeling, E. G.: Gerasa. City of the Decapolis (1938).
Kugler-Schaumberger: Sternkunde und Sterndienst in Babel (1935).

Laible, H.: Jesus Christus im Talmud (1900).
Landay, J. M.: Silent Cities, sacred stones—archaeological discovery in the land of the
    Bible (1971).
Layard, A.: Discoveries in the Ruins of Nineveh and Babylon (1853).
Lefebvre, G.: Romans et contes égyptiens de l'époque pharaonique (1949).
Lentzen, H. J.: Die Entwicklung der Ziggurat (1942).
Lepsius, C. R.: Königsbuch der alten Ägypter (1858), Denkmäler aus Ägypten und
    Äthiopien (1849/56).
Lietzmann, H.: Petrus und Paulus in Rom (1927).
Loud, G.: Megiddo Ivories (1939), Megiddo II (1948).

Macalister, R. A. S.: Gezer I–III (1912), The excavations of Gezer (1912), A Century
    of Excavations in Palestine (1925).
McCown, C. C.: Tell en-Hasbeh. Berkeley, Calif., The Palestine Institute of Pacific
    School of Religion and the American Schools of Oriental Research (1947).
Mari: Archives royales de, ed. Musée du Louvre I–V.
Meyer, Ed.: Der Papyrusfund von Elephantine (1912), Geschichte des Altertums I–III
    (1925/37).
Miller, M. S. and J. L.: Encyclopedia of Bible Life (1944).
Moldenke, H. N. and A. L.: Plants of the Bible (1952).
Montet, P.: Les nouvelles fouilles de Tanis (1929/32, 1933), Avaris, Pi-Ramsès, Tanis
    (Syria XVII 1936), Tanis (1942).
Moret, A.: The Nile and Egyptian Civilisation (1927).
Morton, H. V.: In the Steps of the Master (1953), Through Lands of the Bible
    (1954).
Moscati, S.: Geschichte und Kultur der semitischen Völker (1953).
Mowinckel, S.: Studien zum Buche Ezra-Nehemia I (1964).

Negev, A.: Archäologisches Lexikon zur Bibel (1972).
Newberry, P. E.: Beni Hasan I (1893).
Noth, M.: Die Welt des Alten Testaments (1953), Geschichte Israels (1954).

Origen: Contra Celsum I, 32.
Orlinski, H. M.: Ancient Israel (1954).
Otto, E.: Ägypten (1953).
Otto, W.: Handbuch der Altertumswissenschaft (1928).

Parrot, A.: Mari une ville perdue (1936), Archéologie mésopotamienne, Les Etapes I (1946), Studia Mariana (1950), Déluge et arche de Noé (1952), Découverte des mondes ensevelis (1952).
Petrie, Fl.: Researches in Sinai (1906).
Pfeiffer, R. H.: History of New Testament Times (1949), Introduction to the Old Testament (1948).
Pingré, M.: Cométographie I (1783).
Pius XII., Pope: Die Gottesbeweise im Lichte der modernen Naturwissenschaft (Universitas, Okt. 1952).
Plutarch: Life of Alexander.
Post, G. E.: Flora of Syria, Palestine and Sinai (1933).
Pottier, E.: Musée du Louvre, Catalogue des Antiquités Assyriennes No. 165.
Pritchard, J. B.: Ancient Near Eastern Texts relating to the Old Testament (1950), The Ancient Near East in pictures relating to the Old Testament (1954), Solomon and Sheba (1974).

Ramsay, W. M.: The Cities of St. Paul (1900).
Redford, D. B.: A Study of the Biblical Story of Joseph (1970).
Rehork, J.: Archäologie und biblisches Leben (1972).
Reisner, Th., H. and W. O. E. Oesterley: Excavations at Samaria I–II (1924).
Ricciotti, G.: Storia d'Israele I–II (1949).
Riemschneider, M.: Die Welt der Hethiter (1954).
Rothenberg, B.: Timna—das Tal der biblischen Kupferminen (1973).
Rowe, A.: The Topography and the History of Beth-Shan (1930), The Four Canaanite Temples of Beth-Shan I (1940).
Rowley, H. H.: The Re-discovery of the Old Testament (1945), The Old Testament and Modern Study (1952), From Joseph to Joshua (1948).

Schaeffer, C. F. A.: The Cuneiform Texts of Ras Shamra-Ugarit (1939), Ugaritica I–II (1939/49).
Scharff, A.: Handbuch der Archäologie I (1939).
Scharff, A., Moortgat, A.: Ägypten und Vorderasien im Altertum (1950).
Schmidt, E. F.: The Treasury of Persepolis and other Discoveries in the Homeland of the Achaemenians (1939).
Schmidt, W. H.: Königtum Gottes in Ugarit und Israel (1966).
Schnabel, P.: Berossos u. d. babylon.-hellenist. Literatur (1923).
Schott, A.: Das Gilgamesch-Epos (1934).
Sellin, E.: Wie wurde Sichem israelitische Stadt? (1923), Geschichte des israel.-jüd. Volkes (I–II. 1924/32).
Sethe, K.: Die Achtungstexte feindl. Fürsten, Völker u. Dinge auf altägypt. Tongefässscherben d. Mittl. Reiches (APAW 1926, Nr. 5), Zur Geschichte der Einbalsamierung b. d. alten Ägyptern (1934).
Simons, J.: Opgravingen in Palestina (1935).
Soden, W. v.: Leistung und Grenze sumerischer u. babylon. Wissenschaft, Welt als Geschichte II (1936), Das altbabylon. Briefarchiv v. Mari, Die Welt des Orients (1948).
Speiser, E. A.: Introduction to Hurrian (1941).
Starkey, J. L.: Excavations at Tell ed-Duweir 1933/34 (1934).

Starr, R. F. S.: Nuzi, Report on the Excavations at Yorgan Tepe near Kirkuk, Iraq, I–II (1937/39), Nuzi I (1939).
Steindorf, G., K. C. Seele: When Egypt Ruled the East (1942).
Strabo: Geography.
Sukenik, E. L.: Ancient Synagogues in Palestine and Greece (1934), The Third Wall of Jerusalem (1930) (with L. A. Mayer).
Svenskt Bibliskt Uppslagsverk (ed. I. Engnell and A. Fridrichsen, 1948).

Thompson, Th. L.: The Historicity of the Patriarchal Narratives. The Quest for the Historical Abraham (1974).
Torczyner, H.: Lakish I, The Lakish Letters (1938).
Tzaferis, V.: Jewish Tombs at and near Givat ha-Mivtar (1970).

Unger, E.: Babylon, die heilige Stadt (1931).
Ungnad, A.: Reallexikon der Assyriologie (1938), Die neue Grundlage f.d. alt-oriental. Chronologie (1940).

Vaux, R. de: Histoire ancienne d'Israël (1971).
Vincent, L. H.: Canaan d'après l'exploration récente (1914), Jéricho et sa chronologie (1935), L'Archéologie et la Bible (1945).

Watzinger, C.: Denkmäler Palästinas I–II (1933/35).
Weimar, P. und Zenger, E.: Exodus, Geschichten und Geschichte der Befreiung Israels (1975).
Weissbach, F. H.: Die Keilschriften der Archämeniden (1911).
Wolff, H. W.: Eine Handbreit Erde (1955).
Wood, J. T.: Modern Discoveries on the Site of Ancient Ephesus (1890).
Woolley, C. L.: Abraham, Recent Discoveries and Hebrew Origins (1936), Ur Excavations. V, The Ziggurat and its Surroundings (1939), Ur of the Chaldees (1954).
Wreszinski, Atlas zur ägyptischen Kulturgeschichte I–III (1923/40).
Wright, G. E.: Biblical Archaeology (1962).
Wright, S. E. and Fl. V. Filson: The Westminster Historical Atlas to the Bible (1953).
Würthwein, E.: Die Königsbücher (1976).

Yadin, Yigael: Masada. Der letzte Kampf ... (1967). Hazor (1976).

Journals: Annual of American Schools of Oriental Research (AASOR), Der Alte Orient (AO), American Journal of Archaeology (AJA), Biblical Archaeologist (BA), Bulletin of the American Schools of Oriental Research (BASOR), Beiträge zur Wissenschaft vom Alten u. Neuen Testament (BWANT), Illustrated London News, Israel Exploration Journal, Journal of the Society of Oriental Research (JSOR), Picture Post, London, Zeitschrift des Deutschen Palästinavereins (ZDPV), Revue Biblique (RB), Syria, Zeitschrift für alttestament. Wissen (ZAW).

INDEX

The Golden Spurs

The Western Writers
of America Present

The Golden
Spurs
The Best of
Western Short Fiction

Foreword by Elmer Kelton

Edited by Dale L. Walker

A TOM DOHERTY ASSOCIATES BOOK
NEW YORK

THE GOLDEN SPURS

Copyright © 1990 by Western Writers of America, Inc.

A Tor Book
Published by Tom Doherty Associates, Inc.
49 West 24th Street
New York, N.Y. 10010

Library of Congress Cataloging-in-Publication Data

The Golden spurs: the best of Western short fiction / introduction by
  Elmer Kelton; edited by the Western Writers of America.
    p.   cm.
  ISBN 0-312-85251-7
  1. Western stories.   I. Western Writers of America.
PS648.W4G65   1991
813'.0874—dc20   91-21172
                                                            CIP

First Edition: December 1991

Printed in the United States of America

0 9 8 7 6 5 4 3 2 1

Contents

Foreword

The short story seems to be an endangered art form. To those of us who can remember its glory days, when it flourished in all types of subject matter including the Western, that is indeed unfortunate.

When I was a boy, growing up on a Texas ranch far from town, every drugstore had a magazine rack taller than I was, crowded with pulp magazines of every kind: Western, mystery, romance, science fiction, and all-around adventure. These offered short stories and novelettes in such profusion that no one could possibly read them all, though some of us tried. Most of the major "slick" magazines also featured short stories in every issue. These stories carried us to other worlds, other times. They offered us experiences we could otherwise not have known. They made our imaginations soar.

My old friend and mentor Paul Patterson, a beloved Texas folklorist, was not only one of my teachers but summerworked as a cowboy when I was growing up. He has regaled folklore audiences with his recollection of seeing me serving as a horse jingler on a McElroy Ranch roundup, the most responsible job I was capable of holding at the time, looseherding the remuda of horses on grass until the cowboys came in off drive needing fresh mounts. There, he says, was as splendid a Western scene as ever inspired an artist, nearly two hundred saddlehorses spread out across the West Texas sandhills under an open blue sky, a spectacle thousands would have paid good money to see. And there, oblivious to this grand reality, I sat with my leg hooked over the saddlehorn, my eyes glued to the pages of a Western fiction magazine.

Those magazine stories, both pulp and slick, were not

only a fine entertainment medium but—at their best—taught us more than we realized about the world around us. They stimulated mental images far grander than any that can ever be captured on a small screen.

My own favorite genre was, of course, the Western. I knew the works of many writers and sought their names on the covers or on the contents pages before I plunked down my dime. It was my great privilege in later years to get to know many of these writers personally and be uplifted by their friendship. Several of those who inspired me are represented in this book.

Some critics lazily dismiss the Western without bothering even to read it, regarding it as juvenile and endlessly repetitive. This collection, chosen from among past winners of the Western Writers of America Spur award, illustrates how myopic such a viewpoint can be. These stories are widely varied in background and theme, ranging from the Indians before the white man's intrusion to rural problems in modern times, from the classic gunbarrel confrontation to a man's endurance against nature at her most murderous.

In the classic Western action mold are Thomas Thompson's retired marshal resisting the community's need for him to wear the badge again; Wayne Barton's old mountain man trying to live out his final years quietly in town; Oakley Hall's horseman seeking redemption for a costly mistake; S. Omar Barker's lad facing the temptation of the outlaw trail. Wagon trains west are touched upon by Bill Gulick, and Robert J. Conley tells about the tragedy of the Cherokees. Dorothy Johnson and Fred Grove spin gripping stories about women in—and out of—Indian captivity.

James Bellah tells of a man to whom honor is of more worth than life. Will Henry spins a tale of mysticism in the context of a classic cowman-sheepman conflict. Carla Kelly's offbeat story about a white officer and a black sergeant touches upon a chapter of frontier army life rarely examined. Folklorist Bill Brett gives us a glimpse of family loyalties in the East Texas piney woods. Bill Bragg describes the strange bond that develops between a hungry wolf and a mail carrier trapped by a Wyoming blizzard. Loren D. Estleman's tale of an oldtime bandit at the prison gate is both wry and ironic. Paul St. Pierre tells why the sale of a ranch is much more than simply a financial transaction.

That, friends, is variety, and the Western short story at its best. Enjoy, for it has become a rare thing.

Elmer Kelton
San Angelo, Texas

Acknowledgments

"Gun Job" by Thomas Thompson, from *Collier's*, © 1953, by permission of the author.

"Bad Company" by S. Omar Barker, from *The Saturday Evening Post*, © 1955, by permission of the Estate of S. Omar Barker, Robert Phillips, executor.

"Lost Sister" by Dorothy Johnson, from *Collier's*, © 1956, by permission of the Estate of Dorothy Johnson, Raymond J. Fox, executor.

"Thief in Camp" by Bill Gulick, from *The Saturday Evening Post*, © 1958, by permission of the author.

"Isley's Stranger" by Henry Wilson Allen, from *Legends and Tales of the Old West* (Doubleday & Co.), © 1962, by permission of the author.

"Comanche Woman" by Fred Grove, from *Pick of the Roundup* (Avon Books), © 1963, by permission of the author.

"A Season for Heroes" by Carla Kelly, from *Far West*, © 1978, by permission of the author.

"Jason Glendauer's Watch" by James Bellah, from *Far West*, © 1979, by permission of the author.

"One Man's Code" by Wayne Barton, from *Far West*, © 1980, by permission of the author.

"Horseman" by Oakley Hall, from *The Antioch Review*, © 1982, by permission of the author.

11

"The Ten Sleep Mail" by William F. Bragg, Jr., from *Wyoming Wild and Wooly* (Pruett Publishing Co.), © 1983, by permission of the Estate of William F. Bragg, Rita Bragg, executor.

"Sale of One Small Ranch" by Paul St. Pierre, from *Smith and Other Events* (Beaufort Books), © 1984, by permission of the author.

"The Way It Was Told to Me" by Bill Brett, © 1985, by permission of Texas A&M University Press and the author.

"The Bandit" by Loren D. Estleman, from *Best of the West* (Doubleday & Co.), © 1986, by permission of the author.

"Yellow Bird: An Imaginary Autobiography" by Robert J. Conley, from *The Witch of Goinsnake and Other Stories* by Robert J. Conley, © 1988, by the University of Oklahoma Press, by permission of the University of Oklahoma Press and the author.

The editor gratefully acknowledges the special assistance of these WWA members in the making of this book: Elmer Kelton, Bill Pronzini, Jeanne Williams, David Dary, Stan Paregien, and Richard C. House.

And special thanks to Harold Kuebler, wagon boss.

Introduction

In June 1981, at the Western Writers convention in Santa Rosa, California, I sat around a table in the tiny bar of the Tropicana Motel with Thomas Thompson, William R. Cox, and Brian Garfield. Tommy and Bill were holding court—telling outrageously funny stories of editors and editorial atrocities, whatever-became-of- reminiscences of great writers missing or dead, and lamenting the golden, lost days of the pulps, of the TV and movie Western.

Garfield, the much younger and quieter member of this triumvirate, content to give those elders full rein, was no less a wonder to me—the author of *Wild Times,* one of the best Western novels of all time, also the writer of such non-Western thriller-classics as *Death Wish, Death Sentence, Hopscotch,* and *Recoil.*

A man dressed in Western duds—a plaid lumberjack shirt, Levis, and boots—sat on a bar stool a few feet from our table and periodically swiveled around and looked toward us, then swiveled back to chat with the bartender. Eventually he came over. "Are you guys with the Western Writers group meeting here?" he asked with a big grin. We nodded. He said he read nothing but Westerns and stuck out his hand. We all introduced ourselves, each name, especially mine, drawing an obvious blank until Tommy stood up and announced loudly, "Well, I'm just damned glad to meet you. Just call me Zane!"

The man stared seriously at Tommy for a beat, then broke into a broad smile, said, "Aw, hell, glad to meet you guys," and made his way back to the bar.

"It's only in times like these," Bill Cox said after the man was out of hearing range, "when I want to be Louis L'Amour."

13

*   *   *

My best memories and most fun in thirty years of freelance
writing are traceable to that wonderful organization which
Tommy Thompson cofounded back in 1952, the organization of which both Bill Cox and Brian Garfield served as
president—Western Writers of America, Inc. Through
WWA, the warmest and most accessible writer's organization of them all, I've drunk beer and eaten supper with,
swapped information and stories with, gone on bus rides,
bookshop expeditions, and midnight flapjack hunts with,
and been privileged to call friend many, maybe most, of the
finest Western writers of our time and a good many Western
editors, publishers, and literary agents as well.

I should have taken more notes, although it is awkward to
do so in bars, where so much of the really important business of WWA conventions is conducted, but such moments
as these are indelible in my memory:

—Standing silently with Dee Brown at the rail surrounding the cemetery at the Custer Battlefield in Montana and
later watching my wife, Alice, and British Western writer
Robin May dancing with the Crow Indians at a WWA welcome feast on their reservation;

—Chatting with Iron Eyes Cody in a San Diego motel
ballroom; spending an afternoon at Will Henry's home in
Encino;

—Standing at the bar on the sternwheeler Columbia Gorge
on the Columbia River during the Portland convention in
1989 and meeting there Glendon Swarthout, author of The
Shootist, Bless the Beasts and Children, and They Came to
Cordura, then retiring to the top deck to spend a breezy hour
of talk and scenery-admiration with Don Coldsmith of Em-
poria, Kansas, medical doctor and author of the "Trail of the
Spanish Bit" novels;

—Searching for all-night restaurants in Amarillo with
Loren Estleman and Brooklyn Western writer Bob Randisi
("I think I see some lights over there at about 3 o'clock," I

told Loren from the backseat of his rental car. "Sorry, I've got a digital watch," he said), trying to satiate Randisi's new-found passion for chicken-fried steaks. (He also saw actual beef cattle in the pasture for the first time during this first trip to Texas.);

—Drinking beer in the Menger Hotel in San Antonio with Wally Clayton, editor of the *Tombstone Epitaph*, and gazing at the framed photographs on the walls of Lt. Col. Teddy Roosevelt and his officers of the Rough Rider regiment who, in 1898, used the hotel as their headquarters;

—Perching on the edge of a bed in a motel room in Fort Worth during the end-of-convention "Campfire" gathering while that splendid Arkansas novelist and Spur-winner (*Gone the Dreams and Dancing*) Douglas C. Jones cussed and wrestled with the spur part of my Golden Spur Award, which had sprung loose from its moorings.

Thomas Thompson of California and Nelson Nye, the prolific "Baron of Blood and Thunder" Western novelist in Arizona, launched Western Writers of America, Inc., toward the end of 1952 after Tommy wrote Nels bemoaning the drying up of Western story markets as the pulp magazines fell one by one with their bellies up. Tommy contacted Anthony Boucher, then president of the affluent Mystery Writers of America, borrowed a copy of MWA's charter, and Nels wrote WWA's preamble while Norman Fox, another veteran Western writer, in Great Falls, Montana, hammered out a constitution.

Dwight Newton, up in Bend, Oregon, agreed to serve as the original secretary-treasurer, Wayne Overholser of Colorado joined in to help, Nye agreed to serve as first president and also wrote, edited, mimeographed, and mailed (in April 1953) the first issue of *Roundup* (still WWA's official publication, though now a spiffy quarterly journal).

The charter members of WWA were a roll-call of the greatest names in the business: Frank Bonham, Giff Cheshire, Dan Cushman, Harry Drago, Leslie Ernenwein, Steve Frazee,

Luke Short, Bill Gulick, Roe Richmond, Chuck Martin, Charles L. Heckelmann, Garland Roark, Noel M. Loomis, Frank C. Robertson, L. P. Holmes, Lewis B. Patten, John L. Sinclair, Thomas Thompson, Norman Fox, Wayne D. Overholser, D. B. Newton, Nelson Nye, and Walker Thompkins, and from "Publisher's Row," Ian Ballantine, Raymond Bond, Clarkson Potter, William Clifford, W. Hughes-Hanna, Bernard Shir-Cliff, and Don Ward.

By the end of 1954, WWA not only had produced its first anthology (*Good Men and Bad*) but had held its first annual convention, at the Shirley-Savoy Hotel in Denver, and distributed its first Spur awards.

Thompson recalls the naming of this prestigious award:

"Les Ernenwein, a fine writer and editor who succeeded Nels Nye on the *Roundup*, suggested we call them 'Ernies' after Ernest Haycox; Norman Fox thought up 'Charlies' after Charlie Russell. We had a small civil war over it, with Nye joining Ernenwein and Harry Drago joining Fox's side.

"Then, in the middle of the night, a thought struck me: Why not call them 'Spurs'? I told my warring pals, 'A spur is definitely Western and if you win one it would spur you on the way to bigger and better things.'

"There was a long silence after I said that and then the sound of six-shooters being dropped back into their holsters was heard in the land. They had bought my idea."

The Spurs awarded at the Denver convention (for work published in 1953) went to Lee Leighton for Best Novel (*Lawman*), to Lucia Moore for Best Historical Novel (*The Wheel and the Hearth*), to Frank C. Robertson for Best Juvenile (*Sagebrush Sorrel*), to Hoffman Birney of the *New York Times* for Best Reviewer—and, with justice to a first-rate *Saturday Evening Post* story and for drawing a royal flush of an award name, to Thomas Thompson for Best Short Story ("Gun Job," which leads off this anthology).

While Spur categories have been added (and dropped, as

in the case of "Reviewer") and refined over the thirty-seven years since the first WWA Spurs were awarded, the prestigiousness of the Spur has not diminished. It is awarded after judging by panels of active (published, professional) WWA members; any published Western work fitting the various categories, by any writer—whether a WWA member or not—is eligible to be nominated and judged.

As editor of WWA's then-monthly magazine The Roundup for five years and fifty issues between 1980 and 1985, I could drop a note or get on the phone and talk Elmer Kelton, Will Henry, Nelson Nye, Bill Gulick, Omar Barker, Jeanne Williams, Doc Sonnichsen, Dee Brown, Don Worcester, Steve Frazee, Wayne Lee, Mel Marshall, Dwight Newton, Eve Ball, Fred Grove, Tommy Thompson, Bill Cox, Brian Garfield, Ben Capps, Nellie Yost, Dorothy Johnson, Lew Holmes, Wayne or Steve Overholser, Max Evans, Jory Sherman, Dick Wheeler, Bob Randisi, Loren Estleman, Matt Braun, Phil Ault, Lucia Robson, Frank Roderus, Judy Alter, Don Coldsmith, Nancy Hamilton, Francis Fugate, Leon Metz, Dick House, Gordon Shirreffs—or Joe Rosa, J. T. Edson, or Peter Watts (in England), Finn Arnesen (in Norway), Tom Jeier (in West Germany), and in Los Angeles, even the redoubtable Louis L'Amour—all the finest writers in the Western field—into writing something for their magazine.

Nobody ever turned me down; their loyalty to WWA was constant and touching.

Because of my own indebtedness to WWA, my own memories of and associations with the marvelous people of the organization, it is a privilege to be able to gather together these Golden Spur Award stories.

—Dale L. Walker
El Paso, Texas

THOMAS THOMPSON

Gun Job

Thomas ("Tommy") Thompson, one of the founders of Western Writers of America, was born in Dixon, California, in 1913. In 1940 he began writing short stories for the pulp magazines, and also contributed to the "slicks"—*The Saturday Evening Post, Collier's, American Magazine.* To date he has written some 500 short stories; his first novel, *Range Drifter*, was published in 1948 and his most recent one, *Outlaw Valley*, in 1988.

Tommy is a veteran of television as well. He wrote scripts for "Wagon Train," "Cimarron City," "The Rifleman," and served fourteen years as associate producer and scriptwriter for one of the most successful TV series of all time, "Bonanza."

In 1954, at the first national WWA convention in Denver, Tommy was awarded the first Western short story Golden Spur for "Gun Job."

He was married in June and he gave up his job as town marshal the following September, giving himself time to get settled on the little ranch he bought before the snows set in. That first winter was mild, and now, with summer in the air, he walked down the main street of the town and thought of his own calf crop and of his own problems, a fine feeling after fifteen years of thinking of the problems of others. He wasn't Marshal Jeff Anderson any more. He was Jeff Anderson, private citizen, beholden to no man, and that was the way he wanted it.

He gave the town his quick appraisal, a tall, well-built man who was nearing forty and beginning to think about it, and every building and every alley held a memory for him, some amusing, some tragic. The town had a Sunday-morning peacefulness on it, the peacefulness Jeff Anderson had worked for. It hadn't always been this way. He inhaled deeply, a contented man, and he caught the scent of freshly sprinkled dust that came from the dampened square of street in front of the ice-cream parlor. There was a promise of heat in the air and already the thick, warm scent of the tarweed was drifting down from the yellow slopes back of the town. He kept to the middle of the street, enjoying his freedom, not yet free of old habits, and he headed for the marshal's office, where the door was closed, the shade drawn.

This was his Sunday-morning pleasure, this brief tour of the town that had claimed him so long. It was the same tour he had made every Sunday morning for fifteen years; but now he could enjoy the luxury of knowing he was making it because he wanted to, not because it was his job. A man who had built a bridge or a building could sit back and look at his finished work, remembering the fun and the heartache that had gone into it, but he didn't need to chip away personally at its rust or take a pot of paint to its scars.

In front of the marshal's office Anderson paused, remembering it all, not missing it, just remembering; then he turned and pushed open the door, the familiarity of the action momentarily strong on him. The floor was worn and his boot heels had helped wear it; the desk was scarred and some of those spur marks were as much his own as his own initials would have been. He grinned at the new marshal and said, "Caught any criminals lately?"

The man behind the desk glanced up, his face drawn, expressionless, his eyes worried. He tried to joke. "How could I?" he said. "You ain't been in town since last Sunday." He took one foot off the desk and kicked a straight chair toward Jeff. "How's the cow business?"

"Good," Jeff said. "Mighty good." He sat down heavily and stretched his long legs, pushed his battered felt hat back on his thinning, weather-bleached hair, and made himself a cigarette. He saw the papers piled on the desk, and glancing at the clock, he knew it was nearly time to let the two or three prisoners exercise in the jail corridor. A feeling of well-being engulfed him. These things were another man's responsibility now, not Jeff Anderson's. "How's it with you, Billy?" he asked.

The answer came too quickly, the answer of a man who was nervous or angry or possibly both. "You ought to know, Jeff. The mayor and the council came to see you, didn't they?"

Annoyance clouded Jeff Anderson's gray eyes. He hadn't liked the idea of the city fathers going behind the new marshal's back. If they didn't like the job Billy was doing they should have gone to Billy, not to Jeff. But that was typical of the city council. Jeff had known three mayors and three different councils during his long term in office and they usually ran to a pattern. A few complaints and they got panicky and started going off in seven directions at once. They seemed to think that because Jeff had recommended Billy for this job the job was still Jeff's responsibility——

"They made the trip for nothing, Billy," Jeff said. "If you're worried about me wanting your job you can forget it. I told them that plain."

"They'll keep asking you, Jeff."

"They'll keep getting 'no' for an answer," Jeff said.

Billy Lang sat at his desk and stared at the drawn shade of the window, the thumb of his left hand toying nervously with the badge on his calfskin vest. He was a small man with eternally pink cheeks and pale blue eyes. He wore a full white mustache and there was a cleft in his chin. He was married and had five children, and most of his life he had clerked in a store. When Jeff Anderson recommended him for this job, Billy took it because it paid more and because the town was quiet. But now there was trouble and

Billy was sorry he had ever heard of the job. He said, "You can't blame them for wanting you back, Jeff. You did a good job."

There was no false modesty in Jeff Anderson. He had done a good job here and he knew it. He had handled his job exactly the way he felt it should be handled and he had backed down to no one. But it hadn't been all roses, either. He grinned. "Regardless of what a man does, there's some who won't like it."

"Like Hank Fetterman?"

Jeff shrugged. Hank Fetterman was a cattleman. Sometimes Hank got the idea that he ought to take this town over and run it the way he once had. Hank hadn't gotten away with it when Jeff was marshal. Thinking about it now, it didn't seem to matter much to Jeff one way or the other, and it was hard to remember that his fight with Fetterman had once been important. It had been a long time ago and things had changed—— "Hank's not a bad sort," Jeff said.

"He's in town," Billy Lang said. "Did you know that?"

Jeff felt the old, familiar tightening of his stomach muscles, the signal of trouble ahead. He inhaled deeply, let the smoke trickle from his nostrils, and the feeling went away. Hank Fetterman was Jeff Anderson's neighbor now and Jeff was a rancher, not a marshal. "I'm in town, too," he said. "So are fifty other people. There's no law against it."

"You know what I mean, Jeff," Billy Lang said. "You talked with Rudy Svitac's boy."

Jeff moved uneasily in his chair. Billy Lang was accusing him of meddling, and Jeff didn't like it. Jeff had never had anything to do with the marshal's job since his retirement, and he had promised himself he never would. It was Billy's job, and Billy was free to run it his own way. But when a twelve-year-old kid who thought you were something special asked you a straight question you gave him a straight answer. It had nothing to do with the fact that you had once been a marshal——

"Sure, Billy," Jeff said. "I talked to Rudy's boy. He came

to see me about it just the way he's been coming to see me about things ever since he was big enough to walk. The kid needs somebody to talk to, I guess, so he comes to me. He's not old-country, like his folks. He was born here; he thinks American. I guess it's hard for the old folks to understand him and it's hard for the boy to understand them. I told him to have his dad see you, Billy."

"He took your advice," Billy Lang said. "Three days ago." He turned over a paper. "Rudy Svitac came in and swore out a warrant against Hank Fetterman for trespassing. He said his boy told him it was the thing to do."

Jeff had a strange feeling that he was suddenly two people. One was Jeff Anderson, ex-marshal, the man who had recommended Billy Lang for this job. As such, he should offer Billy some advice right here and now. The other person was Jeff Anderson, private citizen, a man with a small ranch and a fine wife and a right to live his own life. And that was the Jeff Anderson that was important. Jeff Anderson the rancher grinned. "Hank pawin' and bellerin' about it, is he?"

"I don't know, Jeff," Billy Lang said. "I haven't talked to Hank about it. I'm not sure I'm going to."

Jeff glanced quickly at the new marshal, surprised, only half believing what he had heard. He had recommended Billy for this job because he figured he and Billy thought along the same lines. Surely Billy knew that if you gave Hank Fetterman an inch he would take a mile——

He caught himself quickly, realizing suddenly that it was none of his business how Billy Lang thought. There were plenty of businessmen in town who had argued loudly and openly that Jeff Anderson's methods of law enforcement had been bad for their cash registers. They had liked the old days when Hank Fetterman was running things and the town was wide open. Maybe they wanted it that way again. Every man was entitled to his own opinion and Billy Lang was entitled to handle his job in his own way. This freedom of thought and action that Jeff prized so highly had to work for everyone. He stood up and clapped a hand affectionately on Billy Lang's shoulder, anxious to change the conversation. "That's up to you, Billy," he said. "It's sure none of my affair." His grin widened. "Come on over to the saloon and I'll buy you a drink."

Billy Lang stared at the drawn shade, and he thought of Hank Fetterman, a man who was big in this country, waiting over at the saloon. Hank Fetterman knew there was a warrant out for his arrest; the whole town knew it by now. You didn't need to tell a thing like that. It just got around. And before long people would know who the law was in this town, Hank Fetterman or Billy Lang. Billy colored slightly, and there was perspiration on his forehead. "You go ahead and have your drink, Jeff," he said. "I've got some paperwork to do——" He didn't look up.

Jeff went outside and the gathering heat of the day struck the west side of the street and brought a resinous smell from the old boards of the false-fronted buildings. He glanced at the little church, seeing Rudy Svitac's spring wagon there, remembering that the church hadn't always been here; then he crossed over toward the saloon, the first business building this town had erected. He had been in a dozen such towns, and it was always the same. The saloons and the deadfalls came first, the churches and the schools later. Maybe that proved something. He didn't know. He had just stepped onto the board sidewalk when he saw the druggist coming toward him. The druggist was also the mayor, a sanctimonious little man, dried up by his own smallness. "Jeff, I talked to Billy Lang," the mayor said. His voice was thin and reedy. "I wondered if you might reconsider——"

"No," Jeff Anderson said. He didn't break his stride. He walked by the mayor and went into the saloon. Two of Hank Fetterman's riders were standing by the piano, leaning on it, and one of them was fumbling out a one-finger tune, cursing when he missed a note. Hank Fetterman was at the far end of the bar, and Jeff went and joined him. A little cow talk was good of a Sunday morning and Hank Fetterman knew cows. The two men at the piano started to sing.

Hank Fetterman's glance drifted lazily to Jeff Anderson and then away. His smile was fleeting. "How are you, Jeff?"

"Good enough," Jeff said. "Can I buy you a drink?"

"You twisted my arm," Hank Fetterman said.

Hank Fetterman was a well-built man with a weathered face. His brows were heavy and they pinched together toward the top, forming a perfect diamond of clean, hairless skin between his deep-set eyes. His voice was quiet, his manner calm. Jeff thought of the times he had crossed this man, enforcing the no-gun ordinance, keeping Hank's riders in jail overnight to cool them off. . . . He had no regrets over the way he had handled Hank in the past. It had nothing to do with his feeling toward Hank now or in the future. He saw that Hank was wearing a gun and he smiled inwardly. That was like Hank. Tell him he couldn't do something and that was exactly what he wanted to do. "Didn't figure on seeing you in town," Jeff said. "Thought you and the boys were on roundup."

"I had a little personal business come up," Hank Fetterman said. "You know about it?"

Jeff shrugged. "Depends on what it is."

The pale smile left Hank Fetterman's eyes but not his lips. "Rudy Svitac is telling it around that I ran a bunch of my cows through his corn. He claims I'm trying to run him out of the country."

Jeff had no trouble concealing his feelings. It was a trick he had learned a long time ago. He leaned his elbows on the bar and turned his shot glass slowly in its own wet circle. Behind him Hank Fetterman's two cowboys broke into a boisterous, ribald song. The bartender wiped his face with his apron and glanced out the front window across toward the marshal's office. Jeff Anderson downed his drink, tossed the shot glass in the air, and caught it with a downsweep of his hand. "You're used to that kind of talk, Hank." He set the shot glass on the bar.

"You're pretty friendly with the Svitacs, aren't you, Jeff?" Hank Fetterman asked. He was leaning with his back to the bar, his elbows behind him. His position made the holstered gun he wore obvious.

Again, just for a moment, Jeff Anderson was two people. He remembered the man he wanted to be. "I don't reckon anybody's very friendly with the Svitacs," he said. "They're hard to know. I think a lot of their boy. He's a nice kid."

Slowly the smile came back into Hank Fetterman's amber eyes. He turned around and took the bottle and poured a drink for himself and one for Jeff. "That forty acres of bottom land you were asking me about for a calf pasture," he said. "I've been thinking about it. I guess I could lease it to you all right."

"That's fine, Hank," Jeff Anderson said. "I can use it." He doffed his glass to Hank and downed his drink. It didn't taste right but he downed it anyway. The two cowboys started to scuffle and one of them collided with a table. It overturned with a crash.

"Please, Hank," the bartender said. "They're gonna get me in trouble——" His voice trailed off and his eyes widened. A man had come through the door. He stood there, blinking the bright sun out of his eyes. Jeff Anderson felt his heart start to pump heavily, slowly, high in his chest. "Morning, Mr. Svitac," the bartender mumbled.

Rudy Svitac stood in the doorway, a thick, dull man with black hair and brows that met across the bridge of his nose and a forehead that sloped. Jeff saw the rusty suit the man wore on Sundays, the suit that had faint soil stains on the knees because this man could not leave the soil alone, even on Sundays. He had to kneel down and feel the soil with his fingers, feeling the warmth and the life of it; for the soil was his book and his life and it was the only thing he understood completely and perhaps the only thing that understood him. He looked at Jeff, not at Hank Fetterman. "Is no good," Rudy Svitac said. "My son says I must talk to Billy Lang. I talk to Billy Lang but he does nothing. Is no good."

A thick silence settled in the room and the two cowboys who had been scuffling quit it now and stood there looking at the farmer. Hank Fetterman said, "Say what's on your mind, Svitac."

"You broke my fence," Rudy Svitac said. "You drive your cows in my corn and spoil my crop. All winter I wait to plant my crop and now is grown fine and you drive your cows in."

"Maybe you're mistaken, Svitac," Hank Fetterman said.

"My boy says is for judge to decide," Rudy Svitac said. "My boy tell me to go to Billy Lang and he will make a paper and judge will decide. My boy says is fair. Is America." Rudy Svitac stared unblinkingly. He shook his head slowly. "Is not so. I want my money. You broke my fence."

"You're a liar, Svitac," Hank Fetterman said. He moved away from the bar, slowly. He looked steadily at Jeff Anderson, then he glanced across the street toward the marshal's office. The door was still closed, the shade still drawn. Hank Fetterman smiled. He walked forward and gripped Rudy Svitac by the shirt front. For a moment he held the man that way, pulling him close, then he shoved and Rudy Svitac stumbled backward, out through the door, and his heel caught on a loose board in the sidewalk. He fell hard and for a long time he lay there, his dull steady eyes staring at Jeff Anderson; then he turned and pushed himself up and he stood there looking at the dust on his old suit. He dropped his head and looked at the dust and he reached with his fingers and touched it. One of Hank Fetterman's cowboys started to laugh.

Across the street Jeff Anderson saw the blind on the window of the marshal's office move aside and then drop back into place, and immediately the door opened and Billy Lang was hurrying across the street. He came directly to Rudy Svitac and put his hand on Svitac's arm and jerked him around. "What's going on here?" Billy Lang demanded.

"Svitac came in looking for trouble," Hank Fetterman said. "I threw him out." Hank was standing in the doorway, directly alongside Jeff. For a brief moment Hank Fetterman's amber eyes met Jeff's gaze and Jeff saw the challenge. *If you don't like it, do something about it, Hank Fetterman was saying. I want to know how you stand in this thing and I want to know now....*

There was a dryness in Jeff Anderson's mouth. He had backed Hank Fetterman down before; he could do it again. But for what? One hundred and fifty dollars a month and a chance to get killed? Jeff had had fifteen years of that. A man had a right to live his own life. He looked up toward the church and the doors were just opening and people were coming out to stand on the porch, a small block of humanity suddenly aware of trouble. Jeff saw his wife, Elaine, and he knew her hand was at her throat, twisting the fabric of her dress the way she did. He thought of the little ranch and of the things he and Elaine had planned for the future, and then he looked at Billy Lang and he knew Billy wasn't going to buck Hank Fetterman. So Jeff could make a stand, and it would be his own stand and he would be right back into it again just the way he had been for fifteen years. There was a thick line of perspiration on Jeff's upper lip. "That's the way it was, Billy," Jeff said.

He saw the quick smile cross Hank Fetterman's face, the dull acceptance and relief in Billy Lang's eyes. "Get out of town, Svitac," Billy Lang said. "I'm tired of your trouble-making. If Hank's cows got in your corn, it was an accident."

"Is no accident," Rudy Svitac said stubbornly. "Is for judge to decide. My son says——"

"It was an accident," Billy Lang said. "Make your fences stronger." He didn't look at Jeff. He glanced at Hank Fetterman and made his final capitulation. "Sorry it happened, Hank."

For a long moment Rudy Svitac stared at Billy Lang, at the star on Billy's vest, remembering that this star somehow had a connection with the stars in the flag. His son Anton had explained it, saying that Jeff Anderson said it was so, so it must be so. But it wasn't so. Hank Fetterman wasn't in jail. They weren't going to do anything about the ruined corn. The skin wrinkled between Rudy Svitac's eyes and there was perspiration on his face and his lips moved thickly but no sound came out. He could not understand. Thirteen years he had lived in this America, but still he could not understand. His son had tried to tell him the things they taught in the schools and the things Jeff Anderson said were so; but Rudy had his soil to work and his crops to plant, and when a man's back was tired his head did not work so good. Rudy Svitac knew only that if the Jimson weed grew in the potato patch, you cut it out. And if the wild morning glory climbed the corn, then the wild morning glory must be pulled out by the roots. No one came to do these things for a man. A man did these chores himself. He turned and walked stolidly up the street toward where he had left his spring wagon by the church.

His wife, Mary, was there, a thick, tired woman who never smiled nor ever complained, and watching them, Jeff saw Anton, their son, a boy of twelve with an old man's face, a boy who had always believed every word Jeff Anderson said. Jeff saw young Anton looking down the street toward him and he remembered the boy's serious brown eyes and the thick black hair that always stood out above his ears and lay rebelliously far down his neck. He remembered the hundred times he had talked to young Anton, patiently explaining things so Anton would understand, learning his own beliefs from the process of explaining them in simple words. And Anton would listen and then repeat to his parents in Bohemian, telling them this was so because Jeff Anderson said it was so. A bright boy with an unlimited belief in the future, in a household where there was no future. At times it seemed to Jeff almost as if God had looked upon Rudy and Mary Svitac and wanted to compensate in some way, so he had given them Anton.

Jeff saw Rudy reaching into the bed of the wagon. He saw Mary protest once; then Mary stood there, resigned, and now the boy had his father's arm and there was a brief struggle. The father shook the boy off, and now Rudy had a rifle and he was coming back down the street, walking slowly, down the middle of the street, the rifle in the crook of his arm.

Billy Lang moved. He met Rudy halfway, and he held out his hand. Jeff saw Rudy hesitate, take two more steps; and now Billy was saying something and Rudy dropped his head and let his chin lay on his chest. The boy came running up, and he took the rifle out of his father's hand and the crowd in front of the saloon expelled its breath. Jeff felt the triumph come into Hank Fetterman. He didn't need to look at the man. He could feel it.

The slow, wicked anger was inside Hank Fetterman, goaded by his ambition, his sense of power—and the catlike eagerness was in his eyes. "No bohunk tells lies about me and gets away with it," he murmured. "No bohunk comes after me with a gun and gets a second chance." His hand dropped and rested on the butt of his holstered six-shooter, and then the thumb of his left hand touched Jeff Anderson's arm. "Have a drink with me, Jeff?"

Jeff saw Elaine standing in front of the church and he could feel her anxiety reaching through the hot, troubled air. And he saw the boy there in the street, the gun in his hand, his eyes, bewildered, searching Jeff Anderson's face. "I reckon I won't have time, Hank," Jeff said. He walked up the street and now the feeling of being two people was strong in him, and there was a responsibility to Billy Lang that he couldn't deny. He had talked Billy into taking this job. It was a lonely job, and there was never a lonelier time than when a man was by himself in the middle of the street. He came close to Billy and he said, "Look, Billy, if you can take a gun away from one man you can take a gun away from another."

Billy looked at him. Billy's hands were shaking, and there was sweat on his face. "A two-year-old kid could have taken that gun away from Rudy, and you know it," he said. He reached up swiftly and unpinned the badge from his vest. He handed it across. "You want it?"

Jeff looked at that familiar piece of metal and he could feel the boy's eyes on him; and then he looked up and he saw Elaine there on the church porch, and he thought of his own dreams and of the plans he and Elaine had made for the future. "No, Billy," he said, "I don't want it."

"Then let it lay there," Billy Lang said. He dropped the badge into the dust of the street and hurried off, a man who had met defeat and accepted it, a man who could now go back to the clothing store and sell shirts and suits and overalls because that was the job he could do best. There was no indignity in Billy Lang's defeat. He had taken a role that he wasn't equipped to handle, and he was admitting it.

The boy said, "Mr. Jeff, I don't understand. You told me once——"

"We'll talk about it later, Anton," Jeff said. "Tell your dad to go home." He walked swiftly toward Elaine, swallowing against the sourness in his throat.

They drove out of town, Jeff and Elaine Anderson, toward their own home and their own life; and now the full heat of the day lay on the yellow slopes and the dry air crackled with the smell of dust and the cured grass, and the leather seat of the buggy was hot to the touch. A mile out to town Jeff stopped in the shade of a sycamore and put up the top. He moved with dull efficiency, pausing momentarily to glance up as Hank Fetterman and his two riders passed on their way back to the ranch. He got back into the buggy and unwrapped the lines from the whip stock and Elaine said, "If there's anything you want to say, Jeff——"

How could he say it? He couldn't, for the thing that was most in his mind had nothing to do with the matter at hand, and yet it had everything to do with it and it couldn't be explained. For he was thinking not of Hank Fetterman nor of Rudy Svitac, but of a colored lithograph, a town promotion picture that had once hung on every wall in this town.

It showed wide, tree-lined streets, a tremendous townhouse with a flag half as large as the building flying from a mast, and lesser pennants, all mammoth, rippling from every building. Tiny men in cutaway coats and top hats leisurely strolled the avenues, and high-wheeled bicycles rolled elegantly past gleaming black Victorias on the street of exclusive shops, while three sleek trains chuffed impatiently at the station. The railroad had put on a large land promotion around here when the road was first built. They had offered excursion trips free so that people could see the charms of New Canaan. They had handed out these lithos of the proposed town by the bushel. For a while New Canaan bustled with activity, and men bought town lots staked out in buffalo grass. And then the bubble burst and New Canaan settled back to what it was before—a place called Alkali at the edge of open cattle range. And young Anton Svitac had come to see Marshal Jeff Anderson for the first time and he had come about that picture——

Jeff remembered how the boy had looked that day, no more than six years old, his eyes too large for his old man's face, his voice a mirror of the seriousness of thought that was so much a part of him. He had come to Jeff Anderson because Jeff Anderson was authority, and already young Anton had learned that in America authority was for everyone. "My father and mother do not understand," he said. "They do not speak English. . . ." He unrolled the lithograph and put his finger on it, and then indicated the town of Alkali with a spread hand. "Is not the same," he said. "Is not so."

There were dreams in that boy's eyes, and they were about to be snuffed out; and Jeff Anderson didn't want it to happen. "Sure it's so, Anton," he heard himself saying. "It's not what it is today; it's what's going to be tomorrow, see?" He remembered the trouble he had had with the words, and then it was all there and he was telling it to Anton, telling it so this boy could go home and tell it to a workbent man and a tired woman. "It's like America, see? Some of the things aren't right where you can touch them. Maybe some of the things you see are ugly. But the picture is always there to look at, and you keep thinking about the picture, and you keep working and making things better all the time, see? America isn't something you cut off like a piece of cake and say, 'There it is.' You keep on looking ahead to what it's going to be, and you keep working hard for it all the time, and you keep right on, knowing it's going to be good because you've got the picture there to look at. You never stop working and say, 'Now the job is done,' because it never is. You see that, Anton?''

The boy hadn't smiled. This was a big thing and a boy didn't smile about big things. He rolled the lithograph carefully. "I see," he said. "Is good. I will tell my father. We will keep the picture. . . . ''

Those were Jeff Anderson's thoughts, and how could he tell them, even to Elaine? For they had so little to do with the matter at hand and yet they had everything to do with it.

And Elaine, looking at her husband now, respected his silence. She remembered the three long years she was engaged to this man before they were married, years in which she had come to know him so well because she loved him so well. She knew him even better now. He was a man who was born to handle trouble, and a piece of tin on his vest or a wife at his side couldn't change the man he was born to be. She knew that and she didn't want to change him, but a woman couldn't help being what she was, either, and a woman could be afraid, especially at a time like this, when there was so much ahead. She wanted to help him. "Maybe the Svitacs would be better off someplace else," she said. "They never have made the place pay."

And that was exactly the same argument he had used on himself, but now, hearing it put into words, he didn't like the sound of it and he wanted to argue back. His voice was rough. "I reckon they look on it as home," he said. "The boy was born there. I reckon it sort of ties you to a place if your first one is born there."

She closed her eyes tightly, knowing that she was no longer one person but three, knowing the past was gone and

the future would always be ahead, and it was her job to help
secure that future as much as it was Jeff's job. She opened
her eyes and looked at her husband, still afraid, for that was
her way; but somehow prouder and older now. She folded
her hands in her lap and the nervousness was gone. "I suppose we'll feel that way, too, Jeff," she said. "It will always
be our town after our baby is born here. I talked to the doctor
yesterday . . ."

He felt the hard knot in the pit of his stomach. Then the
coldness ran up his spine, and it was surprise and fear and
a great swelling pride; and the feeling crawled up his neck,
and every hair on his head was an individual hair, and the
hard lump was in his throat——He moved on the seat, suddenly concerned for her comfort. "You feel all right, honey?
Is there anything I can do?"

She didn't laugh at him any more than Anton had laughed
at him that day in the office. She reached over and put her
hand on his hand, and she smiled. As they drove down the
lane the great pride was inside him, swelling against him
until he felt that the seat of the buggy was no longer large
enough to contain him. He helped her out of the buggy, his
motions exaggerated in their kindness; and he took her arm
and helped her up the front steps.

The coolness of the night still lingered in the little ranch
house, for she had left the shades drawn; and now she went
to the west windows and lifted the shades slightly, and she
could see down the lane and across the small calf pasture
where a thin drift of dust from their buggy wheels still lingered. There was a loneliness to Sunday after church, a
stillness on the ranch. She glanced toward the barn and Jeff
was unharnessing the mare and turning her into the corral,
his back broad, his movements deliberate; and she saw him
stand for a moment and look down the creek toward where
Rudy Svitac's place cornered on Hank Fetterman's huge,
unfenced range.

He came into the house later, into the cool living room, and
he sat down in his big chair with a gusty sigh and pulled off

his boots and stretched his legs. "Good to be home," he said. "Good to have nothing to do." He raised his eyes to meet hers and they both knew he was lying. There was always something to do.

The moment he was sure she knew, it was easier for him, but he still had to be positive that she understood that now it was different. Once he made this move there would be no turning back. She had to see that. An hour ago the town had been a town, nothing more; and if certain merchants felt business would be better with Hank Fetterman running things, that was their business; and if Billy Lang wanted to go along with that thinking or go back to the clothing store, that was his business. Jeff Anderson hadn't needed the town. It was a place to shop and nothing more, and a man could shop as well with Hank Fetterman running things as he could with Jeff Anderson running things. But now, suddenly, that had changed, and there was tomorrow to think about, and it was exactly as he had explained it to Anton. Now, one day soon, Jeff Anderson might be explaining the same things to his own son; and a man had to show his son that he believed what he said, for if he didn't there was nothing left——"I was wrong about Billy Lang," Jeff Anderson said. "He's not going to stand up to Hank Fetterman."

She looked into his eyes and saw the deep seriousness and knew his every thought, and in this moment they were closer than they had ever been before; and she remembered thinking so many times of men and women who had been married for fifty years or more and of how they always looked alike. She said, "I have some curtains I promised Mary Svitac. Will you take them to her when you go?"

She didn't trust herself to say more and she didn't give him a lingering embrace as a woman might who was watching her man go off to danger; but she pretended to be busy and turned her head so that his lips just brushed her temple, and it was as casual as if he were only going to his regular day's work. "And thank her for the pickles," she said.

He stalked out of the house as if he didn't like having his

Sunday disturbed by such woman nonsense, but when he was halfway to the barn his stride lengthened and she saw the stiffness of his back and the set of his shoulders. She sat down then and cried.

Anton, the boy, was pouring sour milk into a trough for the pigs when Jeff rode into the Svitac yard. The world could collapse but pigs had to be fed, and the boy was busy with his thoughts and did not see Jeff ride up. The door of the little house that was half soddy, half dugout, opened, and Mary Svitac called something in Bohemian. The boy looked up, startled, and Jeff smiled. "Will you ride my horse over and tie him in the shade, Anton?"

The flood of hope that filled the boy's eyes was embarrassing to a man, and Jeff dismounted quickly, keeping his head turned. He took the bundle of curtains from behind the saddle and handed the reins to the boy; then walked on to the sod house, where Mary Svitac stood, the shawl tied under her chin framing her round, expressionless face. He handed her the curtains. "Those pickles you gave us were fine, Mrs. Svitac. Elaine wanted me to bring these curtains over."

Mary Svitac let her rough fingers caress the curtain material. "I will give you all the pickles," she said. "We don't need the curtains. We don't stay here no more."

Rudy's thick voice came from the dark interior of the sod house; and now Jeff could see him there, sitting in a chair, a man dulled with work and disappointments, a man with a limited knowledge of English who had come to a new country with a dream, and found grasshoppers and drought and blizzards and neighbors who tried to drive him out. He looked up. "We don't stay," he said.

"Can I come in for a minute, Mrs. Svitac?" Jeff asked.

"I make coffee," she said.

He stooped to pass through the low door, and he took off his hat and sat down. Now that his eyes were accustomed to the darkness of the room he saw the big lithograph there on the wall, the only decoration. Rudy Svitac stared unblinkingly at the floor, and a tear ran unashamed down the side of his nose. "We don't stay," he said.

"Sure, Rudy," Jeff Anderson said softly. "You stay."

Mary Svitac started to cry. There were no tears, for the land had taken even that away from her. There were just sobs—dry, choking sounds as she made the coffee—but they were woman sounds, made for her man; and she was willing to give up fifteen years of work if her man would be safe. "They will fight with us," she said. "They put cows in my Rudolph's corn. They tear down our fence. Soon they come to break my house. Is too much. Rudolph does not know fight. Rudolph is for plant the ground and play violin——"

"You stay, Rudy," Jeff Anderson said. "The law will take care of you. I promise you that."

Rudy Svitac shook his ponderous head. "Law is for Hank Fetterman," he said. "Is not for me."

"It's not so, Rudy," Jeff said. "You ask Anton. He knows."

"I ask Anton," Rudy Svitac said. "He says I am right. Law is for Hank Fetterman."

The boy came to the door and stood there, peering inside the room. His face was white, drawn with worry; but the hope was still in his eyes and a confidence was there. He didn't say anything. He didn't need to. Jeff could hear the sound of horses approaching. . . . Jeff stood up and the feeling that was in him was an old and familiar feeling—a tightening of all his muscles. He went to the corner of the room and took Rudy Svitac's rifle from its place, and he levered in a shell, leaving the rifle at full cock. He stepped through the door then, and he put his hand on the boy's head. "You explain again to your father about the law," he said. "You know, Anton, like we talked before."

"I know," Anton Svitac said.

Jeff stepped swiftly through the door into the sunlight, and he saw Hank Fetterman and the same two riders who had been with him at the saloon coming toward the soddy. Only Hank was armed, and this could be handy later, when Hank talked to the judge. *If we had expected trouble all three of us would have been armed, Judge, Hank Fetterman could say.* . . . They rode stiffly, holding their horses in. Jeff Anderson stood the cocked rifle by the fence post, placing it carefully. He pushed his hat back on his head and felt the sun on his back as he leaned there, one foot on a fence rail, watching the pigs drink the sour milk.

He knew when the riders were directly beside him, and he turned, his elbows leaning on the top rail of the fence behind him. His hat was pushed back but his face was in shade, for he had moved to where he was between the sun and the riders. Hank Fetterman said, "We're seeing a lot of each other, neighbor."

"Looks that way," Jeff said.

Hank Fetterman quieted his horse with a steady hand. His eyes never left Jeff Anderson's face. "I asked you once today if you was a friend of the bohunk's," he said. "Maybe I better ask it again."

"Maybe it depends on what you've got on your mind, Hank."

"The bohunk's been eating my beef," Fetterman said. "I'm sick of it."

"You sure that's it, Hank?" Jeff asked quietly. "Or is it just that there's something that eats on you and makes you want to tear down things other folks have taken years to build up?"

There were small white patches on either side of Hank Fetterman's mouth. "I said the bohunk was eating my beef," Hank Fetterman said. His lips didn't move. "You doubting my word?"

"No," Jeff said. "I'm calling you a liar."

He saw the smoldering anger in Hank Fetterman, the sore, whisky-nursed anger, and then the cattleman felt the full shock as the flat insult in Jeff's voice reached through to him. He cursed and half twisted in the saddle, blinking directly into the sun. "You forgetting you ain't a lawman any more?" he demanded.

"You decide, Hank," Jeff said.

They looked at each other, two men who had killed before

and knew the meaning of it, two men who respected a gun and understood a gun. They said nothing and yet they spoke a silent language, and the man who had been a lawman said, *I'm telling you to back down, Fetterman,* and the man who wanted to be king said, *You'll have to be big enough to make me.* No actual words, and yet they knew; and they faced each other with muscles tense and faces drawn, and appeared at ease. Jeff Anderson had dealt himself into the game, and he had checked the bet.

Hank Fetterman saw the rifle by the post. He knew it was cocked and loaded. He wondered if Jeff Anderson was actually as quick and as accurate as men said he was; and because he was Hank Fetterman he had to know, because if he backed down now it was over for him and he knew it. He jerked his horse around, trying to avoid that direct glare of the sun, and he made his decision. His hand went for his gun.

Jeff Anderson saw the move coming. It seemed to him that he had plenty of time. He had placed the rifle carefully and now he held it, hip-high, gripping it with one hand, tilting it up and pulling the trigger all at the same time. He didn't hear the sound of the rifle's explosion. You never did, he remembered; but he saw the thin film of gun smoke and he saw Hank Fetterman's mouth drop open, saw the man clawing at his chest. He didn't feel the sickness. Not yet——

Time passed as if through a film of haze, and nothing was real. Then he was gone and a canvas was stretched over the still form of Hank Fetterman and Rudy Svitac was whipping his team toward town to get the coroner. Now the sickness came to Jeff Anderson. He stood by the barn, trembling, and he heard the boy come up behind him. The boy said, "This was in the street in town, Mr. Anderson." The boy held out the tin star. "I told my father how the law was for everybody in America. Now he knows."

Jeff Anderson took the tin star and dropped it into his pocket.

Elaine saw him through the front window. She had been watching a long time and she had been praying, silently;

and now she said, "Thank God," and she went and sat down, and she was like that when he came into the room. She wanted to ask him about it, but her throat kept choking; and then he was kneeling there, his head in her lap, and he was crying deep inside, not making a sound. "It's all right, Jeff," she said. "It's all right."

For that was the thing he had to know—that it was all right with her. He had to know that she loved him for the man he was and not for the man he had tried to become. He couldn't change, any more than Billy Lang could change. She had never told him to take off his gun—not in words—but she had wanted him to, and he had understood, and he had tried. No woman could ask for greater love than that a man try to change himself. And no woman need be afraid when she had such love. She thought of young Anton Svitac and of her own who was to be, and she was calm and sure.

A long time later she picked up Jeff's coat and laid it across her arm. The tin star fell to the floor. For a long time she looked at it, then she bent her knees and reached down and picked it up and put it back into the coat pocket. She went into the bedroom then and hung the coat carefully. From the bureau drawer she took a clean, white pleated-front shirt and laid it out where he could see it. Marshal Jeff Anderson had worn a clean, white pleated-front shirt to the office on Monday morning for as long back as she could remember. She didn't expect him to change his habits now.

S. OMAR BARKER

Bad Company

S. (for Squire) Omar Barker (1894–1985) was one of the most beloved figures in Western writing. Born—literally—in a log cabin in Beulah, New Mexico, he served with the American army in France during World War I, and afterwards was a forest ranger, schoolteacher, and high school principal.

Beginning in the early 1920s, and throughout his long life, he contributed stories and verse to virtually every major magazine and newspaper in the country. "The Old S.O.B.," as he sometimes signed his letters, became a fixture in *The Saturday Evening Post* for such short, wistful, always clever verses as:

> Oh, sing me a song of the Western range—
> A good one or even a bad one,
> But sing, oh sing me, just once for a change
> A cheerful, instead of a sad, one!

"Bad Company" earned the Golden Spur Award at the Santa Fe WWA convention in 1956.

"Swaller big, kid," said Chugwater. "That panther milk will put whiz in your gizzard!" The straw-haired youngster on a sweaty cow pony hesitated. For two days he had been

41

out whooping around with this curly-wolf cowboy from Wyoming and the two Bonnadeen boys, and he had a pretty good idea what punishment his Uncle Tate would have in store for him when he got back to the ranch. Uncle Tate was a quiet-spoken, gristle-necked old bachelor with stern, old-fashioned ideas about how a boy should be raised, and he had promised this one a walloping the next time he ran off to "hell around," as he called it, with Chet and Smoky Bonnadeen.

Willie Shelton knew he would be needing some "whiz in his gizzard" when he got back to the T 8, but he soberly doubted if the kind that came in a bottle would help very much. Yet sometimes nothing can seem more important to a nearly-sixteen-year-old than not to be tagged as a sissy. Willie leaned his lankness from the saddle and took the proffered bottle.

"Here's to long ropes and loose hobbles!" he proclaimed. "Let the he-wolves howl and the pant'ers prowl!"

Big-enough talk, just right for a bold, booted buckaroo. At least he hoped it sounded that way. He stuck the neck of the bottle inside his mouth and pretended to swallow a lot more than he actually did.

"Woo-haw!" With a sudden squall, Chet Bonnadeen poked the chestnut horse in the flank with the butt end of his quirt.

The four of them had spent a good part of the day match-roping on T 8 yearlings over on Potrillo Creek and their horses were pretty well ridden down. But the chestnut pony still had enough life in him to jump almost from under his rider when Chet poked him.

"You get me throwed, you bangtailed buck idiot," said Willie, "and I'll come over you like a bullwhacker's bad dream!"

He made it sound tough, but there was no real anger in it—just the kind of rawhide talk Chet and Smoky were always swapping around. It gave him a swaggery feeling to be able to swap it right back at them.

Chet and Smoky were local cowboys, around nineteen and twenty, with restless black eyes and wildcat ways. In Uncle Tate Murdock's tally book they were bad companions for the nephew he had taken to raise after an epidemic of typhoid fever had orphaned him some three years before. But Willie, with the disquiet of oncoming manhood in his blood, had lately taken to running with them anyway, just as any high-spirited colt may take to running with the wild bunch. They called him "Bill," not "Willie," and he liked that, too.

Chugwater was older, a ruddy, moonfaced cowpoke with a sandy bristle of mustache and yellow-green coyote eyes. He hadn't been around the Black Mesa country more than a few weeks. If he had any name but Chugwater, he had never bothered to mention it. He said he owned a horse ranch up in Wyoming, and was just out on a *pasear* to see what kind of cayuses grew in New Mexico, and maybe kick up his heels a little in fresh pasture. He rode a fancy rig and had money to spend. He carried a long-reach lass rope and was just as handy with it as he seemed to be with six-gun, rawhide talk, and rye whisky. It never occurred to Willie that there might be anything odd about a stranger of Chugwater's age taking up so readily with the much younger Bonnadeens, whooping around with a trio of youngsters as if they were just as much man as he was.

Now, after a couple of days of comparatively harmless high jinks, Willie was headed for home, the others on their way back to Black Mesa.

When they came in sight of the Otis place on Tusa Creek, Willie challenged Smoky to a race, saddle-stand style, as far as the bridge beyond the Otis house.

"Shucks, you couldn't stand up in a wagon bed!" scoffed Smoky.

So Willie showed him. His chestnut pony was half a length ahead as they fogged past the Otis gate. Willie let out a long-drawn cowboy yell. He couldn't see whether Letha Otis was watching from a window or not, but he couldn't help hoping she was.

Where the road turned off to the T 8, Chugwater offered his bottle again, but Willie shook his head.

"Too close to home base, Chug." His grin had an uneasy look about it. "Uncle Tate'll be mad enough as it is!"

"Here, Bill!" Smoky Bonnadeen handed him a piece of gum. "Chaw that if you're scared the ol' gristle-neck will sniff likker on your wind!"

"Let him sniff," shrugged Willie. "If he gets too rollicky, I'll quit him and take out for Texas!"

"Make it Wyoming," said Chet, with a wink at Chugwater, "and you might have company. I hear that's curly-wolf country up there."

"But tough on pups!" Chugwater batted his coyote eyes at Willie as if sizing him up for caliber.

"You ain't talkin' about me!" Willie batted boyish blue ones right back at him. "I'm a growed he-wolf with a hanker to howl!"

"Then maybe you'd just as well ride on in with us. There ain't no law says you got to check in ever' few minutes, is there?"

Willie sensed challenge in it, but he hesitated only a second. "No law, I reckon," he said. "But I'm goin' to—this time, anyway. So long, you saddle bumpers!"

"So long, gopher gizzard!" Chet poked Willie's chestnut in the flank again. "See you in Wyoming!"

Willie wondered about that Wyoming talk as he rode away from them. Maybe it was all just cowboy hurrawing, maybe it wasn't. He wished he knew. He wondered some about himself, too, trying to remind himself that he ought to be grateful to Uncle Tate for furnishing him with bed, board, and a place on the ranch roller towel for the past three years. In those three years Uncle Tate and his right bower, a wizened old *vaquero* named Policarpio Mascareñas, had somehow made him over from a raw kid roustabout into a copper-bradded cowhand, ready and able to ride for the brand. For that he owed them.

But he wished Uncle Tate could get it through his head

that he was now old enough, and man enough, to pick his own company—and too old to take a whipping. Not that Uncle Tate had walloped him any more than his own father probably would have if he had lived; five or six times in three years, mostly for bad talk, and all but one of those wallopings had been more than a year ago. That was all right. He'd been just a kid then, and maybe needed that kind of daddying. But Uncle Tate's last application of a doubled lead rope, only three weeks ago, had been for drinking beer with Chet and Smoky Bonnadeen. Willie had wanted mighty bad to warn Uncle Tate right then that the next time he tried it he'd have a fight on his hands. But he had lacked enough courage to get it said.

All right, Uncle Tate. You've got your ideas, and I've got mine. I reckon you might as well find out right now that they don't always tally. That was what he was planning to say this time.

The man waiting by the saddle-shed door with a doubled lead rope in his hand was medium tall, built like a thong of rawhide, with a bony, weather-leathered face. There was little about his appearance to remind Willie of his dead mother except the quiet, steady look that stayed in his deep-set blue eyes, no matter what kind of humor he was in. Right now they looked at the sweat-caked horse more than at the boy.

"Willie," he said, "you been helling around with them no-account Bonnadeens again?"

He didn't raise his voice any more than if he had been asking about some stray cow he'd sent a cowhand out to look for. But Willie knew what was up. He got off and un-laced his saddle without answering. He wished he knew some way to make Uncle Tate understand about the big feeling it gave him to be accepted by Chet and Smoky and Chugwater as their rough, rawhide equal. But it wouldn't be any use to try.

He put up his saddle and started to go turn his pony out.

"Poley will turn out your horse, Willie," said Uncle Tate quietly. "You come here."

"I'll turn out my own horse," said Willie. "I ain't crippled."

He started off with the pony, but old Policarpio came hobbling over from where he was wedging rags into a leak in the water trough and took the reins.

"Take easy, Weellie," he advised. "More queeck you cry, more queeck he don't wheep no more!"

"Cry, my foot!" The boy turned and went back to the saddle-shed, flapping his chaps defiantly.

"Willie," said Uncle Tate, so quietly that his voice almost sounded kind despite its sternness, "I promised your mother I'd try and make a man out of you, but I won't never get the job done as long as you slip off and run around with rubbish."

"They ain't rubbish! They're——"

"I know what they are. You want to stand for your whippin' or have I got to hold you?"

"Neither one, Uncle Tate." Willie was tall enough to meet the older man's eyes almost on the level. "I've took my last whippin'. I'm headin' out for Wyoming—and you've lost you a cowhand!"

The look in Uncle Tate's eyes betrayed neither anger nor surprise.

"All right, Willie," he began, "if that's——"

"That's another thing!" the boy broke in hotly. "A man old enough to punch cows don't have to be called 'Willie'!"

"Willie," said Uncle Tate slowly, "I've broke a heap of broncs in my time, but I never did whip a horse except to learn him right from wrong—nor a boy, either. Only a whippin' won't do you no good if you don't know you need it." He tossed the rope inside the saddle shed. "If that's the way you see it, you might as well saddle you a horse and git goin'!"

"Never mind a horse!" Willie tried to put all the man-sized don't-give-a-hoot into his voice that he could. "I'll make out afoot till I get one!"

"No, by ginger, you won't!" It was the first time Willie

had ever heard Uncle Tate sound sure-enough mad. "I never
have set a cowhand afoot, and I don't aim to start now! Ol'
Gravy's your horse. You take him—and that duckfoot dun to
pack your bedroll on if you want him." He fished out a
pocket-worn wallet. "Here's fifty dollars due you in wages.
I don't give a hoot how you spend it, but I won't have no
nephew of mine sneakin' off broke and afoot like a hobo
sheepherder! Either you leave the T Eight up in the saddle
like a white man, or else you stay and take your whippin'.
And remember what I tell you: whatever trail you take from
now on out, you've got to pick it yourself!"

Willie wound up by taking Gravy and the fifty dollars, but
not the pack horse. He already had his own saddle.

After Uncle Tate went in the house, old Poley came out to
where Willie was saddling up, with some cold biscuits in a
flour sack.

"Gwyoming putty far place," he said.

"So's the hot place," shrugged the boy, "but I reckon the
trail's open!"

"The Ol' Man don't got no keeds hees own, Weellie!"

"Well, that ain't my fault!"

"You be good boy, Weellie. Someday you come back *mu-
cho hombre!*"

"Don't look for me right quick!" Willie managed to put on
a good-by grin. This horse-warped old *Mejicano* had been
mighty good to him.

Old Boojum Johnson, the cook, and a T 8 cowboy called
Tack Akers stood in the cookshack door and watched him
bundle his war bag on behind the saddle, but neither of
them made any comment.

It was around sundown when Willie came riding past the
Otis place. Letha Otis was standing just inside the gate,
teasing a pup with a long switch. She kept her back turned
to the road, as if she didn't see him. Willie leaned over the
gate and gave one of her gold-yellow braids a yank. She
whirled around and whacked him, not very hard, with the
switch.

"Shame on you, Willie Shelton!" she said. "Don't you ever do that again!"

"Likely I won't, taffy-top," Willie told her. "I'm quittin' the country—for good."

Letha was just a little ranch girl, hardly a day over fourteen, with freckles and a snubby nose, but the surprised way her big blue eyes looked up at him gave Willie's heart a twist.

"Don't talk silly!" she said.

"Silly, my foot! Me and Uncle Tate had a showdown, and I'm on my way!"

"Good riddance!" Letha flipped her braids in a sassy gesture, then abruptly sobered. "Not—not sure 'nough, Bill?"

"Sure as cockleburs on a coyote!" Willie sat straight in the saddle. "A man's got to pick his own trail, Letha, and I'm Wyoming-bound!"

The girl didn't say good-by, but when he looked back from on down the road, she waved to him.

Chet and Smoky Bonnadeen had folks over on Tejón Creek, but they didn't stay with them much. They had a little shack on the outskirts of Black Mesa where they batched most of the time, and where Chugwater had thrown in with them the past several weeks. Willie felt sure he would be welcome there.

But first he rode into town. At Horseshoe Higgins' store he bought a couple of soogans, a horsehide jacket with fringes on it like the one Chugwater wore, a secondhand .45 in a black leather holster, and some cartridges. Horseshoe Higgins hesitated a little about selling the gun.

"Your uncle know you're buyin' this weapon?" he asked. Willie shrugged. "He will when you tell him."

"You sure you know which end the bullets come out of?"

"I'm fixin' to study up on it," Willie told him. "You goin' to sell me this pistol, or ain't you?"

The fat storekeeper shrugged and let him have it. Willie added some dry salt pork, sardines, crackers, and dried prunes to his purchases. Welcome or not, he didn't intend to sponge on anybody.

He thought about stopping at the Bullhorn Saloon for a bottle of whisky, but he was afraid Brocky Jones might not sell him hard liquor, and there might be cowboys around to josh him about it. Besides, now that he was riding his own trail, with no one to forbid him, he had already decided it might be a good idea not to drink much more than might be necessary to keep from looking like a sissy.

It was dark when he rode up to the Bonnadeen shack. Even with his horse loaded like a sheepherder's burro with soogans and sacks, it gave him a big feeling to arrive well supplied and with a six-shooter on. He reined up and let out what the cowboys call a squall. Both the Bonnadeens came out.

"You holler wicked for a tenderfoot," grinned Smoky. "Fall off your horse, so we can drag you in and see how bad you're shot!"

"Woo-haw-w-w-w!" squalled Willie again. He stepped off his horse, drew his new gun, and banged away a couple of times in the air.

"You want Constable Ellers rompin' out here to see who's shootin' off firecrackers?" Chet demanded.

Willie waited till he had put up his horse and sat down to biscuits and gravy before he told them how he had slipped his hobbles and come to throw in with them.

"Big feller!" Chet walloped him on the back. "Let's have a drink of bob-wire extract on it!"

Smoky got a jug out from under one of the bunks.

"Here's to the three muskrat ears!" he declaimed. "One for all, all for one—unless he gets caught!"

Brash, breezy talk. Willie liked it, but he made his turn at the jug a light one.

"Chet," he inquired, "where's ol' Chugwater?"

"Gone to the wilderness to look for the ol' gray mare," said Chet. "We're fixin' to meet him at some old corrals at the mouth of Torcido Canyon about Sunday mornin', with our beds all rolled and grub in a sack."

"What about Wyoming?"

"Why? You goin' with us?"

"Try and stop me!"

"All right, but don't go blabbin' it around, you savvy?"

Willie wondered if he ought to tell them that he had already bragged to Uncle Tate and Poley and Letha Otis about being Wyoming-bound, but as long as they hadn't robbed a bank or anything, he couldn't see that it mattered.

He and Chet and Smoky spent part of the next few days shoeing horses, rigging pack-saddles, readying gear for packing, and spent part of it in Black Mesa. No high jinks that would get Constable Ellers after them. Just Junin' around, as the cowboys say.

His first afternoon in town, Willie saw Boojum Johnson with the T 8 supply wagon. On a sudden impulse he helped the old cook load some hundred-pound sacks of salt. For a while Chet and Smoky stood around, hurrawing him for being a flunky, then strutted off, spurs ajingle, to the Bullhorn Saloon.

"I heard you and them two no-accounts had took out to Wyoming, Willie," Boojum grinned. "You back already?"

"You can hear a heap of things when you got big ears," shrugged Willie.

The next morning Willie came across Tack Akers just lighting down at the Bullhorn hitch rack.

"Hi, Tack," Willie said. "How come you townin' on a weekday?"

"I come lookin' for an egg to suck," grinned Tack. "How's Wyoming?"

"A foot wide and open in the middle," Willie breezed back at him. "Same as a cowboy's mouth. How's the ranch?"

"Better," said Tack. "I ain't seen a dirty place on the roller towel since you left. Say, you wouldn't know the whereabouts of a feller called Chugwater, would you?"

"He's gone to the wilderness to look for the old gray mare. You want him for somethin'?"

"Nothin' important," Tack shrugged. "I punched cows up around the Chugwater country one summer. Just wonderin'

if he was some jasper I'd met up there. You headin' for
Wyoming west of the mountains or east up the flats?''

Willie couldn't think of any reason why Tack might want
to pump him, but he remembered what Chet had said about
keeping his blab shut.

"Who wants to know?" he asked.

"Not me, Willie." The T 8 cowboy shrugged and went on
into the Bullhorn.

That night after supper Chet saddled up and rode away by
himself. After he was gone, Willie asked Smoky where Chet
was headed for, that he had to ride by night.

"To help Chug look for the ol' gray mare," said Smoky.

"Doggone it, Smoky!" Willie flared up at him. "You talk
riddles to me and I'll come over you like a wet saddle blanket! What's all this about the old gray mare?"

"Keep your shirt on," Smoky advised him with a grin.
"Chet's gone to help gather some horses Chug's been buying
for us to take along to Wyoming, whenever we go."

"Buyin'?"

"What else? You don't think a big ranch owner like Chug
would be borrowin' 'em, do you?"

Willie didn't know for sure what to think. But what he did
know was that he had thrown in with this outfit of his own
free will, and as long as they continued to treat him good, he
sure didn't aim to raise a fuss over something that really was
none of his business.

"It ain't nothing to me where Chugwater gets his horses,"
he said. "Let's wander down to Brocky's and shake for the
beers."

The next afternoon the two young cowboys met Tate Murdock and old Poley coming out of Horseshoe Higgins' store.
Uncle Tate nodded to him as casually as if he were a stranger
and walked on down the street. Old Poley didn't even nod.

"Ol' gristle-gut!" shrugged Smoky. "You're lucky you quit
him!"

Willie restrained an unaccountable impulse to warn
Smoky to mind his tongue where Uncle Tate was concerned.

"Sure," he said, instead. "You ain't heard me cryin' about it, have you?"

He was trying a new saddle blanket on his horse out back of the store a few minutes later when old Poley showed up with a brand-new rope in his hand. Smoky was still inside the store, probably teasing Horseshoe's none-too-pretty daughter.

"How you makin', Weellie?" The old *vaquero's* sharp black eyes seemed to be appraising the boy's new six-shooter in its black leather holster. "Whassamatta you don't went to Gwyoming?"

Willie started to say "None of your business," but something like shame stopped him. This was a man who had never spoken an unkind word to him in his life.

"We'll be pullin' out," he said instead, "as soon as Chug-water finds the ol' gray mare. How's things at the ranch?"

"Joost same. Water trough still leakin'." Poley shrugged, batting wrinkle-bound black eyes. "Señor Chugwater, he's nize man, eh? Geeve you good job in Gwyoming, Weellie?"

One thing sure, Willie didn't want Poley—or anybody else—feeling sorry for him.

"Sure," he said. "On his horse ranch. Forty a month. Same as he's payin' me to help trail a bunch with us. We're fixin' to pick 'em up at Torcido Canyon, Sunday mornin'. I'm my own man now, Poley, and—— Hey, what you think you're doin' with that rope?"

Poley finished tying a fine new lariat on Willie's saddle.

"Leetle borthday's present, Weellie," he grinned. "You forget you sixteen years today?"

Willie gulped. "I sure had," he said. "Gosh! Much obliged! I'll sure try to keep the kinks out of it!"

"*Buen cabestro, vaquero honesto!*" Policarpio Mas-careñas spoke the words with a certain dignity. "*Adiós, Weellie!*"

Good rope, honest cowboy. He don't have any call to preach at me, thought the boy. *I'm a man grown now, and able to pick my own trail.*

He hadn't meant to blab, but he was tired of getting gigged about still not being gone to Wyoming. Anyhow, why should it matter?

That night he and Smoky got to trying to see which one could do a better job of tilting a jug one-handed, with the result that Willie swallowed a little more barbed-wire extract than he meant to. He woke up the next morning with a ratty taste in his mouth and all his clothes on, and for the first time, stayed away from the two dusty streets of Black Mesa all day.

Both Willie and Smoky were surprised when Chugwater and Chet came riding in late Saturday evening. Chet said they had got the old corrals patched so they would hold the ol' gray mare overnight and so had decided they might as well ride in and help pack out.

Chugwater's ruddy face bristled like a porcupine with a week's growth of sandy whiskers. After a long pull at the jug, he lathered up and shaved them off, including his mustache.

"You look like moonrise over a cowpen, Chug," Willie told him.

"You can't insult me, kid." Chugwater's laugh was short. "I wasn't put together for purty, like you. Chet tells me you've slipped your hobbles an' lookin' for passage to Wyoming."

"You heard him right. From now on, I'm skinnin' my own wolf. You see my new six-gun?"

Chugwater took the .45, spun it expertly on his finger, and handed it back.

"Totin' a hogleg don't make you a curl-wolf, kid. Not till you learn when, where, an' how to make it talk for you. You sing the right tune till we git to Wyoming, an' maybe I'll give you a few pointers."

They packed up and pulled out by moonlight, leading three pack horses. From the wrecked condition in which Chet and Smoky left their shack, it looked to Willie as if they were not expecting to come back. Well, neither was he.

It was a twenty-mile ride to where Torcido Canyon twisted its way out of the rimrocks in such poor grass country that nobody had ever bothered to fence it and few stock ever ranged there. Eighteen of those twenty miles were already behind them when sunrise began to spread an orange-red glory over rimrocked buttes and mesas.

Willie had never ridden this far east of the T 8 before, but yonder, westward some fifty miles away, he could recognize La Ceja—the long "eyebrow" of mesa rim that marked off his Uncle Tate's main summer range—with the golden broom of sunrise slowly brushing away its purple haze.

Willie was wondering if sunrise would ever be like this in Wyoming, when, topping a low rise, they came upon a little bunch of loose horses: a mare with a colt, some twos, threes, and full-grown geldings. Eleven head, all golden chestnuts but two. Willie didn't have to look twice to recognize them for T 8 horses, some of Uncle Tate's best. What they were doing off here, forty miles from T 8 headquarters, thirty from the nearest T 8 fence, Willie had no idea. But here they were.

Tate Murdock had never raised his horses wild. These put up their heads and circled a little, but didn't run. When the four riders came close enough to read brands, Chugwater reined up. He looked as surprised as Willie felt.

"Hell's a-hootin'!" he exclaimed. "Where did these nags come from? That T Eight's your uncle's brand, ain't it, kid?"

Willie nodded. He took a deep breath, unconsciously straightening a little in the saddle as he remembered what Uncle Tate had said about picking his own trail.

"Boys," he said quietly, "here's where I quit you. I'm goin' to take these strays back where they belong."

Chugwater swung his horse around to face the boy, a coldly calculating squint in his coyotelike eyes.

"I don't know how these strays got here, kid," he said, "but there ain't no sense kickin' luck in the face. They've got the same brand as the horse you're ridin'. What's to keep us from throwin' 'em up the trail, sell 'em, an' split the take?"

"Not a damn thing," said Willie, "except that I'm takin' 'em home!"

"Don't be a knucklehead, Bill!" That was Chet. "You've done throwed in with this outfit, and by gulliver——"

"I'll 'tend to this, boys," Chugwater cut in dryly. He turned again to Willie. "I ain't foolin', kid. I want these horses. You goin' to be reasonable, or ain't you?"

Willie stared at the six-shooter that had appeared with sudden ease in Chugwater's hand.

His own gun came out of the holster awkwardly. It shook when he tried to point it.

"You horse thieves can go to hell!" he said between white, tight lips. "I'm takin' these horses home!"

"You double-crossin' little so-and-so!" said Chet. "Let him have it, Chug!"

If I shoot first I'll miss, thought Willie grimly. *And if I don't——*

"Chet," said Chugwater without taking his eyes off the white-faced boy in front of him, "if you think I'm fool enough to put myself on the murder list for shootin' a pucker-brained pipsqueak, you're crazy! A few horses just ain't worth it! Let's git goin'!"

They went. So did Willie, in the other direction. He was shaking all over. He wondered how Chugwater knew he hadn't been going to shoot unless he had to. He was short a bedroll and some stuff in the departing packs, but it didn't matter. All he wanted now was to get these strays started back to the T 8.

He pushed them up a little draw, then cut back over the next ridge north and found a rimrock from which he could get a good look down at about twenty horses in the old Torcido Canyon corrals. If he saw even one T 8 chestnut among them, he knew he would have to go back down there. He was glad that he saw none.

Willie ran into some rough country getting back to the T 8, but by using his new rope to catch a fresh mount a couple of times and pushing right on by moonlight, he managed to hit headquarters with his strays a little before sunup the next day. Always an early riser, Uncle Tate saw the drive coming and opened the gates. Willie shoved the horses on into the horse trap beyond the corrals.

"Must be some fence down someplace," said Uncle Tate when he came riding back through the trap gate. "Where'd you find 'em?"

He sounded like a man who had sent a cowhand out to look for some strays and was passably glad he'd found them.

"Over east," Willie told him. " 'Bout a mile south of Torcido Canyon."

"You've made a good ride, Bill." Uncle Tate's leathery face looked no different from what it had as he stood there at the saddle-shed a few days ago, with a rope in his hand. "Turn out your horse and we'll go in to breakfast."

It was the first time, as far as Willie could remember, that Uncle Tate had ever called him Bill. The man-to-man, matter-of-fact sound of it was in itself a promise and a testimony of new understanding between them.

Still the boy stayed on his horse. Blabbing on those he had so lately counted as friends was not going to be easy. But they had picked their own trail, and now he had picked his.

"Some fellers had a bunch of horses penned in them old corrals, Uncle Tate," he said. "I reckon maybe——"

"Sheriff Ortega's keepin' tabs on 'em," Tate Murdock broke in quietly. "It ain't your fault if everybody can't be honest, Bill."

He didn't say "like you," but Willie knew what he meant. If it turned out that some of those horses were stolen, he hoped the law wouldn't be too hard on Chet and Smoky—specially Smoky.

But now he still had his own gully to jump. He got off his horse and took down the new rope old Poley had given him.

"I'm still due that whippin', Uncle Tate," he said. "Here's a rope."

Uncle Tate didn't take the rope, nor even look at it. It was almost the first time Willie had ever seen anything like a twinkle in his eye.

"Horse or man," he said, "sixteen is too damned old to whip! Let's go in to breakfast. Then you better rest up awhile."

Along toward noon Willie took a notion to ride over to the Otis place and see how Letha was making out with her pup. Old Poley was out there, wedging rags in a water-trough leak, when he came out to saddle up.

"How you makin', Beel?" he grinned. "Those new rope ketch putty good?"

"It sure did," said Willie earnestly.

Because now he understood how it was: why Boojum and Tack and Poley had tried to pump him; why those T 8 strays had turned up where they were—not wholly by accident. And when an old gristleneck like Uncle Tate would risk losing some of his best horses on the chance that a runaway kid's finding them would put him back on the right trail, it sure did give a man a fine, big feeling!

DOROTHY M. JOHNSON

Lost Sister

In 1984, when 100 members of Western Writers of America contributed their lists on the best Western short stories ever written, Dorothy Johnson emerged as the hands-down favorite of them all: "A Man Called Horse" was judged the best Western story of all time, and three of her other tales, "The Hanging Tree," "The Man Who Shot Liberty Valence" and "Lost Sister" (which earned the Golden Spur for 1956) were also on the list of the "21 Best."

Born in Iowa, Johnson grew up in Montana, worked as a stenographer and magazine editor in New York and returned to her adopted home state in 1950. She began publishing her stories in the 1930s and devoted many years to studying the history and cultures of the Plains Indians and writing effectively of them in her stories, novels (*Buffalo Women, All the Buffalo Returning*), and in such nonfiction books as *The Bloody Bozeman* and *Sitting Bull: Warrior for a Lost Nation*.

Dorothy Johnson died on November 11, 1984, at her home in Missoula, Montana.

Our household was full of women, who overwhelmed my uncle Charlie and sometimes confused me with their bustle and chatter. We were the only men on the place. I was nine years old when still another woman came—Aunt Bessie, who had been living with the Indians.

When my mother told me about her, I couldn't believe it. The savages had killed my father, a cavalry lieutenant, two years before. I hated Indians and looked forward to wiping them out when I got older. (But when I was grown, they were no menace any more.)

"What did she live with the hostiles for?" I demanded.

"They captured her when she was a little girl," Ma said. "She was three years younger than you are. Now she's coming home."

High time she came home, I thought. I said so, promising, "If they was ever to get me, I wouldn't stay with 'em long."

Ma put her arms around me. "Don't talk like that. They won't get you. They'll never get you."

I was my mother's only real tie with her husband's family. She was not happy with those masterful women, my aunts Margaret, Hannah, and Sabina, but she would not go back East where she came from. Uncle Charlie managed the store the aunts owned, but he wasn't really a member of the family—he was just Aunt Margaret's husband. The only man who had belonged was my father, the aunts' younger brother. And I belonged, and someday the store would be mine. My mother stayed to protect my heritage.

None of the three sisters, my aunts, had ever seen Aunt Bessie. She had been taken by the Indians before they were born. Aunt Mary had known her—Aunt Mary was two years older—but she lived a thousand miles away now and was not well.

There was no picture of the little girl who had become a legend. When the family had first settled here, there was enough struggle to feed and clothe the children without having pictures made of them.

Even after army officers had come to our house several times and there had been many letters about Aunt Bessie's delivery from the savages, it was a long time before she came. Major Harris, who made the final arrangements, warned my aunts that they would have problems, that Aunt Bessie might not be able to settle down easily into family life.

This was only a challenge to Aunt Margaret, who welcomed challenges. "She's our own flesh and blood," Aunt Margaret trumpeted. "Of course she must come to us. My poor, dear sister Bessie, torn from her home forty years ago!"

The major was earnest but not tactful. "She's been with the savages all those years," he insisted. "And she was only a little girl when she was taken. I haven't seen her myself, but it's reasonable to assume that she'll be like an Indian woman."

My stately aunt Margaret arose to show that the audience was ended. "Major Harris," she intoned, "I cannot permit anyone to criticize my own dear sister. She will live in my home, and if I do not receive official word that she is coming within a month, I shall take steps."

Aunt Bessie came before the month was up.

The aunts in residence made valiant preparations. They bustled and swept and mopped and polished. They moved me from my own room to my mother's—as she had been begging them to do because I was troubled with nightmares. They prepared my old room for Aunt Bessie with many small comforts—fresh doilies everywhere, hairpins, a matching pitcher and bowl, the best towels, and two new nightgowns in case hers might be old. (The fact was that she didn't have any.)

"Perhaps we should have some dresses made," Hannah suggested. "We don't know what she'll have with her."

"We don't know what size she'll take, either," Margaret pointed out. "There'll be time enough for her to go to the store after she settles down and rests for a day or two. Then she can shop to her heart's content."

Ladies of the town came to call almost every afternoon while the preparations were going on. Margaret promised them that, as soon as Bessie had recovered sufficiently from her ordeal, they should all meet her at tea.

Margaret warned her anxious sisters, "Now, girls, we mustn't ask her too many questions at first. She must rest for a while. She's been through a terrible experience." Margaret's voice dropped 'way down with those last two words, as if only she could be expected to understand.

Indeed Bessie had been through a terrible experience, but it wasn't what the sisters thought. The experience from which she was suffering, when she arrived, was that she had been wrenched from her people, the Indians, and turned over to strangers. She had not been freed. She had been made a captive.

Aunt Bessie came with Major Harris and an interpreter, a half-blood with greasy black hair hanging down to his shoulders. His costume was half army and half primitive. Aunt Margaret swung the door open wide when she saw them coming. She ran out, with her sisters following, while my mother and I watched from a window. Margaret's arms were outstretched, but when she saw the woman closer, her arms dropped and her glad cry died.

She did not cringe, my aunt Bessie who had been an Indian for forty years, but she stopped walking and stood staring, helpless among her captors.

The sisters had described her often as a little girl. Not that they had ever seen her, but she was a legend, the captive child. Beautiful blond curls, they said she had, and big blue eyes—she was a fairy child, a pale-haired little angel who ran on dancing feet.

The Bessie who came back was an aging woman who plodded in moccasins, whose dark dress did not belong on her bulging body. Her brown hair hung just below her ears. It was growing out; when she was first taken from the Indians, her hair had been cut short to clean out the vermin.

Aunt Margaret recovered herself and, instead of embracing this silent, stolid woman, satisfied herself by patting an arm and crying, "Poor dear Bessie, I am your sister Margaret. And here are our sisters Hannah and Sabina. We do hope you're not all tired out from your journey!"

Aunt Margaret was all graciousness, because she had been assured beyond doubt that this was truly a member of the family. She must have believed—Aunt Margaret could believe anything—that all Bessie needed was to have a nice nap and wash her face. Then she would be as talkative as any of them.

The other aunts were quick-moving and sharp of tongue. But this one moved as if her sorrows were a burden on her bowed shoulders, and when she spoke briefly in answer to the interpreter, you could not understand a word of it.

Aunt Margaret ignored these peculiarities. She took the party into the front parlor—even the interpreter, when she understood there was no avoiding it. She might have gone on battling with the major about him, but she was in a hurry to talk to her lost sister.

"You won't be able to converse with her unless the interpreter is present," Major Harris said. "Not," he explained hastily, "because of any regulation, but because she has forgotten English."

Aunt Margaret gave the half-blood interpreter a look of frowning doubt and let him enter. She coaxed Bessie. "Come, dear, sit down."

The interpreter mumbled, and my Indian aunt sat cautiously on a needlepoint chair. For most of her life she had been living with the people who sat comfortably on the ground.

The visit in the parlor was brief. Bessie had had her instructions before she came. But Major Harris had a few warnings for the family. "Technically, your sister is still a prisoner," he explained, ignoring Margaret's start of horror. "She will be in your custody. She may walk in your fenced yard, but she must not leave it without official permission.

"Mrs. Raleigh, this may be a heavy burden for you all. But she has been told all this and has expressed willingness to conform to these restrictions. I don't think you will have any trouble keeping her here." Major Harris hesitated, remembered that he was a soldier and a brave man, and added, "If I did, I wouldn't have brought her."

There was the making of a sharp little battle, but Aunt Margaret chose to overlook the challenge. She could not overlook the fact that Bessie was not what she had expected.

Bessie certainly knew that this was her lost white family, but she didn't seem to care. She was infinitely sad, infinitely removed. She asked one question: "Ma-ry?" and Aunt Margaret almost wept with joy.

"Sister Mary lives a long way from here," she explained, "and she isn't well, but she will come as soon as she's able. Dear sister Mary!"

The interpreter translated this, and Bessie had no more to say. That was the only understandable word she ever did say in our house, the remembered name of her older sister.

When the aunts, all chattering, took Bessie to her room, one of them asked, "But where are her things?"

Bessie had no things, no baggage. She had nothing at all but the clothes she stood in. While the sisters scurried to bring a comb and other oddments, she stood like a stooped monument, silent and watchful. This was her prison. Very well, she would endure it.

"Maybe tomorrow we can take her to the store and see what she would like," Aunt Hannah suggested.

"There's no hurry," Aunt Margaret declared thoughtfully. She was getting the idea that this sister was going to be a problem. But I don't think Aunt Margaret ever really stopped hoping that one day Bessie would cease to be different, that she would end her stubborn silence and begin to relate the events of her life among the savages, in the parlor over a cup of tea.

My Indian aunt accustomed herself, finally, to sitting on the chair in her room. She seldom came out, which was a relief to her sisters. She preferred to stand, hour after hour, looking out the window—which was open only about a foot, in spite of all Uncle Charlie's efforts to budge it higher. And she always wore moccasins. She never was able to wear shoes from the store, but seemed to treasure the shoes brought to her.

The aunts did not, of course, take her shopping after all. They made her a couple of dresses; and when they told her, with signs and voluble explanations, to change her dress, she did.

After I found that she was usually at the window, looking across the flat land to the blue mountains, I played in the yard so I could stare at her. She never smiled, as an aunt should, but she looked at me sometimes, thoughtfully, as if measuring my worth. By performing athletic feats, such as walking on my hands, I could get her attention. For some reason, I valued it.

She didn't often change expression, but twice I saw her scowl with disapproval. Once was when one of the aunts slapped me in a casual way. I had earned the slap, but the Indians did not punish children with blows. Aunt Bessie was shocked, I think, to see that white people did. The other time was when I talked back to someone with spoiled, small-boy insolence—and that time the scowl was for me.

The sisters and my mother took turns, as was their Christian duty, in visiting her for half an hour each day. Bessie didn't eat at the table with us—not after the first meal.

The first time my mother took her turn, it was under protest. "I'm afraid I'd start crying in front of her," she argued, but Aunt Margaret insisted.

I was lurking in the hall when Ma went in. Bessie said something, then said it again, peremptorily, until my mother guessed what she wanted. She called me and put her arm around me as I stood beside her chair. Aunt Bessie nodded, and that was all there was to it.

Afterward, my mother said, "She likes you. And so do I." She kissed me.

"I don't like her," I complained. "She's queer."

"She's a sad old lady," my mother explained. "She had a little boy once, you know."

"What happened to him?"

"He grew up and became a warrior. I suppose she was proud of him. Now the Army has him in prison somewhere. He's half Indian. He was a dangerous man."

He was indeed a dangerous man, and a proud man, a chief, a bird of prey whose wings the Army had clipped after bitter years of trying.

However, my mother and my Indian aunt had that one thing in common: they both had sons. The other aunts were childless.

There was a great to-do about having Aunt Bessie's photograph taken. The aunts, who were stubbornly and valiantly trying to make her one of the family, wanted a picture of her for the family album. The government wanted one too, for some reason—perhaps because someone realized that a thing of historic importance had been accomplished by recovering the captive child.

Major Harris sent a young lieutenant with the greasy-haired interpreter to discuss the matter in the parlor. (Margaret, with great foresight, put a clean towel on a chair and saw to it the interpreter sat there.) Bessie spoke very little during that meeting, and of course we understood only what the half-blood *said* she was saying.

No, she did not want her picture made. No.

But your son had his picture made. Do you want to see it? They teased her with that offer, and she nodded.

If we let you see his picture, then will you have yours made?

She nodded doubtfully. Then she demanded more than had been offered: If you let me keep his picture, then you can make mine.

No, you can only look at it. We have to keep his picture. It belongs to us.

My Indian aunt gambled for high stakes. She shrugged and spoke, and the interpreter said, "She not want to look. She will keep or nothing."

My mother shivered, understanding as the aunts could not understand what Bessie was gambling—all or nothing.

Bessie won. Perhaps they had intended that she should. She was allowed to keep the photograph that had been made of her son. It has been in history books many times—the half-white chief, the valiant leader who was not quite great enough to keep his Indian people free.

His photograph was taken after he was captured, but you

would never guess it. His head is high, his eyes stare with boldness but not with scorn, his long hair is arranged with care—dark hair braided on one side and with a tendency to curl where the other side hangs loose—and his hands hold the pipe like a royal scepter.

That photograph of the captive but unconquered warrior had its effect on me. Remembering him, I began to control my temper and my tongue, to cultivate reserve as I grew older, to stare with boldness but not scorn at people who annoyed or offended me. I never met him, but I took silent pride in him—Eagle Head, my Indian cousin.

Bessie kept his picture on her dresser when she was not holding it in her hands. And she went like a docile, silent child to the photograph studio, in a carriage with Aunt Margaret early one morning, when there would be few people on the street to stare.

Bessie's photograph is not proud but pitiful. She looks out with no expression. There is no emotion there, no challenge, only the face of an aging woman with short hair, only endurance and patience. The aunts put a copy in the family album.

But they were nearing the end of their tether. The Indian aunt was a solid ghost in the house. She did nothing because there was nothing for her to do. Her gnarled hands must have been skilled at squaws' work, at butchering meat and scraping and tanning hides, at making tepees and beading ceremonial clothes. But her skills were useless and unwanted in a civilized home. She did not even sew when my mother gave her cloth and needles and thread. She kept the sewing things beside her son's picture.

She ate (in her room) and slept (on the floor) and stood looking out the window. That was all, and it could not go on. But it had to go on, at least until my sick aunt Mary was well enough to travel—Aunt Mary, who was her older sister, the only one who had known her when they were children.

The sisters' duty visits to Aunt Bessie became less and

less visits and more and more duty. They settled into a bearable routine. Margaret had taken upon herself the responsibility of trying to make Bessie talk. Make, I said, not teach. She firmly believed that her stubborn and unfortunate sister needed only encouragement from a strong-willed person. So Margaret talked, as to a child, when she bustled in:

"Now there you stand, just looking, dear. What in the world is there to see out there? The birds—are you watching the birds? Why don't you try sewing? Or you could go for a little walk in the yard. Don't you want to go out for a nice little walk?"

Bessie listened and blinked.

Margaret could have understood an Indian woman's not being able to converse in a civilized tongue, but her own sister was not an Indian. Bessie was white, therefore she should talk the language her sisters did—the language she had not heard since early childhood.

Hannah, the put-upon aunt, talked to Bessie too, but she was delighted not to get any answers and not to be interrupted. She bent over her embroidery when it was her turn to sit with Bessie and told her troubles in an unending flow. Bessie stood looking out the window the whole time.

Sabina, who had just as many troubles, most of them emanating from Margaret and Hannah, went in like a martyr, firmly clutching her Bible, and read aloud from it until her time was up. She took a small clock along so that she would not, because of annoyance, be tempted to cheat.

After several weeks Aunt Mary came, white and trembling and exhausted from her illness and the long, hard journey. The sisters tried to get the interpreter in but were not successful. (Aunt Margaret took that failure pretty hard.) They briefed Aunt Mary, after she had rested, so the shock of seeing Bessie would not be too terrible. I saw them meet, those two.

Margaret went to the Indian woman's door and explained volubly who had come, a useless but brave attempt. Then she stood aside, and Aunt Mary was there, her lined white face aglow, her arms outstretched. "Bessie! Sister Bessie!" she cried.

And after one brief moment's hesitation, Bessie went into her arms and Mary kissed her sun-dark, weathered cheek. Bessie spoke. "Ma-ry," she said. "Ma-ry." She stood with tears running down her face and her mouth working. So much to tell, so much suffering and fear—and joy and triumph, too—and the sister there at last who might legitimately hear it all and understand.

But the only English word that Bessie remembered was "Mary," and she had not cared to learn any others. She turned to the dresser, took her son's picture in her work-hardened hands, reverently, and held it so her sister could see. Her eyes pleaded.

Mary looked on the calm, noble, savage face of her half-blood nephew and said the right thing: "My, isn't he handsome!" She put her head on one side and then the other. "A fine boy, sister," she approved. "You must"—she stopped, but she finished—"be awfully proud of him, dear!"

Bessie understood the tone if not the words. The tone was admiration. Her son was accepted by the sister who mattered. Bessie looked at the picture and nodded, murmuring. Then she put it back on the dresser.

Aunt Mary did not try to make Bessie talk. She sat with her every day for hours, and Bessie did talk—but not in English. They sat holding hands for mutual comfort while the captive child, grown old and a grandmother, told what had happened in forty years. Aunt Mary *said* that was what Bessie was talking about. But she didn't understand a word of it and didn't need to.

"There is time enough for her to learn English again," Aunt Mary said. "I think she understands more than she lets on. I asked her if she'd like to come and live with me, and she nodded. We'll have the rest of our lives for her to learn English. But what she has been telling me—she can't wait to tell that. About her life, and her son."

"Are you sure, Mary dear, that you should take the responsibility of having her?" Margaret said dutifully, no
doubt shaking in her shoes for fear Mary would change her
mind now that deliverance was in sight. "I do believe she'd
be happier with you, though we've done all we could."

Margaret and the older sisters would certainly be happier
with Bessie somewhere else. And so, it developed, would
the United States Government.

Major Harris came with the interpreter to discuss details,
and they told Bessie she could go, if she wished, to live with
Mary a thousand miles away. Bessie was patient and willing, stolidly agreeable. She talked a great deal more to the
interpreter than she had ever done before. He answered at
length and then explained to the others that she had wanted
to know how she and Mary would travel to this far country.
It was hard, he said, for her to understand just how far they
were going.

Later we knew that the interpreter and Bessie had talked
about much more than that.

Next morning, when Sabina took breakfast to Bessie's
room, we heard a cry of dismay. Sabina stood holding the
tray, repeating, "She's gone out the window! She's gone out
the window!"

And so she had. The window that had always stuck so
that it would not raise more than a foot was open wider
now. And the photograph of Bessie's son was gone from the
dresser. Nothing else was missing except Bessie and the
decent dark dress she had worn the day before.

My uncle Charlie got no breakfast that morning. With Margaret shrieking orders, he leaped on a horse and rode to the
telegraph station.

Before Major Harris got there with half a dozen cavalry-
men, civilian scouts were out searching for the missing
woman. They were expert trackers. Their lives had depended, at various times, on their ability to read the meaning of a turned stone, a broken twig, a bruised leaf. They
found Bessie had gone south. They tracked her for ten miles.

And then they lost the trail, for Bessie was as skilled as they were. Her life had sometimes depended on leaving no stone or twig or leaf marked by her passage. She traveled fast at first. Then, with time to be careful, she evaded the followers she knew would come.

The aunts were stricken with grief—at least Aunt Mary was—and bowed with humiliation about what Bessie had done. The blinds were drawn, and voices were low in the house. We had been pitied because of Bessie's tragic folly in having let the Indians make a savage of her. But now we were traitors because we had let her get away.

Aunt Mary kept saying pitifully, "Oh, why did she go? I thought she would be contented with me!"

The others said that it was, perhaps, all for the best. Aunt Margaret proclaimed, "She has gone back to her own." That was what they honestly believed, and so did Major Harris.

My mother told me why she had gone. "You know that picture she had of the Indian chief, her son? He's escaped from the jail he was in. The fort got word of it, and they think Bessie may be going to where he's hiding. That's why they're trying so hard to find her. They think," my mother explained, "that she knew of his escape before they did. They think the interpreter told her when he was here. There was no other way she could have found out."

They scoured the mountains to the south for Eagle Head and Bessie. They never found her, and they did not get him until a year later, far to the north. They could not capture him that time. He died fighting.

After I grew up, I operated the family store, disliking store-keeping a little more every day. When I was free to sell it, I did, and went to raising cattle. And one day, riding in a canyon after strayed steers, I found—I think—Aunt Bessie. A cowboy who worked for me was along, or I would never have let anybody know.

We found weathered bones near a little spring. They had a mystery on them, those nameless human bones suddenly come upon. I could feel old death brushing my back.

"Some prospector," suggested my riding partner.

I thought so too until I found, protected by a log, sodden scraps of fabric that might have been a dark, respectable dress. And wrapped in them was a sodden something that might have once been a picture.

The man with me was young, but he had heard the story of the captive child. He had been telling me about it, in fact. In the passing years it had acquired some details that surprised me. Aunt Bessie had become once more a fair-haired beauty, in this legend that he had heard, but utterly sad and silent. Well, sad and silent she really was.

I tried to push the sodden scrap of fabric back under the log, but he was too quick for me. "That ain't no shirt, that's a dress!" he announced. "This here was no prospector—it was a woman!" He paused and then announced with awe, "I bet you it was your Indian aunt!"

I scowled and said, "Nonsense. It could be anybody."

He got all worked up about it. "If it was *my* aunt," he declared, "I'd bury her in the family plot."

"No," I said, and shook my head.

We left the bones there in the canyon, where they had been for forty-odd years if they were Aunt Bessie's. And I think they were. But I would not make her a captive again. She's in the family album. She doesn't need to be in the family plot.

If my guess about why she left us is wrong, nobody can prove it. She never intended to join her son in hiding. She went in the opposite direction to lure pursuit away.

What happened to her in the canyon doesn't concern me, or anyone. My aunt Bessie accomplished what she set out to do. It was not her life that mattered, but his. She bought him another year.

BILL GULICK

Thief in Camp

Bill (actually Grover Cleveland) Gulick has, since the early 1940s, compiled an enviable record as a Western novelist, story writer, and dramatist—especially of outdoor plays and musicals. Missouri-born but now a resident of Walla Walla, Washington, in recent years he has turned to pictorial histories, such as *Snake River Country* and *Chief Joseph Country*.

Gulick's first novel, *Bend of the Snake*, published in 1950, was made into a successful film. His good-natured *Hallelujah Trail* (1963), which concerned a liquor shipment to Denver and the unlikely involvement of Indians, a woman's temperance organization, and the U.S. Cavalry, was filmed in 1965.

"Thief in Camp" earned the Golden Spur Award for best Western short story of 1958 at the Oklahoma City WWA convention.

The morning after the wagon train went into camp on the plain near Fort Laramie, Jimmy Coleman saddled his paint pony Cherokee and was fixing to go for a ride when that nuisance of a Ben Frankfort showed up. Being two years older and a head taller than Jimmy, Ben Frankfort had been making life miserable for him ever since the wagon train left Independence. What started it was that Jimmy's mother had bought him a fine pony to ride to Oregon, while Ben's pa had said riding in the wagon was good enough for any youngster, which had made Ben so jealous he spit green.

"Where do you think you're going?" Ben said.

"Guess that's my business, not yours."

"You know what Pa said. Kids aren't supposed to go out of sight of camp without there's a man along."

"Aw, your pa can't boss me."

"Pa's wagon captain."

"What of it?"

"And you don't even have a pa."

"Well, you don't have a ma, so that makes us even."

Ben took hold of the pony's reins. "Let me ride Cherokee twice around the camp and I won't tell no matter what you do."

"No."

"I whipped you once. I could do it again."

"Not today you couldn't."

Ben shot a look down the slope toward camp. Nobody was watching, but still he hesitated. "Heck, if I did whip you, you'd tattle."

"Only girls tattle. Now get out of my way."

Jimmy gave Ben a shove. Ben shoved back. Tripping, Jimmy fell down, bounced to his feet, and charged at Ben. He managed to catch Ben a good one on the temple, but the older boy's weight and reach soon proved too much for him. Next thing he knew he was lying flat on his back and Ben was swinging aboard Cherokee.

"*Yipee!*" Ben yelled. "Let's go!"

Cherokee went. His head went down, his back went up, and Ben went sailing through the air, hitting with a thump that knocked all the wind out of him. Jimmy grabbed a stick and made for him. A couple of wild whacks were all he got time for, then Ben got his feet under him and made fast and frequent tracks for camp.

Sobbing with frustrated anger, Jimmy dropped the stick

and leaned against the pony's neck. "Big old bully! Someday I'll peel him good! Someday——"

Before he could name half the unpleasant things he was
going to do to Ben Frankfort, a quiet voice said, "Howdy,
youngster. Kind of a rough game you two was playin', wa'n't
it?"

Jimmy turned and stared up at the man, who was tall,
gray-eyed, dressed in buckskin, and riding a good-looking
sorrel horse. Jimmy brushed hastily at his eyes. "We weren't
playing. We were fighting."

"Kind of outmatched yourself, didn't you?"

"I'd fight anybody tried to ride Cherokee without my say-
so."

The gray eyes were sympathetic. "Can't say I blame you a
mite fer that. Tell me, son, you know whar I kin find a gent
name of Theodore Frankfort?"

"Sure, I can take you right to him."

"I'd be obliged, boy, I truly would."

Riding down to camp, Jimmy covertly eyed the man, who
had a long-barreled rifle slung across his back, a pistol and
knife in his belt, and a powder horn and bullet pouch
hung from one shoulder. He was clean-shaven, handsome
in a rugged sort of way, and appeared to be the same age as
Mr. Frankfort, which would be in the middle thirties. A
pungent smell, which Jimmy had noted before as an occu-
pational mark of men who trapped for a living, emanated
from him.

When they rode into the enclosure, Jimmy said, "That's
Mr. Frankfort. The big man with the black hat."

The man rode up to where Mr. Frankfort was bossing a
crew removing a wagon wheel. "Mr. Frankfort?"

"Yes?"

"Heerd tell you're lookin' fer a guide."

"We are."

The man swung off his horse. "Name's Buff Shelley.
Rate's five dollars a day."

Mr. Frankfort gave him an appraising look. "Are you acquainted with the trail?"

"Been over it a few times, yeah."

The men crowded in, asking questions, which Buff Shelley answered with calm brevity. Mr. Frankfort nodded. "I guess you'll do. But we'd better have an understanding. I'm wagon captain. You'll take orders only from me. Agreed?"

By now, news that a guide was being hired had spread through the camp, and everybody had come over for a look. Feeling a hand on his shoulder, Jimmy looked up to see his mother standing behind him. She was slim and dark-haired, still pretty enough to turn the head of any man. Jimmy saw Buff Shelley's eyes pause for a moment on his mother's face, saw Mr. Frankfort's sudden frown, then Buff was looking at Mr. Frankfort and nodding.

"That's fine with me. You boss the wagons. I'll guide 'em. Long as it's left that way we'll have no trouble."

As everyone went back to their interrupted chores Jimmy started to ride off on Cherokee, but his mother suddenly noticed the way his clothes and face were dirtied. "Jimmy!" she scolded. "What have you been doing?"

"I sort of fell down."

"After I just put clean clothes on you!"

"It was an accident. I didn't go to do it."

She dusted him off, her tongue clucking chidingly. "You're getting to be a regular little savage, do you know that?"

"You want me to be a sissy?"

"Not at all. But your father was a gentleman. I want you to grow up to be a gentleman too."

"Dad got dirty sometimes. When we went camping——"

"I'm not asking you to stay clean all the time, Jimmy. But surely you could make some effort to keep your clothes nice. Other boys do. Look at Ben Frankfort."

"You looked at him lately?"

"No, why?"

Jimmy started to say that Ben had fallen a sight farther and harder than *he* had, but he knew if he told his mother that he'd have to tell why Ben had fallen. So he let it go.

The wagon train lined out for Oregon next morning, and for the next week or so Jimmy spent most of his waking hours with Buff Shelley. He learned a pile of things, too. Like how you trapped beaver, how you lifted a scalp, how you hunted antelope and such. Unconsciously he began to imitate the guide's manner of riding, walking, and speaking. Buff seemed to enjoy his company and they talked about every subject under the sun. One day Buff said, "Your ma's a widow, I take it?"

"Yes, sir. Dad died a year ago."

"Whar you from?"

"Virginia. We're going out to Oregon to live with my uncle—till Mom gets married again, anyhow."

"Oh, yore ma's gettin' married agin?"

"Well, people back home say she's bound to."

"Got a man picked out, has she?"

"Nobody particular. But I guess she's looking around."

Buff's gray eyes twinkled. "What kind of man is she lookin' around fer?"

"A gentleman, I guess. At least she's always talking about how Dad was a gentleman and how I got to grow up to be a gentleman, so I guess that's what she's after."

Buff looked thoughtful. "Would a well-fixed widower like Mr. Frankfort fit the bill?"

"I suppose so," Jimmy mumbled without enthusiasm.

"You don't take to Mr. Frankfort, do you?"

Jimmy scratched Cherokee's neck disconsolately. "He's kind of bossy. But I guess he's all right."

"How'll it suit you to have Ben for a stepbrother?"

"Aw, I ain't afraid of Ben. He's bossy, too, but only because he's bigger'n me."

"Kind of a bully, is he?"

"Tries to be. But I'll show him who lays the chunk."

Buff laughed heartily. "That's the spirit, boy. Size ain't

everything. Why, I recollect a leetle booger I used to know, name of Kit Carson. Regular runt of a fella, he was, but one time when a great big hunk of Injun jumped him . . .''

Buff was just full of stories about Kit, and that evening Jimmy repeated them to his mother, while she sat listening with a growing look of concern on her face.

". . . an' then this big jigger of an Injun comes bilin' at Kit, fixin' to cut out his gizzard. But you know what ol' Kit done? He jest tripped the booger, jumped astraddle of his back, sunk his knife in clean up to Green River, then—whack—he's lifted hisself a piece of hair! An' another time——''

"Jimmy!"

"Huh?"

"Where on earth did you hear such horrible stories? And where did you pick up such abominable English?"

"Why, me and Buff was jest talkin' and Buff——''

"Mr. Shelley, you mean? Buff Shelley, the guide?"

"Yes'm."

His mother's lips tightened. "Is that all he has to do, fill young minds with fantastic, terrible stories?"

"But they're all true! Buff swears they're true! He's been all over the West and seen all kinds of things!"

"Indeed!"

"Sure! Buff knows more than anybody."

"About what?"

"Why, Injuns and trapping and trailing and hunting—there's nothing he don't know."

His mother frowned. "Jimmy, I'm afraid there are a lot of very important things Buff Shelley doesn't know. Things such as proper grammar, good manners——''

"Aw——''

"And those awful buckskin clothes he wears. Why, they actually smell!"

"All trappers' clothes smell that way. I asked him about it and he told me. It's the medicine they use."

" 'Medicine'?"

"That's what they call the bait for their beaver traps. You see, what they do is——"

Mr. Frankfort strode into the circle of light shed by their fire before Jimmy could tell all the details of what trappers did. His mother looked relieved. Removing his hat, Mr. Frankfort smiled graciously at her.

"I don't want to alarm you, Mrs. Coleman, but I feel I should warn you. We're getting into dangerous Indian country. You'd better keep Jimmy close to the wagon."

"Thank you, Mr. Frankfort," his mother said gratefully. "I appreciate your thoughtfulness." She looked at Jimmy. "Tomorrow you must ride in the wagon, dear."

"But, Mom——"

"You heard what Mr. Frankfort said. There are dangerous Indians about."

"Shucks, they're just Crows. Buff says they're harmless as flies, if you handle them right."

Mr. Frankfort bowed. "I felt I should warn you, Mrs. Coleman. Good night."

When Mr. Frankfort had gone, Jimmy's mother gazed at him reproachfully. "Jimmy, that was very impolite."

"What'd I do?"

"You know very well what you did. You flatly contradicted Mr. Frankfort. You should be ashamed of yourself. After all, he has been very kind to us and is only doing his duty."

"But Buff says——"

"You've been seeing a great deal too much of Buff Shelley," his mother cut in sharply. "Now remember, tomorrow you ride in the wagon."

The thing Jimmy suddenly remembered was that tomorrow when the train halted for its nooning, Buff had promised to take him on an antelope hunt. So he swallowed hard and said, "All day?"

"Well . . ."

Well, next day was as peaceful as could be, with not an Indian in sight, so when the wagons stopped at noon Jimmy's mother said she guessed it would be all right if he exercised Cherokee a little bit. So he hurriedly lugged his saddle out to the horse herd and saddled up, fearful that Buff would ride off without him. How Ben Frankfort happened to get wind of their expedition, he never knew, but he'd no more than got the saddle clinched up than there was Ben at his elbow.

"Where are you riding off to?" Ben asked suspiciously.

"Nowhere."

"Bet I know. Bet you're going hunting with Buff."

"Well, what if I am?"

"Your ma will tan you, she finds out."

"How's she going to find out?"

"Pa will tell her."

"How's he going to find out?"

"I'll tell him."

Heated remarks were exchanged, but before they could tangle Buff rode up. "C'mon, boy, time's a-wastin'."

They rode off, got their antelope, and were back with the wagon train in practically no time at all. But Mr. Frankfort was fit to be tied. Jimmy's mother had been worried sick, he claimed, and who did Buff think he was, anyway, taking a child out into dangerous country without the wagon captain's say-so? Buff listened indifferently until Mr. Frankfort had run out of breath, then he said, "C'mon, Jimmy, we'll go make peace with yore ma."

Jimmy's mother stared accusingly at him as they rode up. "Jimmy, I thought I told you——"

"Ma'am," Buff cut in, touching the rim of his slouch hat carelessly, "don't jaw at the boy. I took him huntin' with me 'cause I figgered he was due fer some fun. You want to lay on blame, lay it on me. But don't chew on him."

It wasn't often Jimmy's mother looked taken aback. But she sure looked that way now. Her cheeks colored angrily. "I'm quite capable of raising my son without any advice from you, Mr. Shelley. Furthermore——"

" 'Tain't advice I'm givin' you, ma'am. I'm jest a-tellin'

you some facts of nature as I've observed 'em. This is a prime colt you got here. But you can't picket a yearlin' on a short rope an' expect him to build up his legs an' wind."

And with that, Buff wheeled his horse around and rode off.

While his mother stood in stunned silence, Jimmy tied Cherokee to the tailgate of the wagon and then went to her, ready to take his tongue-lashing. But she was still staring after Buff Shelley. "What a rude man!"

"I don't think so," Jimmy said humbly. "I think he's the nicest man I know."

"You call him nice after hearing how he spoke to me?"

Jimmy scuffed the dirt with a toe. "Well, he takes me hunting and lets me ride with him and he talks to me and answers questions—just like Dad used to do. And when he saw you were mad at me, he tried to get you mad at him instead—just like Dad always did."

The funniest look came over his mother's face. All of a sudden she put an arm around him and pulled him close. "Oh, Jimmy, I'm sorry! You do need a father so!" She gazed into his eyes. "Would it hurt you terribly, dear, if I were to marry again?"

"Guess that's according to who you picked."

"I'd make sure you approved, of course," she said, trying to make a joke of it. "So if you have anyone you'd like to recommend——"

He stared off in the direction Buff had just ridden. "Well, since you asked me——"

Saturday afternoon they camped in a fine valley where there was plenty of grass, wood, and a clear-water stream. It was decided that they would lie over here for the Sabbath. Buff brought in enough fresh meat for a real feast that evening, and as soon as supper was over out came the fiddles and couples began dancing around a big bonfire. Jimmy was standing watching the fun when he heard Ben Frankfort whisper at his elbow, "Psst, c'mere a minute."

Jimmy followed him off into the shadows and asked him what he wanted. Ben looked around to make sure nobody could overhear, then he muttered, "How'd you like to go hunting with me tomorrow?"

"Just you and me, you mean?"

"And Cherokee."

"What would we do for a gun?"

Ben led him to his father's wagon, rummaged in it, and brought out a brand-new Henry rifle. "Guess we can kill any old antelope in the world with this, can't we?"

"Did your pa say you could use it?"

"He'll be too busy bossing things to notice it's gone."

"But if he finds out——"

"What tattletale is going to tell him?"

It was a sneaky thing to do, but the way Jimmy reasoned, it was Ben who was being sneaky, not him. And it was a compliment, in a way, Ben's asking him to go along, though the main reason he'd done it, Jimmy guessed, was that he didn't know the first thing about hunting antelope so just naturally had to come to somebody that could show him how it was done.

"Well?" Ben demanded. "You wanta go?"

"Sure," Jimmy said. "Why not?"

It being Sunday and a day of rest, everybody slept later than usual next morning and the sun was an hour high before the breakfast fires began to crackle. Jimmy had done battle in dreams with his conscience all night long, his conscience losing every round, and it was still getting the whey beat out of it now as he sat waiting for the breakfast call. Suddenly there came a clatter of hoofs, and Mr. Tracy, who had been riding guard over the horse-and-cattle herd outside the enclosure, galloped up, shouting excitedly, "Indians! Indians!"

The camp panicked. Women were screaming at children, men were running every which way, but Mr. Frankfort knew exactly what to do. Standing in the center of camp, he roared, "Women and children inside the wagons. Lige, Sam, Ned—take your men and guard the sides you've been assigned to! Step lively, men! It's our lives we're fighting for!"

There was a frenzied scramble for positions. Suddenly Jimmy heard Buff's sharp voice ring out, "Hold it, men! They's no call to spook!"

The Indians were in sight now, some fifty of them, streaming down a grassy slope to the northwest. Mr. Frankfort seized Buff's arm. "Are you crazy? Can't you see they're attacking us?"

"I kin see real good," Buff said imperturbably. "They're Crows an' friendly. Ain't a bit of harm in 'em."

"How do you know?"

"See that Injun leadin' the pack? He's an old side-kick of mine. Slept in his lodge many's the time."

As the Indians came galloping down the slope their leader was reining his horse this way and that, twisting his body about and waving his arms around in an odd fashion. Buff was doing queer things with his hands and arms, too, Jimmy noticed, and he suddenly remembered what Buff had told him about the way Indians had of making sign talk with one another as far off as they could see or be seen. Buff grinned at Mr. Frankfort.

"Jest tell yore boys to hold their fire. I'll go out an' palaver with the jiggers."

While Mr. Frankfort and the other men watched suspiciously, Buff climbed over a wagon tongue and walked out and greeted the Indians as calmly as you please, paying no mind to the way they came charging at him. Seeing he wouldn't scare, they pulled up and milled their horses around him, while he and their head man shook hands. Presently the Indian slid off his horse and Buff led him into the enclosure, where Mr. Frankfort was waiting.

"This here is Wolf Runner," Buff said. "Seen our dust yesterday he says, and decided to ride down fer a look."

"He's a Crow, you say? I've heard the Crows are born thieves and murderers."

"Man's apt to hear most anything, he listens to the wrong people."

"Well, if his intentions are friendly he's welcome. But tell him I won't have his people in camp. Tell him to make them keep their distance or I'll be obliged to——"

Right about then, Mr. Frankfort looked around. The Crows had gotten off their horses and were swarming into the enclosure from every direction. They were friendly, all right, grinning at everybody, lifting up wagon covers to peer inside, stooping to see what was in pots and pans simmering over the fires, fingering knives and axes and anything lying around loose with monkeylike curiosity. Mr. Frankfort frantically tried to put a stop to it.

"Don't do that!" he exclaimed, rushing over to a grinning buck who had lifted a steaming coffeepot off a fire. "Put that back!" he cried, wresting an ax out of the hand of another brave, who was testing its edge. "Leave that rifle alone!" he shouted, snatching his new Henry away from still a third Indian, who was hefting it admiringly. Tossing the gun back into the wagon, he turned in desperation to Buff. "Clear them out of here before they steal us blind!"

Buff made sign talk with Wolf Runner, who issued a guttural order. Spoons, knives, and a miscellaneous collection of small items magically reappeared from their hiding places upon the persons of the Indians and were returned to their owners. "They don't mean no harm," Buff said. "Give 'em some breakfast an' they'll be on their way."

"You mean we've got to feed this whole mob?"

"A hungry Indian's apt to turn mean. Feed him an' he'll ride away happy. It's a cheap way to buy friendship."

The Indians were fed, though from the nervous way his mother and the other whites in the party acted, Jimmy guessed that the hosts enjoyed the meal a good deal less than their visitors did. When breakfast was over the band of Crows rode on its merry way, except for Wolf Runner, whom Buff had persuaded to travel with the wagon train for a few days.

"He's a top dog in the Crow tribe," Buff explained to Mr. Frankfort. "Long as he's with us the Crows won't give us no trouble."

"They had better not," Mr. Frankfort said, tight-lipped.

Now that the excitement had simmered down, the men went to work at their repairing chores and the women settled down to baking and washing. Ben swiped the rifle and handful of cartridges out of his pa's wagon, Jimmy saddled Cherokee, and the two boys made for the river. The willows growing along the south shore soon hid them from the camp. What they would do, Ben said, was go a mile or so downstream, cross the river, then make their hunt in the hilly country on the far side.

Ben was afoot, carrying the rifle, while Jimmy rode Cherokee. Finding a place where it looked like the river could be forded without too much trouble, they paused. Ben didn't like the thought of getting his feet wet.

"Cherokee will carry double, won't he?"

"Don't know," Jimmy said dubiously. "But we can try him."

Taking the rifle, Jimmy lifted his left foot out of the stirrup and talked soothingly to Cherokee while Ben climbed aboard. Cherokee didn't like it much, but he stood quietly enough. "I'll take the rifle now," Ben said. "Make him go easy."

Jimmy passed the rifle back and urged Cherokee into the water. The current was a sight stronger than it looked. Not liking the feeling of the slick rocks underfoot, Cherokee stopped in midstream.

"Make him go!" Ben commanded.

"Keep your shirt on. He'll go when he's ready to."

"Well, if you won't make him go, I will!" Ben said, and booted Cherokee good with both heels.

Next thing Jimmy knew Cherokee was pitching, then falling. Ice-cold water closed over him. He came up spluttering, caught Ben—who was wrong side up—by the collar, and made for the bank. Mighty disgusted with it all, Cherokee plunged up out of the river. Dumping Ben to the ground, Jimmy went over and calmed the pony down. Ben spit out a mouthful of water and glared at Cherokee.

"Fool horse! Why didn't you tell me he wouldn't carry double?"

"He was doing all right till you kicked him."

"Lucky he didn't drown us both!" Ben complained. Suddenly he remembered something. "Where's the rifle?"

"I dunno. I gave it back to you."

"That's right, you did." He gazed around him. "It's gone!"

Well, they looked for it. First they looked along the bank, but it wasn't there, so then they took off their clothes and waded out into the river and felt around among the rocks with their bare feet. It wasn't there either. Just a few feet downstream from where they had tried to cross was a deep hole that the current had washed out as it swirled against a steep gravel bluff. The water was 'way over their heads and the current was so swift that though they dived time after time it was impossible to examine the bottom with any thoroughness.

They kept trying till they were both near drowned. Finally they sat down on the bank, spent and gasping. Jimmy shot Ben a look. "Must be in that hole. Isn't that what you figure?"

"Yeah. But we'll never find it. It's gone for good."

"What'll you tell your pa?"

Ben looked scared. "I dunno. But I'll think of something." He started pulling on his wet clothes. "First thing I got to do is slip back to the wagon and get into some dry clothes. Pa finds out I fell in the river, he'll skin the hide off me."

"If he'll skin you for falling into the river, what'll he do to you for losing his new rifle?"

Ben's lower lip quivered. "He didn't see me take it, did he?"

"Well, you got to tell him, don't you? 'Cause he's bound to find out it's gone."

Ben looked mighty sick. While Jimmy dressed, he just

stood staring down at that deep hole, as if wishing he had
drowned in it, then he turned and gave Jimmy a stricken
look. "You won't tell him, will you, Jimmy?"

"Me tell him? Why should I?"

"Cross your heart and hope to die?"

Jimmy made the sign and said the words. Then they went
back to camp.

If he had tried hard enough, Jimmy might have been able to
change into some dry clothes before his mother saw him,
but, never having made a practice of lying to her, he went to
the wagon wet and dripping and told her the truth. Part of it,
anyway.

"Sorry, Mom. I fell in the river."

She frowned at him. "What were you doing down by the
river?"

"Trying to cross it."

"Jimmy! You might have drowned!"

"Yes'm. But I didn't."

She sighed and dug out some dry clothes. "Well, at least
you're truthful. Now please try to behave yourself for a little
while, dear."

He tried. He wandered around the camp, keeping as far as
possible from the Frankfort wagon, where he figured an explosion was due 'most any time now. Inevitably he ended
up squatting beside Buff, who was sitting in the shade of a
wagon exchanging grunts and hand talk with Wolf Runner.
Buff grinned at him.

"Wolf Runner had himself a nap a few minutes ago an'
dreamed a queer dream. Seen a couple of white young'uns
playin' in the river like they was beaver, he says. Only they
was so anxious to git at their game they forgot to take off
their clothes."

"Aw, he didn't dream that. You saw Ben and me come
back to camp in wet clothes."

"So I did. What happened?"

Jimmy had promised Ben he wouldn't tell Mr. Frankfort

but he hadn't said a word about not telling Buff. So he told Buff now, though first he made Buff promise *he* wouldn't tell Mr. Frankfort. Buff scowled and shook his head.

"That's a bad thing, boy, stealin' a gun an' goin' huntin' on yore lonesome. You an' Ben shouldn't've done it."

"I know that now," Jimmy said contritely. "But what's Mr. Frankfort going to do to Ben when he finds out that the rifle is gone?"

"The world'll bring you trouble enough, without you go borrowin' somebody else's. Ben made his bed, now he kin lie in it. Let this be a lesson to you."

Right then Jimmy saw Mr. Frankfort climb out of his wagon, call sharply to Ben, and talk to him for a spell. There wasn't much doubt what they were talking about, because Mr. Frankfort kept gesturing at the wagon and Ben kept shaking his head violently. Jimmy saw Mr. Frankfort stride to the front of the wagon and pick up the bull whip lying on the seat. He felt kind of sick.

But instead of going to work on Ben, Mr. Frankfort called out something to a man working near by, turned, and walked across camp toward the spot where Jimmy, Buff, and Wolf Runner were sitting. Buff grunted something to Wolf Runner and they both got to their feet. The look on Mr. Frankfort's face brought Jimmy to his feet in a hurry, too.

"I'll mince no words, Shelley," Mr. Frankfort snapped. "A brand-new Henry rifle belonging to me has been stolen. Tell your thieving Crow friend I want it back—and quick."

All work in camp had ceased. As the crowd gathered around Mr. Frankfort all eyes were on the tall, silent Crow and the stony-faced white man who stood beside him. The silence was so complete Jimmy could hear his own heart thumping against his ribs. He shot a look at Ben, who had followed his father and was staring glassy-eyed at Wolf Runner. *It's him or me*, Ben must be thinking, *and he's nothing but an Indian.*

Buff said quietly, "You're barkin' up the wrong tree, Frankfort. Wolf Runner didn't steal yore rifle."

"Then some of his people did."

"You're wrong there, too."

"I'm not asking your opinion. I'm telling you. You vouched for him. But the rifle is gone. Now I want you to tell him that I'm going to have him tied up and guarded until the gun is returned to me. He knows where his people have gone and who stole it. He can tell you and you can ride after them." Mr. Frankfort paused, letting the coils of the whip drop free of his hand. "Give him my message."

"No."

Mr. Frankfort beckoned to the men standing behind him. "Joe, Frank, Lige, Ned—seize this Indian and tie him up. Maybe a touch of the whip will make him admit the truth—even to his softhearted friend."

The four men moved forward uneasily, then stopped as Buff said, "You lay hands on Wolf Runner, you'll buy yore-self a bigger hunk of trouble than you kin eat. He didn't steal yore blame rifle, Frankfort, an' neither did his bucks. Put that whip away 'fore you make a fool of yoreself."

"Shelley, you're discharged!"

"All right. But when I ride out of this camp Wolf Runner is ridin' with me. Any man tries to lay a hand on him is goin' to have big trouble with me."

Jimmy's mother had joined the crowd and was standing with an arm around him, looking on with a puzzled light in her eyes. He felt weak clean down to his toes. He knew that all he would have to do would be to point a finger and say one word and Ben would blubber out the whole story. Or Buff could do it. But they had both promised.

"Men," Mr. Frankfort said, "I gave you an order. Carry it out."

Shaking his head, one of the men muttered, "It's your gun and your quarrel, Frankfort. Reckon we'll let you kill your own snakes."

Mr. Frankfort went livid. "That's just what I will do!" he exclaimed, and raised the whip.

Jimmy heard his mother gasp. He saw Buff grab the upraised arm and twist the whip out of Mr. Frankfort's hand. Stumbling backward, Mr. Frankfort fell to the ground. For a moment he lay there, and then, cursing Buff with words Jimmy had never known existed, he leaped to his feet and charged Buff as if intending to kill him with his bare hands.

There came a sharp pistol-like crack as Buff's right fist landed, then Mr. Frankfort sagged to the ground like a sledged ox. Rubbing his knuckles and looking sorrowful, Buff stared down at him for a moment, then he turned to Jimmy's mother and said apologetically, "Shore hated to do that, ma'am, but it didn't seem fittin' language fer a lady er young boys to listen to."

Then he went over to Ben Frankfort, put an arm around his shoulders, and said kindly, "No need to blubber, son. C'mon, we'll go down to the river an' you kin show me whar you lost it. Wolf Runner here is one half beaver an' t'other half fish. He'll find the fool thing fer you."

While they were gone, Jimmy went back to the wagon with his mother and told her the whole story. He expected to get a good scolding, but when he was done she didn't have a word to say. She just stood gazing off into the distance with a funny look in her eye, and when Ben, Wolf Runner, and Buff came back to camp a while later with the rifle she still had that look. Buff walked over, took off his hat, and stood sheepishly before her, shuffling his weight from one foot to the other as he glanced at Jimmy out of the corner of his eye.

"Mrs. Coleman," he said finally, "I s'pose Jimmy's already told you, but——"

"Yes, he's told me."

"Wal, I know it must seem queer to you, him not sayin' anything when he knowed the truth an' me not sayin' anything, but the way of it was——"

"We'd promised," Jimmy blurted out.

Buff nodded solemnly. "That's right, ma'am. We'd promised. Kind of gave our word of honor as gentlemen, so to speak. Now I ain't meanin' to give you no advice on how to raise a young'un, 'cause it's plain to see he's gettin' fine raisin' jest the way things stand. But I—wal, I wanted you to know how things are with us men. An' if there's any blame to be laid——''

Jimmy's mother smiled and shook her head. There was a glow in her eyes, a gentle kind of glow that he couldn't remember having seen there since his father had died. "You men!" she scolded, as if she didn't mean to scold at all. "You foolish men!"

Something told Jimmy that when they got to Oregon they wouldn't be living with his uncle very long. Which was fine with him.

WILL HENRY

Isley's Stranger

No western writer matches the beloved Henry Wilson Allen in accomplishments and honors. No less than three of his fifty novels (*No Survivors*, *From Where the Sun Now Stands*, and *I, Tom Horn*) appear in WWA's all-time "Best Western Novels" list; and four of his stories—"The Trap" (under his second best-known pen name, "Clay Fisher"), "Lapwai Winter," "The Tallest Indian in Toltepec," and this story (which earned the 1962 Golden Spur)—have been judged among the twenty-one best of all time.

Allen, who is best known to friends and fans by his "Will Henry" pen name, has written Western historical novels about Butch Cassidy, Wyatt Earp, Jesse James, Luther Sage, "Yellowstone" Kelly, Lewis and Clark, Tom Horn, and Chief Joseph, and such renowned novels-into-movies as *Santa Fe Passage*, *The Tall Men*, *MacKenna's Gold*, and *Journey to Shiloh*.

He rode a mule. He was middling tall, middling spare, middling young. He wore a soft dark curly beard. His bedroll was one thready army blanket wound round a coffee can, tin cup, plate, razor, camp ax, Bible, copy of the *Rubáiyát*, a mouth harp, some other few treasures of like necessity in the wilderness.

Of course, Isley didn't see all those things when the drifter rode up to his fire that night on Wolf Mountain flats. They came out later, after Isley had asked him to light down and dig in, the same as any decent man would do with a stranger riding up on him out of the dark and thirty miles from the next shelter. Isley always denied that he was smote with Christian charity, sweet reason or unbounding brother love in issuing the invite. It was simply that nobody turns anybody away out on the Wyoming range in late fall. Not with a norther building over Tongue River at twilight and the wind beginning to snap like a trapped weasel come full dark. No, sir. Not, especially, when that somebody looks at you with eyes that would make a kicked hound seem happy, and asks only to warm his hands and hear a friendly voice before riding on.

Well, Isley had a snug place. Anyway, it was for a line rider working alone in that big country. Isley could tell you that holes were hard to find out there in the wide open. And this one he had was ample big for two, or so he figured.

It was a sort of outcrop of the base rock making a three-sided room at the top of a long, rolling swell of ground about midway of the twenty-mile flats. It had been poled and sodded over by some riders before Isley, and was not the poorest place in that country to bed down by several. Oh, what the heck, it wasn't the Brown Hotel in Denver, nor even the Drover's in Cheyenne. Sure, the years had washed the roof sods. And, sure, in a hard rain you had to wear your hat tipped back to keep the drip from spiking you down the nape of your shirt collar. But the three rock sides were airtight and the open side was south-facing. Likewise, the old grass roof, seepy or not, still cut out ninety-and-nine percent of the wind. Besides, it wasn't raining that night, nor about to. Moreover, Isley was a man who would see the sun with his head in a charcoal sack during an eclipse. It wasn't any effort, then, for him to ease up off his hunkers, step around the fire, bat the smoke out of his eyes, grin shy and say:

"Warm your hands, hell, stranger; unrope your bedroll and move in!"

They hit it off from scratch.

While the wanderer ate the grub Isley insisted on fixing for him—eating wasn't exactly what he did with it, it was more like inhaling—the little K-Bar hand had a chance to study his company. Usually, Isley was pretty fair at sizing a man, but this one had him winging. Was he tall? No, he wasn't tall. Was he short, then? No, you wouldn't say he was exactly short either. Middling, that's what he was. What kind of face, then? Long? Thin? Square? Horsey? Fine? Handsome? Ugly? No, none of these things, and all of them too. He just had a face. It was like his build, just middling. So it went; the longer Isley looked at him, the less he saw that he could hang a guess on. With one flicker of the fire he looked sissy as skim milk. Then, with the next, he looked gritty as fish eggs rolled in sand. Cock your head one way and the fellow seemed so helpless he couldn't drive nails in a snowbank. Cock it the other and he appeared like he might haul hell out of its shuck. Isley decided he wouldn't bet either way on him in a tight election. One thing was certain, though. And that thing Isley would take bets on all winter. This curly-bearded boy hadn't been raised on the short grass. He wouldn't know a whiffletree from a wagon tongue, or a whey-belly bull from a bred heifer. He was as out of place in Wyoming as a cow on a front porch.

Isley was somewhat startled, then, when his guest got down the final mouthful of beans, reached for a refill from the coffeepot and said quietly:

"There's bad trouble hereabouts, is there not, friend?"

Well, there was for a fact, but Isley couldn't see how this fellow, who looked like an out-of-work schoolteacher riding a long ways between jobs, could know anything about *that* kind of trouble.

"How come you to know that?" he asked. "It sure don't look to me like trouble would be in your line. No offense, mind you, mister. But around here—well, put it this way—there ain't nobody looking up the trouble we got. Most of us does our best to peer over it, or around it. What's your stake in the Wolf Mountain War, pardner?"

"Is that what it's called?" the other said softly. Then, with that sweet-sad smile that lighted up his pale face like candle shine, "Isn't it wonderful what pretty names men can think up for such ugly things? *'The Wolf Mountain War.'* It has alliteration, poetry, intrigue, beauty—"

Isley began to get a little edgy. This bearded one he had invited in out of the wind was not quite all he ought to be, he decided. He had best move careful. Sometimes these nutty ones were harmless, other times they would kill you quicker than anthrax juice.

He tried sending a return smile with his reply.

"Well, yes, whatever you say, friend. It's just another fight over grass and water, whatever you want to call it for a name. There's them as has the range, and them as wants the range. It don't change none."

"Which side are you on, Isley?"

"Well, now, you might say that—" Isley broke off to stare at him. "*Isley?*" he said. "How'd you know my name?"

The stranger looked uncomfortable, just for a moment. He appeared to glance around as though stalling for a good answer. Then, he nodded and pointed to Isley's saddle propped against the rear wall.

"I read it on your stirrup fender, just now."

Isley frowned. He looked over at the saddle. Even knowing where he had worked in that *T-o-m I-s-l-e-y* with copperhead rivets and a starnose punch, he couldn't see it. It lay up under the fender on the saddle skirt about an inch or so, purposely put there so he could reveal it to prove ownership in case somebody borrowed it without asking.

"Pretty good eyes," he said to the stranger. "That's mighty small print considering it's got to be read through a quarter inch of skirting leather."

The stranger only smiled.

"The skirt is curled a little, Isley, and the rivets catch the firelight. Call it that, plus a blind-luck guess."

The small puncher was not to be put off.

"Well," he said, "if you're such a powerful good blind-luck guesser, answer me this: how'd you know to call me Isley, instead of Tom?"

"Does it matter? Would you prefer Tom?"

"No, hell no, that ain't what I mean. Everybody calls me Isley. I ain't been called Tom in twenty years." His querulously knit brows drew in closer yet. "And by the way," he added, "while it ain't custom to ask handles in these parts, I never did cotton to being put to the social disadvantage. Makes a man feel he ain't been give his full and equal American rights. I mean, where the other feller knows who you are, but you ain't any idee who he might be. You foller me, friend?"

"You wish me to give you a name. Something you can call me. Something more tangible than friend."

"No, it don't have to be nothing more tangle-able than friend. Friend will do fine. I ain't trying to trap you."

"I know you aren't, Isley. I will tell you what. You call me Eben."

"Eben? That's an off-trail name. I never heard of it."

"It's an old Hebrew name, Isley."

"Oh? I ain't heard of them neither. Sounds like a southern tribe. Maybe Kioway or Comanche strain. Up here we got mostly Sioux and Cheyenne."

"The Hebrews weren't Indians exactly, though they were nomadic and fierce fighters. We call them Jews today."

"Oh, sure. Now, I knowed that."

"Of course you did."

They sat silent a spell, then Isley nodded.

"Well, Eben she is. Eben, what?"

"Just Eben."

"You mean like I'm just Isley?"

"Why not?"

"No good reason." Isley shrugged it off, while still bothered by it. "Well," he said, "that brings us back to where we started. How come you knowed about our trouble up here? And how come you got so far into the country without crossing trails with one side or the other? I would say this would

be about the unhealthiest climate for strangers since the
Grahams and Tewksburys had at it down in Arizony Territory. I don't see how you got ten miles past Casper, let alone
clear up here into the Big Horn Country."

Eben laughed. It was a quiet laugh, soft and friendly.

"You've provided material to keep us up all night," he
said. "Let us just say that I go where trouble is, and that I
know how to find my way to it."

Isley squinted at him, his own voice soft with seriousness.

"You're right; we'd best turn in. As for you and finding
trouble, I got just this one say to say: I hope you're as good
at sloping away from it as you are at stumbling onto it."

The other nodded thoughtfully, face sad again.

"Then, this Wolf Mountain War is as bad as I believed,"
he said.

"Mister," replied Isley, "when you have put your foot
into this mess, you have not just stepped into *anybody's*
cow chip; you have lit with both brogans square in the middle of the granddaddy pasture flapjack of them all."

"Colorful," smiled Eben wryly, "but entirely accurate, I
fear. I hope I'm not too late."

"For what?" asked Isley. "It can't be stopped, for it's already started."

"I didn't mean too late to stop it, I meant too late to see
justice done. That's the way it was in Pleasant Valley: too
late, too late—"

He let it trail off, as Isley's eyes first widened, then narrowed, with suspicion.

"You was *there?*" he said, "in that Graham-Tewksbury
feud?"

"I was there; I was not in the feud."

"Say!" said Isley enthusiastically, curiosity overcoming
doubt, "who the hell won that thing, anyways; the sheepmen or the cattlemen? Naturally, we're some interested, seeing how we got the same breed of cat to skin up here."

"Neither side won," said Eben. "Neither side ever wins a
war. The best that can be done is that some good comes out

of the bad; that, in some small way, the rights of the innocent survive."

Isley, like most simple men of his time, had had the Bible
read to him in his youth. Now he nodded again.

"You mean 'the meek shall inherit the earth'?" he asked.

"That's close," admitted his companion. "But they never
inherit anything but the sins of the strong, unless they have
help in time. That's what worries me. There's always so
much trouble and so little time."

"That all you do, mister? Go around looking for trouble to
mix into?"

"It's enough, Isley," smiled the other sadly. "Believe me it
is enough."

The little cowboy shook his head.

"You know something, Eben," he said honestly. "I think
you're a mite touched."

The pale youth sighed, his soft curls moving in assent.

"Do you know something, Isley?" he answered. "I have
never been to any place where the men did not say the same
thing. . . ."

Next morning the early snow clouds were still lying heavy
to the north, but the wind had quieted. Breakfast was a lot
cheerier than last night's supper, and it turned out the new-
comer wasn't such a nut as Isley had figured. He wasn't
looking for trouble at all, but for a job the same as everybody
else. What he really wanted was some place to hole in for
the winter. He asked Isley about employment prospects at
the K-Bar, and was informed they were somewhat scanter
than bee tracks in a blizzard. Especially, said Isley, for a boy
who looked as though he had never been caught on the
blister end of a shovel.

Eben assured the little rider that he could work, and Isley,
more to show him to the other hands than thinking Old Man
Reston would put him on, agreed to let him ride along in
with him to the homeplace. Once there, though, things took
an odd turn and Isley was right back to being confused
about his discovery.

As far as the other hands went, they didn't make much of the stranger. They thought he looked as though he had wintered pretty hard last year, hadn't come on with the spring grass. Most figured he wouldn't make it through another cold snap. To a man, they allowed that the Old Man would eat him alive. That is, providing he showed the gall to go on up to the big house and insult the old devil's intelligence by telling him to his bare face that he aimed to hit him for work. A cow ranch in October is no place to be looking for gainful employment. The fact this dauncy stray didn't know that, stamped him a real tinhorn. Naturally, the whole bunch traipsed up to the house and spied through the front-room window to see the murder committed. Isley got so choused up over the roostering the boys were giving his protégé that, in a moment of sheer inspiration, he offered to cover all Reston money in the crowd. He was just talking, but his pals decided to charge him for the privilege. By the time he had taken the last bet, he was in hock for his wages up to the spring roundup. And, by the time he had gotten up to the house door with Eben in tow, he would have gladly given over twice that amount to be back out on the Wolf Mountain flats or, indeed, any other place as many miles from the K-Bar owner's notoriously lively temperament.

He was stuck, though, and would not squeal. With more courage than Custer's bugler blowing the second charge at the Little Big Horn, he raised his hand and rapped on the ranchhouse door. He did bolster himself with an under-breath blasphemy, however, and Eben shook his head and said, "Take not the name of the Lord thy God in vain, Isley. Remember, your strength is as the strength of ten." Isley shot him a curdled look. Then he glanced up at the sky. "Lord, Lord," he said, "what have I done to deserve this?" He didn't get any answer from above, but did draw one from within. It suggested in sulfuric terms that they come in and close the door after them. As well, it promised corporal punishment for any corral-mud or shred of critter-matter stomped into the living-room rug, or any time consumed, past sixty seconds, in stating the grievance, taking no for an answer, and getting the hell back outside where they belonged.

Since the offer was delivered in the range bull's bellow generally associated with H. F. Reston, Senior, in one of his mellower states, Isley hastened to take it up.

"Mr. Reston," he said, once safe inside and the door heeled shut, "this here is Eben, and he's looking for work."

Henry Reston turned red, then white. He made a sound like a boar grizzly about to charge. Then he strangled it, waited for his teeth to loosen their clamp on one another, waved toward the door and said, "Well, he couldn't be looking for it in better company, Isley. Good luck to the both of you."

"*What?*" said Isley in a smothered way.

"You heard me. And don't slam the door on your way out."

"But Mr. Reston, sir—"

"Isley." The older man got up from his desk. He was the size of an agey buffalo, and the sweetness, too. "You remember damned well what I told you when you drug that last bum in here. Now, you want to run a rest camp for all the drifters and sick stock that come blowing into the barnyard with every first cold spell, you hop right on it. I'm trying to run a cow ranch, not a winter resort. Now, you get that pilgrim out of here. You come back in twenty minutes, I'll have your check."

Isley was a man who would go so far. He wasn't a fighter but he didn't push too well. When he got his tail up and dropped his horns, he would stand his ground with most.

"I'll wait for it right here," he said.

"Why, you bandy-legged little sparrowhawk, who the hell do you think you're telling what you'll do? *Out!*"

"*Mr. Reston*—" The stranger said it so quietly that it hit into the angry air louder than a yell. "Mr. Reston," he went on, "you're frightened. There is no call to take out your fears on Isley. Why not try me?"

"You?"

The Old Man just stared at him.

Isley wished he was far, far away. He felt very foolish right then. He couldn't agree more with the way the Old Man had said, "You?" Here was this pale-faced, skinny drifter with the downy beard, soft eyes, quiet voice and sweet smile standing there in his rags and tatters and patches and, worst of all, his farmer's runover flat boots; here he was standing there looking like something the cat would have drug in but didn't have the nerve to; and here he was standing there with all that going against him and still telling the biggest cattleman in Big Horn basin to wind up and have a try at *him!* Well, Isley thought, in just about two seconds the Old Man was going to tie into him with a list of words that would raise a blood blister on a rawhide boot. That is, if he didn't just reach in the desk drawer, fetch out his pistol and shoot him dead on the spot.

But Isley was only beginning to be wrong.

"Well," breathed Henry Reston at last, "try you, eh?" He rumbled across the room to come to a halt in front of the slight and silent mule rider. He loomed wide as a barn door, tall as a wagon tongue. But he didn't fall in on the poor devil the way Isley had feared. He just studied him with a very curious light in his faded blue eyes, and finally added, "And just what, in God's name, would you suggest I try you *at?*"

"Anything. Anything at all."

Reston nodded. "Pretty big order."

The other returned the nod. "Would a man like you take a small order?"

The owner of the K-Bar jutted his jaw. "You ain't what you let on to be," he challenged. "What do you want here?"

"What Isley told you—a job."

"What brought you here?"

"There's trouble here."

"You like trouble?"

"No."

"Maybe you're a troublemaker."

"No. I make peace when I can."

"And when you can't?"

"I still try."

"You think me giving you a winter's work is going to help you along that path?"

"Yes. Otherwise, I wouldn't be here."

Again Henry Reston studied him. Reston was not, like Tom Isley, a simple man. He was a very complicated and powerful and driving man, and a dangerous man, too.

"I make a lot of noise when I'm riled," he said to the drifter. "Don't let that fool you. I'm a thinking man."

"If you weren't," said the other, "I wouldn't be asking to work for you. I know what you are."

"But I don't know what you are, eh, is that it?"

"No, I'm just a man looking for work. I always pay my way. If there's no work for me, I travel on. I don't stay where there's no job to do."

"Well, there's no job for you here in Big Horn basin."

"You mean not that you know of."

"By God! Don't try to tell me what I mean, you ragamuffin!"

"What we are afraid of, we abuse. Why do you fear me?"

Reston looked at him startled.

"I? Fear you? You're crazy. You're not right in the head. I'm Henry F. Reston. I own this damned country!"

"I know; that's why I'm here."

"Now, what the devil do you mean by that?"

"Would the men in the valley give me work? They're poor. They haven't enough for themselves."

"How the hell do you know about the men in the valley?"

"I told you, Mr. Reston. There's trouble here. It's why I came. Now will you give me work, so that I may stay?"

"No! I'm damned if I will. Get out. The both of you!"

Isley started to sneak for the door, but Eben reached out and touched him on the arm. "Wait," he said.

"By God!" roared Reston, and started for the desk drawer. But Eben stopped him, too, as easily as he had Isley.

"Don't open the drawer," he said. "You don't need a pistol. A pistol won't help you."

Reston came around slowly. To Isley's amazement, he showed real concern. This white-faced tumbleweed had him winging.

"Won't help me what?" he asked, scowlingly.

"Decide about me."

"Oh? Well, now, you ain't told me yet what it is I've got to decide about you. Except maybe whether to kill you or have you horsewhipped or drug on a rope twice around the bunkhouse. Now you tell me what needs deciding, past that."

"I want work."

Henry Reston started to turn red again, and Isley thought he would go for the drawer after all. But he did not.

"So you want work?" he said. "And you claim you can do anything? And you got the cheek to hair up to me and say, slick and flip, 'Try me.' Well, all right, by God, I'll do it. Isley—"

"Yes, sir, Mr. Reston?"

"Go put that Black Bean horse in the bronc chute. Hang the bucking rig on him and clear out the corral."

"Good Lord, Mr. Reston, that outlaw ain't been rode since he stomped Charlie Tackaberry. He's ruint three men and—"

"You want your job back, Isley, saddle him."

"But—"

"Right now."

"No, sir," Isley began, hating to face the cold with no job, but knowing he couldn't be party to feeding the mule-rider to Black Bean, "I don't reckon I need your pay, Mr. Reston. Me and Eben will make out. Come on, Ebe."

He began to back out, but Eben shook his head.

"We need the work, Isley. Go saddle the horse."

"You don't know this devil! He's a killer."

"I've faced them before, Isley. Lots of them. Saddle him."

"You, a bronc stomper? Never. I bet you ain't been on a bucker in your whole life."

"I wasn't talking about horses, Isley, but about killers."

"No, sir," insisted the little cowboy stoutly, "I ain't a'going to do it. Black Bean will chew you up fine. It ain't worth it to do it for a miserable winter's keep. Let's go."

Eben took hold of his arm. Isley felt the grip. It took him like the talons of an eagle. Eben nodded.

"Isley," he said softly, *"saddle the horse."*

The K-Bar hands got the old horse in the chute and saddled without anybody getting crippled. He had been named Black Bean from the Texas Ranger story of Bigfoot Wallace, where the Mexican general made the captive rangers draw a bean, each, from a pottery jug of mixed black and white ones; and the boys who got white beans lived and the boys who got black ones got shot. It was a good name for that old horse.

Isley didn't know what to expect of his friend by now. But he knew from long experience what to expect from Black Bean. The poor drifter would have stood a better chance against the Mexican firing squad.

The other K-Bar boys *thought* they knew what was bound to take place. This dude very plainly had never been far enough around the teacup to find the handle. He was scarce man enough to climb over the bronc chute to get on Black Bean, let alone to stay on him long enough for them to get the blindfold off and the gate swung open.

But Isley wasn't off the pace as far as that. He knew Eben had *something* in mind. And when the thin youth had scrambled over the chute poles and more fallen, than fitted, into the bucking saddle, the other hands sensed this too. They quit roostering and hoorawing the pilgrim and got downright quiet. One or two—Gant Callahan and Deece McKayne, first off—actually tried helping at the last. Gant said, "Listen, buddy, don't try to stay with him. Just flop off the minute he gets clear of the gates. We'll scoop you up 'fore he can turn on you." Deece hung over the chute bars and whispered his advice, but Isley, holding Black Bean's head, heard him. What he said was, "See that top bar crost the gateposts? Reach for it the minute Isley whips off the blind. Hoss will go right on out from under you, and all you got to do is skin on up over the pole and set tight. You'll get spurred some by the boys, but I don't want to be buryin' you in a feedsack, you hear?"

Fact was, that between Gant and Deece giving him last-minute prayers and the other boys getting quiet, the whole operation slowed down to where the Old Man yelled at Isley to pull the blind, and for Wil Henniger to jerk the gate pin, or get out of the way and leave somebody else do it—while they were on their way up to the big house to pick up their pay. Being October and with that early blizzard threatening, he had them where the hair was short. Wil yelled out, "Powder River, let 'er buck!" and flung wide the gate. Isley pulled the blind and jumped for his life.

Well, what followed was the biggest quiet since Giggles La Chance decided to show up for church on Easter Sunday. And seeing that Giggles hadn't heard the preacher, wore a hat, or been seen abroad in daylight for six years, that was some quiet.

What Black Bean did, sure enough deserved the tribute, however. And every bit as much as Giggles La Chance.

Moreover, there was a connection between the two: the Devil seemed involved, somehow, with both decisions.

That old horse, which had stomped more good riders into the corral droppings than any sun-fisher since the Strawberry Roan, came out of that bucking chute in a side-saddle trot, mincy and simpery as an old maid bell mare. He went around the corral bowing his neck and blowing out through his nostrils and rolling back those wally-mean eyes of his, soft and dewy as a cow elk with a new calf. He made the circuit once around and brought up in front of the chute gate and stopped and spread out and stood like a five-gaited Kentucky saddlebred on the show stand; and that big quiet got so deep-still that when Dutch Hafner let out his held wind and said, "*Great Gawd A'mighty!*" you'd have thought he'd shoot off a cannon in a cemetery four o'clock of Good Friday morning.

Isley jumped and said, "Here, don't beller in a man's ear trumpet thataway!" and then got down off the chute fence and wandered off across the ranch lot talking to himself.

The others weren't much better off, but it was Old Man Reston who took it hardest of all.

That horse had meant a lot to him. He'd always sort of looked up to him. He was a great deal the same temperament as Old Henry: mean and tough and smart and fearing neither God nor Devil nor any likeness of either which walked on two legs. Now, there he was out there making moony-eyes at the seedy drifter, and damn fools out of Henry F. Reston and the whole K-Bar crew.

It never occurred to Old Henry, as it later did to Isley, that Eben had done about the same thing to him, Reston, in his living room up to the ranch house, as he'd done to Black Bean in the bucking chute: which was to buffalo him out of a full gallop right down to a dead walk, without raising either voice or hand to do it. But by the time Isley got this figured out, there wasn't much of a way to use the information. Old Henry, cast down by losing his outlaw horse and made powerful uneasy by the whole performance, had given Isley his pay, and Eben fifteen dollars for his ride—the normal fee for bronc breaking in those parts—and asked them both to be off the K-Bar by sunset. Eben had offered the fifteen dollars to the Old Man for Black Bean, when he had heard him order Deece and Gant to take the old horse out and shoot him for wolf bait. Old Henry had allowed it was a Pecos swap to take anything for such a shambles, by which he meant an outright steal. But he was always closer with a dollar than the satin over a Can-Can dancer's seat, and so he took the deal, throwing in the bucking saddle, a good split-ear bridle and a week's grub in a greasy sack, to boot. It was maybe an hour short of sundown when Isley, riding Eben's mule, and Eben astride the denatured killer, Black Bean, came to the west line of the K-Bar, in company with their escort.

"Well," said Dutch Hafner, "yonder's Bull Pine. Good luck, but don't come back."

Isley looked down into the basin of the Big Horn, sweeping from the foot of the ridge upon which they sat their horses, as far as the eye might reach, westward to Cody, Pitchfork, Meeteetse and the backing sawteeth of the Absoroka Range. The little puncher shook his head, sad, like any man, to be leaving home at only age forty-four.

"I dunno, Dutch," he mourned, "what's to become of us? There ain't no work in Bull Pine. Not for a cowhand. Not, especially, for a K-Bar cowhand."

"That's the gospel, Isley," said Deece McKayne, helpfully. "Fact is, was I you, I wouldn't scarce dast go inter Bull Pine, let alone inquire after work."

Gant Callahan, the third member of the honor guard, nodded his full agreement. "You cain't argue them marbles, Isley. Bull Pine ain't hardly nothing but one big sheep camp. I wish there was something I could add to what Dutch has said, but there ain't. So good luck, and ride wide around them woolies."

Isley nodded back in misery. "My craw's so shrunk it wouldn't chamber a piece of pea gravel," he said. "I feel yellow as mustard without the bite."

"Yellow, hell!" snapped big Dutch, glaring at Deece and Gant. "These two idjuts ain't to be took serious, Isley. Somebody poured their brains in with a teaspoon, and got his arm joggled at that. Ain't no sheepman going to go at a cowboy in broad day, and you'll find work over yonder in the Pitchfork country. Lots of ranches there."

"Sure," said Isley, "and every one of them on the sharp lookout for a broke-down line rider and a pale-face mule wrangler to put on for the winter. Well, anyways, so long."

The three K-Bar hands raised their gloves in a mutually waved, "So long, Isley," and turned their horses back for the snug homeplace bunkhouse. Isley pushed up the collar of his worn blanket coat. The wind was beginning to spit a little sleet out of the north. It was hardly an hour's ride down the ridge and out over the flat to Bull Pine. Barring that, the next settlement—in cow country—was Greybull, on the river. That would take them till midnight to reach, and if this sleet turned to snow and came on thick—well, the hell with that, they had no choice. A K-Bar cowboy's chances in a blue norther were better than he could expect in a small-flock sheeptown like Bull Pine. Shivering, he turned to Eben.

"Come on," he said, "we got a six-hour ride."

The gentle drifter held back, shading his eyes and peering out across the basin. "Strange," he said, "it doesn't appear to be that far."

"Whoa up!" said Isley, suddenly alarmed. "What don't appear to be that far?"

"Why, Bull Pine, of course," replied the other, with his sad-soft smile. "Where else would we go?"

Isley could think of several places, one of them a sight warmer than the scraggly ridge they were sitting on. But he didn't want to be mean or small with the helpless pilgrim, no matter he had gotten him sacked and ordered off the K-Bar for good. So he didn't mention any of the options, but only shivered again and made a wry face and said edgily:

"I'd ought to know better than to ask, Ebe; but, why for we want to go to Bull Pine?"

"Because," said the bearded wanderer, "that's where the trouble is."

Eben was right. Bull Pine was where the trouble was.

All the past summer and preceding spring the cattlemen had harassed the flocks of the sheepmen in the lush pastures of the high country around the basin. Parts of flocks and whole flocks had been stampeded and run to death; some had been put over cliffs; some cascaded into the creeks; others just plain chased till their hearts stopped. Nor had it been all sheep. A Basque herder had died and five Valley men had been hurt defending their flocks. So far no cattleman had died, nor even been hit, for it was they who always made the first jump, and mostly at night. Now the sheepmen had had all they meant to take.

Those high country pastures were ninety percent government land, and the sheep had just as much right to them as the cattle. More right, really, because they were better suited to use by sheep than cattle. But the country, once so open and free and plenty for all, was filling up. Even in the twenty years since Isley was young, the Big Horn basin had grown six new towns and God alone knew how many upcreek, shoestring cattle ranches. The sheep had come in late, though, only about ten years back. Bull Pine was the first, and sole, sheep town in northwest Wyoming, and it wasn't yet five years old. The cattlemen, headed by Old Henry Reston, meant to see that it didn't get another five years older, too. And Isley knew what Eben couldn't possibly know: that the early blizzard, threatening now by the hour, was all the cattlemen had been waiting for. Behind its cover they meant to sweep down on Bull Pine in a fierce raid on the haying pens and winter sheds along the river. These shelters had been built in a community effort of the valley sheep ranchers working together to accomplish what no two or three or ten of them could do working alone. They were a livestockmen's curiosity known about as far away as Colorado, Utah and Montana. They had proved unbelievably successful and if allowed to continue uncontested, it might just be that the concept of winter-feeding sheep in that country would catch on. If it did, half the honest cattlemen in Wyoming could be out of business. On the opposite hand, if some natural disaster should strike the Bull Pine feedlots—say like the fences giving way in a bad snowstorm—why then the idea of winter-feeding sheep in the valley would suffer a setback like nothing since old Brigham Young's seagulls had sailed into those Mormon crickets down by Deseret.

Knowing what he knew of the cattlemen's plan to aid nature in this matter of blowing over the sheepmen's fences during the first hard blizzard, Isley followed Eben into Bull Pine with all ten fingers and his main toes crossed.

By good luck they took a wrong turn or two off the trail on the way down off the ridge. Well, it wasn't exactly luck, either. Isley had something to do with it. But, no matter; when they came into Bull Pine it was so dark a man needed both hands to find his nose. Isley was more than content to have it so. Also, he would have been well-pleased to have been allowed to stay out in front of the General Store holding the mounts, while Eben went within to seek the loan of some kind soul's shearing shed to get in out of the wind and snow for the night. But Eben said, no, that what he had in mind would require Isley's presence. The latter would simply have to gird up his courage and come along.

Groaning, the little K-Bar puncher got down. From the number of horses standing humpback to the wind at the hitch rail, half the sheepmen in the basin must be inside. That they would be so, rather than home getting set to hay their sheep through the coming storm, worried Isley a great deal. Could it be that the Bull Piners had some warning of the cattlemen's advance? Was this a council of range war they were stepping into the middle of? Isley shivered.

"Ebe," he pleaded, "please leave me stay out here and keep our stock company. Me and them sheepmen ain't nothing in common saving for two legs and one head and maybeso a kind word for motherhood. Now, be a good feller and rustle on in there by yourself and line us up a woodshed or sheep pen or hayrick to hole up in for the night."

Eben shook his head. "No," he insisted, "you must come in with me. You are essential to the entire situation."

Isley shivered again, but stood resolute. "Listen, Ebe," he warned, "this here blizzard is a'going to swarm down the valley like Grant through Cumberland Gap. We don't get under cover we're going to be froze as the back of a bronze statue's lap. Or like them poor sheep when Old Henry and his boys busts them loose in the dark of dawn tomorry."

"It's Old Henry and the others I'm thinking of," said Eben quietly. "We must be ready for them. Come along."

But Isley cowered back. "Ebe," he said, "I know that kicking never done nobody but a mule no good. Still, I got to plead self-defense here. So don't crowd me. I'm all rared back, and I ain't a'going in there conscious."

He actually drew up one wrinkled boot as though he would take a swing at the drifter. But Eben only smiled and, for the second time, put his thin hand on Isley's arm. Isley felt the power of those slender fingers. They closed on his arm, and his will, like a Number 6 lynx trap.

"Come on, Isley," said the soft voice, "I need your testimony." And Isley groaned once more and put his head down into his collar as deep as it would go, and followed his ragged guide into the Bull Pine General Store.

"Friends," announced Eben, holding up his hands as the startled sheepmen looked up at him from their places around the possumbelly stove, "Brother Isley and I have come from afar to help you in your hour of need; please hear us out."

"That bent-legged little stray," dissented one member immediately, "never come from no place to help no sheepman. I smell cowboy! Fetch a rope, men."

Eben gestured hurriedly, but it did no good. A second valley man growled, "Ain't that Tom Isley as works for Henry Reston?" And a third gnarled herder rasped, "You bet it is! Never mind the rope, boys; I'll knock his head open, barehanded."

The group surged forward, the hairy giant who had spoken last, in the lead. Eben said no more, but did not let them beyond him to the white-faced K-Bar cowboy.

As the burly leader drew abreast of him, the drifter reached out and took him gently by one shoulder. He turned him around, got a hip into his side, threw him hard and far across the floor and up against the dry-goods counter, fifteen feet away. The frame building shook to its top scantling when the big man landed. He knocked a three-foot hole in the floor, ending up trapped in a splintered wedging of boards from which it took the combined efforts of three friends and the storekeeper's two-hundred-pound daughter to extract him.

By the time he was freed and being revived by a stimulant-

restorative composed of equal parts of sheepdip and spirits
of camphorated oil, the rest of the assemblage was com-
mencing to appreciate the length and strength of the drifter's throw. And, realizing these things, they were politely
moving back to provide him the room he had requested in
the first place. Eben made his address direct and nippy.

They had come down out of the hills, he said, bearing
news of invading Philistines. They were not there to become
a part of the Wolf Mountain War, but to serve in what small
way they might, to bring that unpleasantness to a peaceful
conclusion, with freedom and justice for all. Toward that
end, he concluded, his bowlegged friend had something to
say that would convince the sheep raisers that he came to
them, not as a kine herder bearing false prophecies, but as a
man of their own simple cloth, who wanted to help them as
were too honest and God-fearing to help themselves at the
cattlemen's price of killing and maiming their fellowmen by
gunfire and in the dead of night when decent men were
sleeping and their flocks on peaceful, unguarded graze.

This introduction served to interest the Bull Pine men
and terrify Tom Isley. He was not up on kine herders, Philistines and false prophets, but he knew sheepmen pretty
well. He reckoned he had maybe thirty seconds to fill the
flush Eben had dealt him, before somebody thought of that
rope again. Glancing over, he saw Big Sam Yawkey—the
fallen leader of the meeting—beginning to snort and breathe
heavy from the sheepdip fumes. Figuring Big Sam to be
bright-eyed and bushy-tailed again in about ten of those
thirty seconds, it cut things really fine.

Especially, when he didn't have the least, last notion what
the heck topic it was that Eben expected him to take off on.
"Ebe!" he got out in a strangulated whisper, "what in the
name of Gawd you expect me to talk about?" But the Good
Samaritan with the moth-eaten mule and the one thin army
blanket wasn't worried a whit. He just put out his bony
hand, touched his small companion on the shoulder and
said with his soft smile, as the sheepmen closed in:

"Never fear, Isley; you will think of something."

And, for a fact, Isley did.

"Hold off!" he yelled, backing to the hardware counter and picking himself a pick handle out of a barrel of assorted tool hafts. "I'll lay you out like Samson with that jackass jawbone!"

The sheepmen coagulated, came to a halt.

"Now, see here," Isley launched out. "Ebe's right. I'm down here to do what I can to settle this fight. There's been far too much blood spilt a'ready. And I got an idee, like Ebe says, how to stop this here war quicker'n you can spit and holler, 'Howdy.' But it ain't going to be risk-free. Monkeying around with them cattlemen is about as safe as kicking a loaded polecat. They're touchier than a teased snake, as I will allow you all know."

Several of the sheepmen nodded, and one said, "Yes, we know, all right. And so do you. You're one of them!"

"No!" denied Isley, "that ain't so. Mr. Reston thrun me off the K-Bar this very day. Ebe, here, made him look some small in front of the boys, and the Old Man ordered us both took to the west line and told to keep riding. I got included on account I drug Ebe in off the range, and Old Henry, he said I could keep him, seeing's I'd found him first."

His listeners scowled and looked at one another. This bowlegged little man had been punching cattle too long. He had clearly gone astray upstairs and been given his notice because of it. But they would hear him out, as none of them wanted to be flung against the dry-goods counter, or skulled with that pick handle.

"Go ahead," growled Big Sam Yawkey, coming up groggily to take his place in front of the Bull Piners. "But don't be overlong with your remarks. I done think you already stretched the blanket about as far as she will go. But, by damn, if there's a sick lamb's chance that you do have some way we can get back at them murderers, we ain't going to miss out on it. Fire away."

"Thank you, Mr. Yawkey," said Isley, and fired.

The idea he hit them with was as much a surprise to him as to them. He heard the words coming out of his mouth but it was as though somebody else was pulling the wires and making his lips flap. He found himself listening with an interest equal to that of the Bull Pine sheepmen, to his own wild-eyed plan for ambushing the cattlemen in Red Rock Corral.

It was beautifully simple:

Red Rock Corral was a widened-out place in the middle of that squeezed-in center part of Shell Canyon called the Narrows. If you looked at the Narrows as a sort of rifle barrel of bedrock, then Red Rock Corral would be like a place midways of the barrel where a bullet with a weak charge had stuck, then been slammed into by the following, full-strength round, bulging the barrel at that spot. It made a fine place to catch range mustangs, for example. All you had to do was close off both ends of the Narrows, once you had them in the bulge. Then just leave them there to starve down to where they would lead out peaceful as muley cows.

Isley's idea was that what would work for tough horses would work for tough men.

The sheepmen knew for a fact, he said, that the hill trail came down to the basin through Shell Canyon. Now, if added to this, they also knew for a fact, as Isley did, that Old Henry and his boys were coming down that trail early tomorrow to knock over their winter feed pens and stampede their sheep into the blizzard's deep snow, why then, they would be catching up to the first part of the Isley Plan.

Pausing, the little cowboy offered them a moment to consider the possibilities. Big Sam was the first to recover.

"You meaning to suggest," he said, heavy voice scraping like a burro with a bad cold, "that we bottle them cattlemen up in Red Rock Corral and starve them into agreeing to leave us be? Why, I declare you're balmier than you look, cowboy. In fact, you're nervier than a busted tooth. You think we need you to tell us about ambushing? That's the cattlemen's speed. And you can't go it without people getting hurt, kilt likely. Boys," he said, turning to the others, "some deck is shy a joker, and this is him. Fetch the rope."

"No! Wait!" cried Isley, waving his pick handle feebly. "I ain't done yet."

"Oh, yes you are," rumbled Big Sam, moving forward.

Yet, as before, he did not reach Tom Isley.

Eben raised his thin, pale hand and Big Sam brought up short as though he had walked into an invisible wall.

"What the hell?" he muttered, rubbing his face, frightened. "I must be losing my marbles. Something just clouted me acrost the nose solid as a low limb."

"It was your conscience," smiled Eben. "Isley has more to say. Haven't you, Isley?"

The little cowboy shook his head, bewildered.

"Hell, don't ask me, Ebe; you're the ventrillyquist."

"Speak on," nodded his friend, "and be not afraid."

"Well," said Isley, "I'll open my mouth and see what comes out. But I ain't guaranteeing nothing."

Big Sam Yawkey, still rubbing his nose, glared angrily.

"Something better come out," he promised, "or I'll guarantee you something a sight more substantial than nothing; and that's to send you out of town with your toes down. You've got me confuseder than a blind dog in a butcher shop, and I'm giving you one whole minute more to hand me the bone, or down comes your doghouse."

"Yeah!" snapped a burly herder behind him. "What you take us for, a flock of ninnies? Jest because we run sheep don't mean we got brains to match. And you suggesting that we set a wild hoss trap for them gunslingers and night riders of Old Man Reston's is next to saying we're idjuts. You think we're empty-headed enough to buy any such sow bosom as holding them cattlemen in that rock hole with a broomtail brush fence on both ends?"

"No," said Isley calmly and to his own amazement, "but you might try doing it with blasting powder."

"What!" shouted Yawkey.

"Yes, sir," said Isley meekly, "a half can of DuPont Number 9 at each end, touched off by a signal from the bluff above. When all of them have rode into Red Rock Corral, down comes the canyon wall, above and below, and there they are, shut off neat as a newborn calf, and nobody even scratched. I'd say that with this big snow that's coming, and with the thermometer dropping liko a gut chot elk, they'd sign the deed to their baby sister's virtue inside of forty-eight hours."

There was silence, then, as profound as the pit.

It was broken, presently, by Big Sam's awed nod, and by him clearing his throat, shaky and overcome as though asked to orate in favor of the flag on Independence Day.

"Great Gawd A'mighty, boys," he said, "it might work!"

And the rush for the front door and the horses standing back-humped at the hitch rail, was on.

As a matter of Big Horn basin record, it did work.

The Bull Piners got their powder planted by three A.M., and about four, down the trail came the deputation from the hills. The snow was already setting in stiff, and they were riding bunched tight. Big Sam Yawkey fired his Winchester three times when they were all in the middle of Red Corral and Jase Threepersons, the storekeeper, and Little Ginger, his two-hundred-pound daughter, both lit off their respective batches of DuPont Number 9 above and below the Corral so close together the cattlemen thought it was one explosion and Judgment Day come at last.

Well, it had, in a way.

And, as Isley had predicted, it came in less than forty-eight hours.

The sheepmen were mighty big about it. They lowered down ropes with all sorts of bedding and hot food and even whiskey for the freezing ranchers, as well as some of their good baled sheep hay for the horses. But they made it clear, through Big Sam's bellowed-down advice, that they meant to keep their friends and neighbors from the hills bottled up in that bare-rock bulge till the new grass came, if need be.

They wouldn't let them starve, except slowly, or freeze, unless by accident. But they had come out from Bull Pine to get a truce, plus full indemnity for their summer's sheep losses, and they were prepared to camp up on that bluff—in the full comfort of their heated sheep wagons—from right then till Hell, or Red Rock Corral, froze over.

That did it.

There was some hollering back and forth between the two camps for most of that first day. Then it got quiet for the better part of the second. Then, along about sundown, Old Henry Reston yelled up and said: "What's the deal, Yawkey? We don't get back to our stock, right quick, we won't have beef enough left to hold a barbecue."

Big Sam read them the terms, which Isley wasn't close enough to hear. Reston accepted under profane duress and he and Big Sam shook on the matter. Naturally, such a grip had the force of law in the basin. Once Old Henry and Big Sam had put their hands to an agreement, the man on either side who broke that agreement might just as well spool his bed and never stop moving.

Realizing this, Isley modestly stayed out of the affair. There were other inducements toward laying low and keeping back from the rim while negotiations went forward and concluded. One of these was the little cowboy's certain knowledge of what his fellow K-Bar riders would think of a cowman who sold out to a bunch of sheepherders. Even more compelling was the cold thought as to what they would do to such a hero, should they ever catch up to the fact he had plotted the whole shameful thing. All elements, both of charming self-effacement and outright cowardice, considered, Isley believed himself well-advised to saddle up and keep traveling. This he planned to do at the first opportunity. Which would be with the night's darkness in about twenty minutes. It was in carrying out the first part of this strategy—rounding up Eben and their two mounts—that he ran into the entertainment committee from the Bull Pine camp: three gentlemen sheepherders delegated by their side to invite Isley to the victory celebration being staged in his honor at the Ram's Horn Saloon later that evening.

Isley, confronted with this opportunity, refused to be self-ish. He bashfully declined the credit being so generously offered, claiming that it rightfully belonged to another. When pressed for the identity of this hidden champion, he said that of course he meant his good friend Eben. "You know," he concluded, "the skinny feller with the white face and curly whiskers. Ebe," he called into the gathering dusk past the hay wagon where they had tied Black Bean and the mule, "come on out here and take a bow!"

But Eben did not come out, and Jase Threepersons, the chairman of the committee, said to Isley, "What skinny feller with what white face and what curly whiskers?"

He said it in a somewhat uncompromising manner and Isley retorted testily, "The one that was with me in the store; the one what thrun Big Sam acrost the floor. Damn it, what you trying to come off on me, anyhow?"

Jase looked at him and the other two sheepmen looked at him and Jase said, in the same flat way as before, "You thrun Big Sam agin that counter. There wasn't nobody in that store with you. What you trying to come off on us, Tom Isley?"

"Blast it!" cried Isley, "I never laid a finger on Big Sam. You think I'd be crazy enough to try that?"

The three shook their heads, looking sorrowful.

"Evidently so," said Jase Threepersons.

"No, now you all just hold up a minute," said Isley, seeing their pitying looks. "Come on, I'll show you. Right over here ahint the hay wagon. Me and Ebe was bedded here last night and boilt our noon coffee here today. I ain't seem him the past hour or so, and he may have lost his nerve and lit out, but, by damn, I can show you where his mule was tied and I'll fetch him for you, give time."

They were all moving around the wagon as he spoke, Isley in the lead. He stopped dead. "No!" they heard him say. "My God, it cain't be!" But when they got up to him, it was.

There was no sign of a double camp whatever. And no sign of the bearded stranger, nor of his moth-eaten mule. "He was right here!" yelled Isley desperately. "Damn it, you saw him, you're just funning, just hoorawing me. You seen him and you seen that broke-down jackass he rides; who the hell you think I been talking to the past three days, *myself?*"

" 'Pears as if," nodded Jase sympathetically. "Too bad, too. Little Ginger had kind of took a shine to you. Wanted me to see you stuck around Bull Pine a spell. But, seeing the way things are with you, I reckon she'd best go back to waiting out Big Sam."

"Yes sir, thank you very much, sir," said Isley gratefully, "but I still aim to find Ebe and that damn mule for you." He bent forward with sudden excitement. "Say, lookit here! Mule tracks leading off! See? What'd I tell you? Old Ebe, he's ɐ shy cuss, and mightily humble. He didn't want no thanks. He'd done what he come for—stopped the trouble—and he just naturally snuck off when nobody was a'watching him. Come on! we can catch him easy on that stove-up old jack."

The three men came forward, stooped to examine the snow. There were some tracks there, all right, rapidly being filled by the fresh fall of snow coming on, but tracks all the same. They could have been mule tracks, too. It was possible. But they could also have been smallish horse tracks. Like, say, left by Pettus Teague's blue-blood race mare. Or by that trim Sioux pony belonging to Charlie Bo-peep, the Basque half-breed. Or by Coony Simms's little bay. Or Nels Bofors's slim Kentucky-bred saddler. Or two, three others in the camp.

Straightening from its consideration of the evidence, the committee eyed Tom Isley.

"Isley," said Jase Threepersons, "I'll tell you what we'll do. All things took into account, you've been under considerable strain. Moreover, that strain ain't apt to get any less when word gets back up into the hills that you come down here and hatched this ambush idea. We owe you a'plenty,

and we ain't going to argue with you about that there feller
and his mule. But them cowboys of Old Henry's might take
a bit more convincing. Now, suppose you just don't be here
when Big Sam and the others come up out of the corral with
the K-Bar outfit. We'll say you was gone when we got here
to the hay wagon, and that you didn't leave no address for
sending on your mail. All right?"

Isley took a look at the weather.

It was turning off warmer, and this new snow wouldn't
last more than enough to cover his tracks just nice. The
wind was down, the sun twenty minutes gone and, from the
rim of the bluff above the corral, sounds were floating which
indicated the roping parties were pulling up the first of the
K-Bar sheep raiders. To Isley, it looked like a fine night for
far riding. And sudden.

He pulled his coat collar up, his hat brim down, and said
to Jase Threepersons, "All right."

"We'll hold the boys at the rim to give you what start we
can," said Jase. And Isley stared at him and answered. "No,
don't bother; you've did more than enough for me a'ready.
Goodbye, boys, and if I ever find any old ladies or dogs that
need kicking, I will send them along to you."

Being sheepherders, they didn't take offense, but set off to
stall the rescue party at the rim, true to their word.

Isley didn't linger to argue the morals of it. He got his
blanket out from under the hay wagon, rolled it fast, hurried
to tie it on behind old Black Bean's saddle. By this time he
wasn't even sure who *he* was, but didn't care to take any
chances on it. He just might turn out to be Tom Isley, and
then it would be close work trying to explain to Dutch and
Gant and Deece and the rest, what it was he was doing
bedded down in the sheep camp.

He had the old black outlaw swung around and headed in
the same direction as the fading mule tracks—or whatever
they were—in something less than five minutes flat. The
going was all downhill to the river, and he made good time.
About eight o'clock he came to the Willow Creek Crossing of

the Big Horn, meaning to strike the Pitchfork Trail there. He
was hungry and cold and the old black needing a rest, so he
began to look around for a good place to lie up for the night.
Imagine his surprise and pleasure, then, to spy ahead, the
winky gleam and glow of a campfire, set in a snug thicket of
small timber off to the right of the crossing. Following its
cheery guide, he broke through the screening bush and was
greeted by a sight that had him bucked up quicker than a
hatful of hot coffee.

"Ebe!" he cried delightedly. "I knowed you wouldn't run
out on me! God bless it, I am that pleased to see you!"

"And I likewise, Isley," smiled the gentle-voiced drifter.
"Alight, and thrice welcome to my lowly board."

Well, he had a wind-tight place there. It was nearly as
warm and shut in from the cold as the old rock house out on
Wolf Mountain flat, and he had added to it with a neat
lean-to of ax-cut branches, as pretty as anything Isley had
ever seen done on the range. And the smell of the rack of
lamb he had broiling over the flames of his fire was enough
to bring tears to the eyes of a Kansas City cow buyer.

Isley could see no legitimate reason for declining the invitation.

Falling off Black Bean, he said, "You be a'saying Grace,
Ebe, whilst I'm a'pulling this hull; I don't want to hold you
up none when we set down—"

While they ate, things were somewhat quiet. It was very
much the same as it had been when Eben came in cold and
hungry to Isley's fire out on the flats. Afterward, though,
with the blackened coffeepot going the rounds, Isley rolling
his rice-paper smokes and Eben playing some of the lone-
somest pretty tunes on his old mouth harp that the little
cowboy had ever heard, the talk started flowing at a better
rate.

There were several things Isley wanted to know, chief
among them being the matter of the Bull Pine men letting on
as if he had jumped his head hobbles. But he kept silent on
this point, at first, leading off with some roundabout inquir-

ies which wouldn't tip his hand to Eben. These were such
things as how come he didn't recognize any of the tunes
Eben was playing on the harp? Or how did Eben manage to
evaporate from the sheep camp at Red Rock Corral without
any of the Bull Piners seeing him? Or why didn't he let Isley
know he was going? And how come him, Eben, to have lamb
on the fire in October, when there wasn't any lamb?

To this tumble of questions, Eben only replied with his
soft laugh and such put-offers as that the tunes were
sheepherder songs from another land, that the fresh snow-
fall had hidden his departure from the hay wagon bed
spot, that he knew the Bull Piners planned a party for Isley and didn't wish to stand in his way of enjoying the
tribute due him, and that for him, Eben, lamb was always
in season and he could put his hand to some just about as
he pleased.

Well, Isley was a little mystified by this sort of round-
the-barn business. But when Eben made the remark about
the Bull Pine party being due him, Isley, he quit slanting his
own talk, off-trail, and brought it right to the bait.

"Ebe," he said, "I'm going to ask you one question. And
you mighten as well answer it, for I'm going to hang onto it
like an Indian to a whiskey jug."

"Gently, gently," smiled the other. "You'll have your answer, but not tonight. In the morning, Isley, I promise you."

"Promise me what?" demanded the little cowboy. "I ain't
even said what I wanted."

"But I know what you want, and you shall have it—in the
morning."

Isley eyed him stubbornly.

"I'll have what in the morning?" he insisted.

Eben smiled that unsettling sad-sweet smile, and shrugged.

"Proof that I was with you all the while," he said.

Isley frowned, then nodded.

"All right, Ebe, you want to save her for sunup, that's fine
with me. I'm a little wore down myself."

"You rest, then," said the drifter. "Lie back upon your

saddle and your blanket, and I will read to you from a book
I have." He reached in his own blanket, still curiously unrolled, and brought forth two volumes: one a regular-sized
black leather Bible, the other a smallish red morocco-bound
tome with some sort of outlandish foreign scripting on the
cover. "The Book of the Gospel," he said, holding up the
Bible; then, gesturing with the little red book, "the Rubáiyát
of Omar Khayyám: which will you have, Isley?"

"Well," said the latter, "I can tell by some of your talk,
Ebe, that you favor the Good Book, and I ain't denying that
it's got some rattling-tall yarns in it. But if it's all the same
to you, I'll have a shot of the other. I'm a man likes to see
both sides of the billiard ball."

Eben nodded soberly, but without any hint of reproval.

"You have made your choice, Isley," he said, "and so be
it. Listen. . . ."

He opened the small volume then and began to read selected lines for his raptly attentive companion. Lazing back
on his blanket, head propped on his saddle, the warmth of
the fire reflecting in under the lean-to warm and fragrant as
fresh bread, Isley listened to the great rhymes of the ancient
Persian:

> . . . And as the Cock crew, those who stood before
> The Tavern shouted—"Open then the Door!
> "You know how little while we have to stay
> "And once departed, many return no more! . . . "

> . . . Come, fill the Cup, and in the fire of Spring
> Your winter-garment of Repentance fling:
> The Bird of Time has but a little way
> To flutter—and the Bird is on the Wing. . . .

> . . . A Book of Verses underneath the Bough,
> A Jug of Wine, a Loaf of Bread—and Thou
> Beside me singing in the Wilderness—
> Oh, Wilderness were paradise enow! . . .

. . . Yesterday this Day's Madness did prepare,
Tomorrow's Silence, Triumph, or Despair:
   Drink! for you know not whence you came, nor why:
Drink! for you know not why you go, nor where. . . .

   The Moving Finger writes; and, having writ,
Moves on: nor all your Piety nor Wit
   Shall lure it back to cancel half a Line,
Nor all your Tears wash out a Word of it. . . .

The poetry was done, then, and Eben was putting down the little red book to answer some drowsy questions from Isley as to the nature of the man who could write such wondrously true things about life as she is actually lived, just on a piece of ordinary paper and in such a shriveled little old leather book.

Eben reached over and adjusted Isley's blanket more closely about the dozing cowboy, then told him the story of Omar Khayyám. But Isley was tired, and his thoughts dimming. He remembered, later, some few shreds of the main idea; such as that Old Omar was a tentmaker by trade, that he didn't set much store by hard work, that he didn't know beans about horses, sheep or cattle, but he was a heller on women and grapejuice. Past that, he faded out and slept gentle as a dead calf.

The sun was an hour high and shining square in his eye when he woke up. He lay still a minute, not recalling where he was. Then it came to him and he sat up with a grin and a stretch and a "Morning, Ebe," that was warm and cheerful enough to light a candle from. But Eben didn't answer to it. And never would. For, when Tom Isley blinked to get the climbing sun out of his eyes and took a second frowning look around the little campsite, all he saw was the unbroken stretch of the new snow which had fallen quiet as angel's wings during the night. There was no Eben, no mule, no threadbare army blanket bedroll. And, this time, there were not even any half-filled hoofprints leading away into the snow. This time there was only the snow. And the stillness. And the glistening beauty of the new day.

Oh, and there was one other small thing that neither Tom Isley, nor anybody else in Big Horn basin, was ever able to explain. It was a little red morocco book about four-by-six inches in size, which Isley found in his blanket when he went to spool it for riding on. Nobody in northwest Wyoming had ever heard of it, including Tom Isley.

It was called the *Rubáiyát* of Omar Khayyám.

FRED GROVE

Comanche Woman

Fred Grove's father was a trail driver and rancher, and his mother was of Osage and Sioux blood. Born in Hominy, Oklahoma, in 1913, and now a resident of Silver City, New Mexico, Grove began his career as a journalist, editor, and public relations man. His first appearance as a Western writer was in 1958, and in the past thirty years he has earned two Wrangler Awards from the Cowboy Hall of Fame and five Golden Spurs for his novels and stories.

Grove is an authority on old-time match racing, and has written five novels on the subject (among them *The Great Horse Race*, *Match Race*, and *Search for Breed*), with a continuing cast of Runyonesque racetrack characters. In addition, he is the author of other notable books, such as *Comanche Captives*, *Warrior Road*, and most recently, *Bitter Trumpet*.

"Comanche Woman" was awarded the Golden Spur for 1963.

A brazen sun beat down on the figures strung out across the yellow prairie, their long travois poles raising puffs of smoky dust. They rode warily, on horses worn thin, as strangers in a land they had once known and claimed. They followed a single warrior toward the company of cavalry drawn up outside the stone fort.

"Think they mean trouble?" the young lieutenant in charge said nervously, turning to the weathered man whose ragged moustache drooped in its white oxbow over broad lips, whose get-up struck the lieutenant as extremely outlandish for a government scout—greasy blue britches, calfhide vest, calico shirt and that ridiculous floppy hat banded with frayed beaver skin, worn as though a special mark or badge.

The old man—far older than he would admit to the officers at the fort—was shading one hand against the glare, squinting. He grew more intent, stiffly erect. His eyes weren't much by now, but he knew this band, these Antelope people. He watched the warrior leading them in. The broad, high-boned Comanche face, and the hair as fair as corn silk.

"No trouble," he replied after some moments, stifling the disgust he longed to express. "They wouldn't bring their families along an' start a fight. You're lookin' at the last Comanche band, Lieutenant. Remember that. Buff'lo's gone. The war's over." And a good deal more, he thought, his mind retreating suddenly to dwell on dim shapes and sunlit buttes and curly grasses that rolled away like an ocean, on these same whirlwind people and the dreaming white woman who had lived among them so long ago.

It was late afternoon, while the women gathered mesquite wood for the supper fires, before Emily could approach the small white girl brought in that morning as Kill Bears' captive.

The girl whirled, an instant fear climbing high in her small, taut face. "Let me be!" she cried and shrank away. Her skin, too light for the Texas sun, had peeled on her nose and cheeks. Her hair was the color of flax and needed washing; even so, it managed to curl softly along the temples. But what held Emily rigid and aching was the terror she saw blazed in the thin face, in the enormous blue eyes that seemed too large for the rest of her. She was only nine or ten.

"No hurt . . . you," Emily said, forming the awkward words. Over the years she had made herself speak English so she would not forget how her people at the stockade had talked.

She put out a tentative hand, and wasn't surprised when the girl struck it aside.

"No hurt . . . no hurt."

"Git away—you dirty Injun!" The girl snatched up her bundle of wood and ran.

Emily caught her easily. The captive whimpered and twisted, and in that brief struggle Emily felt a sickening knowledge. This little white girl wasn't strong enough for camp work. Not as Emily had been when captured. Once winter came she would die like a young quail caught in a blizzard.

"Me white—me white," Emily said, desperate to be understood, holding her firmly, but not hurting. She pointed to her own blue eyes and yellow hair. "See? Me white—like you."

The captive dropped her sticks. Some of her terror edged away, then suddenly all of it, as she seemed to notice Emily's features for the first time. Her mouth twisted and she came sobbing into Emily's arms, and Emily was murmuring words she hadn't said in years.

"Your name, child?" she asked after a bit.

"Mary . . . Mary Tabor."

"Where is your home?"

"Down river from Fort Belknap."

"That's on the Salt Fork of the Brazos."

Mary displayed a small, pleased, wet-eyed smile. "You've been there?"

"A long time ago," Emily lied, wanting to humor her.

"My folks . . ." Mary began and trailed off, lips quivering.

Emily shook her head. "Don't talk now. Go back to camp. Don't let the Indians see you crying. Be brave."

That evening she spoke to Jumping Bull. "The little *Tejano* girl Kill Bears captured. I want her for a slave in our lodge."

"She is not strong. You would have to take care of her."

"She's not strong now because Kill Bears is mean to her. She goes hungry. She longs for her people. I could teach her many things. She will grow strong. She will be like a little sister to me."

Across the soft gloom in the tipi, Emily saw her husband's dark gaze play over her; it gave her a warm feeling. She could not forget how he had paid Runs Antelope, her captor, many horses for her. She was proud of him, in a way. Jumping Bull was a rising warrior who never lacked followers when he led war parties against the Utes or *Tejanos*. And even when she knew he was raiding the settlements, she wanted him to return. She wondered why, as a wealthy man who had only one son, he hadn't taken another woman into his lodge. A skilled hunter, he could provide for several wives and many children.

But for her, always, between them, lay the wedge of her massacred people, so distant and lost in time they might never have existed save in a dream, even though he had been too young to go on that raid.

He didn't answer and she, wanting this as nothing she had asked before, wisely forced down her eagerness.

Two days passed. Then she noticed that Jumping Bull's horse herd appeared smaller. Certain swift buffalo runners were missing. She said nothing and waited.

On the third day Mary Tabor came to live in the lodge.

"Now tell me about your kinfolks," Emily said.

Mary stared at the toe of her rawhide moccasin. "Wiped out. 'Less Uncle Amos got away." She shuddered and Emily saw the fear again, livid as a quirt slash in the pale face.

"Some day you will go back," Emily said gravely, sad for her. "Don't ever quit hopin'. I ain't."

Mary's large eyes showed a searching, inquisitive look, older than her years. "Mean you'd leave Jumping Bull if you could?"

Emily averted her eyes, somehow annoyed and surprised.

"He's mighty good for an Injun," Mary went on. "Gave

good horses for me. He ain't mean like Kill Bears, who beats his womenfolks. Reckon I'm lucky; I know that. And you—you're so good to me, Emily. Now you show me how to do Injun chores. I got to earn my keep. I can sew a mite. I can cook. I can make cornbread."

"There's no corn meal," Emily said, smiling, knowing Mary would be no bother. First, she washed and braided Mary's light hair; by that afternoon she had lost the driven look. Soon Emily dressed her in buckskins, after working the hides until they were soft and smooth and buff in color, and adding bright bead designs and fringes on sleeves and hems.

Having Mary close and hearing her speech awakened in Emily sleeping words and expressions. Homesickness seized her. She saw as never before the cool spring beyond the stockade where the children had played, the red plum bushes heavy with fruit, the sweet, dim faces of her mother and the neighbor women. She thought of her father, away when the Indians struck. Was he alive? Had he searched for her or offered ransom? She felt the strength of a new determination. She spent more time instructing Yellow Bird, her son.

"Peace is better than war," she would say when Jumping Bull wasn't around. "It is not right to kill."

"*Tejanos* kill us," the boy said. He was brown as any Comanche and he had the proud, high cheekbones of his father, but you couldn't mistake the white cast of his mouth, or the blue eyes and yellow hair. Trouble was, he thought like a Comanche.

"It takes a brave man to follow the peace road," she said, "when the others howl to fight."

The boy looked puzzled. "My father is brave. He fights."

When they reached a stopping place in their discussions, he would leap up with relief and run out. Emily, left to her dreaming, could see him grown up as a white man and living in a wooden house with windows.

By the time the band trailed out on the vast prairie floor

of the Staked Plains for summer trading, she was thinking
of home with an increasing sick desperation. Her resolve
deepened.

They drew up to a place called *Casas Amarillas*—the Yellow Houses—a high bluff in which caves had been cut.
There the *Comancheros* waited with their familiar high-
wheeled *carretas*.

Emily's usual excitement was missing. She moved dully.
Mary helped her raise the long cedar tipi poles and lift the
cover of dressed buffalo skins against the framework, fasten
the small wooden pins and pound the pegs. That done, Mary
joined the other youngsters curiously observing the trade
people and the many bright goods.

Soon she came flying back. "There's a white man out
there!"

"White man!" Emily looked up. "No white man has ever
come here." She shook her head; it wasn't possible.

"He's a trader," Mary insisted, impressed, and her hands
framed the shape of a large man. "Black boots . . . buckskins
and a big round hat with beaver skin around it. The children
call him Beaver Hat."

Emily got up. "He's white? You're certain?"

"I heard him talkin' to Jumping Bull. I saw him as close as
I am to you."

"Then he will come here," Emily said, more to herself.
There would be much palavering and smoking and feasting
before Jumping Bull, who owned more horses than any warrior in the band, struck his trade. Excitement swept her.

To her disappointment, Jumping Bull returned alone. He
looked pleased and secretive as he reached inside his blanket and held out something that shone.

She caught her breath. It was a silver necklace, turquoise
set in each link, very bright and pretty in the sun; his first
real gift for her, worth many horses. She considered it long-
ingly, in confusion. She took the necklace and spread it out
in her hands, and started to slip it over her head. As she did,
a thought arrested her. Jumping Bull didn't know she was

going to tell the white trader about her people. Therefore, it would be unseemly for her to wear his gift. Yet she couldn't refuse it.

"It's too pretty to wear now," she said, instead, and saw the flicker of hurt deep in his brown eyes before he walked away.

Afterward, she placed the necklace among her things—with the hand mirror, the colored beads left over from making Mary's dress, awls and needles of sharpened bone, a pair of thin, shell earrings obtained from the *Comancheros*, and a broken comb found in the litter of an old camp ground.

Near evening the next day she took a buffalo paunch to the water hole below the yellowish cliffs. Coming back, she looked about and stopped suddenly. Tiny tremors raced through her.

A rawboned white man in a broad hat was walking beside Jumping Bull. She delayed, until they passed her and entered the lodge. Had the white man noticed her pale skin? Her yellow hair?

She hung up the water paunch and when she came to the lodge door, carrying a kettle of meat, she paused desperately so Beaver Hat could see her framed there in the full light. Going in, she saw her husband on his robes, facing the door. Beaver Hat sat on his left, in the place of honor. She lingered so long while placing the kettle and wooden bowls and spoons that Jumping Bull threw her a questioning look.

Beaver Hat seemed not to notice.

She stood outside, slumped in dejection. As a Comanche woman she couldn't approach the white man in camp. People would laugh at Jumping Bull, whose wife talked to strangers. Yet why should she, a captive, think of him and his reputation as a warrior? She didn't understand herself.

Yellow Bird ran in to eat. She fed him and watched him run off into the dusky light. She sent Mary to play and sat motionless, listening to the murmuring voices inside the tipi. A thought settled; it kept growing, stirring her. She emptied the paunch into a large kettle and went unhurriedly to the spring and opened the bag, letting it fill slowly while she watched.

When she could wait no longer, when evening's haze masked the brown land and her long absence would be noted, she saw a figure leave the lodge and start toward the trader's camp.

She rose at once, the water bag forgotten, and stepped away, striding to intercept him. But the fine feeling of anticipation with which she had begun deserted her suddenly. She slowed her step, uncertain. What if he pretended again not to see her?

She could hear his bootsteps, heavy, steady. Not once did his head turn in her direction. His gaze seemed fixed afar. His beaver hat made him look taller.

She walked faster and turned to stand across his path. He couldn't miss her now! She saw his eyes stray over her, and she waited for some sign that she existed. He came on, just a few steps away. Still, he gave no awareness of her.

Her head lifted. She was white, not Comanche! She posted herself squarely. Facing him, she saw him swing his glance right and left. To her astonishment and relief, he halted and said, low, "I know, ma'am . . . you're white." She heard nothing but pity as he spoke, pity and helplessness.

She touched her breasts. "Me Emily—Emily Bragg," she said, and suddenly she became angry with herself. She had thought so long over the impressive way she would speak, the rehearsed white man's words. Now, in her anxiety, she was falling back on the old, halting, Indian-camp English, which she'd come to despise since Mary came.

"Bragg? Bragg?" He pulled on his chin and mulled the name around on his tongue. He shifted one high shoulder and inclined his head in the manner of one who listens. A tawny moustache fell down the slopes of his broad mouth. His eyes, almost white against the brownness of his face, squinted in at the corners. The eyes were wise, but missing was the shrewd glint of a *Comanchero*.

"My father's name was Josiah Bragg. He built a fort on a river." She could never think of him as dead; at last the words were rising off her tongue. "The settlers called it Fort Bragg. There was a massacre—ever'body killed—"

"On the Navasota, wasn't it?" he interrupted, and nodded reminiscently, in sympathy. "I recollect that. You been all this time with the Antelope-Eaters?"

"Since I was ten."

He hesitated, not meeting her eyes. "They didn't swap you off none . . . nor trade you around to other bands or tribes?"

"No," she replied and drew herself straighter.

He appeared relieved, though his pity slid back as he said, "Now you're Jumping Bull's woman?"

"*His wife,*" she said, surprised at her instant sharpness. "Listen to me! I still have people. I know. They'll pay ransom."

"Thought you said everybody was rubbed out?"

"My father wasn't there. He was east in the settlements." She spoke in a torrent, in confusion, and a pang of guilt pressed her. She'd meant to tell him first about Mary. "Listen! There's a little *Tejano* girl here—Mary Tabor. Her folks lived on the Brazos Salt Fork. Maybe she's got kin left—somebody. The pony soldiers at Fort Belknap will know. Somebody'll remember that raid . . . just last summer. Her folks had stock." Emily didn't know whether Mary's people possessed wealth or not; as she remembered, everybody on the frontier was poor. She'd said that on impulse; anything to stir up the greed in this white trader who didn't look or act like a *Comanchero.* "Her people, my people, I know will pay ransom. Many guns, many blankets."

"What about your boy?" he asked. "Figure Jumping Bull'd give up you an' the boy together?"

She shook her head evasively and touched his arm with a pleading gesture. "All I know I've dreamed about goin' home ever since they took me. You will take word?"

She waited, feeling her throat muscles tighten. Waves of

purple twilight thickened across the open land and lay banked in darker shadows against the foot of the bluff. Camp sounds fell away.

"Ma'am," he said, finally, "true, I brought some trade goods. But no guns. I ain't a real *Comanchero*. I'm a scout for the state of Texas. There's a big war comin' between the states." When her brows knitted in puzzlement, he tried to explain and pointed. "Americans agin Americans. North and South. A brother-killin' war. Mighty bad. Texas wants to keep the Comanches peaceful. That's why I'm here."

"You take word?" she said, slipping into the sparse, hated camp lingo.

He didn't answer at once. "I'll try. Maybe I can locate somebody. If I can, I'll send a rider back. My man can say the *Tejanos* are lookin' for two whites like you an' Mary. That there'll be ransom goods." She was thanking him with her eyes, her throat too full for speech. "Ma'am, you're a mighty brave woman. Only don't get your hopes too high now. If I can't find anybody—well. Could be, too, the band won't let you go."

"I am Jumping Bull's *wife*," she said. "Not *their* slave."

Beaver Hat's eyes looked thoughtful, but Emily no longer saw pity. He had that expression as he walked off.

Emily clung to it, trusting it, as the slow days wore away and the fickle band shifted from one scattered watering to another. By late summer, as restless as the whirlwinds that played across their shimmering world, the Antelope-Eaters had returned to the Yellow Houses, where the constant *roo-roo-oo* of bellowing buffalo bulls meant winter meat ranged nearby.

That was when the dark-skinned rider found them. Emily felt the hot clutch of excitement as she gave him food and fought down her questions. Was her father alive? Was Mary's uncle?

The rider and Jumping Bull talked, and then the man went to his picketed horse and waited.

It seemed a long time before Jumping Bull called her,

before she stood in the gloom of the lodge. She had never feared him. Except now she had to will herself to meet his eyes.

"Beaver Hat," he said, expressionless, "sends me word from the *Tejano* chiefs. They want to buy you and the little white slave."

She stared into her hands, ashamed for him to see her naked elation.

"Your home is here," he told her.

"I am not Comanche," she said, looking up. "I want to go back to my people."

"It would not be the same. Your skin is white, but your heart is Comanche."

"I am a white woman. I want my son to live as a white man."

His dark eyes flashed a baffled anger.

"My father is rich. He will pay much for me."

He flinched as if struck. His eyes locked on her, in them something she had never seen until now. He strode past her, gone.

White-faced, standing in the lodge door, she saw him go out and speak to the rider. What was he saying?

He told her nothing, and the following morning, taking only his medicine bundle, he rode off alone. He returned after three days, lean and hollow-eyed.

Soon she heard the camp crier calling: "You friends of Jumping Bull—come to his lodge tonight. He will lead a war party against the Utes."

Emily's heart turned cold. In that moment she became a Comanche woman again, fearing for her warring husband. She watched with dread as the warriors hung up their shields to absorb the powerful sun medicine and readied weapons. All except Jumping Bull, who chose only his long *bois d'arc* lance, which only the bravest carried. A war-lance man never retreated, and the feeling spread through her that he would not return.

All during the hot afternoon she heard him singing and

drumming songs in the lodge. Near sundown the war party paraded through the village. They would leave tonight, for it was bad to go in daylight. As darkness fell, the old men beating the drums struck up a throbbing song.

Now the departing warriors began choosing women partners for the dance.

Emily waited. Always before he had danced with her.

His gaze brushed her, just once. He wheeled swiftly by. That was all. He danced on and she knew that he had shut her out of his heart.

Living was dreading and dreaming and instructing young Yellow Bird. *Is it good to see friends in their grief slashing themselves? Is it good to see old people without sons, no one to kill meat for them? Is the war way good?*

Several times a day she climbed the bluff to catch the first signs of distant movement, hoping to see low puffs of dust, or dark figures crawling through the glazy heat waves.

On the afternoon that she sighted the bobbing shapes in the west, she thought first of the war party. She watched a long time; they were so far away and the sun burned her eyes.

Of a sudden she dropped her head. There was no war party. The figures out there were mainly mules pulling high-wheeled carts. But remembering Mary, she felt a warm triumph and she ran toward camp.

They stood outside the lodge and waited for Beaver Hat to make his way through the Comanches swarming around the carts. He came quickly. As he approached, Emily took Mary's hand.

"It's all right," he announced, displaying the engulfing smile of one bringing good news. "Got plenty of things—blankets, calico, tobacco, coffee, kettles."

Mary uttered a small cry and Emily held her harder.

"Ma'am," Beaver Hat said, his eyes fixing Emily alone, "your father is still living. There's a little town growed up there now close to the fort."

Emily felt her throat lump. A mist crossed her eyes. She

fought a sudden trembling. "Is . . . is he old?" she asked, and the fort and its phantom people and the Navasota and its postoak hills swam in a sweet haze. "I mean . . . does he look old?" In truth, she didn't know what she meant.

"His hair is snow-white. A hardy man for his age, though. Handles stock. Raises cotton. He's well-to-do."

"Did he . . . is he? . . ." Again, Emily faltered.

"He never married again, if that's what you mean. Lives by himself. He wants you back, ma'am. Says you're all he's got. He's never quit lookin' for you." His voice changed. "I figure we'd better pull out tomorrow."

Emily didn't understand. She stared into his face. "Pull out? My husband is making war on the Utes." She hesitated even more and when she spoke, her voice sounded other than her own. "And my son?" Her gaze broke away from his.

"Mean Jumping Bull didn't tell you?" he demanded, astonished. "Why, he gave his word to my man last summer. You can go home now. You an' Mary. With me. As for the boy, it's his choice to go or stay. What's more, Jumping Bull didn't want any ransom goods. Your father sent 'em just the same—for good will."

"My husband is gone," she said again, dully. "I can't go now. His war party's been out a long time."

Beaver Hat pulled on his beard, and she could see the wise eyes thoughtfully upon her. He said, "That's not all. About that fight on the Salt Fork, ma'am. All Mary's kin got wiped out. I'm mighty sorry."

Mary's fingers were clawing into Emily's palm. But Emily didn't whimper as she would have months ago.

"Now, ma'am," he said earnestly, "set your mind to this. I can wait a few days. No longer. I won't ever be back here again." He turned away.

Emily heard shouts on the afternoon of the second day after Beaver Hat's arrival. She ran out to the shrillness of wailing voices and, hurrying to the camp's edge, she recognized a warrior who had traveled with the war party. His face was painted black. Scattered behind him trailed a small band of riders. Sixteen men had gone to war; not half that many were returning. Jumping Bull, she saw, wasn't among them.

She stumbled. The sky was spinning. As she swayed upward, she noticed, just now, the cedar-pole travois.

Running, running, she found him upon it. His long spear lay beside him, unbroken. A red, wicked slash ran crookedly across his chest. His dark eyes, open, took no notice of her even when she bent over him. She heard a warrior say:

"He counted many coups with the war lance before he went down. He told us to leave him, but we put him on the drag. His spirit wants to stay in his body, but his heart is on the ground."

She followed them, holding herself tightly, as if she might fall apart if she did not, followed as they carried him inside the lodge. Seeing him on the buffalo robes, she thought, "He tried to die; only he was too strong, too brave." And she was proud.

Yellow Bird sat at his warrior father's feet to watch and worship. Mary Tabor, big-eyed, silent, slipped to Emily's side, intent on the rise and fall of Jumping Bull's heavy breathing. And in the wide eyes Emily saw again the fear that Mary had when she first came to the Indian camp.

In a little while Emily felt Mary touch her arm. She turned to find Beaver Hat standing back from the doorway. Emily stepped outside, Mary close on her heels.

"I saw them bring him in," Beaver Hat said, nodding his regret. He paused. "I'll have to know now, ma'am. Hard time for you to decide. I understand that."

Emily felt Mary's hand creep inside hers, and the calling images of her father and the fort and the people seemed to float again before her, revealed in soft sunlight, forever there, forever secure. She could see each face, each remembered woodland path and hill shape.

"No harder," she said then, shaking her head. "Guess I decided the other day; just didn't know. My home is here." And suddenly: "But Mary will go! My father is old—she will make him a good daughter."

At that, Mary sobbed and Emily felt her fierce, small grasp.

Beaver Hat's jaw hung. His broad lips opened, closed. His eyes ran over her, thoughtfully, a blend of sadness behind them. And he did a strange thing. He swept off his hat. For her, she knew, some *Tejano* sign she didn't remember. But she sensed it was good, and without pity.

Mary couldn't stop sobbing. "Emily, don't make me leave you!"

Emily grew firm. She took Mary's arm, just as she had that first day, and led her the few steps to Beaver Hat.

"Go now—be brave," Emily said, and kissed one wet cheek. "Don't look back. I don't think I could stand that."

She watched them walk off. Once Mary seemed to lag, to falter, to cry. But she didn't look back.

Emily turned. She went inside and searched among her scant possessions and found the necklace, which she looped around her neck.

She saw Jumping Bull look up as she faced around. His dark, warm gaze came over her.

"There will never be another woman in this lodge," he said.

She inclined her head, indicating approval. The faces in the old dream had gone. Only those of her husband and son were real. Yet, for Yellow Bird, because he was young, she could dream of the peace road.

CARLA KELLY

A Season for Heroes

Twice winner of the Golden Spur Award (for this story, she received WWA's 1978 Golden Spur), Carla Kelly began her Western writing after two years as seasonal ranger and historian for the Fort Laramie National Historic Site.

At present Kelly is a public information officer for a large hospital in Springfield, Missouri, and has completed a collection of "Fort Laramie Stories."

For some years, Kelly has been writing Regency romances for Signet Books and in 1989 was named by *Romantic Times* as "Best Regency Writer of the Year."

Ezra Freeman died yesterday. I don't usually read the obituaries, at least I didn't until after Pearl Harbor. With four grandsons in the service now and one of them missing over a place called Rabaul, or some such thing, I generally turn to the obituaries after the front page and the editorials.

There it was, right at the bottom of the column, in such small print I had to hold the paper out at arm's length . . . Ezra Freeman. There was no date of birth listed, probably because even Ezra hadn't known that, but it did mention there were no surviving relatives and the deceased had been a veteran of the Indian Wars.

And when I thought about Ezra Freeman, I ended up thinking about Mother and Father. Still carrying the newspaper, I went into my bedroom and looked at the picture of Mother and Father and Company D hanging on the wall next to the window. It was taken just before Father was assigned to 10th Cav headquarters, so he is still leaning on a cane in the picture. Mother is sitting on a bench holding quite a small baby and next to her, his shoulders thrown back and his feet together, is Sergeant Ezra Freeman.

The picture was taken at Ft. Bowie, Arizona Territory. I was ten or eleven then and that garrison was the first memory that really stuck in my mind. It was where Dad nearly got killed and my little brother was born, and where I discovered a few things about love.

My mother was what people call lace-curtain Irish. She was born Kathleen Mary Flynn. Her father owned a rather successful brewery in upstate New York and Mother was educated in a convent where she learned to speak French and make lace. She never owned up to learning anything else there, although she wrote a fine copperplate hand and did a lot of reading when Father was on campaign. The nuns taught her good manners and how to pour tea the right way. Father could always make her flare up by winking at her and saying in his broadest brogue, "What'll ye hev to dhrink now, Kate Flynn?"

She had beautiful red hair that curled every which way. Little springs of it were forever popping out of the bun she wore low on her neck. She had a sprinkling of light brown freckles which always mystified the Indians. I remember the time an old reservation Apache stopped us as we were walking down Tucson's main street. He spoke to Father in Apache. Dad answered him, and we could see he was trying to keep a straight face.

We pounced on him when the Indian nodded and walked away.

"What did he say, Dad? What did he say?"

Father shook his head and herded us around the corner where he leaned against the wall and laughed silently until tears shone on his eyelashes. Mother got exasperated.

"What *did* he say, John?"

"Oh, Kate Flynn," he wheezed and gasped, "he wanted to know . . . Oh God . . ." He went off into another quiet spasm.

"John!"

Mother didn't approve of people taking the Lord's name in vain (which made garrison life a trial for her at times).

"Sorry, Kathleen," Dad looked at her and winked. I could feel Mother stiffening up. "He wanted to know if you had those little brown dots all over."

We children screamed with laughter. Mother blushed. A lesser Victorian lady would have swooned, but Tucson's streets were dusty then, and Father was laughing too hard to catch her on the way down.

Mother and Father met after Father's third summer at West Point. He had been visiting friends of his family in Buffalo and Mother had been a guest of one of the daughters. They had spent a week in each other's company, then Mother had gone back to the convent. They had corresponded for several months, then Father proposed during Christmas furlough and they were married after graduation in June.

There had been serious objections from both sides of the family. Papa Flynn made Father promise to raise any children as Catholics, and Grandpa Stokes wanted to be assured that he and Grandma wouldn't be obliged to call on the Flynns very often.

Father agreed to everything and he would have raised us as Catholics, except that we seldom saw a priest out on the plains; besides, Mother wasn't a very efficient daughter of the church. I think she figured she'd had enough, what with daily Mass at the convent for six years straight. But she always kept her little ebony and silver rosary in her top drawer under her handkerchiefs and I only saw her fingering it once.

I don't really remember what my father looked like in those early years. I do remember that he wasn't too tall (none of the horse soldiers were) and that the other officers

called him Handsome Johnny. Mother generally called him
"the Captain" when we were around. "The Captain says
you should do this, Janey," or "Take the Captain's paper to
him, Gerald." When he was promoted, she called him "the
Major," and the last name before he died was "the Colonel."
Fifteen years later, just before she died, she had started over
and was calling him "the Lieutenant" again.

I was born in Baton Rouge about a year after they were
married, where the 10th Cavalry was serving Reconstruction duty. Pete came along two years later at Ft. Sill and
Gerald was born at Ft. Robinson in the Black Hills.

When I was ten, we were assigned to Ft. Bowie, Arizona
Territory. That was in the fall of 1881, more than sixty years
ago.

Dad commanded Company D of the 10th Cavalry. The 9th
and 10th Cavalry were composed entirely of Negro enlisted
men, serving under white officers. The Indians called them
Buffalo Soldiers, I suppose because their kinky black hair
reminded them of the hair of a buffalo. Father always swore
they were the best troops in the whole U.S. Army and said
he was proud to serve with them, even though some of his
fellow officers considered such duty a form of penance.

My favorite memory of Company D was listening to them
riding into Ft. Bowie after duty in the field. They always
came in singing. The only man who couldn't carry a tune
was my father. I remember one time right before Christmas
when they rode out of Apache Pass singing "Star of the
East." Even Mother came out on the porch to listen, her
hand on my shoulder.

Company D had two Negro sergeants. Master Sergeant
Albert Washington was a former slave from Valdosta, Georgia. He was a short, skinny little man who never said very
much, maybe because he was married to Clara Washington
who did our washing and sewing, and who had the loudest,
strongest voice between the Mississippi and the Pacific.

The other sergeant was Ezra Freeman. Ezra wasn't much
taller than my father and he had the biggest hands I ever

saw. They fascinated me because he was so black and the
palms of his hands were so white.

Ezra had a lovely deep voice that reminded me of choc-
olate pudding. I loved to hear him call the commands to the
troops during Guard Mount and I loved to watch him sit in
his saddle. My father was a good horseman but he never sat
as tall as Ezra Freeman, and Father's shoulders got more and
more stooped as the years passed. Not Ezra. Last time I saw
him, sitting in his wheelchair, his posture was as good as
ever, and I think he would have died before he would have
leaned back.

Once I asked Ezra about his childhood. He said that he
had been raised on a plantation in South Carolina. At the
age of twelve, he and two sisters and his mother and father
had been sold at the Savannah auction to help pay off his
master's gambling debts. He never saw any of them again.

He was bought by a planter from Louisiana and stayed a
field hand until Admiral Farragut steamed up the Mississippi and ended that. He sometimes spoke a funny kind of
pidgin French that made my mother laugh and shake her
head.

But she never got too close to Ezra, or to any of Father's
other troopers. None of the other white ladies of the regiment did either. Mother never would actually pull her skirts
aside when the colored troopers passed, as some of the ladies did, but she had a formality about her in the presence
of the Buffalo Soldiers that we weren't accustomed to. At
least, she did until the summer of 1882, when we came to
owe Ezra Freeman everything.

That was the summer Ignacio and his Apaches left the
San Carlos Agency and raided, looted, burned and captured
women and children to enslave or sell in Mexico. The troops
garrisoned at Bowie knew that Ignacio's activities would
touch them soon, and the early part of the summer was
spent in refitting and requisitioning supplies and ordnance
in preparation for the orders they knew would come.

Mother was not receiving any callers that summer. That

was how we put it then. Or we might have said that she was "in delicate health." Now, in 1942, we say "she is expecting," or "she is in the family way." But back then, that would have been altogether too vulgar and decidedly low class.

Neither of them told us. I just happened to notice Mother one morning when I burst into her room and caught her in her shift. She bulged a little in the front and I figured we were going to have another baby brother sometime. They never seemed to have girls after me. She didn't say anything then and I didn't either. Later on in the week, when we were polishing silver, she paused, put her hand on her middle and stared off in space for a few moments, a slight smile on her face.

At breakfast a few mornings later, Father asked Mother if she wanted to go home for the summer to have the baby. The railroad had been completed between Bowie and Tucson, and it would be a much less difficult trip.

"Oh, no, I couldn't, John," she had replied.

"Well, why not? I'll probably be gone all summer anyway." Dad wiped up the egg on his plate with one swipe of his toast and grinned when Mother frowned at him.

"Oh, I just couldn't, John," she repeated, and that was the end of that.

About two weeks later, three of the cavalry companies and two of the infantry were detached from Bowie to look for Ignacio.

Mother said her goodbyes to Father inside their bedroom. As I think of it, very few of the wives ever saw their husbands off from the porch, except for Lieutenant Grizzard's wife, and everyone said she was a brassy piece anyway.

But we kids followed Father out onto the porch. My little brother Pete wore the battered black felt hat Dad always took on campaign and Gerald lugged out the sabre, only to be sent back into the house with it. Father let me bring out his big Colt revolver and I remember that it took both hands to carry it.

He took the gun from me and pushed it into his holster.
He put his hand on my head and shook it back and forth.
Then he knelt down and kissed me on both cheeks.

"Keep an eye on Mother for me, Janey," he said.

I nodded and he stood up and shook my head again. He
plucked the black hat off Pete's head and swatted him lightly
with it. He knelt down again, and both Pete and Gerald
clung to him.

"Now you two mind Janey. She's sergeant major."

Company D rode out at the head of the column after Guard
Mount, and the corporal who taught school for the officers'
children was kind enough to dismiss us for the day.

Summers are always endless to children, but that summer
of 1882 seemed to stretch out like cooling taffy. One month
dragged by and then two, and still the men didn't return. In
fact, another company was sent out and Bowie had only the
protection of one understrength troop of infantry and the
invalids in the infirmary.

The trains stopped running between Bowie and Tucson
because of Ignacio and his warriors, and I recall how irritated Mother was when the last installment of a serial in
Frank Leslie's *Illustrated Weekly* never showed up. The
only mail that got through was official business the couriers
brought in.

But then Mother was irritated with many things that summer. She usually didn't show at all until the eighth month,
but this time she had Clara Washington sew her some new
Mother Hubbards before her sixth month was over. And her
ankles were swollen too. I rarely saw Mother's legs, but once
I caught her out on the back porch one evening with her
dress up around her knees.

"Oh, Mama!" was all I said.

It startled her and she dropped her skirts and tucked her
feet under the chair.

"Jane, you shouldn't spy on people!" she scolded, and
then she smiled when she saw my face. "Oh, I'm sorry, Jane.
And don't look so worried. They'll be all right again soon."

Toward the middle of August we began to hear rumors in the garrison. Ordinarily we just shrugged off rumors, but the men were now quite overdue and still Ignacio hadn't been subdued. One rumor had the troops halfway across Mexico pursuing Apaches, and another rumor had them in San Diego waiting for a troop train back.

On the 18th of August (I remember the date because it was Gerald's fifth birthday), the rumor changed. A couple of reservation Apaches slouched in on their hard-bitten ponies to report a skirmish to the south of us, hard on the Mexican border. Captain Donelly, B Company, 4th Infantry, was senior officer of the fort then and he ignored the whole thing. The Indians weren't scrupulous about the truth and they often confused Mexican and U.S. soldiers.

I mentioned the latest rumor to Mother, who smiled at me and gave me a little shake. I went back outside to play but I noticed a look in her eyes that hadn't been there before.

Two days later the troops rode in. They were tired, sunburned and dirty, and their mounts looked mostly starved. Mother came out on the porch. She leaned on the porch railing and stood on one foot and then the other. I saw that she had taken off her wedding ring and Dad's West Point ring that she wore on her first finger. Her hands looked swollen and tight.

The troops assembled on the parade ground and some of the women and children ran out to them. We looked hard for Company D but it wasn't there. Mother sat down on the bench under the parlor window.

Several of the officers dismounted and stood talking together. One of them gestured our way and Mother got up quickly. When Major Connors started walking over to our quarters, she backed into the house and jerked me in with her.

"Listen to me, Jane Elizabeth," she hissed and her fingers dug into my shoulders until I squirmed in her grasp. "You take their message."

"But Mother," I whined, trying to get out of her grip. "Why don't you?"

"It's bad luck," she said, and turned and went into the parlor, slamming the door behind her.

Major Connors didn't seem too surprised that Mother wouldn't come out to talk to him. I backed away from him a little myself, because he smelled so awful.

"Jane, tell your mother that Company D and A are both a bit overdue but not to worry because we expect them anytime."

After he left I told Mother, but she wouldn't come out of the parlor until supper time.

Several days passed, and then a week and still no sign of either company. None of the other officers' wives said anything to Mother about it but several of them paid her morning calls and brought along baked goods.

"Why are they doing this, Mama?" I asked her, after Captain O'Neill's wife left an eggless custard.

Mother murmured something about an early wake. I asked her what she meant but she shook her head. My brothers and I downed all the pastries and pies but Mother wouldn't eat any of it.

One night when I couldn't sleep because of the heat, I crept downstairs to get a drink of water from the pump. Mother was sitting on the back porch, rocking slowly in the moonlight. She heard me and closed her fist over something in her lap, but not before I'd seen what it was . . . the little ebony rosary she kept in her drawer. I could tell by the look in her eye that she didn't want me to say anything about it. She rocked on and I sat down near her on the porch steps.

"Mother, what happens if he doesn't come back?"

I hadn't meant to say that. It just came out. She stopped rocking. I thought she might be angry with me but she wasn't.

"Oh, we just manage, Jane. It won't be as much fun, but we'll just manage."

She rocked on in silence and I could hear above the creak of the rocking chair the click of the little ebony beads. I got up to go and she took my hand.

"You know, Jane, there's one terrible thing about being a woman."

I looked down at her. Her ankles and hands were swollen, her belly stretched against the nightgown that usually hung loose on her and her face was splotched.

"What's that, Mama?"

"The waiting, the waiting."

She didn't say anything else, so I went back upstairs and finally fell asleep after the duty guards had called the time from post to post all around the fort.

Another week passed and still no sign of the companies. The next week began as all the others had. The blue sky was cloudless and the sun beat down until the whole fort shimmered. Every glance held a mirage.

It was just after Stable Call that I heard the singing. The sound came up faintly from the west, and for a few moments I wasn't sure I heard anything except the wind and the stable noises to the south of us. But there it was again, and closer. It sounded like "Dry Bones," and that had always been one of Dad's favorite songs.

I turned to call Mother, but she was standing in the doorway, her hand shading her eyes as she squinted toward Apache Pass.

People popped out of houses all along Officers' Row, and the younger children began pointing and then running west past headquarters and the infirmary.

There they were, two columns of blue filing out of the pass, moving slowly. The singing wasn't very loud and then it died out as the two companies approached the stables.

Mother took her hand away from her eyes and walked over to the edge of the porch.

"He's not there, Jane," she whispered.

I looked again. I couldn't see Father anywhere.

She stood still on the porch and shaded her eyes again, then she gave a sob and began running.

So many nights in my dreams I've seen my mother running across the parade ground. She was so large and clumsy then, and as I recall, she was barefoot, but she ran as lightly as a young child, her arms held out in front of her. In my dreams she runs and runs until I wake up.

I was too startled to follow her at first and then I saw her run to the back of the column and drop down on her knees by a travois one of the horses was pulling. The animal reared back and then nearly kicked her but I don't think she even noticed. Her arms were around a man lying on the travois. As I ran closer, I could see him raise his hand slowly and put it on her hair.

I didn't recognize my father at first. His hair was matted with blood and it looked as though half his head had been blown away. There was a bloody, yellowish bandage over one eye and his whole face was swollen.

He turned his head in my direction and I think he tried to smile, but he only bared his teeth at me and I stepped back. I wanted to turn and run and I didn't see how Mother could stand it.

But there she was, her head on his chest. She was saying something to him but I couldn't hear, and all the while he was stroking her hair with that filthy, bruised hand.

I backed up some more and bumped into Ezra Freeman. I tried to turn and run but he held me.

"Go over to him, Janey," he urged and gave me a push. "He wants you."

I couldn't see how Ezra could interpret the slight movement of Father's hand but he kept pushing me toward the travois.

"Pa? Pa?" I could feel tears starting behind my eyelids.

He said something that I couldn't understand because it sounded as if his mouth was full of mashed potatoes. I leaned closer. He smelled of blood, sweat, dirt and woodsmoke. As I bent over him, I could see under the bandage on his face and gasped to see teeth and gums where his cheek should have been.

Mother was kneeling by him now, her hand on his splinted leg. She took my hand in her other hand and placed it on his chest. He tried to raise his head and I leaned closer. I could make out the words "Janey" and "home," but what he was saying was unimportant. All of a sudden I didn't care what he looked like. He was my father and I loved him more than words could say.

He must have seen my feelings in my eyes because he lay back again and closed his eyes. His hand relaxed and let go of mine.

I helped Mother to her feet and we stood back as two orderlies lifted him off the travois and onto a stretcher. He moaned a little and Mother bit her lip.

They took him to the infirmary and Ezra Freeman walked alongside the stretcher, steadying it. Mother would have followed him but the post surgeon took one look at her and told her to go lie down, because he didn't have time to deliver a baby just then. Mother blushed and the two of us walked back to our quarters hand in hand.

Mother spent an hour that evening in the infirmary with Father. She came home and reported he looked a lot better and was asleep. We went upstairs then and, while she tucked Gerald and Pete in bed, I sat on the rag rug by Pete's army cot, and she told us what happened.

"The two companies had separated from the main detachment and, after a couple days, they found an Apache rancheria. It was at the bottom of a small canyon near Deer Spring; when they tried to surround it before daybreak, they were pinned down by rifle fire from the rim of the canyon."

Mother paused and I noticed that she had twisted her fingers up in the afghan at the foot of Pete's bed. He sat up and prodded her.

"And what happened, Ma? What happened?"

He pulled on her arm a little and his eyes were shining. He had been down at the creek that afternoon and hadn't seen Father yet. The whole thing was still just a story to him.

While the candle on the night stand burned lower and lower, Mother told how Father had been shot down while trying to lead the men back to the horses. He had lain on an exposed rock all morning until Ezra Freeman had crawled out and pulled him to safety. The two companies had stayed in a mesquite thicket, firing at the Apaches until the sun went down. They withdrew in the dark.

Pete was asleep by then but Mother went on to say that the men had holed up for several days about sixty miles south of us because they were afraid Father would die if they moved him. When it looked like he would make it, they started for the fort.

Gerald fell asleep then and as Mother pulled the sheet up around him, she said to me,

"I can't understand it, Jane. Everyone else thought the Captain was dead. Why did Sergeant Freeman do it?"

Then she tucked me in bed.

But I couldn't sleep. Every time I closed my eyes, I kept seeing Father on that travois and the look in Mother's eyes as she knelt by him. I got out of bed and started into Mother's room.

She wasn't there. The bed hadn't even been slept in. I tiptoed down the stairs, stepping over the third tread because it always squeaked. As I groped to the bottom in the dark, I saw the front door open and then close quietly.

I waited a few seconds, then opened it and stood on the porch. Mother was dressed and wrapped in a dark shawl, despite the heat, and walking across the parade ground. She wasn't going toward the infirmary so I trailed her, skirting around the parade and keeping in the shadow of the officers' quarters. I didn't know where she was going but I had a feeling that she would send me back if she knew I was following her.

She passed the quartermaster's buildings and the stables, pausing to say something to the private on guard, who saluted her and waved her on. I waited until he had turned and walked into the shadow of the blacksmith shop before I continued.

I could see now that she was heading for Suds Row, where

the enlisted and their families lived. She walked to the end of the row and kept going, toward the Negro soldiers' quarters at the edge of the fort. Halfway down the row of attached quarters she stopped and knocked on one of the doors. I ducked behind the row until I came to tho baok of the place where she had knocked. There was a washtub in the yard and I dragged it to the window and turned it over and climbed up.

It was Ezra Freeman's quarters. He lived there with his friend Jackson Walter of Company A, Jackson's wife, Chloe, and their two children.

Mother and Ezra were standing in the middle of the room. She had taken off her shawl. Freeman offered her the chair he had been sitting in but she shook her head. I could see Chloe in the rocking chair by the kitchen, knitting.

Mother was silent for a few moments. Then,

"I just wanted to say thank you, Sergeant Freeman," she said finally. Her voice sounded high and thin, like it did after Grandpa Flynn's funeral three years before.

"Oh . . . well . . . I . . . Jeez, ma'am, you're welcome," stammered Ezra.

She shrugged her shoulders and held her hands out in front of her, palms up. "I mean, Sergeant, you didn't even know if he was alive and you went out there anyway."

He didn't say anything. All I could hear was the click of Chloe's bone needles. I barely heard Mother's next word.

"Why?"

Again that silence. Ezra Freeman turned a little and I could see his face. His head was down and he had sucked in his lower lip, and he was crying. The light from the kerosene lamp was reflected in his tears and they shone like diamonds on his black face.

"Well, hell, ma'am . . . he's the only man I ever served of my own free will." He paused. "And I guess I love him."

Mother put her hands to her face and I could see her shoulders shaking. Then she raised her head and I don't think she ever looked more beautiful.

"I love him too, Ezra. Maybe for the same reasons."

Then she sort of leaned against him and his arms went around her and they held onto each other, crying. She was patting him on the back, like she did when Father hugged her, and his hand was smoothing down her hair where it curled at the neck.

I am forever grateful that the white ladies and gents of Ft. Bowie never saw the two of them together like that, for I'm sure they would have been scandalized. But as I stood there peeking in the window, I had the most wonderful feeling of being surrounded by love, all kinds of love, and I wanted the moment to last and last.

But the moment soon passed. They both backed away from each other and Mother took out a handkerchief from the front of her dress and blew her nose. Ezra fished around in his pocket until he found a red bandanna and wiped his eyes. He sniffed and grinned at the same time.

"Lord almighty, ma'am. I ain't cried since that Emancipation Proclamation."

She smiled at him and put her hand on his arm, but didn't say anything. Then she nodded to Chloe, put her shawl around her head again and turned to the door.

"Good night and thank you again," she said before she went outside.

I jumped off the washtub and ran down the little alley behind the quarters. Staying in the shadows and watching out for the guards, I ran home. I wanted to be home before Mother because I knew she would look in on us before she went to sleep.

She did. She opened the door a crack, then opened it wider and glided in. I opened my eyes a little and stretched, as if she had just wakened me. She bent down and kissed me, then kissed Gerald and Pete. She closed the door and soon I heard her getting into bed.

One week later a couple of troopers from Company D carried Father home on a stretcher. The doctor insisted on putting him in the parlor on the daybed because he didn't want him climbing the stairs.

The post surgeon had done a pretty good job on Father's face. The bandages were off so the air could get to his cheek, which was a crisscross maze of little black sutures. He had lost his left eye and wore a patch over the socket. (Later on he tried to get used to a glass eye but never could get a good fit. He gradually accumulated a cigar box-full of glass eyes, and we used to scare our city cousins with them and play a kind of lopsided marbles game.)

His mouth drooped down at one corner and made him look a little sad on one side, and none of the other officers called him Handsome Johnny again.

The day after he had been set up in the parlor, Mother went into labor. The post surgeon tried to stop him but Father climbed the stairs—slowly, hand over hand on the railing and sat by Mother until her third boy was born.

An hour later the doctor motioned me and my brothers into the room. Mother was lying in the middle of the bed, her red hair spread around the pillow like a fan. Her freckles stood out a little more than usual, but she was smiling. Father sat in an armchair near the bed, holding the baby, who had a red face and hair to match.

"What are you going to name him?" I asked, after giving him a good look.

Mother hesitated a moment, then looked over at the baby and Father.

"Ezra Freeman Stokes," she replied quietly, her eyes on Father.

He said something to her that I couldn't understand because his face was still swollen. But Mother kept her eyes on his and snapped back to him in a low voice that sent shivers down my back.

"I don't give a damn what the garrison thinks! He's going to be Ezra Freeman!"

None of us had ever heard Mother swear and Father nearly dropped the baby.

So that was how Ez got his name.

About a month later Father was promoted to major and

given the Medal of Honor for "meritorious gallantry under fire at Deer Spring." I remember how he pushed that little medal around in its plush velvet case, then closed the box with a click. "I'm not the one who should be getting this," he murmured. No one could ever prevail upon him to wear it. Even when he was laid out in his coffin years later, with his full dress uniform and all his medals, I never saw that one.

Father was transferred to 10th Cavalry headquarters, then in San Antonio, and given a desk job. We didn't see much of Ezra Freeman after that and never did correspond with him because he couldn't read or write. But somehow we always heard about him from the other officers and men of Company D, and every year at Christmas, Mother sent him a dried-apple fruitcake and socks she had knitted. We knew when he retired twenty-five years later and learned in 1915 that he had entered the Old Soldiers' Home in Los Angeles.

Before Father's stroke, he paid him one visit there. I remember that it was 1919 and Father went to tell him that Captain Ezra F. Stokes had died in France of Spanish influenza.

"You know, Janey," he told me after that visit, "Ez may have been my son but I ended up comforting Sergeant Freeman. I almost wish I hadn't told him."

After Father passed away, Mother paid Ezra the yearly visit. She insisted on going alone on the train up from San Diego but when her eyesight began to fade, she finally relented and let me come with her once.

As it turned out, it was her last trip. I think she knew it.

Sergeant Freeman was in a wheelchair by then and, after giving me a nod and telling me to wait there, Mother pushed Ezra down the sidewalk to a little patio under the trees. She sat next to him on a bench and they talked together. After about half an hour she took an object out of her purse, leaned toward Ezra and put something on the front of his robe. I couldn't see what it was but I could tell that Ezra was protesting. He tried to push her hands away, but she went ahead and put something on him. It flashed in the sunlight but I was too far away to make out what it was.

Then she took a handkerchief out of her pocket and wiped his eyes. She sat down again beside him and they sat there together until his head nodded forward and he fell asleep. She wheeled him back to the far entrance of the building and I never had a chance to say good-bye.

She was silent on the trip home; after we got to my house, she said, "Jane, I feel tired," and went to bed. She drifted in and out of sleep for the next two days and then she died.

After the funeral I was going through her things when I came across the plush velvet case containing the Medal of Honor Father had been awarded at Ft. Bowie. I snapped it open but the medal was gone. I think I know where it went.

And now Ezra's dead. Well.

I can see that I've spent more time on this than I intended. I hear the postman's whistle outside. I hope there's a letter from my daughter Ann. Her oldest boy Steve has been missing over the Solomons for more than a month now. I don't suppose I can give her much comfort but I can tell her something about waiting.

Jason Glendauer's Watch

James Bellah is the son of James Warner Bellah (1899–1976), the Western writer whose stories were transformed by John Ford and other directors into such films as *Fort Apache, She Wore a Yellow Ribbon, Rio Grande,* and *Sergeant Rutledge.*

The younger Bellah, who lives in Tarzana, California, completed this story in 1962 and saw it rejected by a number of magazines before its publication in *Far West* seventeen years after it was written.

The wait was worth it and Bellah's persistence and belief in the worth of his story was vindicated when it received the 1979 Golden Spur Award from Western Writers of America.

Martin Wilkards had not yet passed his tenth birthday when he first encountered death. He died a little then with the emptiness of it and he died in particles many times thereafter, but as a child, when he was first introduced to the Grey Jurist, he learned that a man's life is his final coin and that when a gentleman makes his barter, he must honor his bid.

It was May, and the lust and laziness of summer were in Sacamore. The world had stopped and the heady warmth of spring still wrapped its invisible blanket over and around all things.

Young Martin had come home from school and was sitting at the table in his father's waiting room when the front door opened and a stranger entered. He was a thin man who somehow carried with him the illusion of having stepped from another time. He stood easily erect and was dressed in a fashion popular before Martin's birth. His frock coat was worn, but not quite frayed, at the cuffs and his boned boots were almost cracked across the insteps.

The stranger stood on the threshold, silhouetted gold against the afternoon sun. He looked directly at the boy. "Good day," he said after a particularly long moment. "Is the doctor in?"

Despite a certain vague feeling of having been displaced in time, Martin was able to command himself sufficiently to tell the man his father would probably be available in a moment.

The stranger thanked the boy and closed the door. He moved with an easy grace which could perhaps have marked him as an actor or a soldier on parade. Yet Martin noticed almost immediately that the man's face showed none of the femininity of theatrical men any more than it mirrored the flat, ovine quality he had seen in so many of the soldiers stationed at Fort Wimiwa.

The man crossed the room and sat at the table opposite Martin. Then, for the first time, the boy noticed the stranger's right hand hung limply at his side. It was swollen to almost double its normal size.

Dr. Wilkards stayed in his inner office for some time. From beyond the closed door there came the sounds of shuffled movements and the occasional groans of a male patient. Charles Wilkards was the only doctor in Sacamore then. His son was used to such sounds and, if he found them unusual or upsetting in any way, the stranger gave no sound. He seemed preoccupied with some vague or profound thought. He held his injured hand under the table and showed no indication either of pain or discomfort. He simply stared out the window beyond the mud of High Street.

From time to time, the boy would glance from his McGuffey's Reader and, almost furtively, snatch an impression of the man. He wore his copper hair to his shoulders. The light of afternoon played on the few silver strands in it. His face, although strong and masculine, might have been a cameo cut of onyx. Its form was similar to many seen on old and foreign coins.

As the two waited, young Martin was again struck by the fact the man was not really there at all. He was some form of ghost. Yet the boy felt neither fear nor any sense of apprehension. He sensed no threat in the man. There was no anger, only a deep and all-pervading sadness—perhaps a brooding nostalgia.

From where they sat, both the man and the boy could hear Dr. Wilkards's final words to his patient in the next room and the squeak of a turning doorknob. Suddenly, however, it was apparent the doctor changed his mind. Footsteps retreated from the waiting room door. For some reason, the doctor ushered his patient out through the kitchen.

A moment later, Dr. Wilkards stepped into the waiting room. He was a stooped man aged beyond his actual years by the world's madness and his own personal tragedies. His tired, bearded features showed both a kindness of soul and a weariness of heart, but still, in his eyes, there flickered the memory of a young man's mischievous twinkle.

The stranger rose as the doctor entered the room. He took a pace away from the table and bowed. "Dr. Wilkards?"

"Yes."

"Your servant, sir. My name is Glendauer. It seems I have injured my hand."

The doctor squinted as a man might stare at a horse he contemplated buying. He nodded very profoundly twice until the twinkle in his eyes could be buried no longer. He smiled very broadly and sincerely. "Come in," he said. "I've been expecting you."

They went into the dressing room and were gone for almost an hour. During that time, the boy tried to concentrate on his lessons but he was listless with spring fever and, consumed by youth's curiosity, much more interested in the soft muffles of conversation coming from beyond the closed door.

When it finally opened, Glendauer came into the waiting room first. He wore a new bandage over his right hand and supported his forearm in a sling.

The doctor followed him, closed the door and asked if he would like a drink.

Glendauer bowed again. The movement was quite formal but lacked any stiffness. It was an easy gesture he was obviously quite used to making. "It is one of the few pleasures left," he said.

Dr. Wilkards removed his new copy of Howe's Surgery from the book cabinet and reached into the space for his bottle. Almost ignoring his son's presence, he placed the bottle and two glasses on the table beside the open McGuffey's Reader.

The two men poured and toasted one another as if they had been quite alone and the boy in another world entirely. But he watched them and, as he did, a strange thing happened. It seemed to Martin Wilkards, aged nine, that an invisible cloak fell from his father's shoulders. He had never known his father as a young man, but seeing him then with Glendauer, he watched his father change from the serious, gentle parent he knew to a still handsome shadow of the young man his mother had married. Something disappeared from the doctor's face and the lines around his eyes and mouth appeared to soften. In the glow of the afternoon sun and the almost unreal play of light in the waiting room, it seemed the gray left the doctor's hair and beard, and his back and shoulders no longer stooped with age and responsibility.

Young Martin's feeling that the man with the broken hand could only be a ghost became stronger than ever. He stared intently at the two men and tried to recall every word they spoke to one another.

Although strangers to one another only an hour before, their shared bond was the spiritual amalgam of veterans. Dr. Wilkards had served with Thomas Jackson and, when the general had been shot at Chancellorsville, had been with him to the last, hopelessly praying for some miracle he and his medicine could not bring about.

Jason Glendauer was a Virginian who had attended West Point. After the secession, he had resigned his commission and raised a regiment of cavalry, maintaining it at his own expense throughout the war. After Appomattox, he had returned to the water-filled cellars and war-pocked, overgrown fields of his home. He had seen rats scurrying over the broken boards of the bed in which he had been born.

He had turned his back on what had once been a home worth dying to preserve and had ridden west.

He had heard of the '87 gold scare in Sacamore Valley and had wandered there because it had seemed as good or bad a place as any other. Technically, his occupation was "gambler." Actually, he was a gentleman without property—a vagabond.

His hand had been broken in a political discussion and Dr. Wilkards, despite his medical sympathies, found the injury amusing. Ed Tirowen, his earlier patient, had come to him with a broken nose.

As time passed, Glendauer returned to the office for new dressings and, finally, to have the last of his bandages removed. Although he was always quite pleasant to young Martin, he never quite lost the quality of having stepped out of the past. Often, Jason Glendauer would stay for dinner or, if he had won at cards that day, would treat the doctor and Martin to a meal at Mrs. Fairwright's boarding house.

Long before the end of summer Jason Glendauer and Dr. Wilkards had become the best of friends. Even young Martin had taken to calling the strangely enigmatic man "Uncle Jason" and accepting the now traditional Wednesday meeting of his father and the Virginian. One of the boy's chores on that day was to take a dollar from the box in the top drawer of his father's desk and walk to Little Gomorrah for a bottle of whiskey.

Little Gomorrah was a street of tents and board-fronted shanties pitched on Watson's Knoll overlooking the first six miles of the Sacamore Valley. During the gold scare, it had been a jumping-off spot for prospectors and, naturally, the bartenders and the gamblers and the whores had located there. The little town traced along a muddy street for half a mile on either side of Isaac Larson's Sutler's Shop. It was already dying of starvation, although it still managed to grub some bare sustenance from the soldiers at Fort Wimiwa and the sporting men of Sacamore.

Martin had heard the ladies at church and other citizens call the place sinful and terrible, but with the confidence of youth and the trust of one loved and respected, he was sure that, if his father sent him to hell for a bottle, hell couldn't be such a bad place after all.

It was on a particularly humid and sweltering July day he took the usual coin from his father's cash box and walked through town, along the old Wagon Road to the Sutler's Shop in Little Gomorrah. Ordinarily, he would simply have bought the whiskey and left but he happened to meet Jason Glendauer inside the shop. The man was exercising the fingers of his right hand by manipulating a deck of cards. Despite the unusually sluggish heat, he was dressed in his frock coat and his linen showed no signs of wilt.

Glendauer greeted the boy with his usual formality and started to ask him his plans for the rest of the afternoon when a dark-haired man in his early twenties pushed between them.

"All right, Glendauer," the man announced. "Now's as good a time as any."

Jason Glendauer glanced briefly at the younger man but did not speak. Instead he looked beyond him to the boy. "It's been pleasant seeing you again, Martin," he said. "Please give my respects to your father."

He turned his back to the man. His face was calmly unemotional. "Poker?"

Tight-lipped, the man nodded and, leaving the boy by the counter, he and Glendauer left the Sutler's Shop.

Martin Wilkards watched them cross the rutted street and enter a tent over which hung a crude sign: *Faro Pit*. Many years later, as an old and much wiser man, he would often remember that syrupy July afternoon. He stood just outside the Sutler's Shop holding a bottle of whiskey by the neck and wondering how his Uncle Jason Glendauer managed to keep his boots so clean in that awful mud.

But he did not speculate long. He had the whiskey and his duty was to return home. He turned back to Sacamore, but hadn't traveled ten yards before he heard the single shot. For a moment there was absolute deathly silence, then the murmur of hushed and angry voices.

Martin stopped. He was sure the sound was coming from the Faro Pit. Then he went on. He was even more sure no one on earth would dare disturb his Uncle Jason while he was playing cards.

That evening Glendauer arrived as usual and the doctor himself opened the door. Martin was upstairs. He heard the door open and started down to greet the visitor but was stopped at the very top of the flight by some inexplicable quality in Glendauer's manner. The boy watched the two men speak. He could hear their serious exchange of whispers but not their words. Then he saw his father move away from the front door. He heard the opening and closing of a desk drawer and saw his father return holding the dragoon pistol he had carried during the war.

Through the banister posts, the boy saw his father inspect the cylinder and check the priming. Then he began to hear the voices. They started as a soft murmur coming from the direction of Watson's Knoll, then grew to a great babbling swell like a chopping tide.

Seated, his knees hunched under his chin, the boy worked his way down one, then another step. His father and Glendauer were standing by a front window. Martin could see the flicker of torches outside and knew by the shouts the crowd was just before the house.

Then a rock crashed through the window exactly between the two men.

As quietly as he had ever done anything, Jason Glendauer took the pistol from his friend's hand and, holding it almost casually behind his back, opened the front door. He and Dr. Wilkards walked onto the porch and stood under the gingerbread hangings.

The boy crept farther down the stairs until he could see half of each man's back and the angry faces gathered below the front steps. The leader was Edward Tirowen, father of the young man who had gone with Jason Glendauer to the Faro Pit.

Tirowen stood with his legs apart, pointing to Glendauer. He spoke through his teeth, his once-broken nose making him sound as though he had a bad cold.

"Fancy Mister Jason Glendauer," he sneered. "A rebel—now a murderer!"

Glendauer's hands remained behind his back. His posture was erect, yet appeared quite relaxed. "Mister Tirowen," he said very quietly, "you're an ass. I've broken your head once, I'll not hesitate to do it again."

"Too late for fancy talk, Glendauer. You stuck your foot in it this time. You're going to hang."

"I don't hang for swine, Mister Tirowen."

Ed Tirowen motioned to the men behind him. "We're not having a murderer loose in this town. Get him, boys!"

Three of the men started up the stairs, then stopped. Suddenly the evening was silent as death. Glendauer's hands were no longer behind his back. Three unholy snicks of a cocking revolver hammer tapped into the night.

The men stopped. They were looking eye-to-barrel into Dr. Wilkards's dragoon pistol.

Ed Tirowen remained where he had been standing. He lifted his arm and pointed a fat finger at the armed man. "Glendauer!" His voice was hatred itself. "You murdered my boy. You're a traitor and a cheat and you're going to hang."

"I'll not lynch, Mr. Tirowen—now or ever."

"You're yellow, Glendauer—just like the rest of your rebel scum. You'll hide behind a gun so you won't have to face the truth like a man. Fine old Southern gentry—cream of Virginney! Fancy Jason Glendauer! Gentleman. Ha! You're a liar and a coward, afraid to stand trial for murder!"

Jason Glendauer's already straight back appeared to stiffen even more. The pistol remained level and motionless as he took an almost leisurely breath. "I'll stand trial," he announced. "You get a qualified judge and a jury and I'll be there."

"Then come down here," Tirowen snapped, "and give up that pistol."

"The pistol stays with me, Mister Tirowen. You may call it my bail—my assurance against a lynch mob. You let me know the date of the trial, Mister Tirowen. You may rest completely assured I shall be there."

Jason Glendauer turned his back to the mob and, followed by Dr. Wilkards, entered the house and closed the door.

Outside the crowd murmured for a few moments, then slowly dispersed and, in groups of three or four, scattered away.

Glendauer returned the pistol to his friend as casually as if the weapon had been a walking stick. He appeared completely unaffected by the incident. His hands remained absolutely steady as he set two glasses on the waiting room table.

Dr. Wilkards took the bottle his son had brought from Little Gomorrah. Martin watched through the banister rails as his father filled both glasses and raised his. "Jason," the doctor said, "that took a great deal of courage."

Glendauer stared at his liquor for a moment. "I don't know," he said at length. "Is life so precious, really?"

Both men were silent a long time before the doctor looked up. "And the trial, Jason? You know the trial will be no better than that mob. Tirowen is powerful—an influential man. You mustn't stand trial."

"Mustn't?" Glendauer seemed genuinely puzzled.

"You can't, Jason. You must leave—"

Jason Glendauer put his glass down. He seemed utterly shocked. "Of course I'll stand trial," he said. "Don't you understand, Charles? I gave my word."

The circuit judge wasn't due in Sacamore until late August. Because of the anger of the townsmen and the talk being spread by Ed Tirowen, Dr. Wilkards asked Glendauer to stay with him and, as the hot and sticky days passed, constantly begged him to leave town altogether. At first, the gambler would answer. Then he would shake his head. Finally he refused to discuss the matter entirely.

While Dr. Wilkards was busy with his patients, Glendauer would amuse himself by reading or playing cards. Often he and the boy would talk. That summer, a deep and very important friendship grew between Martin Wilkards and his Uncle Jason.

One day as the two sat in the waiting room listening to the rain patter into the mud of High Street and watching it slither down the windows, Martin suddenly looked up. "Why did you go to war?" he asked.

Jason Glendauer had been watching the rivulets of water sliming the window panes and almost obscuring the green of trees beyond. He inspected the boy. "One day," he said very slowly, "you'll understand it all, Martin. We went to war because of the law. You see, we had made a monster and the monster began to eat us. Finally, there was no choice. It's better to die in the field than to live with the pain of an empty belly."

"But, you lost," the boy said. "They say the whole South is starving even now."

Glendauer almost smiled but his pale eyes remained quite serious. "Of course," he said in an almost matter-of-fact tone, "but that's because the dragon killed St. George." He looked out the window again and drew a deep breath. "Do you know," he said more seriously, "it was raining just like this at Appomattox. Just like this." Abruptly he got up, crossed the room and left through the front door.

Martin stared after him, not knowing what he had said or done to offend. Only after many years had passed did he come to understand why Jason Glendauer had walked into the rain that afternoon.

Ezekiel Wingate was the circuit judge. He arrived in Sacamore on the 24th of August to try all misdemeanors, thefts and other crimes. The trial of Jason Glendauer was saved for last.

The day before the trial, Glendauer asked young Martin a strange question. "Martin," he said, "how would you like to be a gambler?"

Not quite sure what the man meant, the boy told him he would like that.

Jason Glendauer took Martin by the shoulders. His expression was quite serious and determined. "Very well," he said. "You must stay exactly by my side during the entire trial. No matter what happens, or what I say or do, you mustn't be afraid. I promise no harm shall come to you."

The boy didn't know what Glendauer meant but he saw the almost feral determination in his eyes and he trusted him absolutely.

The trial was held on the 28th day of August, 1888, in the Episcopal Church on High Street. It was a hot day, fuming and blustering and gasping impotent against the thickness of air. The nave was strong with the sweat of men and the sweet smell that seeps from under the glaze of women's perfumes. Everyone from town and Little Gomorrah and almost all the people from the valley were crowded into the church, most obviously more interested in the life of one gambler than in caring for their own souls on Sunday.

Jason Glendauer was the first man to rise when Judge Wingate came in. He put his hand gently on Martin's shoulder as the judge sat down behind the pulpit and nodded to the jurors sitting in the choir.

Years before, Edward Tirowen had been a lawyer in Philadelphia. He acted as prosecuting attorney. Jason Glendauer told the court that he would defend himself. The trial lasted for three days.

On the first day, Tirowen told how the accused, although masquerading as a gentleman, was actually a man of low habits who made his living as a gambler in the saloons and brothels of Little Gomorrah. He was a man no self-respecting citizen would be seen with and was known to have an extremely short and violent temper.

"Why, Your Honor, the accused even threatened to kill me!"

He also claimed that Glendauer and the deceased had never been friendly, despite the noble character of the deceased, and that, on the 11th of July, with several witnesses present, Jason Glendauer had shot and killed Mr. Arnold Tirowen during a game of cards being played at the Faro Pit.

When Tirowen finished his opening address, Jason Glendauer rose. He told the court that he had not threatened to kill Ed Tirowen, but rather had mentioned his intention to break Tirowen's head. He said that Tirowen Senior had persisted in discussing political issues which were offensive to him, and the lawyer, drunk and in the presence of a lady, had used offensive language. He told the court he had been obliged to order Mr. Tirowen to stop his swearing. When the lawyer refused he had struck him across the face. At that time, Tirowen had threatened to have him killed, "one way or another."

He went on to say that the deceased, the son of Ed Tirowen, had, on several occasions, solicited his company for the purpose of gambling and that when he finally accepted on the 11th of July, the deceased had cheated at cards. When he had admonished the man, Tirowen the younger drew a revolver and cocked it. He admitted to killing him in self-defense.

The second day of the trial there were several witnesses. Genny Liggate was the first. She claimed she was an actress although there was no theater closer than Chicago.

Miss Liggate mentioned that Mr. Glendauer was a heavy drinker and at one time had struck Mr. Edward Tirowen across the face.

"And was my language offensive, Miss Liggate?"

"Hell, honey. It didn't bother me none."

"Mr. Glendauer?"

"No questions, Your Honor."

The second witness was Bartram Stubbs, proprietor of the Faro Pit. He told the court that Mr. Glendauer was in the habit of drinking and gambling at his establishment. He said Mr. Glendauer had showed a distinct dislike for both Mr. Tirowen and his deceased son, but he did not know the cause. Mr. Stubbs told the court that, on the 11th of July, he had seen Arnold Tirowen and Mr. Glendauer rise from the table at which they had been playing poker and had heard a shot. He saw the accused with a small pistol in his hand as Mr. Tirowen Junior fell to the floor.

Ed Tirowen put both thumbs into his waistcoat pockets. He thrust his head toward the witness and spoke through his broken nose. "And did the deceased have a weapon?"

"No, Ed. Can't say as he did."

"Mr. Glendauer?"

The Virginian rose and crossed the church to the chair that had been placed beside the pulpit.

"You're the proprietor of the Faro Pit, Mr. Stubbs?"

"I am."

"Isn't it true, Mr. Stubbs, that Edward Tirowen is the owner of that tent, its contents and the property on which it stands?"

"Well, sir, I—"

"Is it true?"

"Yes."

"And isn't it true that, on the 11th of July, Mr. Tirowen took the revolver that his son had drawn and, in my presence, gave it to you and informed you I had shot and killed an unarmed man?"

Bartram Stubbs looked at Ed Tirowen for a moment. He seemed worried but he faced the courtroom. "No, it's not! I seen you shoot him with that derringer of yours. It was murder."

Glendauer didn't move. His only expression was a slight tightening of his jaw muscles. "Thank you, Mr. Stubbs. No further questions."

Four other witnesses took the stand. They were all from Little Gomorrah and they all said the same thing.

On the third day, Ed Tirowen made his speech to the jury. He started soft and spoke for almost half an hour. But as he warmed to his subject, the sweat began to pour off him. It stained his armpits and wilted his collar.

"This man's a murderer!" he screamed. "He shot down my son in cold blood. If we allow him to live, he'll kill again. Your sons and brothers will die and God alone knows what he'll do to your daughters. He's a traitor and a killer and we don't need his kind in Sacamore. He needs hanging and hanging *now!*"

The people began to murmur as so many of them had on the night a month before. Judge Wingate was banging his gavel on the pulpit but no one seemed to pay attention. Three or four of the men who had been sitting in pews rose and started up the aisle toward Jason Glendauer and the boy.

Both rose to face them.

Still the men walked toward them. Their words were angry and confused. Only Ed Tirowen could be heard above the mumbles of the crowd.

"Get him, boys. We all know the verdict—Guilty! We'll string him up now!"

Before either Glendauer or the boy could move, two of the bigger men grabbed the gambler's arms and pinned them to his sides. He didn't struggle. Instead he looked directly at Ed Tirowen and said something that seemed almost ludicrously out of place.

"Mister Tirowen—you're violating the law."

Tirowen laughed. "Fancy talk for a murderer," he said. "Come on, boys. Let's hang the son of a bitch!"

Abruptly Jason Glendauer jerked himself free of the two men who had been holding him, but instead of backing away, he stepped forward and with the hand that had so recently been injured, lashed Ed Tirowen across the face.

The fat man almost went down under the force of the blow as Glendauer moved to Martin Wilkards's side. One hand went around the boy's shoulders. The other held the same small weapon that had killed Arnold Tirowen.

"Back!" he said through clenched teeth. "Back or the boy dies!"

The church hushed. Amazement or terror marked every face, but none more deeply than that of old Dr. Wilkards who stared in complete shock at his best friend now threatening to kill his only son.

In the hush, Jason Glendauer's quiet voice might have come from a sepulcher. "This is a court of law," he said. The barrel of his tiny pistol didn't move against the boy's head. "We are attempting *some* form of justice here. I killed Arnold Tirowen in self-defense. The man cheated at cards. I called him out and he drew a revolver. I'll not hang without an honest verdict."

One could almost hear the squeeze of perspiration oozing from every pore. Jason Glendauer was the only person in the building who appeared calm. He stood tall, impassive with one arm around the boy's shoulders and the other calmly holding a derringer to Martin's head.

Judge Wingate was the first to make a sound. He cleared his throat, then cleared it again. As Glendauer held the boy, the judge finally addressed the jury. He explained their duty and finally instructed them to ignore the outburst and to bring back a just verdict.

Slowly, awkwardly, the twelve men rose. Some turned to stare at Glendauer and the boy. Others obviously tried to avoid glancing in that direction as they adjourned to the vestry. Only after the door closed behind them did the whispers begin.

Jason Glendauer did not move. He held the boy and the pistol. His eyes never left the crowd.

The jury wasn't gone five minutes before they returned to

the choir. Judge Wingate looked to Glendauer and then to the jury foreman. "Have you reached a verdict?"

The foreman seemed nervous. He looked to the crowd and then to Glendauer. "He'll kill the boy."

"I'll not murder a child for a verdict." For the first time, there was an edge of contempt in Glendauer's voice.

The foreman swallowed. "On your word?"

"Yes. On my word."

The foreman swallowed again. "Guilty," he said. "We find the defendant guilty."

Martin could feel Glendauer stiffen slightly behind him. Then the man's hand fell away from his shoulders and the pressure of the derringer left the boy's head. Glendauer turned from Martin and, still carrying the pistol, walked to Judge Wingate. No one in the church dared breathe as the gambler raised the pistol to the judge. He held it before the jurist for a long second before he laid it on the pulpit.

Judge Wingate pulled the derringer nearer and wiped the gloss of perspiration from his very high forehead with an already dank bandanna. He took a deep breath, let it out and breathed again. He stared at the weapon before him and then frowned. "Why—" He seemed perplexed. "—it's not even primed."

Jason Glendauer shook his head.

"Is . . . is it—loaded?"

Again Glendauer shook his head. And again, the judge wiped at his forehead and pate as the murmurs began to whisper through the church. He put the bandanna down, raised his gavel and rapped twice on the pulpit for order.

"Jason Glendauer," he said, "you have been duly tried and have been found guilty of murder. Under the laws of this state, my duty is clear. It is the judgment of this court that you shall be taken hence and hanged by the neck until dead."

Jason Glendauer was confined to the guardhouse at Fort Wimiwa that night because there was still no jail in Sacamore. Charles Wilkards rode there with him after ordering his son to return home.

The boy did as he was told and with the emotional and physical resilience of youth even managed to gain a night's sleep. Still, with morning, he awoke confused, then afraid. He called for his father, but his voice rang empty in the old house. The boy looked into his father's bedroom and then downstairs before finally accepting the fact he was gone.

The fear within him grew to a horrid terror. The stark reality of the trial came back to him. The people of Sacamore were going to kill his Uncle Jason and, that frightening morning, he was sure they intended to hang his father as well.

As quickly as he could, Martin Wilkards dressed, then ran through town all the way to the fort. He talked to two of the soldiers there and, because discipline was slack and no one was a stranger, the sergeant of the guard not only let Martin into the guardhouse but into Glendauer's cell as well.

The condemned man and Dr. Wilkards were sitting at the single table. Except for the dimness of morning light and the bars on the window, they might have been in the waiting room on High Street. It was obvious they had been there all night.

As the boy came into the cell, Glendauer rose and, with his usual easy formality, bowed. "Good morning, Martin."

The boy was so relieved to find him alive he rushed to him and threw his arms around the man's waist. "Oh, Uncle Jason," he gasped. "Oh, Uncle Jason—"

Very gently, yet firmly, the condemned man took the boy by the shoulders and pushed him away. He looked down at him for a moment until he was sure the near-hysteria had broken, then, apparently satisfied, he reached into his waistcoat pocket, withdrew a large gold watch and snapped the hunting case open.

"Nine fifteen," he said almost absently. He snapped the hunting case shut, then looked to the boy again. "Martin," he said, "I should like you to have this watch. My father gave it to me when I went to war. He was a very wise man."

The boy could not speak. He could only stand holding the

watch in both hands as the guard came to the cell again and opened the door. Somehow, as though in a heavy-footed dream, he was able to leave the guardhouse and follow the men through the fort and over the rutted road to the single oak tree just below Watson's Knoll. His father, preoccupied with the condemned man, barely noticed the boy.

A small group of men had already gathered around the tree and a single horse pawed away its nerves under the dangling noose.

Jason Glendauer took Dr. Wilkards's hand. "Goodbye, Charles," he said. "There's a better land, I'm sure." Then he turned to the boy. "Goodbye, Martin." He smiled very sincerely and in the gesture the boy again saw the ghostly memory of other days. Again, as it had been the first time they met, he was convinced Jason Glendauer had stepped from the past.

"You will understand all this one day, Martin." He patted the boy on the head, then turned and, without orders or assistance, walked directly to the horse.

Jason Glendauer put his left foot in the stirrup and swung his right over the saddle as if he were preparing to lead a cavalry charge. He did not move or speak as his hands were bound behind him and the noose slipped over his head. When they slapped the horse from under him, he made no sound.

The boy turned away and clenched his teeth against a pain within his soul which was almost physical in intensity. His head was bowed and he held Jason Glendauer's watch in both hands. His father stood beside him, helpless to offer relief. He put one arm around the boy's shoulders and held him against his side.

The world might have stopped. No one there made a sound. It was the boy who was the first to move. He pressed the stem of Jason Glendauer's watch. The hunting case snapped open and he looked inside. There was an inscription etched within but he could not understand the characters. He handed the watch to his father.

The doctor glanced at it, then looked up to the slender body dangling from the tree. His expression, which a moment before had been bitter, painful and angry, changed. It was apparent he had seen some great truth and the knowledge of it had soothed him and washed away some of the agony of his sorrow.

The boy didn't understand. He stared at his father in silent wonderment.

Dr. Wilkards returned the watch to his son. "It's Greek," he told the boy. "It's the inscription on the tomb of the six hundred Spartans who died at Thermopylae." He glanced again at the dangling body, then back to the watch. " 'Stranger,' it says, 'you who pass by, take this message to the Spartans, that we lie here obedient to their laws.' "

The boy closed the hunting case and looked again to the body of his Uncle Jason. Strangely, perhaps, his eyes were clear. The entirety of the scene and of all life itself seemed in precise focus. Perhaps that is why he noticed something he had never seen before.

There were holes in the bottoms of Jason Glendauer's boots. They looked as if a pebble had been dropped and the swirling circles of water had suddenly been frozen.

But on that day, Martin Wilkards noticed something else and throughout the rest of his life he never forgot it. Jason Glendauer's boots were polished. There wasn't the slightest fleck of mud on the gleaming leather.

WAYNE BARTON

One Man's Code

A petroleum engineer for a Midland, Texas, oil company, Wayne Barton sold a dozen or so stories to *Far West*, the now sadly defunct California-based Western fiction magazine, among them this 1980 Golden Spur Award winner.

Barton's first novel, *Ride Down the Wind*, also appeared in 1980 and has been followed by such excellent book-length Westerns as *Return to Phantom Hill*, *War Horse*, and *Live by the Gun*.

At present he is collaborating with Stan Williams of Odessa, Texas, on a series of Western novels.

Heavy footsteps on the boardwalk woke Seth Gatlin from a dream of the mountains. For a moment he sat motionless, holding the picture behind his closed eyelids. Lately, he dreamed more and more often of the old days, of the chill bite of a beaver stream around his thighs or the warmth of his Crow wife, Sun Woman, beside him in the night. And lately, he was strangely reluctant to awaken.

"Mr. Gatlin?"

Seth had expected Marshal Calloway's quiet voice. He shook off the dream and opened his eyes, an old man drowsing beside the doorway of his livery stable, in a town where the mountains weren't even a blue shadow on the horizon.

"Good morning, Mr. Gatlin. I hope you're feeling better today."

"Tolerable. Just tolerable."

Seth's tone was sharper than he'd intended. He'd never had much meat on his bones, but he'd been gifted with a wiry strength that enabled him to best larger men. Now he was scrawny as a buffalo wolf in winter, and he felt his strength failing almost day by day.

He shook his head sharply. He was alive, and he could do for himself. He didn't need sympathy. Almost angrily, he squinted up at Calloway.

"What can I do for you, Marshal?"

"It's about Lonnie Weaver. I'd thought you might be coming to me."

"Now, why might that be?"

"I'm told you saw Lonnie shoot Steve Hubbard. I want you to testify about it in court."

Seth rubbed his stubbly chin. "Nigh half the town saw the killing. What makes this child so special?"

"Well—" Calloway hesitated, gestured to the boardwalk. "Mind if I sit down?"

Seth shrugged, and Calloway dropped down beside him. The marshal was a broad, dark-haired man, slow of speech and movement. He took his time getting settled against the splintery wall before he spoke again.

"I'll tell you, Mr. Gatlin," he said at last. "Half those so-called witnesses are afraid to say good morning. The other half would swear Lonnie shot Abe Lincoln, if it would get him hung." Calloway spread his big hands. "You're about the only man in town who isn't either feuding with the Weavers or scared green of them. Your word would carry weight."

"I can't see it, Marshal. The reason I ain't feared of the Weavers is I let them be. They let me be. I got no call to change."

"Neighbors should stand together, Mr. Gatlin. You were one of the first settlers here in Dryden."

That puzzled Seth. It was true he'd come to Dryden when it was little more than a stage stand and a tent saloon. He had spent the previous summer hunting buffalo, had guessed the price of hides was about to crash. He'd had a few dollars and a string of horses—he'd always been good with animals—and Dryden looked like a place that would need a livery stable. Before winter set in, he built a pole corral from willows cut along the creek and hired a couple of drifters to help him put up a barn.

That had been seven years ago. The town had a few hundred people now, with a hotel and a bank, and merchants who talked about a city of the future. And Seth had a place where he could live out his time. It was poor bull beside the mountains, but it was his. He wouldn't be a burden on anybody.

"Lots of folks came here after I did," he told the marshal. "But I didn't ask 'em to stay, and it ain't my part to watch after them. I'm not beholden to the town."

Calloway smiled a little. "Figured you might feel that way. I can't say I blame you much." He levered himself to his feet, hesitated. "Oh. I don't suppose you've seen my boy today?"

"Young Toby?" Seth hid his surprise. He suspected that the marshal and his son didn't talk much at home, but that was their business. "He hasn't been here. Wouldn't be surprised if he turned up later. Should I send him home?"

"No." Calloway frowned for a moment, shook his head. "You think on what I said, Mr. Gatlin, about neighbors helping each other."

"I don't ask help and I don't offer it. It ain't my way."

"Ways change, Mr. Gatlin. Good day."

The marshal tipped his hat and strode away. For a minute, Seth stayed motionless, casting his mind back to the fight of three days before. He'd been sitting in that same spot, enjoying the warmth of the afternoon sun, when Lonnie Weaver pushed out through the batwing doors of the saloon. As the marshal said, Seth had seen the whole thing.

Lonnie was the youngest of Sam Weaver's three sons. Just over nineteen, he had curly hair and a smile the local girls liked. He'd been smiling as he came toward the livery stable.

"Weaver!"

Lonnie spun around. Steve Hubbard slammed out of the saloon, stopped on the boardwalk.

"Weaver! I mean to talk to you."

"All right." Lonnie was still smiling, but his voice had a scornful bite. "You want to complain about losing your money or your girl?"

"Leave her out of this."

Hubbard stepped down into the street. He'd been drinking, Seth could see. Lonnie stood waiting for him, hands on his hips.

"Hurry up, cowpuncher. Cindy's expecting me."

"You're a liar!" Steve Hubbard yelled. "Just because—"

Lonnie's cold voice cut him off. "Nobody calls me a liar, mister." The easy smile was gone. "Are you too yellow to back that up?"

The warning in his words was clear enough even for Hubbard. The big cowboy hesitated. Lonnie grinned.

"Reckon so. I'll tell Cindy hello for you."

Hubbard let out a roar and charged, swinging wildly for Lonnie's head. Lonnie sidestepped and hooked hard into his belly, then smashed him in the mouth as he doubled over. Hubbard was tough enough to grab his opponent's arm for support and drive home one blow, but then Lonnie clubbed him to the ground.

The cowboy hit on his back with an impact that sent his sixgun flying from its holster. Lonnie kicked him in the ribs. His nose was bleeding from Hubbard's punch, and rage twisted his face.

Hubbard groaned, managed to sit up. "I'll get you Weaver," he muttered thickly. He groped for his gun, got hold of the barrel, and started it back toward its holster. "This don't end it."

Looking down at him, Lonnie smiled. "Then I guess we better end it right now," he said.

Hubbard understood. Desperately, he scrambled to one knee, trying to shift his grip on the pistol. Lonnie's sixgun came up smooth and easy. He waited until Hubbard found the butt of his Colt and started to raise the gun. Then he fired.

The bullet took Hubbard full in the chest. He fell back, still clutching the pistol, and tried to raise himself. Deliberately, Lonnie shot him again. Then he holstered his pistol and walked casually toward the livery stable.

"Saddle my horse, old man."

Seth led the animal out. Lonnie mounted, then tossed him a silver dollar.

"You saw that was self-defense. Be sure you tell the marshal that, hear?"

Seth closed his hand over the coin, squinted up at Lonnie. "That critter's mouth is cut up some," he said. "You oughtn't to use a spade bit on him."

Lonnie blinked uncertainly, laughed, and rode out. A crowd was gathering around Steve Hubbard's body. Seth ignored them, walked back toward his living quarters. It wasn't his affair.

Looking at it now, he still felt the same way. Marshal Calloway had brought Lonnie in, figuring to hold him in jail until the judge came through. And the whole town was worried about what Sam Weaver and his sons might do.

Seth had no doubts on that score. In a way, he understood the Weaver clan better than he understood townsfolk like the marshal. The Weavers were like the men he'd trapped with in the mountains, throwbacks to a time when the law was whatever a man had the strength to back up. He knew that as long as one of them was alive, Grady or Mase or the old man, they'd never let Lonnie stand trial for murder.

Bracing his hand against the wall, Seth rose and passed between the stalls to the back door. As he'd half expected, Toby Calloway was there, feeding bits of carrot to a colt penned in the small corral. He looked up.

"You were right about his leg, Seth. It looks 'most as good as new."

"Weren't really broke. His bones are still green." Seth jerked his head toward the doorway. "Come in here. I got something to say."

Toby's eyes narrowed slightly at the command. He reached out with another slice of carrot, letting the colt's velvet nose brush his palm. He was twelve, dark and stocky like his father, but there was a rebellious quirk to his mouth and a touchy pride inside him that must have come from his mother. Maybe that was what made Seth put up with him and his questions.

The carrot gone, he wiped his hands and followed Seth back to the living quarters adjoining the stable. The rooms were built neat and tight, with bits of furniture bought or built as they'd been needed. Seth didn't hold with pictures or other foofaraw, but he'd hung his old Sharps rifle on a couple of pegs over his cot, and the beaded belt that held his Bowie and its sheath was looped over one of the pegs. Those were about the only solid things he had to show for his thirty years as a free trapper, and he liked them where he could see them.

"Your pa was looking for you," Seth said. "Likely you should get home."

"Aw, he's busy now. He's always busy." The boy's voice was at once disappointed and proud. "He brought in Lonnie Weaver. Arrested him."

"Should've shot him," Seth muttered. "It would've saved a power of trouble."

Toby was shocked. "He couldn't do that. Not if Lonnie gave up. He's a lawman."

There it was again, the difference Seth could never quite pin down. Calloway believed Lonnie was a murderer, but he couldn't step outside the rigamarole of laws to settle it.

"Reckon you're right, young hoss. It was different in my day."

"Did you ever shoot anybody?" the boy asked quickly.

"That ain't a proper question, Toby. You don't want to just up and ask a man that."

"You've told me before about fighting Indians."

"Ain't rightly the same," Seth maintained.

He'd talked a lot to the boy, about his own green years, about the first trip with Carson on the Santa Fe trail and the later days in the north country with Bridger and Fitzpatrick and Black Jim Beckwourth. He knew it was foolish, but talking to someone seemed to bring the old times back, and the boy liked to listen. Seth had spun stories of Indian fights and the last great rendezvous in 1837 and the killing of the buffalo. Once, he'd even told about living with the Crows, and about Sun Woman.

"You had an Indian wife? What was she like?"

"Small, and didn't have much to say—quietlike, and she didn't run to fat like some of their women. And she had quick hands. Her sewing was always the best, and our lodge was the first with a cookfire after a move."

"Why did you leave?"

"We were in hunting camp. A trader from down-river brought the smallpox. I'd had it, but a heap of the People died. She died."

"My—my ma's dead, too. I don't even remember her. But I miss her, sometimes, anyway."

Seth knew now it was as well that Sun Woman had died. He could never have brought her to live among white men, and time had run out on the Crows even as it was running out on him.

That reminded him of Toby, and the reason he'd called him in here. He frowned at the boy.

"You tended the critters last week while I was ailing."

Toby's mouth pulled into a stubborn set that Seth had seen before. He folded his arms and looked at the floor.

"Somebody had to do it. They needed water. And you were sick."

"I'll pay you for it."

"Didn't do it for pay."

"I don't rightly care, boy. I won't be beholden." He crossed to the chest, took out a silver dollar—the same one Lonnie

had given him, he guessed. Brusquely, he held it out to
Toby. "Take this. Then git before your pa skins me."

For a moment, he thought the boy would refuse. Then
Toby reached out and took it, his eyes burning with hurt
anger. He thrust the money into his pocket and ran out,
banging the door behind him.

Seth shook his head. "That boy beats all," he growled. But
there was something about it that pleased him, and he
chuckled softly as he went about his chores.

Toward midday he cleaned up and had a bite to eat. Then
he went out for his daily turn around the town. He'd fallen
into the habit of walking every day, not because he craved
company but to ease the restless longing for the high country that rose in him now and again. Today his steps took him
up the main street. He nodded shortly to the banker, touched
his hat to a pair of ladies shopping. He was almost surprised
when he found himself pausing before the marshal's office.

Calloway might have seen him there, or maybe he was
just setting out on a routine round, for he opened the door a
moment later and stepped out onto the boardwalk.

"Why, Mr. Gatlin. Did you want to see me?"

"Just walking, Marshal. Just walking."

"Too bad. I'd hoped you might decide to testify, after all."

Seth looked at him shrewdly. "Suppose I saw it as self-
defense?"

"Mr. Gatlin, the Weavers are a pack of thieves and killers." The marshal's voice had a hard edge to it. "But I'm a
peace officer, and Lonnie's on trial for one shooting. If he's
guilty, he should hang. If not, he should go free. I want the
truth."

"Truth's a hard cat to skin, Marshal." Seth rested his hand
against the wall for a moment. "Your young'un stopped in.
I told him to get along home."

Calloway nodded soberly. "Thank you." He made to move
away.

"Marshal? If'n you're not set on hanging Lonnie, you
might think on letting him go. Likely his kin will take this
pretty bad."

"Likely," Calloway said dryly.

"They'll come looking to lift your hair. Best you swear in some help, at least."

"Scared deputies are worse than none at all, Mr. Gatlin. Nobody wants to face the Weavers if it comes to gunplay."

Calloway smiled suddenly, and Seth was surprised by the resemblance to young Toby. There was a difference, though. The boy had a sullen streak, an unformed stubbornness. In his father, it showed as a cool, rockbound determination.

"Not even me," Calloway said. "But it's my job."

Seth trudged back home, cranky and out of sorts. He'd babbled on like a greenhorn, over something that didn't touch him. Worse, it hadn't done a lick of good.

Customers were waiting for him just inside the big double doors of the stable. There were three of them: old Sam Weaver, gaunt and bearded like a prophet, taciturn Grady, Mase with his go-to-hell grin and his two tied-down guns. They were leading an extra horse. Sam Weaver passed the reins to Seth.

"Keep them inside. Don't unsaddle them." He laughed, showing yellowed teeth. "We may want to leave in a hurry."

He jerked his head at Grady and Mase. They followed him into the street, turning left toward the jail.

Not until Seth led the horses back toward their stalls did he see Toby. The boy was standing in the shadows, his eyes wide.

"Those were the Weavers," he said. "They're—everybody's saying—they're going to take Lonnie out of jail."

"Reckon so."

"But you don't understand!" Toby caught Seth's arm. "My pa doesn't have anybody to help him. They're all afraid. You've got to do something."

Seth made a quick negative motion. "Nothing I can do. It ain't my fight."

"But they'll kill him!"

"Reckon they might, if he tries to meet them head-on. I

hope he's smarter than that." He saw the look on Toby's face and tried to explain. "Listen, son, it ain't the way to do. Your pa nor the Weavers never mixed in my troubles. It ain't fitting I should mix in theirs."

The boy wasn't listening. "You're just like the others," he yelled. For some reason, Seth was surprised to see tears in his eyes. "I thought you were different. But you're scared, too."

"No such thing," Seth said flatly. He gave a yank on the reins. "Now I got work to do. See yourself out."

He tended to the horses, then snatched up a pitchfork and went furiously to work cleaning the empty stalls. The young'un should have been able to understand. In the mountains, you tended your own traps, made your own way, paid your rightful debts. That was how Seth had learned, and that was how he lived. Toby was 'most a man. He should be able to see the right in that.

The sound of a slamming door brought Seth out of his thoughts with a start. It sounded like the street door to his rooms. The boy must have done it, but he had no business in there.

For a moment, Seth went on with his work. Then a sudden fear struck him, and he laid the fork aside and hurried toward his quarters. As soon as he opened the door, he knew he'd guessed right. The Bowie knife still hung in its beaded sheath, but the pegs above it were empty. The old carbine was gone.

"That young scamp," Seth muttered. He remembered with complete clarity the day he'd showed Toby how to work the gun.

"Seth, is that a buffalo gun?"

"I've killed buffer with it, but that don't make it a buffalo gun. That's a Sharps U.S. Government carbine. I got it when I scouted for Gen'l Carleton."

"Can I see it? Please?"

"Well—this one time, I reckon."

"I can't hold it still. It wobbles."

"Loosen up some with your left hand, hoss. This old gun, it does things its own way. You just hold easy, and let it shoot when the sights line up."

"Boom! Right behind the shoulder. That's where you shoot a buffer, isn't it?"

"Certain sure. Then you pull down on the trigger guard and slide in another round. Leastways, you do that after you get up."

"Get up? Up from where?"

"From where the kick knocked you. Those old shells carry a heap of powder. I reckon I still have a box of them around here someplace."

Seth turned toward the chest where he'd kept the shells, but he already knew they would be gone. As he reached toward it, something on its top caught his eye. A silver dollar lay there, gleaming against the dark wood.

For a moment, Seth froze, his hand poised in midair. Then he picked up the coin, turned it in his fingers.

"That young—" Seth began. But it was just as he had said. A man took care of his own, and he paid his debts. He'd taught Toby that himself.

Hurling the dollar aside, Seth snatched the Bowie from the wall. He cinched the belt about his waist so that it was hidden by his shirt. Then he jerked open the door and ran.

He circled behind the general store, figuring to come up the alley and put himself between the Weavers and the marshal's office. He was afraid he might already be too late. As he slowed at the mouth of the alley, he heard Sam Weaver's shout.

"Calloway! Stand aside! We're taking Lonnie!"

The marshal's office was directly across from Seth. Calloway stood like an idiot out front, his pistol still in his holster. The Weavers were a few yards up the street, spread out so that Calloway couldn't cover them all. Grady, nearest the mouth of the alley, was barely twenty feet from the place where Seth stopped. He gave Seth a quick look, then shifted his gaze back to the marshal.

"Toby." Calloway was watching Sam Weaver, but something kept pulling his eyes away. "Toby, get out of here."

The boy didn't answer. He was in front of the saloon to Seth's left. The long stock of the Sharps was tucked awkwardly under his arm, and he was looking over the sights at the Weavers.

Sam Weaver grinned. "Don't try it, Marshal," he said. "We're coming in."

"Toby—"

Calloway broke off as Sam Weaver took a step forward. The marshal hesitated, and Mase and Grady edged a little farther onto his flank.

"Hold on!"

Seth's piercing voice startled everybody. Grady turned to look straight at him this time, and old Sam's cold eyes flicked that way.

"You want something, hostler?"

"That whelp has my gun. I aim to get it, right now. You've got no business with me, nor with the boy."

"Not a chance, old man." Weaver laughed. "I guess the marshal won't shoot if his cub's in the middle."

Seth looked toward Calloway. The lawman had made up his mind. There was no give in his face. He still meant to fight.

"Then I'm taking up the quarrel," Seth said quietly.

"Are you?" Sam Weaver frowned, some instinct warning him that here was a man like himself. Then Calloway stepped down into the street, and Weaver's attention snapped back to him.

"Grady, slap that old fool out of the way. We've waited long enough."

Grady moved across, grabbed Seth's shirt with his left hand. He drew his pistol, swinging up the barrel to club Seth aside.

Seth stepped into him. As smoothly as ever, his right hand swept up. He plucked the Bowie from its sheath, turned it, driving it up and home against sudden resistance until the guard thunked against Grady's breastbone.

For a moment, nothing happened. Grady gave a little surprised cough, then began to crumple. Seth grabbed for the pistol, but the dying man's hand was locked around it. Then Mase Weaver was turning, his hands flashing down for his guns.

"Pa, look out!"

Seth wrenched the pistol away just as the first bullet smashed into his ribs. He staggered back. Both Weavers were shooting now. Something hit him hard in the belly, and he went to his knees.

He was seeing everything with the unnatural clarity he remembered from fights in the old days. Sam and Mase seemed suddenly to remember the marshal. They started to turn, guns coming into line. But Calloway had been moving, too. His long-barreled Colt crashed twice, and Mase jackknifed forward in the street. A bullet plowed the ground at Calloway's feet. He fired again, but the sound was lost in the roar of the old Sharps.

Sam Weaver's head snapped back as if he'd been kicked by a horse. He slammed backward into a post, spun away, and sprawled on the boardwalk in front of Levy's store.

The echoes of the shots died away, leaving a shocked silence. Calloway glanced quickly toward Toby, saw the boy was all right. The Colt balanced in his hand, he went cautiously toward the Weavers.

Seth Gatlin leaned over the cold numbness in his middle, folding his arms tightly across himself. He didn't hurt at all, and he knew how bad that was. The belly wound didn't seem to be bleeding, and that was bad, too.

Someone caught his shoulders, turned him gently. He saw Marshal Calloway leaning over him. A crowd was gathering, now that the danger was past, but Seth saw only Toby.

"That was a fool trick, young hoss," he said.

"I did just like you said, Seth." The boy's face was wet with tears. "Held easy and let the rifle shoot when it wanted to."

He looked toward the still form on the boardwalk and swallowed convulsively, but his voice was steady.

"I hit him, too."

"Don't talk, Seth," Calloway urged. "You shouldn't have done it."

Seth chuckled, found the effort brought the taste of blood to his mouth. "A man's got to pay his debts." His eyes sought Toby again. "The old days are gone beaver, hoss. Likely your pa's way is best now." He paused a moment, rested. "You'd best keep the Sharps. A man needs a good rifle."

He closed his eyes. Doc Ainslee was pushing through the crowd, pausing as the marshal whispered something to him. Toby was speaking, too, but Seth Gatlin paid them no mind.

He was alone now, the dust of the street far behind him. His pack rode high and heavy on his shoulders, and he held his rifle easy in the crook of his arm. Sunlight struck down through the trees as he led his horse across the divide. Hunting had been good. Rendezvous was near, and somewhere Sun Woman waited.

Ahead of him, clothed in virgin green and alive with beaver, the mountains reached up until they touched the sky.

OAKLEY HALL

Horseman

Born in San Diego in 1920, Oakley Hall is a Marine Corps veteran of World War II and a former member of the Iowa State University's prestigious Writer's Workshop. His first novel (as "O. M. Hall"), a mystery story, was published in 1949, and his first Western novel, *Warlock*, in 1958. It was subsequently made into a Twentieth Century-Fox film by the same title in 1959. Hall's other Western novels include *Adelita* and *The Badlands*.

"Horseman," originally published in *The Antioch Review* in the fall of 1982, earned WWA's Golden Spur Award for best short Western story for that year.

In my life I have been a fool with liquor and a wise man with horses. I was born on a horse, or just off one anyway, for my mother died in a fall a month before she was due to be light of me, and they cut me from her there. Which was the last time I was throwed, except by whiskey.

In those days before the Big Dry-up, I rode for the Castle Hundred and proud of it. That was when the Squire's lands comprised a third of the Territory, who went to smash with the rest of the foreign owners when the country turned to desert.

I know that a man's memory will confuse him, and there is a true saying that the past has a rosier bottom than the present, but I can remember well the assemblies at the Castle, and the beautiful women, so fair-fleshed, with hair piled up to gleam like gem stones in the light of a thousand candles. You will ask if I remember the general at those affairs, and I will answer that he was only another youngster of an officer, though he had a powerful carriage even then. He was a hotheaded young fellow, and I am sure no better at fighting temptation than I have been in my life, and there was temptation and plenty amongst those ladies at the Castle.

The Hundred was green then, trees everywhere, and grassy meadows that would be a blanket of flowers in the spring. I remember the Squire and his guests hunting through the woods and meadows with that pack of white-and-liver-spotty hounds, the fox flying hell-for-leather with the dogs bellowing, and after them the riders coming. I was chief horsebreaker, and came to be trusted with more than mustangs, as I will relate. And did betray my trust which I would never have done if the liquor hadn't turned me into nothing more than a beast, as I will relate as well.

In those old times I remember the fat cattle, belly-down in grass like they were afloat in it. Cattle trailed down to the bottoms to drink at creeks that ran clear and fast and two yards wide. Those were prime days for man and beast, then.

The Dry-up came like a curse. The creeks dried up, and the Sweetwater turned to dry sand. Then you would see cattle baked into lumps of hide and horn in the dry bottoms, and all the fine foreign landowners, the Squire among them, went back to where they had come from, and their foremen and cowboys turned into rustlers and desperados, and I will not deny I was among them.

Those were terrible times, with all men at their worst. Water was brought in in tank cars on the railroad until the railroad stopped running. Prospectors searching for the Lost Dutchman Mine died of thirst and you would find dried lumps of hide and hair in the bottoms that was man and donkey. But others died beside prospectors, and of lead, and scalping knives. For it seemed all men were turned into

outlaws preying on each other, with Kimanches raiding out
of the mountains to pick off stragglers, and not just stragglers. Many times the cavalry was too few to drive them off.

But little by little the general began beating them back.
There would be a truce, then the hatchet dug up and more
fighting, and another truce. In the main the general won the
scraps, and that was a time when he was acquiring the litle
spreads that the Hundred had been cut up into. Putting it
back together by hook and crook; for there were some to say
that if a man didn't sell out cheap, that would be the next
place Kimanche would come down on, and the cavalry slow
to show.

I was riding with a bunch of turned-bad hands then, no
better than the fellows next to me. But I saw what the general was doing was right, putting things back together the
way it used to be, and so I went to him and threw in with
him.

So I became a horsebreaker, and trusted man besides. He
confided in me secrets that will never pass my lips, and I
was a help to him in many ways putting the Castle back in
trim. Besides the Kimanche beat to where they scarcely troubled any more, it even rained a time or two, as it had not
done in a coon's age. The grass came back a little, and Putaw
Creek even ran a trickle, though the Sweetwater never did,
and Bright City, where the fort was, became a considerable
town.

And then the general asked me to undertake a task for
him. I was to go east for a lady, and I knew that lady from the
old days. I promised I would bring her safely back to him.

For I thought I saw that it was all coming around again,
the great days returning. First the Kimanche beat back, then
the rains coming, and the fine ladies and gentlemen returning to the Castle. For I know it can come round again if the
right man shows up with his good sense, courage, and
strength.

When I came to the place where the general had sent me,
it was as though I had walked up to a mirror, spit and image

of the Castle in the old days. There was green river bottom, and forests sweeping down from the hills, so that it seemed any minute there would be a horn call, and a fox streaking out with the hounds and riders after it. A great stone mansion lay on the far side of a creek with a covered bridge over it, and a road spiraling tan against the green hillside.

A plump fellow in a uniform of red trousers and striped vest showed me up some stairs to where she was standing in a slant of sun from a window behind her, in a velvet gown with crisp ruching down the bosom and white lace at the sleeves. I thought she didn't remember me at first, but then she did, her rosebud mouth puckering once as though to blow a feather, and then softening into the winningest of smiles. All around her head was black hair in long sweet waves.

I told her what I had come for, and she nodded as though she knew it already. She said that we must hurry.

She went out of the room and came back with a carpet bag which she tossed some clothing into. She put on a hat that had a feather on it, and swung a cape over her shoulders.

I followed her carrying the carpet bag, which was heavy to pull my arm from its socket. Outside I swung the team around with the tassels on their harness nodding, while she whispered, "Hurry! Please hurry!" Then we were flying down the winding road. She never looked back one time.

She couldn't have said a dozen words to me on the long way to Cenotaph, where we booked seats on the train to San Hedrin and the Territory.

Jolting along the river and then through plains country in that coach, she watched out the window with her little chin braced on her hand like if she took her eyes off those mountains they would disappear.

For company we had a fat man and his fat wife in a poke bonnet, and a tall old drummer with hair like he'd been lightning-struck, and with him a pretty young woman with black hair, very demure most of the time looking down at her hands in black net gloves, though once in awhile her eye would catch mine sideways and smoulder like a hot coal. The other men would snicker and nudge each other whenever the drummer called her "daughter."

There were two prospectors with skin like bootleather, and those far-off-looking chips of eyes; a half-grown boy playing cards with his old lady aunt; and a blind man with black-lensed spectacles and a terrible scar twisted across his forehead at the hairline like a pink centipede. He sat his seat with a very military bearing, both hands clasped on his long stick.

Once my lady took a sewing kit from her reticule to fasten a button back to her sleeve. When it was done she cut the thread with a tiny curved blade she sprung from her finger ring, like a cat's claw coming out. She showed it to me, a ring with a pale face in cameo on it. I couldn't make out where the shiny little blade had come from, which pleased her.

When a new conductor came on my heart sank, for it was Dan Slagle from the Castle Hundred crew that I knew well, stepping along the aisle with his eyes slitted at the fat couple, the drummer and his daughter, and me and my lady, like tallying stock. He gave me a nod.

"Well, hello, Dan," I said, and he said, "Well, hello, J.D."

When he'd gone on I eased my piece in its leather and never rested easy for a moment, for if it was Dan Slagle, King Mac was probably nearby.

And all of a sudden there was a jolt that flung everybody out of his seat. Another jolt tipped the coach up. It went over on its side with screeching metal, women squalling, and men shouting. My lady and I were tangled together from the wreck, and we extricated each other, moving a limb here and another there. The screaming had stopped and all through the car people were sorting themselves out. No one seemed much hurt. The coach being on its side, fellows climbed on the seats to try to open the windows. Just then glass was smashed with a boot kicking it in, and a man dropped through. It was Red Hoskins I had known all my life. As I reached for my revolver Jack Carew ducked in from the forward passage with a gun in either hand. My lady stood holding onto my arm as we faced these two fellows, and I was in a cold sweat over my task of bringing her safe back to the general.

We made our way outside with the rest, Jack relieving me of my revolver as I went by him, saying, "There's a good fellow, J.D." Outside, and right side up again, I saw they had broken the two coaches and the caboose off from the locomotive like wolves cutting a calf out of a herd.

King Mac was sitting on a big black looking over the scene, with a dozen riders in a half-circle with him. The coaches had been laid on their side by a log stabbed across the rails as I have seen done more times than I care to remember. All this while my lady kept her hand on my arm, not tight but reminding me I was responsible for her safety.

King Mac slumped on that seventeen-hands black, the corners of his mouth turned down steep and his eyes sleepy like he had seen everything there was to see and it bored him to extinction, but here it all came past again. His chins ran down to his neck, his belly hung out before him, and his black hat was turned down all around to keep the sun off his face that was scabby with sun sores and bristled with beard.

He didn't seem to take any notice of anything in particular, though some of his riders nudged each other to see me and my lady, and one or two nodded to me not unfriendly.

My lady leaned against me like she was taken faint, and whispered, "Who is that man?"

And I told her he was King Mac.

Just then she cried out in a muffled way when Jack Carew came up behind her to stick his ugly face against her neck.

"Oh, this one do smell so *good*, J.D.!"

I hit him, but he bounced back with his revolver out and slashed me across the face so I thought I was blinded and sank to me knees. My lady helped me up and daubed at my bloody face with a handkerchief. King Mac must have signaled Jack off, for he did no more.

They tied my hands behind my back then, with a chunk of sapling through the elbows, and tied hers too, though I noticed they were gentler with her than with the other women. Very nasty they were with the drummer's daughter, sticking dirty hands down the neck of her dress until she flinched back, then Red coming up behind to make her scream and jump forward. They were vile men that rode for King Mac out of Putaw Crossing.

They said he himself was not interested in women in a natural way but could only watch others in the exercise of their lusts, though I have also heard he could take his revolver barrel so cunning and skillful to those Putaw women they would beg him never to stop.

We set out with some of his riders alongside, up a stretch of dry creek, and then turned north through winding washes and big boulders. My lady looked elegant even with her hat gone and her hair loose and her cheeks streaked with sweat. Her bosom stuck out proud from the way her hands were tied behind.

King Mac rode drag, hulking along with the motion of his gelding. Once my lady whispered to ask where they were taking us, but I shook my head I didn't know. I thought she and the other women were headed for Putaw Crossing, with some stops along the way. The men would be lucky to get much further at all. Though I noticed they had left the blind man his stick.

My lady spoke up to ask Jack Carew where we were going, and with a wink at me he said, "Oh, you'll find out soon enough, ma'am."

And she asked him who they were.

"Oh, just some fellows out rounding up the estrayed mares," he said, and grinned like he was the cleverest fellow alive.

The blind man had listened to this, and after it attached himself alongside us. I was able to help him step out faster by warning him what to watch out for in the path.

But the old woman, aunt to the boy, plumped herself

down on a little pile of rocks with the boy crying and trying to tug her to her feet. She announced that she would just as soon die here as further along. Red Hoskins drew his rifle from its boot and laid it across the saddlehorn aimed at her. She folded her arms and gazed back at him, while the boy ran a few steps away, and then ran back. I saw nothing pass between Red and King Mac except that Red shrugged and put his piece away. We all marched on past where she sat straight-backed, with her arms folded. The boy kept sobbing and looking back until Red told him to shut up, which he did.

At sundown we came to sheds and a big corral, with a low adobe wall on two sides, and, rising from that, posts with barb wire strung between, and branches woven through the wire. In the corral we all sat on bales and gunnybags that were scattered around, and waited for what was to happen next. And I waited with my heart in my boots.

King Mac strolled by us, rolled by, I guess I should say, in his bulk. He wore a greasy cowhide jacket with fringes on it everywhere. Whenever he moved there was a haze of motion, so it seemed he moved swifter than another. He stood bellied out in front of us, scratching inside two buttons of his shirt and chewing on something like a cud, while he looked my lady over with his black-glass chips of eyes in his scabby, bristly face.

"You have brought us a rare one, fellow," he said, in his high voice.

I said I was bringing her to the general, whose guest she was to be, and who would not take it lightly that we had been interfered with.

"What'll he do about it, do you suppose?" King Mac said, taking a good toothpick from his pocket and jabbing between his jagged, stumpy teeth with it. He scratched a thumbnail through the scabs of his chin, and asked if my lady had been educated.

She said she had.

"You know men's preferences, then, ma'am?"

She blushed very hot and did not answer him.

"Sometimes we must send the ladies to school for their lessons," King Mac said. "Other times it is unnecessary." There was a round of loutish laughter, to which he closed his eyes as though offended. When it was quiet he said to my lady, very low, "I will give you your freedom if you can discover mine. And much besides."

"Your what?" she said.

"My preferences." He swung away with his fringes all in blurry motion, and minced over to where the drummer's daughter was sitting, with men crowding around him as men will around a bully. My lady was looking at me with her hot black eyes.

"You will tell me who he is," she said.

She pried at me until I told her he was in the business of seizing women and selling them into a certain slavery, but I did not tell her that Putaw Crossing was the call station for every kind of rustler, deserter, miner, trapper, and every other hard, lonely, and desperate man, and every color of nigger, breed, greaser, and Chinaman too. Nor that it was said King Mac sold women to the Kimanches, who paid well for white women.

All she said was, "I see."

The blind fellow, who was seated nearby, said, "He is not an entirely heartless man. Do not despair."

"Thank you," my lady said, as though she had taken comfort from that.

Dark came like a curtain let down. King Mac's people had made a bonfire in the center of the corral, dragging in branches and pine knots, and my lady and I sat together on a pile of sacking as close to the adobe wall and fence as we could get, with the blind man next to us. On a post nearby, but high up, I could see the rusty handles of a pair of wire-cutters, though there was no way I could have reached them anyway, with my arms tied back aching as they were.

My lady moved closer as she was doing something behind me. She had the knifeblade out of her ring and was sawing rope, stopping once to catch her breath from exertion. Below us King Mac had climbed into a big highchair affair, like a judge's stand at a rodeo, made of saplings rawhided together. He had a jug which he lifted to his shoulder to suckle from, and, in the flickering of the bonfire, he cast a shadow over all that was a fearsome brooding thing.

When my lady sawed I could feel the heat of her breath on my ear. Then my hands were loosed, and in an instant I had the rope off, and her hands untied as well. Still I could not reach the wirecutters until my lady whispered to the blind man and borrowed his stick, and carefully I prized the cutters loose from their nail with the tip, flipped them toward me, and caught them as they fell. Squeezed up close to my lady and the blind man on the pile of sacking, I managed to clip one of the wires behind me with what seemed the loudest snap in the world. I clipped another, and another, finally turning to push a hole in the brush and loose wire. I helped my lady crawl through, and she dropped to the ground outside. Then I whispered to the blind fellow that it was his turn.

His fingers touched my face, quick and soft as the ghosts of fingers, exploring my features. "Do not worry about me," he whispered, "for men like these take me for good luck and will not molest me."

I swung through the wire after my lady, and we waited there, hardly breathing, but it didn't seem we had been missed.

There was a whicker, a horse tied to a post nearby. I helped my lady up behind the saddle, and swung up myself. I reined the animal away, whispering to him how I was counting on him, for likely he was one I had broke and trained myself like most in the Territory. He jerked his head like he understood, and we moved away from the big corral with my lady's arms locked around my waist. Then I touched my bootheel in and whispered again, and we made tracks away.

But as though King Mac, in his cunning, had laid a trap

for my downfall, looped on the saddlehorn by its thong, was a leather-covered flask. And of course I must sample what was in it, and go on sampling. With whiskey-heat in my belly, and my lady pressed up against me, before much of that night of riding was gone we had tumbled off the horse to rut like beasts on the bare ground.

In full light she cried out my name. I came to my feet still drunken. There were two of them not fifty yards away, Jack Carew and another, with his rifle slanted at us, a rat-jawed dirty face showing under his hat brim.

Jack said, "Well, J.D., I allus said you was one selfish son-a-bitch. Now!"

There wasn't a thing in the world I could do while my lady scrambled to cover her limbs, except to back on over to the paint horse that had carried us here, with my hands raised to satisfy Rat-jaw, who kept his rifle trained on me. Just then Jack Carew started to swing out of his saddle.

Well, there are those who say I can talk to a horse and know what the horse replies. I have had a hand in the gentling of most all the riding stock in the Territory; if I don't know each one by name, I know most, and Jack Carew's mare was called Magpie for her thieving habits. A horse will remember me because I chose to train him with words and whistles instead of hitting him over the face with a rope end like some ham-handed busters will do. Once I could whistle to bring in a horse at a gallop from a mile off.

So I called "Magpie!" just as Jack started to swing down. She jerked toward me, and Jack yelped as he started to fall. I whistled, not loud, and Magpie began trotting in a big arc, Jack with his boot caught in the stirrup bumping on the ground and squalling. The other fellow took up the chase, yelling to Jack to hold on and let go all at the same time. I had the lariat off the saddlehorn in a second, swinging a loop while Rat-jaw raced up beside Magpie, grabbing for her bridle. I settled a loop over him and with a yelp he came out of the saddle and hung in the air about a minute before he came down with a jar to shake his grandmother. I sprinted barefoot through thorns and sharp pebbles for the rifle he had dropped, and laid it in on him, his neck was broke where he sprawled there. His horse was high-tailing away, and Magpie had stopped to graze the dry grass. Jack Carew had managed to break his boot out of the stirrup. I took his revolver away from him while he sat there groaning. His face was scraped to raw bacon. "Jayd—Jayd—Jayd—."

I grabbed his hair and shook him hard, calling him an evil toad who had once been a decent man. "Jayd—" he kept saying, "Jayd—" until I blew his brains out.

I took Magpie's reins and, with the revolver and rifle, tender-footed back to where my lady, with her clothing all together, stood watching me with those great dark eyes I would drown in every time I looked into them.

I got my clothes on to cover my nakedness, with Magpie pulled between us like a curtain. She mounted the other pony while I tended to the horses, feeling their legs and lifting each foot to look at shoe and hoof, talking to them both the while so they would know how we were depending on them. Then I swung up on Magpie and we made ourselves scarce from there.

My lady and I never spoke a word of what had happened that night I got into the whiskey. We never spoke of that or much else either in those days of riding and nights with a little cookfire, she sleeping on one side of it, and I pretending to on the other, staring at a red coal gleaming in the ashes and listening to the small sound of her breath. It was in small roundabout ways that we came to know each other, both of us, it seemed like, afraid of speaking more than good mornings and good nights, or how many days now? and maybe a word or two when I had shot a little game for supper and we sat braising bits of meat over the fire.

So I brought her safe to the Castle, which had been my charge. I had done the best I could, but failed in what the general might never come to know of, and I'll never know myself whether he did or didn't. He could see, on the outside of it anyway, that she was worn to a frazzle. He greeted

her and me from the veranda of the Castle, very grateful to
me, shaking my hand, and courtly with her, putting an arm
around her and pecking at her cheek. And at that moment
she looked past him at me, opening her eyes wide so I fell
into them drowning, and smiled at me once and forever.

I had sworn off strong spirits and stuck with it for a long
time after the flask was left on that pony's saddlehorn. I
lived in the foreman's quarters just back of the Castle, and
often, despite myself, dreamed of those nights with my lady
across the cookfire, a little red coal winking a warning.

And one night when I was half-asleep, half-dreaming, I
knew there was someone in the room with me. I jerked a
hand for my revolver in its holster hanging from the bedpost, but did not touch it. There was a sniff of flowergarden
in the room.

In the morning it seemed to me it must have been one of
those dreams a man will have when he has been long without a woman and cannot control himself, until I got up from
my bed with the covers thrown back, and there was a white
flower with its petals mashed brown, one of the kind that
grew in pots in the solarium of the Castle and that I had seen
my lady wear in her hair.

After that once, though I would lie awake at night shivering to jar to pieces, it never happened again. Sometimes I
would almost weep in my disappointment, and in the end I
all but forgot it, as though it had been the dream I had first
thought it was.

Meanwhile my lady became plumper and plumper until
it was certain she was carrying child, and very near her
term. And one day riding in from the corral I saw clouds
rolling up black this side of the feathery clouds that hung
over the Bucksaws. These had flashes of lightning streaking
through them and were blackbelly rainclouds building up,
so high all at once their shadow came sweeping over everything. And in the first real rainstorm for as long as anybody
could remember, my lady was delivered of the most beau-

tiful girl child as this world has ever seen. They called her
Flora.

Before she was three she was sitting a mare fine as you
please, a good seat on her, straight little back, and a commanding way she had of looking at you with her chin set
and those eyes that seemed to gather in right away just what
you were or weren't, but pink lips smiling as though to
show she understood and forgave. She was her mother's
very light and life when in her pinafore and a pink ribbon in
her golden hair she ran to my lady, who would snatch her
up to cover her with kisses. And the general's also, who
often sat in the solarium when he was at the Castle, with his
book, and a blanket over his knees, and Flora standing beside his chair touching his medals and asking about each
one.

When it came time for the child to learn the ways of
horses, it was me that was turned to. First, in the little ring
I had had built, I would let her turn and turn at the end of
a rope on the gentle mare Jessie, sidesaddle in her velvet
riding habit like her mother's riding dress, and her black
velvet cap with a feather in it. Then, with me beside her we
rode close around the Castle, and later down the hill and
splashing through Putaw Creek where water ran now.

I would only have to tell her once to hold the reins higher
or tip her quirt a hair straighter, and she had done it and
kept it that way, her mouth tight with her concentration.
Now there was peace in the Territory, when we passed a
band of Kimanche she would raise her quirt just so, while
the young chief returned her greeting just the same, raising
his rifle or spear as she had raised her quirt. The same with
a squadron of cavalry, who would salute her very formal
and as though she had been the general himself. Once we
saw a pack of black riders off to the north that must be King
Mac's, a great rush of hooves and dust and jammed-together
men, too far off to make much out of, although I felt my
blood turn to whey at the sight of them. But they showed no

interest in us, and came no closer so that I thought we were safe from them here because of the general and cavalry at the fort.

But another time when we were out together we saw four riders trotting along a ridge line. At the distance we could make out that one of them was so small it might've been a monkey sitting his pinto horse, and another much bigger than the other two. Closer, they reined up to look us over, and I spurred Billy-bub so as to get between them and Flora. For the big one was King Mac, in a black slouch hat and about an acre of fringed white buckskin; with him one of the black riders, a boy that looked no older than Flora, with a mean, squinched face glowering down at us, and a woman seated sidesaddle, all in black velvet, with a cap of black feathers over a white face. It was the Drummer's daughter from the train. I didn't get my breath right until the four of them had swung away to disappear over the ridge, and we had got distance between us in the opposite direction.

Flora asked who they were, and I replied that they were from Putaw Crossing, which was on the other side of Helix Hill from the Castle, and was a place I hoped she would never see, for it was a filthy place.

"Are those bad people, J.D.?" she asked me.

"Yes. Bad."

"How can you tell?"

"For one, they have got different ways of looking at you, kind of sideways instead of straight on."

"But could you tell that from here?"

"So could you, which is why you asked about them."

The whiskey was after me again. It would gripe my insides like a halfhitch on the strain for one swallow of the stuff. I had sworn I would not drink in my room, and I did not, but I began to stash bottles here and there, one in a cairn of stones in a place Flora and I would pass when we rode out. I made sure we rode close by there, and with the excuse that I must relieve myself, which was true enough, walk down into the bottom and around a crag of rock, where I would take out my bottle and have a swig or two of whiskey.

And so I did this one day, taking the bottle from its hidey-hole with the glass blister-hot where the sun had got to it, and uncorked it, and knocked back a long pull, standing there panting and hating myself and everything else. I tipped the bottle up for another dose to wash out the fire, and a third to drown the ashes, when there was a heavy drumming I could feel through my boot soles, like a flash flood bearing down from a cloudburst in the mountains. Then it was hooves, a herd of buffalo it seemed, so many, building and building but whatever it was invisible except for a rise of dust coming on. I began to run back to where I had left Flora, so slowfooted it was like running in quicksand, and my shouting drowned out by those beating hooves. Then they passed and went on, and the dust cloud passed along. I ran on panting and knowing I was too late. She was gone, with only the tracks of a great bunch of horses heading off to the north where the dust was still moving.

I set off riding hard following those tracks. The dust faded away before me. There was stony ground, and then a place where some tracks swung off to the left while the others ran straight ahead, and further along another party veering to the right. I didn't know what to do but keep spurring after the main body, though what I would do if I caught up I didn't know. Then there was hard ground for a spell, and a tangle of rocky draws, and night coming, and that was the end of it.

I rode back to the Castle with a half-moon sailing in scud clouds above me, slow and slower up the winding road toward the lights of the Castle windows. I dismounted there and climbed the steps with my hat in my hand.

Inside my lady came running toward me, with the general behind her, and two officers from the fort with him. "Where is my child?"

When I told her what had happened she didn't speak a word, and the officers made a great hubbub that they would ride out, they would find her and bring her back, though I saw the general only crossed his arms on his chest in that way they lay dead men out sometimes. My lady crouched back against the marble fireplace there. She said, "It is a judgment on me!"

The two officers stopped their foolish talk and turned to try to comfort her. But she burst past them with the poker raised high to brain me, her face as fierce as a tigress. I did not even put up my hands to protect myself.

But she did not bring that poker down to kill me for my sins, for just then the general fell. He fell like a tree falling, not even trying to ease it, just toppling straight over with a crash on the parquet, like a dead man.

In the months of my wandering I took the pledge and failed, and pledged again and failed again in drunken shame, and misused myself in many ways. And one day, through an old acquaintance met by chance in a saloon in some trailhead town, I learned that my lady had never got over her grieving, that the Castle had been abandoned and was run down to ruin, and she and the general were moved into Bright City, where he never rested sending out cavalry troops to search for the band of renegade Kimanche that had stolen his daughter. But I knew it was not Kimanche that had taken Flora.

And so it was I returned to Bright City, coming in past the adobe fort, where a trooper with a rifle paced before the open gate and a bit of striped color hung from the flagpole as limp as I felt; and on along past the dump and Boot Hill, and into the town square with the dust from Blackie's hooves itching on my face. A carriage drawn by a fine team of grays came at me swaying on its thoroughbraces, a big sergeant with yellow chevrons on his sleeve up on the box. Seeing the two gold stars on the door I brought a hand up to jerk down on my hat brim, for I knew the general was inside that carriage, though I could not see him through the window.

I sat Blackie with my hand still pulling on my hat brim as

though saluting, dust settling over me as the carriage jounced on by—heading for the fort where my lady was.

I gave Blackie a low whistle to start him along. For I knew I had not come back to Bright City, nor the fort either, but to Putaw Crossing where I must find Flora, and if King Mac decided to put me under for shooting Jack Carew and Rat-jaw that time when I snatched my lady free of him, why that was all right; and if I had to go into harness like those other fellows I had known in the old days, in order to snatch Flora free, then that was as it must be too.

It was sunset, with the sun sinking blood red into the western clouds when I rode out along the railroad tracks, the rails with rusty flashes of light along them. Coming into Putaw Crossing, the air was filled with dust mingled with smoke and the open-sewer stench that seemed to get caught in my clothes so that I could smell it on myself even when the breeze veered around.

At the crossroads I turned Blackie uphill, a bridge sounding hollow as a coffin beneath his hooves. In black night we mounted a pot-holed road past a solid front of storefronts under a wooden awning. There was a creak of a shutter in a wind I couldn't feel, and once a caterwauling and two cats tearing across the way in front of us. Blackie jumped pole-legged and then stood steady, shivering, while I patted and whispered to him.

There were sounds in the silence now, a voice raised somewhere, and laughter and a spate of tinny music shut off like a door had closed. I could remember when there'd been no more than a dozen adobe and tin shacks at the Crossing, and now the hill was thick with them.

Pretty soon I could make out dark forms of men, and lights showed where the road narrowed between two squatty 'dobes, with candles or lanterns inside. Women leaned out of windows, many of them in their bare flesh, calling out to the men passing, me among them, sometimes sweetly but more often coarse to chill your belly.

There was a big horse-barn at one of the turnings, there

must have been a hundred horses stalled inside, and I left
Blackie with the one-armed hostler there. King Mac's "palace" was on up the narrow, curving way another half a mile,
he told me.

More men crowded the way, some few in town clothing,
most in rough dress and many in leather jackets aping King
Mac's buckskin fringes. There were hardrock miners in their
sashes, working men in heavy boots, skinners, drifters, ruf-
fians, and hardcases of every shade of color. From a window
above me a redheaded woman opened the blouse of her
dress to scoop her breasts at me. " 'Ey, 'andsome, you come
see me, eh? Further up they's all clappy." When I went on
past she spat down at me.

I could not even look down the side streets of cribs,
though I knew I might have to before I was through here.

The cobbled street led along a ridge where there was a
breeze with the sewer stink blown away for a spell. Above
the slot of a canyon a black peak towered, which, as I came
up further, I saw was not a part of the hill but a tented,
sprawling structure with lights piercing its sides. Just here
three of the black riders leaned together like blackbirds
watching me come past them. One of them was Jim Eggers,
who chose not to recognize me, nor I him.

There was another cross-street of cribs, with the whores
hanging out the tops of the dutch-doors, and as I hurried on
past I wondered if each one of the black riders had come
here in this same way, with a blight on his conscience and
no decency left him, or on some hunt that put a good face on
his coming to Putaw Crossing and King Mac's service.

So at last I reached the top with the "palace" piled up
before me in a confusion of lights and shadows. Nearer was
a long building that had burned, with the roof timbers fallen
in; all at once, like a kick in the belly, I understood that the
"palace" was no less than the Castle, for Putaw Crossing
had grown up and over Helix Hill. Coming up the back way
I had not realized that until now.

I stood there trying to catch my breath, staring at the Castle which was so changed, with the outbuildings burned. On a broad veranda I could make out the pale glow of cheroots where men lounged on benches. Someone sent a butt spinning sparks out into the dark. Each of the steps up to the veranda seemed three feet high as I climbed them.

The first person I saw, sitting above the pack of people inside, was a big, wall-eyed shotgun, slumped on his lookout stand between the faro layouts. He nodded to me just as though he had been certain I would come in the door at that very moment. Beyond him stairs curved to a landing. Walls had been knocked out to make the ballroom bigger, while the height seemed lower, as though the Castle had slumped down somehow.

I was nervy as a spooked horse as I made my way through bunches of men who paid me no attention, and whores with their bogus smiles and winks, until I came to the bar, where first I ordered a whiskey, then changed my mind. I jumped half out of my skin when there was a slap on my back.

"Well, hello, J.D.!"

It was Bobby Kettle from the old Hundred, in the rusty black the hands all seemed to wear here, scratchy little beard with a thin dark mouth grinning out of it.

"Well, hello, Kett," I said.

"Whiskey with an old pard, J.D.?"

I said I had taken the pledge, and he shrugged and set about swinging his elbows to clear a space for us among the men ganged around the bar. Those who weren't black-dressed were quick to make way for one who was, and the barkeep hurried to bring whiskey and a glass.

"Come out to join the boys, have you?" Bobby Kettle said.

"Just thought I'd look in, Kett. How is everybody?"

"Oh, everybody is healthy and prosperous," he said with a wink.

All at once there was shouting that shrilled to a screech, mixed with a snarling rousting. I switched around to see a man hurl himself out the door with a great black hound on his heels. There was laughter like the toadying laughter for

a bully at another's expense. King Mac stood spread-legged
on the landing, big as a grizzly in his pale buckskins, hat
brim pulled down and a cigar stuck in his jaw. Beside him
was a redheaded boy in a kind of dickey-shirt, with a nasty,
freckled, squinched-up face. I had seen him with King Mac
once before, and I looked for the drummer's daughter in the
half-open door behind them, but didn't see her.

With a stirring and pushing this way and that, the black
hound trotted back inside, nails clattering on the floor. He
raced up the steps and haunched down beside the boy, who
patted him and in the silence, in a shrill, mean voice, said,
"Good dog, sir!"

"That's a big dog," I said to Kett.

"He will just take out after a man for no reason sometimes," he said, and giggled.

The boy took something from his pocket and dropped it
bouncing down the stairs—a red ball. The hound lit out
after it, down and across the room with people piling out of
the way, some of them falling, and women squealing, until,
with a scraping clatter, the dog caught the ball and trotted
back up the stairs to return it to the boy, who patted him
some more. All the while King Mac stood there sucking on
his cigar and glancing around, so that I found myself sidling
to get behind Kett.

Another rusty-black fellow clapped me on the shoulder
and called me by name, though I couldn't recall his. Others
came up to shake hands, and more whiskey was poured
with me still managing to refuse a glass. And when I glanced
back toward the landing, King Mac, the boy, and the hound
were gone.

One of the fellows asked if I wasn't the one that was
supposed to be able to talk to horses. "How about mules?"
another wanted to know.

They were a hard-eyed, sharp-jawed bunch, dirty-faced
like they hadn't washed this month. They were quick to
nudge one another and have the laugh on someone else.
Now they kept after me very scornful, who was the one

supposed to be able to talk to horses, and I pretended to think it as funny as they did, though finally I said there might come a day and a reason for me to call in all the riding stock in the Territory, and then we'd see who was on foot.

This gave them a great laugh. They quieted down when a tall, bare-headed fellow came toward us. He had black spectacles on and swung a stick out before him, saying "Pardon. Pardon, gentlemen." He was greeted very polite by those around me, and called Lute. He was the blind man from the train, with that twisted scar on his forehead.

He came close to me and asked me my name, and, when I told him, if I would mind his touching my face: "For I must have other means of seeing than the sight of my eyes."

His fingers, that I remembered, chased over my features, light and quick, and like he was remembering me, too.

"Think you'll know him next time you see him, Lute?" Kett said, to snickers. And I heard another fellow whisper, "Damn-all how he knows when there's a stranger showed up."

"J.D. used to ride with the old Hundred bunch one time, Lute. Come back to join up again."

The blind man looked like a young fellow who had been struck old in an instant, his face young and old at the same time. A pulse ticked in the scar.

He said, "If you gentlemen would pardon us, I'd like to have a word with your friend. What I have felt in his features may be of value for him to know."

Kett said, "Lute can tell a man's fortune fine as any gypsy woman!"

"Do you see a table where we can have privacy?" the blind man said in a low voice. He took my arm, and I led him to a table in the corner. When we had seated ourselves he commanded me to put out my hand.

Leaning forward he made to be tracing lines in my palm, whispering, "You must tell me why you are here!"

I told him that I had come to find a child who had been stolen, a girl I thought must be in this place; and that her mother, who was out of her senses with grief, was the woman who had been with me when King Mac had derailed the train.

"And you are the father?"

I said that the general was the father.

He folded my fingers into my palm as though finished reading what was there, and leaned back with the round black lenses of his spectacles fixed on me. He said, "The child is here. She is an influence for the good."

My heart began to bang on my ribs. "It was my fault she was taken, you see," I said. He was silent, considering, his mouth a flat line. "The mother—" I started, but did not go on, for he had nodded in decision.

"Very well," he said. "I can help you take her from here. But how will you escape from the Crossing? There would be two hundred riders after you."

"You can leave that to me," I said.

"Very well. Listen to me: in five minutes' time you will leave this room. There is a door at the end of the veranda that will be unlocked. I will meet you inside." His chair jarred back as he rose. Without another word he headed across the room, stick flicking ahead of him, a head taller than anyone else there: "Pardon, please, gentlemen; ladies!"

I wandered among the gambling layouts, watching a play then moving along. One of the fancy-dressed women attached herself to my arm, but I shook her off, saying, "Later." When I judged five minutes had passed I strolled on outside, as though I was just stepping out for a breath of fresh air.

I opened the door at the end of the veranda on pitchy blackness. My arm was caught and I was pulled inside, the door closing behind me, a bolt rattling home. Lute thrust a bit of leather into my hand, the end of his belt.

"Hold to that. I know these passages well."

He set off at a good clip, pulling me behind him. I brushed a wall of splintery wood, then one of dressed stone. We were in a long passageway, very narrow. I remembered in the old days hearing of secret ways about the Castle.

"Steps," Lute said. It was a long flight up, making a right turn and then another. Once there were glimmers of dusty light from cracks in the wall, so that I had a glimpse of him climbing before me, holding the other end of the belt. Then there was another long passageway, and more stairs, until I had lost all sense of direction. At last he halted, so abruptly I banged into him from behind. He worked at something in the wall and became visible again in a dim square of light. It was a judas window. He pulled me to it.

In the exact center of a room Flora sat on the floor with her back to me. She was wearing a pinafore, and her long blonde hair, caught up in a blue bow, hung down her back. Squatting facing her was the redheaded boy. The big dog sat, tongue lolling, beside an open door in which the drummer's daughter stood, sumptuously dressed in black velvet with white lace, bare shoulders gleaming. Her lips were moving; she and Flora seemed to be conversing past the boy and the dog. I could make out voices, but not the words.

"Tell me what you see!" the blind man whispered in my ear.

I described the room and the people in it. Meanwhile the woman disappeared with a flick of her black skirt.

Flora gestured with her hand and the boy rose and retreated across the room. A shelf there held dolls seated against the wall. He brought one of these back to Flora, who incorporated it into some game she was playing, which was invisible to me. He squatted before her again.

Tapping my arm, Lute demonstrated that the square of smoked glass could be slid to one side, and that we stood behind a secret door into the room, which was secured by bolts at the top and bottom.

Flora gestured again, I heard the distant voices again, there was considerable more back and forth talk, and the boy, hands in his pockets, stalked out of the room.

"The boy's gone," I whispered to Lute. "Now there is only the hound."

He nodded as though that was to be expected, and pressed

something round into my hand. It was a red ball like the one
the boy had tossed down the stairs. "You must be certain it
goes out the far door," he whispered, and slid the glass
aside.

I aimed the ball, flipped my wrist several times to limber
it, and tossed the ball through the judas window. It flew
over Flora's blonde head, bounced past the hound and out
the door. The dog leaped after it, skidding around the corner
and out of sight. Lute had slid the bolts and I pushed the
door open. Flora's astonished face swung toward me.

"J.D.!" She scrambled to her feet and ran to me. I caught
her in my arms, pulled her back through the door while Lute
swung it closed behind us and threw the bolts just as the
hound slammed into the door. I pressed my finger to Flora's
lips in the dust-smelling dark.

Now the boy's voice was audible; "*Florrie*. You come out
from where you're hiding, you hear—" Then Lute slid the
judas window closed.

We hurried blind along the dark passageway, me holding
to Lute's belt end with one hand and pulling Flora along
with the other. "Step!" Lute whispered to me, and I whispered "Step down!" to Flora. We shuffled down the first
stairs.

"Are you taking me to my mother and the general, J.D.?"
Flora asked, and I said I was.

I touched dressed stone again, but Lute continued to de-
scend, a ramp now instead of stairs, raw rock walls, mossy
and damp. Further along I heard water trickling, and there
was a feel of other passages drifted off this one, with puffs of
cooler air sometimes and once a swatch of starry sky giving
light enough for me to see the blind man hurrying along in
the lead, and Flora's pale face behind, her tight hand gripping mine. We had to halt to pick our way over a rock fall.

"I knew you'd come, J.D.," Flora panted. "I'll be so happy
to see my mother and the general again! Have they been very
worried?"

"Very worried," I said, and asked if those people had
been bad to her.

"They were as nice as they knew how to be. But they are a different kind of people, you see. They look at you out of the corners of their eyes the way you said, but then if you are straight with them they stop doing it."

"We must move swiftly," Lute said, and we hastened on. All at once we were under the stars again, with all around us the feverish clamor of Putaw Crossing. I saw we were not a hundred steps from the big stable where I had left Blackie. The blind man remained behind the pile of rubble, where the tunnel had come out. When I said he must come with us, he only shook his head.

"Others may need me here. But you must hurry. There will be many men in pursuit."

"You can trust me now," I said, clasped his hand once, and hurried Flora down to the corral. There was no light, but I found Blackie quickly and boosted Flora up behind the saddle. I gave a low whistle, and heard the answering stirring and whickering of the other animals in that place.

I swung up and cautioned Flora to hold on tight. Her arms came around me, and I could feel her warm face pressed to my back. I jammed my knuckles to my lips and blew such a blast as I had never blown before.

Behind us in the corral a terrific racket began, and the one-armed hostler, hurrying up with a lantern, gawked open-mouthed at Flora and me and the open doors of the horsebarn behind us. He backed away, swinging the lantern like a railroad switchman.

I pushed Blackie into a hard trot down the cobbled street, men jumping aside with yells and curses. I blew another whistle to rattle the windows. Just then one of the rusty-black riders leaped out to try to catch Blackie's reins, and I jerked out my piece and cold-cocked him with the barrel. We rode rattling on downhill.

The whole stampede of us, Blackie in the lead, and all the horseflesh of Putaw Crossing swarming after, surged on down the street between the dark shacks and storefronts, thundered across the bridge, and swung north on the road

for Bright City. When I looked back over my shoulder it
seemed that all the horses in the world were galloping after
us in the starlight. Far back I saw a rider, but he had disappeared before I could unship my revolver. Her arms clasped
around my waist, Flora spoke to me sometimes, but I
couldn't make out what she said for the pounding of the
hooves. Horses had caught up on either side of us, a big bay
named Lopey on the right, and on the left a black and white
pinto I couldn't recall the name of. Others were saddled,
and many trailed ropes. I gave a whistle from time to time to
keep them coming.

When we reached the fort a white quarter-moon hung
over the Bucksaws and the sky was paling for dawn. The
trooper at the gate stood with his carbine at a half-ready,
gaping out at Blackie and me with Flora pillion, and most of
an acre of horses crowding around us. I swung out of the
saddle to lift Flora down, so tired she could hardly stand.

"Take Miss Flora to the general, pronto!" I said, and the
guard gasped. He clutched for her arm.

Flora said, "J.D., you just wait right there till my mother
comes!"

"No," I said. No, I just wanted to secure these animals
inside, for I'd bet the cavalry could use some remount. Then
I'd be on my way.

The trooper rushed her inside the gate, with her little face
turned back toward me and a hand raised up and waving to
me to wait.

It took me some time to chouse those Putaw horses inside
the fort, and swing the gate to, and mount up on Blackie
again. My lady came running outside in her long wrapper,
with her hair up in a cloth, to stop by me with her breast
heaving and a hand held there, and those black discs of her
eyes fixed on my face. The white knot of her hand sought
mine where I held the reins. And she said, "You have
brought me back my child!"

I said I had brought her back, who had lost her in the first
place.

I drowned again in those black eyes, and she whispered the name of a place in Bright City. Just then the general trotted outside holding Flora by the hand. I raised up an arm in greeting to him, pulled Blackie to his haunches, whistled to make him jump, and lit out of there.

I found the place in town she had whispered to me, which was a hotel, and I lay there on the bed with my hands locked beneath my head staring up at the waterstains on the ceiling. Then I went down the street to buy a glass of whiskey for my dry throat, and ended up bringing the bottle back to my room.

The next morning I woke up not even sober yet, to smell on the pillow beside my face the scent of a white blossom laid there by someone who had come, and gone.

WILLIAM F. BRAGG, JR.

The Ten Sleep Mail

Like James Bellah, Bill Bragg was the son of a noted Western writer (Williäm Frederick Bragg, Sr., author of such novels as *Outlaw Moon, Buzzard's Roost, Texas Fever,* and twenty others published between 1936 and 1959) and like that of his father, Bragg's life and work were centered in Wyoming.

Bill, Jr., a one-time prizefighter, served in the Marine Corps in World War II, and was widely known in Wyoming as a state historian, teacher, public speaker, radio talk show host, and public information officer for Casper College.

"The Ten Sleep Mail" earned the Golden Spur Award for 1983.

Bragg died on May 10, 1988.

Sam Stringer had been a Confederate soldier in the Civil War. As a Johnny Reb, he really was in the freighting end of the war because he was an expert with a team of mules and therefore wound up hauling supplies to the hard-fighting Stonewall Jackson in the early stages of the conflict. When Jackson was killed, Sam fell heir to the job of supplying the dashing Confederate cavalry commander, J.E.B. Stuart.

When the war was over, Sam drifted West. The South that he knew had disappeared in shot and shell—in flame and smoke. So he moved out West just in time to get a job helping haul supplies for Colonel Henry B. Carrington's long soldier column on their way past Fort Laramie in the summer of 1866 to build Forts Reno, Phil Kearny, and C. F. Smith along the Bozeman Trail.

Good teamsters were in demand, so Sam had no trouble landing a job. Oh, he took a lot of kidding from the infantry and cavalry soldiers with Carrington because he, Sam, had lost the war. But with the war in the South behind him and a new, red enemy in the offing in the form of Arapaho, Cheyenne, and Sioux led by Chief Red Cloud, Sam knew he was really being joshed. Besides, a good many Southerners were "joined up" with the Yankee soldiers, or "walk-a-heaps," as the Indians were apt to call the infantry, and "yellow-legs," or cavalry, a term given them by the Indians because of the yellow stripe running down the horse soldiers' legs.

When Sam pulled his four-mule team and big old freight wagon into the Crazy Woman Creek and Clear Creek country around Buffalo, he knew he had found the country where he wanted to live the rest of his life.

The grass was belly-deep to a tall horse, and antelope, deer, elk, and buffalo were everywhere. The creeks were alive with wary native trout, and the towering Big Horn Mountains to the west produced a breathtaking backdrop to the whole panoramic vista.

"Only one thing wrong," Sam thought, "too many Indians." And every single one of them seemed to be on the warpath that summer and fall of 1866. Sam was in the burial detail of wagoneers who hauled in the remains of Captain Fetterman and his entire command, eighty-one men who had been wiped out by Red Cloud December 21, 1866. Sam said later, " 'Twas the grisliest job I ever got, picking up the dead, and then haulin' 'em back to Fort Phil Kearny and trying to dig graves in the ground all froze plumb solid."

Sam got to know Jim Bridger, the old mountain man, real well that winter. He was at Fort Kearny, too. The next summer Sam was at the same post when Major Powell and his small contingent of men held off thousands of Red Cloud's best warriors in the Wagon Box Fight in August. But even though the army won, the treaty signed gave the land back to the Indians. Later on Sam helped Bridger dismantle the forts and haul them off to the North Platte to help build a new post called Fort Fred Steele on the Union Pacific Railroad.

Time went by, and finally after ten years of drifting from one area to another, always hauling freight, Sam heard of Custer's defeat and the Dull Knife Battle near Kaycee later on that fall of 1876. Sam knew then that it would only be a short time before the Powder River region would be taking on settlers, cow companies and towns. So he went back to the country that he had fallen in love with, and in the fall of 1877 Sam moved into the area between Buffalo and Sheridan.

Sam was near forty years old then. He hadn't taken a wife and seemed to like the solitary life, even though he was always welcomed at lonely ranches as he pulled in with supplies that they had ordered from the railroad clear down at Medicine Bow or Rock River.

You see, Sam knew the art of range conversation—gossip some would call it. When he drew up at a ranch he was not only loaded down with salt, sugar, flour, beans, and other supplies, but he was also carrying the latest news of what was happening around the country and in the territory. He also knew about cattle prices, who had married into what family, that a new baby was born at such-and-such a ranch, courthouse news, of county situations, and lots and lots of just plain good humorous stories.

In place of a newspaper, Sam was like a towncrier.

So—Sam was looked forward to by most everybody and didn't really have any enemies—just friends.

But as he grew older, he got tired of loading up tons and tons of supplies, and then off-loading them, ranch-by-ranch, town-by-town, and rattling and rumbling over winding trails called roads in those days where wagon breakdowns were common. So he applied for a star route hauling mail from Sheridan to Buffalo with a side trip once a month west over the Big Horn Mountains from Mayoworth to Ten Sleep and back.

One fall day in late October, just before Wyoming became a state, Sam and his span of long-eared Missouri mules pulled into Mrs. Worthington's ranch, where she handled the post office duties. The post office was named after her daughter May. An "O" was added to the first part of the last name; thus, May-O-Worth.

Folks from other ranches drifting into the post office that day visited with Sam and warned him not to try to slip over Hazelton Pass to the post office at Ten Sleep, fifty miles west. One old-timer said, "I git the ache in my bones, Sam, whin she's gonna storm. My big toe's hurting like hell! Storm is a'comin'."

But Sam allowed as he had traveled the route dozens of times, that he was prepared for the trip. And the next morning, after feeding his mules and getting himself on the right side of a couple of stacks of Mrs. Worthington's best flapjacks, Sam pulled out. He loaded in a couple of bales of hay and some grain for his mules, and Mrs. Worthington gave him a big sack lunch.

Sam loved the fall, especially in the mountains. As he traveled along, bump-bumping over rocks and ruts in the narrow mountain road, he marveled at the riot of yellows, browns, oranges, and reds that the aspens and cottonwoods had taken on. At each small mountain stream he pulled up and let his mules suck in the clean, crystal-clear mountain water. Then he'd nicker them along, whistling a small tune under his breath.

Higher and higher Sam and the mules climbed from the 5,000-foot ranch; 6,000 feet, then 7,000, then 8,000—and he was nearing the 9,000-foot pass. He was now crossing wide, high-country meadows guarded by islands of Englewood spruce and lodgepole pine.

Not much wild game up this high this time of year, nor any cattle. They had drifted down and were ready for the first onslaught of winter at lower elevations where they could find feed, cured by the warm summer sun.

It was late in the afternoon of that first day. Sam was dozing in the seat of his wagon, letting the fall sun seep into his bony body, when a large wet snowflake hit him on the face and woke him up.

Sam wiped his face and sat straighter, taking stock of just where he was. Seemed like he wasn't more than seven to eight miles below the pass. But, looking up at the long climb ahead, he saw the spiny ridges of granite guarding the pass disappear behind a solid wall of snow flurries, whipping down the mountain meadow right at him.

Within minutes what had been a quiet, warm October afternoon had turned into a blinding fall blizzard as the wet flakes flung themselves at Sam and his wagon, plopping and smashing at first with a wet hissing sound, then stinging Sam and his mules as they turned into icy pellets driven by the fury of the freezing mountain wind.

So, plastered now with snow that was sticking to his hat and coat, Sam drove his team under the spreading arms of some giant pine, where the trees offered protection from the blinding storm. There he took some old gunnysacks and wiped the mules down, unharnessed them, filled nosebags with some grain, and fed his two long-eared friends. Then Sam pulled out his own suggins, a sort of bedroll covered with a heavy canvas tarpaulin, and rolled it out under the wagon bed. Safe and snug in his bedroll, Sam soon went to sleep, cozy and warm while the storm raged past him and the mules.

When morning came, Sam woke to a white wilderness. The storm, as he looked out past the trees, was still howling along over the flats, past the rocky crags, and filling the air not only with snow from above, but also from the surface, until it was nearly impossible to see.

But Sam had his mail sack with him and mail for Ten Sleep. Besides, he had been through many a fall storm. They mostly quit after a day or so. Thus, he spent the morning waiting for the storm to abate. Along about noon, he ate part of the lunch, scattered the hay for his mules, and made certain that they were well-tied to the trees. Then he fished around in the wagon and found his "webbs"—homemade snowshoes. He strapped them on, cut a staff from the limb of a tree to help him walk, slung his mail sack over his shoulder, and took off for the pass.

Sam figured, "If'n I kin just get over the pass, why then, I'll be headin' downhill all the way to the Bay State Cow Company line shack 'bout ten miles away." Yep, Sam figured on spending a night there, and on the third day drifting down to Ten Sleep on top of a cow pony that he knew he'd find at a line shack at the head of Ten Sleep Canyon.

For four hours Sam struggled gamely into the buffeting blizzard. Head down, neckerchief tied over his ears to hold his hat on, and gloves keeping his hands from freezing, Sam staggered onward and upward. The snow wasn't really deep, but it had filled every little draw. When Sam stumbled into one of them, he would sink down, lose his balance, and fall. So it wasn't long before Sam's wool coat and wool California pants were snow covered, and little by little they built sheets of ice over them. And—remember—Sam wasn't any kid, or young man. He was nearly fifty-five years old, and he soon grew very tired and leg-weary.

Then he stepped into a deep draw and broke the right webb in half. He could have cried out with the pain of twisting an ankle, but more than that, Sam knew that he was really a cripple now, since he only had one snowshoe to support him over the crusted snow, which was getting deeper. Also, he was getting numb from the cold wind whipping into his face, and his gloves, coat, and pants were wet and ice-covered. Worse—it was growing dark!

Sam was in big trouble, and he knew it. So he picked out a small granite shelf sticking up in the snow with a stand of dead aspen and pine trees about a hundred yards from the rocky ridge. He stumbled over to the rocks and, using the snowshoe as a shovel, dug right down to bedrock and piled and banked the snow in a semicircle all around, building a kind of igloo without a roof. Just before the sunlight completely left Sam, he struggled through the snow to the dead trees, broke off a number of limbs, and painstakingly hauled them back to his icy little camp. He made five trips before he thought he had enough wood for fuel and heat to last him the night through.

Then, slowly, he fumbled through his pockets with nearly frozen fingers for matches to start the fire from the dry needles and grass he had scooped up from under a fallen pine tree. At last he found his matches and scratched one against a rock. The head of the match just crumbled off. No fire. He tried another. But it was the same. His matches were plumb wet. He tried a third, then a fourth. Then he gave up. He knew he'd have to build a fire some other way. Either that, or freeze.

The only trouble was that he didn't have any flint to strike a spark to create a fire. Still, he took his belt knife and stabbed it against the granite rock, hoping to create a spark. But nothing came from it.

Now Sam was a guy who would sing a little tune under his breath when he was worried. Right now he was humming out loud, proving that he was worried alright. But old as he was and the experiences he had been through in his life gave him a cool head under pressure. So he just sat real still in his small ice cove while the wind whistled all around and above him, and he tried to reason a way out of his predicament. He remembered Jim Bridger showing him how Indians made fire, but he didn't have the right tools for that. And then the germ of an idea gave a glint to his eye as he remembered back to the Civil War days when General Sherman was chasing Sam's outfit through Georgia. One wet, cold night, a stringy old horse soldier from Texas shoved the muzzle of a big revolver into a pile of dry moss and pulled the trigger. The fire and flame from the blast made a spark or two in the moss, and a soft breath blowing on the moss soon ignited it into a flame. The net result was a fine roaring fire.

Sam pulled back his overcoat and unholstered the six-shooter he always carried as part of his equipment as a U.S. mailman on a star route to guard the mail. In the dimness of the small, cold camp, Sam leaned over and built a pyramid of twigs and laced it with needles. As an afterthought, he pulled the silk neckerchief from around his neck and shredded it with his belt knife. This lint he carefully tucked into the pyramid, which was braced in the crack of the bedrock of the wall behind him. Then he cocked the six-shooter, turned his head, and let the hammer drop.

"Blamm-ammm!" The roar of the revolver had no sooner died away than Sam was kneeling forward scanning the crack for a spark—a sign of fire. Sure enough, a couple of sparks were glowing in the lint. Sam leaned into them and very, very softly increased their size by blowing his controlled breath on them. He kept feeding tiny twigs and pine needles on them until a flame burst into being.

Well. It wasn't long before Sam had stuck a forked stick over a fine warm fire with his pants and coat roasting and drying out as he munched some more of Mrs. Worthington's fine and vital lunch.

That night as he struggled back into his clothes and settled down to sleep, he sure guessed that the red eye of life was fire. In fact, he knew it.

Once or twice during the night he woke up and fed the fire more wood and then slept some more as the wind howled and moaned all around him, carrying more snow and stinging ice pellets a half dozen feet above. But Sam was snug, protected, and reasonably warm. Alive at least, he mused as he dropped back to sleep.

Near dawn Sam woke once more, built up the fire, and went back to sleep again. Tired as he was, and with the fire growing smaller as it ate merrily through the dry wood, Sam unconsciously inched closer and closer to the fire. Soon his coat and the seat of his pants got too hot and dry and ignited, bringing Sam out of his sleep yelping and crowhopping over the top of his snowy parapet into the dim dawn of the third day on the trail.

Like a crazy dancer among the Indians, Sam scooted, stomped, and hopped around in circles and zig-zagging patterns until he finally figured out that if he sat down, his rear end would be cooled off. Then he got up and made his way back to the camp. He sadly surveyed his still-smoking tail and bitterly gave himself a talking to.

"Look at that." He was right indignant. "Worse'en a dang pilgrim." He saw that the firewood was nearly gone and that the storm was still as bad, if not worse, than the night before. "Burn up the wood. Burn up his tail end. Got dry, then got wet all over again putting out the fire." He shook his grizzled head back and forth. But he knew he'd have to make more trips to the dead trees—his wood pile—a hundred yards away.

So, bundling up best as he could, he plowed to the timber and dragged back dead branches and limbs. It was tough work, and the snow was now three feet deep on the level and hard to walk through, let alone to drag uneven limbs over. But he worked and struggled back and forth, four times. He figured that one more trip would do it—give him enough fuel to last him all day and through the night—if he was careful. As he trudged down his trail, head down, he suddenly had an eerie feeling creep over the skin at the nape of his neck, sending shivers up and down his spine as his skin crawled and his hair seemed to stand on end. He looked up—stopped—and there standing on the trail about twenty yards ahead was a great, grey timber wolf.

For a frozen split second Sam saw the pale yellow eyes staring back at him, the long fangs and sharp, dull, ivory-colored teeth, row on row, marching back into the big, yawning mouth, out of which the wolf's long tongue was hanging. The whole wolf's head seemed to give Sam a malevolent grin, scaring the old freighter—but not enough to stop him from clawing his overcoat back, dragging the six-shooter out, and, using both hands to cock it, dropping the hammer.

The wolf had been ready to leap at the old man, but when he saw the gun come up, he recognized what it meant and leaped back into the timber just as the hammer fell—"Click"—on a bad round!

Well, Sam just stood there holding the gun out sort of paralyzed as he watched the grey beast disappear into the dead timber. Slowly, he lowered the six-shooter and holstered it, and then, like a man coming to from a deep sleep, he numbly turned and made tracks back to his small, enclosed camp.

There he ejected the faulty cartridge from the cylinder of his revolver and inspected it in the late afternoon light. He saw where the hammer had nicked a dent into the base of the cartridge that should have caused the bullet to explode. Then he ejected the other three rounds.

You see, Sam carried the hammer down on an empty chamber in the cylinder of the revolver which fired six shots. He had fired the first one the night before into the small bits of wood and pine needles to make a fire. This one evidently was damaged, frozen, or faulty. That left three to kill the wolf, or at least hold him off until Sam could quit this camp and head to Ten Sleep with the mail. He carried no extra ammunition in his gun belt.

He pondered on that quite a bit that evening as he finished off the last of the lunch. He lay back and looked up at the black sky, which was white-streaked from the fast-flying snow still scooting along with the icy blasts that were pouring over the rim of the Big Horn Mountains. He shivered, stuck another limb into the small fire, and thanked his good luck for his small cockpit of safety instead of being out in the bitter wilderness driven by the long-lasting blizzard.

Once or twice during the night Sam woke up, fed the fire into life again, and peered out into the edge of the light cast from his camp, looking for the wolf. But he didn't see the big predator. Still, in his mind's eye, he could plainly see those yellow fangs, the long tongue, the flat yellow eyes, and the gaunt, big frame, lean from hunger.

When dawn arrived on the fourth day, Sam saw that his wood was nearly gone again, and he knew with certainty that he was going to have to make more trips to his standing fuel depot a hundred yards away. He figured that the wolf might still be in the vicinity, but it was a chance he was going to have to take.

Sam remembered back talking with Bill Cody, the army scout who had helped guide the Grand Duke Alexis from Russia fifteen to twenty years before. Cody had asked the duke if wolves really ate people. The heir to the Romanov crown had answered with an affirmative, "Certainly. If they are hungry enough, the beasts will eat anything—dead or alive!"

Sam thought to himself that the wolf he had seen was lean enough, and with cattle, elk, and deer down in the lowlands now, he was hungry enough to eat anything, including Sam! Those thoughts were percolating through Sam's mind as he wallowed down to the timber in the deep snow and brought more limbs and small trees back to his camp. Only this time, Sam carried the six-shooter in one hand, so the effort of snapping off big limbs with one hand while he covered himself with the gun was extra hard.

Sure enough, he was nearly through when, turning around to give an extra yank and tug to a big limb, he spied the lank wolf sitting down on his skinny haunches, studying Sam with his unblinking yellow eyes. Sam merely swung the six-shooter up, thumbed back the hammer, and dropped it on the cartridge.

"Click!" For the second time nothing happened except that the wolf leaped away and trotted out of sight again, wary and gunwise. Sam doggedly stuck the gun into his holster and pulled the limb back to his camp, then sat down to try to dry his pants, boots, and coat once more in the frigid air. While he was roasting his backside, he used the tip of his knife to pry the lead nose of the bullet loose from the brass case of the cartridge. No powder poured out. It was frozen inside and so hadn't been able to be ignited into action when the hammer struck the shell.

He tossed it into the fire and watched it with disdain as it fizzled like a badly built firecracker. And as he pulled on his pants again, and stuck his feet into his boots, Sam decided that he was going to have to roast the remaining two bullets slowly over the fire if he had any hopes of them saving his life.

That fact was driven home as he stood tucking in his shirttails and looked out across the hundred-yard expanse to the dead timber, and saw the wolf sitting halfway, stoically studying Sam. It was afternoon now, and Sam hadn't had a thing to eat all day long. He rummaged around in his coat pocket and came up with the stub of a tallow candle. So he stuck that into his mouth and slowly masticated it as he stared back at the wolf.

Also, Sam was humming right pretty now, which showed that he was still worried. The Cody-Romanov conversation began to prey on his mind, and the more he thought about it, the more worried he got. He purely didn't like the idea of a wolf eating him. He had figured on all sorts of ways of meeting his maker, and not once had the idea of Sam ending his life as wolf bait crossed his mind. He didn't like it at all, and so he got down to the serious business of fixing up a roasting fork for his two remaining bullets.

The storm that night seemed to build up into hurricane-like winds, and it caused Sam to have a miserable time as he stayed awake most all night long, guarding his small fire of life, protecting it from the sifting snow drifting over the edges of his dug-in camp. When the dim morning of the fifth day announced daylight to Sam, it found the old freighter worn out, terribly hungry, and jumpy as hell. His wood supply was nearly gone. He didn't dare let the fire die out, since he wasn't sure that the bullets could be fired to make a new fire. So he had to go to the stand of timber for more fuel, and the wolf was still there where Sam had last seen him late the previous afternoon. If anything, the wolf was a few yards closer.

Casting around in his mind for something to gnaw on, Sam jerked off the rattlesnake band that he had around his old hat. He bit it off in chunks, tearing it into pieces like he was chewing on jerky. While there wasn't much there, it gave Sam's jaws something to do.

He scooped handfuls of snow into his mouth to help salivate the dry, tough skin, and finally, after much gulping, he finished off his slim, snaky skin breakfast and decided to head right at the wolf.

Grabbing a burning brand from the fire, and with the six-shooter in his other hand, Sam headed right at the wolf and the stand of trees beyond the grey intruder. The wolf just sat there, seeming to measure Sam as he plowed step-by-step closer. Finally, Sam swung up the gun, thumbed back the hammer once more, and pulled the trigger.

The hammer descended with a dull metallic "Click!" And this time the wolf flinched but didn't run away. He was standing now, and it looked like he might make a lunge at Sam. So the exasperated old man reared back and threw the smoking limb cartwheeling directly at the wolf.

That did it. The wolf jolted away once more, and Sam sighed a breath of relief as he stumbled forward into the trees and broke off more limbs. His six gun holstered and nearly useless, Sam worked as fast as he could in the wind-swept area, dragging more limbs back to his camp. Each time that he wearily crawled back up over the crusted parapet of snow surrounding the camp, he carried with him another burning and smoking stick. It was, he figured, his only real protection.

Then the snow seemed to increase, and a curtain settled down so that Sam seemed to work in a fantasy of snowy gusts driven by the bitter wind as he heedlessly dragged back limb after limb. Dogged and determined, he knew that his survival now depended upon wood and upon the fire that would consume it—the fire that would protect him not only from the polar-like storm, but from the tearing tusks and fangs of the great grey timber wolf.

On his last trip through the falling snow, Sam saw the wolf appear once more on the trail. This time, he saw the wolf behind him as he pulled a crooked limb back to camp. The wolf was only a few yards behind Sam, and without the use of a smoking stick for protection, Sam didn't dare stop. But he did yell and curse at the wolf, hoping that the sound of his voice would hold the animal at bay until he could fall safely down into his camp and grab another stick with cherry-red embers to throw at the wolf.

The noise of his voice and the final act of rearing back up with the red-hot limb and throwing it at the wolf worked for Sam. He threw the stick and saw the wolf jump back, then sit down. The sharp ears pointed forward, his eyes staring at Sam, the wolf held his ground, and Sam lost his temper.

He yelled, "Lissen here, old wolf! I ain't gonna be your supper. Only one of us is gonna get et, and it's gonna be you."

The wolf just sat there. And he stayed there for a long spell as Sam cast several more sticks his way. Just as the last light of day passed into the black night, the wolf left. And Sam finally got to sit down. He was bone weary, hungry, and scared plumb through.

He hummed louder than ever as he stuck the remaining bullet in the fork of a stick and tried to figure out a way to get the wolf. He didn't know it, but back at the post office ranch, Mrs. Worthington had just received a message from one of her cowboys, whom she had sent to Buffalo the day before to send a wire to Ten Sleep. The message was that Sam hadn't yet made an appearance in that tiny hamlet on the west side of the Big Horns. The message had been sent from Buffalo to Sheridan, up into Montana, and back down the other side of the mountains to Worland, then to Ten Sleep. It took all of two days for the message to be carried by horseback to a telegraph station, then relayed back by horse to the ranch.

Mrs. Worthington organized a search party for Sam. It was to leave the next morning, the sixth day that Sam had been gone.

Well, that was a day Sam would rather forget than remember. He spent most of the sixth day leaning against his snow parapet watching for the wolf out of red-rimmed eyes. Then, when he would spy the big gaunt beast, he would yell and shake his fists at the animal. But nothing seemed to shake or sway the wolf. He wasn't impatient. He just sat there, about halfway between Sam and the timber. As the snow coasted along the surface of the snowfield, the wolf would nearly disappear from sight. Then, as the wind would let up, the wolf would reappear. Once or twice that long morning, the wolf trotted away. Then Sam would make ready to crawl back up the side of his snow wall and to go after wood. Taking a smoking stick with him, Sam was able to forage a couple of loads of firewood in the morning, and he did about the same that afternoon.

It was just nearly enough to keep his fire going, and maybe to last all night. It was while Sam was hurrying along as fast as he could that the idea of killing the wolf grew on Sam. In fact, he had just finished cutting off the fingers of his lefthand glove to chew on for food, such as it was, that Sam hit on the idea of trapping the wolf, Indian style.

He had heard about eagle trapping by the Indians, where they would dig a pitfall and cover it with a willow roof upon which they had placed bait. When an eagle spied it from high above and landed on the roof to tear at the bait, the Indian would reach through the willows, drag the eagle into the pitfall, and try to strangle or otherwise kill it. More than one would-be eagle trapper among the Indians wore scars from the razor-sharp talons of an angry eagle that refused to be taken that way. Still, more times than not, an eagle was trapped.

So that night Sam crawled twenty yards away from his camp in the crusted snow and proceeded to dig a pitfall for himself. It was going to be about seven feet long and about three to four feet wide. He'd use his big knife to dig it down about another three feet. Fact is, the pitfall looked more like a winter coffin for Sam than anything else.

Cold as it was, Sam could only work so long, and then

he'd scuttle back to the fire and rub his hands and arms, bringing circulation back to them. Then, once the numbing cold had left and he could wiggle his fingers once more, he'd crawl back out to his icy grave and dig some more.

As he scraped and dug, he kept a wary eye out for the wolf, and several times he saw the twin orbs of red reflecting the flickering firelight off the wolf's eyes watching him. So Sam knew that he had an audience. And that caused him to keep right on digging and figuring.

He'd hum, too. Talking to himself, he'd remind himself time and time again that he was smarter than the wolf. Finally, he was through.

When dawn came the seventh morning, the storm lifted. The sky was pale pink at first, then orange-colored as the sun peered across the snowy wastes that the storm left in its wake. Sam was oblivious to the pristine beauty of the color of that dawn as he made his way to his pitfall. There, he wrapped his overcoat around his throat. Then, holding the six-shooter in one hand with the one untested round in it, and belt knife in the other hand, he sank back into the grave, pulling dry branches over himself.

There he lay, peering up at the new dawn from his grave in the ice and snow. He waited and waited and held his breath, cocking an ear for a sound indicating that the wolf was coming after him. But nothing happened. The wolf wouldn't take the bait. Sam slowly raised up and saw the wolf looking at him from the edge of the timber. So Sam crawled out of the pitfall and made his way back to his fireplace. Warming himself, it dawned on Sam why the wolf wouldn't come to him. He needed the smell of blood to draw him to Sam. That's what was needed. Blood for bait. Just Sam lying there wasn't bait enough. Even the Indians had used a bait outside their pitfall.

So, as much as Sam hated it, he went back to his grave in the snowfield, and there, sitting on the side of it with his overcoat wrapped once more around his throat for protection from the terrible fangs, Sam drew his sharp knife across his left forearm, trying to cut and draw blood.

But it was easier said than done, cutting himself to draw blood. It was repugnant to Sam, until he just shut his eyes and brutally sawed back and forth, cutting several deep gashes in his arm. Then, when the blood ran free, Sam swung his arm all around the edge of the pitfall, scattering bright red drops of blood in profusion on the branches of his cover and on the snow. Then he lay back down, face-up, once more, and drew the branches over his face to hide wide-open eyes.

Now, as he lay real still, clutching the six-shooter in his left hand and with his right hand holding the bloody knife, Sam tensed as he heard the soft crunching of snow from the big pads of the wolf's feet drawing up to the edge of the trap.

Sam lay like death itself. Rigid, silent, holding his breath, and hoping the wolf would jump down on top of him. Then, he would pull the trigger and gut-shoot the wolf. If that didn't work, he would rip upwards with the deadly knife, and tear the wolf's innards right out.

He heard the wolf move again, and he was certain that he heard the soft rhythm of the wolf panting, but he never saw the wolf peer over the edge of the coffin-like pitfall. Now, Sam was nearly freezing again, and if the wolf didn't make a move soon, he would start to shake so bad his teeth would chatter, giving him away.

The longer Sam lay there, the madder he got. He wasn't afraid any longer. Nope. Just mad. Here he had gone and dug this trap. Worked his fingers to the bone. Nearly froze himself. Then, to bait the trap, he'd sawed his own arm until the blood ran.

So, when Sam thought he heard the wolf retreat, he lost all control of himself. He jumped straight up, branches going one way, his head and shoulders emerging from the thick cover of the dead wood, and with the coat still wrapped around him, his eyes bulging and glaring, Sam saw the startled wolf about twenty-five yards away standing stock-still.

Sam scrambled up over the edge of the trap and stumbled

right at the startled animal. Then he pulled the trigger on his old six-shooter.

"Blaaammm!" The last round was a good one. Sam's heart fairly leaped as he felt the six-shooter action jump familiarly in his left hand, rocking up with the force of the explosion, then settling down. Only his eyes registered the fact that Sam had missed the wolf with that shot. The wolf skittered to one side, tucked his rear legs under his body, and lunged away rapidly, pumping with forefeet and hind legs for his life as he really lit out. He disappeared once more into the narrow draw holding the dead timber.

Sam stood there, unbelieving that he had missed at such close range. Slowly, he let his gun arm and hand holding the gun down to his side. Then, sort of unconsciously, he pulled the overcoat from around his shoulders and neck, pulled it on, and stumbled back to his camp. He came to the edge of the parapet and let himself slide back down to the black-crusted area where the little fire smoked.

As far as Sam was concerned, that did it. He'd fought the good battle. He'd lasted seven days without anything to speak of to eat. He'd built a fire without matches to save his life. He'd lasted through a terrible blizzard. Then, to top it off, he'd eyeballed a hungry wolf for four days with a use-less six-shooter, and lost the last bet as he threw all his chips in the pot trying to outwit the wolf.

Sam lay down, a tired, thoroughly exhausted old man, and clutching the big knife, he fell fast asleep. He reminded himself that when the wolf did come for him, he'd still try to knife him. But he knew that he just wasn't strong enough to put up much of a fight.

What Sam didn't know was that the round fired from the six-shooter had let loose an echo that bounced off the walls above Sam and carried clear down to the stand of timber, where a bobsled drawn by several big draft horses had just pulled up to find Sam's mules still safe. The two men driving the horses heard that solitary shot a long way off and turned their team in that direction. In an hour, the sled pulled up on the edge of Sam's camp.

Looking down on the old man, they saw a sleeping and nearly frozen Sam. His whiskers were plumb white and his face beet red and dirty black from the exposure and from the act of hanging over the fire as he tried to keep warm. Fishing some whiskey from the sled, one of the men forced a bit of it into Sam's mouth, bringing the old one to life. Then they lifted Sam tenderly and carefully into the straw-covered floor of the sled, wrapped him up in blankets, and turned the team around and headed down the mountain.

Once, a long way off, they saw the old grey wolf. They stopped the sled, and the younger man levered a round into his carbine and fired at the wolf. That shot brought Sam up, clawing to the edge of the bobsled. Seeing that the younger man was going to take a second shot, Sam grabbed his coat just as he fired, causing him to miss the wolf now loping away from them to safety.

"Hey Sam!" the younger man said, "what'd you do that for?"

Sam said wearily, "Didn't want you to kill him. He saved my life."

"Huh?" the younger one asked. "What's that mean?"

Then Sam related how the wolf kept eyeing Sam for four days. "I was too scart to die," Sam said. "I purely didn't want that wolf to eat me. So I kept on fighting to stay alive." Sam lay back down, thoroughly relaxed now as the sled bumped along. "Yes, sir. That old wolf kept me alive, and I didn't want you to kill him."

Late that evening they had Sam hauled all the way down to the ranch. His hands and feet were in terrible shape. But constant dousing and soaking in coal oil saved them.

When they finally got some soup into Sam and had him tucked into a big featherbed, Mrs. Worthington nodded at the mail sack hanging from the bedpost. She said, "I wonder?" She took it into the big kitchen and absently looked inside to see the mail that Sam was delivering to Ten Sleep. There was one letter. That's all. Just one letter for Ten Sleep.

PAUL ST. PIERRE

Sale of One Small Ranch

A newspaperman for over thirty years (mostly with the Vancouver, B.C., *Sun*), member of the Canadian Parliament, parliamentary secretary for external affairs in Ottawa, and police commissioner for British Columbia, Paul St. Pierre has also served in the Royal Canadian Air Force and written numerous plays and fiction and nonfiction stories. Among his books are *Boss of the Namko Drive*, *British Columbia Our Land*, *Cholcotin Holiday*, and *Breaking Smith's Quarter Horse*.

"Sale of One Small Ranch," which earned the 1984 Golden Spur Award, appeared in the author's *Smith and Other Events* (Beaufort Books).

When Norah came downstairs, Smith was leaning with folded arms on the kitchen counter, looking out the window whose panes were rimmed with heavy frost. He had not set the coffee on to boil nor lit the fire.

"What are you doing, Smith?"

"Nothing."

"I can see that."

She waited for him to say more, but he didn't. She shaved three feathersticks, there being no newspaper with which to fire kindling. She lit these, crammed some split jack pine

into the stove, filled the coffee kettle, and shouted upstairs
to wake the boys. She brought pancake batter down from the
cupboard and beat it in a pan, whittled some rashers off a
slab of bacon and cut up meat for frying, sometimes working
on one side of Smith and sometimes on the other at the
linoleum topped counter. He never moved. The two older
boys came down, fetched wood and water and lit the oil
drum heater in the living room. He ignored them, too.

"What are you doing, Smith?" she asked.

His answer, as usual, was mild. "I am just looking at the
mountain," he said.

"Exactly how long do you plan to spend looking at the
mountain?"

"Well, it ain't much of a mountain, not really. I would say
that another five to ten minutes would take care of it pretty
well."

Norah and the boys had almost finished breakfast when
he joined them at the table.

"She's gonna be a bad winter," said Smith.

"Can you tell that by looking at the mountain, Smith?"
said Sherwood.

"No, it's a combination of a lot of things. How the leaves
blow off, when the first frost bites in, fur on the horses. You
can feel it. Can't you feel it?"

"No," said Sherwood, "I don't feel anything."

Smith looked at him in some surprise. Now and then he
encountered evidence that not everybody in the world
thought exactly as he did and it invariably surprised him.
"You'll pick up the idea as you go along," he said.

"What are we gonna do today, Smith?" asked Roosevelt.

"We'll pull the shoes off all the horses we can catch. You
guys run in the bunch from the horse pasture."

"Pull the shoes," said Norah. "What for?"

"Don't I usually pull the shoes off all the horses before the
snow hits?"

"But what do you want to do it now for? Today, I mean."

"Because it might snow tomorrow. And stop looking at
me that way, the light hurts my eyes."

"You two boys get out quick and do what your father says," said Norah. She walked over to the stove and found something unnecessary and noisy to do until Sherwood and Roosevelt were gone. At the slam of the door she came back to the table, hooked her elbows into the linoleum and stared at Smith, who continued chewing his bacon, slowly. He was a slow feeder.

"I never told the boys about us selling."

"Uh-huh."

"Did you?"

"Me? No. Why should I? There is no sense getting them upset; I am upset enough myself."

"Then what is all this business about taking shoes off the horses? The horses will go with the ranch, won't they?"

"Could be."

"Goddam it, Smith, why can't you ever give a straight answer to anything? It's always maybe, could be, might be. I get goddam sick of it."

"Nothing is certain in this world, Norah, except death and taxes. God and the government have decided they should be permanent. Coffee?"

She brought him more coffee.

"You said you was gonna sell, you know."

"If I get my price."

"And the price was thirty thousand."

"Well, I don't remember saying exactly the price. But if the price is good enough, we will sell her out."

"Well, you will never get more than thirty."

"No, I s'pose not. Mind you, a man could say that thirty thousand is not much to show for most of his working life. But then no doubt I am prejudiced."

"What have we got to show now, for God's sake? An old log cabin and no running water. A lot of fence around swamp meadow that nothing ever wants to get into in the first place. A bunch of cayuses that nobody in his right mind wants to buy and some beef for a falling market."

"And a discontented woman," said Smith. "Don't forget

to add that." He went to the peg on the wall, took his hat, held it at arm's length above his head, placed himself under it, dropped it on his head and went out to where the wind was talking about the dreadful things it planned for the winter ahead.

Twenty minutes later, when he drew the leg of the first horse between his knees and grabbed the worn, silver-bright shoe with the tongs, Sherwood said, "You ain't gonna sell out, are you, Smith?"

"No," said Roosevelt. "He ain't gonna sell. If we was gonna sell out, we wouldn't be getting the horses ready for winter."

Smith pulled off the shoe, examined it and threw it to the ground six feet away. "That pile will be for the ones too much worn to be put on again. I will make another pile to the right of ones we keep."

"And we put them on again next spring," said Roosevelt.

"No, stupid," said Sherwood. "When we get spring ice, we put ice shoes on them."

"All depends on whether there is ice," said Smith.

"Then you ain't gonna sell, are you?"

Smith said, "You boys have been listening to conversations that don't concern you."

"Sure as hell does concern me," said Sherwood.

Smith, about to start on the second foot, let the horse's leg back on the ground and looked at the boy. "You are right, Sherwood. It does concern you. I apologize about that."

He addressed them both. "I been planning to say something to you for a while," he said.

"Mum wants you to sell, but you don't want to," said Roosevelt.

"You boys should know that your mother is right about some things," said Smith. "Sometimes a woman sees what a man won't let himself see."

"Then what does she see?"

"What she sees is that this ranch is on the fiftieth parallel north latitude and thirty-five hundred feet elevation. Do you know what that means? No, I s'pose not. Well, what it means is that nobody should have started trying to make a ranch out of this country in the first place."

"We done alright," said Sherwood.

"Lots of horses," said Roosevelt.

"And beef is going up next spring," said Sherwood. "I heard a guy on the radio say it."

"I admire your style," said Smith, "but there comes a time to look at facts. The facts are, the winters are too long and my life is too short."

He looked the two boys over. "So that's the way it is," he said. He returned his attention to the horse with some sense of satisfaction. Normally, he didn't talk to his kids much, any more than his father had talked to him; but now and then, he knew, a good, long, heart-to-heart talk was a big help to a boy. He felt a certain gratification at having contributed so much of his morning to them.

"He still hasn't said he is goin' to sell out," said Roosevelt to Sherwood.

"Is my mare among the bunch?" asked Smith.

"Bringing her in is like herding a cougar," said Sherwood.

Smith gave a short laugh. "Yeah, she is difficult."

"Are you gonna sell out or not?" asked Roosevelt.

"We have talked that subject out," said Smith. His voice was sharp; they knew the tone. The matter was not raised again and they spun out the morning pulling shoes, filing hoofs and stacking usable shoes in the barn.

Norah spent the morning shining tables, counters, windows and the floor. For all the good it will do, she said. The buyer would be interested in the grass and how it grew and the water and how it flowed. The condition of the house would mean nothing to him. The living room might as well be strewn with saddles and horse buns. They were all the same, the men of this country, the dull sons of bitches. She had both barrels loaded and cocked by the time Smith and the boys came in to dinner; to placate her he went upstairs and put on his best pants, his ten-dollar shirt and his Llama boots. The boots were the most expensive articles of personal adornment he had ever bought and were known to the household as the Bull-Buying Boots. They were too fine to work in, but he always put them on when going to a bull sale.

"Is he buying me, is he buying my clothes, or does he have some idea of buying the place?" he said to her in the bedroom.

"I'm going to get the boys clean, too," she said. "I'm going to wear a dress, too. We may be poor but there's no sense in giving him the advantage of seeing it. He'll talk more money the better we look."

"I rather doubt that," he said.

"Don't be so down in the mouth. We'll have money to buy a house, a real house in Prince George. And a guy that can do anything, like you ... do you know what cat operators are getting at Prince?"

"More than I am, I'm sure of that."

"Right. A lot more. You will get real money."

"And I will be working for somebody else."

"And there's the boys. They'll go to school. They'll be in hockey clubs and stuff."

"And they will grow up to work for somebody else."

"Smith, almost everybody in the country works for somebody else now."

"Just because you see a lot of guys jumping into the river, it don't mean you got to jump in, too."

"Hey. There's somebody coming in."

They stood and heard heavy steps at the doorway. "Oh, my God," she said, "and my hair isn't done."

Smith walked to the top of the stairs, steep as a ship's ladder, which connected the upstairs loft with the ground floor. "It's Larsen," he said. "Hello, Ken."

"You got a hand pump, Smith?"

"I guess. You got troubles?"

"Truck stalled about half a mile past your gate. I figure I got a blockage in the gas line. Maybe I can blow it through with a pump."

"Wait a minute; I'll give you a hand."

He stepped up the ladder stairs and spoke to Norah. "I'm gonna give Ken a hand," he said. "He is no good with machinery anytime."

This was a slander they all passed upon one another in the Namko Country. Oddly enough, each man believed it when he said it and had a curious faith in his own exemption from the general rules of carelessness and neglect with trucks, tractors, diesel power plants or any other manifestation of the internal combustion engine. If Canadian law provided fines or jail terms for wanton cruelty to mechanical equipment, most men in Namko would have been hanged. They were adept at fixing equipment after it broke, but they would seldom avert breakdown by so much as regular oiling and greasing, or the checking of antifreeze. They could understand that horses, even the poorest of them, responded well to attentiveness, care, even a bit of affection, but they had never been able to transfer this thinking to machinery or, often as not, to their wives.

"Ken has no feel for equipment." Feeling that something more was expected of him, he went on, "If the buyer shows up, he can't miss us."

"Not unless he comes in the other road."

"In that case, won't take ten minutes to get us. Or he won't mind waiting. If he's come this far by car, he must be a man with time for spending."

When he was about to leave, she came over and stood in front of him. There were shadows in her eyes.

"There's something I haven't told you . . . ," she said.

"Tell me after."

"No. I am telling you now, Smith. I want you to get this through your head, all the way through it."

"What is it, Norah?"

"Maybe you don't really plan to sell this place for any price. I don't know. I can't read you. But whether you do or whether you don't, I am going to Prince George, Smith."

He looked at her a long time. Then he dropped his head and looked at the floor. He scratched his ear.

"I'll take the baby with me. As for the boys, we can figure out about them later. But by this week's end, I am gone from this place. You can sell and come or keep it and stay."

He shook his head, twice, up and down. "I hear you, Norah," he said.

"Smith," came Ken's voice from the kitchen. "Just tell me where to find the pump. No need for you to come out."

"No, I'll give ya a hand," said Smith. "Might as well be doing something useless this afternoon."

He left before Norah realized that he was in his best clothes, his only good clothes, and it occurred to her that engine oil would never come out of the Bull-Buying Boots.

After a time she relented. She took off the print dress, got into slacks, her second-best outfit, threw Smith's old clothes and boots into a gunny sack and went down the road to find the truck. She rode a Tennessee Walking Horse named The Colonel. He paced instead of trotting and although she was only average as a rider, he made her look good because of the side-to-side gait. His long legs were driving as they came down the road, the thin, cold dust rising behind them. Norah's hair, freshly curled, blew in the breeze of their passage and there was a delicate flush on her cheeks. On The Colonel, drudgery, children, husband, money, all the several woes of womankind fell away from her and she was again young, warm as the breath of spring, even lovely.

"Pretty," said Larsen as she came up. "Pretty. Pretty."

"He's showy," said Smith, "but he ain't much for working cows. Won't lift his feet enough."

Norah hit him with the bundle of clothing. "For God's sake, get out of your good clothes," she shouted.

"In a minute," he said, throwing them to the side of the road.

Norah might have persisted but at that moment she saw Margaret Larsen in the cab of the truck. She stepped lightly off The Colonel and let his lines drop to the ground, so that he stood. She ran across to the other woman. Months sometimes passed between their meetings.

"You're all dressed up, Norah," said Margaret.

Norah was startled by the reminder of the larger affairs of that day, but recovered. "We're expecting someone from town."

"Anyone we know?"

"Prob'ly not. It's a Mr. MacKenzie."

"No. I guess not."

The matter was dropped. Selling out was like divorce; you did not discuss it with neighbors until the hard part was over.

"Come up to the house. You can't sit here. You'll catch your death."

"They say it'll be fixed in a few minutes."

"Like hell it will," said Smith. He and Larsen expressed the wish that the women would leave them to their unique and powerful sorrows and, with the usual yeaing and naying with which such simple requests are commonly surrounded, Norah and Margaret finally left, The Colonel stepping sedately behind them on the lead.

Within an hour the two women were joined at the ranch house by Morton Dilloughboy who was hunting for his horses. Since most of his horses were lost most of the time, Morton had an ever-available excuse for visiting most of his neighbors most of the time.

In late afternoon, Frenchie Bernard, accompanied by his wife, towed Larsen's truck into the Smith yard behind his own. He had come to return some borrowed wrenches and accept the loan of others.

As darkness was rushing down on the ranch from the grey hills of the west, Henry James rode in on a buckskin mare, loaded with half of a deer which he had shot the day before and the freight of loneliness earned by five unbroken weeks of riding the Ildash Meadows.

Thus did a small back-eddy of the great river of time catch up these human morsels in the great emptiness of the range country. None were surprised or questioned the process. It was the way life flowed in that land, particularly in the winter, whose breath they now felt for the first time in that year.

Similarly, without comment or question, the women collectively prepared dinner. Frenchie's wife made a mountain of golden-yellow potato salad. Margaret cut meat from Henry's haunch of mowitch, doing it Chilcotin style—no chops, no steaks, no roasts of any name, but chunks which would become the staple fare of the country—fried meat.

Finding her regular cooking duties relieved by two other women, Norah found time to make two dozen baking powder biscuits and two pies filled with raisins and canned peaches. From the porch she brought four quart sealers of canned, smoked trout which she had prepared the previous summer. They were a dusky rose in color, firm and well chilled.

The liquor was not in good supply. Morton, who seldom traveled without the necessities of life, had half a bottle of rye left when he reached the ranch and Ken had a mickey of rum under the seat of his truck. The Smiths had one bottle of Liquor Control Board rye, the seal of which they had planned to break when the buyer arrived. Smith, who foresaw a long night, poured it all into a large bowl and added three quarts of grape drink, mixed from powder, and the juice from the pie peaches.

On the top he floated slices of lemon. They were old and evil lemons, dark, small and hardened by months of neglect. But the brew seemed to revive their spirits and the lemon slices made a handsome garnish. The taste of the punch was dreary, but the older men spoke well of it, comparing it with the home brew they made during the Depression, the drink of youth, Peaches Wine.

The party, for such it had become, burned brighter as the cold October wind beat stronger against the little log house, the flame of it fed by the sums of all their individual loneliness. The process resembled that of the fire which had burned that summer on a corner of the Long Jim Meadow. For weeks that fire had smoldered in the peat, revealed only

here and there by a thin strand of blue smoke. A sudden
chill wind came down from the snow mountains one afternoon and the whole upper end of the meadow burst into a
yellow flame which swept grandly, wildly, across the grass,
caring not where it was taken or what was in its path.

When MacKenzie, the buyer, drove into the ranch yard,
no one noticed his car lights and when he knocked on the
door no one answered. He stepped inside, as he should have
done after the first knock anyway. He found them dancing
while the dinner steamed on the old McClary range. Larsen
was playing his push-button accordion which, by chance,
had been in his truck; Morton blew his mouth organ and
Margaret Larsen was beating time with two spoons. Smith
was dancing with Frenchie's wife and Norah with Frenchie.
Frenchie had in his big feet all the grace which God had
failed to put into his face and the pair spun about the
crowded little room as lightly as soap bubbles. When she
saw MacKenzie, Norah broke away from Frenchie and stood
a moment, unable to move toward the man at the door. The
color went down from her red cheeks and a crease appeared
on the top of her nose. MacKenzie could not be sure if she
was frightened or angry, but he knew that in that split second he had seen the face of a woman dreadfully dismayed.
Damn, he said to himself, Smith wants to sell and the wife
doesn't; I'm into the middle of a family fight.

"You're Mrs. Smith? I'm Aaron MacKenzie." He held out
his hand. Damn, he thought, and pretty too. Worn, but pretty
still. The kind who makes the family decisions.

Before he retired and became a part-time real estate sales-
man, MacKenzie had been a B.C. provincial policeman and
he had a reputation of being a good judge of men. He was
not, however, a good judge of women; police work, during
his active years, hadn't much involved women.

She poured apologies all over him. They hadn't seen his
lights. They thought maybe he wasn't coming until tomorrow. Had he been knocking on the door? Was he cold? Was
he tired? Smith, who had joined them, was introduced by

Norah. "We're dancing away a hard winter," Smith said. "It's an old tribal custom in these parts."

The buyer was introduced as "Aaron MacKenzie from Town" and no one asked more about him. The occasional stray from Williams Lake drifted through the country from time to time. They were acceptable, sometimes interesting. The music started again. MacKenzie went back to his car and brought, as his contribution, a bottle of Glenfiddich single-malt Scotch. "Much too fine to mix with anything," said Smith, holding the pale, straw-colored fluid up to the light of the hissing gas lantern. "But," he added, "this is a communist society." He poured the Scotch into the punch bowl. MacKenzie burst into tears, but not so that it could be noticed.

"You'll be staying the night, of course," said Smith.

"Well, thanks, yes. I guess we can talk business tomorrow morning."

"Oh, I don't doubt we'll talk over our business tonight. It won't take long. I'm a very simple man. Maybe the simplest man you ever did business with."

"You want to talk right now?"

"Sure. Why not?"

"Smith," shouted Morton from across the room, "I was telling Ken . . . what was the year you and I had the Great Goose Hunt?"

" 'Forty-nine," said Smith, "God, what a shoot." He smiled at the memory, collected himself for a moment, long enough to dip MacKenzie a drink from the punch bowl and addressed the room at large about that memorable occasion. "It was right this time of year, but even colder. The country was almost seized up. There was only open water left on the Big Slough and not much of that."

"And you froze a finger," said Morton.

"Froze *two* fingers."

Morton held two arms aloft. "We never got a single bird," he cried.

"Not a one," said Smith. "They were coming down out of

the north like fleets of bombers and we were right where
they wanted to sit. Every time they came in I'd say, 'Morton,
be calm. Don't get excited.' All of a sudden my gun would
be empty and I couldn't remember firing a shot.''

"We were too cold and stiff to swing the gun," said
Morton.

"*Of course* we were. And too dumb to know it. I think
myself our brains had curdled that day. You were firing that
old Damascus twist . . .''

". . . with light shot, so it wouldn't bust its gut . . .''

"That's right. Light shot." Smith turned to MacKenzie. "I
asked Morton how he could expect to reach out for a goose.
Morton says, 'When I pull the trigger, I give just a little push,
with my shoulder.' ''

"Oh God, we're into hunting stories," said Norah. She
took MacKenzie's arm. "Come and eat," she said. "Those
stories are never exactly the same twice, but when you've
heard them fifty or so times they seem to be all the same. I
have heard all fifty varieties of the Big Goose Hunt.''

In line for the buffet, which had been laid out on the
counter in the kitchen, MacKenzie found himself flanked by
the two Smith boys. He introduced himself, but they admitted nothing except that he was probably who he claimed to
be. This bothered MacKenzie, who prided himself on understanding kids almost as well as he understood men.
When he dipped the ladle in the gravy bowl and found a
spoon had dropped into it, he offered it up as a small joke.
"I don't know if that spoon is cooked enough." He laid it on
Sherwood's plate. "What do you say? Is it tender? A spoon
takes a lot of cooking.''

Sherwood did not look at the spoon. He stared directly at
MacKenzie. "It's cooked all you can cook a goddamned
spoon," he said.

"Sherwood!" said Norah.

"That's alright; he's exactly right in what he says," said
MacKenzie.

"That was rude, Sherwood.''

"Rude but right, you know," said Smith. "It won't improve with any more cooking, Norah. Help yourself to them biscuits, Aaron; they're homemade, but they're good."

MacKenzie found himself surrounded by Smiths as he ate. Smith himself sat beside him on the sagging sofa while Norah ate nearby, standing, there being no chairs, stools or other places for sitting left in the living room. The two Smith boys sat nearby on the floor, cross-legged, watching him as they ate. If I make a sudden move, thought MacKenzie, one of those little buggers is going to bite my ankle.

"You'll be wanting a horse to ride around and look the place over tomorrow," Norah suggested.

"There is no place on this ranch his people ain't ridden over," said Smith, shortly.

"That's right," said MacKenzie, "we know about as much about this place as you do."

"Not quite as much. If you knew as much, you wouldn't be willing to buy it."

"Don't sell yourself short. You've done a lot of work on these meadows."

"That is true," said Norah.

"Who is buying, anyhow?" said Smith.

"The name you'll see on the papers is just a holding company and doesn't mean a damn thing."

"In other words, a big outfit."

"Yes. They want it for summer range. They have the idea they can truck cattle here for summer feeding and take them out in the fall."

"Then the house will be empty all winter?" said Norah.

"It'll be empty all summer, too," said MacKenzie. "There'll be a couple of cowboys under canvas on the range. That's all."

"You mean, there won't be anybody living in this place?"

"They've got no use for the house. They'd pay you as much if it wasn't here. It's the grass they want. I suppose they might use it for an equipment shed."

"A toolshed!"

MacKenzie saw in her face the same wan terror that had showed, briefly, when he first came to the ranch-house door.

Smart man, MacKenzie, he told himself. To this woman and the kids, you're a son of a bitch who's coming to throw them out, and you help it all along by telling her the house is only good for a toolshed.

"Not that it matters," Norah said. "It's just, gosh, I think of the work that went into varnishing these logs."

"It's a shame, Mrs. Smith," said MacKenzie. "This is a handsome little place. But it's a small rancher's house and the small rancher is going out in this country. We might as well all be honest about this. Only the big outfits can make a go of it at today's beef prices."

"That is absolutely true," said Smith.

"And it's better that way, really," said MacKenzie. "The little man is going to earn a far better living at something else."

"Earn a lot more money," said Smith. "There is not a doubt in God's green world about that."

"So I'm told to bid twenty thousand," said MacKenzie.

"Smith," called Morton from across the room, "I'm right, ain't I? It was Jerome and Thaddeus Eriksen who homesteaded on Big Creek."

"Jerome and Thaddeus? No, that was the names of the brothers that started the Gang Ranch."

"Mind you, twenty thousand is our starting figure," said MacKenzie.

"Jerome and Thaddeus Harper," said Smith, "they must have been big men. Drove cattle all the way from the Gang to Ogden, Utah, one time. Fifteen hundred miles. A fifteen-hundred-mile drive." He turned back to MacKenzie. "Excuse me, you were saying something?"

"I said twenty-five," said MacKenzie.

"What about Norman Lee's drive from the Chilcotin to the Klondike?" said Larsen.

"He never got them to the Klondike," said Smith. "They had to butcher them on Lake Bennett and try floating the meat down on rafts."

MacKenzie smiled and kept eating. He had seen these men do business before.

Early in his acquaintance with them he had attended a sheriff's auction and joined a knot of ranchers who were surrounding two cases of beer with conversation. They drank it all and told wonderful stories and the last cow in the auction had been sold before he realized that his companions had been bidding and buying at the same time they were drinking and telling stories. Their ways were their own, private and personal possessions which he had no license to disturb. He sat back and watched the many conversations run. The ghosts of old ranchers whose bones were now mixing with the pale, yellow earth of these hills were brought into the room and vastly admired. There were stories about old practical jokes, about rank horses and cold winter camps. Smith's favorite saddle horse was compared with a camel, unfavorably, but all insults appeared to translate into praise within the mind of Smith. They played penny stook, they danced some more. The boys were herded to their tiny upstairs bedroom, stacked together in one narrow cot so that the other bed should be left for MacKenzie. When MacKenzie himself made his slow passage to the bedroom, Morton, who had been most often to the well, was asleep on the sofa, but all the others remained in full cry; Norah was making yet more coffee and Frenchie and Larsen were shouting at one another in an argument about the merits of the McClellan cavalry saddle.

MacKenzie had, as far as he knew, done no business. But then you could never be sure. There was the problem of the woman. Always the woman, irrational, illogical and, for all their winsome ways, inflexible in purpose.

It was, as it turned out, a woman who interrupted the negotiations next morning, but she was not human but horse: Smith's old mare. The mare had immense stamina, but not much else. She was an ugly animal with a matching temperament. Smith's pride in her was, typically, perverse. "She has never let me lose my respect for her," he would tell people. "Even after fourteen years together, I cannot approach her without whistling or talking first or she will nail me with her feet or her teeth."

She was not in evidence when MacKenzie came downstairs for breakfast in the middle of a grey and shabby morning. Nothing much moved outside the cabin. It had rained during the night, freezing as it fell. All the land was sheathed in pewter. Larsen's truck was in the yard. "Leave her lay where fate has flang her," he had said, while he and his wife rode home with the Bernards. Young Henry James was beside the drum stove, preparing reluctantly for a slow and hard ride back to the Ildash.

Old Morton had a hangover and said his hair ached. Norah had taken pity on him and poured him a shot of brandy from the medicine chest stock; this revived him sufficiently to take coffee, provided it was uncontaminated with cream or sugar. The boys had been herded to a corner of the living room with their correspondence school textbooks. The baby slept in his crib. Smith was looking at his mountain. Norah was busy.

When the men sat for breakfast, Morton went outside, revolted by the smell of food. He would saddle up, he said; when the ice softened he would pick his own way home.

Henry brought forth grizzly bears, the previous year's stampede and next year's stampede as openers for the kind of long, pointless and thoroughly enjoyable conversations which had filled all the previous night. But there were no takers for conversational games and Henry faded to silence. Then Smith casually picked up the thread of old conversation.

"You said twenty-five," he said to MacKenzie.

"Actually, there was something I wanted to say," said Norah.

"You?" said Smith.

"It's kinda dumb, maybe . . . Mr. MacKenzie, you said they wouldn't be using this house?"

"No, they don't care about the house."

"Then do you s'pose they'd mind if, before we moved away, we burned the old place down?"

"There is a woman for you," said Smith. "Always complicate the simple. That way, nobody can ever be sure exactly what is going on."

"I would have to ask them, Mrs. Smith."

"Let's talk in numbers," said Smith.

Every figure at the table was stiff. MacKenzie, for the moment, considered that each of them was encased in the ice of the storm. He also had the sensation of smothering.

Henry James, who couldn't have been more embarrassed if found in a strange bedroom, walked stiffly into the kitchen section to pour coffee for himself and remained there by the window, looking at the mountain and humming loudly and without tune.

"How does twenty-eight sound?" said MacKenzie.

"I can hear it plain," said Smith.

"We figured on thirty," said Norah.

Smith said, "There isn't much difference, really, between twenty-eight and thirty."

"Then if there isn't much difference, they can pay the extra two," said Norah.

Smith spoke sharply. "Am I talking, or are you?"

"Last and final, thirty," said MacKenzie.

"Smith," said Norah.

"Smith," said Morton, standing at the open door, "give me your gun."

"No hangover is that bad, Morton; I know. I have had some bad ones, but it is not that bad."

"Shut up," said Norah. "He isn't joking. Look at his face."

"I'm sorry, Smith," said Morton, "your mare has had it. There isn't any easy way to tell you that."

"Had it how?"

"The ice, I s'pose. Foreleg snapped right through."

"I will take a look at her."

"There is nothing to look at that you want to see, Smith. The bone is out through the skin. She's down by the gate."

"Well," said Smith. "Well, well, well, well, well." He walked across to the gun rack and pulled down the 30-30. "In this country it's like the nightly screw. Everything comes at once."

"I'll take the gun," said Morton, holding out his hand.

Smith ignored him. "Hell of a thing, she had to go with all that pain. I would think God could arrange things better if He would only put his mind to it."

"Give me the gun," said Morton. "You don't want to see her this way."

Smith placed his hand on Morton's chest and gently pushed him away. "I have always shot my own horses," he said.

"Let him go, Morton," said Norah.

"He was always proud of that," she told MacKenzie after Smith walked out. "Everybody usually has to shoot an old horse or two just before winter, the ones that aren't gonna make it. A lot of the ranchers would trade the job so's they shot each other's and not their own, but Smith always done it himself. I think he figures it's a sort of self-discipline."

"I don't think that mare fell at the gate," said Morton. "I think she got to the gate somehow on three legs. I never heard of a horse doing that, but I think it happened."

"Your coffee is cold, Mr. MacKenzie," said Norah. She brought the pot to the table.

After they heard the shot she excused herself and went out into the yard, a heavy sweater flung over her shoulders. He came across the yard with his eyes on the ice. She stood and waited for him. He did not look at her until he was beside her.

"Smith," she said, "there's something I want you to know. I know how you felt about that mare, and I'm sorry she's gone."

"It probably doesn't matter much, really," he said. "I was gonna shoot her when we left the place. There was nobody would have taken her; there wasn't another man in the country would have put up with her biting. And I wasn't going to see her neglected or abused."

He took a step toward the house. She stopped him with a hand on his arm.

"Smith, what I really wanted to say . . . I ain't found life too bad on this place . . ."

He looked at her with half a smile. "When you growl and snap at me, I don't mind, not really. But when you wag your tail, you make me nervous." He slapped her behind, lightly, and walked into the house. There were tears in her eyes as she followed him.

"I'm sorry if you've lost a great horse," said MacKenzie. "They don't come our way very often."

"No. Fact is, she was not a great horse. I got along with her. But she was not great. Not great in any way." He poured coffee and, standing, sipped at it. "You know, Mac, if you wanted a reason to pull out of this country, you had it seeing that old mare.

"Born to a hard life, lived a hard life, died hard. Never praised. Never thanked. And hardly noticed, when she went, by anybody except me.

"I was thinking that when I stood over her with the gun. And a funny thing happened. You know what happened, Mac?"

MacKenzie did not interrupt.

"I was just bringing the gun down on her and she looked me straight in the eye. As straight as she could look, that is. She was walleyed, you know. 'Smith,' she says to me, 'Smith, goddam it all, don't sell.' "

"And you are going to take her advice?"

"She was older than me, as horses' ages go. Years count."

"I can't tell if you are fooling or not," said MacKenzie.

"I couldn't tell with her either," said Smith. "She was a deep one in some ways."

"I'll go back to them and see if they'll go to thirty-five," said MacKenzie.

Smith waved an arm in dismissal. He did not bother to answer.

"I can tell when a man's mind is made up," said Mac-

Kenzie. "When this coffee is done, I'm on my way. Since we can't shake on a deal, let's shake anyway." He shook Smith's hand, and then Norah's. To her he said, "I tell you this sincerely, Mrs. Smith. I hope you winter well. I wish you both the best of luck."

"We'll winter alright," she said.

But Smith, at the counter, looking again at his mountain, was somber when he spoke. For the first time in their marriage, his wife could hear all the years of Smith's life in his voice. "We are gonna need all the luck there is to winter this year," he said. "She is gonna be a bad one. You can feel it, comin' at you."

BILL BRETT

The Way It Was Told to Me

Just the titles of Bill Brett's books make you want
to read them: *This Here's a Good 'Un, They Ain't
No Such Animal, The Stolen Steers: A Tale of the
Big Thicket* (which earned Brett the Western Heritage Award from the National Cowboy Hall of
Fame), and *He Wanted To Know, and I Knew, So I
Told Him.* (The latter, Brett says, was supposed to
say "I Knowed," but the publisher couldn't live
with it.)

Brett, born and raised in Daisetta, Texas, two
miles from his present home in Hull, went to school
through the seventh grade and did ranching and
cattle work most of his life. He started writing in
the late 1950s, and began to be published regularly
in the seventies. Brett is a member of the Texas
Institute of Letters.

"The Way It Was Told to Me" earned the Golden
Spur Award for 1985.

That's about the only way I can title this. The man that
told it to me said it wasn't much of a yarn, just started out
and didn't have much of a middle and no endin' to speak of.

See what you think of it.

*   *   *

It use't to be, you know, that lots of people died young, died
young and left small children, and that happened to my

folks and another one of my Grampa's children, and he wound up with four grandsons and one grandaughter for him and Grandma to raise. This was back before they was any orphan homes where we was and we wasn't the only ones they took in. They was a couple sharecroppin' just up the road from us that had a six-year-old boy and when they both died with pneumonia Grampa took him in with the rest of us.

I was grown and then some before it even occurred to me to wonder why the old man went and got him. They was big cotton farmers that was always needin' hands and would take a kid like that and get enough field work out of him to pay for his room and board and enough more to leave a profit but Grampa sure as hell wasn't that kind. He was a carpenter and blacksmith and farmed maybe eighteen or twenty acres, subsistence farmin' I guess you'd call it, but with four grandsons there already to help he sure didn't need another hand. I finally decided the reason he took Joe Ten in—believe it or not his first two names was Joseph Tennessee—was just because my Grampa was a good man. I hope my own grandchildren think the same of me.

Me and Joe Ten—one of the older boys was named Joe and Joe Ten was what we called him so's no mix-up—was the same age about, and me and him growed up closer even than I was to my own kinfolk.

I guess one reason we was close was we was together so much. Grampa blacksmithed and carpentered, like I said, and farmed enough corn for horsefeed and cornbread and Irish and sweet 'taters and Grandma raised a big garden and by time them and my girl cousin and the three oldest boys jumped in and helped they wasn't much left for me and Joe Ten to do except git in stove wood and run the woods. There was more for us to do of course but not really all that much and we had lots of time for just me and him.

When I can first remember, the old man had maybe two hundred head of cows and it was free range and by time we was big enough to work—we was I guess fourteen or fifteen—they'd increased enough that ridin' and workin' cattle took most of our time. Even in the wintertime he had enough hogs in the woods, ridin' and tendin' to them was about all we done. The older boys was married and gone, or off on jobs by then and me and Joe Ten couldn't slack off and let them do it for us like before. We both liked that work though—cowboyin' they call it now—and didn't mind it one bit 'cept when we wanted to go to a dance or something like that.

Well, to git on with it, we'd worked together and slept together and been together since we's five or six, and the year I guess we was twenty he wanted to go off and git a job. One of the old oil towns, Sour Lake, was just about twelve or fourteen miles through the woods east of us and they was still lots of work goin' on and that's where he wanted to go.

I did want to go with him. They was payin' three dollars for twelve hours on them oil rigs and Grampa wasn't payin' us but just a dollar, and lots of times lettin' us work longer than twelve hours to be sure we wouldn't be ashamed to take it. I could just see us gittin' rich over there but right at the time I had the sweetass bad on a girl and I watched Joe Ten ride off one mornin' and didn't go with him.

It was one of them things you do and wonder the rest of your life why you done it.

It was maybe three months before he come back home and had a pocket full of money and we was all glad to see him and the whole bunch gathered up at Grampa's the next Sunday and had a big dinner.

He didn't seem much different—didn't talk much about Sour Lake but didn't seem much different—and went back to ridin' with us like always.

He stayed about a month and one Sunday evenin' told me he wanted to use a horse I had, to ride over to Sour Lake the next day.

Well, borrowin' a horse was a little unusual, since he had three or four good horses of his own, and besides that he wanted to use a little ole horse that'd been motherless and I'd raised in the backyard on a bottle. It wasn't none of my business though and he was welcome to the pony and Monday mornin' he saddled up when we did and went and hugged Grandma and waved at us and rode off.

Tuesday mornin' my horse was standin' at the backyard gate with Joe Ten's saddle still on, the girt slacked a little and the bridle hangin' over the saddle horn and tied on with the pommel string. I was two or three days admittin' it but I knew right then he'd borrowed the little horse because he was the only one on the place he could depend on comin' home when he's turned loose.

We all of course had this on our minds all day but nothin' jelled 'til that evening Grandma was in her sewin' bucket for something and found stuff he'd left in it. They was some money and a note sayin' it was for her and he loved her and a note for Grampa, and the old man never did say what he'd wrote him but I imagine the same thing. Back then men lovin' men wasn't talked about much, even when it was appreciated. He'd also wrote who got what of his stuff—his horses and his saddle and eighteen or twenty head of cows and a few other things he'd accumulated. I got a good pocket knife and carried it for years 'til it wore out and I've still got a fiddle back there he said was mine. Me nor him neither coulda carried a tune in a corked jug but he knew I'd appreciate it.

One of the other boy's children still laugh and tell about their daddy keepin' the cattle he got for them and how they'd look forward to new clothes and things when "Uncle Joe Ten's" calf crop was sold. One of the other boys got the saddle and wore it slam out but long as he lived he kept it hung up and greased like a new one.

Well, to git on with it, it was dark after when Grandma found that stuff and nothin' we could do then.

Next mornin' though before good daylight Grampa left for Sour Lake on a big sorrel horse that was the roughest and best traveler I ever seen and I knew the old man was in a hurry because he did hate to ride that old horse.

That was Wednesday mornin' and whilst he was saddlin' he told me what horses to leave in the trap and to git word to the other boys that he might need us and then I was to go to the depot and wait, he'd either send a telegram or come home. Him goin' didn't bother me much, I knew he'd do that, but Grampa had a six-shooter in his saddle pocket when he left.

We had a cousin a little way up the road and I got my blowin' horn and blowed two shorts and a long a time or two—three of any was you needed help and I didn't specially—and in a little bit here come a eight- or ten-year-old boy and I asked him would he, for a dime and not tell his daddy about gittin' it, take a horse and tell the others. He would, and I bridled the same one that'd brought Joe Ten's saddle in and throwed him up bareback and he left. I saddled me one and left for the depot.

You got good service for a dime then. It wasn't more'n an hour before I saw one of the grandsons comin' at a lope. I was glad to see him 'cept he had a Winchester on his saddle and he wanted to know what'd Grampa say for us to do and I said wait.

Directly here come another'n leadin' a horse, and told the first'n "I knowed you was as bad off for saddle stock as I was, and I come by Grampa's and got me and you both somethin' fit to ride." He had a Winchester on his saddle like the first.

Well, it was maybe another thirty or forty minutes before the boy that lived furtherest showed up and he was ridin' a pretty good horse and leadin' one a damn sight better. He didn't have a Winchester, just had a shotgun. Just a double-barreled Remington 10-gauge and I seen right then this thing might be a damn sight more serious than I thought.

Well, we set there. Set there all day and waited and when the station agent left at 5 o'clock we did too and went to Grampa's.

We had a bunch there. The two oldest was married and their wives, when they left, had hooked up the wagons and loaded the young'uns and whatever they had to eat and come. The other boy was ridin' for a cattleman not far up the road and he'd sent word if he could help to let him know.

I wasn't the only one that thought this might be gittin' serious. I seen the oldest one's wife hand him a box of 44-40 Winchester cartridges and say "You forgot these."

I don't know whether I as yet understood our attitude. We certainly wasn't the wild west. Southeast Texas had in seven counties more marketable cattle at one time than the rest of Texas put together, the first trail herds started east out of here in 1830 and went until more than two million head had left Texas. The worst boomtown in the world, oil, gold, silver or precious stones, was Batson, just seven or eight miles up the road from us and we had the free range until 1956 that the rest of Texas has just talked about since maybe 1900. What I don't understand is, why us? We was good, hardworkin' respectable people, was ready to go to the next county and go to war if Grampa said so. Maybe I guess because we was kinfolk, but I ain't really sure why, even now.

Anyways, for whatever reason, the next mornin' when us four rode out, I had a old .41 single-action Colt that'd belonged to my Papa in a saddle pocket and a single-barrel 12-gauge I'd swapped for hangin' by my pommel string. (I wouldn't 'specially want this told, but I'd eased out to Grampa's shop the night before and sawed the barrel off that old thing to maybe 15 or 16 inches. If I'd ever shot it, long as my arms was, I bet I'd'uv slid my left hand out too far and shot a finger or two off.)

The other three still had their weapons and we was ridin' four as good a horses as there was in the county, and when we got to the depot we set. I don't guess I've ever had a harder job than that. I was ready to jump on one of the others and take my behind-whippin', and they was ready to give it, when we got a telegram from Grampa. All it said was "Leavin' here now." Three words, and he fussed for years about them chargin' him for ten.

We went on home and it wasn't two hours before Grampa rode in. It was a good twelve miles to Sour Lake but none of the creeks was swimmin' and I told you that ole big sorrel was a road horse. You ought to heard Grampa cussin' about how rough he was, though, while he was unsaddlin'.

He hadn't found out nothin'. He seen my little horse's tracks two or three times in the woods goin' there, and thought maybe he'd seen them just before he'd got to Sour Lake but wasn't sure, and outside of that Joe Ten had just disappeared from the earth.

My Grandma wouldn't hear to that. Something had happened to that boy between home and Sour Lake in them big woods and she wanted him found.

Nothin' Grampa said changed her one bit and the next mornin' him and us four rode out to comb them woods, and my girl cousin come in the wagon to keep camp for us so's we wouldn't have to come home ever' night.

We put in four days ridin' and lookin' and watchin' for buzzards and then give up and went home. Found several of Grampa's cows that had strayed off and went back later and got them, but no sign of Joe Ten.

Grandma long as she lived always believed something had happened to him there in the woods but Grampa never did. Told me years later he'd found out that the day Joe Ten left for Sour Lake, that night a man there had been called out on his front porch and killed with a shotgun. Grampa said he believed Joe Ten had done that and left so's not to git his family, which was us, mixed up in it. Said he didn't know why he'd done it, but leavin' that stuff in Grandma's sewing basket and borrowin' my ole comin-home horse showed he didn't intend to come back.

We never did find out anything for sure, heard rumors a time or two. Heard he was in Cuba once, and again real strong he was in Louisiana and Grampa send me and the next oldest over there but there wasn't nothin' to it. I told you this yarn didn't have much of an endin.'

Or maybe it does. The whole family remembered and

talked about Joe Ten often and me and the girl cousin is the only ones left now and we still do and love him.

"And that's it, he says."

I found one thing wrong with this story and that's him sayin' there wasn't no endin' or "maybe" there was an endin'.

There ain't no way him bein' loved and remembered ain't one hell of an endin'.

LOREN D. ESTLEMAN

The Bandit

A rare writer who has built a solid reputation in two genres—he is also author of the acclaimed "Amos Walker" detective series—Michigander Loren D. Estleman also has the distinction of winning Golden Spurs in the Western historical novel category (for his Wild Bill Hickok novel *Aces and Eights* in 1981) and for this short story (for 1986).

His first novel was published in 1976, his first Western in 1978, and Estleman has deftly switched between mysteries and Westerns ever since. In the latter category are such books as *This Old Bill* (about Buffalo Bill Cody), *Bloody Season* (on the O.K. Corral gunfight), and such traditional Westerns as *The Hider*, *The Wolfer*, *The Stranglers*, and *Murdock's Law*. He is also author of a nonfiction book on Western fiction classics, *The Wister Trace*.

They cut him loose a day early.

It worried him a little, and when the night captain on his block brought him a suit of clothes and a cardboard suitcase containing a toothbrush and a change of shirts, he considered bringing it up, but in that moment he suddenly couldn't stand it there another hour. So he put on the suit and accompanied the guard to the administration building, where the assistant warden made a speech, grasped his hand, and presented him with a check for $1,508. At the gate he shook hands with the guard, although the man was new to his section and he didn't know him, then stepped out into the gray autumn late afternoon. Not counting incarceration time before and during his trial, he had been behind bars twenty-eight years, eleven months, and twenty-nine days.

While he was standing there, blinking rapidly in diffused sunlight that was surely brighter than that on the other side of the wall, a leather-bonneted assembly of steel and inflated rubber came ticking past on the street with a goggled and dustered operator at the controls. He watched it go by towing a plume of dust and blue smoke and said, "Oldsmobile."

He had always been first in line when magazines donated by the DAR came into the library, and while his fellow inmates were busy snatching up the new catalogs and finding the pages containing pictures of women in corsets and camisoles torn out, he was paging through the proliferating motoring journals, admiring the photographs and studying the technical illustrations of motors and transmissions. Gadgets had enchanted him since he saw his first steam engine aboard a Missouri River launch at age ten, and he had a fair idea of how automobiles worked. However, aside from one heart-thudding glimpse of the warden's new Locomobile parked inside the gates before the prison board decided its presence stirred unhealthy ambitions among the general population, this was his first exposure to the belching, clattering reality. He felt like a wolf whelp looking on the harsh glitter of the big world outside its parents' den for the first time.

After the machine had gone, he put down the suitcase to collect his bearings. In the gone days he had enjoyed an instinct for directions, but it had been replaced by other, more immediate survival mechanisms inside. Also, an overgrown village that had stood only two stories high on dirt streets as wide as pastures when he first came to it, had broken out in brick towers and macadam and climbed the hills across the river, where an electrified trolley raced through a former cornfield clanging its bell like a mad mother cow. He wasn't sure if the train station would be where he left it in 1878.

He considered banging on the gate and asking the guard, but the thought of turning around now made him pick up his suitcase and start across the street at double-quick step, the mess-hall march. "The wrong way beats no way," Micah used to put it.

It was only a fifteen-minute walk, but for an old man who had stopped pacing his cell in 1881 and stretched his legs for only five of the twenty minutes allotted daily in the exercise yard, it was a hike. He had never liked walking anyway, had reached his majority breaking mixed-blood stallions that had run wild from December to March on the old Box W, and had done some of his best thinking and fighting with a horse under him. So when at last he reached the station, dodging more motorcars—the novelty of that wore off the first time—and trying not to look to passersby like a convict in his tight suit swinging a dollar suitcase, he was sweating and blowing like a wind-broke mare.

The station had a water closet—a closet indeed, with a gravity toilet and a mirror in need of resilvering over a white enamel basin, but a distinct improvement over the stinking bucket he had had to carry down three tiers of cells and dump into the cistern every morning for twenty-nine years. He placed the suitcase on the toilet seat, hung up his hat and soaked coat, unhooked his spectacles, turned back his cuffs, ran cold water into the basin, and splashed his face. Mopping himself dry on a comparatively clean section of the roller towel, he looked at an old man's unfamiliar reflection, then put on his glasses to study it closer. But for the mirror in the warden's office it was the first one he'd seen since his trial; mirrors were made of glass, and glass was good for cutting wrists and throats. What hair remained on his scalp had gone dirty-gray. The flesh of his face was sagging, pulling away from the bone, and so pale he took a moment locating the bullet-crease on his forehead from Liberty. His beard was yellowed white, like stove grime. (All the men inside wore beards. It was easier than trying to shave without mirrors.) It was his grandfather's face.

Emerging from the water closet, he read the train schedule on the blackboard next to the ticket booth and checked it against his coin-battered old turnip watch, wound and set for the first time in half his lifetime. A train to Huntsford was pulling out in forty minutes.

He was alone at his end of the station with the ticket agent and a lanky young man in a baggy checked suit slouched on one of the varnished benches with his long legs canted out in front of him and his hands in his pockets. Conscious that the young man was watching him, but accustomed to being watched, he walked up to the booth and set down the suitcase. "Train to Huntsford on schedule?"

"Was last wire." Perched on a stool behind the window, the agent looked at him over the top of his *Overland Monthly* without seeing him. He had bright predatory eyes in a narrow face that had foiled an attempt to square it off with thick burnsides.

"How much to Huntsford?"

"Four dollars."

He unfolded the check for $1,508 and smoothed it out on the ledge under the glass.

"I can't cash that," said the agent. "You'll have to go to the bank."

"Where's the bank?"

"Well, there's one on Treelawn and another on Cross. But they're closed till Monday."

"I ain't got cash on me."

"Well, the railroad don't offer credit."

While the agent resumed reading, he unclipped the big watch from its steel chain and placed it on top of the check. "How much you allow me on that?"

The agent glanced at it, then returned to his magazine. "This is a railroad station, not a jeweler's. I got a watch."

He popped open the lid and pointed out the engraving. "See that *J.B.H.*? That stands for James Butler Hickok. Wild Bill himself gave it to me when he was sheriff in Hays."

"Mister, I got a scar on my behind I can say I got from

Calamity Jane, but I'd still need four dollars to ride to Huntsford. Not that I'd want to."

"Problem, Ike?"

The drawled question startled old eardrums thickened to
approaching footsteps. The young man in the checked suit
was at his side, a head taller and smelling faintly of lilac
water.

"Just another convict looking to wrestle himself a free
ride off the C.H.&H.," the agent said. "Nothing I don't handle twice a month."

"What's the fare?"

The agent told him. The man in the checked suit produced a bent brown wallet off his right hip and counted four
bills onto the window ledge.

"Hold up there. I never took a thing free off nobody that
wasn't my idea to start."

"Well, give me the watch."

"This watch is worth sixty dollars."

"You were willing to trade it for a railroad ticket."

"I was not. I asked him what he'd give me on it."

"Sixty dollars for a gunmetal watch that looks like it's
been through a thresher?"

"It keeps good time. You see that J.B.H.?"

"Wild Bill. I heard." The man in the checked suit counted
the bills remaining in his wallet. "I've got just ten on me."

He closed the watch and held it out. "I'll give you my
sister's address in Huntsford. You send me the rest there."

"You're trusting me? How long did you serve?"

"He's got a check drawn on the state bank for fifteen hundred," said the agent, separating a ticket from the perforated
sheet.

The man in the checked suit pursed his lips. "Mister, you
must've gone in there with some valuables. Last I knew,
prison wages still came to a dollar a week."

"They ain't changed since I went in."

Both the ticket agent and the man in the checked suit
were staring at him now. "Mister, you keep your watch.
You've earned that break."

"It ain't broke, just dented some. Anyway, I said before I don't take charity."

"Let's let the four dollars ride for now. Your train's not due for a half hour. If I'm not satisfied with our talk at the end of that time, you give me it to hold and I'll send it on later, as a deposit against the four dollars."

"Folks paying for talking now?"

"They do when they've met someone who's been in prison since Hayes was President and all they've had to talk to today is a retiring conductor and a miner's daughter on her way to a finishing school in Chicago." The man in the checked suit offered his hand. "Arthur Brundage. I write for the *New Democrat*. It's a newspaper, since your time."

"I saw it inside." He grasped the hand tentatively, plainly surprising its owner with his grip. "I got to tell you, son, I ain't much for talking to the papers. Less people know your name, the less hold they got on you, Micah always said."

"Micah?"

He hesitated. "Hell, he's been dead better than twenty-five years, I don't reckon I can hurt him. Micah Hale. Maybe the name don't mean nothing now."

"These old cons, they'll tell you they knew John Wilkes Booth and Henry the Eighth if you don't shut them up." The ticket agent skidded the ticket across the ledge.

But Brundage was peering into his face now, a man trying to make out the details in a portrait fogged and darkened with years.

"You're Jubal Steadman."

"I was when I went in. I been called Dad so long I don't rightly answer to nothing else."

"Jubal Steadman." It was an incantation. "If I didn't fall in sheep dip and come up dripping double eagles! Let's go find a bench." Brundage seized the suitcase before its owner could get his hands on it and put a palm on his back, steering him toward the seat he himself had just vacated.

"The Hale-Steadman Gang," he said, when they were seated. "Floyd and Micah Hale and the Steadman brothers

and Kid Stone. When I was ten, my mother found a copy of
the *New York Detective Monthly* under my bed. It had Floyd
Hale on the cover, blazing away from horseback with a six-
shooter in each hand at a posse chasing him. I had to stay
indoors for a week and memorize a different Bible verse every day."

Jubal smiled. His teeth were only a year old and he was just
a few months past grinning like an ape all the time. "Them
dime writers made out like Floyd ran the match, but that was
just because the Pinkertons found out his name first and told
the papers. We all called him Doc on account of he was always full of no-good clabber and he claimed to study eye doc-
toring back East for a year, when everyone knew he was in the
Detroit House of Corrections for stealing a mail sack off a railroad hook. He told me I'd never need glasses." He took his off
to polish them with a coarse handkerchief.

Brundage had a long notepad open on his knee. He
stopped writing. "I guess I should have accepted that watch
when you offered it."

"It ain't worth no sixty dollars. I got it off a fireman on the
Katy Flyer when we hit it outside Choctaw in '73."

"You mean that was a story about Wild Bill?"

"Never met him. I had them initials put in it and made up
the rest. It pulled me through some skinny times. Folks
appreciated a good lie then, not like now."

"Readers of the *New Democrat* are interested in the truth."

He put his spectacles back on and peered at the journalist
over the rims. But Brundage was writing again and missed it.

"Anyway, if there was someone we all looked to when
things went sore, it was Doc's brother Micah. I reckon he
was the smartest man I ever knew or ever will. That's why
they took him alive and Doc let himself get shot in the back
of the head by Kid Stone."

"I always wondered if he really did that just for the reward."

"I reckon. He was always spending his cut on yellow silk
vests and gold hatbands. I was in prison two years when it

happened so I can't say was that it. That blood money busted up all the good bunches. The Pinks spent years trying to undercut us with the hill folk, but it was the rewards done it in the end."

"The Kid died of pneumonia three or four years ago in New Jersey. He put together his own moving picture outfit after they let him go. He was playing Doc Holliday when he took sick."

"Josh always said Virge was a born actor. Virgil, that was the Kid's right name."

"I forget if Josh was your older or your younger brother."

"Older. Billy Tom Mulligan stabbed him with a busted toothbrush first year we was inside. They hung him for it. Josh played the Jew's harp. He was playing it when they jumped us after Liberty."

"What really happened in Liberty?"

Jubal pulled a face. "Doc's idea. We was to hit the ten-twelve from Kansas City when it stopped to water and take on passengers, and the bank in town at the same time. We recruited a half dozen more men for the job: Creek Eddie, Charley MacDonald, Bart and Barney Dee, and two fellows named Bob and Bill, I never got their last names and couldn't tell which was which. Me and Josh and my kid brother Judah went with Micah and Charley MacDonald on the bank run and the rest took the train. Bart and Barney was to ride it in from Kansas City and sit on the conductor and porters while Doc and them threw down on the engineer and fireman and blew open the express car with powder. Doc said they wouldn't be expecting us to try it in town. He was dead-right there. No one thought we was that stupid."

"What made Micah go along with it?"

"Fambly bliss. Doc was threatening to take Kid Stone and start his own bunch because no one ever listened to them good plans he was coming up with all the time, like kid-napping the Governor of Missouri and holding him for ransom. Creek Eddie learned his trade in the Nations, so when we heard he was available, Micah figured he'd be a good

influence on Doc. Meantime Creek Eddie thought the train
thing was a harebrained plan but figured if Micah was saying yes to it, it must be all right." He showed his store teeth.
"You see, I had twenty-nine years to work this all out, and
if I knew it then—well, I wouldn't of had the twenty-nine
years to work it all out.

"Micah and Charley and Josh and Judah and me, we slid
through that bank like a grease fire and come out with seven
thousand in greenbacks and another four or five thousand in
securities. And the bank president and his tellers and two
customers hollering for help on the wrong side of the vault
door on a five-minute time lock. We never made a better or
a quieter job. That was when we heard the shooting down at
the station."

"A railroad employee fired the first shot, if I remember my
reading."

"It don't matter who fired it. Bart and Barney Dee missed
the train in Kansas City, and the conductor and a porter or
two was armed and free when Doc and the rest walked in
thinking the opposite. Creek Eddie got it in the back of the
neck and hit the ground dead. Then everybody opened up,
and by the time we showed with the horses, the smoke was
all mixed up with steam from the boiler. Well, you could see
your hand in front of your face, but not to shoot at. That
didn't stop us, though.

"Reason was, right about then that time lock let loose of
them folks we left in the bank, and when they hit the street
yammering like bitch dogs, that whole town turned vigi-
lante in a hot St. Louis minute. They opened up the gun
shop and filled their pockets with cartridges and it was like
Independence Day. I think as many of them fell in their own
crossfire as what we shot.

"Even so, only six men was killed in that spree. If you was
there trying to hold down your mount with one hand and
twisting back and forth like a steam governor to fire on both
sides of its neck and dodging all that lead clanging off the
engine, you'd swear it was a hundred. I seen Charley take a

spill and get dragged by his paint for twenty feet before he cleared his boot of the stirrup, and Judah got his jaw took off by a bullet, though he lived another eight or nine hours. Engineer was killed, and one rubbernecker standing around waiting to board the train, and two of them damn-fool townies playing Kit Carson on the street. I don't know how many of them was wounded; likely not as many as are still walking around showing off their old gall-bladder scars as bullet-creases. I still got a ball in my back that tells me when it's fixing to rain, but that didn't give me as much trouble at the time as this here cut that kept dumping blood into my eyes." He pointed out the white mark where his hairline used to be. "Micah took one through the meat on his upper arm, and my brother Josh got it in the hip and lost a finger, and they shot the Kid and took him prisoner and arrested Charley, who broke his ankle getting loose of that stirrup. Doc was the only one of us that come away clean.

"Judah, his jaw was just hanging on by a piece of gristle. I tied it up with his bandanna, and Josh and me got him over one of the horses and we got mounted and took off one way while Doc and Micah and that Bill and Bob went the other. We met up at this empty farmhouse six miles north of town that we lit on before the job in case we got separated, all but that Bill and Bob. Them two just kept riding. We buried Judah that night."

"The posse caught up with you at the farmhouse?" asked Brundage, after a judicious pause.

"No, they surprised Josh and me in camp two nights later. We'd split with the Hales before then. Micah wasn't as bad wounded as Josh and we was slowing them down, Doc said. Josh could play that Jew's harp of his, though. Posse come on afoot, using the sound of it for a mark. They threw down on us. We gave in without a shot."

"That was the end of the Hale-Steadman Gang?"

A hoarse stridency shivered the air. In its echo, Jubal consulted his watch. "Trains still run on time. Nice to know some things stay the same. Yeah, the Pinks picked up Micah posing as a cattle-buyer in Denver a few months later. I heard he died of scarlatina inside. Charley MacDonald got himself shot to pieces escaping with Kid Stone and some others, but the Kid got clear and him and Doc put together a bunch and robbed a train or two and some banks until the Kid shot him. I reckon I'm what's left."

"I guess you can tell readers of the *New Democrat* there's no profit in crime."

"Well, there's profit and profit." He stood up, working the stiffness out of his joints, and lifted the suitcase.

Brundage hesitated in the midst of closing his notebook. "Twenty-nine years of your life a fair trade for a few months of excitement?"

"I don't reckon there's much in life you'd trade half of it to have. But in them days a man either broke his back and his heart plowing rocks under in some field or shook his brains loose putting some red-eyed horse to leather or rotted behind some counter in some town. I don't reckon I'm any older now than I would of been if I done any of them things to live. And I wouldn't have no youngster like you hanging on my every word neither. Them things become important when you get up around my age."

"I won't get that past my editor. He'll want a moral lesson."

"Put one in, then. It don't . . ." His voice trailed off.

The journalist looked up. The train was sliding to a stop inside the vaulted station, black and oily and leaking steam out of a hundred joints. But the old man was looking at the pair of men coming in the station entrance. One, sandy-haired and approaching middle age in a suit too heavy for Indian summer, his cherry face glistening, was the assistant warden at the prison. His companion was a city police officer in uniform. At sight of Jubal, relief blossomed over the assistant warden's features.

"Steadman, I was afraid you'd left."

Jubal said, "I knew it."

As the officer stepped to the old man's side, the assistant

warden said, "I'm very sorry. There's been a clerical error. You'll have to come back with us."

"I was starting to think you was going to let me have that extra day after all."

"Day?" The assistant warden was mopping his face with a lawn handkerchief. "I was getting set to close your file. I don't know how I overlooked that other charge."

Jubal felt a clammy fist clench inside his chest. "Other charge?"

"For the train robbery. In Liberty. The twenty-nine years was for robbing the bank and for your part in the killings afterward. You were convicted also of accessory in the raid on the train. You have seventeen years to serve on that conviction, Steadman. I'm sorry."

He took the suitcase while the officer manacled one of the old man's wrists. Brundage left the bench.

"Jubal—"

He shook his head. "My sister's coming in on the morning train from Huntsford tomorrow. Meet it, will you? Tell her."

"This isn't the end of it. My paper has a circulation of thirty thousand. When our readers learn of this injustice—"

"They'll howl and stomp and write letters to their congressmen, just like in '78."

The journalist turned to the man in uniform. "He's sixty years old. Do you have to chain him like a maniac?"

"Regulations." He clamped the other manacle around his own wrist.

Jubal held out his free hand. "I got to go home now. Thanks for keeping an old man company for an hour."

After a moment Brundage took it. Then the officer touched the old man's arm and he blinked behind his spectacles and turned and left the station with the officer on one side and the assistant warden on the other. The door swung shut behind them.

As the train pulled out without Jubal, Brundage timed it absently against the dented watch in his hand.

ROBERT J. CONLEY

Yellow Bird: An Imaginary Autobiography

A Cherokee Indian, scholar, teacher, poet, and novelist, Robert J. Conley was born and raised in Oklahoma, educated there and in Texas, and until recently served as associate professor of English at Morningside College in Sioux City, Iowa.

The author of such novels as *Back to Malachi*, *The Actor*, and *Killing Time*, Conley is also a widely published poet.

"There is a movement among contemporary Cherokee writers to produce more indigenous literature. Robert J. Conley is a leader of that movement," says Wilma P. Mankiller, Principal Chief of the Cherokee Nation.

"Yellow Bird," from Conley's *The Witch of Goinsnake and Other Stories* (University of Oklahoma Press), received the Golden Spur Award for 1988.

The year is 1867. I am forty years old, and I am writing from Grass Valley, in the state of California—the state called by my people Adel' juhdluh, "They get money from out of there." I am lying in what I know will soon be my deathbed. The physicians have diagnosed my illness as "a softening of the brain," but I alone know its source. I am in no pain, although I have gone through much intense suffering. It has passed, however, and now I am calm and reasonably comfortable. I am weak and I know that I am dying, but my mind and body alike are reconciled to the inevitable. My only regret is for my poor wife, Elizabeth. She will suffer greatly, for I know that she loves me, and I know that she will never understand what has happened to me, much less the reasons underlying my—and her—present circumstances. I am much to blame, for I should never have convinced the poor woman to share a miserable life with me. But soon she will be set free, and I pray that she will in time overcome her grief and begin her life anew. My only hope for myself is for time and strength to finish this sorry tale before I am taken away to the Darkening Land.

The blood of two races flows in my veins. My mother, Sarah Bird Northrup, was a good, old Connecticut family, a white woman whose parents strenuously objected to her marriage to my father. My father, known to the world as John Ridge, was named *Skah-tle-loh-skee* in the Cherokee language. When I was born, I was given two names—John Rollin Ridge and *Tsisqua Dahlonageh*—according to current Cherokee practice. The latter name means "Yellow Bird," or, because English is backward to Cherokee, "Bird Yellow."

To be totally honest and forthright, I should mention that had I been born at an earlier time in history I could not justifiably claim my father's heritage as my own. I could not, that is, claim my own Cherokee blood, because under our ancient traditions a child belongs to its mother and, by extension, to her clan. Since my mother was a white woman, I have no clan. Some years ago a man without a clan could not be a Cherokee except by adoption into a clan. However, at about the time of my birth our Nation adopted the manner, customs, and style of European nations. I was born a Cherokee citizen under the Cherokee Constitution and laws, and I was brought up among my people—the Cherokee people. I have ever been Cherokee, and whatever befalls me in the future, I shall ever remain Cherokee.

But perhaps I have started ahead of my story. My life in itself is of little moment, and it would be a monstrous presumption on my part to present the world with the story of my life as something to take note of, were it not for the fact that my story is a part of the story of my people. A man does not exist alone and apart, though in times of trial it may seem so. I am a Cherokee, and my story is of the Cherokees.

At the time of my birth, in 1827, in what is now called the state of Georgia, the Cherokees were living in our ancient homelands. The land has now been taken from us and carved up into the states of Georgia, North and South Carolina, Tennessee, Kentucky, Alabama, and West Virginia. It is a mountainous country and heavily wooded. It is a beautiful land, and though it was stolen from us, it is Cherokee land, for it has been nourished for hundreds, perhaps thousands, of years by the flesh and blood of Cherokee people, and Cherokee spirits will forever inhabit its hills and valleys.

This is how the old ones tell us that the world is made: Everything that we know, the world in which we exist, was originally covered by water. But there are two other worlds, and they have always existed. They are spiritual worlds inhabited by spiritual beings. One is beneath us, and its seasons are exactly opposite ours. It is chaotic and unpredictable—a world in which anything can happen—a world in which the unexpected is commonplace. The other world is above us, atop a great Sky-Vault made of rock. It is calm, orderly, and predictable. Neither of these worlds is either good or bad, but because their powerful spiritual forces are exactly opposite one another, there exists a constant and tremendous spiritual conflict between them, and this world on which we live and breathe and go about our daily chores is set directly in the center of that turmoil. Our task, we are told, is to live our lives in such a way as to maintain a constant and precarious balance between these powerful opposing forces.

The stories that are told, a few of which I shall here relate, lay down the rules of life. They tell us where we came from, how to live, and why. They constitute our Bible, if you will, and lately I have given them much thought. For years they had not been much with me, having been replaced by the dogma of the missionaries. Perhaps that is the whole source of the troubles, and perhaps, if you read my story through, you will begin to understand.

Once, they say, there was no middle world, but only water. All forms of life we know on earth today, and even some we know no longer, existed in their primal forms on high. They lived atop the Sky-Vault. The life forms on the Sky-Vault became too populous, so they looked around for someplace else to go. They came to the water of the middle world, where, of course, they could not stand. They wondered if perhaps there might be something down beneath the water. Dayunisi (Beaver's Grandchild), the water beetle, volunteered to go down and see. He dived headlong into the waters, and he was gone so long that the others thought him lost. They had given up hope for his return and were about to leave when he emerged and brought forth from the depths some mud. They spread the mud on the surface of the water; then, to dry it so they could stand on it, the Great Buzzard flew back and forth, flapping his wings. The motion of his wings as he flew close to the mud created the mountains and the valleys of the land the Cherokees would learn to love.

   The time or space that followed was what we know in Cherokee as the Ancient Time, the time in which the universal rules were made. The first man and woman, for instance, had plenty to eat, and they had perfect health, but then, they say, some things took place that changed all that, and the universal laws were made that apply to all of us for all time to come.

The first man was called Kanati, the Perfect Hunter, and his wife was Selu, Corn. They had one son. Every day Kanati brought home fresh game, and every day Selu had fresh corn and beans. One day Selu washed off some meat in the river that ran near their house. A few days later their son went out to play, and he went to the river. After a while Kanati and Selu heard the voices of two boys at play. When their son came home, they asked him about the other voice.

"A boy came out to play with me," he said, "and he said that he's my brother."

"Then bring him home with you tomorrow," the mother said.

Next day after play the boy came home alone.

"He wouldn't come," he said. "He said that you threw him away."

Then Selu knew that he had grown from the blood of the meat she had washed in the river.

"Tomorrow when you go to play," Kanati said, "your mother and I will follow and hide. Wrestle with him and hold him down and then call out to us."

The next day the boy did as he was told, and when he got the other boy down, he called his parents out.

"We don't want to hurt you," said Kanati.

"Come home with us. We'll care for you," said Selu.

But the strange boy struggled to get free.

"Let me go," he cried. "You threw me away."

At last, however, they prevailed upon him and took him home. They found him to be so mischievous that they called him the Wild Boy. And the Wild Boy constantly led his brother into mischief and trouble.

The two boys followed their father to hunt one day, though he had strictly forbidden them to do so. They hid and watched as he moved a large rock from in front of a cave. Out ran a deer. Kanati quickly shot the deer and put the rock back in place. He shouldered the deer and headed for home. The boys ran fast to move the rock, and when they did the deer came running out. The boys were nearly trampled by the stampede of the deer. And the deer were followed by other animals: raccoons, foxes, wolves, and 'possums, even buffalo (a few), and, finally, the birds. So many birds came out that the sky was black, and the noise of their wings was tremendous.

Kanati heard the commotion, and he rushed back to the cave. He saw what his boys had done and in a rage went into the cave and kicked over some jars. Bees, mosquitoes, wasps, gnats, and all kinds of flying, buzzing insects swarmed from the jars and out of the cave and began stinging and biting the two bad boys. They ran. They swatted. They screamed. They fell to the ground, rolling over and over. At last Kanati drove the swarms away.

Because of what the boys did, the game was all let loose, and hunters now must work much harder on the hunt to bring home game.

One day not too long after that, Kanati brought home no meat. Selu was not upset. She went outside behind the house to a shed, and she returned again with a large basket filled with corn and beans. The Wild Boy watched her intently, and then he pulled aside his brother.

"Where does our mother get all that food?" he asked.

The next time they needed corn and beans, the boys ran and hid behind the shed and found a crack in the wall and peeked through. As they watched, Selu got down on her knees in the center of the floor. She placed the large basket in front of her knees. She rubbed her stomach with her hands, and the basket was filled with corn. She rubbed her sides below her arms, and beans filled the basket to overflowing. Wild Boy whispered to his brother.

"Our mother is a witch, and we must kill her."

They ran and got an axe and waited for her just inside the house. When Selu stepped inside the doorway and saw the boys, she knew just what they had in mind.

"I see that you bad boys intend to kill your mother," she said.

"We watched you," said the Wild Boy, "and we know that you're a witch."

"First listen to what I have to say, so that when I am gone you will still have food to eat."

She told the boys that after they had done their deed, they should clear a space in the shape of a circle in front of the house. Then they should drag her body seven times across it. In the morning they would have ripe corn to eat. The boys killed her, and they cleared the space, but, tired of the dragging, they failed to do it seven times. Because of that the corn takes longer to mature and must be tended carefully. Just like the hunters, farmers today have a harder life because of those two boys.

When Kanati returned and saw what the boys had done, he left them and went back to his original home on the Sky-Vault in the West, in a place called the Darkening Land. There he found Selu, his wife, awaiting him. But the two bad boys even followed him there. And today Kanati is Thunder, whom we also call Gigage Asgaya, or Red Man, and the boys are the Little Thunders or the Thunder Boys.

From time to time, Thunder returned to this world for visits, and often when he did, he left behind a woman pregnant with his child. One such woman never married. She raised her child, a son, alone, and as the boy grew he developed ugly sores over all his body. He was ashamed and stayed in the house all the time.

One day his mother took pity on his condition, and she called him to her.

"I never told you this before," she said, "but your father is Thunder. He is a great doctor, and I know he can cure you."

She made her son some new clothes, made him some parched corn, and sent him on his way.

"Thunder lives to the west," she said.

The boy traveled for many days and nights. Everywhere he found anyone, he asked the way to Thunder's house.

"To the west," they always said.

At last he came to a house owned by a man called Untsaiyi. This name means "Brass," and the man was made of brass, but he was also called the Gambler. Brass had invented a gambling game, which we call Gatayusti. It is played on a large, round field, and Brass's playing field was there in front of his house. As the boy approached the house, he found Brass in his playing field with his stone wheel and his throwing stick.

"Hello there, boy," said Brass. "Come on and play a game with me."

"Hello. I haven't time," replied the boy. "I'm looking for the house of Thunder. Can you tell me how far it is?"

"Why, your journey is almost over," said Brass. "He lives just over that hill. I hear him every now and then rumbling away. Play me a game before you go."

"No. I really have to hurry on. Besides, I have nothing to bet."

"I'll play for your pretty spots," said Brass.

The boy's cheeks grew hot and flushed, for he knew that Brass was making fun of his sores.

"I have to go," he said, "but I'll stop and play you on my way back."

Now, word had come to Thunder that the boy was coming. Thunder knew he had left some sons behind in the middle world, but he had a suspicious mind. Any boy would like to say he was Thunder's son.

"I'll have to test this boy," he thought.

So when the boy arrived, Thunder told him to sit down and showed him a chair. The chair was made of long, sharp thorns, but Thunder had it covered with a blanket so the boy wouldn't know. The boy sat on the chair and was comfortable. Thunder stroked his chin and watched.

"Perhaps this is my boy," he thought.

"What is it that you want of me?" he said out loud.

"My mother told me that you are my father," the boy said. "She also told me that you are a great doctor. I came to ask you to cure me of these sores."

"I can do that," Thunder said.

He called his wife and had her build a fire and set a pot of water on to boil. Then Thunder got some herbs and threw them in the water and let them boil awhile. Then he picked up the boy. The boy showed no fear, and when Thunder dropped him into the pot of boiling water, he showed no pain.

"Carry this pot down to the stream," Thunder told his wife, "and throw it in."

She did. She threw the heavy pot, with boiling water, herbs, boy and all into the stream, and when it hit, a giant cloud of steam went up. The stream began to boil. And when the stream cleared, the boy was in the water, clinging to the roots of a tree growing on the bank. His spots were gone. Then Thunder's wife gave him a hand and helped him out of the water. With his sores gone, the boy was handsome.

"Listen to me," said Thunder's wife. "Your father is suspicious. He has more tests for you, but while we walk back to the house, I will tell you what to expect and what to do."

When they arrived back at the house, the boy was prepared.

"Well," said Thunder, "you look new. You need some new clothes."

He gave the boy a new deerskin dress and had him put it on. Then he placed a large box in the center of the room and told the boy to pick his ornaments from there. The boy looked into the box and saw that it was filled with writhing snakes. He shoved his arm into the box all the way to the bottom (as he had been told to do) and pulled out what he found there. It was a rattlesnake. He wrapped it around his neck for a necklace. He reached in again and brought out a copperhead, which he put on his right arm for a bracelet. A third time he plunged his arm into the box, and he brought out another copperhead. This one he put on his left arm.

"Now," said Thunder, "I want you to play ball with your brothers."

He handed the boy two ballsticks and sent him to the field. There the Thunder Boys showed up. And as the game progressed, the thunder cracked and rolled, and then, as the new boy ran back and forth across the field, the lightning began to flash, for the boy was Thunder's son, and he was Lightning.

When Lightning tired of the game, he struck a tree beside the field (Thunder's wife had told him of this tree—Thunder's favorite), and Thunder stopped the game for fear that Lightning would kill his favorite tree.

Then Lightning told his father of the promise he had made to stop and play a game with Brass, the Gambler. But Thunder was acquainted with the Gambler.

"He cheats," he said. "He can't bear to lose. But he won't be able to beat you, and you'll have an endless string of beads to bet."

He gave Lightning a gourd with a hole in its end and a string of beads dangling out through the hole.

"He will bet more and more each time he loses until he will bet his own life. Still you will win. Then call your brothers to help you kill him."

Lightning went to the home of Brass and found him waiting there ready to play. Lightning began walking around the field, pulling the string of beads from the gourd. At last the beads encircled the playing field and still there was no end to the string. Brass wanted that gourd. But every time he rolled his stone and Lightning threw his stick, when the stone stopped rolling and the point of the stick sank into the ground, the stone and the stick were touching. Finally Brass had nothing left to bet.

"We'll play for my wife against your beads," he said.

He lost again.

"Another game," he said. "If I lose this time you can kill me."

And Lightning won the game.

"Just let me go inside my house and tell my wife what's happened here," said Brass.

Brass went inside, but he didn't come back. Lightning went inside the house and found a back door opened. He called his brothers, who came with their dog, but the dog was a beetle. They all got on the trail of Brass. When they had gone a ways, they came across an old man sitting beside the road carving a pipe from stone. They told him they were following the trail of Brass.

"He hasn't been by here," the old man said. "I've been here all day at my work."

Just then the beetle flew high into the air and made a fast dive straight for the old man's head. It struck him hard in the center of the forehead and bounced off with a ping. The beetle's head was green where it had struck the old man's head, and a spot of brass showed through the brown of the old man's skin. Then, there before their eyes, the old man became Brass, and he ran. The boys and the dog ran after him, but Brass ran fast and soon was out of sight.

The boys slowed down, and as they walked along the road, they saw an old woman standing there.

"Have you seen Brass go by this way?" they asked.

"No," she said, "and if he had come by this way, I would have surely seen him. I've been here all day long."

The beetle made his dive again and hit again with a ping. The old woman changed into Brass and ran, but this time the boys stayed close behind. Soon they came to the edge of the world. There was nothing beyond but water. The boys drove a long, sharp stake through the Gambler's chest, ran with him into the water and pinned him there to the ocean floor. They say that Brass will be there until the end of the world, because he cannot die.

Now here's what happened on another trip that Thunder made to the middle world. One time, still in those Ancient Times, a Cherokee boy went out to hunt. He was deep in the woods, far from his home, when he heard a tremendous commotion like the sounds of giant trees cracking, breaking, and crashing to the ground. There were very loud growling and scuffling sounds. And there was popping and crackling of thunder. The boy looked in the direction of the sounds and saw coming from the far side of a hill a great cloud of dust and debris. He hurried to that hill and climbed it, and when he reached the top, this is what he saw:

There was a powerful and handsome man locked in a death struggle with a creature known as Uk'ten. The Uk'ten came from the lower world, and he was a giant snake, but he had wings, and on his head were antlers. Fire came out of the Uk'ten's mouth, and on his forehead was a great and shiny crystal. They say that he could kill a man with a look or with his breath. When the boy came over the hill, the Uk'ten saw him and saw that he carried a bow and some arrows.

"Boy," the Uk'ten cried, "shoot this man for me and I'll forever be your friend."

But the man shouted out to the boy, "Don't listen to this Uk'ten. If you kill me for him, he'll just kill you. Shoot him instead, and you'll have me for a friend."

The boy shot an arrow, and it sank into the Uk'ten's flesh but did no harm.

"Shoot him in the seventh spot," the man said.

The boy looked, and sure enough, the Uk'ten had seven spots along his body. The boy took aim again and this time sent his arrow right into the seventh spot. The Uk'ten roared and writhed in pain, then went rolling down the hill, ripping up all the trees in his path until finally he came to rest at the bottom of the hill—still and dead.

The man whom the boy saved was Thunder, and because of what the boy did, Thunder has always been a friend of the Cherokees.

There are many other stories about the Ancient Time that tell us how things came to be the way they are, how we should conduct our lives, and how to maintain the balance in this world. I heard these stories many times as a child, and they have helped to shape my character, even though I pushed them to the back of my mind for a number of years. As I have said, I heard the ancient stories, told by the old ones, many times as a child, but the world of the Cherokees was changing rapidly at the time of my birth. I was taught by the missionaries, as was my father. My Grandfather Ridge had grown to manhood under the ancient ways, but he had consciously rejected them and eagerly embraced what he called the civilizing influence of the white man. I was told the story of Adam and Eve and taught that all men came from their union. I was taught to believe that our ancient tales were nothing but childish fancy. I was taught, in short, that our entire ancient civilization was childlike. And Grandfather Ridge was determined that his offspring would be "Christian" and "civilized." It was during this time that he took the English translation of his Cherokee name, "I Came Walking Along the Ridge" and changed it into an English surname, Ridge. For a Christian name he later took the rank he had earned fighting in the white man's army, and he became Major Ridge. He gave his children Christian names (my father was John), after the style of the white man, and, usurping the power of the clan matron, he made himself the head of his family.

So the ancient tales, though known to me, were known as fairy tales, while the white man's Bible was known as the Word of God. And the old men who told the tales in earnest, who continued to dance and sing the old songs, were spoken of in our home as ignorant and superstitious. And the conjurers, whose power was still feared by my venerable grandfather—so far as any belief in their power was retained—were believed to be in league with the forces of Satan.

So the world of the Cherokees became two worlds, and the delicate balance, which had been maintained for so long, was lost. There were some who fought bravely and desperately to regain the balance and even forfeited their lives for the effort, and yet they lost. Those on the opposite side were convinced that salvation for the Cherokees lay at the end of the white man's road. They, too, fought and died—and they, too, lost. And here is the way it came about.

Neither my strength nor my knowledge will allow me to chronicle the entire history of the Cherokee people, but I cannot tell my own story without at least a summary of the major events that led up to it. Do not lose patience with me or think that I am delirious. My mind is clear, more so, perhaps, than ever before in my life, and everything that I am writing is related to my present condition—is a part of my impending death. The chronicle that follows is a tale of the loss of balance and the chaos that resulted from that loss, and though white man's blood, too, flows in my veins, I believe that the loss was caused by the entry of the white man into our precarious world. The major events in this story are chronicled below.

The Cherokee people lived in about fifty towns throughout the land that now makes up parts of North Carolina, South Carolina, Georgia, Alabama, Kentucky, West Virginia, and Tennessee. They walked in balance.

1540: Europeans visited our land. They were Spaniards, led by De Soto. We welcomed them and gave them dogs to eat. We called them *ayonega*, or *yonegs*, "white people."

1673: The English came. They came from a colony they had established, called Virginia.

1693: The English sold some Cherokees, just as they did blacks and cattle, as slaves.

1711: We fought the Tuscaroras. Then we discovered, along with the Tuscaroras, that the *yonegs* had tricked us both into the war. We fought the *yonegs*.

1715: Again we had a war with them—the whites.

1721: The *yonegs* took some land from us.

1736: A little man from England, whose name was Coming, talked our leaders into designating one man "Emperor" of all the Cherokees. This was agreed upon because the English liked to have only one man with whom to deal on matters of trade and treaties. We agreed for those purposes, but the English never understood that he was not an emperor in the sense that they understood the word. The man so designated was named Amaedohi, meaning "the Water Walker." The English wrote his name down in their books as "Moytoy."

1738: The yonegs gave us smallpox. One-half our people died.

1761: We had another war with them.

1771: My grandfather was born. He was called, for a time, Nung-noh-hut-tah-hee, or "He Who Slays the Enemy in the Path." In English this name is usually called "Pathkiller." Later his name became Kah-nung-dah-clah-geh, because of my grandfather's frequent statement, "I Came Along the Top of the Mountain." It was this latter name that he eventually modified to "Ridge."

1773: The yoneg missionaries came and told us we were praying to the devil. We did not even know the devil.

1775: Some of our chiefs gave in to pressure from the whites and sold some of our land. One of the whites involved was Daniel Boone, and he made money speculating on that land. One of our greatest patriots, Dragging Canoe, and his followers, known as the Chickamaugans, believing that land to still be ours, fought with the yonegs from that day until he died.

1783: They sent us smallpox yet again and wiped out many more of our people.

1785: The Treaty of Hopewell established peace between the Cherokees and the newly formed United States. It was the first of many treaties that nation would demand of us. They took more land, and they promised to remove the whites who had squatted on our land. They never kept that promise.

1791: The Treaty of Holston was signed. Three thousand whites were living on our land, and since the United States had failed to keep its promise, Dragging Canoe fought to drive them out. The new treaty established peace again, took more of our land, provided some payment for it, repeated the same promise regarding whites on Indian land, and made provisions to lead the Cherokees "to a greater degree of civilization."

1792: Dragging Canoe died that year.

1794: Chief Bowl and others who were dissatisfied with the encroachment of the whites onto our lands went to Arkansas. Then they went to Texas, where many of them, including Bowl, were later killed.

1801: The Moravians established a mission school amongst us.

1802: President Jefferson signed an agreement with the state of Georgia promising to take from us all the lands which Georgia claimed. The Cherokees did not know about this agreement, but looking on it today, we can see that the U.S. Government deliberately deceived us with every treaty we signed after that date, for they agreed with us in treaties to leave us in peace forever on our remaining lands.

1807: Grandfather Ridge was selected by the Cherokee National Council as one of the men to execute Doublehead, one of our town chiefs, for having betrayed our people and sold our land.

1808: Tahlonteskee and other Cherokees moved west to Arkansas. We call them the Old Settlers.

1813: Grandfather Ridge became Major Ridge while fighting in the army of Andrew Jackson against the Creek Red Sticks. Other Cherokees fought with Jackson in that war.

1821: Sequoyah gave our people the syllabary with which to write in Cherokee.

1822: Our Nation established a Supreme Court.

1827: I was born. In this same year the Cherokee Nation adopted its first written constitution and elected John Ross as its principal chief.

That completes my outline of the history of the Cherokee people up until the date of my birth. Here I will insert some verse on the same subject, which I have on hand but have never published.

The Migrations of the Cherokees

1.

The Migration of Legend

Once, in times of history lost, they say,
a large group of Cherokees found their way

across the Mississippi, there—somewhere—
to make new homes, but legend says that there,
in the west, in the place of darkness, they
can but wander. Forever lost their way.
For in the west dwells death, and even the sun
dies there, but the first migration was done.

2.

Chief Bowl

For twenty years in seventeen-ninety-four
the Cherokees and whites had been at war—
had fought with one another, when Chief Bowl,
with a small band, captured at Muscle Shoals
the boat of William Scott and killed that day
six men and took for captives, for his pay,
three women, four children, twenty-one slaves.
Bowl knew his success would be met with waves
of indignation from the other chiefs,
for they were engaged at the time in peace
talks with the whites. He led his men not home
but down the Tennessee, and then they roamed
west to the Saint Francis River, then more west
to Arkansas, before coming to rest
in Texas.
               And these were not lost to those
back home in the east, as the others who chose,
according to legend, to go west had been.
They made their homes on the River Red, then
protected the Texans from Indians
who'd attack from the north, while Mexicans
came from the south. In trade for this aid
Sam Houston, acting for Texas, made
a treaty with Bowl, which took the stand
of the Cherokees' right to live on the land.
Well, it wasn't the first time, nor was it
the last, that white men's words proved worth
not a whit. Texans elected Lamar in eighteen-
thirty-eight, and Mirabeau didn't mean
for Indians, not Cherokee nor any kind,
to live within the new republic's lines.

He sent an army to drive them across
the Red. The Cherokees suffered a loss,
and they moved again, but without their Chief:
Bowl lay dead in Texas, clutching the sheaf
of paper Houston'd signed.

3.

Tahlonteskee

        Meanwhile back east
the United States, growing like bread with yeast,
put pressure on the Cherokees to move
the entire Nation, to drop into the groove
already cut out for them in the west.
Some brothers had gone before: now the rest
should join them there. And the government urged
them to go. The white population surged
'round the Cherokee Nation. Land and game
were getting scarce.
        Then from Arkansas came
word from Bowl and his band: hunting was good:
the hilly land was covered with woods:
no white men were there. A leading chief,
Tahlonteskee, decided to seek the relief
of western wilderness.
        (Besides, he had
with Chief Doublehead made a very bad
decision two years past by signing
his name to a treaty redefining
Cherokee boundaries in favor of whites.
Some had then killed Doublehead, and they might
do so to Tahlonteskee, too.)
        He set out,
summer of eighteen-oh-nine, on a route,
with a few hundred folks, for Arkansas.

4.

John Jolly

In the east, the year eighteen-eighteen saw
around the Nation, which once covered vast

areas of Appalachia, a fast-
tightening band drawing close and closer 'til the guest had surrounded the host—
'til the once-powerful Nation was confined
to a small area in North Carolina,
Tennessee, and Georgia.
                              On Hiwasee
Island, Houston's boyhood home, Oolooteskee,
foster father of the future father
of Texas, watched the growing fuss and bother
of white menace in his land. Oolooteskee,
he who was known to whites as John Jolly,
though loath to leave homeland, wanted more
room.
He feared that already was sealed the doom
of the Nation.
                    Tahlonteskee, his brother,
had gone on before. Before he smother
under the rising white tide, perhaps he,
too, should move on. West, the traps would be
full once again.
                        Then came from Washington
an official visit from his foster son.
And even Houston thought it would be best
for John Jolly to lead his people west.
And so, persuaded by his son, Houston,
Chief Jolly took his people and moved them.

5.

The Treaty Party

And still continued the great debate
between the U.S. and the tiny state
of Cherokee. On one side the greedy
red-necks, wanting Indian land—seedy
people—have-nots who, since they had nothing,
wanted to steal from others to bring
themselves up out of the mire. And standing
firmly behind them, also demanding
Cherokee dispossession, were Lumpkin,

Georgia's governor, and another bumpkin
who'd made it big, Old Hickory himself,
Andrew Jackson.
                        The Cherokees were elves
in the woods against the giant Jackson.
This man, once friend of the Raven, Houston,
rose to fame in war with Creeks, then turned
his back on those who'd helped him to the win—
    spurned
them for causes more politic. Judas
of the wilderness, or, at least, Brutus,
sat in the president's chair when Jackson
was loosed in the White House.
                        But the sun
had not yet set on the tiny Nation
of Cherokees, struggling to keep their station
in the east. There were voices strong raised in
their behalf—voices of men of reason,
compassion, and justice—voices which cried
that their country had lost its way—had lied
once again to steal land from the people
who lived on it first. There were Ralph Waldo
Emerson, David Crockett, Francis Scott
Key, three who tried hard to rub out the blot
that Jackson would smear on history's page.
The debate went to court, and there the sage
justice, Marshall, declared it illegal
for Lumpkin and Jackson to move the people
from their ancestral home.
                        But Jackson's men
had persuaded certain Cherokees then
that removal west, though sad, would be
the wisest of moves for the Cherokee.
On the twenty-ninth day of December
(a day Cherokees all will remember),
in eighteen-and-thirty-five, at a place
called New Echota, on treaty were traced
the following names: John Ridge and Major
Ridge, Elias Boudinot, James Starr, Sr.,
and Stand Watie. Though they had not the right

to speak for their Nation, there was the might
of Jackson which gave them authority.
So in spite of justice, morality,
and the highest court of the land, Jackson
ordered the army on down to pack them
out of the Nation.
              And those who had signed
had agreed to go in very short time
to join the others out west. The trek
for the signers was not all that bleak;
they were helped on their way in exchange for
all the events their names had arranged for.
And when they left home, they took west with them
more of the people away from the din.

6.

The Trail of Tears

John Ross was Chief of the Cherokees, and
he and his followers stayed on the land.
They refused to allow that the treaty
signed at Echota had any validity.
In response, King Andy said that John Ross
was not the legal chief, and, as he was boss
of the U.S. Army, he sent it out
to corral all Cherokees, completely rout
them out of their homes and out of the hills.
In the meantime, Lumpkin loosed for the kill
red-necks from all over Georgia to take
what they wanted by force. Free to make
havoc, they did. Like a hungry wolf pack
with a peaceful fold of sheep to attack
and no watchful shepherd to interfere,
the red-necks descended. From front and rear
they raced in, and they lifted the cattle,
the sheep, and the pigs. It was no battle,
but ruffianism on a grand scale
sanctioned by Washington—a shameful tale—yet it is
   just begun.
        The Cherokees

were hunted down and rounded up to be
placed in pens like wild animals until
the job was done. Who resisted was killed.

There was one called Tsali, who told his sons
to die on the land before being run
west with the rest like cattle. A soldier,
come to round them up, acted bolder
than he ought—rudely pushed at Tsali's wife,
pushed at her with bayonet, threat'ning life.
In righteous indignation, Tsali struck
down the wretch who dared so far push his luck
as poke at Tsali's wife.
                                Others found him,
though, and took him in. They tried him, bound him,
placed him before their firing squad, and shot.
Tsali's family escaped, and they got
with other stubborn ones into the hills
and hid, and to this day Cherokees still,
descended from those hardy ones, remain
in the eastern hills.

My father's father was known as Major Ridge, and this is
how he came to have that name. Major Ridge was the older
of two brothers. He was first known as Nung-noh-hut-tah-
hee, or the Pathkiller, and his brother was Oowatie, the
Ancient One. As he grew older, my grandfather was often
heard to reply, when asked whence he came, "I came along
the top of the mountain." This reply, shortened and put into
English, became his name. And he became the Ridge.

When the Cherokees went to war against the whites in
1788 because of the murder of our great Chief Old Tassel,
my Grandfather Ridge was one of the foremost warriors,
though he was but seventeen years of age. I wish I could
have seen him in those days—head shaved, scalp lock tied
with red and white feathers, face painted, and clad only in
moccasins and breechclout. I know that he presented a formidable figure to his enemies. And in the wars that followed, he did his part. These wars were ended by

negotiations in Philadelphia with George Washington in 1794. During the relatively peaceful years that followed, Grandfather Ridge became a prominent Cherokee council-man, due in part to his tremendous oratorical skills. It was also during this time that he married the woman who be-came my grandmother, Sehoya, whose English name was Susanna Wicket.

During this time, due partly to the influence of our Indian agent, Benjamin Hawkins, but largely because of the con-viction held by certain Cherokees that doing so would allow us to remain peacefully in our ancient homelands, many Cherokees began to adapt to the ways of the white man. My grandmother became a spinner and a weaver. Grandfather Ridge built a large house like a white man's, cleared his fields, grew cotton, and raised horses, cattle and hogs. I still can almost see the extensive fields of cotton and corn and the beautiful apple and peach orchards he maintained. It was in this setting that my father, John Ridge, the second of five children, was born, in the year 1803.

Another important event in the life of the Ridge, and one that carried ominous overtones, occurred in 1807. A prom-inent Cherokee named Doublehead accepted bribes from the U.S. Secretary of War and negotiated away by treaty vast acres of our best lands. This was not the first time Double-head had betrayed his people, but it was to be the last, for our leaders determined to put an end to his chicanery. Alexander Saunders, James Vann, and Grandfather Ridge were selected to execute Doublehead for his crimes against the people. On the way to fulfill their sacred obligation, Vann became ill, but my grandfather and Saunders went ahead. In Hiwasee, at a tavern, they waited for Doublehead. The wretch was already drunk when he arrived at the tavern and sat down at the table. Saunders thrust a candle in front of Doublehead's face. Grandfather, having got a good look at Doublehead, rushed over, blew out the candle, and fired his pistol into the side of the traitor's head just below the ear. Grandfather and Saunders then left the tavern, thinking they had accomplished their task, but soon they heard that the bullet had passed through Doublehead's jaw and not killed him. The wounded man had been taken to the loft at the home of a man named Black. Saunders and Grandfather recruited two additional men to accompany them, and the four of them broke into Mr. Black's loft. Grandfather and Saunders aimed pistols simultaneously at Doublehead and pulled the triggers, but both pistols misfired. Doublehead, wounded though he was, sprang from his bed, but his heels caught in the sheets. As he fell forward, he clutched at Grandfather Ridge, and the two of them engaged in desperate hand-to-hand combat. Saunders reprimed his pistol, while the two other men merely stood by observing. Saunders fired a shot, which went through Doublehead's hips, and the struggle continued. Then Saunders pulled out his war axe and drove it with all his might into Doublehead's skull. The old chief at last collapsed on the floor.

For nearly a decade and a half following this incident, all the most strenuous efforts of my grandfather were directed at preserving the homelands of our people. At the suggestion of President Jefferson, the Council of the Cherokee Nation determined to develop a set of written laws, and to this end they appointed a national committee of thirteen. The Ridge was one of that number.

When General Andrew Jackson moved his army against the Red Stick Creeks, the Ridge, with many other Cherokees, including the adopted Cherokee Sam Houston, joined the U.S. Army as volunteers. It was during this action against the Creeks that Grandfather achieved the rank he adopted as part of his name and became Major Ridge.

My grandfather's brother, Oowatie, had also by this time Anglicized his name and was known as Stand Watie. Uncle Stand had a son whom he named Buck. Buck Watie and his cousin, my father, were about the same age, and their fathers, being convinced that the path to success for the Cherokees was the white man's way, sent them both away to school. They both returned home well educated and with white wives. Uncle Buck also came home with a new name. He was calling himself Elias Boudinot. For several years these four men were the strongest voices on behalf of our people in the struggle against the government of Georgia and the U.S. government's removal policy. However, they came to believe that the struggle was hopeless, and that further resistance would only make the sufferings of our people more intense. They began to counsel our people to accept the inevitable, but they were much misunderstood, and they were strongly opposed by Principal Chief John Ross. Finally, the four men signed the treaty that Jackson wanted, and my grandfather, upon signing, said, "I feel as if I had just signed my own death warrant." No doubt he recalled at that time what he had helped do to Doublehead for the crime of selling tribal lands. Soon after that we moved west and joined the Old Settlers.

Chief Ross and his followers remained behind, refusing to acknowledge the validity of the treaty. Later when President Jackson's patience ran out, they were rounded up like cattle, held in pens, and forcibly removed from the old lands to the west. Many of them died, and the survivors blamed the treaty signers as much as they did the United States.

Father had been extremely ill with fever, chest pains, and violent coughing fits, and, at his own insistence, Mother had made him a bed in the living room. I was sound asleep in my own bed the awful night that Father met his end. But it was not the sickness that killed him. It was the far greater sickness of our Nation. I was but twelve years old at the time.

I remember hearing the sound of many horses riding up the road to our house, but I did not quite come out of my slumber until I heard a loud crash, the sound of someone smashing in our door. I saw my mother run past me to the door that led to the room where Father was sleeping. When she reached the doorway, I saw her stopped abruptly by the rough, dark hands of a stranger. She screamed. I jumped out of bed and ran to her side. Mother grabbed me with both her hands and tried to hold me behind her to shield from me the awful spectacle in the next room. But I saw.

I saw a crowd of men with guns and knives. I saw two men dragging my father across the room. Each had him by one of his arms, and they thrust him viciously against the wall. No sooner had they done that than another man stepped forward and plunged a knife deep into my father's chest.

"Stop it!" I shouted.

Mother screamed and held me more tightly. Then another knife flashed, and another. Blood spattered across the room. I do not know how many men were in the room or how many of them stabbed and slashed my father as he was held helpless against the wall. It seemed an eternity to me, and it seemed as if the blood would never stop. Finally, the men ran back outside, dragging Father with them. I jerked desperately and tore myself loose from my mother's grasp.

She shouted my name, but I kept running until I had reached the front door. There I stopped in horror. I saw my father flying up into the air. They had apparently tossed him with all their might. He fell back to the ground and landed with an awful thud. Screaming and shouting, the assassins ran one at a time and stamped on his helpless body as they made their way back to their horses to make good their escape.

My mother shoved me aside as she ran through the door and rushed to my father's side. I ran after her. She fell to her knees as she reached him, and she gathered his bloody head in her arms.

"John. John."

I saw him try to answer her, but the only sound he could make was a ghastly gurgling noise as blood bubbled out from between his lips. At last I was overcome, and I covered my eyes and ran crying into the woods.

I remember the terrifying events of that awful night as clearly as if they had occurred only yesterday; for night after night, year after year, I have been forced to relive them in vivid, chilling nightmares.

We later discovered that at about the same time my father had been murdered, Uncle Elias had been chopped in the head with a hatchet, and Grandfather Ridge had been shot from his horse in an ambush. It became apparent to us all that the Ross people intended to murder everyone who had signed the treaty on that fateful December day at New Echota. And not only the signers but their friends and political associates—even their families—were in danger. It had long been rumored that the Ross people planned to slaughter all of the male Starrs. They had killed James, Sr., who had been one of the signers, but his son, Tom, had escaped, and Tom Starr was engaged in massive retaliation. The Cherokee Nation rapidly became embroiled in a bloody civil war. My mother took me to Arkansas to safety and from there sent me north to school. I did not like the north and did not like the school. Perhaps under different circumstances I would have, but I was having recurrent nightmares about my father's death, and I was consumed with an overwhelming desire for revenge. I longed to be with Tom Starr, killing the Ross people to avenge my father's death. I wrote to my mother that the climate disagreed with me and that I was constantly ill. She finally gave in to my pleas and allowed me to return to Arkansas. I finished school in Arkansas. All the while I burned with a secret hatred and a bitter desire for revenge. I grew sullen and morose. I did not play with other children. I sulked by myself, read tales of high adventure, and imagined myself engaged in deadly combat with my enemies.

I was not yet twenty years old when I had my one and only chance to live out my fantasies. I was at a dance in Fayetteville when one of the Ross men showed up and, upon discovering my identity, began to taunt me. I soon discovered his political affiliations, called him some filthy names in turn, and challenged him to fight with me outside. No sooner had we rounded the corner behind the big dance barn than he grabbed me by the collar with both hands. Nothing was further from my mind than the notion of a fair fight, and as he pulled me toward him by my collar, I drew my long "Arkansas toothpick" from inside my jacket and sliced his belly open from one side to the other. I stood over him, watched the lifeblood flow out of him, and listened to his death rattles. I exalted in my triumph—and never once have I felt the slightest twinge of regret for this deed. To avoid prosecution and retaliation from his friends and relatives, however, I left the state of Arkansas and relocated to Springfield, Missouri.

But I had tasted the blood of my enemies, and I thirsted for more. I decided, though, that the blood of minions was not enough. I thirsted for the blood of John Ross himself. At that time John Ross symbolized to me all that was evil in the Cherokee Nation. I devised a scheme to form a small army to invade the Cherokee Nation from Missouri and capture and kill John Ross, but for my plan to succeed, I needed help from within the Cherokee country—and some good military advice. I therefore attempted to enlist the aid of my kinsman Stand Watie, but he refused to involve himself in my effort. Nothing came of it. I spent my time in Missouri scheming and dreaming and accomplishing nothing, and so when a party of local residents announced their intentions of emigrating to California in search of gold, I joined them. That was in 1850, and from that date until this, I have lived my life as an expatriate.

The events of my life in California are of little moment, so I will spend little time and effort outlining them here. I did put forth some small efforts in the goldfields but shortly determined that to be a waste. I decided to expend my efforts in another direction and began seeking and finding small writing jobs with various newspapers around the state. I soon managed to make a living for myself with my pen. When the United States Civil War broke out, I found myself viewing that disaster as another opportunity to attack John Ross and his government. Ross was for the Union

initially, and Stand Watie had formed a regiment of Cherokee Confederates. My plots in this direction, however,
amounted to nothing more than those I had hatched in Missouri.

While I was writing for a living in California, a remarkable
thing took place. There were bandits all around the state,
many of them Mexican, and each of the Mexican bandits
was referred to as "Joaquín." I found myself fascinated by
these Joaquíns. From time to time I even imagined myself to
be Joaquín. California had once belonged to Mexico, and the
Mexicans were, after all, American Indians. Their land had
been invaded by the ever-greedy whites. The story was the
same. There was no way to escape it. And while I was writing poems and stories for the amusement of the conquering
whites, and while my father's murderers were going unpun-
ished, and while my own beloved Cherokee Nation was in
the grip of corrupt politicians, these Joaquíns were killing
and robbing and raping the whites. I was envious of them. In
my mind all the Joaquíns became one, and the one became
a great symbol of a kind of brown-skinned avenging angel. I
conceived the character and wrote the book *The Life and
Adventures of Joaquín Murieta*, and all the while I was engaged in this task, I was vicariously living the action. The
white men of California were, in my mind, John Ross,
Andrew Jackson, Wilson Lumpkin, and all the red-necks of
Georgia and the Ross men of the Cherokee Nation. With my
imagination and my pen I did the things that I could not, or
would not, do in real life but that I felt I should be doing.
Joaquín Murieta was, for a time, my salvation.

But only for a time. When I had been away from the Cherokee Nation for several years, and when I had finished my
work on *Joaquín Murieta*, I found myself with time to reflect
on the past, to analyze events, and to sort out my thoughts.
And I realized that by hating the Ross people, I was hating
most of my own people. I tried to tell myself that they were
ignorant, that they were pawns of Chief John Ross. If I could
believe that, then I could focus all my hatred on John Ross,

who, after all, was seven-eighths *yoneg*. John Ross, I told myself, was the murderer of my father and my kinsmen. Then I recalled my Grandfather Ridge's fateful words as he signed the Treaty of New Echota. I recalled his part in the execution of Doublehead. I wondered if Doublehead had left a son and a grandson, and, if so, if they were today, like me, longing for revenge. If my grandfather was justified in slaying Doublehead, then would the Ross men not be justified in slaying my grandfather and the others? It was logical, but my emotions would not allow me to accept it. Still, the thoughts plagued my mind. Again I became morose and sullen. My poor wife—ah, I have but mentioned my wife, but perhaps that is for the best. I pray that when I am gone, she will be able to put me out of her mind and begin her life anew. She began to worry about me. She asked what was troubling me, but I could not tell her. She, being white, would never understand. My mind was all confusion. My soul was ill at ease.

I was sick at heart. My country had been devastated. My people were being persecuted. They had been ripped asunder and were sniping at each other, and although it seemed to me that they were in their death throes, I could not even return to my homeland to suffer with them. They suffered there—I here. I was sick. I suffered alone. I suffered not for myself alone but for my people. I no longer found any joy in life. The malaise that had infected me was beginning to create physical symptoms. I was sick at heart and sick in my body. I was plagued by almost constant headaches. My wife endured with me, and because of her suffering, I began to wish that my life would end.

But worst of all were the dreams I had been having and the thoughts those dreams created which plagued my waking hours. Rare was the night when, in my troubled sleep, I was not visited by the old Conjurer. He would walk into my room; I would awaken and sit upright in my bed. I would sweat as if I had run long in the hot sun of my home in the Cherokee Nation. My heart would pound and my eyes, opened wide, would not blink; they would burn. The Conjurer would stand just inside my room. He wore buckskin leggings and mocassins decorated with porcupine quills. His long shirt was of buckskin, and he wore an old-fashioned headdress on his shaven head. His face was tattooed and his ears were slit and decorated. He was flanked by two huge, ferocious-looking, black wolves, their lips curled tight in a snarl, saliva dripping from their mouths. After what seemed an interminable silence, his black eyes all the while boring into me, I would find my voice.

"What do you want?" I would ask, my voice trembling, and though I spoke in English, he would answer in Cherokee.

"Burn your big houses," he would say. "Throw away your guns and your steel knives and pots. Kill your cats. Destroy everything you have that came from the white man."

"But why?" I would ask, still speaking in English, and he would answer, again in Cherokee.

"If you forget the ways of your fathers and your fathers' fathers and become like the white man, soon there will be no Cherokees. You are bringing destruction to our people."

"You are a superstitious old fool!" I would shout in English, and suddenly I would no longer be myself. I would have become my Grandfather Ridge, and I would be standing on my bed and waving my arms as if I were delivering a public oration.

"Our path to salvation," I would shout, "is the white man's education! It is the only way!"

"You are doomed," the Conjurer would say in Cherokee, and his old, bony finger would point at me. "If you do not heed my warning, you will be driven westward until you reach the edge of our world and the great sea. There will be no place left to go."

Suddenly there would be thunder and lightning. The wind would begin to blow and rain would fall, and before me I would see the wagons, the horses, the soldiers, and the people—hundreds and hundreds of Cherokee people—

walking along the trail to the west. Many would be lying dead beside the trail, and as I watched, others would fall by the wayside. There would be more thunder and lightning. Then, as suddenly as before, the sky would be clear and blue, and I would look up at it and around me and find myself alone. I would look down and discover that I was standing barefoot in hot sand, and as I raised my eyes to look ahead, I would discover that I was standing on the California beach with nothing before me but the vast and endless ocean. I would scream and wake, sitting up in my bed, covered with sweat. I wonder—was it a dream? This morning I believe there were grains of sand between my sheets where my feet had been.

Was my grandfather wrong? Were he and my father and the rest of their kind to blame for the sufferings of all of my people? Were they at fault? If they had killed their cats and done the other things the old Conjurer told them to do, if they had remained true to the ways of their fathers, would all be well for the Cherokees today? Would we be at home in Georgia and Tennessee raising our children in peace and harmony? I do not know. I have never known life untouched by the white man. All the food I have eaten all my life has been cooked in steel pots. I do not know, but the dream frightened me.

I was afraid, and my headaches continued. Last night my dream was different. I did not scream on the beach and wake up. Instead, as I stood there, the lightning flashed once more, and I beheld a tremendous rattlesnake. He was coiled, his head was erect, his tail was rattling, his tongue was flickering, and his eyes were fixed on me. I believed that I was looking at the Grandfather of all the rattlesnakes that ever lived.

Today I recalled a story that the old ones used to tell. I have not heard it told for many years. One day, the story goes, a hunter was out in the woods. Suddenly he found himself surrounded by rattlesnakes. There was no way he could turn. As he stood there trying to decide what to do,

one very large rattlesnake came forward and raised itself up
to speak.

"Just now," said the rattlesnake, "your wife has killed my
brother near your house. When you go home, send your wife
outside to fetch fresh water. I will be waiting for her there to
get revenge for the life of my brother. If you do not agree to
this, we will kill you here and now."

The hunter agreed, and he went home and did as he had
promised. He sent his wife outside, and she was killed by
the rattlesnake.

> Down from a world on top of the sky
> down to a world of water
> to a world where Beetle brought mud
> from somewhere beneath the waves
> and spread it on top to dry
> and be hurried along in the drying
> by Buzzard's flapping great wings,
> the first of the Cherokees came.

In my lifetime I have been thoroughly indoctrinated by the
missionaries with the story of Adam and Eve (Red Clay and
First Woman). I have been taught to believe that the stories
my people have told for centuries are childish superstition
and prattle. But lately, here on the western edge of my
world, dreams and visitations have been hammering the old
prophecies back into my head. The world that the missionaries built in my mind has been crumbling. I have been
forced to think about these things. I do not know. I do not
know. The missionaries' stories sound to me like fables. I
cannot conceive of the notion that my Grandfather Ridge or
the old man who now haunts my sleep descended from
Adam and Eve. But that the Ridge and the old Conjurer,
with his two black beasts, are children of those first men and
women who came down from the world on top of the sky
seems as natural to me as my own skin.

I got up from bed this morning and did not dress, for I

expected to be back in bed before long. I went to my closet and found my rifle. I checked it and started for my yard. Just as I put my hand on the door, something stopped me. I went through the house to the back door and went outside. Out in the yard, I took my rifle by the barrel, and swinging it round my head let it fly as far as I could fling it. I went back in. In the bedroom I found my wife still fast asleep.

"Thank God," I said to myself. "How could I begin to explain to her?"

I went to the closet in the hall, removed a few things that were in my way, and then brought down from the top shelf a long bundle, which I carefully unwrapped. It was my old bow. I strung it and tested the string. It was good. From the same bundle I removed an arrow. I sighted and found it straight. Then, taking the bow and the arrow, I went outside again, this time through the front door. I had taken but four steps away from my porch when I saw it. It was not as big, certainly, as the one in my dream, but it was huge, and it was poised in exactly the same way. We looked at one another for a moment, then I nocked the arrow, pulled the string, and sighted. The great snake rose higher and his mouth opened wider and I let fly the arrow straight into his gaping maw.

I returned to bed and lay down and immediately felt all my strength leave my body. My fear and my headache left with my strength. Now I am quite at peace. My dear wife is very much concerned and is constantly attending to me. I think she will not be required to do so much longer.